APPLIED BUSINESS STATISTICS

Applied Business Statistics

Methods and *Excel*-based Applications

Second edition

TREVOR WEGNER

Applied Business Statistics
Methods and Excel-based Applications
Second edition

First edition 1993
Reprinted 1995, 1998, 1999, 2000, 2002, 2003, 2005, 2006
Second edition 2007
Reprinted 2007
Revised reprint 2008
Reprinted 2009

Juta & Co.
Mercury Crescent
Wetton, 7780
Cape Town, South Africa

ISBN 978-0-70217-286-1

Typeset in 11/13 Adobe Caslon Pro

Project Manager: Sarah O'Neill
Editor: Mariaan Nel
Typesetter: Lebone Publishing Services
Cover concept: Maryanne Wegner
Cover designer: Martingraphix
Printed in South Africa by Creda Communications, Cape Town

Preface

This text is aimed at students of management who need to have an appreciation of the role of statistics in management decision making. The statistical treatment of business data is relevant in all areas of business activity and across all management functions (i.e. marketing, finance, human resources, operations and logistics, accounting, information systems and technology). Statistics must be seen as an important decision support tool in management.

This text has two primary aims: it seeks to present the material in a non-technical manner to make it easier for a student to grasp the subject with a basic mathematical background; and to develop an intuitive understanding of the techniques by giving explanations of methods and interpretations of the solutions. Its overall purpose is to develop a management student's statistical reasoning and statistical decision making skills which will give him or her a competitive advantage in the work place.

A new feature of this edition is the introduction of Microsoft Excel as a computational tool to perform statistical analysis. This allows a student to examine problems with larger, more realistic datasets and to allow a student to focus more on the interpretation of the statistical results and less on the number-crunching aspects.

To emphasise the relevancy of statistical methods in practice, each method is illustrated by a number of practical examples from the South African business environment. These worked examples are solved both manually (to highlight the rationale of the technique) and using Excel (to emphasise the ease with which analyses can be performed in practice).

Each chapter is prefaced by a set of learning objectives to focus the learning process. There are also numerous exercises at the end of each chapter (to be solved either manually or using Excel) to develop analytical skills and build confidence in solving business problems statistically. There is also strong emphasis on providing clear and valid management interpretation of the statistical findings.

The text is organised around the following themes of introductory statistics:

(i) setting the statistical scene in management (i.e. reviewing the importance of statistical reasoning / understanding in management practice; and appreciating the importance of data quality in statistical analysis);
(ii) observational decision making (using exploratory data analysis methods);
(iii) statistical decision making (using various inferential techniques); and
(iv) exploring statistical relationships (using statistical modelling tools).

The final chapter covers financial calculations (interest, annuities and NPV) which are appropriate for many business students, particularly those in financial management.

This text is intended to cover the statistics syllabi of a number of Management diploma courses of tertiary institutions and of Professional Institutes. It is also suitable for a semester course in introductory business statistics at Universities; and for delegates on general management development programmes. The practical, management-focused treatment of the discipline of statistics in this text makes it suitable to all students of management.

Trevor Wegner

January, 2007

To

Shirley, Sally and Maryanne

and my parents (Sief and Sheila)

Contents

PART 1

Setting the Statistical Scene

Chapter 1

Statistics in Management

Objectives

This chapter sets the scene for data analysis within the context of management decision making.

After studying this chapter, you should be able to:

- define the term "management decision support system"
- explain the difference between data and information
- explain the role of Statistics in management decision making
- explain the basic terms and concepts of Statistics
- provide examples of each of the basic statistical terms and concepts
- recognise the different symbols used to describe statistical concepts
- explain the different components of Statistics
- identify some applications of statistical analysis in business practice.

1.1 The Context of Statistics in Management

A course in business statistics is part of virtually every management education programme offered today by academic institutions, business schools and management colleges worldwide. Why?

Management Decision Making

The reason lies in the term "management decision support systems". Decision making is central to every manager's job. Managers must decide, for *example*: which products to sell; which advertising media is the most effective; who are the company's high-value customers; which machinery to buy; which equities to purchase; whether a consignment of goods is of acceptable quality; where to locate stores for maximum profitability; whether females buy more of a particular product than males.

Information

To make sound business decisions, a manager needs good, quality information. Information must be timely, accurate, relevant, adequate and easily accessible. However, information to support decision making is seldom readily available in the format, quality and quantity required by the decision maker. More often than not, information needs to be generated.

Data

What is more readily available, from a variety of sources and of varying quality and quantity, is *data*. Data consists of individual values (observations or measurements) on an issue. Individually, data values convey no useful or usable information.

The following are all examples of data:

	Characteristic of Interest (random variable)	**Data Value**
(i)	value of a single clothing transaction at Edgars	R324,65
(ii)	time taken by a seamstress to sew a pair of jeans	8 minutes
(iii)	economic sector in which Absa operates	Financial
(iv)	number of cars in a parking lot on a given day	56 cars
(v)	a consumer's usage level of the Internet	Heavy
(vi)	an employee's support for a new pay scheme	Disagrees
(vii)	number of sick leave days taken by an employee last year	18 days
(viii)	gross monthly salary of a grade 4 bank employee	R9 450

Statistics

It is only when a large number of such individual data values are recorded, collated, summarised, analysed and presented in an easily understood format that useful information for decision-making results.

Statistics can therefore be defined as a set of *mathematically-based methods and techniques* which *transform* sets of *raw* (unprocessed) *data* into a few meaningful *summary measures, relationships, patterns* and *trends,* which then convey useful and usable *information* to support effective *decision making.*

Statistics concerns itself with *describing profiles*, *analysing patterns*, *testing relationships* and *identiftying trends* in sample data, which have been drawn from a larger population, to support management decision making. Figure 1.1 illustrates this transformation process from data to information.

Figure 1.1 Statistical analysis in management decision making

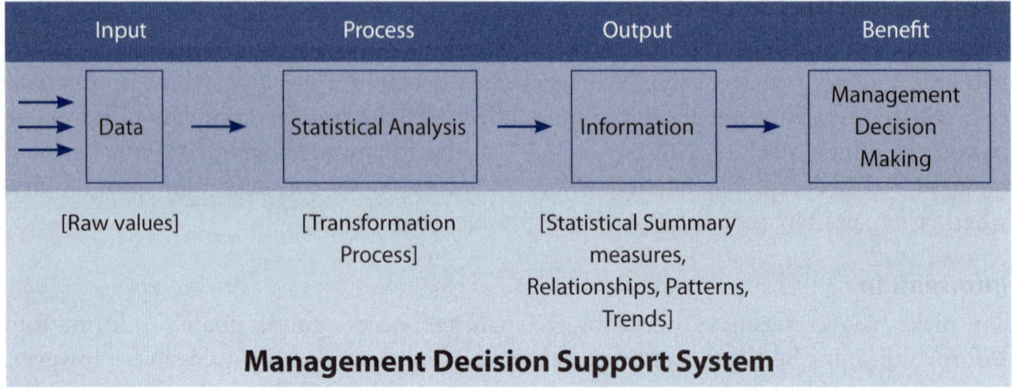

Statistical methods can be applied to any management area where data exists or is generated (i.e. Human Resources, Marketing, Finance, Operations, etc.), in a **decision support role**. Statistics supports the decision process by strengthening the quantifiable basis from which a well-informed decision can be made. *Quantitative information allows a decision maker to justify a chosen course of action more easily and with greater confidence.*

Business statistics is not an obscure, esoteric discipline with little practical value. In many instances managers have been applying statistical principles unknowingly. Much of business statistics is "common sense" translated into formal mathematical and statistical terminology and formulae so that these can be replicated and applied consistently in similar situations elsewhere. A course in Statistics for management students serves to demonstrate this link between the discipline and "common sense".

There are further practical reasons why managers in general should develop an appreciation of statistical methods and thinking. It allows a manager to:

(i) *recognise situations* in which statistics can be applied to enhance a decision process
(ii) *perform simple statistical analyses* in practice – using computer software such as *Microsoft Excel* – to extract additional information from business data
(iii) *interpret, intelligently*, management reports expressed in numerical terms
(iv) *critically assess the validity* of any statistical findings before basing decisions on the statistical information
(v) *initiate research studies* with an understanding of the statistical process involved, and
(vi) *communicate effectively* with statistical analysts.

An appreciation of statistical methods can result in new insights into a decision area, reveal opportunities to exploit, and hence promote more effective business decision making.

This text aims to make a manager an *active participant* rather than a *passive observer* when interacting with statistical findings, reports and analysts. Understanding and using statistical methods therefore **empowers** a manager with **quantitative reasoning skills**, which enhances their decision-making capabilities and gives him or her a competitive advantage over colleagues who do not possess these skills.

1.2 An Overview of Statistics

The Language of Statistics

A number of important terms, concepts and symbols are used extensively in Statistics. Understanding and using these from an early stage in the study of Statistics will make it easier to grasp the subject. The most important of the terms and concepts are:

- a *random variable* and its *data*
- a *sampling unit*
- a *population* and its measures, called *population parameters*
- a *sample* and its measures, called *sample statistics.*

Random variable

A **random variable** is any attribute or characteristic being *measured* or *observed.*

Since a variable can take on different (random) data values at each measurement or observation, it is termed a **random** variable.

Statistical methods analyse the data of a random variable to describe its properties, as well as to draw inferences about its behaviour in practice.

Some examples of random variables are:

(i) *ages* of employees in a company
(ii) *distance travelled* per day by delivery vehicles
(iii) daily *occupancy rate of hotels* in the Western Cape
(iv) *country of origin* of foreign tourists to South Africa, and
(v) *preferences* of employees for a particular remuneration plan.

Data

Data are the *actual values* (numbers) or *outcomes* recorded on a random variable.

Examples of illustrative data for the following random variables are:

(i) *distance travelled* per courier delivery (km). {22; 7; 45; 9; 6; 26; 33; 8; 31}
(ii) Western Cape hotels' daily *occupancy rate* (%). {66; 53; 68; 94; 72; 59; 86; 64; 74}
(iii) "*Do you own Old Mutual Shares*?" {1 = Yes; 2 = No}
(iv) *job satisfaction levels* of Eskom employees {1 = Poor; 2 = Average; 3 = Good; 4 = Excellent}.

Sampling unit

A **sampling unit** is the *item* being measured, observed or counted with respect to the random variable(s) under study.

The item being measured could be *individuals* such as consumers, employees, professional sportspersons, households, etc., or *objects* such as products, companies, equities, schools, etc.

Examples of the appropriate sampling units for the above four random variables are:

- *courier vehicles*; *Western Cape hotels*; *investors in JSE shares*; and *Eskom employees.*

More than one random variable can be defined for a given sampling unit. For example, an *employee* (sampling unit) can be measured in terms of *age* (random variable 1), *qualifications* (random variable 2) and *years of experience* (random variable 3).

Population (or universe)

A **population (or universe)** represents *every possible item* that contains a *data value* (measurement or observation) of the random variable under study.

A population must be defined in very specific terms to include only those sampling units (items) that possess the characteristics that are relevant to the problem.

For the above four random variables, the appropriate populations could be:

(i) *all courier vehicle trips* over a period of, say, one month
(ii) *all hotels* registered with FEDHASA (Western Cape) last year
(iii) *all private investors* in shares of the JSE
(iv) *all* Eskom *employees.*

The following illustrations are further examples of populations.

(i) To research the age, gender and frequency of visits of Virgin Active health club members, the population is represented by *all Virgin Active members.*
(ii) To investigate Gauteng train commuters' views (for or against) on a change in train timetables, the population will consist of *all Gauteng train commuters.*
(iii) In a banking audit at First National Bank, the population would consist of *all financial transactions last year* (all deposits, withdrawals, transfers, investments).
(iv) *All insurance policy holders in South Africa* would represent the population in a survey conducted by the Financial Services Board (FSB) into consumer satisfaction with insurance benefit payouts.

Population parameter

A **population parameter** is the *actual value* of a random variable in a population.

A population parameter value is derived from *all the data values* on the random variable in the population. For this reason, a population parameter value is a fixed (or *constant*) value, as long as the population remains unchanged.

For the random variables above, the following statements identify relevant population parameters:

(i) the *actual average distance per trip* for *all* deliveries in January was 23,5 km
(ii) *all* Western Cape Hotels had an *average occupancy rate* of 68,8% last year
(iii) *17% of all private investors* on the JSE hold Old Mutual shares
(iv) *38% of all* Eskom *employees* rated their job satisfaction as poor.

Population parameter values are seldom known. Instead they are always estimated by sample statistics.

Sample

A **sample** is a *subset* of items drawn from a population.

Samples are drawn because it is often not possible to record every data value of the population, mainly for reasons of *cost*, *time* and, possibly, *item destruction*.

A sample should be drawn to be *representative* of all the members of the population. This ensures that conclusions based on sample analysis will be *valid* when generalised to the broader population.

Examples of samples for the above four random variables could be:

(i) a simple random sample of 215 deliveries is selected and the *actual distance* of each of these trips is recorded
(ii) a proportional stratified random sample of forty 3-star, twenty-five 4-star, and thirty 5-star hotels in the Western Cape is selected and, for each, their *daily occupancy levels* are recorded for last year
(iii) a random sample of 340 private JSE investors from the investors register is selected and their *shareholding* of Old Mutual shares is identified
(iv) a stratified (by job grade) random sample of 540 Eskom employees are surveyed and their *attitude* with regard to job satisfaction is recorded.

Table 1.1. Further illustrative examples of populations and associated samples

Random Variable	Population	Sampling Unit	Sample
Size of bank overdraft	All current accounts with Absa	An Absa client with a current account	400 randomly selected clients' current accounts
Mode of daily commuter transport to work	All commuters to Cape Town's CBD	A commuter to Cape Town's CBD	600 randomly selected commuters to Cape Town's CBD
TV programme preferences	All TV viewers in the KZN area	A TV viewer in the KZN area	2 000 randomly selected TV viewers in the KZN area

Sample statistic

A **sample statistic** is a *value* of a random variable derived from *sample data*.

The value of a sample statistic for a given random variable is *not constant*. Its value will vary from sample to sample, because different data values will be included in each separately drawn sample. Thus, a sample statistic will always assume different values, depending on how the sample was drawn. Sample statistics are used to estimate the unknown population parameters of a random variable.

Scenario to illustrate statistical terms and concepts

Scenario 1.1 Daily Fuel Transactions Analysis at all Service Stations in Durban

Random variable Monetary value (in Rand) of fuel transactions.
Data Value of each fuel transaction (e.g. R125,6; R240,3; R63,6).
Sampling unit A service station in Durban.
Population Every fuel transaction at all service stations in Durban.
Population parameter The *actual* average value of a fuel transaction is R146,7.
Sample 780 randomly selected fuel transactions at 18 service stations.
Sample statistic The *sample* average value of a fuel transaction is R157,6.

Refer to Table 1.2 for a selection of commonly used terms and symbols to distinguish a sample statistic from a population parameter for the given statistical measure.

Table 1.2 Symbolic notation for sample and population measures

Statistical Measure	Sample Statistic	Population Parameter
Mean	$\bar{x}$	μ
Standard deviation	s	σ
Variance	s^2	σ^2
Size	n	N
Proportion	p	π
Correlation	r	ρ

1.3 Components of Statistics

There are three components to Statistics. They are:

- *Descriptive statistics* used for observational decision making
- *Inferential statistics* used for rigorous statistical decision making, and
- *Statistical modelling* used to build relationships between variables.

Descriptive statistics

Descriptive statistics condense *large volumes* of data *into a few summary measures.*

When large volumes of data have been gathered, either from a survey or extracted from a database, there is a need to distil (organise, summarise and extract) the essential information (profiles, patterns and trends) contained within this data for communication to management. This is the role of descriptive statistics (also called **exploratory data**

analysis) – it seeks to paint a picture of a management problem scenario. This is achieved through summary measures such as tables and graphic displays.

Descriptive statistics are *interpreted* by an *inspection* of the summary measures and can therefore be referred to as *management decision making by observation.*

Inferential statistics

Inferential statistics *generalises* sample findings to the broader population.

Descriptive statistical findings are usually based on an analysis of sample data only. However, managers are seldom interested in sample findings alone. They are more interested in the "bigger picture", which refers to the behaviour and characteristics of a random variable in the population from which the sample was drawn. *Inferential statistics* is that area of Statistics that extends the information extracted from a sample to the actual population in which the problem arises.

Statistical inference uses rigorous statistical test procedures to allow managers to establish, with given levels of confidence, the degree of precision of their sample findings when generalising these findings to the population. Thus, inferential statistics provide managers with a *statistically verified basis for decision making.*

Statistical modelling

Statistical modelling builds *relationships* between variables to make predictions.

Many variables in business are either known or assumed to interact with each other. *Statistical modelling* is that area of statistics where mathematical equations are used to build relationships between these variables. These equations (called **models**) are then used to *estimate* or *predict* values of one or more of the variables under different management scenarios.

Figure 1.2 overleaf schematically shows the different components of Statistics.

Figure 1.2 Conceptual overview of the components of Statistics

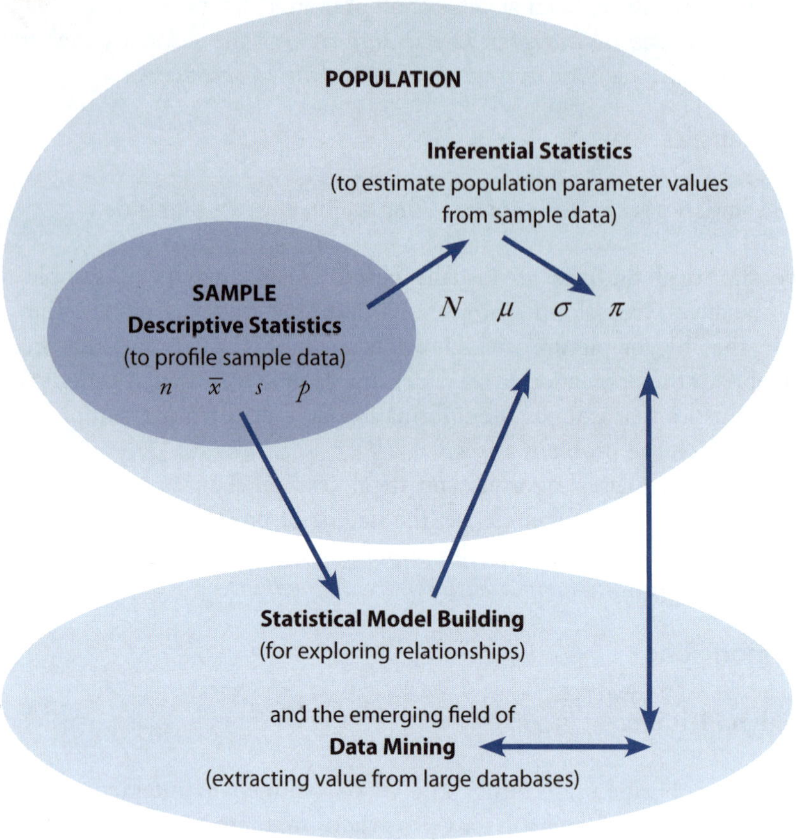

Data Mining – A New Emerging Field

Data mining is a new dimension emerging in the field of quantitative methods. Its primary focus is the analysis of *very large company-wide databases* (consisting of tens of thousands, or even a few million records) to extract strategic value for an organisation.

The advanced statistical techniques of data mining – called **multivariate methods** – are designed to "mine" databases in order to uncover interesting profiles, patterns and useful relationships to identify new business opportunities. Despite their complex nature, data mining techniques draw on many of the principles of basic statistical techniques covered in this text.

Scenarios to illustrate descriptive and inferential statistics

Scenario 1.2 A Proposed Flexi-hours Working Policy study

The human resources management of a large organisation plans to introduce a flexi-hours working system as a means of enhancing employee productivity. Before proposing this new HR policy to its board of directors, the HR management wants to establish the level of support such a system will enjoy amongst the 5 758 employees of the organisation. A random sample of 218 employees is surveyed in the study.

Descriptive statistics can be used to analyse and profile the perceptions and intention-to-support responses of the 218 randomly sampled employees only.

An illustrative sample finding could be:

- 64% of the sampled female employees support the proposal, while support from the sampled male employees is only 57%.

Inferential statistics can be used to project the sample findings derived from the 218 respondents to the population of all company employees. These techniques estimate and hypothesise the likely response profiles of *all* employees to the issues investigated in the study with respect to the proposed flexi-hours working arrangement.

The following two statistical conclusions could be made with respect to all employees (based on the sample findings):

- there is a 95% chance that the actual percentage of all employees who would support this new flexi-hours working arrangement will lie between 58% and 63%.

Further:

- there is a 95% chance that there is no difference in the percentage of males and females who will support this proposal.

Scenario 1.3 A New Product Test-market Adoption study

Consider a new-product adoption study for a hot-wax car shampoo aimed at all car owners. The study seeks to identify attitudes of car owners towards car body protection and their willingness to buy this new hot-wax car shampoo. Before proceeding with a product launch, management is interested in finding out how often car owners wash their cars – providing opportunities to use the new product – and whether there is regular usage of car body protection products (by at least 25% of car owners). A random sample of 326 car owners is interviewed in this study.

Descriptive statistics can be used to analyse and profile the perceptions (attitudes) and intention-to-buy responses of the 326 sampled car owners only.

An illustrative sample finding could be:

- The sample of car owners interviewed washed their cars, on average, 8,2 times per year. In addition, only 18% of the sampled car owners regularly used specialised car body protection products on their cars.

Inferential statistics on the other hand, can be used to project the sample findings derived from the 326 respondents to the population of all car owners. These techniques estimate and hypothesise the likely response profiles of *all* car owners to the issues investigated in the study with respect to hot-wax car shampoo.

The following two statistical conclusions could be made with respect to all car owners (based on the sample findings):

- There is a 95% chance that car owners wash their cars, on average, between 7 and 10 times per year.

In addition, it can be stated that:

- At the 5% level of significance, there is insufficient sample evidence to conclude that at least 25% of all car owners use car body protection products regularly.

Note: The reliability and precision of such estimates and generalisations are always conditional upon the *sampling process* used and the appropriate application of *probability concepts*.

Probabilities provide the basis for conducting inferential analysis. Probabilities quantify the confidence that decision makers who use this inferential information can have in the reliability of the population estimates. Probabilities are considered in Part 3.

1.4 Statistics and Computers

Almost every manager today has access to computing capabilities (desktop and/or laptop computers) in the work environment. This, together with the availability of user-friendly statistical software such as *Microsoft Excel*, has placed the capability of statistical analyses within easy reach of all managers.

This text will draw on the statistical capabilities of *Microsoft Excel* to illustrate the practical use of statistics in management. While *Excel* is not a complete statistical package, it does provide an adequate selection of statistical tools and techniques to cover most basic statistical analysis requirements. For more advanced statistical analyses – beyond the scope of this text – a user must migrate towards one of the more widely accepted, commercially available statistical software packages such as *SAS*, *SPSS*, *S-Plus*, *Minitab*, *Number Cruncher NCSS*, to name a few.

1.5 Statistical Applications in Management

Statistical methods can be applied in any business management area where data exists or is generated. This covers the entire spectrum of business. A few examples follow for illustrative purposes.

Finance

Stock market analysts use statistical methods to predict share price movements; financial analysts use statistical findings to guide their investment decisions in bonds, cash, equities, property, etc. At a company level, statistics is used to assess the viability of different investment projects, to project cash flows, and to analyse patterns of payment by debtors.

Marketing

Market research uses statistical methods to sample and analyse a wide range of consumer behaviour and purchasing patterns. Market segmentation studies use statistical techniques to identify viable market segments, while advertising research makes use of statistics to determine media effectiveness.

Human Resources

Statistics is used to analyse human resources issues, such as training effectiveness, patterns of absenteeism and employee turnover, compensation planning and manpower planning. Surveys of employee attitudes to employment issues use similar statistical methods to those in market research.

Operations/Logistics

Production managers rely heavily on *statistical quality control* methods to monitor both product and production processes for quality. In the area of production planning, managers use statistical forecasts of future demand to determine machine and labour utilisation over the planning period.

Economics

The performance of the economy is studied and analysed, using statistical methods by economists and government organisations such as the Reserve Bank, the Department of Trade and Industry, and Stats South Africa (www.statssa.gov.za). Statssa, for *example*, conducts a wide range of statistical studies (over 270 publications in 2005) – mostly through sampling – to measure the performance of the economy in terms of, *inter alia*, unemployment, Gross Domestic Product (GDP), Producer Price Index (PPI) and Consumer Price Index (CPI, Inflation indicator). Economic data is also used as the basis for economic forecasting of such measures as interest rates and foreign reserves. Economists use economic data to build statistical models – called **econometrics** – of the economy, mainly to prepare forecasts of future economic activity and to inform government policy making.

1.6 Summary

This chapter has set the scene for the use of statistical analysis as a support tool in management decision making. Managers need to be familiar with the language of Statistics if they are to understand reports containing statistical findings and interact effectively with statistical analysts.

The chapter introduced the most commonly used terms, notation and concepts in statistical analysis and described the major components of the field of statistics.

Finally, the inclusion of a few illustrative applications of the use of Statistics in management and economics are given to highlight how important it is for managers to have a basic understanding of applied business statistics.

Exercises

1.1 A survey amongst a random sample of 68 human resources (HR) managers of JSE-listed companies were asked to identify the *performance appraisal system* their company used. The options were: 1 = a *trait* method; 2 = a *behavioural* method; and 3 = a *results* method. The survey found that only 15% used the *trait* method; 39% used the *behavioural* method; and 46% used the *results* method. The study aims to describe the profile of performance appraisal systems used by all JSE companies.

Define the random variable of interest?
What is the population of interest?
What is the sample?
What is the sampling unit in this scenario?
Is the 46% who use the *results* method a parameter or a statistic?
Why is it important that the sample of 68 HR managers be *randomly* selected?

1.2 The *Fair Lady* magazine believes that it has a 38% share of the national female readership market of female magazines. When 2 000 readers of female magazines were randomly selected and interviewed, 700 stated that they read *Fair Lady* regularly. Does the sample evidence support their claim?

What is the random variable of interest?
What is the population of interest?
What is the sample?
What is the sampling unit in this scenario?
What percentage of readers interviewed read *Fair Lady* regularly? Is this a statistic or a parameter? Explain.
Does the problem scenario require inferential statistics or only descriptive statistics to answer the question? Explain.

1.3 The marketing director of a company selling portable DVDs wants to determine the effectiveness of their recent advertising strategy. Over the past 6 months they had varied both the number of ads placed per week and the advertising media (press, pamphlets, magazines) used each week. *Weekly sales volume* data was recorded as well as the *number of ads placed per week* and the *advertising media used* each week.

How many random variables are there in this study? Name them.
Which is the random variable being predicted?
Which random variables are assumed to be related to the predicted variable?
Which area of statistical analysis is suggested by this management scenario?

1.4 For each of the following scenarios, identify, with reasons, whether it is adequate to use only *descriptive statistical* methods to address the problem situation or whether *inferential statistical* methods are also needed.

Scenario 1

South Coast Estate Agency wants to determine the *average selling price per square metre* and *size of accommodation* of *all residential properties* in Margate, KwaZulu-Natal. The 25 residential property sales by their agents out of the 230 total sales in the area recorded so far this year, were analysed from deeds of sale documents.

Scenario 2

The Alabama Restaurant's owner asked a sample of 18 patrons who ate at the restaurant on a particular Saturday evening to complete a short questionnaire to determine their perception of the *quality* of *service* and *food* received that evening.

Scenario 3

The organisers of the "Design for Living" Exhibition held annually at the Good Hope Centre, Cape Town conducted a survey during the latest exhibition by randomly selecting 544 visitors as they left the exhibition hall. The survey's objective was to give the organisers some insight into what the sample of visitors found worthwhile about the exhibition and what new innovations, if any, they would like to see at future exhibitions.

Scenario 4

An environmental awareness NGO was conducting a study into Nelspruit consumers' attitudes towards "green" (i.e. environmentally friendly) household products. A randomly selected sample of 196 shoppers was interviewed on their attitudes towards purchasing 'green' household products. The objective was to estimate the likely percentage of households in Nelspruit who would buy "green" household products.

Scenario 5

Metro Rail, the train commuter service in Cape Town, has been working on improving service to its commuters. A random sample of 875 commuters were interviewed recently on trains over a period of a week and asked their opinion on issues of personal safety on trains, comfort, cleanliness, convenience and punctuality. The results of the sample are to be used to measure the improvement in service.

Scenario 6

Metro Rail also recently conducted a campaign to attract road (bus, taxi and car) commuters to using their rail service. Metro Rail's management commissioned a survey one month after the campaign ended to find out the success of their campaign. The brief of the researchers was to estimate the percentage of road commuters that converted to train commuting as a result of the campaign.

Scenario 7

The Star newspaper in Gauteng conducted a survey amongst a random cross-section of its subscriber readers to identify the popularity of the various sections of the newspaper amongst *all its readers.*

Chapter 2

Data – Types, Sources and Collection Methods

Objectives

The quality of data used in statistical analysis affects the validity of the statistical findings. Data quality is influenced by the *type of data* used, the *source* of the data and the *methods* used to *gather* the data.

After studying this chapter, you should be able to:

- understand and illustrate the different types of data
- explain the importance of data types in choosing a data analysis technique
- explain the difference between secondary and primary data sources
- understand the benefits and drawbacks of gathering data from each source
- identify useful secondary data sources in South Africa
- distinguish between the various forms of primary data collection
- understand the advantages and disadvantages of each form of primary data collection
- understand the important requirements of questionnaire design
- identify the steps in data preparation prior to data analysis.

2.1 The Importance of Data

Data is the *raw material* of statistical analysis.

Managers who use statistical information should understand the factors that influence the quality of the data on which they base their important management decisions. A useful acronym to remember in Statistics is GIGO, meaning *garbage in, garbage out*. If the data quality is poor (i.e. too much "noise" – errors and unexplained variability – in the data), irrespective of the sophistication of the statistical analysis, the results may be meaningless. This has the effect of lowering user confidence in statistical findings.

Data quality is influenced by three important factors:

- the *type of data* available for analysis
- the *source* from which that data comes, and
- the *data collection method(s)* used to record the data.

The *type of data* available – together with the purpose of the management problem to be addressed – determines the choice of the appropriate statistical method to use. Particular statistical methods are valid for certain data types only and an incorrect choice of a statistical method for a given data type can produce invalid findings to the management problem. The other two factors, namely the *source of data* and the *method(s) used to capture data,* impact on the accuracy and reliability of the data, which influence user confidence in the statistical findings. A critical understanding of data is therefore essential in order to generate user confidence in the findings.

2.2 Data Types

Data can be classified in three ways:
Classification 1: Categorical versus numeric (or qualitative versus quantitative)
Classification 2: Nominal; ordinal; interval and ratio-scaled
Classification 3: Discrete versus continuous.

Classification 1: Categorical versus Numeric Data

(i) Categorical data

Categorical data (or qualitative data) refers to data representing *categories* of outcomes of a random variable. Categorical data are *number-like codes* arbitrarily assigned to different category labels.

Table 2.1 overleaf provides examples of random variables that generate categorical response data for arbitrarily assigned codes.

These codes have *no numerical properties* other than to distinguish one category from another. The coded values therefore cannot be manipulated using normal arithmetic operations. They are used merely for ease of tabulation (counting purposes only). As a general rule of thumb, if a response can only be *counted*, the data type is *categorical.*

Table 2.1 Examples of random variables of categorical data

Random variable	Categories	Codes
Gender	Female Male	1 2
Country of origin	Kenya Angola Namibia Botswana	1 2 3 4
Managerial level	Supervisor Section head Department head Division head	1 2 3 4
Company sector	Manufacturing Financial Retailing	1 2 3
Highest qualification achieved	School certificate Diploma Degree	1 2 3
Do you exercise regularly?	Yes No	1 2

(ii) Numeric data

Numeric data (or quantitative data) are *real numbers* that can be manipulated using arithmetic operations (i.e. addition, subtraction, multiplication and division) to produce meaningful results.

As a general rule, if the outcome of a random variable can be "measured", the data type is *numeric.*

Table 2.2 shows examples of numeric random variables. In each case, the random variable could be "measured".

Table 2.2 Examples of random variables of numeric data

Random variable	Numeric response range (illustrative)	Numeric data value (illustrative)
Employee years of service (in years)	1–45 years	18 years
Hourly rate for cleaners (R/hour)	R21,40–R34,80	R26,74
Number of days absent per month	0–20 days	4 days
Children under 10 years in a family	0, 1, 2, 3, 4, 5, 6	2 children
Number of company employees	1–500 workers	128 workers
Annual rate of inflation (%)	0–20%	6,9% p.a.

Classification 2: Nominal, Ordinal, Interval and Ratio Scales of Measurement

Data can also be defined by its *scale of measurement* which indicates how much numeric information is contained in the data. This determines which statistical methods are appropriate in order to produce valid results.

There are four scales of measurement:

- nominal-scaled data

- ordinal-scaled data
- interval-scaled data
- ratio-scaled data.

(i) Nominal-scaled data

Nominal-scaled data is a sub-classification of categorical data. If the categories are of *equal importance*, then the data is termed nominal-scaled. No response category in nominal-scaled data is more, or less, important than any other category.

Table 2.3 shows examples of nominal-scaled data for categorical random variables.

Table 2.3 Examples of nominal-scaled data for categorical random variables

Random Variable	Nominal-scaled Response Categories (with arbitrarily assigned numeric codes)
Gender	1 = Female 2 = Male
City of residence	1 = Cape Town 2 = Durban 3 = Johannesburg 4 = Nelspruit
Home language	1 = Xhosa 2 = Zulu 3 = English 4 = Afrikaans 5 = Other
Commuter transport type used	1 = Car 2 = Train 3 = Taxi 4 = Bus
Cereal brand names	1 = Kelloggs 2 = Bokomo 3 = ProNutro
Makes of car owned	1 = Toyota 2 = VW 3 = Ford 4 = Opel 5 = Nissan 6 = Renault 7 = Other
"Are you a M-Net subscriber?"	1= Yes 2 = No
Type of dwelling	1 = House 2 = Flat 3 = Informal dwelling
Engineering profession	1 = Civil 2 = Electrical 3 = Mechanical
"Is our local public transport system efficiently run?"	1 = No 2 = Yes 3 = Don't know

The number-like values assigned to the various response categories are only arbitrary *codes* (e.g. *gender*: 1 = female; 2 = male) and therefore possess *no numerical properties*. Statistically, nominal-scaled data is the *weakest* form of *data* to *analyse*. At most, these coded response values can be *counted* (or tabulated). This limits the range of statistical methods that can be applied to nominal-scaled data to only a few techniques.

(ii) Ordinal-scaled data

Ordinal-scaled data is another sub-classification of *categorical* data. It differs from nominal-scaled data in that there is an *implied ranking* between the categories (e.g. *dress size*: 1 = small; 2 = medium; 3 = large). Each consecutive category possesses either *more,* or *less,* than the previous category of a given characteristic.

The *implied ranking* between consecutive categories could apply to, for *example*, increasing (or decreasing) age, preference, satisfaction, size, weight, responsibility, authority, or strength.

In market research studies, ordinal-scaled data is also generated when consumers are asked to *rank* objects (e.g. products, brands, companies) or product attributes (e.g. taste, packaging, price, staff friendliness, size, etc.) from *most preferred* to *least preferred* or from *most important* to *least important*. The assigned ranks of 1, 2, 3, 4, etc., are ordinal-scaled data.

Table 2.4 shows examples of ordinal-scaled data for categorical variables.

Table 2.4 Examples of ordinal-scaled categorical random variables

Random Variable	Ordinal Categories	Ranked Codes
Company size (showing increasing turnover)	Small Medium Large	1 2 3
Income group (showing decreasing wealth)	Upper Middle Lower	1 2 3
Exercise (showing increasing frequency)	Light Moderate Heavy	1 2 3
Magazine preference (rank the top three womens' magazines)	*O* *Cosmopolitan* *Fair Lady*	1 (top) 2 (2nd) 3 (3rd)

While there is an *implied ranking* between the categories, this *numeric difference can neither be measured* exactly *nor assumed to be equal*. The coded values only indicate the *order* in which the categories appear. Such data is still numerically weak, as it simply possesses the numeric property of *order*. However, in addition to *counting* these data values as a form of analysis, there is a wider range of valid statistical methods (from the field of non-parametric statistics) available for the analysis of ordinal-scaled data than there is for nominal-scaled data.

(iii) Interval-scaled data

Interval-scaled data is a sub-classification of *numeric* data. It is generated mainly from *rating scales* which are used in survey questionnaires to measure respondents' *attitudes*, *motivations*, *preferences* and *perceptions*.

Rating scales commonly range from 1 to 5 (or 1 to 7) and are designed to capture preferences/perceptions on a scale from one extreme position (e.g. *1 = strongly dislike*) to an opposite extreme position (e.g. *5 = strongly like*).

Table 2.5 illustrates examples of interval-scaled numeric random variables.

Table 2.5 Examples of interval-scaled numeric random variables

"How would you rate your chances of promotion after the next performance appraisal?"				
Very Poor	Poor	Unsure	Good	Very Good
1	2	3	4	5
"How satisfied are you with your current job description?"				
Very Dissatisfied	Dissatisfied	Satisfied	Very Satisfied	
1	2	3	4	
Rate your opinion of the latest "Idols" series on TV.				
Very Boring	Dull	OK	Exciting	Fantastic
1	2	3	4	5

"The performance appraisal system is biased in favour of technically oriented employees."				
Strongly Disagree	Disagree	Unsure	Agree	Strongly Agree
1	2	3	4	5

The first three examples in Table 2.5 illustrate the use of a *semantic differential* rating scale (which uses *bipolar adjectives* to label the extremes of the scale), while the last example illustrates the use of a *Likert rating scale* (which measures the degree of *agreement or disagreement* with a *statement*).

Interval-scaled data has no absolute starting point of zero. They can start at any arbitrary value such as 1, which is a numerical drawback. However, interval-scaled data is designed to possess both the numeric properties of *order* (implied ranking) and *distance* (by assuming a constant difference between successive rating scores), but with an arbitrary value as its origin.

To illustrate, on a 1 to 5 rating scale, for *example,* a 4 is considered to reflect a stronger perception (or preference) than a 2. This is the property of *order.* Also, the differences between the ratings are assumed to reflect equal differences in perceptions or expressed preferences. It is possible to conclude that the difference in perception (or preference) between ratings of 3 and 4 is the same as between ratings of 1 and 2. This is the property of *distance.*

However, because there is no absolute origin of zero (the origin is arbitrarily set to 1), it is not possible to meaningfully compare the ratio of interval-scaled values to one another. For *example,* it is not valid to conclude that a rating of 4 is twice as important as a rating of 2, or that a rating of 3 is three times more important than a rating of 1. Only absolute differences make sense between interval-scaled data values.

Thus, while rating scale data is not fully numeric, the two properties of *order* and *constant distance* gives interval-scaled data adequate numeric properties to allow it to be treated statistically as numeric data. It should be noted that the wider the rating scale (e.g. 1–10 as opposed to 1–5), the more valid the distance property between data values and, hence, the more meaningful it is to perform numeric operations on interval-scaled data.

From a statistical analysis perspective, a wide spectrum of statistical techniques can be applied to interval-scaled data as it possesses most of the numeric properties.

(iv) Ratio-scaled data

Ratio-scaled data is pure numeric data. Numeric data values are derived from direct *measurement* where there is an absolute origin of zero.

Such data values can be any valid number on the number line. For *example,* the *age of an employee* can be any data value between 18 and 65 years.

Such data is the strongest type of statistical data possible, as it possesses all arithmetic properties, i.e. *order, distance* and an *absolute origin* of *zero.* The zero origin indicates the absence of the attribute being measured and permits relative comparisons through ratios (e.g. 5 is half of 10; 4 is a quarter of 16, 36 is twice as great as 18, etc.). Such data can therefore be manipulated using all arithmetic operations (addition, subtraction, multiplication and division).

Table 2.6 illustrates random variables with ratio-scaled values.

Table 2.6 Examples of ratio-scaled numeric random variables

Random Variable	Illustrative Numeric Data Values
Length of service	56 months
Distance to work	2,4 km
Number of working hours lost due to illness	115 working hours
Employee salary per month	R8 265
Price of milk per litre	R9,85
Actual tyre pressure	1,67 millibars
Number of children in household	4 children

Statistically, ratio-scaled data is the *strongest* and *most desirable data* to gather, as it lends itself to the widest range of statistical methods. Almost all statistical methods are valid for ratio-scaled data. In addition, the greatest degree of insight into data and its behaviour results from the statistical analysis of ratio-scaled data.

Grouping of ratio-scaled data

If ratio-scaled data is grouped into categories – as is often the practice in survey questionnaires for ease of data collection – the gathered data type becomes either *ordinal-scaled* if the categories are of *unequal width*, or *interval-scaled* if the categories are of *equal width*. Since a weaker form of data is captured, this reduces the scope for statistical analysis on the random variable.

Table 2.7 illustrates the difference in data type, depending on the question format.

Table 2.7 Grouping of ratio-scaled data

<table>
<tr><th rowspan="2">Random Variable</th><th colspan="2">Question format for</th></tr>
<tr><th>Ratio Data</th><th>Interval Data</th></tr>
<tr><td>Shopper's age (Clothing Survey)</td><td>How old are you? ☐☐ years</td><td>Indicate the age group to which you belong (Tick only one block.)
16–25 ☐ 26–35 ☐
36–45 ☐ 46–55 ☐
56–65 ☐ Over 65 ☐</td></tr>
</table>

When designing data-capturing instruments, such as questionnaires, to record specific data, care must be exercised to structure the questions (random variables) in such a way that the most useful data type – for the intended analysis – is captured. Failure to capture the appropriate data type could later prevent the use of certain desired statistical analyses to generate the findings needed to address the particular management problem. This may compromise the value of statistical analysis.

Classification 3: Discrete versus Continuous Data

(i) Discrete data

Discrete data consists of *whole numbers* (integers) only.

Many numeric random variables assume whole number data values only, as illustrated in Table 2.8. Categorical data is also discrete data, since only integer codes are used. However, as mentioned earlier, categorical data lacks numeric properties.

Table 2.8 Examples of discrete data types of random variables

Random Variable	Discrete Values (illustrative)
Discrete Numeric	
Number of children in a family	0, 1, 2, 3, 4
Number of 500 g tins of Milo bought monthly	0, 1, 2, 3, 4, 5
Number of sales transactions per day	43, 86, 118, 203
Number of employees in a company	27, 75, 435, 3 023
Number of cars sold per month by a dealer	4, 12, 20, 24
Number of life policies sold last year by Sanlam	2 814, 6 543
Discrete Categorical	
Gender	1 = Male; 2 = Female
Do you exercise regularly?	1 = No; 2 = Yes
At what level of management are you?	1 = Junior; 2 = Middle; 3 = Senior

(ii) Continuous data

Continuous data is numeric data that can validly take on *any value in an interval.* This means that any value between a *lower limit* and an *upper limit* is valid data.

Table 2.9 shows examples of continuous type random variables.

Table 2.9 Examples of continuous data types of random variables

Random Variable	Valid Interval (illustrative)	Data Values (illustrative)
Age of an employee	18–65 years	34,3 years
Time to process a claim	1–26 days	7,25 days
Check-out time at a till	1–15 minutes	3,74 minutes
Distance from home to work	0–30 km	6,68 km
Mass of a caravan	350–1 200 kg	655 kg
Monthly medical subscription	R100–R2 650	R834

The distinction between discrete and continuous data is significant. Certain types of statistical techniques assume only discrete data, while other techniques assume that the data being analysed is continuous in nature. These differences apply to various probability distributions.

Figure 2.1 overleaf diagrammatically summarises the classification of data.

Figure 2.1 Classification of Data types and influence on Statistical Analyses

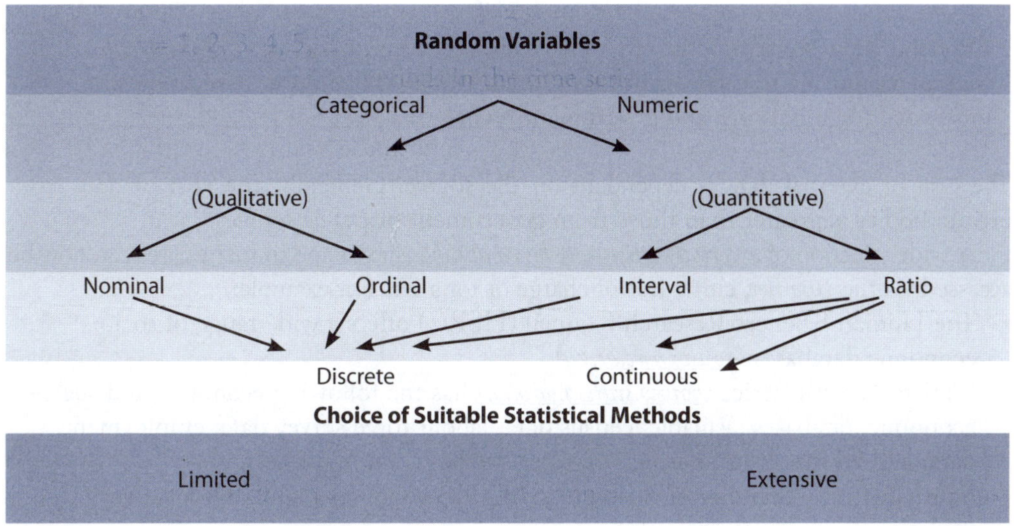

The following sections cover *data sources* and *data collection methods,* two further important determinants of *data quality*. An understanding of the sources and methods of data collection assists in the assessment of data quality.

2.3 Data Sources

Data for statistical analysis is available from many different sources. There are two classification types of data sources:

- internal versus external sources, and
- primary versus secondary sources.

Internal versus External Sources

(i) Internal data sources

Internal data refers to the availability of data from *within an organisation*. It is generated during the normal course of business activities and is relatively inexpensive to gather.

Internal data consists of, *inter alia:*

- *Financial data,* for example, sales vouchers, credit notes, accounts receivable, accounts payable, asset register.
- *Production data,* for example, production cost records, stock sheets, downtime records.
- *Human resource data,* for example, time sheets, wages and salaries schedules, employee personal employment files, absenteeism records.
- *Marketing data,* for example, product sales data, advertising expenditure data.

(ii) External data sources

External data sources refers to data available from *outside an organisation.* Such sources are private research institutions, trade/employer/employee associations, profit-motivated organisations, and government bodies.

The cost of external data is dependent on the source. Generally, the cost of data from private bodies is greater than those from government or public sources.

A wide selection of *external statistically based databases* exist and in many cases can now be accessed via the *Internet*, either free of charge or for a fee. For example:

- The Human Sciences Research Council (HSRC) offers a wide range of socio-economic databases (*www.hsrc.ac.za*).
- Statistics South Africa (*www.statssa.gov.za*) has the following economic and socio-economic databases available: census data; labour force survey data; employment data; and an integrated business register database, among others.
- South African Chamber of Business (SACOB) conducts regular trade surveys (*www.sacob.co.za*).
- Company-level performance data is available from a variety of web sites, depending on the nature of data required. To *illustrate*:
  - *Financial data* can be accessed through I-Net Bridge (*www.inet.co.za*) and the Johannesburg Securities Exchange (JSE) – *www.jse.co.za*.
  - *Marketing data* on product surveys from the All Media Products Surveys (AMPS) conducted by the South African Advertising Research Foundation (SAARF) can be obtained at *www.saarf.co.za*.
  - Consumer research studies conducted by research houses such as Research Surveys in SA (*www.researchsurveys.co.za)* and AC Nielsen internationally (*www2.acnielsen.com)*.
  - *Human resource* data is available through the Institute of Personnel Management (IPM) at *www.ipm.co.za* – the institute also offers its members a People Management Resource Centre.
- Academic university libraries (UCT, Wits, Stellenbosch, Pretoria, University of Johannesburg, Unisa) and research bureaux (Bureau of Economic Research, or simply BER, in Stellenbosch); Bureau of Market Research (Pretoria); Bureau of Financial Analysis (Pretoria); SA Labour Development Research Unit (SALDRU, UCT, Cape Town) are all useful sources of secondary business-relevant data.
- On the Internet, the use of a keyword search on a search engine (such as Yahoo, Google or Aardvark) will uncover numerous potentially useful sources of business data for statistical analysis to address management problems.

Primary versus Secondary Sources

(i) Primary data sources

Primary data is data which is captured at the *point where it is generated.* Such data is captured for the first time and with a specific purpose in mind.

Examples of primary data sources are largely the same as those listed for internal data sources, but in the case of primary sources the list would also include *surveys* (e.g. human resource surveys; salary surveys; economic surveys; and consumer surveys through market research).

Advantages of primary data:
- Primary data are directly *relevant* to the problem at hand.
- They generally offer greater control over *data accuracy*.

Disadvantages of primary data:
- Primary data could be *time consuming* to collect.
- They are generally *more expensive* to collect (e.g. market research).

(ii) Secondary data sources

Secondary data is data collected and processed by others for a purpose other than the problem at hand.

Such databases *already exist*, either within or outside an organisation, i.e. one can get both internal secondary data and external secondary data. The problem at hand (purpose of study) determines whether data is primary or secondary. All external data sources listed are sources of secondary databases and reports.

Advantages of secondary data:
- Secondary data already exists.
- Access time is relatively short, especially if the data is accessible through the Internet.
- Secondary data is generally less expensive to acquire than primary data.

Disadvantages of secondary data:
- Secondary data may not be problem specific (relevancy).
- Currency of data: data may be dated ("old") and hence inappropriate.
- It may be difficult to assess data accuracy.
- Secondary data may not be subject to further manipulation, or may not be at the right level of aggregation.
- Combining various secondary sources could lead to errors of collation and introduce bias.

Despite such shortcomings, an analyst should always consider relevant secondary database sources before resorting to primary data collection.

2.4 Data Collection Methods

There are three approaches to data gathering for statistical analyses:
- through *observation*
- by conducting *surveys*
- through *experimentation*.

Observation Methods

(i) Direct observation

Primary data can be collected by *directly observing* the respondent or object in action.

Examples of *direct observation* approaches include: vehicle traffic surveys; pedestrian flow surveys; observation of the purchase behaviour of consumers in a store or work practices in a production process; and quality control inspection.

The following is an advantage of direct observation:
The respondent is generally not aware of being observed and therefore behaves more naturally or spontaneously. This reduces the likelihood of gathering *biased* data.

A disadvantage of direct observation:
Direct observation is a *passive form* of data collection. There is no opportunity to probe for reasons or to further investigate underlying behaviour and motivating factors.

(ii) Desk research (abstraction)

Extracting *secondary data* from a variety of source documents is a form of data gathering through observation. A wide variety of organisations and individuals use secondary data for decision making or opinion forming.

People or groups who might conduct desk research to find and use secondary data include: economists; financial planners; politicians; senior executives; research groups; and scenario planners, to name but a few.

The *advantages* and *disadvantages* of desk research or abstraction are the same as those listed for *secondary data sources* in the previous section.

Survey Methods

Survey methods gather *primary data* through the *direct questioning* of respondents.

This is the most common form of data collection in the field of marketing and socio-economic research. It takes the form of surveys that use a *questionnaire* to gather the data and structure the data collection process. Surveys mainly capture data on *attitudes,* such as opinions, awareness, knowledge, preferences, perception, intentions and motivations.

There are four approaches to gathering survey data: *personal interviews, postal surveys, telephone surveys* and *e-surveys.*

(i) Personal interviews

A *personal interview* is face-to-face contact with a respondent during which a questionnaire is completed.

Some advantages of personal interviews:
- A higher response rate is generally achieved.
- Questioning allows further probing into reasons.
- Data collection is immediate and the data is current.
- Greater data accuracy is generally ensured.

- Useful when the required data is of a technical nature.
- Non-verbal responses (body language; facial expressions) can be observed and noted.
- Generally more questions can be asked.
- Responses are spontaneous and therefore more likely to be valid.
- The use of aided-recall questions and other visual prompts is possible.

Disadvantages of personal interviews:
- The method is time consuming.
- It requires trained interviewers, and is therefore more expensive.
- Generally, fewer interviews are conducted because of cost and time constraints.
- The possibility of gathering biased data is introduced by interviewer influence.

(ii) Postal surveys

When the target population from which *primary data* is required is large and/or geographically dispersed, then the use of mailed questionnaires is considered most suitable.

Advantages of postal surveys:
- A larger sample of respondents can be reached.
- Postal interviews are more cost effective.
- Interviewer bias is eliminated as there is no direct questioning by an interviewer.
- Respondents have more time to consider their responses.
- Anonymity of respondent is assured, generally resulting in more honest responses.
- Respondents are more willing to answer personal and sensitive questions.

Some disadvantages of postal surveys:
Postal surveys suffer from the lack of personal communication between the researcher and the respondent. The researcher has less control over the data collection procedure than during a personal interview. Other disadvantages of postal surveys include:
- Response rates are very low (mostly below 10%).
- The respondent cannot clarify questions.
- Of necessity, mailed questionnaires must be shorter and simpler to complete, hence less data on the management issues are gathered.
- The opportunity of probing or investigating further is limited.
- Data collection takes a long time (possibly weeks), which reduces currency of data.
- There is no control over who actually answers the questionnaire, which increases the chances of non-sampling error.
- There is no possibility of "checkbacks" to check the validity of responses.

The above advantages and disadvantages apply to any *self-administered* questionnaire. Self-administered questionnaires need not necessarily be posted. They could be handed out randomly in shopping malls, car parks, schools, offices, or wherever the target population can be most readily reached. The respondent is requested to complete the questionnaire and to return it by mail or hand it in at a specified venue.

(iii) Telephone interviews

The interview is conducted telephonically with the respondent. A telephone interview combines many of the advantages of personal interviews and postal surveys and overcomes many of the disadvantages of the latter two approaches. Telephone interviews are used extensively in *snap (straw)* opinion polls, but they can also be used for lengthier, more rigorous survey studies.

Advantages of the telephone interview:
- It allows quicker contact with geographically dispersed respondents.
- Callbacks can be made if the respondent is not available right away.
- The cost is relatively low compared with personal surveys.
- People are more willing to talk on the telephone, from the security of their home.
- Interviewer probing is possible.
- Questions can be clarified by the interviewer.
- The use of aided-recall questions is possible.
- A larger sample of respondents can be reached in a relatively short time.

Disadvantages of a telephonic interview:
- Respondent anonymity is lost.
- Non-verbal responses (body language) cannot be observed.
- Trained interviewers are required, which increases costs.
- Interviewer bias is possible.
- The respondent may terminate the interview prematurely by ending the telephone call, i.e. putting down the telephone.
- Sampling bias is introduced if significant numbers of the target population do not have access to a telephone.

(iv) E-surveys

An **e-survey** is an electronic or e-mail based survey and/or online web-based survey.

E-surveys are becoming *increasingly popular* for the following reasons:
- An e-survey *automates* the process of *collating data,* thus eliminating data capturing errors.
- E-surveys are significantly *cheaper and faster* than personal or postal interviews.
- It is possible to reach local, national and international target populations.
- The data is therefore *highly current* and more likely to be *accurate.*

The primary drawback of e-surveys is twofold at present:
- There is a lack of comprehensive sampling frames (e-mail address lists) targeting specific user groups.
- Not all potential target populations have access to e-mail or Internet facilities.

Questionnaire design

A **questionnaire** is a data collection instrument used to gather data in all *survey-based* studies.

The *design* of a questionnaire is critical to ensuring that the questions asked are *relevant* to the management problem being studied; and that *accurate and appropriate data* for statistical analysis are collected. The design (structure) and length of a questionnaire affects the response rate to the survey.

When designing a questionnaire, a number of design criteria must be considered. Questionnaire design is guided largely by the *purpose of the study* and the *type of data required* to answer the research question statistically.

Structure

A questionnaire should consist of three sections:

(i) *Administrative section*: identifies the respondent (if not anonymous) and the interviewer by name and contact details, and where the interview was conducted. This section is used for checkbacks, to confirm the validity of the recorded data.

(ii) *Demographic* (or *classification) section*: records respondent details by a number of personal demographics (e.g. age, gender, residential location, marital status, language, qualifications, etc.) for consumers, or company demographics (e.g. company size, economic sector, managerial level, functional area, etc.) for employees. These demographic characteristics are used to statistically classify the research data into segments for ease of interpretation.

(iii) *Information section*: makes up the major portion of the questionnaire and consists of all the questions that will extract data from respondents to address the research objective. This section may be subdivided in order to group questions into categories dealing with different aspects of the study. For example, a consumer behaviour questionnaire would have subsections with questions relating to product awareness, product usage, buying behaviour, attitude to product and lifestyle patterns.

Design

A number of criteria should be borne in mind when designing a questionnaire, to ensure that accurate, unbiased and relevant data of the correct type is gathered in line with the research objective(s), which must always be clearly defined and documented. Designing a well-structured, unambiguous and undisguised questionnaire requires close attention to the:

(i) *type* of question to include

(ii) *order* of the questions, and

(iii) *structure* and *wording* of questions.

The following are a number of specific design pointers:

- Include a question only if it contributes to the research objectives.
- Avoid redundant questions.
- Avoid ambiguous questions.
- Avoid leading questions, because they generate biased responses.

- Wherever possible, particularly in the case of self-administered questionnaires, *fixed alternative* questions are recommended. Open-ended questions may add richness to the findings, but they are difficult to analyse statistically, so use them sparingly.
- Arrange questions in a logical sequence.
- Keep questions as short and as simple as possible.
- Avoid technical jargon in consumer-based surveys.
- Questions should not require calculations by the respondents.
- Use filter questions to guide the respondent through various sections of the questionnaire; this helps to prevent the gathering of inconsistent data.
- Instructions must be clear and explicit.
- Questions must be specific and address only one issue. Vague questions result in "noisy", meaningless data.
- To prevent biased responses, do not use emotive language in questions.
- Questions dealing with sensitive issues should be carefully worded so as not to offend or encourage non-response.
- The ability of the target population to understand and respond adequately to the questionnaire should be considered when wording questions.
- Word questions carefully to ensure that you capture the appropriate type of data for the envisaged statistical analyses.
- Finally, always *pilot a questionnaire* before carrying out the full survey. A pilot survey often highlights weaknesses in a questionnaire, which can then be corrected or improved upon.

This list is by no means complete. The design stage is only one of a number of steps in the overall *research design process* of a survey-based study. Each of the steps in the research design process will have an impact on the final format of a questionnaire. Refer to *Research Methodology* texts for a full discussion on the stages of the sample survey approach, which is used in all survey-based studies.

Experimentation

Primary data can also be generated by conducting experiments. This means that the researcher *manipulates certain variables* under *controlled conditions.* Data on the primary variable under study can then be monitored and recorded, while the researcher makes conscious efforts to control the effects of a number of influencing factors.

Examples of the manipulation of variables under controlled conditions:

- *Demand elasticity* for a product can be determined by manipulating the price of the product over time or between various regions or outlets.
- *Advertising effectiveness* can be measured by manipulating the frequency and choice of various *media.*

Some advantages of experimentation as a means to gathering data:

- Quality, "noise-free" data is collected on the research problem if the experiment is correctly designed and executed.
- The results of such studies are generally more objective and valid than other approaches.

Disadvantages of experimentation as a means to gathering data:

- Running an experiment is a costly and time-consuming exercise.
- It may be impossible to control certain extraneous factors, which may confound the results.

Statistical methods – called **experimental design models** – exist to analyse the effects of this manipulation on a response variable. Their purpose is to identify whether the manipulated variables have had any meaningful effect on the response variable under study.

For a fuller discussion on the use of experimentation as a data collection technique, consult market research texts pertaining to *experimental design* models and the use of appropriate statistical methods.

2.5 Data Preparation for Statistical Analysis

Data is the lifeblood of statistical analysis. As such it must be *relevant, "clean"*, and in the *correct format* for statistical analysis if it is to address the particular management problem.

Data Relevancy

It is important to select the most appropriate measures by which the management problem can be addressed. The variables and the data must be *problem-specific*. Variables and data that are not relevant to the management question are likely to produce findings that cannot be used meaningfully to draw conclusions about the management problem.

An analyst would be well advised to consult domain experts who generally know:

- the *kinds of measures that are appropriate* to the business problem under investigation which narrows the search for relevant and appropriate data
- where the necessary *data resides* and how it can best be accessed.

Data Cleaning

Available data is often "dirty" when captured – for example, data can be incomplete, come in varying formats, or contain errors or extreme values (outliers). "Clean" data is essential for valid statistical findings. An analyst must therefore look for the following:

(i) *Missing data*: What percentage of cases does the missing data represent? How serious is the problem? How will the missing percentage affect the validity of the overall results?

(ii) *Valid ranges*: Are values within valid ranges? (e.g. between, say, 20 and 60 years)?

(iii) *Outliers (or extreme values)*: How many are there? What are their magnitudes? Are they influential or inconsequential? How should they be treated once identified?

In **exploratory data analysis**, outliers must be retained in the analysis and be included as part of the discussion of the profile of the data. They may either represent *opportunities* (e.g. high-value customers) to be exploited by the organisation for strategic advantage, or *problem areas* (e.g. under-performing employees) requiring closer examination and intervention.

In **inferential statistics**, however, outliers must be identified, treated (e.g. removed and/or replaced with the average value for the related variable), or grouped into a sub-sample (if sufficiently large) and analysed separately. This ensures that the inferential statistical findings are not distorted by a few extreme values in the data set. Alternatively, the sub-sample can be more closely examined with a view to appropriate management action. However, outliers must *always* be reported in findings.

Data Enrichment

Data can often be made more relevant to the management problem by transforming it into more meaningful measures. For example: turnover and size of store can be expressed more meaningfully as *turnover per square metre*; closing share prices can be more usefully analysed as *daily percentage returns*. Data enrichment can also take place by combining categories (e.g. combine the age categories (21–25); (26–30) into (21–30)); or by aggregating values (e.g. data on individual household expenses can be aggregated to give *total* household expenses).

2.6 Summary

This chapter has examined data as the raw material of Statistics. An understanding of data is useful in the assessment of its quality and, hence, the validity of the statistical findings on which it is based.

Data quality is influenced by three important factors, i.e. the data type; the data source, and the method(s) used to gather the data. Data can be classified by a number of *different types*. The manner in which each data type influences the choice of an appropriate statistical method will be addressed more fully in later chapters. As shown in this chapter, *data sources* and *data gathering methods* all have an influence on the quality of data, and hence the *reliability* and *validity* of statistical findings.

Finally, to conclude Part 1 of the text, the importance of *data preparation* and *data cleaning* were shown to be essential prerequisites to conducting data analysis.

The remainder of the text, Parts 2 to 5, describe the manipulation of gathered data through various *statistical methods* with the purpose of generating useful information to support management decision making.

Exercises

2.1 For each of the following random variables, state the *data type* of each random variable (i.e. categorical or numeric); the *measurement scale* (i.e. nominal, ordinal, interval, or ratio scaled); and whether it is discrete or continuous. Also give two illustrative data values for each of these random variables.

(i) The *ages* of athletes in a marathon
(ii) The *floor area* of Foschini stores
(iii) The *highest qualification* of employees in an organisation
(iv) The *marital status* of employees
(v) The *different types of aircraft* used by SAA for domestic flights
(vi) The types of *child abuse* (physical, sexual, emotional, verbal)
(vii) The *performance appraisal rating scores* assigned to employees
(viii) The *ranked preferences* of employees to three different pay schemes.
(ix) Consumer responses to each of the following statements:
  (a) Rank your preferences of the fruit juices that you have just tasted
  Orange [1] Guava [2] Apple [3] Grape [4]
  (b) Do you enjoy your job?
  [Yes] [No]
  (c) Which mode of transport do you mostly use to commute to work?
  Car [1] Bus [2] Train [3] Taxi [4] Motorcycle [5] Bicycle [6]
  (d) "Returns on JSE equities are no better than those on unit trusts"
  Rate your response to this statement using the Likert rating scale:
  Strongly disagree [1] Disagree [2] Unsure [3] Agree [4] Strongly agree [5]
(x) The *weight* (in kg) of bags of potatoes
(xi) The *brand of coffee* you prefer
(xii) The *time taken* (in minutes) to travel to work
(xiii) The *grades* used to classify red meat [Prime, Super, First Grade, Standard]
(xiv) The *monthly premiums payable* on life assurance policies
(xv) The *number of patrons* in a cinema
(xvi) The *number of outlets* owned by a chainstore
(xvii) The *flying time* of an Airbus A-300 between Johannesburg and London
(xviii) How would you rate the *service level* of your bank?
Use the following semantic differential rating scale:
Extremely Poor [1] Very Poor [2] Poor [3] Unsure[4] Good [5] Very Good [6] Excellent [7]
(xix) The *number of copies* of the *Cape Times* sold daily by a café in Paarl
(xx) The *different sectors* of unit trusts.

2.2 Refer to the **Financial Analysis** schedule below. The data captured in this schedule is extracted from financial reports of JSE listed companies and is used to compile a database on the financial status of JSE listed companies.

(i) How many random variables are being studied in the questionnaire?
(ii) For each question, identify:

(a) the name of the random variable being measured;
(b) its data type (categorical or numeric); and
(c) its measurement scale (nominal; ordinal; interval and ratio) and whether it is discrete or continuous.

(iii) Give an illustrative data value for each random variable in the study.

Financial Analysis study

(1) Economic Sector

Mining	☐	Manufacturing	☐
Retail	☐	Insurance	☐
Financial	☐	Computers	☐

Other (specify) ....

(2) Head Office Region:

Gauteng	☐	Western Cape	☐
Free State	☐	Border	☐
Durban/Pinetown	☐	KwaZulu-Natal	☐

Other (specify) ....

(3) Company size (in terms of number of employees) ☐

(4) Turnover (rands per annum):

<1 million	☐	1–<5 million	☐
5–<10 million	☐	10–<20 million	☐
20–<50 million	☐	More than 50 million	☐

(5) Share price (in cents) as at 31 December 2006 ☐
(6) Earnings per share (in cents) for 2006 tax year ☐
(7) Dividends per share (in cents) for 2006 tax year ☐
(8) Number of shareholders as at 31 December 2006 ☐
(9) Return on investment for 2006 tax year ☐ %
(10) Inflation index for your economic sector ☐ %
(11) Year company was established ☐☐☐☐

2.3 Refer to the **Voyager Service Quality questionnaire** below.
(Note: Voyager is an SAA customer loyalty programme)

(i) How many random variables are being studied in the questionnaire?
(ii) For each question, identify:
(a) the name of the random variable being measured;
(b) its data type (categorical or numeric); and
(c) its measurement scale (nominal; ordinal; interval and ratio) and whether it is discrete or continuous.
(iii) Give an illustrative data value for each random variable in the study.

Voyager service quality questionnaire

Section A: Demographics

(1) Gender
Male ☐ Female ☐

(2) Home language
English ☐ Afrikaans ☐ Xhosa ☐ Other ☐

(3) Which of the following best describes your position in your company?
Junior manager ☐ Middle manager ☐ Senior manager ☐
Director ☐

(4) When did you join Voyager?
Pre-2002 ☐ 2003 ☐ 2004 ☐ 2005 ☐ 2006 ☐

(5) What is your Voyager membership status?
Blue ☐ Silver ☐ Gold ☐ Platinum ☐

Section B: Voyager usage level

(6) Have you ever claimed Voyager Awards?
Yes ☐ No ☐

(7) *(a)* Did you encounter any problems in claiming Voyager Awards?
Yes ☐ No ☐
(b) If 'yes', what kinds of problems did you encounter?
....
....
....

(8) How often have you used services by a *Voyager Partner* in the following categories?

	Never	*Rarely*	*Sometimes*	*Often*	*Always*
Airlines	1	2	3	4	5
Car rentals	1	2	3	4	5
Hotels and resorts	1	2	3	4	5
Financial services	1	2	3	4	5
Telecommunications	1	2	3	4	5

2.4 What essential differences are noticed between the **data types** gathered for the *Financial Analysis* database (**Exercise 2.2**) and the *Voyager Service Quality* study (**Exercise 2.3**)?

PART
2

Exploratory Data Analysis

Chapter 3

Using *Excel* for Statistical Analysis

Objectives

Excel has a number of useful, easy-to-use statistical capabilities for the analysis of data. This chapter *introduces* areas of *Excel* where statistical functionality can be found. The focus is on *learning how to use Excel* tools to perform statistical analysis. Interpretation of statistical findings using these tools is covered in later chapters.

After studying this chapter, you should be able to:

- sort, filter and validate data using the Data option in the menu bar
- use the functions key [f_x] to compute various statistical measures
- produce one-way and two-way pivot tables and corresponding charts using the Data option in the menu bar
- explain the meaning of numbers in a pivot table
- use the Data Analysis add-in for more advanced statistical analysis.

3.1 Introduction

This chapter shows how to use *Excel* to perform data analysis. *Excel* is not a comprehensive package for statistical analysis, but it does offer a wide selection of tools and techniques for basic statistical analysis. For more advanced statistical analysis, a user must migrate towards one of the widely accepted *statistics software* packages which are commercially available, such as *SAS*, *SPSS*, *Stata*, *S-Plus*, *Minitab* and *Number Cruncher* (*NCSS*), to name but a few.

There are five sections relevant to statistical analysis as offered by *Excel:*

(i) **Data Capturing**, including Data Validation
(ii) **Data Querying** (Interrogation), which involves sorting and filtering (drilling down)
(iii) The **Functions key** facility for single function operations
(iv) **Summary Tables** (pivot tables) and **Graphing** capabilities
(v) The **Data Analysis** add-in module to extend the range of statistical analysis.

3.2 Data Capture (and Validation)

In *Excel,* data is recorded in a *worksheet* with a maximum of 65 536 rows and 220 columns. Therefore the maximum possible sample size (n) is just over 65 000 records (respondents) with each record having a maximum of 220 variables (responses).

Each row records all the data values for a single respondent and it is usual to use **row 1** to label the variables using **variable names**. Each column, on the other hand, records all the data values for a single variable and, again, it is good practice to use the first column (**column A**) to identify the respondents (i.e. use it for **record identification** purposes).

Figure 3.1 overleaf illustrates a sample database of 25 financial advisors for an insurance company. Refer to the *Excel* file: C3.1 – financial advisors.

The following data is recorded for each advisor: his or her *employee number* (**Advisor ID**) followed by the *insurance product* he or she mostly sells (**Product**) (1 = Life Assurance; 2 = Short-term Insurance); years of *sales experience* (**Experience**); work-related *qualifications* (**Qualification**); (1 = work experience only; 2 = product knowledge training; 3 = financial planning diploma); and his or her annual *performance appraisal score* (**Perform**).

There are four random variables in this database: two are numeric (i.e. *Experience* and *Performance*), as their values are real numbers; and two are categorical (i.e. *Product* and *Qualification*), as only codes are used to represent a particular category. Column A (*Advisor ID*) is not used for analysis purposes as it simply identifies the financial advisor in each row.

Figure 3.1 Data capture of financial advisors' Performance Appraisal database

Advisor ID	Product	Exper	Qualif	Perform
F21	1	12	2	74
M12	2	18	2	78
F53	1	6	1	65
F19	1	8	2	76
M65	2	18	1	66
M36	2	27	2	76
M19	2	21	2	66
F03	1	14	1	82
F65	1	28	3	90
M92	2	22	2	70
M42	2	20	1	65
M16	2	22	1	68
M45	2	16	3	84
F15	1	33	3	90
F50	2	12	1	50
F45	1	5	1	57
F76	1	24	2	68
F28	1	25	3	92
M73	2	16	1	66
F26	2	2	1	56
M36	2	32	1	72
M21	1	27	1	92
F69	1	25	2	78
M56	2	10	1	56
M48	2	26	3	72

Captured data should be clean (i.e. as complete, valid, accurate and error free as possible) before proceeding with statistical analysis. In *Excel*, the Validation option in the Data command (from the menu bar) can be used to restrict data values to within a specified range (e.g. *employee age* to between 18 and 65 years) or to specific values only (e.g. for *gender*, use 1 = male, and 2 = female, only) for any variable. If any data values are entered that fall outside these valid ranges or specified values, an error message will be displayed to alert the data capturer to the invalid entry.

3.3 Data Querying/Interrogation

A preliminary step to performing more formal statistical analysis, is to run a few basic queries on the data set to "get a feel for the data" and to highlight possible errors, either due to data capturing or coding errors. This can be done by sorting the data in ascending (or descending) order and/or scanning subsets of the complete data set (filtering).

Sorting Data

From the menu bar: Data – Sort

A sort of the data set (by selecting a primary sort variable) will identify the **minimum** and **maximum** values in a data set for the sort variable. An *inspection* of the ordered data will highlight *any outliers* (extreme values) and allow an analyst to check their validity before using the data for further analysis.

HOW TO

To sort a database

- Highlight the complete database, including variable names in row 1.
- Select Data (from the menu bar) and then select Sort.
- Select the Sort Variable from the Sort by list and then click OK.

The database will be arranged – by default – in ascending order of the values of the sort variable. If more than one sort variable is selected, the database is sorted first by the primary sort variable, and then by the secondary sort variable(s).

Filtering Data

From the menu bar: Data – Filter – Autofilter

The filter option in *Excel* allows an analyst to view only *subsets of data records* that meet specified criteria. A cursory *inspection* of a sub-sample of the data set provides additional insight into the profile of the data set.

HOW TO

To filter data

- Highlight the complete database, including variable names in row 1.
- Select Data (from the menu bar) and then Filter, followed by Autofilter.
- Each variable name (row 1) will now have a drop-down arrow next to it.
- Choose a Filter Variable by clicking its drop-down arrow.
- Select the data value(s) on which to filter (options exist to choose a range of values).
- To restore the full database to view, select the All option for the filter variable(s).

When filtered by the value(s) of a filter variable, only those records that satisfy the filter conditions are displayed. This represents a sub-sample of the complete database. A visual inspection of these records may highlight some useful patterns (e.g. financial advisors with Qualification 1 may have low performance appraisal scores; those with Qualification 3 may have higher performance appraisal scores).

3.4 Using the Functions Key [f_x]

A wide range of basic mathematical, statistical and financial calculations can be performed using *Excel's Functions key* [f_x] in the toolbar. A function key uses a **single name** to activate a calculation.

For example, the function key SUM will find the sum of a set of values; the function key AVERAGE will find the average of a set of values; and the function key MAX will find the maximum value for a set of numbers.

HOW TO

To view the full list of available functions key operations

- Click on [f_x] in the toolbar and select the All category from the **Function Category** list.
- Scroll down the right-hand side in the **Function name** list, noting the range of analytical operations.

Figure 3.2 illustrates a selection of operations that can be performed in the **Statistical** Function category. Every **Function name** is followed by brackets in which a number of **arguments** are specified. Arguments identify the data required for analysis and any other necessary conditions to activate the function.

HOW TO

To activate a particular function

- Place the cursor in a desired destination cell.
- Highlight the **Function name** (from the right column of Figure 3.2), click OK.
- The specific **arguments** required to execute the function are presented and the user must provide the necessary input.
- When all arguments are given, the result is shown in the specified destination cell.

Alternatively, to use a function key, the function name and its argument(s) can be typed directly into the destination cell (if the analyst knows the syntax). *Note:* The function name *must always* start with an arithmetic operator such as = or +.

Figure 3.2 A selection of statistical operations using the functions key $[f_x]$.

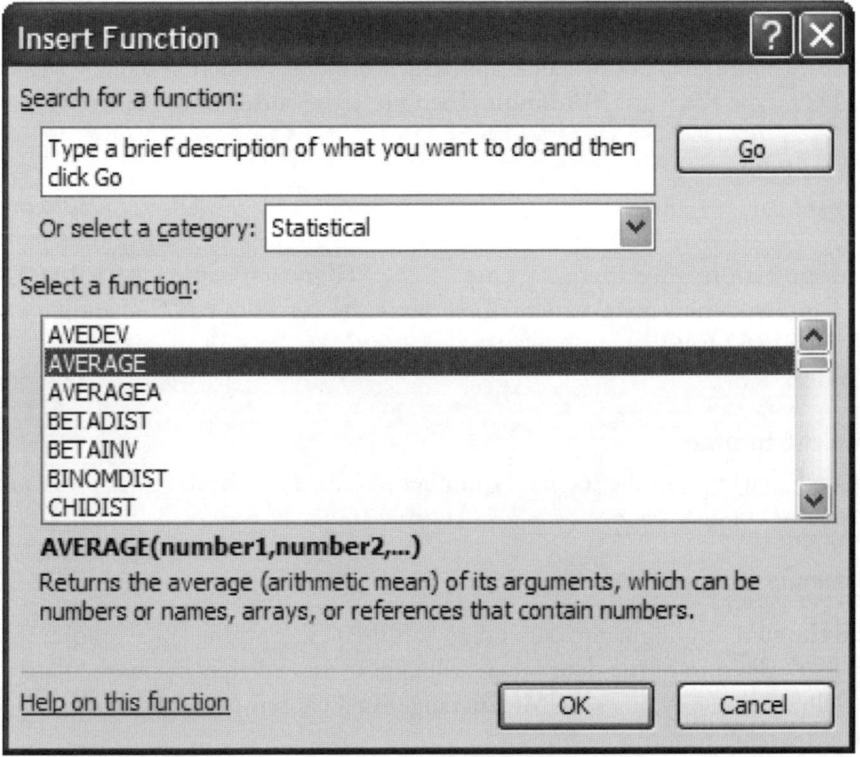

Example 3.1 Financial Advisors – Performance Appraisal study

Refer to the database in Figure 3.1. *Excel* file: **C3.1 – financial advisors**

Management question

Refer to the **Perform** variable in the data range (E1:E26). Use the appropriate functions key to find:

(i) the sum
(ii) the minimum value, and
(iii) the average value

for the scores of the *performance appraisal* variable.

Solution using *Excel*

For each of the examples, select [f_x] from the toolbar to display the **Insert Function** screen. Select **Statistical** from the **Function category** and the appropriate function name from the **Function name** list.

(i) The total (sum) of performance appraisal scores. (Function name = SUM)
In cell D28, type the word **Sum**. Then place the cursor in cell E28 and type:
= SUM(E2:E26)
Press **enter**. Answer = 1 808 score

(ii) The lowest (minimum) performance appraisal score. (Function name = MIN)
In cell D29, type the word **Minimum**. Then place the cursor in cell E29 and type:
= MIN(E2:E26)
Press **enter**. Answer = 50 score

(iii) The average performance appraisal score. (Function name = AVERAGE)
In cell D30, type the word **Average**. Then place the cursor in cell E30 and type:
= AVERAGE(E2:E26)
Press **enter**. Answer = 72,32 score

The [Σ] key in the toolbar

The Summation [Σ] symbol in the toolbar is another *shortcut Function key* to find the *sum of* a column (or row) of *data values.*

HOW TO

To find the sum of data values

To find the sum, highlight the data range and then click on the [Σ] symbol from the toolbar. The sum of the data values will appear immediately below the data range. Alternatively, typing = SUM(data range) in a chosen destination cell will produce the same result.

Example 3.2 Financial Advisors – Experience study

Refer to the database in Figure 3.1. *Excel* file: **C3.1 – financial advisors**

Management question

Use the SUM symbol [Σ] in the toolbar to find the *total number of years of experience* of the 25 financial advisors.

Solution using *Excel*

- Highlight the input data range (C2:C26).
- Select the [Σ] symbol in the toolbar.
- The sum is placed in the destination cell C27. Answer = 469 years

3.5 Tables and Charts

From the menu bar: Data – Pivot Table and Pivot Chart Report

Pivot tables are a very useful *Excel* feature to summarise data into tables and charts. This makes it easier to interpret the data.

Pivot tables are useful for:

(i) *summarising categorical measures* into frequency counts for either a single variable (one-way pivot table) or two variables together (two-way pivot table), and

(ii) *splitting numeric measures* (e.g. sales) into sub-samples (e.g. by stores) to compare various descriptive statistics (e.g. total sales per store; average sales per store).

3.5.1 Constructing a One-way Pivot Table

A one-way pivot table can be constructed only for a single categorical variable. It is called a **frequency table** in statistics, since it *counts* the number (or percentage) of cases in each category of the categorical variable.

HOW TO

To create a one-way pivot table

- Highlight the data range of the categorical variable to be summarised.
- From the menu bar, select Data, then PivotTable and PivotChart Report and follow the three steps of the PivotTable Wizard instructions:
  - At step 1, click **Next >** if the default options **Microsoft Office Excel list or database** and **PivotTable** are both selected (radio buttons on)
  - At step 2, click **Next >** if the **Range** box shows the data range of the selected variable(s) – which it should do if the data range was highlighted upfront.
  - At step 3, select the Layout option to structure the pivot table as follows:
    - Drag the chosen categorical variable icon to the **ROW box**.

- Drag this same variable icon to the **DATA box**.
- "Count of (Variable name)" must appear in the **DATA box**. If not, double click on this box and select "**Count**" from the **PivotTable Field** screen.
- Select OK, then select OK again, and finally select Finish.

The resulting one-way pivot table appears in a separate worksheet and shows the *count of the number of cases* (records) – called **frequency counts** – for each category of the analysed variable.

To convert these frequency counts to *percentages*, right-click anywhere in the count column of the Pivot Table, select Field Settings, then Options and press the down arrow on Show data as: to scroll to the % of total option. Select OK.

Example 3.3 Financial Advisors – Qualifications study

Refer to the database in Figure 3.1. *Excel* file: C3.1 – financial advisors

Management questions

(1) Construct a *one-way pivot table* (of counts only) for the **Qualification** variable.
(2) Show the frequency counts as percentages.

Then answer the following questions:
(i) How many financial advisors had *product knowledge* training only?
(ii) What percentage of financial advisors had *work experience* only?

Solution using *Excel*

Figure 3.3 overleaf shows the **Layout dialog box** to compute the one-way pivot table for the **Qualification** variable, and Figure 3.4 shows the computed one-way pivot table for both *frequency counts* (Table 1) and *percentages* (Table 2).

The answers to the two questions are:
(i) Eight of the 25 financial advisors had *product knowledge* training (see Table 1).
(ii) 48% of the financial advisors had *work experience* only (see Table 2).

Figure 3.3 The pivot table layout dialog box for the **Qualification** variable

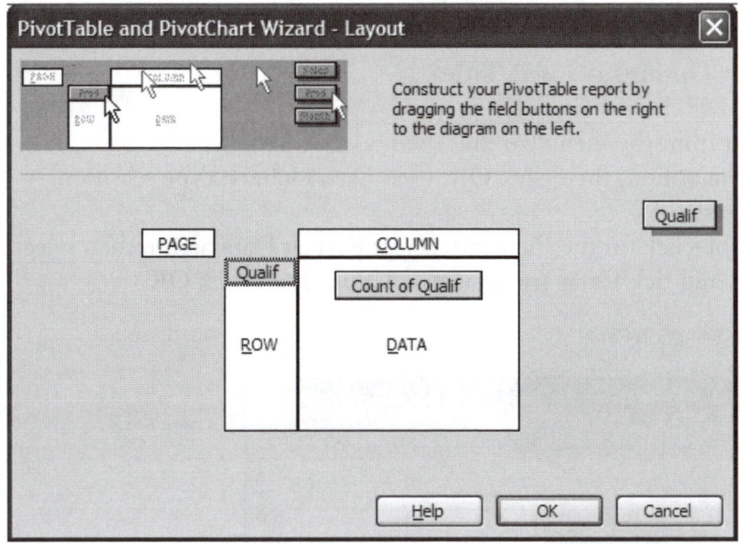

Figure 3.4 One-way pivot table of **Qualification** (counts and percentage)

Qualifications of Financial Advisors

Table 1: Frequency Counts

Count of Qualif	
Qualif	**Total**
Work	12
Training	8
Diploma	5
Grand Total	25

Table 2: Percentages

Count of Qualif	
Qualif	**Total**
Work	48%
Training	32%
Diploma	20%
Grand Total	100%

Note: Category codes can be replaced with labels by typing a suitable text label in each cell. For *example*, **Qualification**: 1 = Work; 2 = Training; and 3 = Diploma.

3.5.2 Constructing Charts of a One-way Pivot Table

The pivot table can be viewed graphically as a **bar chart** or a **pie chart**.

HOW TO

To produce a bar chart from the one-way pivot table

- Right-click anywhere inside the one-way pivot table.
- Select the PivotChart option from the drop-down menu to show a Bar Chart.
- The default Bar Chart can be changed by selecting Chart from the **menu bar**.

- To edit a chart to show the data counts or percentages per bar:
  - Right-click on any bar in the Bar chart
  - Select **Format Data Series** then select **Data Labels** and tick the **Value** box.
  - Select **Chart Options** to insert **Titles**.
- To change the bar chart to a pie chart:
  - Select **Chart** from the menu bar and then select **Chart Type**.
  - Select the **Pie** option, then click **OK**. (See *Excel's* **Chart Type** selection panel in Figure 3.5.)
  - To **edit**, right-click on the Pie chart, select **Format Data Series**, then select **Data Labels** and tick **Category name** and **Value**. Then click **OK.**

Figure 3.5 Excel's Chart Type Selection Panel

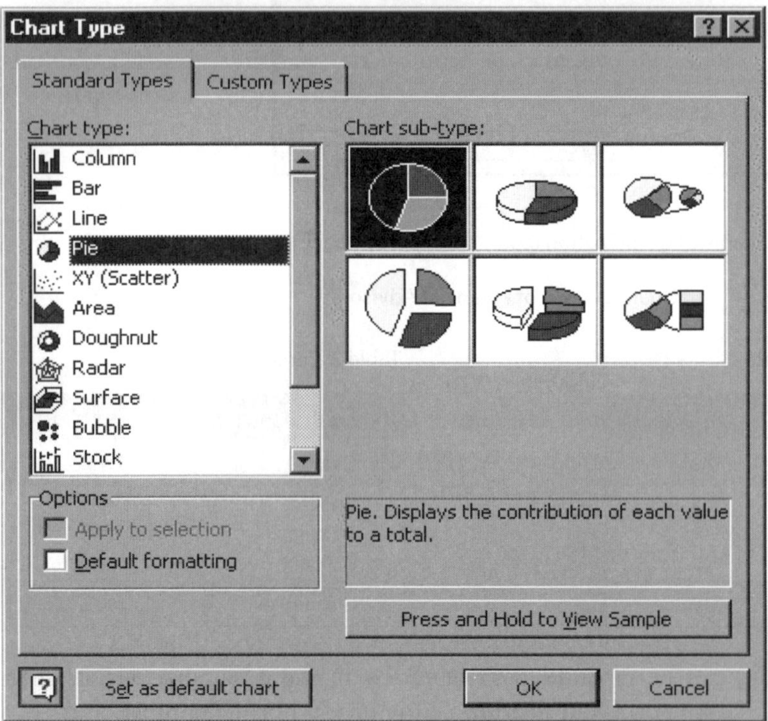

Example 3.4 Financial Advisors – Bar and Pie charts of Qualifications

Refer to the database in Figure 3.1. *Excel* file: **C3.1 – financial advisors**

Management question

Display the *percentage pivot table* for the **Qualification** variable from Table 2 in Figure 3.4 as:
(i) a bar chart, and (ii) a pie chart. Also show the *category percentages.*

Solution using *Excel*

Figure 3.6 below shows the bar chart (Chart 1) and pie chart (Chart 2) for the **Qualification** variable.

Figure 3.6 Graphic Display of Pivot Tables (Bar and Pie charts) for **Qualification**

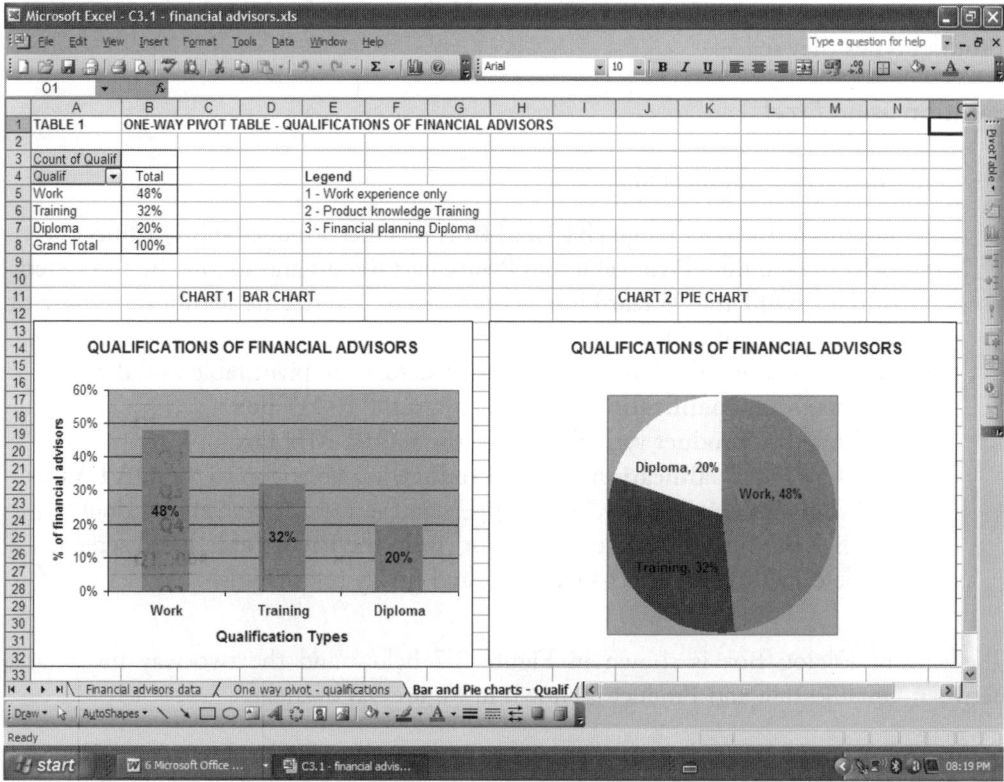

3.5.3 Constructing a Two-way Pivot Table

In statistics, there is often the need to:

- examine the *association* between two *categorical* variables, or
- split a *numeric variable* into a number of *sub-samples* for purposes of comparison.

A two-way pivot table can be used for both purposes.

Examine the association between two categorical variables

When two categorical variables are summarised together in a two-way pivot table, the table shows the number of cases (records) associated with each combination of the outcomes of the two categorical variables.

The same procedure is used to construct a two-way pivot table as was used for a one-way pivot table (see above), except that a second categorical variable is included in the layout table by dragging this second variable to the COLUMN box.

Example 3.5 Financial Advisors – Qualifications by Product Type study

Refer to the database in Figure 3.1. *Excel* file: C3.1 – financial advisors

Management question

Create a *two-way pivot table* between the **Qualifications** of financial advisors and the **Product types** they sell.

Solution using *Excel*

To create a two-way pivot table

- Highlight the data range [B1:E26] (this includes Product and Qualification).
- Select Data, then PivotTable and PivotChart Report and follow the three steps of the **PivotTable Wizard** instructions. Steps 1 and 2 are identical to those of a one-way pivot table.
- At step 3, select the Layout option to structure the pivot table as follows:
  - Drag the **Qualification** variable icon to the **ROW box**.
  - Drag the **Product** variable icon to the **COLUMN box**.
  - Drag the **Qualification** (or the **Product**) variable icon to the **DATA box**.
  - "Count of Qualification" must appear in the DATA box. If not, double click on this box and select "Count" from the **PivotTable Field** screen.
  - Select OK, then select OK again, and finally select Finish.

The Layout Dialog Box is shown in Figure 3.7 below and the two-way pivot table between Qualification and Product is shown in Figure 3.8 overleaf.

Figure 3.7 Two-way Pivot Table Layout Dialog box for **Qualifications** vs **Product Types**

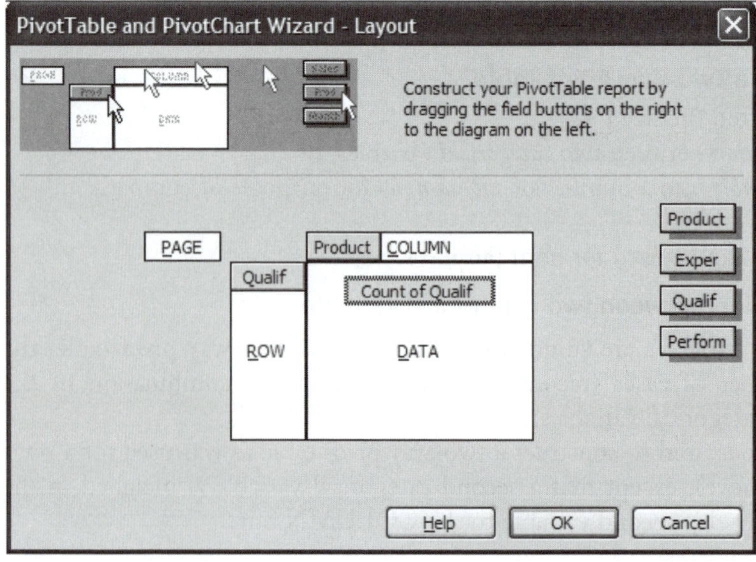

Figure 3.8 Two-way Pivot Table between **Qualifications** and **Product** Type sold

Count of Qualif	Product		
Qualif	Life	Short term	Grand Total
Work	4	8	12
Training	4	4	8
Diploma	3	2	5
Grand Total	11	14	25

Note Labels can replace category codes for both variables by typing suitable text labels into the appropriate cells. For *example,* **Qualification** 1 = Work; 2 = Training; 3 = Diploma. For **Product** type 1 = Life; 2 = Short term.

Management interpretation

The Grand Total column shows the frequency counts for the three categories of qualifications only; the Grand Total row shows the frequency counts for the two product types sold only; the joint frequency counts are shown by the counts between pairs of categories (e.g. there are eight financial advisors who have qualification type 1 (work experience only) and sell product type 2 (short-term insurance).

HOW TO

To change the frequency counts to percentages

- Right-click on any count value in the two-way pivot table.
- Select Field Settings from the drop-down menu, then select Options >>.
- Click on the Show data as: down-arrow and choose one of three possible percentage displays: % of row, % of column, or % of total, whichever interpretation is desired.

3.5.4 Stacked bar charts for a two-way pivot table

The two-way pivot table can be shown graphically as either a **stacked bar chart** or a **multiple bar chart**. A graph could make it easier to see the possible association between the two categorical variables, as shown in a two-way pivot table.

HOW TO

To create a stacked bar chart

- Right-click anywhere inside the pivot table.
- Select PivotChart from the menu bar. A stacked (component) bar chart is produced and shown in a separate worksheet.
- To edit a chart to show the data counts or percentages for each component in a bar:
  - Right-click on any component in a bar in the stacked bar chart.
  - Select Format Data Series then select Data Labels and tick the Value box.

Example 3.6 Financial Advisors – Chart of Qualifications by Product Type

Refer to the database in Figure 3.1. *Excel* file: **C3.1 – financial advisors**

Management question

Construct a *stacked bar chart* between the **Qualifications** of the sample of 25 financial advisors and the **Product** types they each sell.

Solution using *Excel*

Figure 3.9 below shows the stacked bar chart (Chart 1) based on the two-way pivot table in Figure 3.8.

Figure 3.9 Stacked Bar Chart between **Qualifications** and **Product** type sold

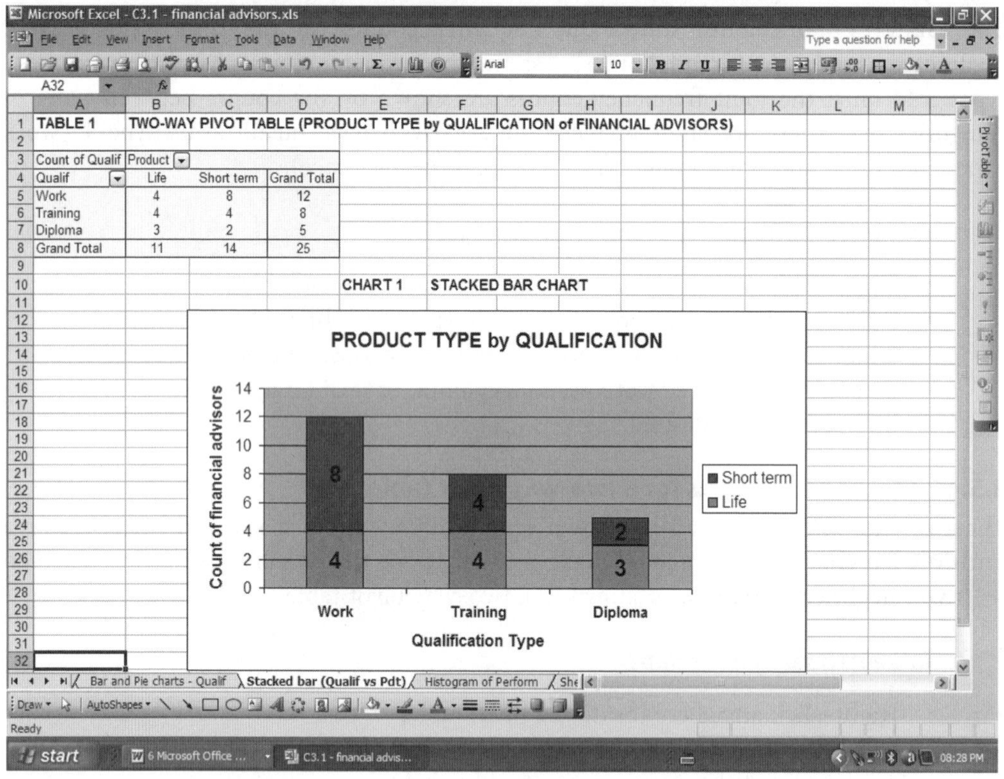

Management interpretation

Each bar shows the total number of financial advisors with each type of *qualification*. Each bar is then split into two components, each showing the number of financial advisors selling *product types* 1 (*life assurance*) and 2 (*short-term insurance*) respectively. For example, there are 12 (4 + 8) financial advisors with *work experience only* (qualification type 1), of whom four are selling *life assurance* products (product type 1) and eight are selling *short-term insurance* products (product type 2).

3.5.5 Splitting a numeric variable into sub-samples

The Pivot Table facility in *Excel* can also be used to split the data values of a *numeric variable* into sub-samples that correspond to categories of a categorical variable. Various descriptive statistical measures (e.g. minimum, sum, count, average, maximum) can then be displayed for each sub-sample. This makes it possible to compare relevant statistics between samples.

HOW TO

To create sub-samples for a numeric variable

- Highlight the database to include the numeric variable to be split into sub-samples and the categorical variable that will define the categories for the different samples.
- Create a two-way pivot table (as above), but with the following procedure at **step 3** of the **PivotTable and PivotChart Wizard**:
  - Drag the *categorical* variable to the ROW box.
  - Drag the *numeric* variable to the DATA box.
  - In the DATA box, double click the operation specified (e.g. Sum of [Numeric variable]) and select the desired descriptive analysis from the **PivotTable Field** screen (i.e. sum, count, average, max, min, etc.)
  - Select **OK**, then **OK** again, and finally **Finish**.

Example 3.7 Financial Advisors – Performance Assessment by Product Type study

Refer to the database in Figure 3.1. *Excel* file: **C3.1 – financial advisors**

Management question

Split the *performance assessment* scores of financial advisors into sub-samples by *product type* and show the **average** *performance assessment* score per *product type.*

Solution using *Excel*

HOW TO

To construct this two-way pivot table:

- Highlight the database from [B1:E26].
- Select **Data** and **PivotTable and PivotChart Report** and follow the Wizard to step 3.
- At step 3:
  - Drag the **Product** variable icon to the ROW box (this creates the sub-samples).
  - Drag the **Perform** variable icon to the DATA box (the numeric variable to split).
  - Double click on the operation in the DATA box and select **average** from the **PivotTable Field** screen list of operations.
  - Select **OK**, then **OK** again and finally **Finish**.

Figure 3.10 below shows the two-way pivot table for the average *performance assessment* scores of financial advisors split into the two *product type* sub-samples.

Figure 3.10 Average **Performance Assessment** scores by **Product Type** sold

Average of *Perform*	
Product	Total
Life	78,545
Short term	67,5
Grand Total	72,36

Note: The product codes (1, 2) can be replaced with labels by typing a suitable text label in each cell (e.g. for **Product** type: 1 = Life; 2 = Short term).

Management interpretation

The ***average*** *performance assessment score* for financial advisors who sell life assurance products (type 1) is 78,545, while those who sell short-term insurance products (type 2) have a much lower average performance assessment score of 67,5.

To create separate data sets for each sub-sample

- Double click on the descriptive statistic for a given sub-sample (e.g. on the average of 67,5 for product type 2).
- This operation will result in a new worksheet being created, containing all the cases (records) belonging only to the sub-sample selected.

By double-clicking on the average performance assessment value of 67,5 for product type 2, a new worksheet is created which contains only the records of financial advisors who sell product type 2. This will allow for separate statistical analysis to be done on this sub-sample of data only.

To create a bar chart for sub-samples of data

Follow the exact same procedure as the one used to construct a bar chart from a one-way pivot table.

3.6 Using Excel's Data Analysis Add-In

Excel has a **Data Analysis add-in** macro, which extends the range of statistical analyses that can be performed to include more advanced techniques. The Data Analysis add-in is provided with the *Excel* software, but needs to be specifically installed before use.

To install** Microsoft Excel's **Data Analysis ToolPak

- Select from the menu bar, **Tools** and then the **Add-Ins** option.
- Tick the **Analysis ToolPak** box. Click **OK**.

To use the Data Analysis Add-In

- From the menu bar, select **Tools** and **Data Analysis**.

Figure 3.11 (a) and (b) shows all 19 statistical techniques available in the **Data Analysis** add-in.

Figure 3.11(a) Data Analysis dialog box (first 10 techniques)

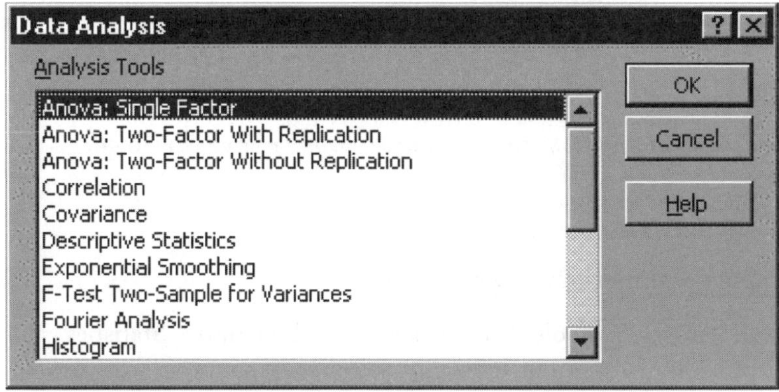

Figure 3.11 (b) Data Analysis dialog box (remaining 9 techniques)

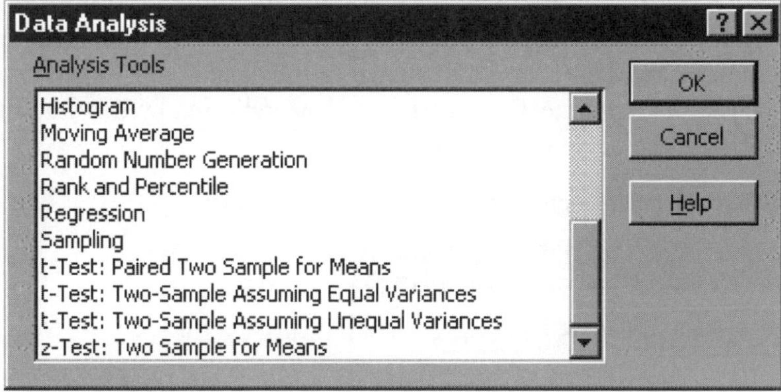

To use a particular data analysis tool, select the required statistical procedure; identify the appropriate input data ranges, output options; and execute. The data preparation and statistical output for two of these data analysis tools, namely **Descriptive Statistics** and **Histogram** are illustrated below.

3.6.1 The descriptive statistics tool

Example 3.8 Financial Advisors – Performance Assessment Descriptive Statistics

Refer to the database in Figure 3.1. *Excel* file: **C3.1 – financial advisors**

Management question

Compute the *descriptive statistics* for the *performance assessment* variable, **Perform.**

Solution using *Excel*

To compute Descriptive Statistics using Data Analysis

- From the menu bar, select **Tools, Data Analysis** and **Descriptive Statistics.**
- At the Descriptive Statistics input screen:
  - enter the data range [E1:E26] in the **Input Range** box
  - tick the **Labels in First Row** box, since the variable name is included in the data range
  - tick the **Summary statistics** box, and click **OK**.

The data preparation screen for the **Descriptive Statistics** tool is shown in Figure 3.12 for the **Performance Assessment** variable (column E) shown in the database of Figure 3.1. The output will be displayed in a separate *Excel* worksheet – as indicated by the Output options in Figure 3.12. This is the default output option.

Figure 3.12 Data preparation screen for descriptive statistics for the **Perform** variable

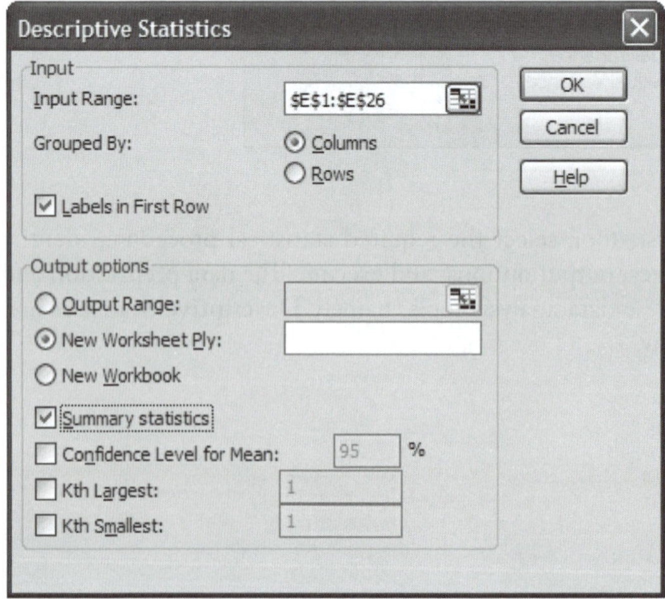

The statistical output is shown in Figure 3.13 overleaf.

Overall, these descriptive measures show how the 25 financial advisors were rated on their *performance assessments*. A full interpretation of these measures is given in later chapters when the various statistical terms and concepts are covered.

Figure 3.13 Descriptive statistics output for the **Performance Assessment** variable

Perform	
Mean	72,36
Standard Error	2,3309
Median	72
Mode	66
Standard Deviation	11,6543
Sample Variance	135,8233
Kurtosis	–0,5687
Skewness	0,1074
Range	42
Minimum	50
Maximum	92
Sum	1 809
Count	25

3.6.2 The histogram tool

A histogram is a *graphic display* of a frequency table for a numeric variable. The frequency table is similar to a one-way pivot table, except that the data values must first be grouped into intervals – called **bin ranges** in *Excel* – before they can be displayed graphically.

Example 3.9 Financial Advisors – Performance Assessment Histogram

Refer to the database in Figure 3.1. *Excel* file: **C3.1 – financial advisors**

Management question

Construct a *histogram* of the *performance assessment* scores of the 25 financial advisors.

Solution using *Excel*

To construct a histogram

- Set up a **bin range** in the same worksheet as the database. The bin range defines the upper limits for each interval into which the data will be grouped. For the **Performance Assessment** variable, these bin upper limits could be: 60; 70; 80; 90; and 100. Enter these limits, together with a bin range name (e.g. **Perform Bin**), in the cell range [E28:E33].
- From the menu bar, select **Tools**, then **Data Analysis** and **Histogram**.
- At the Histogram Input Screen: (as shown in Figure 3.14 below)
  - enter the data range [E1:E26] in the **Input Range** box
  - enter the bin range [E28:E33] in the **Bin Range** box

- tick the **Labels** box, since the variable names are included in both the input range and bin range cell references
- tick the **Chart Output** box (which will show the histogram graphically)
- from the output options, select **Output Range** to show the output in the same worksheet as the database, starting at cell H3. Finally, click **OK**.

The data preparation screen for the histogram is shown in Figure 3.14.

Figure 3.14 Data preparation screen of the histogram for the **Perform** variable

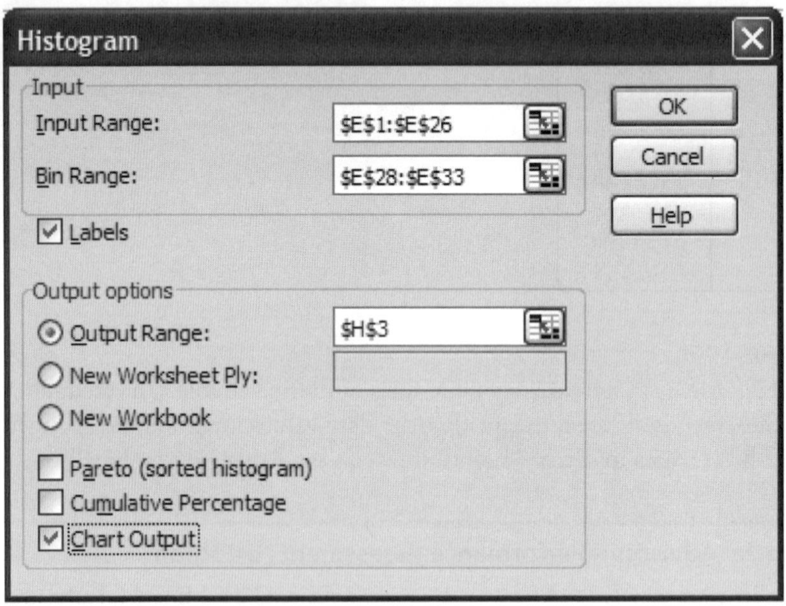

The computed *frequency table* and *histogram* is shown in Figure 3.15 overleaf.

When initially produced, the histogram will have gaps between the bars. There should be no gaps in a histogram. To set the gap to zero, right-click on any bar in the histogram, select **Format Data Series** then **Options** and toggle the **Gap width** box to show 0.

To insert **Data Labels** and **Data Values** on each bar, refer to the steps listed in section 3.5 for pivot tables.

Figure 3.15 Frequency table and histogram for **Performance Assessment**

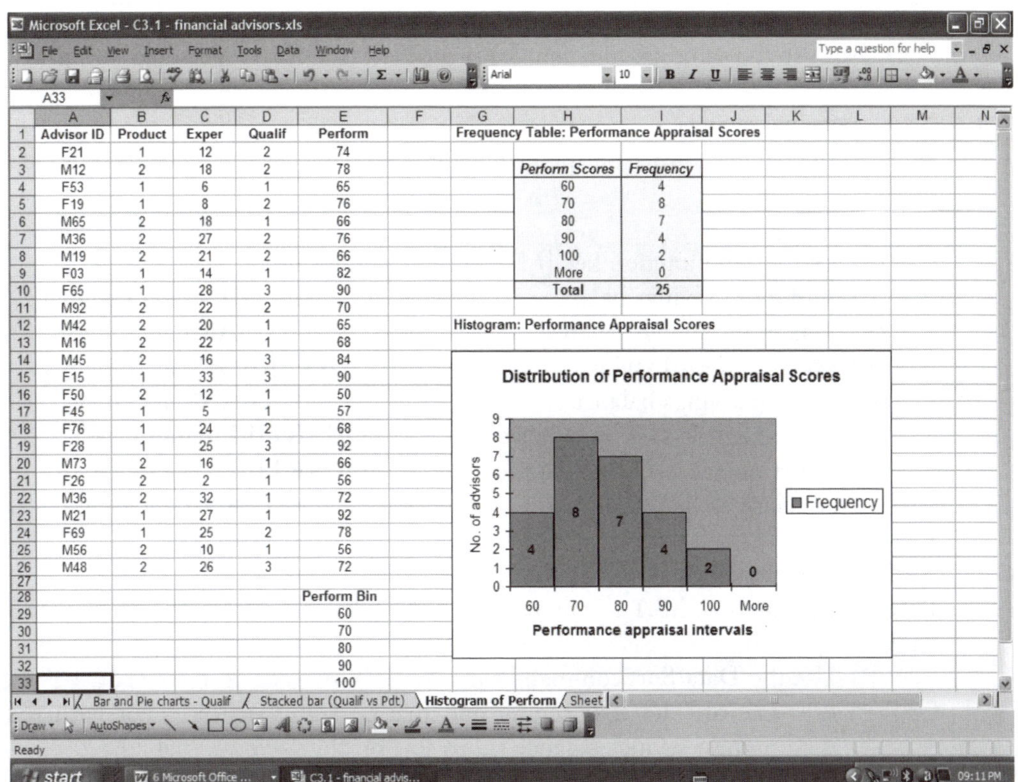

Advisor ID	Product	Exper	Qualif	Perform
F21	1	12	2	74
M12	2	18	2	78
F53	1	6	1	65
F19	1	8	2	76
M65	2	18	1	66
M36	2	27	2	76
M19	2	21	2	66
F03	1	14	1	82
F65	1	28	3	90
M92	2	22	2	70
M42	2	20	1	65
M16	2	22	1	68
M45	2	16	3	84
F15	1	33	3	90
F50	2	12	1	50
F45	1	5	1	57
F76	1	24	2	68
F28	1	25	3	92
M73	2	16	1	66
F26	2	2	1	56
M36	2	32	1	72
M21	1	27	1	92
F69	1	25	2	78
M56	2	10	1	56
M48	2	26	3	72

Perform Bin
60
70
80
90
100

Perform Scores	Frequency
60	4
70	8
80	7
90	4
100	2
More	0
Total	25

Management interpretation

The frequency table and the histogram show that four financial advisors had the lowest performance assessment scores at 60 or below; eight financial advisors had the most common performance assessment scores of between 61 and 70; while two financial advisors had the highest performance assessment scores of between 91 and 100.

The remaining 17 data analysis tools are executed in much the same way as the Descriptive Statistics and Histogram tools illustrated above.

3.7 Summary

This chapter provided a broad overview of *Excel's* statistical capabilities. Many of these techniques will be used in various statistical analyses in the following chapters. A reader should therefore familiarise him or herself with these *Excel* operations and seek to further develop his or her understanding of the use of *Excel* as a tool to performing basic statistical analysis with relative ease. Later chapters place more emphasis on the interpretation of these statistical outputs in a management context.

Exercises

All the exercises use the same sample data from the *Excel* file **X3.1 – personal savings.**

3.1 **X3.1 – personal savings**

Refer to the database **X3.1** on the *personal savings* balances of 25 clients of a local bank.

Use the appropriate function key [f_x] operation to find the:

(i)	minimum savings balance	**=MIN**(data range)
(ii)	maximum savings balance	**=MAX**(data range)
(iii)	average (mean) savings balance	**=AVERAGE**(data range)
(iv)	median savings balance	**=MEDIAN**(data range)
(v)	lower quartile savings balance	**=QUARTILE**(data range,1)
(vi)	upper quartile savings balance	**=QUARTILE**(data range,3)
(vii)	standard deviation of savings balances	**=STDEV**(data range)

3.2 **X3.1 – personal savings**

Refer to the database **X3.1** on the *personal savings* balances of 25 clients of a local bank.

(i) Use the **Data/Sort** command to:

- (a) identify the age, gender and marital status of the client with the highest savings balance (hint: sort on the *savings* variable);
- (b) identify savings balance of the youngest client (hint: sort on the *age* variable).

(ii) Use the **Data/Filter/AutoFilter** command to identify:

- (a) the subset of clients who are *married*
- (b) the subset of clients who are *single* and *female*
- (c) the subset of clients who are *under 30* years of *age*
- (d) the subset of *female clients* with a savings balance of *R5 000 or more*
- (e) clients who are *over 40 years* with a savings balance of *less than R3 000.*

Hint: In (c), (d) and (e), use the **custom** option from the drop-down list.

3.3 **X3.1 – personal savings**

Refer to the database **X3.1** on the *personal savings* balances of 25 clients of a local bank.

(i) Use the **Tools/Data Analysis/Descriptive Statistics** command to produce the summary statistics for the *savings* variable.

(ii) Identify the mean, standard deviation, skewness, range, minimum, and maximum savings values from the output.

3.4 X3.1 – personal savings

Refer to the database **X3.1** on the *personal savings* balances of 25 clients of a local bank.

(i) Use the **Tools/Data Analysis/Histogram** command to construct a *frequency table* and a *histogram* for the *savings* variable.
Hint: Set up a bin range for the intervals {2000, 3000, 4000, 5000, 6000, 7000}.

(ii) Which savings interval(s) has the most number of clients?; three or fewer clients?

3.5 X3.1 – personal savings

Refer to the database **X3.1** on the *personal savings* balances of 25 clients of a local bank.

Use the **Data/PivotTable and PivotChart Report** command to construct each of the following pivot tables.

(i) (a) Construct a one-way pivot table of the *gender* variable.
(b) How many of the clients are male? What percentage of the clients are female?
(c) Show the results of the one-way pivot table graphically as a pie chart.

(ii) (a) Construct a one-way pivot table of the *marital* status variable.
(b) How many of the clients are married? What percentage of the clients are single?
(c) Show the results of the one-way pivot table graphically as a bar chart.

(iii) (a) Construct a two-way pivot table between the *gender* and *marital* status.
(b) How many clients are single males? What percentage of clients are married females?
(c) Show the results of the two-way pivot table graphically as a stacked bar chart.

3.6 X3.1 – personal savings

Refer to the database **X3.1** on the *personal savings* balances of 25 clients of a local bank.

Use the **Data/PivotTable and PivotChart Report** command to split the *savings* variable into different sub-samples as follows.

(i) (a) Construct a one-way pivot table to show the *total savings* between married and single clients.
(b) Which marital status group of clients has the larger total savings with the bank?
(c) Show the results of the one-way breakdown table as a bar chart.

(ii) (a) Construct a one-way pivot table to show the difference between the *average savings* of male and the *average savings* female clients.
(b) Which gender group saves less on average?
(c) Show the results of the one-way pivot table as a bar chart.

3.7 X3.1 – personal savings

Refer to the database **X3.1** on the *personal savings* balances of 25 clients of a local bank.

Use the **Data/PivotTable and PivotChart Report** command to construct the following sub-samples for *savings* variable.

(i) Construct a two-way pivot table (using *gender* and *marital*) to show the *average savings* between single males, single females, married males and married females.

(ii) Which group of clients saves the most, on average? the least, on average?

(iii) Show the results of the two-way breakdown table as a component bar chart (called a **clustered column chart** in the Chart Wizard).

3.8 X3.1 – personal savings

Refer to the database **X3.1** on the *personal savings* balances of 25 clients of a local bank.

(i) Transform numeric data (variable *savings*) into categorical data as follows:

Use the **IF(logical test, Value_if_true, Value_if_false)** function to transform the *savings values* in column D into *savings categories* in column E based on the following decision rule:

If a client's savings balance is less than R4 000, classify the balance as "*Low*"

If a client's savings balance is R4 000 or more, classify the balance as "*High*".

Hint: Type the variable name *Savings_Cat* in cell E1.
In cell E2, type =IF(D2<4000, "Low", "High")
Then copy cell E2 to the data range [E3:E26].

(ii) Use the savings categories from column E and construct a bar chart showing the percentage of clients in each category.

Hint: Use the **PivotTable and PivotChart Report** command and select **"% of total"**.

3.9 X3.1 – personal savings

Refer to the database **X3.1** on the *personal savings* balances of 25 clients of a local bank.

(i) Use the **Chart Wizard** in the toolbar to construct an **X–Y scatter** plot between clients' *ages* and their *savings balances*.

(ii) Does there appear to be any relationship between these two variables?

Chapter 4

Summarising Data – Pivot Tables and Graphs

Objectives

Data gathered from a sample must be organised and displayed in ways that make it understandable to a manager. This chapter examines various data summary methods and graphic displays that will highlight patterns in the sample data and make them discernable at a glance.

After studying this chapter, you should be able to:

- summarise *categorical* data into summary tables, such as *one-way* and *two-way pivot tables*
- interpret the findings in a pivot table
- produce and interpret appropriate graphic displays of each type of pivot table.
- summarise *numeric* data into summary tables, such as frequency tables and cumulative frequency tables (ogives).
- construct and interpret graphic displays of numeric data, such as histograms and cumulative frequency polygons.
- display time series data as line graphs and interpret trends.

4.1 Introduction

Statistical findings are of value to managers only when the information can be easily interpreted and effectively and concisely communicated to them. *Summary tables* and *graphical displays* are commonly used to convey statistical results. A table or a graph can convey information much more vividly and quickly than a written report. For graphs in particular there is much truth in the adage: "a picture is worth a thousand words".

In practice, an analyst should always opt for *summary tables* and *graphs/charts*, instead of written texts, to promote rapid understanding of statistical information to support management decision making.

Summary tables and graphs can be used to *profile the responses* for a *single* random variable, or to examine the *relationship* between *two* random variables. The choice of a summary table and graphic display technique depends on the type of data being analysed (i.e. *categorical* or *numeric*). This chapter demonstrates – both manually and by using *Excel* – how to produce and interpret summary tables and graphs.

For purposes of illustration, a sample data set of the shopping habits of 30 grocery shoppers will be used. Refer to Figure 4.1 and the *Excel* file: **C4.1 – grocery shoppers**.

Figure 4.1 Database of Grocery Shoppers

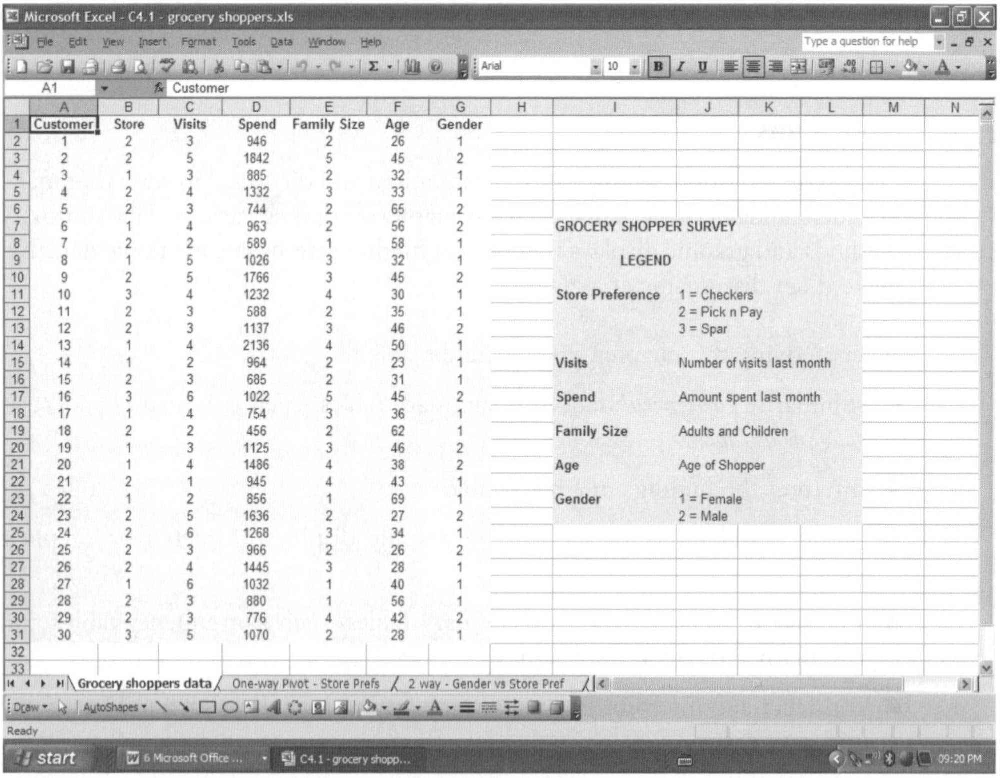

Microsoft Excel - C4.1 - grocery shoppers.xls

Customer	Store	Visits	Spend	Family Size	Age	Gender
1	2	3	946	2	26	1
2	2	5	1842	5	45	2
3	1	3	885	2	32	1
4	2	4	1332	3	33	1
5	2	3	744	2	65	2
6	1	4	963	2	56	2
7	2	2	589	1	58	1
8	1	5	1026	3	32	1
9	2	5	1766	3	45	2
10	3	4	1232	4	30	1
11	2	3	588	2	35	1
12	2	3	1137	3	46	2
13	1	4	2136	4	50	1
14	1	2	964	2	23	1
15	2	3	685	2	31	1
16	3	6	1022	5	45	2
17	1	4	754	3	36	1
18	2	2	456	2	62	1
19	1	3	1125	3	46	2
20	1	4	1486	4	38	2
21	2	1	945	4	43	1
22	1	2	856	1	69	1
23	2	5	1636	2	27	2
24	2	6	1268	3	34	1
25	2	3	966	2	26	2
26	2	4	1445	3	28	1
27	1	6	1032	1	40	1
28	2	3	880	1	56	1
29	2	3	776	4	42	2
30	3	5	1070	2	28	1

GROCERY SHOPPER SURVEY

LEGEND

Store Preference	1 = Checkers 2 = Pick n Pay 3 = Spar
Visits	Number of visits last month
Spend	Amount spent last month
Family Size	Adults and Children
Age	Age of Shopper
Gender	1 = Female 2 = Male

Grocery shoppers data | One-way Pivot - Store Prefs | 2 way - Gender vs Store Pref

4.2 Categorical Data – Summary and Graphic Display

The responses to a *single* categorical variable can be summarised into a one-way pivot table (also called a **categorical frequency table**) and then displayed graphically, either as a *pie chart* or a *bar chart*.

When the responses to *two* categorical variables are jointly summarised, for the purpose of seeking a possible association between them, a two-way pivot table (also called a **cross-tabulation table**) is constructed and displayed graphically, either as a *stacked bar chart* or a *multiple bar chart*.

4.2.1 Profiling a Single Categorical Variable

(i) Categorical frequency table (one-way pivot table)

A **categorical frequency table** (also known as a **one-way pivot table**) shows the *count* (or *percentage*) of responses that belong to each category of a categorical variable.

The actual number of observations that fall into the ith category are referred to as the **count** or **frequency** (f_i) of that category. When expressed as a percentage of the total sample, these category frequencies are called **percentage counts** or **percentage frequencies** ($\%f_i$).

It is always more meaningful to express the counts as *percentages* of the total sample size. Percentages are easier to understand and they allow for comparisons between similar samples of different sizes.

To construct a one-way pivot table, refer to chapter 3, Section 3.5.1.

(ii) Bar chart/pie chart

The one-way pivot table (or categorical frequency table) can be displayed *graphically*, either as **a bar chart** or a **pie chart** as illustrated in chapter 3.

HOW TO

To construct a bar chart

- The categories are shown on the horizontal axis (x-axis).
- The vertical axis (y-axis) is scaled to show either the count (or percentage).
- The height of each bar shows the frequency count (or percentage) of each category.
- The sum of the heights of each bar must sum to the sample size (or 100%).
- The width of the bars must be of equal thickness to avoid distortion of category importances, but neither the order of the categories on the x-axis nor the chosen bar thickness is important – only the height is important.

HOW TO

To construct a pie chart

- Divide a circle into category segments where the size of each segment is proportional to the frequency count (or percentage) of its category (this shows the relative importance of each segment).
- The sum of the segment frequency counts (or percentages) must equal the whole (i.e. sum to the sample size, or to 100%).

- To make interpretation easier and avoid misrepresentation, all charts must:
  - be adequately labelled with headings, axes titles and legends
  - have uniform scales (i.e. equal distance between constant differences)
  - identify, where possible, the source of the data used, to allow a user to assess the credibility and validity of the findings.

Comparison between a bar chart and a pie chart

Bar charts and pie charts display the same information graphically. In a *bar chart*, the importance of a category is shown by the *height of a bar*, while in a *pie chart*, this importance is shown by the *size of each segment* (or slice). The choice of bar chart or pie chart to display information depends on which information an analyst wishes to emphasise. The *contrast between the categories* is more evident in a *bar chart*, while a *pie chart* conveys more of a sense of the *whole*. A limitation of both bar chart and pie chart is that each displays information on only one variable at a time.

Example 4.1 Grocery Shoppers Survey – Store Preference study

Refer to the database in Figure 4.1. *Excel* file: **C4.1 – grocery shoppers**

Management question

Summarise and interpret the number of customers by *store most preferred.*

Solution

The categorical variable to be summarised is **Store Preference.** The response categories are:

1 = Checkers; 2 = Pick 'n Pay; 3 = Spar.

To manually produce the one-way pivot table, **count** how many of the 30 customers shopped at *Checkers* last month, then how many shopped at *Pick 'n Pay* last month, and finally how many shopped at *Spar* last month. Then display the categories and their corresponding counts in a table.

Solution using *Excel*

The **one-way pivot table** option in *Excel* will produce the same result. In the pivot table, the category names can be typed in to replace the codes and make the output more readable.

Figure 4.2 overleaf shows the one-way pivot table both as a *frequency count* table and as a *percentage* table. The percentage bar chart and pie chart are also shown.

Management interpretation

Of the 30 customers surveyed, 17 (or 56,67%) customers prefer to shop at Pick 'n Pay. One third (10 or 33,33%) prefer to shop at Checkers, while only 10% shop mainly at Spar. Overall, most shoppers prefer to shop at Pick 'n Pay.

Figure 4.2 One-way pivot table and charts (bar and pie) for **Store Preference**

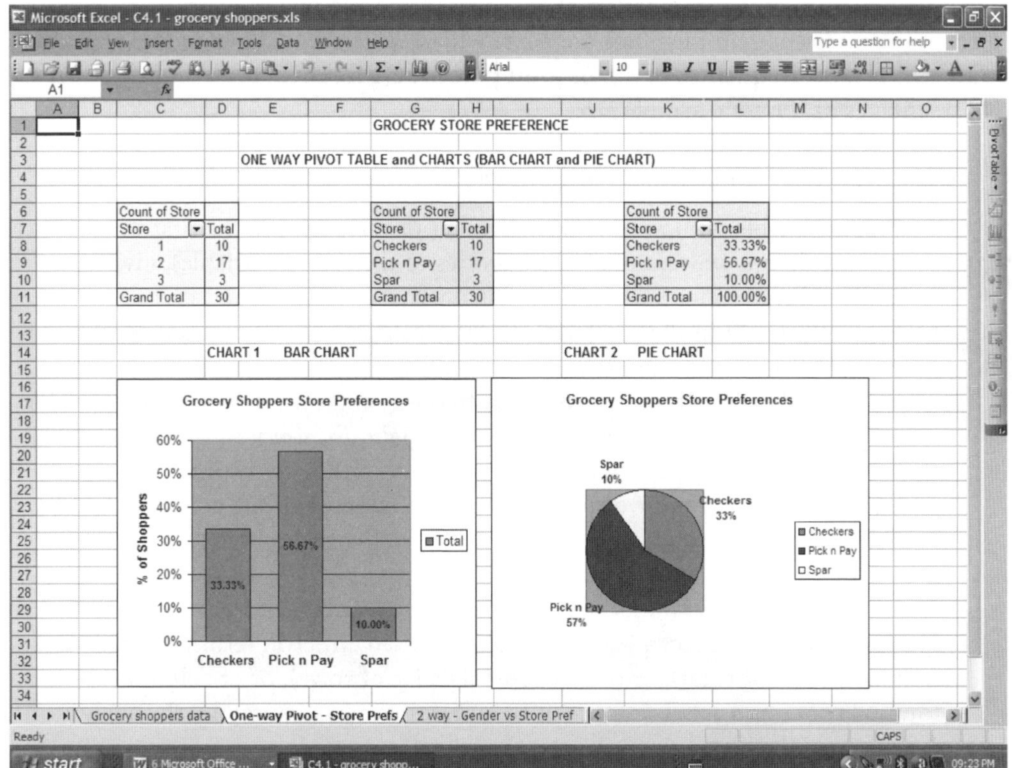

4.2.2 Examine the Association between Two Categorical Variables

The relationship between two categorical random variables can be examined by showing their joint responses in a *summary table*, called a **cross-tabulation table** or a **two-way pivot table,** and displayed *graphically* either as a stacked bar chart or a multiple bar chart.

(i) A cross-tabulation table (two-way pivot table)

A **cross-tabulation table** shows the number (and/or percentage) of observations that *jointly* belong to each combination of categories between *two categorical variables*.

If, for example, the association between *gender* and *gym attendance* is being examined, then:

- The first categorical variable is *gender* with two categories (*male* and *female*).
- The second categorical variable is *gym attendance* with three categories (*seldom*, *often*, and *regularly*).
- The resultant *cross-tabulation table* will consist of six cells (2 × 3), with each cell representing a particular combination of *gender* and *gym attendance*.

- Each cell of a cross-tabulation table shows the *count* (or *percentage*) of responses that jointly represent that combination of categories from the two categorical variables (e.g. 45 or 15% of gym members are *males* who *seldom* attend a gym). These counts are called **joint frequencies** (f_{ij}), or **joint percentage frequencies** ($\%f_{ij}$), if shown as percentages of the total sample size.

HOW TO

To construct a two-way pivot table (manually)

- Prepare a table with m rows (m = number of categories of the first variable) and n columns (n = number of categories of the second variable), giving $m \times n$ cells.
- For each record in the database, allocate each pair of observations for the two variables to the appropriate cell in the table.
- When each record has been assigned to one – and only one – cell in the table, tally the allocations per cell to arrive at the *joint frequency count* for each cell.
- Sum each row to give row totals per category of the row variable.
- Sum each column to give column totals per category of the column variable.
- Sum the column totals (or row totals) to give the grand total (sample size).

These joint frequency counts can be shown as **percentages** for easier interpretation. The percentages could be expressed either in terms of the total sample size (**% of total**), or of row sub-totals (**% of rows**), or of column sub-totals (**% of columns**). The focus of the interpretation required by the analyst determines which way the percentages will be computed.

(ii) Stacked bar chart/multiple bar chart

Cross-tabulations (two-way pivot tables) can be displayed graphically, either as a *stacked bar chart* or as a *multiple bar chart*.

In both stacked and multiple bar charts, the frequency counts (or percentage counts) of each category of one of the variables is split proportionately into the categories of the second variable. The proportional split is based on the frequency counts (or percentage counts) of the second variable.

The charts vary in how they display the relative splits across the different categories.

Stacked bar chart

The *stacked* (or *component) bar chart* is a simple bar chart of the first categorical variable, with the height of each bar split in proportion to the frequency counts of the second variable. This results in a "*stacking*" effect of the categories of the second variable within each category of the first variable.

Multiple bar chart

The *multiple bar chart* displays each category of the first categorical variable as a separate simple bar chart. Each simple bar chart is constructed from the frequency counts of the second categorical variable. It is used when a user wants to *emphasise the difference* between the categories of the second variable for each category of the first variable.

Comparison of a stacked bar chart and a multiple bar chart

The format of the stacked bar chart retains the focus on the relative frequencies between the categories of the first variable, while showing the relative split of each category of the first variable across the categories of the second variable. The intention of the multiple bar chart, on the other hand, is to emphasise the relative difference between the categories of the one variable for each category of the other variable.

Example 4.2 Grocery Shoppers Survey – Store Preference by Gender study

Refer to the database in Figure 4.1. *Excel* file: **C4.1 – grocery shoppers**

Management question

Examine the association between *store preference* and the *gender* of the shoppers surveyed. Show the results in a **cross-tabulation table** and graphically as a **stacked bar chart** and a **multiple bar chart**.

Solution

The cross-tabulation process can be done manually, as explained above, but it is quicker and easier to use the two-way pivot table option in *Excel* (see chapter 3 section 3.5.3).

This will result in the cross-tabulation table of joint frequency counts as shown in **Table 1** of **Figure 4.3**. **Table 2** shows the counts, converted to percentages, of the total number of shoppers surveyed, as well as edited text to make them easier to interpret. Both the percentage stacked bar chart (**Chart 1**) and the percentage multiple bar chart (**Chart 2**) are also shown.

Figure 4.3 Two-way pivot table and charts (stacked and multiple) for **Store Preference** and **Gender**

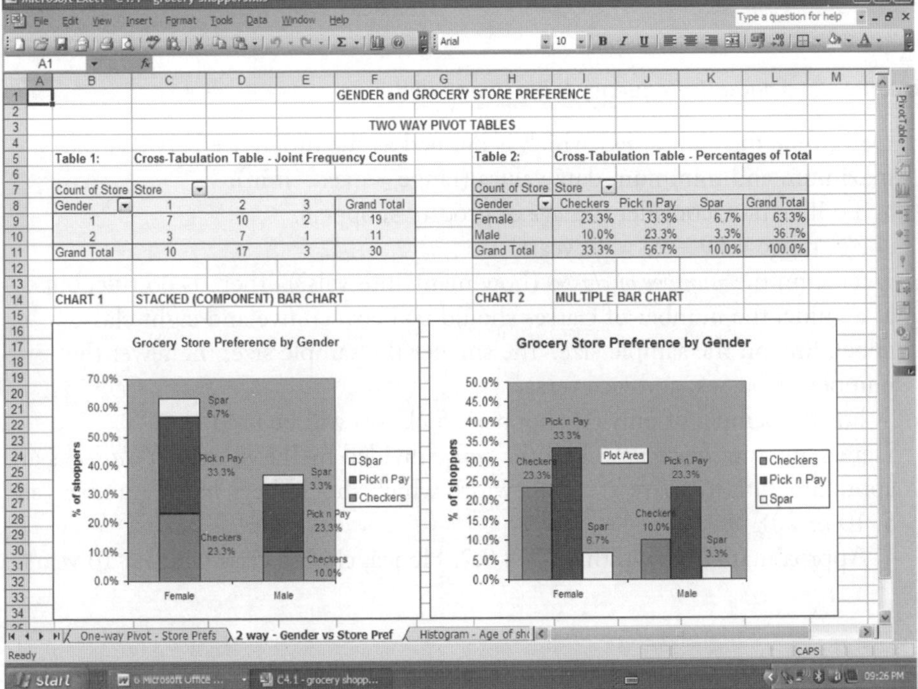
GENDER and GROCERY STORE PREFERENCE

TWO WAY PIVOT TABLES

Table 1: Cross-Tabulation Table - Joint Frequency Counts

Count of Store	Store			
Gender	1	2	3	Grand Total
1	7	10	2	19
2	3	7	1	11
Grand Total	10	17	3	30

Table 2: Cross-Tabulation Table - Percentages of Total

Count of Store	Store			
Gender	Checkers	Pick n Pay	Spar	Grand Total
Female	23.3%	33.3%	6.7%	63.3%
Male	10.0%	23.3%	3.3%	36.7%
Grand Total	33.3%	56.7%	10.0%	100.0%

Management interpretation

(Based on Tables 1 and 2 and Charts 1 and 2 of Figure 4.3)

The most important findings of this survey are that:

- twice as many females (67%) as males (33%) do the grocery shopping
- almost twice as many shoppers (57%) prefer to shop at Pick 'n Pay rather than at Checkers (33%)
- the choice of grocery store is similar for males and females (i.e. their shopping profiles, in terms of store preference, are the same).

Overall, by inspection, there appears to be *no association* between the *gender* of the shoppers surveyed and their *store preference* (since they are the same).

4.3 Numeric Data – Summary and Graphic Display

Numeric data can also be summarised into table format and displayed graphically. Similar methods as for categorical data are used, except that the categories are replaced by *numeric intervals*. Tables and graphs will be shown to *profile* both a *single numeric variable* and to *examine* the *relationship* between *two numeric variables*. Numeric data from the grocery shoppers survey in Figure 4.1, on page 64, will be used to illustrate these techniques.

4.3.1 Profile a Single Numeric Variable

(i) Numeric frequency table

A **numeric frequency table** (or *distribution*) is a summary table which groups numeric data into intervals and reports the frequency count of numbers assigned to each interval.

HOW TO

To construct a numeric frequency table (manually)

- Determine the *data range*, which is defined as the difference between the maximum and minimum data values (range = max – min).

  To illustrate, consider the *age* of grocery shoppers.

  Age range = 69 – 23 = 46 years.
- Decide on the *number of classes* (how many intervals?). There is no rule, but as a guide, the number of classes should be between five and eight classes, depending on the sample size. The smaller the sample size, the fewer the number of classes, and vice versa.

  For the sample of only 30 shoppers, 5 classes will be used.
- Determine the *class width*. Use the *range* divided by the *number of classes* as an approximation to arrive at a class width which should be a "neat" number (e.g. 5, 10 or 20).

  Approximate class width = $\frac{46}{5}$ = 9,2. Hence, choose class width = 10 years.

- Determine *class limits* (class boundaries). The lower limit for the first class should be a value smaller than or equal to the minimum data value, and it should be an easy number with which to work, such as "20" in this example.
- The *lower limits for successive classes* are found by adding the class width to each preceding lower limit. The *upper limits* are chosen to avoid overlaps between adjacent class limits.

Lower Limit	*Upper Limit*
20	< 30 (or 29)
30	< 40 (or 39)
40	< 50 (or 49)
50	< 60 (or 59)
60	< 70 (or 69)

Note: The format of <30 (less than 30) should be used if the source data is continuous, while discrete upper limits such as 29 can be used if the source data is itself discrete.

- Tabulate the data values. Assign each data value in the data set to one and only one class interval.
  A *count* of the number of data values assigned to each class will produce the *summary table,* called the **numeric frequency distribution**.

The following *construction pointers* are worth noting*:*

- Class widths must be constant.
- Adjacent upper and lower class limits must not overlap (i.e. classes must be *mutually exclusive*).
- Each data value must be assigned to only one class interval (i.e. the classes must be *all inclusive*).
- The sum of the frequency counts must equal the total number of observations, *n*.
- The *frequency counts* (f_i) can also be expressed as percentages – called **percentage frequencies** ($\%f_i$). *Percentage frequencies* show the *proportion* of observations within each class interval, while *frequency counts* show the *number* of observations within each class interval.
- The number of class intervals and the class width of each class interval (which must be the same for all class intervals) are guided by the *sample size* (*n*) and the *level of detail required* for interpretation. If too few class intervals are chosen with corresponding wide class intervals, there will be a loss of information, caused by an over-concentration of data values in only a few intervals. Conversely, if too many class intervals are selected with corresponding narrow class intervals, clear patterns (profiles) are difficult to identify. Both extremes limit meaningful interpretations of the summarised numeric data.

(ii) Histogram

A **histogram** is a graphic display of a numeric frequency distribution.

A histogram is computed by *Excel* at the same time as the numeric frequency count table, by ticking the **Chart Output** box in the **Histogram** input dialog box within **Data Analysis** (refer to chapter 3 Figure 3.14). A user must specify the *class limits* into which the data values will be assigned. In *Excel* the class limits are called **bin ranges**. *Excel* requires that a user specify only the inclusive *upper limit for each class* as the bin ranges.

In a histogram, the class intervals – as defined in the frequency table – must be consecutive and continuous. This means they must be arranged consecutively in the order of the increasing class limits – and they must have no gaps between them, as the values are continuous. The height of each bar – as in a bar chart – shows either the frequency count or percentage of observations within each class interval.

The *management interpretation* of a *histogram* is exactly the same as for its corresponding numeric frequency table.

Example 4.3 Grocery Shoppers Survey – Age study

Refer to the database in Figure 4.1. *Excel* file: **C4.1 – grocery shoppers**

Management question

Construct both the numeric frequency table and histogram to describe the *age* profile of grocery shoppers.

Manual solution

The manual approach follows the steps outlined on pages 70 and 71.

Solution using *Excel*

The same steps are used by *Excel,* where both the numeric frequency count table and the histogram are constructed using the **Histogram** tool in the **Data Analysis** add-in. To use *Excel*, the bin ranges for shoppers' *ages* are set at 29, 39, 49, 59 and 69 and represent the inclusive upper limits for each age class. The percentages frequencies are computed separately from the frequency counts. The results are shown in Figure 4.4 below.

Figure 4.4 Numeric frequency table and histogram for shoppers' **Age** profile

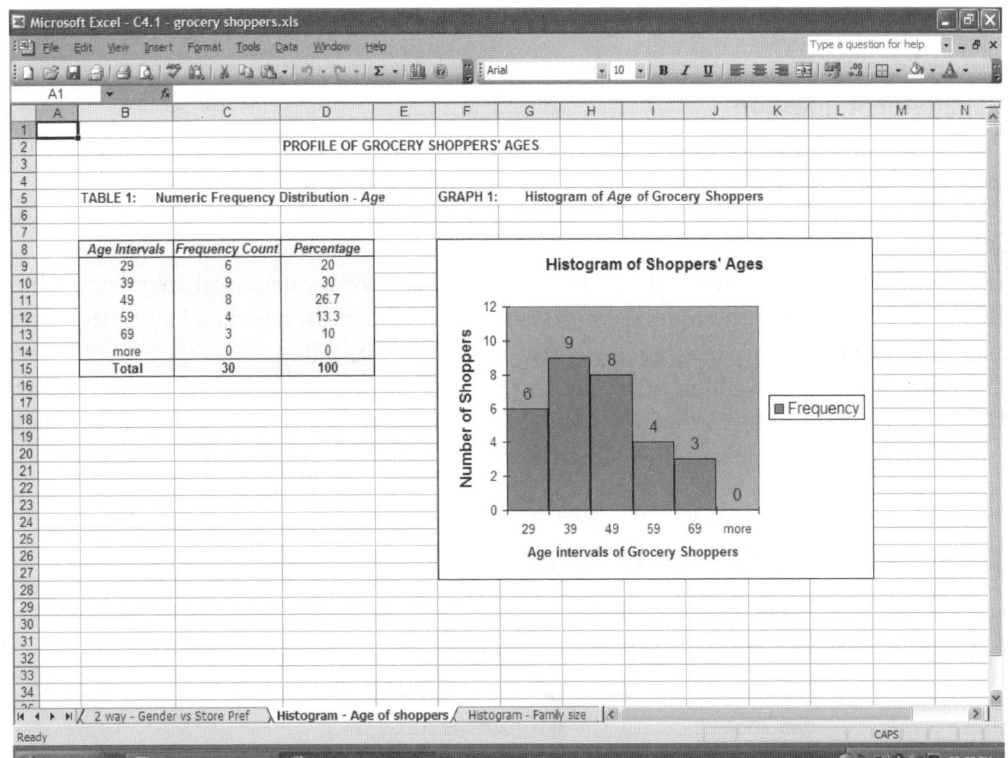

Management interpretation

The most common age grouping of grocery shoppers surveyed are between 30 and 39 years and represent 30% (9/30) of all grocery shoppers. They are followed by the 40 to 49-year age group (26,7%). Less than one quarter of all grocery shoppers (23,3%) are over 50 years of age. Overall, the majority of grocery shoppers tend to be in the middle *age* band.

(iii) Summarising and graphing discrete numeric data

If the numeric data are *discrete values* in a limited range (e.g. 5-point rating scales; number of children in a family, etc.), then the discrete-valued numeric variable can be treated as a categorical measure for pivot table and graphic display purposes. The **Pivot Table and Pivot Chart Report** option, from the **Data** command in the menu bar, can then be used to produce a discrete-valued numeric frequency table and histogram.

Example 4.4 Grocery Shoppers Survey – Family Size study

Refer to the database in Figure 4.1. *Excel* file: **C4.1 – grocery shoppers**

Management question

Profile the *family size* of grocery shoppers by constructing both the numeric frequency table and histogram.

Solution

The manual approach follows the steps outlined above for a categorical frequency table. This involves counting the number of cases for each of the discrete data values (e.g. how many shoppers of *family size 1*? *size 2*?, *size 3*?, *size 4*?, *size 5*?).

Figure 4.5 shows the numeric frequency tables (**Tables 1 and 2**) and histogram (**Chart 1**) for the discrete numeric data of *family size* in the grocery shoppers survey produced using *Excel's* **Pivot Table and Pivot Chart Report** option.

Figure 4.5 Numeric frequency table and histogram for **Family Size**

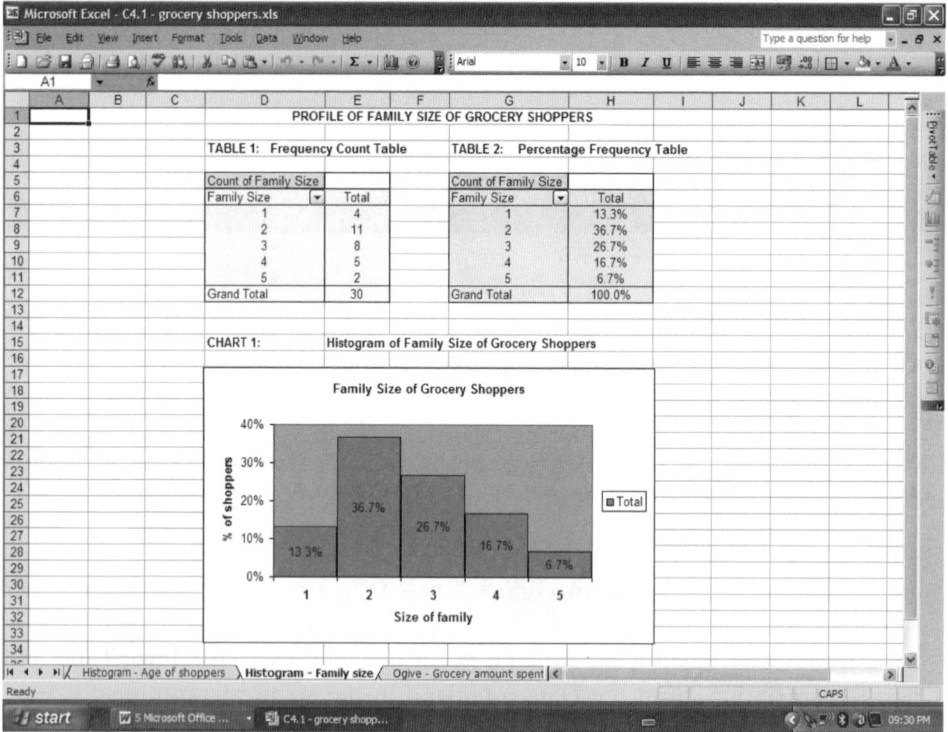

PROFILE OF FAMILY SIZE OF GROCERY SHOPPERS

TABLE 1: Frequency Count Table

Count of Family Size	
Family Size	Total
1	4
2	11
3	8
4	5
5	2
Grand Total	30

TABLE 2: Percentage Frequency Table

Count of Family Size	
Family Size	Total
1	13.3%
2	36.7%
3	26.7%
4	16.7%
5	6.7%
Grand Total	100.0%

Management interpretation

Most grocery shoppers are shopping for either two (36,7%) or three (26,7%) persons. Larger families (size 4 or 5) are less common (23,4%).

(iv) Ogive – the cumulative frequency table

A **cumulative frequency distribution** (or **ogive**) is a summary table of *cumulative frequency counts* which is constructed specifically to answer questions of a *more than* or *less than* nature.

HOW TO

To construct a cumulative frequency table

- Construct an extra class below the lower limit of the first class.
- For each class beginning with this extra class, ask the question: "How many observations fall *below* this class *upper limit*?" The answer is: the sum of *all* frequency counts (or percentages) *below* this current *class upper limit.*
- Each successive cumulative frequency is found by adding the current class frequency to the immediately preceding cumulative frequency.
- The last class's cumulative frequency must equal the sample size (n) (if frequency counts are summed); or 100% (if percentages are summed).

(v) Cumulative frequency polygon

A **cumulative frequency polygon** is a graph of an ogive.

This graph is constructed by plotting the cumulative frequency counts (or cumulative percentages) against the *upper limit* of its *corresponding class interval* (i.e. against the limits defined in the *bin ranges*) and then joining these points to produce a line graph.

The cumulative frequency polygon can then be used to estimate (interpolate) cumulative percentages (of a *less than* or *more than* nature), or estimate values of the variable that matches certain specified cumulative percentages.

Example 4.5 Grocery Shoppers Survey – Amount Spent study

Refer to the database in Figure 4.1. *Excel* file: **C4.1 – grocery shoppers**

Management question

Compute the cumulative frequency table (*ogive*) and its graph (*cumulative frequency polygon*) for the *amount spent on groceries last month* and answer the following questions:

(i) What percentage of shoppers spent less than R1 199 last month?
(ii) What percentage of shoppers spent more than R1 599 last month?
(iii) What proportion of shoppers spent between R800 and R1 600 last month?
(iv) What was the maximum amount spent by the 20% of shoppers who spent the least on groceries? Approximate the answer.

Manual solution

The manual approach follows the steps outlined above for a numeric frequency table and ogive.

Figure 4.6 shows the numeric frequency table (**Table 1**), ogive (**Table 2**) and cumulative percentage polygon (**Graph 1**) for the *amount spent on groceries* last month by the sample of 30 grocery shoppers. The *amount spent* data is reproduced from Figure 4.1 and shown in the data range [A1:A31]. The histogram's **bin range** is shown in [D27: D32].

Solution using *Excel*

The **ogive** (Table 2) is constructed in *Excel* by ticking the **Cumulative Percentage** box in the **Histogram** input dialog box in **Data Analysis.**

The **Cumulative Percentage Polygon** (Graph 1) is then drawn using chart type **XY (Scatter)** and its chart sub-type **Scatter with data points connected by smoothed lines** from the **Chart Wizard** in the toolbar. The data points plotted are the *upper class limits* (bin range limits) and *cumulative percentages* from **Table 2** (data range [I4:J10]).

Figure 4.6 Numeric frequency table, % ogive, cumulative % polygon – **Grocery Spend**

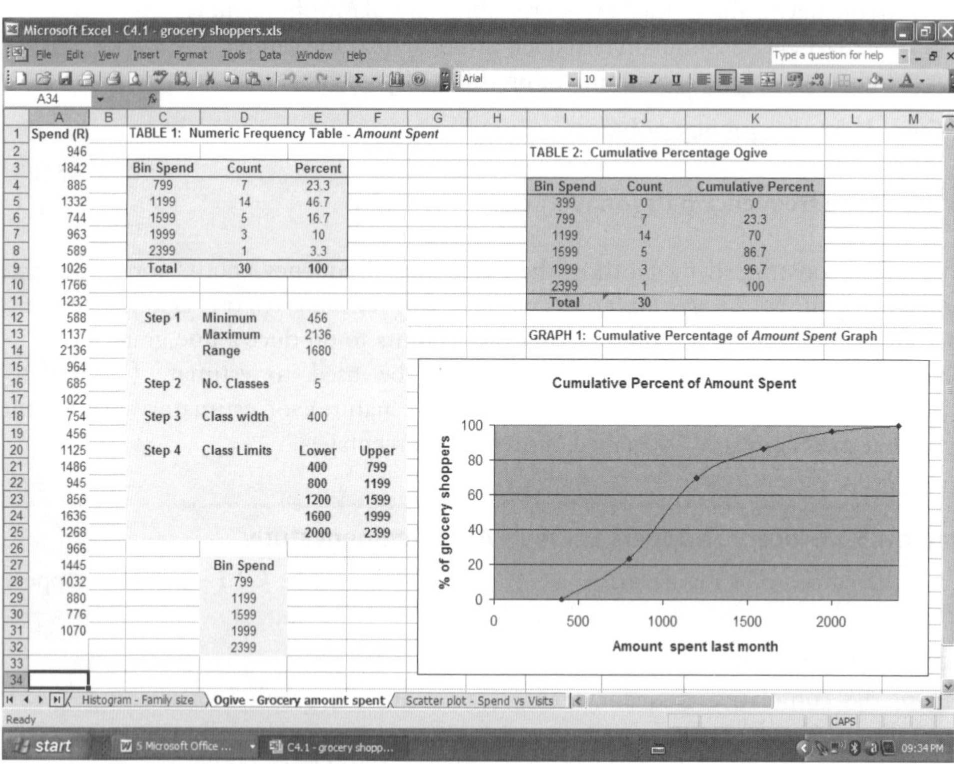

Spend (R): 946, 1842, 885, 1332, 744, 963, 589, 1026, 1766, 1232, 588, 1137, 2136, 964, 685, 1022, 754, 456, 1125, 1486, 945, 856, 1636, 1268, 966, 1445, 1032, 880, 776, 1070

TABLE 1: Numeric Frequency Table - *Amount Spent*

Bin Spend	Count	Percent
799	7	23.3
1199	14	46.7
1599	5	16.7
1999	3	10
2399	1	3.3
Total	30	100

Step 1	Minimum	456	
	Maximum	2136	
	Range	1680	
Step 2	No. Classes	5	
Step 3	Class width	400	
Step 4	Class Limits	Lower	Upper
		400	799
		800	1199
		1200	1599
		1600	1999
		2000	2399

Bin Spend
799
1199
1599
1999
2399

TABLE 2: Cumulative Percentage Ogive

Bin Spend	Count	Cumulative Percent
399	0	0
799	7	23.3
1199	14	70
1599	5	86.7
1999	3	96.7
2399	1	100
Total	30	

Management interpretation

The answers to the questions are read off on **Table 2** and/or **Graph 1**.

(i) 70% of shoppers spent less than R1 199 on groceries last month.

(ii) 13,3% (i.e. 100% – 86,7%) of shoppers spent more than R1 599 on groceries last month.

(iii) 63,4% (i.e. 86,7% – 23,3%) of shoppers spent between R800 and R1 600 on groceries last month.

(iv) The bottom 20% of shoppers spent no more than R750 approximately on groceries last month (found by projecting 20% from the *y*-axis to the polygon graph and reading off the amount spent on the *x*-axis).

Note: The ogive is a *less than* cumulative frequency table, but it can also be used to answer questions of a *more than* nature (by subtracting the *less than* cumulative percentage from 100%).

(vi) Box plot

A **box plot** is a visual display of the *profile of a numeric variable* which shows its *minimum* and *maximum* values and various intermediate descriptive values (such as *quartiles* and *medians*).

The box plot is covered in chapter 6, as it is constructed from descriptive statistical measures for numeric variables that will be derived in chapters 5 and 6.

4.3.2 Exploring Relationship Between Two Numeric Variables

Many *numeric* variables in management practice are potentially related to each other. For example: *advertising expenditure* may have an influence on *turnover*; *training effort* (expenditure) could have a positive influence on *productivity levels*; *hours of driving* could negatively impact on braking *reaction times*, etc.

The value of knowing that two variables are related lies in the fact that the values of the one variable having the influence (x) can be used to predict the outcome of the other variable (y). The x-variable is called the **independent variable**, while the y-variable is labelled the **dependent variable**.

Three graphic displays showing the relationship between two numeric variables are presented. They are: (i) a scatter plot, (ii) a trend line graph and (iii) a Lorenz curve. Each emphasises a different form of the relationship.

(i) Scatter plot

A **scatter plot** is a coordinate plot of the *relationship between two numeric* variables.

A visual inspection of the resultant *scatter plot* will reveal the nature of a relationship between the variables x and y.

HOW TO

To construct a scatter plot

- Select the two numeric variables and identify the *independent variable* (x) and the *dependent variable* (y).
- Plot each pair of data values (x, y) from the two variables on an x–y graph. The x-variable's values are recorded along the horizontal axis, and the corresponding y-variable's values are recorded along the vertical axis.

Example 4.6 Grocery Shoppers Survey – Amount Spent by Number of Visits study

Refer to the database in Figure 4.1. *Excel* file: **C4.1 – grocery shoppers**

Management question

Examine, by inspecting a *scatter plot*, the relationship between the *amount spent on groceries* last month and the *number of visits* to the grocery store by the sample of 30 shoppers surveyed.

Manual solution

The *independent* variable is the *number of visits* and the *dependent variable* is the *amount spent* – as the number of visits is assumed to influence the total amount spent in a month.

Manually, each pair of values for each shopper can be plotted on an x–y graph – with the horizontal axis (x-axis) being the *number of visits*, and the vertical axis (y-axis) being the *amount spent* last month.

Solution using *Excel*

The **Chart Wizard** option in the toolbar can be used to prepare a scatter plot:

- Highlight the data range of the two sets of data (**Visits** and **Amount Spent**).
  Note: Ensure that the two columns of data are adjacent, with the x-variable in the first column and the y-variable in the second column.
- Select chart type **XY (Scatter)** and chart sub-type **Scatter, Compares pairs of values.** Then click **Finish.**

The option to edit the graph interactively also exists when data values are changed. Again, by right-clicking on the graph area and selecting **chart option**, it is possible to insert titles, labels and legends to improve the presentation of the graph.

Figure 4.7 shows the **input data** (data range: [A1:B31]) copied from the data range ([C1:D31]) in Figure 4.1, as well as the resultant **scatter plot** for the *number of visits* (x) versus the *amount spent* (y) on groceries last month.

Figure 4.7 Scatter plot of **Number of Visits** versus **Amount Spent** on Groceries

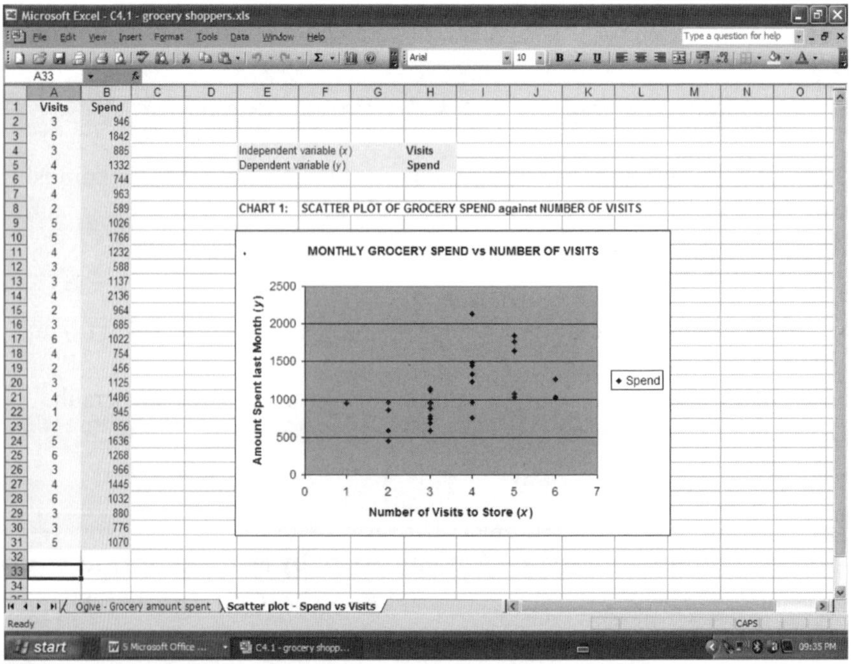

Visits	Spend
3	946
5	1842
3	885
4	1332
3	744
4	963
2	589
5	1026
5	1766
4	1232
3	588
3	1137
4	2136
2	964
3	685
6	1022
4	754
2	456
3	1125
4	1486
1	945
2	856
5	1636
6	1268
3	966
4	1445
6	1032
3	880
3	776
5	1070

Independent variable (x) Visits
Dependent variable (y) Spend

CHART 1: SCATTER PLOT OF GROCERY SPEND against NUMBER OF VISITS

MONTHLY GROCERY SPEND vs NUMBER OF VISITS

Amount Spent last Month (y)

Number of Visits to Store (x)

Spend

Management interpretation

There is a moderate, positive relationship between the *number of visits* to a grocery store in a month and the total *amount spent* on groceries last month. The more frequent the visits, the larger the total grocery bill for the month. This information can assist management to focus on encouraging more frequent shopper visits if they wish to increase turnover in their stores.

(ii) Trend line graph

A **trend line graph** plots the values of a *numeric* random variable *over time.*

Such data is called **time series** data. The x-variable is *time* and the y-variable is a *numeric* measure of interest to a manager (e.g. turnover, unit cost of production, absenteeism, share prices).

HOW TO

To construct a trend line graph

- The horizontal axis (x-axis) records the consecutive *time periods.*
- The values of the *numeric random variable* are plotted on the vertical (y-axis) opposite its respective time period.
- The consecutive points are joined to form a trend line.

Trend line graphs are commonly used to *identify and track trends* in time series data.

Example 4.7 Randburg Municipality Absenteeism Levels study

Refer to the database in Figure 4.8 (overleaf). *Excel* file: **C4.2 – municipal workers**

Figure 4.8 overleaf (data range [B1:B33]) shows the *weekly absenteeism levels* (number of employee-days absent) for the Randburg municipality for a period of 32 weeks.

Management question

Graph and examine the *trend* in weekly *absenteeism levels* within the Randburg municipality over the past 32 weeks.

Solution using *Excel*

Excel offers a line graph facility in the **Chart Wizard** option of the toolbar:

- Highlight only the data range of the y-variable (e.g. absenteeism level) (i.e. data range: [B1:B33] only in Figure 4.8 overleaf).
- Select chart type **Line** and chart sub-type **Line with markers displayed at each data value.**

The option to edit the graph interactively exists when data values are changed. By right-clicking on the graph area and selecting **Chart option,** it is possible to insert titles, labels and legends to improve the presentation of the graph.

Figure 4.8 Line graph of **Absenteeism** Levels – Randburg Municipality

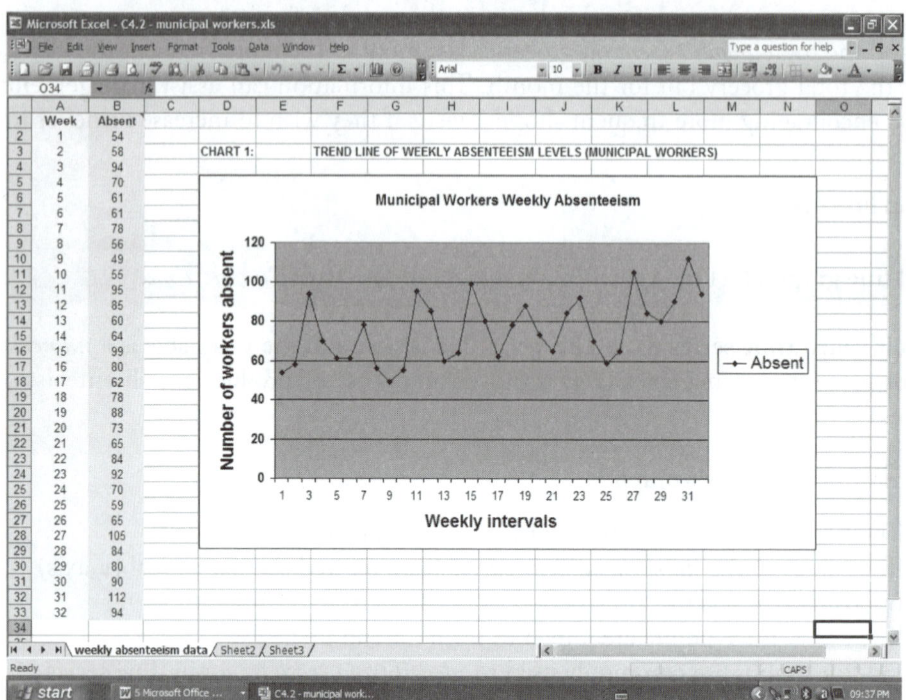

Management interpretation

Over the past 32 weeks, there has been a modest increase in absenteeism, with an upturn occurring in more recent weeks. Evident, is a distinctive "monthly" pattern, with absenteeism in each month generally low in weeks 1 and 2, peaking in week 3, and declining moderately in week 4.

(iii) The Lorenz curve

A **Lorenz curve** shows, graphically, the extent to which the values of two *numeric* random variables have *similar distributions.* It is a plot of the percentage cumulative frequency distributions (i.e. *less than ogives)* of two ratio-scaled random variables against each other.

If the distributions are similar or equal, the Lorenz curve will be represented by a 45°-line from the origin of both axes (line of uniformity or line of equal distribution). The more unequal the two distributions, the more bent (i.e. concave or convex) the curve becomes. A Lorenz curve always starts at coordinate (0 ; 0) and ends at coordinate (100; 100).

A Lorenz curve can be used to show; for example:

(i) the *value* of inventories against the *quantities* of inventories held by an organisation

(ii) the spread of *incomes* amongst various categories of *employees*

(iii) the concentration of *assets* amongst *companies* in a particular industry
(iv) the spread of the *taxation* burden amongst *taxpayers*.

Invariably, a small percentage of *inventories, employees, companies* and *taxpayers* accounts for the bulk of the *value of inventories, incomes, assets* and *taxation*. The degree of concentration or distortion can be clearly illustrated by a Lorenz curve.

Example 4.8 Sunlife Insurance – Employee Income versus Employee Size study

The HR manager of a large insurance company, Sunlife Insurance, studied the distribution of income against the number of employees in each category. She wished to establish whether the distributions were equitable, i.e. equal proportions of income and number of employees per category.

Management questions

(1) Compare the *income* distribution against *employee* distribution across income categories for the HR manager of Sunlife Insurance.
(2) Make a recommendation on the degree of equity between the two distributions.

Solution

The two numeric frequency tables and their respective ogives are given in Figure 4.9. Figure 4.10 overleaf shows the plot of the *less than staff* ogive against the *less than income* ogive.

Figure 4.9 Cumulative distributions of **Income** and **Employee Size**

Income (Monthly)	Number of Staff	Total Income (Monthly)	Staff Ogive %	Income Ogive %
below 0			0	0
0–< 500	12	4 089	19	4
500–< 1 000	18	14 022	47	18
1 000–< 3 000	25	35 750	86	53
3 000–< 5 000	6	24 600	95	78
5 000 or more	3	22 542	100	100
	64	101 003		

Figure 4.10 Lorenz curve of **Employee** distribution against **Income** distribution

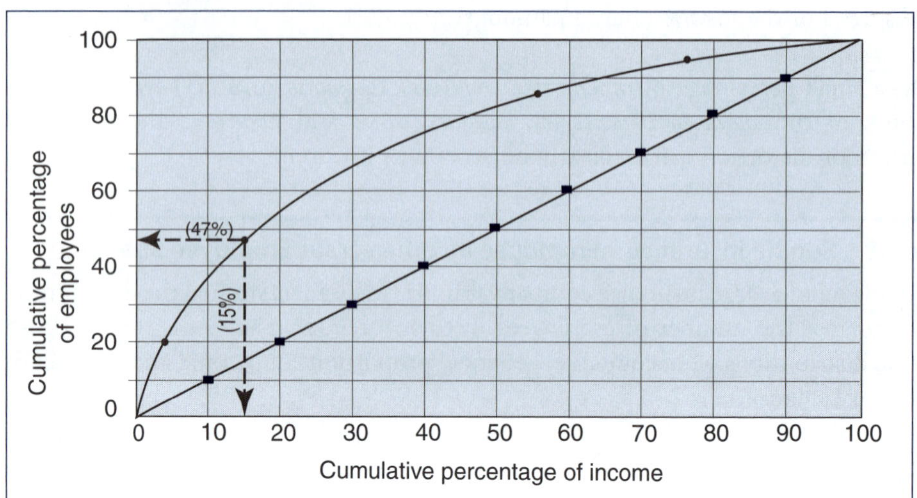

Management interpretation

(1) The diagonal (45°) line shows a distribution of employees across income categories *equal to* the distribution of total income across income categories (equity).

(2) In this illustrative example, an unequal distribution is evident. For *example*, almost half of all employees (i.e. 47%) receive only 15% of all total income. Conversely, the remaining 53% of employees receive 85% of total income.

A larger proportion of low-income employees are receiving a smaller proportion of the total income. Alternatively, a small proportion of high-income employees are receiving a larger proportion of total income.

4.4 Summary

This chapter identified a number of approaches to represent statistical data graphically:

- *Charts,* such as the pie chart, the simple bar chart, the stacked (or component) bar chart and the multiple bar chart, are all used to pictorially display *categorical* data from *qualitative* random variables.
- *Graphs,* on the other hand, are used to pictorially display data from *quantitative* (numeric) random variables (i.e. interval- and ratio-scaled data). Before being able to graphically display numeric data, the data must first be grouped into a *frequency distribution* using *intervals.* The *histogram* and *frequency polygon* are two graphical representations of a numeric frequency distribution.

- *Ogives,* which are derived from frequency distributions, are represented graphically by *cumulative frequency polygons.*
- Other graphical forms are the *line graph*, which is used extensively to display time series data, the *Lorenz curve,* and the *box plot* (to be covered in chapter 6).

When the relationship between *two numeric random variables* is being explored, a *scatter plot* is a suitable graphic display to use. A scatter plots identifies the closeness of a numeric relationship.

This chapter also demonstrated the graphic capabilities of *Excel* to visually display statistical summary tables.

The purpose of each chart and graph was described. The chapter also emphasised that graphical representations should always be considered when statistical data and findings are to be presented to management. A graphical representation promotes more rapid assimilation of the information to be conveyed than written reports and tables.

Exercises

All computational exercises can be performed either manually or using *Excel*.

4.1 Explain at least three differences between a bar chart and a histogram.

4.2 **X4.2 – magazines**
Construct a *pie chart* showing the *percentage* of 500 young female readers surveyed who most prefer each of the following magazines.

Magazine	Count
True Love	95
Seventeen	146
Heat	118
Drum	55
You	86

Insert the **Data Table** from **Chart Options**.
Interpret the findings of the pie chart.

4.3 Refer to Exercise 4.2. Construct a percentage *bar chart* from the frequency table given in Exercise 4.2.
What percentage of young female readers surveyed most prefer *Heat*?

4.4 **X4.4 – job grades**
The *job grade* (A, B, C or D) of 40 clerical employees are as follows:

B	A	A	D	B	D	B	A	D	C
D	A	B	B	C	A	D	C	A	B
B	A	B	C	A	A	C	B	D	D
A	A	B	B	A	D	A	C	A	D

(i) Construct a categorical frequency table of these *job grades*.
(ii) Show the frequency table in *percentage* terms.
(iii) What percentage of employees are in job grade D?
(iv) Show the percentage frequency table as a *pie chart* and a *bar chart*.

4.5 **X4.5 – office rentals**
The monthly rentals per square metre for office space in 30 buildings in Durban central (in Rand) are:

189	156	250	265	195	300
350	315	290	285	165	178
415	280	212	580	395	360
285	225	230	450	185	193
580	248	460	250	520	300

(i) Construct a numerical frequency table of the office rentals by using the classes: 150 – <200; 200 – <250; 250 – <300; etc.

(ii) Compute the *percentage frequencies* and *cumulative percentage frequencies* for office rentals.

(iii) From the frequency table, answer the following questions:
  (a) what percentage of office space costs less than R200/m^2?
  (b) what percentage of office space costs less than R300/m^2?
  (c) what percentage of office space costs more than R400/m^2?
  (d) if a legal company who is looking to hire office space is prepared to pay between R300/m^2 and R400/m^2, how many buildings can they consider?

4.6 X4.6 – storage dams

The capacities (in millions of litres) of each of the four major storage dams that supply the water requirements of Cape Town are shown in the table below.

Storage Dam	Capacity (M!)
Wemmershoek	158 644
Steenbras	95 284
Voelvlei	244 122
Theewaterskloof	440 255

(i) Use *Excel's* **Chart Wizard** to construct a *pie chart* showing the *percentage of water supplied* by each storage dam.

(ii) What percentage of Cape Town's water supply is provided by the Voelvlei dam? By Wemmershoek and Steenbras dams together?

4.7 X4.7 – taste test

A sample of 250 regular fruit juice drinkers were given a *blind taste test* of five different fruit juice brands labelled A, B, C, D and E. Each person was asked to indicate which fruit juice (by the alphabetic label) they most preferred. The results were:

Blind Label	Brand	Number
A	Liqui Fruit	45
B	Fruiti Drink	26
C	YumYum	64
D	Fruit Quencher	38
E	Go Fruit	77

(i) Use *Excel's* Chart Wizard to graphically display these results using:
   (a) a *percentage* bar chart
   (b) a *percentage* pie chart.
(ii) Write a brief report to management explaining your findings.

4.8 X4.8 – annual car sales
Use *Excel's* Chart Wizard to produce separate bar charts showing
(a) the number of passenger cars sold by each manufacturer, and
(b) the percentage market share of the passenger car market held by each of the car manufacturers last year.

Manufacturer	Annual Sales
Toyota	96 959
Nissan	63 172
Volkswagen	88 028
Delta	62 796
Ford	74 155
MBSA	37 268
BMW	51 724
MMI	25 354

What percentage of the total passenger car market is held by the top three car manufacturers?

4.9 X4.9 – half-yearly car sales
Use *Excel's* Chart Wizard to produce a *multiple bar chart* showing the number of new car sales *by manufacturer* between the first and the second half of last year.

Show the **Data Table** from **Chart Options** in the chart display.

Manufacturer	First half	Second half	Annual Sales
Toyota	42 661	54 298	96 959
Nissan	35 376	27 796	63 172
Volkswagen	45 774	42 254	88 028
Delta	26 751	36 045	62 796
Ford	32 628	41 527	74 155
MBSA	19 975	17 293	37 268
BMW	24 206	27 518	51 724
MMI	14 307	11 047	25 354

(i) Which car manufacturers performed better in terms of new car sales in the first half of the year compared to the second half of the year?
(ii) Which car manufacturer showed the largest percentage change (up or down) in sales from the first half to the second half of the year?

4.10 X4.10 – television brands

A survey of a random sample of 125 households recorded the brand of televisions owned.

(i) Construct a *categorical percentage frequency table* of TV brands owned. Use *Excel's* **PivotTable and PivotChart Report** option.
(ii) Show the findings from (i) graphically as a *bar chart.*
(iii) Which brand of TV is least popular amongst households?
(iii) What percentage of households own the most popular TV brand?

4.11 X4.11 – estate agents

The Estate Agents Board analysed the number of residential properties sold by each estate agent in the second half of last year in East London. A random sample of 48 estate agents was selected and the number of houses each sold during this period was recorded. The data are as follows:

5	4	8	4	6	8
7	4	5	4	4	3
6	3	5	3	5	4
3	4	6	4	7	4
8	3	5	6	4	4
3	7	5	3	7	3
4	7	6	3	3	4
3	6	3	4	4	6

(i) Construct a *frequency count table* to show the sales performance of the sample of East London estate agents.
Note: Since the numeric data is discrete and in a limited data range, it is possible to use *Excel's* **PivotTable and PivotChart Report** option.
(ii) Construct a histogram of the frequency count distribution. Show the **Data Table** from **Chart Options** in the display.
(iii) What is the most frequent number of residential properties sold by an estate agent in the second half of last year in East London?
(iv) Repeat (i) and (ii) using the **Tools/Data Analysis/Histogram** option.
Hint: Set a bin range to each discrete value of 3, 4, 5, 6, 7 and 8.

4.12 X4.12 – fast foods

Keen competition exists amongst fast food outlets for the food-spend of consumers. A recent survey established consumers' preferences for various *fast food outlets* and *type of fast foods* (i.e. chicken, pizzas, beef burgers and fish).

Fast Food Outlet	Count
KFC (Chicken)	56
St Elmo's Pizza	58
Steers (Beef Burgers)	45
Nandos (Chicken)	64
Ocean Basket (Fish)	24
Butler's Pizza	78

(i) Use *Excel's* **Chart Wizard** to show customers' preferences for different *fast food outlets* graphically as a bar chart.
(ii) Use *Excel's* **Chart Wizard** to show customer's preference for the different *food types* (chicken, beef, fish, pizzas) graphically as a *percentage* pie chart. Show the **Data Table** from **Chart Options**.
(iii) Write a short note on the findings of this survey to be included in a survey report to be published in an omni-survey on consumer trends.

4.13 **X4.13 – airlines**

A travel agency surveyed 70 passengers to identify which *airline* (Comair, SAA or Nationwide) they prefer to use for domestic travel. The passenger's *purpose of travel*, namely business or tourist, was also recorded.

(i) Construct a two-way pivot table between the *choice of airline* and *purpose of travel.*
(ii) Show the pivot table as a *percentage of each passenger type* per airline.
(iii) Display the percentage pivot table as a multiple bar chart.
(iv) What percentage of passengers prefer to fly with Nationwide?
(v) Which airline is most preferred by tourists?
(vi) Can it be stated that most business travellers prefer to fly with Comair?

4.14 X4.14 – car occupants

A traffic survey was conducted in central Cape Town recently to establish the number of occupants per car commuting into the CBD between 8.00 am and 9.00 am daily from the Northern suburbs. Sixty cars were randomly selected at an entry point into the CBD and the number of occupants was noted. The data were as follows:

1	1	1	5	3	2
3	2	2	5	3	1
2	4	3	2	3	5
1	4	1	1	1	1
5	1	1	1	3	1
1	2	1	1	2	2
3	2	5	2	1	3
1	1	4	1	2	2
2	4	3	1	1	2
2	3	5	4	1	5

(i) Define the *random variable* and the *data type.*

(ii) Use *Excel's* **Tools/Data Analysis/Histogram** option to prepare:
- a numeric *percentage frequency* table (use the discrete values as bins)
- a *histogram* of occupants per car, and
- a *less than ogive* and the cumulative frequency polygon of car occupants.

(iii) From the results, determine:
(a) what percentage of motorists travel alone?
(b) what percentage of vehicles have at least 3 occupants?
(c) what percentage of vehicles have no more than 2 occupants?

4.15 X4.15 – courier trips

The *distance travelled* (in kms) by a courier service motorcycle on 50 trips was recorded by the driver.

24	30	20	6	28
18	19	22	26	31
18	20	34	29	24
19	10	17	11	14
13	28	26	18	16
23	17	16	21	20
21	13	15	20	9
23	25	17	35	29
15	27	18	8	22
27	22	25	14	24

(i) Define the *random variable* and the *data type.*
(ii) Use *Excel's* **Tools/Data Analysis/Histogram** option to prepare:
   - a numeric *frequency* table (use bin ranges: 10, 15, 20, 25, 30 and 35)
   - a *percentage frequency* table, and
   - a *histogram* of the distances traveled by the courier per trip.

(iii) From the results, determine:
   - the percentage of deliveries that were between 25 km and 30 km;
   - the percentage of deliveries within a 25 km radius.
   - the percentage of deliveries beyond a 20 km radius.
   - below which distance (approximately) was 55% of the deliveries made?
   - above which distance (approximately) was the longest 20% of the deliveries made?

(iv) If the company has a policy that no more than 10% of all deliveries should be more than 30 km from their depot, are they adhering to this policy? Justify.

4.16 X4.16 – fuel bills

The monthly expenditures (in Rands) on fuel by 50 randomly sampled motorists in Tshwane are:

289	312	400	368	514
450	330	278	394	662
515	365	460	433	602
385	485	293	646	448
256	680	696	486	356
415	550	348	774	528
380	295	560	360	736
425	265	450	545	414
350	495	864	456	385
390	285	400	408	544

(i) Use *Excel's* **Tools/Data Analysis/Histogram** option to construct a *numerical frequency* table of the monthly fuel expenditure by the sample of 50 Tshwane motorists.
Hint: Use bin ranges of 300, 400, 500, 600, 700 and 800.
(ii) Show the *histogram* of motorists' monthly fuel bills.
(iii) Construct the *percentage frequency* table for monthly fuel bills.
(iv) What percentage of Tshwane motorists spend between R500 and R600 a month on fuel?
(v) Construct the *less than cumulative percentage ogive* for fuel bills and show it graphically as a *cumulative frequency polygon.*

(vi) From the cumulative graph, estimate what percentage of Tshwane motorists spend less R550 on fuel per month.

(vii) What percentage of Tshwane motorists spend more than R500 on fuel per month?

4.17 X4.17 – Corsa car sales

The sales records of an Opel car dealer in Durban show the quarterly sales of the Opel Corsa light passenger vehicle for the past 6 years.

(i) Use *Excel's* Chart Wizard to construct a *time line graph* showing the pattern of quarterly sales of the Corsa vehicle by the dealer.

(ii) If you were the dealer, would you renew your dealership of the Opel Corsa range next year based on past sales performance? Comment.

4.18 X4.18 – market shares

(i) Produce a *trend line graph* showing the trend in market share (%) for Volkswagen and Toyota motor vehicle sales over the past 10 years.

Year	Volkswagen	Toyota
1	13,4	9,9
2	11,6	9,6
3	9,8	11,2
4	14,4	12,0
5	17,4	11,6
6	18,8	13,1
7	21,3	11,7
8	19,4	14,2
9	19,6	16,0
10	19,2	16,9

(ii) Describe the trend in market shares for each car manufacturer over the past 10 years.

(iii) If you were to be offered a 5-year dealership of one of these motor vehicle makes, which one would you choose? And why?

4.19 X4.19 – defects

The production manager of a crockery (cups, saucers, plates, bowls) manufacturer recorded the *inspection time* (in minutes) by the quality controller on each of 30 consignments consisting of 500 items each, and noted the number of *defective items* found in each consignment.

(i) Produce a scatter plot between the *inspection time* (x) and the number of *defects found* (y).
Hint: Use the X–Y (Scatter) plot from *Excel's* Chart Wizard.

(ii) Does there appear to be a relationship between the amount of time spent on inspection of a consignment and the number of defective items founds in the batch? Briefly explain your answer.

4.20 X4.20 – leverage

A financial analyst surveyed 30 JSE-listed companies and recorded the *leverage ratio* (i.e. percentage of capital financed by debt) (x) and their *percentage growth in net profits* (y) over the past year. The analyst wants to know if leverage influences profit growth.

(i) Produce a scatter plot between the *leverage ratio* (x) and the *profit growth* (y) of the JSE-listed companies.
Hint: Use the X–Y **(Scatter)** plot from *Excel's* **Chart Wizard**. Also set the minimum scale on the x-axis to 30.

(ii) Can the analyst conclude that the degree of *leverage* influences a company's *growth in net profits* (as a percentage)? In what way? Explain briefly.

Chapter

5

Descriptive Statistics – Location Measures

Objectives

Summary tables (pivot tables) and graphic data displays provide a broad overview of the profile of random variables. However, more specific, numeric measures are required. These are provided by a set of numeric descriptive statistical measures to describe the *location* of data, the *spread* of data and the *shape* of the data. This chapter introduces the first of these numeric descriptive statistical measures – called measures of **location**.

The **central location** of data is considered first. Different central location measures (arithmetic mean, median, mode, geometric mean) are examined, as are the particular conditions appropriate for the use of each measure. Thereafter various **non-central location** measures (quartiles, percentiles), which describe useful non-central reference values in a data set are considered.

After studying this chapter, you should be able to:

- identify and describe the various central and non-central location measures
- compute each location measure, both manually and using *Excel* functions
- describe the appropriate central location measure for different data types
- interpret the meaning of each central location measure
- interpret the meaning of each non-central location measure.

5.1 Introduction

Summary tables and their graphical displays, as seen in chapter 4, are useful to communicate *broad overviews* of the profiles of random variables. However, managers also need *numerical measures* (called **statistics**) to convey *more precise* information about the behaviour of random variables. This precise communication of data is the purpose of *descriptive statistical measures.*

Three *statistical* measures are commonly used to *quantify* and *describe* the *profile* (behaviour pattern) of a random variable. These are:

- a measure of **location** (both *central* and *non-central* location)
- a measure of **spread** (or dispersion) about the central location value, and
- a measure of **shape** (skewness).

Central location refers to the *most representative value* of all the data values and is generally a "middle" value to represent where the majority of the data values are concentrated.

Non-central location refers to off-centre reference values in the data set used to describe certain data groupings.

A **dispersion** measure describes the extent to which the data values are spread about the central location value.

A **skewness** measure highlights the shape (or degree of symmetry) of the data values about the central location measure for a uni-modal (single peak) distribution.

The following example illustrates the practical use of measures of location, dispersion and skewness:

An electronic goods company has recorded the *value* of its *daily sales* (in Rand) over a 12-month trading period. For this random variable, the marketing manager would like to know:

(i) what the *average daily sales value* has been (a central location measure)

(ii) the extent to which the *individual daily sales values* are grouped around this average value (a measure of dispersion), and

(iii) whether any *exceptionally large* or *small daily sales values*, relative to the average sales, has occurred over this period (a measure of skewness).

This chapter focuses on measures of location (both central and non-central), while measures of dispersion and a measure of skewness for data are described in chapter 6.

5.2 Central Location

A **central location statistic** is a single number that gives a sense of the *concentration of data* values in a sample.

Managers and management reports often make statements containing terms such as:

- the *average* salary per job grade
- the *most popular* health care plan
- the *average* quantity of milk purchased by a household of four persons
- *half* of our employees spend less than R178 per month commuting to work
- the *mean* age of our employees.

These statements all refer to a *typical* or *central data value* used to represent where the majority of data values lie for a given random variable. Data values generally tend to group about some central value (locality) and statistical measures which are used to quantify these positions of data concentration are called **central location statistics**.

Three commonly used central location statistics are the:

(i) *arithmetic mean* (also called the average)
(ii) *mode* (or modal value), and
(iii) *median* (or second-quartile, middle-quartile or 50th percentile).

The choice of a particular central location statistic is determined by the *data type* of the random variable being analysed. All three measures (mean, mode and median) are valid for *numeric* data types, while only the mode is valid for *categorical* data types.

The following section defines each central location statistic, shows how each is derived from raw sample data, and illustrates and interprets the statistic in the context of management-oriented examples.

5.3.1 Arithmetic Mean (Average)

The **arithmetic mean** (or *average*) is that value which lies at the *centre* of a set of data values.

Formula

In general, for *numeric* random variables, the arithmetic mean is formulated as:

$$\bar{x} = \frac{\text{Sum of all the observations}}{\text{Number of observations}} = \frac{\Sigma x_i}{n}$$

Where

$\bar{x}$ = the sample arithmetic mean
n = the number of data values in the sample+
x_i = the value of the ith data value of random variable x
Σx = the sum of the n data values, i.e. $x_1 + x_2 + x_3 + x_4 + \ldots + x_n$

Example 5.1 Machinist Training Days study

The amount of *on-the-job training* (in days) received by 20 randomly selected machine operators in the moulding division of a large ceramics manufacturer was recorded in a recent study conducted by the HR department and shown in Figure 5.1 overleaf.

Refer to the database in Figure 5.1. *Excel* file: **C5.1 – machinists training**

Figure 5.1 Moulding machinist **Training Days** (n = 20 operators)

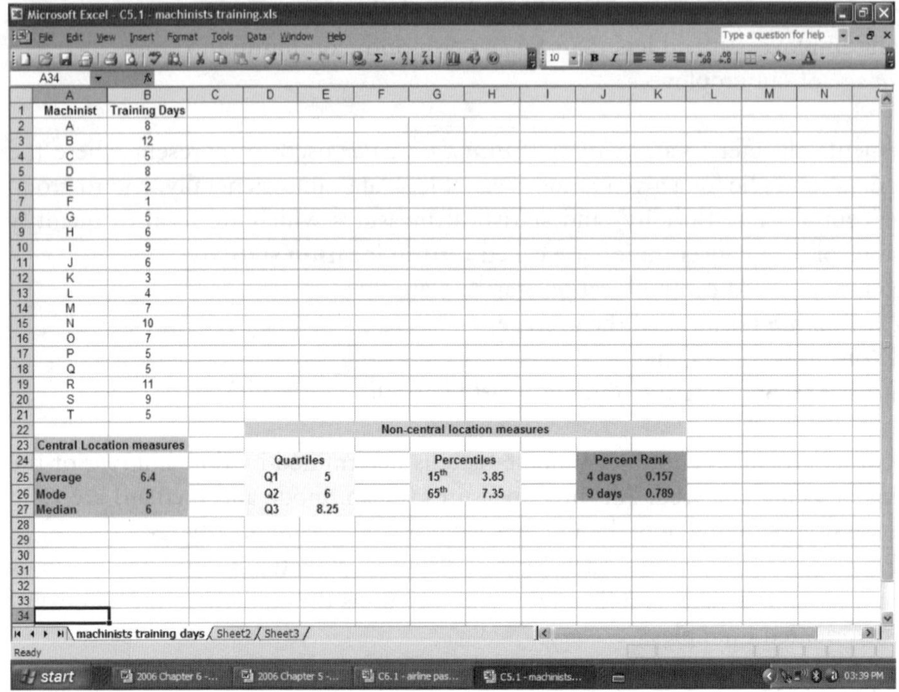

Machinist	Training Days
A	8
B	12
C	5
D	8
E	2
F	1
G	5
H	6
I	9
J	6
K	3
L	4
M	7
N	10
O	7
P	5
Q	5
R	11
S	9
T	5

Central Location measures	
Average	6.4
Mode	5
Median	6

Non-central location measures

Quartiles		Percentiles		Percent Rank	
Q1	5	15th	3.85	4 days	0.157
Q2	6	65th	7.35	9 days	0.789
Q3	8.25				

Management question

Find the **average** *number of training days* received by these 20 machinists.

Manual solution

To find the average, sum the number of training days for all 20 workers ($\sum x = 128$) and divide this total by the number of machine operators ($n = 20$).

Thus $\bar{x} = \dfrac{128}{20} = 6{,}4$ days.

Solution using *Excel*

The data is stored in the *Excel* file: **C5.1 - machinists training**, in the data range [B1:B21].

In cell A25, type the word "Average", and in cell B25 type the following *Excel* function operation:

= AVERAGE(B1:B21).

Press **enter**. The result of **6,4 days** is shown in cell B25.

Management interpretation

Moulding machine operators received an *average* of 6,4 days' training over the past year.

Advantages of using the arithmetic mean:
- It *uses all the data values* in its calculation.
- It is an *unbiased statistical measure*, because the sum of the differences between each data point and the mean always equals zero. This implies that, on average, the mean neither overestimates nor underestimates the actual central value.

The arithmetic mean has two main drawbacks:
- The mean is *valid* only for *numeric* variables of interval-scaled or ratio-scaled data. It is meaningless to compute and interpret an average for categorical data. For *example*, "average" *colour of cars*; or "average" *brand*, or "average" *gender* holds no meaning.
- The mean is *distorted* by *outliers*.
  An outlier is an extreme value relative to the majority of data values in a sample. To *illustrate*, the mean period of employment of four employees with individual employment periods of 3, 4, 6 and 7 respectively, is 5 years. However, if the fourth employee's period of employment was, instead, 39 years, then the "new" average would be 13 years. This "new" average is not representative of the majority's period of employment.

5.2.2 Mode

The **mode** is the *most frequently occurring value* in a sample of *n* data values.

The mode can be found both for *categorical data* (by identifying the most common category) and *numeric data* (after constructing a numeric frequency table).

Illustrative statements that refer to the *mode* as the central location measure are:
- Colgate is the brand of toothpaste *most preferred* by households.
- The *most common* choice of ice-cream flavour is chocolate.
- The *most popular* holiday destination in July is Durban.
- The supermarket *frequented most often* in Kimberley is *Checkers*.

HOW TO

To compute the mode

- *Group the data values* into either a categorical frequency table (if the data type is categorical), or into a numerical frequency table (if the data type is numeric).
  The mode is seldom computed for raw, ungrouped data, as the "most frequently occurring" value is more easily identifiable when data are summarised into a frequency count table.
- Identify either the *modal category* (for categorical data), or the *modal interval* (for numeric data). This is the category or class interval with the highest frequency.
- If the data are numeric, determine the *modal value* within the modal interval. While the midpoint of the modal interval could be used as an approximate measure for the mode, a more representative value can be found using a formula.

Modal value formula

The modal value formula takes into consideration the relative sizes (frequency) of the class intervals immediately adjacent (below and above) to the modal interval. It *weights* the modal value towards the adjacent class interval with the higher frequency count. It "pulls" the modal value from the midpoint of the modal interval to the left (i.e. lower), if the "below" class interval has a higher frequency count than the "above" class interval. Alternatively, the modal value becomes greater than the midpoint if the "above" class frequency is larger than the "below" class frequency.

Thus the *modal value* is *weighted* by the relative frequencies of the adjacent class intervals.

Formula

The formula to accomplish the above is given as:

$$M_o = O_{mo} + \frac{c(f_m - f_{m-1})}{2f_m - f_{m-1} - f_{m+1}}$$

Where

O_{mo} = lower limit of the modal class interval
c = width of the modal class interval
f_m = frequency of the modal class
f_{m-1} = frequency of the class preceding the modal interval
f_{m+1} = frequency of the class following the modal interval

Example 5.2 Courier Delivery Times study

Consider the *time* (in minutes) it takes a courier service to deliver parcels from its depot in Umbilo to its customers in Durban. A sample of 30 delivery times were taken in the last month. The frequency counts and ogive for delivery times is given in Table 5.1.

Table 5.1 Frequency count table and ogive for courier delivery times

Time	Frequency	Ogive
5–<10	3	3
10–<15	**5**	8
15–<20	**9**	17
20–<25	**7**	24
25–<30	6	30
Total	**30**	

Management question

Find the **modal** *time taken* by the courier service company to deliver parcels to its Durban-based customers.

Manual solution

The numeric data of 30 deliveries was grouped into a *frequency count table* – as shown in Table 5.1 – with the following profile:

- The modal interval (interval with the highest frequency) is (15–<20) minutes
- Lower limit of the modal interval O_{mo} = 15 minutes
- The class width c = 5 minutes

- The frequency of the modal class f_m = 9 deliveries
- The frequency of the adjacent lower class interval f_{m-1} = 5 deliveries
- The frequency of the adjacent upper class interval f_{m+1} = 7 deliveries.

Then the *modal delivery time is:*

$$M_o = 15 + \frac{5(9-5)}{2(9)-5-7} = 15 + 3,33 = 18,33 \text{ minutes}$$

Note: *Excel* can only be used if the individual data values are available.

Management interpretation

The *most common* delivery time to customers by the courier service is 18,33 minutes.

Example 5.3 Machinist Training Days study

Refer to the database in Figure 5.1. *Excel* file: C5.1 – machinists training

Management question

Find the **modal** *number of training days* received by the 20 machinists.

Solution using *Excel*

To find the modal days training received, in cell A26 type the word "Mode", and in cell B26 type the following *Excel* function operation:
= MODE(B1:B21).
Press **enter**. The modal value of 5 days is shown in cell B26.

Management interpretation

The most common *number of days' training* received by moulding machine operators is 5 days.

Advantages of the mode:

- The mode is a valid measure of central location for *all data types* (i.e. categorical and numeric). If the data type is categorical, the mode defines the most frequently occurring category. If the data type is numeric, the mode is the most frequently occurring data value (or the midpoint value of a modal interval, if the numeric data has been grouped into intervals).
- The mode cannot be influenced by outliers as it represents the most frequently occurring data value (or response category).

The mode has its disadvantages:

- It is a useful measure of central location only if the shape (distribution) of the numeric random variable is *uni-modal* (i.e. having one peak only). If the shape is *bi-modal*, there is more than one peak, meaning that two possible modes exist, in which case there is no single representative mode.

5.2.3 Median

The **median** is the *middle* number of an ordered set of data. The median is that data value of a numeric random variable that *divides* an *ordered set* of data values into *two equal halves.*

HOW TO

To compute the median – for ungrouped numeric data

- For a set of n data values, sort the data either in *ascending* or *descending* order. Use *Excel's* **Data Sort** option from the menu bar.
- Halve the sample size, n, to identify the middle or median position in the ordered data set, using one of these two methods:
  - If n is *odd*, the *median value* is found in the $\left(\frac{n+1}{2}\right)^{th}$ ordered position.
  - If n is *even*, the *median value* is found by identifying the $\left(\frac{n}{2}\right)^{th}$ data value and averaging it with the next consecutive data value.

Example 5.4 For the unordered data set of $n = 9$ observations

27 38 12 34 42 40 24 40 23

The *ordered* data set becomes:

12 23 24 27 **34** 38 40 40 42

The median position is:

$$\frac{n+1}{2} = \frac{(9+1)}{2} = 5^{th} \text{ position.}$$

The median value is that data value in the 5th position Median = 34

Example 5.5 For the unordered data set of $n = 10$ observations

27 38 12 34 42 40 24 40 23 18

The *ordered* data set becomes:

12 18 23 24 **27** **34** 38 40 40 42

The median position starts at the $\frac{n}{2} = \frac{10}{2} = 5^{th}$ position

The median value is the *average* of the data values in the 5th and 6th positions, i.e.

$$\text{median} = \frac{(27+34)}{2} = 30{,}5$$

To compute the median – for grouped numeric data

- From the numeric frequency table, compute $\frac{n}{2}$ to identify the *median position.*
- Identify the *median interval.* Using the frequency count table, the median interval is that class interval into which the $\left(\frac{n}{2}\right)^{th}$ observation falls. This median interval is found by summing the class frequencies from the lowest class until the cumulative frequencies either equal or just exceed $\frac{n}{2}$ (i.e. half the data values).

- Compute the *median value*. The midpoint of the median interval is the (approximate) median value. Alternatively, a formula can be used which will result in a more representative median value within the median interval:

Median value formula

The formula to accomplish this is:

$$M_e = O_{me} + \frac{c[\frac{n}{2} - f(<)]}{f_{me}}$$

Where

O_{me} = lower limit of the median interval
c = class width
n = sample size (number of observations)
f_{me} = frequency count of the median interval
$f(<)$ = cumulative frequency count of *all intervals before* the median interval

The formula finds the median value by adding a *fraction* $\left(\frac{\frac{n}{2} - f(<)}{f_{me}}\right)$ of the *class width* (c) to the lower limit of the median interval (O_{me}). This *fraction* represents the proportion of observations of the median interval that must be added to the cumulative frequency up to the lower limit of the median interval ($f(<)$) to arrive at the median position.

Thus $(\frac{n}{2} - f(<))$ is the number of additional observations from the lower limit of the median interval to arrive at the median position; and $\left(\frac{\frac{n}{2} - f(<)}{f_{me}}\right)$ is the required median interval fraction.

Example 5.6 Courier Delivery Times study

Refer to Example 5.2, the study of courier delivery times. The *pivot table* and *ogive* for the sample of 30 *delivery times* are given in Table 5.2.

Table 5.2 Frequency count table and ogive for the courier delivery times

Time	Frequency	Ogive
5–<10	3	3
10–<15	5	**8**
15–<20	**9**	**17**
20–<25	7	24
25–<30	6	30
Total	**30**	

Management question

Find the **median** *time taken* by the courier service company to deliver parcels to its Durban-based customers from its Umbilo depot.

Manual solution

From Table 5.2 the following measures can be extracted for the sample of 30 deliveries ($n = 30$):

- The median position is $\frac{n}{2} = \frac{30}{2} = 15^{th}$ position
- The median interval is between 15 and 20 minutes
- The lower limit of the median interval $O_{me} = 15$ minutes

- The class width c = 5 minutes
- The frequency of the median class f_{me} = 9 deliveries
- The cumulative frequency count up to the lower limit of the median interval $f(<)$ = 8 deliveries

Then the *median delivery time is*:

$$M_e = 15 + \frac{5(\frac{30}{2} - 8)}{9} = 15 + 3,89 = 18,89 \text{ minute}$$

Management interpretation

Half the parcels were delivered to the Durban-based customers in under 18,89 minutes.

Example 5.7 Machinist Training Days study

Refer to the database in Table 5.1. *Excel* file: C5.1 – machinists training

Management question

What is the **median** *number of training days* received by the 20 machinists?

Manual solution

First *sort* the 20 data values in ascending (or descending) order, i.e.:

1 2 3 4 5 5 5 5 5 **6** **6** 7 7 8 8 9 9 10 11 12

Now find the middle position for the given sample size n (i.e. $\frac{n}{2} = \frac{20}{2} = 10^{th}$ position).
Count to the 10th position. The 10th rank ordered-data value is the data value "6".

Since n is even, the median is found by averaging the two middle numbers (in this case the 10th and 11th positions), i.e.:

$\frac{(6 + 6)}{2} = 6$ days.

Solution using *Excel*

To find the median days' training received, in cell A27 type the word "Median", and in cell B27 type the following function operation:
= MEDIAN(B1:B21).
Press **enter**. The median value of **6 days** is shown in cell B27.

Management interpretation

The **median** *number of training days received* is six days. This means that half the machinists received 6 days or less on-the-job training while the other half received more than six days on-the-job training.

The median has one major advantage:

- It is *not distorted* by *outliers*. It is therefore the preferred measure of central location when outliers excessively distort the arithmetic mean.

The disadvantage of the median:

- The median is only appropriate (like the mean) for *numeric data*. The median has no meaning in the case of categorical data.

5.3 Non-Central Location Measures (Quartiles, Percentiles)

In addition to finding a central number for a set of numeric data, it is also useful to identify certain non-central reference points in a data set. They add insight into the profile of the sample data. Two sets of *non-central* reference points are *quartiles* and *percentiles*. Quartiles are, in fact, a subset of percentiles, as shown below.

5.3.1 Quartiles

Quartiles are *non-central location measures* that divide an *ordered* data set into quarters (i.e. four equal parts). They can only be computed for *numeric data types*.

Figure 5.2 below graphically illustrates the position of each quartile in an ordered data set.

Lower quartile (Q_1)
The lower quartile (*first quartile*) (*25th percentile*) identifies that data value below which the *lower 25%* of (ordered) data values fall.

Middle quartile (Q_2)
The middle quartile (*second quartile*) (*50th percentile*) identifies that data value which separates the *lower 50%* of data values from the *upper 50%* of data values in an ordered sample. The second quartile is the *median*, as it divides an ordered data set into two equal halves.

Upper quartile (Q_3)
The upper quartile (*third quartile*) (*75th percentile*) identifies that data value above which the *top 25%* of (ordered) data values lie.

Figure 5.2 Graphical illustration of **quartiles** and **percentiles**

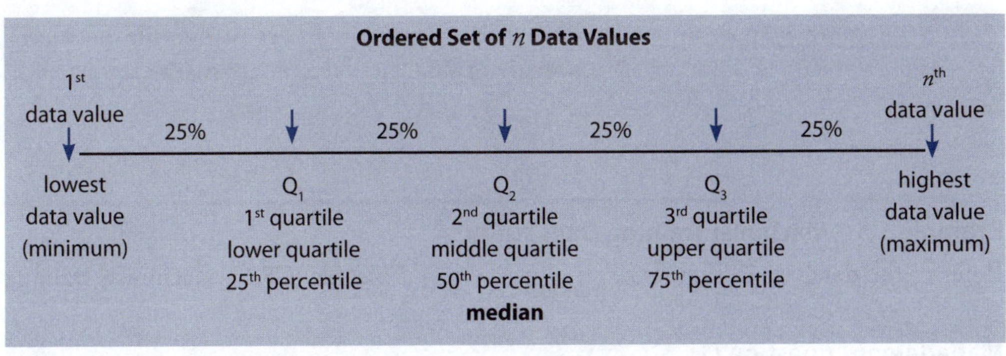

The following is an *illustrative* example of the use of quartiles:
Quartiles are often used to quote *salary scales* in organisations. For a given job grade, the salary scale per month could be:

Lower Limit	R5 250	The minimum salary paid for the job grade.
Lower Quartile	R5 600	The maximum salary received by the lowest paid 25% of employees.
Median	R6 250	The middle salary paid for the job grade.
Upper Quartile	R6 630	The minimum salary received by the highest paid 25% of employees.
Upper Limit	R6 900	The maximum salary paid for the job grade.

Computing Quartiles

Quartiles are computed in a similar way to the median, since the median is itself a quartile (i.e. the second quartile). They can be computed from raw, ungrouped sample data as well as from summarised, grouped data.

HOW TO

To compute quartiles for ungrouped (raw) data

- *Sort the data* either in ascending or descending order. (Use **Data Sort** in *Excel*).
- Identify the *quartile position*. Each *quartile position* is determined as follows, irrespective of whether *n* is even or odd:
  - for Q_1 find the $(n + 1) \times 0{,}25^{th}$ position
  - for Q_2 find the $(n + 1) \times 0{,}5^{th}$ position (same as used in the median)
  - for Q_3 find the $(n + 1) \times 0{,}75^{th}$ position.
- Count to the *quartile position* (rounded down to the nearest integer) to find the (approximate) *quartile value*.

To find a more exact quartile value if the quartile position is not an integer value, multiply the fractional component of the quartile position calculation with the difference between the approximate quartile value and its consecutive value and add it to the approximate quartile value.

Formula

To find a more exact quartile value, use the formula:

Quartile value = approximate quartile value + fractional part of quartile position × (next consecutive value after approximate quartile value – approximate quartile value).

Example 5.8 Machinist Training Days study

Refer to the database in Figure 5.1. *Excel* file: **C5.1 – machinists training**

Management question (1)

Find the **third quartile** *number of training days* received by the 20 machinists.

Manual Solution (1)

For n = 20 operators, the Q_3 position is: (20 + 1) × 0,75 = 15,75.

Thus the upper quartile value lies at the 15,75th position within the ordered set of 20 data values.
The data value in the 15th position is 8, which is the approximate Q_3 value.
The consecutive value in the 16th position is 9.
To find a more exact Q_3 value, which would correspond to the 15,75th position:
add 0,75 × (9 – 8) = 0,75 to the approximate Q_3 value of 8, giving 8 + 0,75 = 8,75.
This is a more likely value of the upper quartile (Q_3).

Management interpretation (1)

75% (or three quarters) of all machinists received *less than 8,75 days* training last year.

Management question (2)

Now use *Excel* to find the **lower**, **middle** and **upper quartiles** for the *number of training days* received by the 20 machinists.

Solution (2) using *Excel*

The **QUARTILE** function can be used to compute all the quartile values.
This function has two arguments:

- "*array*", which defines the *input data range*, and
- "*quart*", which is a *coded integer value* to identify the specific quartile to be found: 0 = minimum data value; 1 = lower quartile; 2 = middle quartile; 3 = upper quartile; and 4 = maximum data value.

To find all the **quartile values** of *days' training received*, type the words:
"Q_1" in cell D25
"Q_2" in cell D26, and
"Q_3" in cell D27

To activate the quartile function, type:
For Q_1 (in cell E25) = **QUARTILE(B1:B21,1)**
Press **enter**. Result: Q_1 = **5 days**

For Q_2 (in cell E26) = **QUARTILE(B1:B21,2)**
Press **enter**. Result: Q_2 = **6 days**

For Q_3 (in cell E27) = **QUARTILE(B1:B21,3).**
Press **enter**. Result: Q_3 = **8,25 days**

Management interpretation (2)

25% of the machinists received no more than 5 days on-the-job training over the past year. Half the machinists received 6 days or less, while another 25% of machinists received the most amount of on-the-job training, namely between 8,25 and 12 days last year.

HOW TO

To compute quartiles for grouped data

If the numeric data values are summarised into a pivot table and corresponding ogive, a formula similar to the median formula (see page 101) for grouped data can be used. The formula is modified to identify the appropriate *quartile position*, which is then used to find the corresponding *quartile interval*. All other terms are identical to those of the median formula.

Formula

Lower Quartile (Q_1): The lower quartile position is $\frac{n}{4}$ and the formula is:

$$Q_1 = O_{q1} + \frac{c[\frac{n}{4} - f(<)]}{f_{q1}}$$

Where

O_{q1} = the lower limit of the Q_1 interval
n = sample size
$f(<)$ = the cumulative frequency of the interval *before* the Q_1 interval
c = class width
f_{q1} = the frequency of the Q_1 interval

Example 5.10 Courier Delivery Times study

Refer to the frequency count data in Table 5.1 on page 98.

Management question

Find the **lower quartile** *time taken* for parcel deliveries to the courier company's Durban-based customers from its Umbilo depot.

Manual solution

From Table 5.1, the following measures can be extracted for the sample of 30 deliveries ($n = 30$):

- the Q_1 position is $\frac{n}{4} = \frac{30}{4} = 7{,}5^{th}$ position
- the Q_1 interval is thus (10 to <15) minutes
- the lower limit of the Q_1 interval O_{q1} = 10 minutes
- the class width c = 5 minutes
- the frequency of the Q_1 class f_{q1} = 5 deliveries
- the cumulative frequency count up to the lower limit of the Q_1 interval: $f(<)$ = 3 deliveries

Then, the Q_1 *delivery time* is:

$$Q_1 = 10 + \frac{5(\frac{30}{4} - 3)}{5} = 10 + 4{,}5 = 14{,}5 \text{ minutes}$$

Management interpretation

25% of deliveries take 14,5 minutes or less.

Formula

Upper Quartile (Q_3): The upper quartile position is $\frac{3n}{4}$ and the formula is:

$$Q_3 = O_{q3} + \frac{c[\frac{3n}{4} - f(<)]}{f_{q3}}$$

Where

O_{q3} = the lower limit of the Q_3 interval

n = sample size

$f(<)$ = the cumulative frequency of the interval *before* the Q_3 interval

c = class width

f_{q3} = the frequency of the Q_3 interval

Example 5.11 Courier Delivery Times study

Refer to the frequency count data in Table 5.1 on page 98.

Management question

Find the **upper quartile** *time taken* for parcel deliveries to the courier company's Durban-based customers from its Umbilo depot.

Manual solution

From Table 5.1 the following measures can be extracted for the sample of 30 deliveries (n = 30)

- the Q_3 position is $\frac{3n}{4} = \frac{3(30)}{4}$ = 22,5th position
- the Q_3 interval is thus (20 to <25) minutes
- the lower limit of the Q_3 interval O_{q3} = 20 minutes
- the class width c = 5 minutes
- the frequency of the Q_3 class f_{q3} = 7 deliveries
- the cumulative frequency count up to the lower limit of the Q_3 interval: $f(<)$ = 17 deliveries

Then, the Q_3 *delivery time* is:

$$Q_3 = 20 + \frac{5(\frac{3(30)}{4} - 17)}{7} = 20 + 3{,}93 = 23{,}93 \text{ minutes}$$

Management interpretation

75% of customers will receive their parcels within 23,93 minutes. Alternatively, 25% of all deliveries will take longer than 23,93 minutes.

5.3.2 Percentiles

A **percentile** is a data value below which a *specified percentage* of data values in an *ordered* data set will *fall.*

Percentiles are used to identify various *non-central location* positions in a sample of data.

Quartiles are examples of specific percentiles:

- the *lower* (or first) *quartile* is the *25th percentile*
- the *median* (or middle, or second, quartile) is the *50th percentile*, and
- the *upper* (or third) *quartile* is the *75th percentile.*

This idea can be extended to *any percentage* of values below a given data value:

- The **30th percentile** would represent that value in an ordered data set such that 30% of all data values will fall below this value and the balance, namely 70%, will lie above it.
- The **80th percentile** is that value in an ordered data set such that 80% of all data values will fall below this value and the balance, namely 20%, will lie above this value.

Refer to Figure 5.3 for a graphical illustration of percentiles.

Figure 5.3 Non-central location measures: **Percentiles**

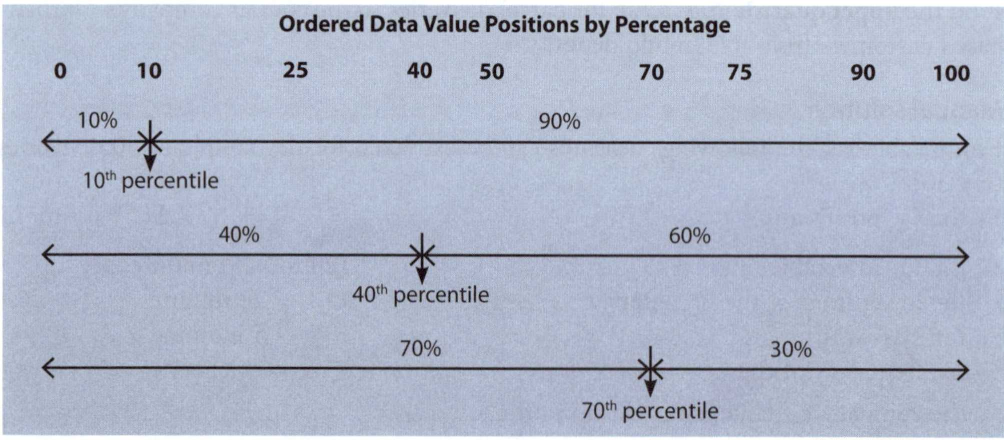

(i) To find percentiles

The logic to finding any percentile is similar to that of quartiles, namely to identify the class interval into which the required percentile position falls (by summing consecutive class frequencies) and then to choose a data value, within this identified class interval, that most closely approximates the desired percentile value.

Formula

The same formula as that applied to the calculations of quartiles (see page 104 for ungrouped data; and page 106 for grouped data) can be used to find the *percentile position* and, subsequently, the *percentile value.*

The *percentile position* is found by multiplying the sample size (n) by the required *percentile.* To *illustrate:*

- For the 90th percentile: the 90th percentile position is found by $((n + 1) \times 0{,}9)$.
- For the 38th percentile: the 38th percentile position is found by $((n + 1)) \times 0{,}38)$.
- For the 16th percentile: the 16th percentile position is found by $((n + 1)) \times 0{,}16)$.
- Thereafter, apply the same rule as for finding quartiles to identify a specific percentile value.

In *Excel*, the **PERCENTILE** function can be used to find the data value associated with a given percentile. The PERCENTILE function has two arguments:

- "*array*", which defines the *input data range*, and
- "*k*", which identifies the desired *percentile. k* lies between 0 and 1.

  If k = 0,25 then this is equivalent to finding the lower quartile.
  If k = 0,5 then the median value is returned by the function.
  If k = 0,75 then the upper quartile value is computed by the function.
  If k = 0,82 then the 82nd percentile value is being found.

Example 5.12 Machinist Training Days study

Refer to the database in Figure 5.1. *Excel* file: C5.1 – machinists training

Management questions

(1) What was the **maximum** *number of days' training* given to the 15% of machine operators who received the *least amount of training*?

(2) How many *days' training* were received by *no more than* 65% of the machinists?

Solution using *Excel*

To find the **15th** and **65th percentile** *training days received*, type the words **"15th Percentile"** in cell G25, and **"65th Percentile"** in cell G26.

To activate the percentile function, type:

For 15th Percentile (cell H25) =PERCENTILE(B1:B21,0.15).
Press **enter**. Result = **3,85** days.

For 65th Percentile (cell H26) =PERCENTILE(B1:B21,0.65).
Press **enter**. Result = **7,35** days.

Management interpretation

(1) 15% of the machinists received less than 3,85 day's training last year.

(2) 65% of the machinists received less than 7,35 day's training last year.

(ii) To find the percentile for a given data value (PERCENTRANK)

It is also useful to know the *percentile associated with a given data value* in a data set. This identifies, in percentage terms, where a given data value lies within an ordered data set.

In *Excel*, the **PERCENTRANK** function computes the *percentile* (%) associated with a specified data value in an ordered data set. The essential arguments for the PERCENTRANK function are:

- "*array*", which defines the *input data range*, and
- "*x*", which identifies the *data value* for which the rank percent is sought.

Example 5.13 Machinist Training Days study

Refer to the database in Figure 5.1. *Excel* file: C5.1 – machinists training

Management questions

What percentage of machinists had received no more than:

(1) 4 days of training over the past year?
(2) 9 days of training over the past year?

Solution using *Excel*

To find the percentile associated, with **4 days'** training and **9 days'** *training received* respectively, type the words **"Percentile 4 days"** in cell J25, and **"Percentile 9 days"** in cell J26. To activate the **percent rank** function:

In cell K25, type =PERCENRANK(B1:B21,4,3).
Press **enter**. Result = 0,157 (15,7%).

In cell K26, type =PERCENRANK(B1:B21,9,3).
Press **enter**. Result = 0,789 (78,9%).

Management interpretation

(1) 15,7% of machinists received four or less days on-the-job training last year.
(2) 78,9% of machinists received up to nine days on-the-job training last year.

5.4 Choosing a Valid Measure of Central Location

The choice of a *representative* central location statistical measure depends mainly on:

- the *data type* of the random variable under study, and
- the presence of outliers in the data set, which is reflected in the *shape* of the *histogram* for numeric random variables.

The influence of data type

The mean and median can only be used for numeric data, while the mode can be applied to both categorical and numeric data types.

The presence of outliers (shape of the frequency distribution)

The shape of the frequency distribution for a numeric random variable – as seen graphically in a histogram – determines the choice of a valid measure of central location.

- If *outliers are not present* in a data set and the shape is uni-modal (i.e. single-peaked distribution), then all three central location measures will give similar results and all are equally representative of the entire sample data set. In these circumstances, the *mean* is the preferred measure of central location.
- If *outliers are present* in a data set, then the arithmetic mean is distorted by the few small (or large) values and will give a misleading central location measure. In these circumstances, the *median* should be chosen as the representative central location measure (in preference to the mode).

Generally, if the numeric frequency distribution is skewed, the *median* is considered the best measure of central location to report, since it is not influenced by the extreme values and it can be used in further data analysis, albeit not to the same extent as the mean. Additionally, the median is not highly influenced by the frequency of occurrence of a single value (as is the mode).

5.5 Other Measures of Central Location

5.5.1 Geometric Mean

When data represents **percentage changes** – such as *indexes*, *growth rates*, or *rates of change* – where each observation is calculated from a different base (usually the preceding value in a time series), then the appropriate measure of central location is the *geometric mean.*

The example below demonstrates this:

The *weekly returns* on a company's share price is found by dividing the weekly change in share price by the previous week's share price. The geometric mean is appropriate if the company wishes to find their average weekly return in the share price over a period of, say, a year of 52 weeks.

HOW TO

To calculate the geometric mean

- Multiply all n observations (which are percentage changes expressed in decimal terms).
- Take the nth root of the product.

Formula

The formula for the Geometric Mean (GM) is:

$$\text{GM} = \sqrt[n]{x_1\, x_2\, x_3 \ldots\, x_n}$$

Note on data format

The percentage changes must be expressed as decimal values. For *example*, a 7% increase must be written as 1,07; a 4% decrease must be written as 0,96.

Example 5.14 Electricity Tariff study

The electricity tariff has increased by 12 per cent, 8 per cent and 16 per cent per annum over a three-year period.

Management question

Find the **average** *annual percentage increase* in the electricity tariff.

Manual solution

Geometric mean = $\sqrt[3]{1,12 \times 1,08 \times 1,16} = 1,1195$
i.e. an 11,95 % average annual increase.

Solution using *Excel*

The GEOMEAN function can be used to compute the geometric mean of a set of percentage change values, as follows:

=GEOMEAN(1.12,1.08,1.16) gives a result = **1.119524**
i.e. an 11,9524% average annual increase.

Management interpretation

The average electricity tariff increases over each of the three years was 11,95% annually.

5.5.2 Weighted Arithmetic Mean

The simple arithmetic mean assumes that each observation is of equal importance in computing the average (i.e. each observation in a sample of n observations is assumed to have a weight of $\frac{1}{n}$. However, if the importance (*weight*) of each observation is *different*, then the appropriate measure of central location for the observations would be the *weighted arithmetic mean*.

To compute the weighted arithmetic mean

- Each observation, x_i, is first multiplied (weighted) by its importance measure, which is generally its frequency, f_i.
- These weighted observations are then summed.
- This sum is then divided by the sum of the weights.

Formula

In formula terms, the **weighted arithmetic mean** is given by:

$$\text{weighted } \bar{x} = \frac{\Sigma f_i x_i}{\Sigma f_i}$$

Example 5.15 Training Consultant's Earnings study

A training consultant is paid R550 per hour for one eight-hour training programme; R420 per hour for a second training programme of six hours, and R800 for a two-hour seminar.

Management question

What is the training consultant's average earnings per hour for the three programmes?

Solution

Weighted arithmetic mean

$$= \frac{[550\ (8) + 420\ (6) + 800\ (2)]}{16} = \frac{8\ 520}{16} = \text{R}532{,}5$$

Management interpretation

The consultant is paid an average hourly rate of R532,5 for the three training programmes.

Note: There is no *Excel* function for the weighted mean.

5.6 Summary

This chapter introduced the first of the numerical measures of descriptive statistics, namely **measures of location**.

Measures of *central location* were examined first. The *mean* (arithmetic), *median* and *mode* are the three most important and commonly used measures of central location and are regularly used to report management information.

In addition, the conditions under which each central location measure would be appropriate to use, were described. The choice of a particular central location measure is influenced by its data type, and the distribution of the data (i.e. skewness) as shown in a histogram. While all three measures can be used for numeric data types, only the mode can be used for categorical data types.

The *geometric mean* was introduced as a measure of central location for percentage change (rate of change) data. The *weighted average* (weighted arithmetic mean) is another useful central location measure, which weights the mean in favour of more important values in a data set (or data values that occur more frequently than other data values).

Non-central location measures for numeric data types were also examined in the chapter. The most commonly used non-central location measures are *quartiles* (i.e. the lower, middle or median, and upper quartiles). *Percentiles* are more general forms of non-central location measures and can be used to exclude outliers beyond certain limits of the data range.

Finally the computation of each of the measures of central and non-central location was illustrated, both manually and using the functions of *Excel*.

Exercises

All computational exercises can be performed either manually or using *Excel*.

5.1 X5.1 – meal values

A restaurant owner randomly selected and recorded the *value of meals* enjoyed by 20 diners on a given day. The values of meals (in Rands) were:

44	65	80	72
90	58	44	47
48	35	65	56
36	69	48	62
51	55	50	44

(i) Define the *random variable* and its *data type*.
(ii) What is the mean *value of a meal* at the restaurant?
(iii) What is the median *value of a meal* at the restaurant? Interpret its meaning.
(iv) What *meal value* occurs most frequently?
(v) Which central location measure would you choose? Why?

5.2 X5.2 – days absent

The human resource department of a company recorded the *number of days absent* of 23 employees in the technical department over the past 9 months.

5	4	8	17	10
9	30	5	6	15
2	16	15	18	4
12	6	6	15	
10	10	9	5	

(i) Find the mean, median and modal *number of days absent* over this 9-month period. Interpret each central location measure.
(ii) Compute the first quartile and the third quartile of the *number of days absent*. Interpret these quartile values for the human resources manager.
(iii) The company aims to keep its absenteeism level to within an average of 1 day per month. Based on the findings in (i), is the company successfully managing its absenteeism level? Explain.

5.3 X5.3 – bad debts

The Gauteng chamber of business conducted a survey amongst 17 furniture retailers to identify the *percentage of bad debts* in each company's debtors' book. The bad debts percentages are as follows:

2,2	4,7	6,3	5,8
5,7	7,2	2,6	2,4
6,1	6,8	2,2	
5,7	3,4	6,6	
1,8	4,4	5,4	

(i) Find the average *% of bad debts* amongst the 17 furniture retailers surveyed.
(ii) Find the median *% of bad debts* amongst the 17 furniture retailers surveyed.
(iii) Interpret the findings from (i) and (ii).
(iv) Is there a modal % of bad debts?
If so, identify it and comment on its usefulness.
(v) Compute the first quartile and the third quartile of the *% of bad debts* amongst the furniture retailers surveyed. Interpret these quartile values.
(vi) The chamber of business monitors bad debt levels based on samples of companies. It will advise an industry to take corrective action if the % of bad debts, on average, exceeds 5%. Should the chamber of business send out an advisory note to all furniture retailers based on these sample findings? Justify your answer.

5.4 X5.4 – fish shop
A fish shop owner recorded the daily turnover of his outlet for 300 trading days as shown in the frequency table.

Daily turnover	**No. of days**
500–< 750	15
750–< 1 000	23
1000–< 1 250	55
1250–< 1 500	92
1500–< 1 750	65
1750–< 2 000	50

(i) Compute and interpret the average *daily turnover* of the fish shop.
(ii) Find the median daily turnover of the fish shop. Interpret its meaning.
(iii) What is the modal daily turnover of the fish shop?
(iv) Identify the maximum daily turnover associated with the slowest 25% of trading days.
(v) What daily turnover separates the busiest 25% of trading days from the rest?

5.5 X5.5 – grocery spend

An economist conducted a study to identify the *percentage of family income allocated to the purchase of groceries*. She surveyed a random sample of 50 families and compiled the following frequency table.

Percent of Income	No. of families
10–under 20%	6
20–under 30%	14
30–under 40%	16
40–under 50%	10
50–under 60%	4

(i) Compute and interpret the mean percentage of family income allocated to grocery purchase.
(ii) What is the maximum percentage of income that is allocated to grocery purchase by the lower 50% of families? By the lower 25% of families?
(iii) 25% of families spend more than a specific percentage of their income on groceries. What is that *percentage of income* value?

5.6 Find the average price paid per share in an equity portfolio consisting of: 40 shares bought for R15 each; 10 shares bought for R20 each; 5 shares bought for R40 each; and 50 shares bought for R10 each.

5.7 Value Cars, a pre-owned car dealership with branches throughout Gauteng, last month sold 5 cars at R25 000 each; 12 cars at R34 000 each; and 3 cars at R55 000 each. What was the average price per car sold by Value Cars last month?

5.8 Office rental agreements contain escalation clauses. For a particular office complex in the Nelspruit CBD, the escalation rates based on the previous year's rental over 4 years were 16%, 14%, 10% and 8% respectively. What was the *average annual escalation rate* in office rentals for this office complex over this 4 year period?

5.9 The price of a kilogram of sugar increased by 5%, 12%, 6%, 4%, 9% and 3% over the past 6 years. Find the *average annual percentage increase* in the price of sugar (per kg).

5.10 Which of the following statements are true and which are false. Give a reason for your answer:
If the *median* mass of 5 parcels for delivery by a courier service is 6,5 kg and one further 7 kg parcel is added to the consignment, then:

(i) the new median mass will be about 6,6 kg
(ii) the median will increase
(iii) it is impossible for the new median mass to be less than it was

(iv) it is impossible for the new median mass to stay exactly at 6,5 kg
(v) the median may increase, but that depends on the actual masses of all 6 parcels.

5.11 For which of the following statements would the *arithmetic mean* be an *inappropriate* measure of central location (give a reason). State which measure of central location would be more appropriate, if necessary.
(i) the ages of children at a playschool
(ii) the number of cars using a parking garage daily
(iii) the brand of cereal preferred by consumers
(iv) the value of transactions in a clothing store
(v) the weight of hand luggage carried by airline passengers
(vi) your preference of daily newspapers available in your city
(vii) the responses by citizens on a 5-point rating scale to the statement: "*South Africa should be divided into two time zones*".

5.12 The following measures of central location were calculated for a distribution of the number of persons per household in Mossel Bay:
mode = 2 persons; mean = 4,1 persons; median = 3 persons

If there are 9 245 households in the municipal district of Mossel Bay, which of the following procedures is appropriate to calculate the likely total number of persons living in Mossel Bay.
(i) multiply the number of households by 2
(ii) multiply the number of households by 4,1
(iii) multiply the number of households by 3.

5.13 **X5.13 – water usage**
Thirty households in a Paarl suburb were surveyed to identify their average water usage per month (in kilolitres (kl)). The usage per household was:

10	18	30	13	42
14	9	15	19	20
25	15	24	12	15
16	22	22	8	33
50	26	16	32	25
26	16	26	25	12

Use *Excel's* **Tools/Data Analysis/Descriptive Statistics** option and, where necessary, the function keys (**AVERAGE, MEDIAN, MODE, QUARTILE**) to answer the following questions.
(i) Find the mean, median and modal *water usage* across the 30 households surveyed.
(ii) Find the first and the third quartile of water usage amongst the 30 households.

(iii) Interpret the findings from (i) and (ii) for the municipal officer who conducted this survey.
(iv) If there are 750 households in the Paarl suburb, what is the *most likely total* water usage (in kl) amongst all these households in a month? In a year?

5.14 X5.14 – veal dishes

The price of a *veal cordon bleu* meal (in rand) was taken from the menus of 28 Durban restaurants in a survey conducted by *Lifestyle* magazine into the cost of "dining out". The prices are:

48	66	60	90
58	68	53	63
64	55	64	58
54	72	56	80
55	62	75	48
55	45	48	72
52	68	56	70

(i) Define the *random variable* and its *data type*.

Use *Excel's* **Tools/Data Analysis/Descriptive Statistics** option and, where necessary, the function keys (AVERAGE, MEDIAN, MODE, QUARTILE, PERCENTILE, PERCENTRANK) to answer the following questions.

(ii) Find the mean and median price of a *veal cordon bleu* meal. Interpret each measure.
(iii) Can you identify a modal price? Give its value and discuss its usefulness.
(iv) Which central location measure would you choose to report in the article on 'dining out'? Why?
(v) What is the least price that a patron to one of these restaurants would pay if they dined out at any one of the most expensive 25% of restaurants?
(vi) The least expensive 25% of restaurants do not charge above what price for the veal cordon bleu meal?
(vii) What is the least price to be paid for the most expensive 10% of cordon bleu meals?
(viii) Find and interpret the percentile ranks for cordon bleu meals costing R70; R52 and R64, respectively.

5.15 X5.15 – rose buds

A commercial flower grower in Hazyview sells fresh-cut rose buds to retailers in Johannesburg. The unit price per rose bud (in cents) varies according to supply and demand. The grower has recorded the unit selling price for 100 transactions over the past two months.

(i) Define the *random variable* and its *data type*.

Use *Excel's* **Tools/Data Analysis/Descriptive Statistics** option and, where necessary, the function keys (**AVERAGE, MEDIAN, MODE, QUARTILE, PERCENTILE; PERCENTRANK**) to answer the following questions.

(ii) What was the average unit selling price per transaction? Interpret.
(iii) What was the median unit selling price of transactions? Interpret.
(iv) Which measure of central location would you choose, and why?
(v) What was the highest unit selling price for the cheapest 25% of transactions?
(vi) What was the minimum unit selling price received from the highest priced 25% of the transactions?
(vii) What was the lowest unit selling price received for the highest-valued 10% of transactions?
(viii) What was the highest unit selling price received for the lowest-valued 10% of transactions?
(ix) Briefly describe the profile of unit selling prices for fresh-cut rose buds received over the past two months by the commercial flower grower.
(x) Find and interpret the percentile ranks for transactions where fresh-cut rose buds were sold for 58c each and 64c each respectively.

Chapter 6

Descriptive Statistics – Dispersion and Skewness Measures

Objectives

Central location measures are inadequate to fully describe the profile of a random variable. A measure of the spread of data values (dispersion) and their shape (skewness) is also required if a complete picture is to emerge. The latter two descriptive statistical measures are covered in this chapter. In addition, the chapter brings all descriptive measures together and shows how to use them to fully interpret a set of data. Another graphic display, the *box plot*, is introduced to capture, completely, the profile of a numeric random variable.

After studying this chapter, you should be able to:

- identify the various measures of dispersion (spread)
- describe the dispersion measures appropriate for the different data types
- compute and interpret each dispersion measure
- identify and compute measures of skewness in data
- construct and interpret a box plot
- integrate your understanding of all descriptive statistical measures.

6.1 Introduction

Chapter 5 identified the three descriptive statistical measures that fully describe the profile of a random variable. They are a:

- measure of *central location* (and *non-central locations*)
- measure of *dispersion* (or spread), and
- measure of *skewness.*

The various measures of central and non-central location were examined in chapter 5. Chapter 6 now describes measures of *dispersion* and *skewness*. These two measures are valid for *numeric* random variables only. They are meaningless for categorical random variables.

6.2 Measures of Dispersion

Dispersion (or spread) refers to the extent to which the data values scatter about their central location value.

Figure 6.1 shows that a random variable, *x* (e.g. the *ages of persons*), representing three separate populations (A = age pattern of MBA students; B = age pattern of mineworkers, and C = age pattern of spectators at a sports event), can have the same central location value (e.g. *mean age = 32 years*), but different measures of dispersion (e.g. for graph A, *spread = 3 years*; for graph B, *spread = 5,2 years*; for graph C, *spread = 9,4 years*).

Figure 6.1 Varying spreads for three groups with same central location

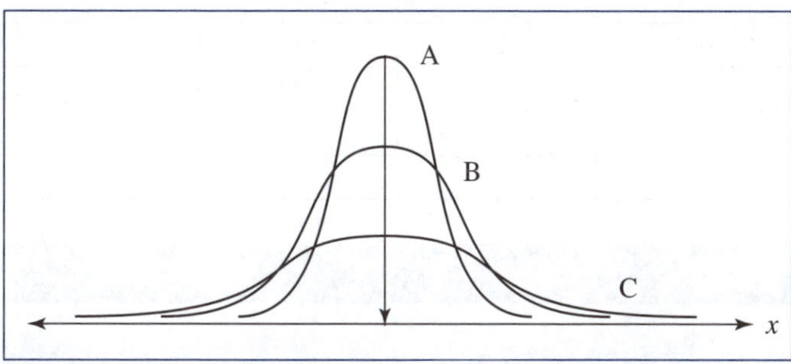

Why measure dispersion?

Dispersion is a measure of *data variability*. This influences the *confidence* that an analyst can have in the *representativeness* and *reliability* (stability) of central location measures. Widely dispersed data values indicate low reliability and less confidence in the central location as a representative measure for a sample of data. Conversely, a high concentration of data values about their central location indicates high reliability and greater confidence in the representativeness of the central location value.

Types of dispersion measures

The measures that are commonly used to describe data dispersion are:

- range
- inter quartile range
- quartile deviation
- variance, and
- standard deviation.

The following example of a problem scenario will be used to illustrate the computation and interpretation of the various dispersion measures.

Problem Scenario 6.1 Aircraft Passengers – Luggage Weights study

The weight profile of passengers' luggage is important in balancing aircraft. Hence commercial airlines have a luggage weight limit of 20 kg per passenger. The *luggage weights* of 30 randomly selected passengers were recorded in Table 6.1 and analysed by a particular airline. The airline's management required statistical evidence to better understand the distribution of luggage weights.

The *Excel* data file is: **C6.1 – airline passengers**, as shown in Figure 6.2 below. The *luggage weights* data is shown in the data range [A2:A32], together with statistical analysis, which is covered in this chapter.

Table 6.1 Airline passengers' Luggage Weights (kg) (n = 30 passengers)

22,4	22,5	19,3	19,8	16,8	13,8
22,1	19,8	19,6	**13,2**	19,6	18,2
21,7	16,7	16,5	16,2	19,9	16,9
18,5	**25,2**	19,3	16,9	18,4	24,3
19,6	16,8	16,9	19,4	19,4	18,8

6.3 Range (R)

The **data range** is the *difference* between the *highest* and *lowest* data values in a data set.

Range identifies the **interval of values** between the highest and lowest data values. The greater the interval, the wider the range; the smaller the interval, the narrower the range.

Formula

Range = max value – min value + 1 $\qquad R = x_{max} - x_{min} + 1$

Figure 6.2 Excel database and analysis for airline passengers' **Luggage Weights**

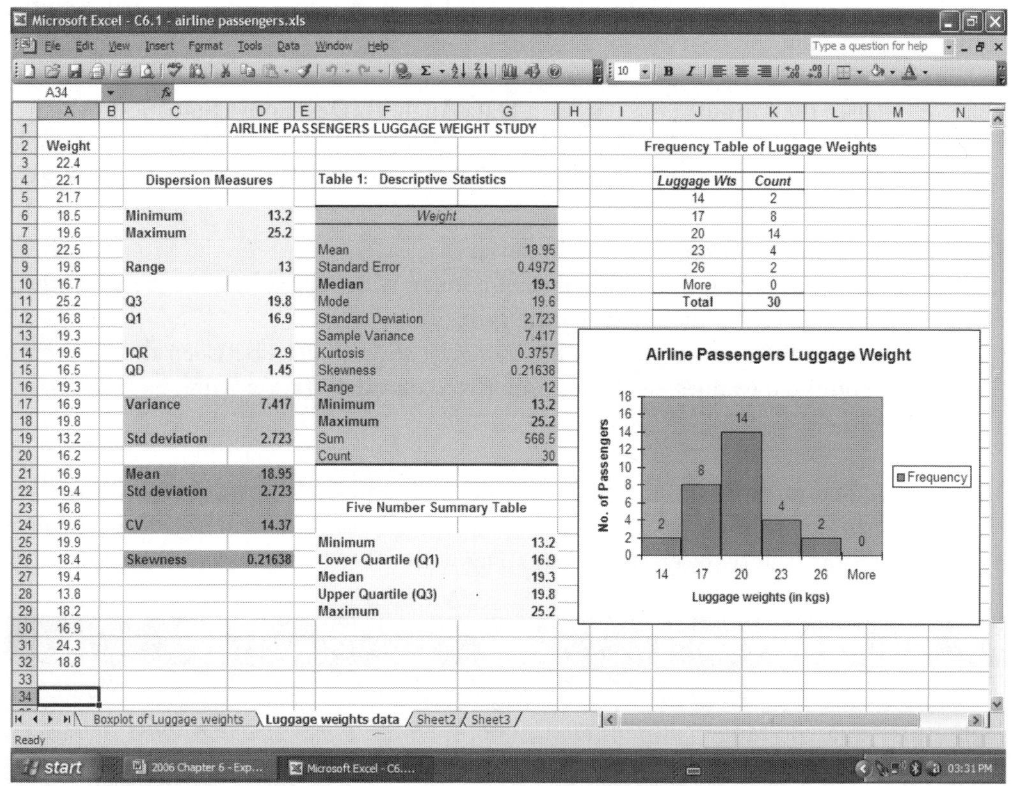

Example 6.1 Aircraft Passengers – Luggage Weights study

Management question

Find the **range** of the 30 sampled passengers' *luggage weights*.

Solution

From Table 6.1, identify x_{max} = 25,2 kg and x_{min} = 13,2 kg

Then the *range* R = 25,2 – 13,2 + 1 = 13 kg

(Refer to cells [C6:D9] for the *range* calculation in Figure 6.2.)

Management interpretation

Luggage weights ranged from 13,2 kg to 25,2 kg. This gives a spread of 13 kg between the lightest luggage and the heaviest luggage.

Note: *Excel* uses the formula ($x_{max} - x_{min}$) in **Data Analysis (Descriptive Statistics)**, which is *not inclusive* of the maximum value in the data set. Thus *Excel's* ***range*** answer would be 12 kg (see Table 6.2 in Section 6.11 below or cells [F16:G16] in Figure 6.2)

The range is a ***crude measure*** of spread because:

- *outliers* distort it, giving the impression of a much wider spread of data between the majority of data values than is really the case.
- range provides *no information about the clustering of data values* between the minimum and maximum data values, as it uses only two data values (i.e. x_{max} and x_{min}) to calculate it.

The range, therefore, is an unstable, volatile and unreliable measure of dispersion. However, it is always a useful first indication of the spread of data in a data set. It must be viewed with care and always examined along with other measures of dispersion.

6.4 Inter Quartile Range

The **inter quartile range** is the difference between the *upper* and *lower quartiles* in a set of sample data values.

It therefore identifies the range (distance) of data values between the *lower quartile* and *upper quartile* positions only.

Formula

$$\text{Inter Quartile Range (IQR)} = Q_3 - Q_1$$

Since the interval between Q_1 and Q_3 covers the **middle 50%** of data values, the inter quartile range identifies the spread of the middle 50% of data values.

Advantage of the inter quantile range:

The inter quartile range removes some of the instability inherent in the range if outliers (or extreme data values) are present. This modified range excludes these outliers and focuses on the spread of the middle 50% of the data values. It is therefore a more stable measure of dispersion than the range.

Disadvantages of the inter quantile range:

- The inter quartile range also only uses two values in its construction (Q_1 and Q_3) and therefore provides no information on the clustering of data values within the interval between the quartiles.
- It excludes the outer 50% of the data values (25% below Q_1, and 25% above Q_3).

Example 6.2 Aircraft Passengers – Luggage Weights study

Management question

Find the **inter quartile range** of the 30 sampled passengers' *luggage weights.*

Solution using *Excel*

Refer to the *Excel* database file: **C6.1 – airline passengers** in Figure 6.2.

Using the *Excel* function =QUARTILE(A2:A32,1) gives Q_1 = 16,9 kg
Similarly =QUARTILE(A2:A32,3) gives Q_3 = 19,8 kg

These quartile values can also be found using the method described in chapter 5, section 5.2.3.

Then, the Inter Quartile Range (IQR) = 19,8 – 16,9 = 2,9 kg
(Refer to cells [C11:D14] for the IQR calculation in Figure 6.2.)

Management interpretation

The *middle 50%* of *luggage weights* spans an interval of 2,9 kg between the lower quartile value of 16,9 kg and the upper quartile value of 19,8 kg.

6.5 Quartile Deviation

The **quartile deviation** is a measure of *spread* of the data values *about the median.*

The quartile deviation approximates the distances of the minimum, lower quartile, upper quartile and maximum values from the central location measure of the median.

Formula

$$\text{Quartile Deviation (QD)} = \frac{\text{(Inter Quartile Range)}}{2}$$

Interpretation of the Quartile Deviation

Since the IQR covers the middle 50% of data values, the QD can be used to find limits within which approximately each 25% of data values can be found.

Thus

- Median – (2 × QD) = (approximately) the minimum data value (50% below the median)
- Median – QD = (approximately) the lower quartile (25% below the median)
- Median (the middle data value)
- Median + QD = (approximately) the upper quartile (25% above the median)
- Median + (2 × QD) = (approximately) the maximum data value (50% above the median)

The shorter the distance between consecutive 25% limits, the smaller the spread of data, and vice versa.

For the *luggage weights* study, the quartile deviation is 1,45 kg. (Refer to cells [C15:D15] in Figure 6.2 on page 123.) This means that there is an approximately 1,45 kg difference between consecutive quartiles.

6.6 Variance

The most useful and reliable measures of dispersion to *capture variability* are those that:

- take *every data value* into account in their calculation, and
- are based on an *average measure of deviation* from the central value.

The *variance* is such a measure of dispersion (or spread). It is the most commonly used measure of dispersion and is a powerful statistic used extensively to capture variability. In *financial analysis*, for *example*, variance is universally used as a *measure of risk* in portfolios.

HOW TO

To calculate the variance

(i) Compute the sample mean $\bar{x}$

(ii) Compute the deviation of each data value from the mean $(x_i - \bar{x})$

(iii) Square these deviations (to avoid positive and negative deviations cancelling each other when they are summed) $(x_i - \bar{x})^2$

(iv) Sum these squared deviations $\Sigma(x_i - \bar{x})^2$

(v) Finally, average the squared deviations by dividing (iv) by $(n - 1)$.

This measure is called the **variance**. It is a measure of *average squared deviation*. It is identified as σ^2 for populaton data, and s^2 for sample data.

Formula

In formula terms, the variance for sample data can be expressed as:

$$\text{Variance } (s^2) = \frac{\text{Sum of squared deviations}}{(\text{sample size} - 1)} = \frac{\Sigma(x_i - \bar{x})^2}{(n - 1)}$$

Note: Division by the sample size, n, would be logical, but the variance statistic would then be a *biased* measure of dispersion. It is unbiased (desirable) when division is by $(n - 1)$. For large samples $(n > 40)$, this distinction becomes less important.

Example 6.3 Aircraft Passengers – Luggage Weights study

Management question

Find the **variance** of the 30 sampled passengers' *luggage weights*.

Manual solution

(Refer to Table 6.1 on page 122.)

- The sample mean = $\frac{568{,}5}{30} = 18{,}95$ kg
- Sum and square all deviations from the sample mean
  $(22{,}4 - 18{,}95)^2 + (22{,}1 - 18{,}95)^2 + (21{,}7 - 18{,}95)^2 + (18{,}5 - 18{,}95)^2 + \ldots$
  $+ (18{,}8 - 18{,}95)^2 = 215{,}095$
- Average the sum of these squared deviations
  $s^2 = \frac{215{,}095}{(30 - 1)} = 7{,}417$

Solution using Excel

Refer to the *Excel* database file: **C6.1 – airline passengers**.
Using the *Excel* function **=VAR(A2:A32)** gives s^2 = **7,417**
(Refer to cells [C17:D17] for the *variance* calculation in Figure 6.2.)

Management interpretation

The ***variance*** of *luggage weights* is 7,417 kg^2.

Variance is a measure of average *squared* deviation about the arithmetic mean. It is expressed in squared units. Consequently, its meaning – in a practical sense – is obscure. To provide meaning, the dispersion measure should be expressed in the original units of measure of the random variable. This is provided by a measure of dispersion called the **standard deviation**.

6.7 Standard Deviation

Standard deviation expresses dispersion – as computed by the variance – in the *original units* of the random variable.

A standard deviation is found by taking the *square root* of the *variance, i.e.*:

$$\text{Standard deviation} = \sqrt{\text{variance}}$$
$$s = \sqrt{s^2}$$

σ identifies a population standard deviation, while s describes a sample standard deviation.

Formula

Thus the mathematical formula for a standard deviation of sample data is the square root of the variance formula, as follows:

$$s = \sqrt{\frac{\Sigma(x_i - \bar{x})^2}{(n-1)}}$$

Example 6.4 Aircraft Passengers – Luggage Weights study

Management question

Find the **standard deviation** of the 30 sampled passengers' *luggage weights.*

Manual solution

Given the sample variance $s^2 = 7{,}417$

Then the sample standard deviation $s = \sqrt{7{,}417} = 2{,}723$ kg

Solution using *Excel*

Refer to the *Excel* database file: **C6.1 – airline passengers.**

Using the *Excel* function **=STDEV(A2:A32)** gives s = **2,723 kg**

(Refer to cells [C19:D19] for the *standard deviation* calculation in Figure 6.2.)

Management interpretation

The *standard deviation* of the sample of luggage weights is 2,723 kg.

A fuller interpretation follows.

To interpret a standard deviation

If the frequency distribution of the *numeric* random variable is *symmetrical*, the following interpretation can be applied to the standard deviation:

- **68,26%** of all data values can be expected to lie within **one standard deviation** of the mean,
  i.e. between the lower limit of $(\bar{x} - s)$ and the upper limit of $(\bar{x} + s)$.
- **95,44%** of all data values can be expected to lie within **two standard deviations** of the mean,
  i.e. between the lower limit of $(\bar{x} - 2s)$ and the upper limit of $(\bar{x} + 2s)$.
- **99,73%** (almost all) of the data values can be expected to lie within **three standard deviations** of the mean,
  i.e. between the lower limit of $(\bar{x} - 3s)$ and the upper limit of $(\bar{x} + 3s)$.

Figure 6.3 below shows the areas under a bell-shaped (normal) distribution associated with one, two and three standard deviations about the mean.

Figure 6.3 Percentage (%) of data values within 1, 2, and 3 standard deviations of the mean

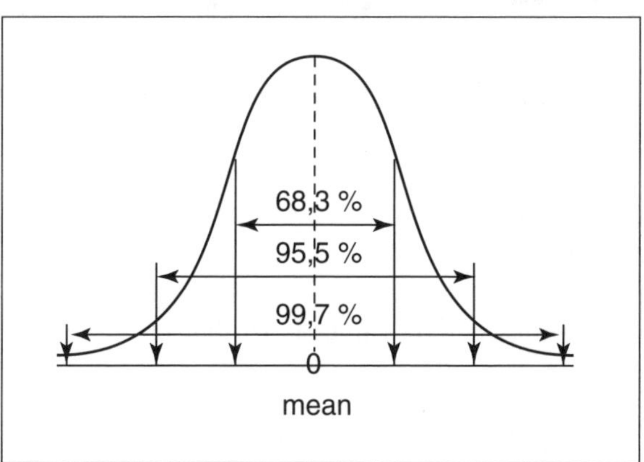

Example 6.5 Aircraft Passengers – Luggage Weights study

Mean weight of luggage = 18,95 kg. Standard deviation of luggage weights = 2,723 kg

Management question

Interpret the **spread** of the sampled *luggage weights* about their mean.

Management interpretation

The *frequency table* (cells [J4:K11]) and *histogram* in Figure 6.2 show that *luggage weights* are almost *symmetrically distributed* about the mean weight of 18,95 kg. Hence the use of the standard deviation to interpret the *spread of luggage weights* is meaningful and valid.

Thus with $\bar{x}$ = 18,95 kg and s = 2,723 kg, and assuming a symmetrical (normal) pattern of data values (outcomes) about the mean, the following can be stated:

(i) Approximately 68,26% of all passengers' luggage can be expected to weigh between 16,227 kg and 21,673 kg.

(ii) Approximately 95,44% of all passengers' luggage can be expected to weigh between 13,508 kg and 24,396 kg.

(iii) Almost all passengers' luggage (99,73%) can be expected to weigh between 10,781 kg and 27,119 kg.

Advantages of the standard deviation measure:

- It *gives more insight* into the *spread* of all the data values about the mean than any other measure of spread.
- It is a relatively *stable measure of dispersion* across different samples of the same random variable. It is therefore a rather powerful descriptive statistic.

Disadvantage of the standard deviation measure:

- The standard deviation (and variance) is distorted by *outliers*.

6.8 Coefficient of Variation

The **coefficient of variation (CV)** is a measure of *relative variability*.

The standard deviation is a measure of absolute variability, which means that the spread of data values can only be measured in relation to its own arithmetic mean. On its own, the standard deviation conveys no meaningful information.

To illustrate:
An $s = 10$ can be large if the arithmetic mean of the data values is 15, but an $s = 10$ can be small if the arithmetic mean is 250.

Formula

To interpret the magnitude of a standard deviation, the standard deviation must be compared to its own mean. This is expressed in the *coefficient of variation:*

$$\text{Coefficient of variation (CV)} = \frac{\text{standard deviation}}{\text{mean}}\%$$
$$= \frac{s}{\bar{x}}\%$$

The coefficient of variation is interpreted as a *percentage*.

The *smaller* the CV, the *more concentrated* the data values are about their mean; conversely, a *large* CV implies that the data values are more *widely dispersed* about their mean value. The lower limit of a CV is zero, but there is no upper limit.

Example 6.6 Aircraft Passengers – Luggage Weights study

Mean weight of luggage = 18,95 kg. Standard deviation of luggage weights = 2,723 kg.

Management question

Compute and interpret a measure of **relative variation** in *luggage weights*.

Solution using *Excel*

Refer to the *Excel* database file: **C6.1 – airline passengers**.

The **coefficient of variation** of *luggage weights* = (2,723/18,95) % = 14,37%
(Refer to cells [C21:D24] for the *coefficient of variation* calculation in Figure 6.2.)

Management interpretation

Passenger *luggage weights* are closely concentrated about the mean weight of 18,95 kg.

HOW TO

To compare variability between random variables

The coefficient of variation can also be used to compare the relative variability of data values between two or more *different* random variables. For *example*, does the *weight* of passengers show greater variability than their *height*?

Example 6.7 Airline Passengers – Weight and Height study

Assume the following descriptive measures are given for a sample of 30 passengers:

	Passenger Weight	Passenger Height
Mean	78 kg	166 cm
Standard Deviation	16,4 kg	20,1 cm

Management question

Compare the **relative variability** between *passenger weights* and *passenger heights*. Which characteristic shows greater *relative variability*?

Solution

Compute the CV for each variable, *weight* and *height*.

	Passenger Weight	Passenger Height
Mean	78 kg	166 cm
Standard Deviation	16,4 kg	20,1 cm
Coefficient of Variation (CV)	21,03%	12,11%

Management interpretation

Passengers' *weights* show *greater variability* than their *heights* about their respective arithmetic means.

6.9 Measure of Skewness

The **skewness statistic** describes the *shape* of a uni-modal *distribution* of numeric data values.

The Importance of Skewness

The shape of uni-modal distribution of data values influences an analyst's choice of central location and dispersion measures to validly describe the profile of a data set. It also influences the choice of an appropriate statistical technique in the field of inferential statistics.

Types of Skewness – assuming a uni-modal distribution

Three common shapes can generally be observed in sets of numeric data:

- Symmetrical shapes
- Positively skewed shapes (skewed-to-the-right)
- Negatively skewed shapes (skewed-to-the-left)

(i) Symmetrical shapes

Symmetrical frequency distributions of data sets have a *single central peak* and *mirror image slopes* on either side of the central value. (See Figure 6.4 overleaf.)

Figure 6.4 Symmetrical distribution of data

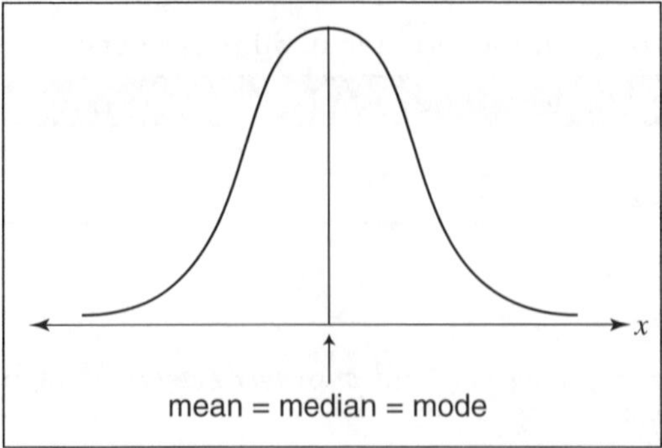

If a distribution is symmetrical, all three *central location* statistical measures (i.e. mean, mode and median) will have the *same value.* All three central location measures are therefore equally valid to use for the description of the central location of a symmetrical set of sample data.

For *example*, the *volume of juice* in 1-litre cartons is generally symmetrical about a mean fill of 1 litre.

(ii) Positively skewed shapes

A frequency distribution is positively skewed (or skewed-to-the-right) when there are a *few extremely large data values* (outliers) relative to the other data values in the sample.

A positively skewed distribution will have a "long" *tail* to the *right,* as shown in Figure 6.5.

For example, the *duration of stay of foreign visitors* to Cape Town may well exhibit positive skewness, since the majority are likely to spend no more than a few days, with a small number spending a few weeks or even months in Cape Town.

Figure 6.5 Positively skewed distribution of data

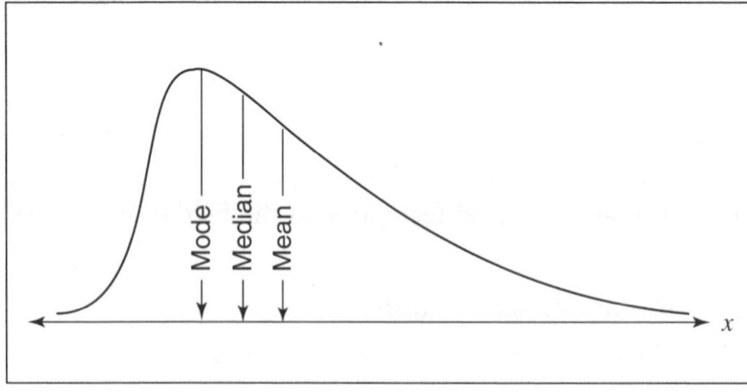

(iii) Negatively skewed shapes

A frequency distribution is negatively skewed (or skewed-to-the-left) when there are a *few extremely small data values* (outliers) relative to the other data values in the sample.

A negatively skewed distribution will have a "long" *tail* to the *left*, as seen in Figure 6.6.

For example, the *lead time (in days) of selling houses* may well exhibit negative skewness. Only a few are likely to be sold within a few days, while the majority are usually sold after lengthy periods of time (even a few months).

Figure 6.6 Negatively skewed distribution of data

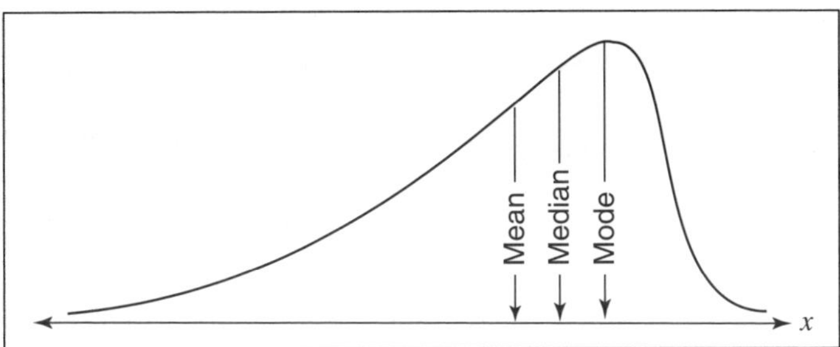

In both a negatively skewed distribution and a positively skewed distribution, the mean will be most influenced (distorted) by the extremely small or large outliers. It should therefore not be regarded as a representative central location measure. The median and the mode, on the other hand, are not affected by outliers and either of these can therefore be used as a valid measure of central location for this skewed distribution of data. In general, the median is the preferred measure of central location with skewed distributions.

A Measure of Skewness

Pearson's coefficient of skewness (Sk_p) is the statistic which measures skewness in a sample of numeric data.

Formula

The coefficient of skewness is computed as follows (although the formula is seldom manually calculated):

$$\text{Pearson's Skewness coefficient } (Sk_p) = \frac{n\Sigma(x_i - \bar{x})^3}{(n-1)(n-2)s^3}$$

Interpretation of the formula

If $Sk_p = 0$ this shows complete *symmetry* in the sample data set. It will also be seen that mean = median = mode.

If $Sk_p > 0$ this implies that the distribution of data values is *positively skewed*. In these instances, it will be noted that mean > median value.

If $Sk_p < 0$ this implies that the distribution of data values is *negatively skewed*. In these instances, it will be noted that mean < median value.

Note: While Pearson's coefficient of skewness can assume, in theory, any value from $-\infty$ to $+\infty$, most skewness coefficients have values within a narrow interval around zero, which represents perfect symmetry. The further the skewness coefficient deviates from zero (in either a negative or a positive direction), the more skewed the distribution. This will also be seen in a large difference between the mean and the median values.

A Decision Rule of Thumb

To facilitate measurement of skewness, the following decision rule may applied:
If only slight (**marginal**) skewness is present, the skewness coefficient is likely to lie between –0.5 and +0.5. **Moderate** skewness will be reflected in an Sk_p value of between –1 and +1. Skewness coefficients outside this range (< –1 and > +1) indicate **excessive** skewness in the data.

The sign of the skewness coefficient is evidence of the *direction* of skewness. If Sk_p is negative (e.g. $Sk_p = -0{,}84$), the distribution is moderately skewed to the left, implying a few low-valued outliers. Alternatively, if Sk_p is positive (e.g. $Sk_p = 0{,}32$), the distribution is only marginally skewed to the right, implying a few high-valued outliers.

The impact of skewness is also determined by the sample size. The smaller the sample size, the larger the absolute value of the skewness coefficient needs to be to be significantly skewed; the larger the sample size, the smaller the absolute value of the skewness coefficient needs to be to be significantly skewed.

An Approximation Test for Skewness

A quick test can be done for the presence of skewness in a data set, by comparing the *mean* and the *median* values, relative to the standard deviation. The further apart these two measures are, the greater the skewness in the sample data set in the direction in which the mean has moved relative to the median value.

Formula

A useful *approximation formula* for skewness is: $\dfrac{3\,(\text{mean} - \text{median})}{\text{standard deviation}}$

The approximation formula is interpreted in the same way as the decision rule for skewness measurement above.

Example 6.8 Aircraft Passengers – Luggage Weights study

(Refer to Table 6.1 on page 122.)
Mean weight of luggage = 18,95 kg. Standard deviation of luggage weights = 2,723 kg.
Median weight of luggage = 19,3 kg.

Management question

Determine the **degree of symmetry** (*skewness*) in the distribution of *luggage weights.*

Solution using *Excel*

Refer to the *Excel* database file: **C6.1 – airline passengers.**

Using the *Excel* function =**SKEW(A2:A32)** gives Sk_p = 0,21638
(Refer to cells [C26:D26] for the *skewness coefficient* calculation in Figure 6.2.)

Management interpretation

The distribution of airline passenger *luggage weights* is only slightly *positively skewed.*

This means that there are only a few passengers with luggage of excess weight. The majority of passengers' luggage is below the weight allowance limit.

6.10 Review of Descriptive Statistics

Chapters 4, 5 and 6 covered a range of graphical and descriptive statistical measures to profile any random variable. A manager needs to understand how to choose the right mix (combination) of statistical displays and descriptors to validly describe the profile of a particular random variable. This choice is determined by two main criteria: the *data type* of the random variable, and the pattern of *skewness* in the summarised data profile.

The following section serves, first of all, to summarise the various graphical displays and descriptive statistical measures and, finally, to provide useful guidelines for the choice of valid measures for any given random variable.

6.10.1 Summary of all the Descriptive Statistical Measures

(i) Five-number summary table

A complete profile of any numeric random variable can be summarised in terms of five descriptive statistical measures known as the *five-number summary table*:

Five-number Summary Table		
(i)	The minimum data value	x_{min}
(ii)	The lower quartile	Q_1 or the 25th percentile
(iii)	The median	M_e or Q_2 or the 50th percentile
(iv)	The upper quartile	Q_3 or the 75th percentile
(v)	The maximum data value	x_{max}

Example 6.9 Aircraft Passengers – Luggage Weights study

(Refer to the data in Table 6.1 on page 122.)

Management question

Prepare a **five-number summary table** for the distribution of *luggage weights.*

Solution using *Excel*

Refer to the *Excel* database file: C6.1 – airline passengers.

Excel offers a summary of **Descriptive Statistics** in the **Data Analysis** add-in:

To activate the Descriptive Statistics tool, select Tools, then Data Analysis and finally Descriptive Statistics from the Data Analysis menu (refer to chapter 3 for the instructions).

Table 6.2 shows the descriptive statistics for *luggage weights* of airline passengers. Also refer to Table 1 (cells [F6:G20]) in Figure 6.2 above.

Table 6.2 Descriptive statistics for Luggage Weights of airline passengers

Luggage Weight (kg)	
Mean	18,95
Standard Error	0,4972
Median	**19,3**
Mode	19,6
Standard Deviation	2,723
Sample Variance	7,417
Kurtosis	0,3757
Skewness	0,21638
Range	12
Minimum	**13,2**
Maximum	**25,2**
Sum	568,5
Count	30

Note: All the descriptive statistics (except Standard Error and Kurtosis) in Table 6.2 were computed (either manually or with the *Excel* function [f_x] using the formulae given in the appropriate section in chapters 5 and 6. In addition, the quartile values (Q_1 and Q_3) can be computed using the *Excel* function [f_x] operation (see chapter 5, section 5.6).

The ***five-number summary table*** can be computed from the descriptive statistics given in Table 6.2 and is shown in Table 6.3 (also shown in cells [F25:G29] of Figure 6.2).

Table 6.3 Five-number summary table for passengers' Luggage Weights

Luggage Weight (kg)	
Minimum (x_{min})	13,2
Lower Quartile (Q_1)	16,9
Median (also Q_2)	19,3
Upper Quartile (Q_3)	19,8
Maximum (x_{max})	25,2

Management interpretation

The lightest luggage weighed 13,2 kg, and the heaviest luggage weighed 25,2 kg. Fifty per cent of all luggage weighed 19,3 kg or less, while 25% of all luggage weighed more than 19,8 kg. The middle fifty per cent of luggage weighed between 16,9 kg and 19,8 kg – a range of 2,9 kg. Finally, 75% of all luggage weighed less than 19,8 kg.

In examining for possible symmetry or skewness in the data, the wider interval at the top end of the profile (of 5,4 kg between Q_3 and x_{max}), compared to the smaller interval (of 3,7 kg between x_{min} and Q_1) at the lower end of the profile, indicates only slight positive skewness (i.e. only a few passengers had luggage which was over-weight). This was confirmed by the skewness coefficient of 0,21638.

To provide a quick and easy visual reference to the profile of a numeric random variable, this *five-number summary table* can be displayed graphically in the form of a *box plot*.

(ii) Box plot

In one, easy-to-view graph, the **box plot** shows the range of the data, various central and non-central location points and possible skewness in the data values of a numeric random variable.

It is *constructed* from the *five-number summary table*.

Based on a number line, the limits of the "box" are Q_1 and Q_3. The median is shown *inside the box*. The distance from the minimum data value to Q_1 and the distance from Q_3 to the maximum data value are shown as a *straight line*.

Excel does not have a box-plot facility, so a user will have to construct the box-plot graph manually. However, various commercially available statistical software packages such as *Mini-Tab*, *NCSS (Number Cruncher)*, *SPSS*, and *SAS* do have the capability to construct box plots.

The box plot for *luggage weight* is shown in Figure 6.7 (contructed using a commercially available *Excel* add-in).

The box plot conveys the same *information pictorially* as the five-number summary table. The slight positive skewness is evident by the two outliers at the upper end of the box plot.

Figure 6.7 Box plot of **Luggage Weights** (kg)

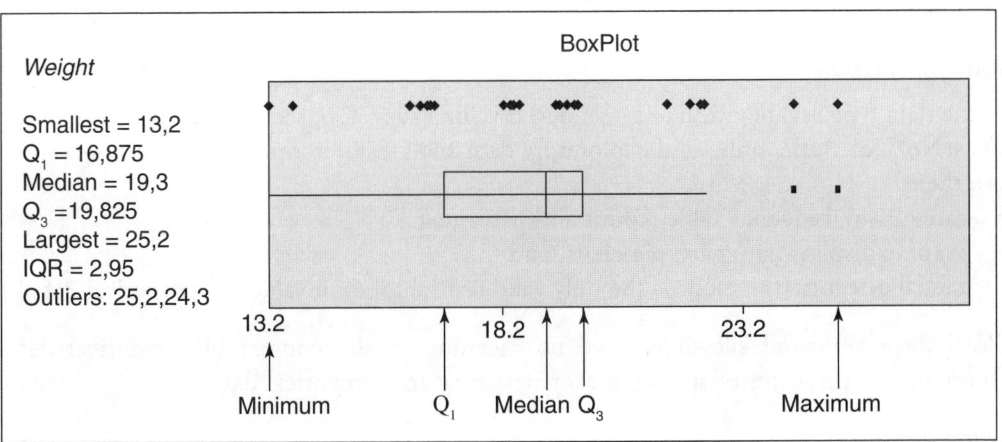

HOW TO

To observe skewness in a box plot

- If a box plot was *symmetrical* about the median (i.e. the quartiles and the minimum and maximum are approximately equidistant from the median in both directions), *no skewness* exists. The box plot profile is symmetrical.
- However, if there is a "*long tail*" at the *lower end* of the box plot, relative to the tail at the upper end, then the data profile is *negatively skewed.* There are a few extremely small data values in the data set.
- Alternatively, if there is a "*long tail*" at the *upper end* of the box plot, relative to the tail at the lower end, then the data profile is *positively skewed.* This means that there are a few extremely large data values in the data set.

HOW TO

To identify outliers using the box plot

- If one or more data values lie more than (1,5 × inter quartile range) [i.e. 1,5 × $(Q_3 - Q_1)$] away from either the lower quartile or the upper quartile, the data value(s) are considered to be outliers (extreme values). These outliers will result in skewness in the distribution in the direction in which they lie.
- In this situation, the box plot ends, either above or below, at the position of (1,5 × $(Q_3 - Q_1)$). Any data value that lies beyond this limit is shown as a separate data point and labelled as an outlier (or extreme value). Two outliers can be seen at the upper end of the box plot in Figure 6.7.

6.10.2 Choosing Valid Descriptive Statistical Measures

As indicated earlier, the choice of an appropriate set of statistical descriptors to produce a valid profile of a random variable is determined mainly by its *data type* and the *shape* of its frequency distribution (its *skewness*), if the variable is numeric.

(i) The effect of data type

Categorical data

If the data type is categorical (e.g. gender, dwelling type, job, sector, "Are you employed? (Yes/No)", etc.), the only valid exploratory data analyses (descriptive statistical measures) are the:

- categorical frequency table (count and percentage)
- graphic display: bar chart; pie chart, and
- modal category (the mode is the only valid central location value for categorical data).

Both dispersion and skewness have no meaning in the context of categorical data. Therefore no measures of spread or skewness exist for categorical data.

Numeric data

A much wider selection of descriptive statistical measures are available, if the data type is numeric. To fully describe a numeric random variable, the available exploratory data analyses are:

- numeric frequency table (counts and percentages) and ogives
- graphic display: histogram and frequency polygons
- all central location measures: mean, median and mode

- all non-central location measures: quartiles and percentiles
- all measures of dispersion: range, variance, standard deviation
- a measure of skewness (Pearson's coefficient of skewness)
- graphic of descriptive statistics measures: the box plot.

(ii) The influence of skewness on the choice of a central location measure

If the profile of a numeric random variable is symmetrical, all three measures of central location (i.e. mean, median and mode) are valid and representative measures of the central focus of the data values. In this instance, it is recommended that the mean be quoted when reporting statistical findings.

If the profile of the data is significantly skewed (either negatively or positively), the mean is not a representative measure of central location. In this instance, one of two courses of action is available to the analyst:

- *Option 1:* Select the median as the more representative measure of central location.
- *Option 2:* Remove the outliers from the data set and recompute the mean, which can now be quoted in statistical reports as it is no longer distorted by the (excluded) extreme data values. The presence and magnitude of the outliers must however, also be reported.

(iii) How to deal with outliers

In descriptive statistics

Outliers should be identified, ***retained*** as part of the analysis, and discussed in the findings, since they shape the profile of the database.

In inferential analysis

The identified outliers can be treated in one of two ways:

- They can be ***removed*** from the database, as they will potentially distort the findings of inferential tests and estimates based on model building. Their *presence must be reported separately* in the findings, however.

  or
- The database (or sample) can be stratified to create a separate sub-sample of outlier values (if their sample size is sufficiently large), which can then be separately analysed.

6.11 Summary

Summary tables (pivot tables), frequency graphs and the three descriptive statistical measures (covered in chapters 4, 5 and 6) fully describe the behaviour of any random variable, qualitative or quantitative. All random variables have a measure of central location. Only quantitative random variables, however, can be described by a degree of dispersion (spread) about the central value, and a measure of skewness.

All provide information to assist in the decision whether the central location value can be regarded as a reliable, representative value of all the observations in a sample of data. A good, representative, reliable central measure has a low measure of dispersion (a small s, as reflected both in absolute terms and in relative terms through the coefficient of variation), and a symmetrical shape of distribution.

These terms – particularly the mean, standard deviation (variance) and concept of symmetry – are important in more advanced statistical analysis (inferential analysis in particular) and will be referred to again in later chapters. For categorical data types, the available exploratory data analysis methods are limited, while those valid for numeric data types are more numerous. Only the modal category is of value for qualitative data.

Chapter 6 ended with an overview of all the exploratory data techniques combined – in terms of a five-number summary table and box plot – and fully describing the profile of a numeric random variable.

This concludes Part 2 of the text, in which the focus was on descriptive statistics and the use of *Excel* functions, including the *data analysis options* available in *Excel* for the performance of various statistical analyses. Part 3, consisting of chapters 7, 8 and 9, investigates the foundation of statistical inference: probability and sampling.

Exercises

All computational exercises can be performed either manually or using *Excel.*

6.1 X6.1 – luggage weights

The weight (in kg) of the hand luggage of 7 air passengers was as follows:

11	12	8	10	13	11	9

(i) Find the average and standard deviation of the *weight of hand luggage.*
(ii) Interpret the meaning of each descriptive statistic in (i).
(iii) Find the coefficient of variation of the *weight of hand luggage.*
(iv) Is there high relatively variability in the *weight of hand luggage* between passengers? Explain briefly.

6.2 X6.2 – bicycle sales

The *number of bicycles sold monthly* by a bicycle dealer was:

25	18	30
18	20	19
30	16	
36	24	

(i) Find the mean and median *number of bicycles sold monthly.* Interpret each descriptive statistics measure.
(ii) Find the range, variance and standard deviation of the *number of bicycles sold monthly.* Interpret the range and standard deviation measures.
(iii) Identify the inter quartile range and interpret its meaning.
(iv) Use the approximate skewness formula to estimate the degree of symmetry in the distribution of monthly bicycle sales. Interpret its meaning.
(v) Construct a *box plot* of monthly bicycle sales. Interpret the plot.
(vi) If the dealer uses the formula: "mean + one standard deviation" to decide on the opening stock level of bicycles at the beginning of next month, will he run out of stock during the month if he receives orders for 30 bicycles next month? Assume no extra bicycles can be ordered.

6.3 X6.3 – setting times

The setting time for ceramic tile glue is an important quality feature of the product. A manufacturer of ceramic tile glue tested a sample of 9 batches from a large consignment and recorded the *setting times* (in minutes) of each batch.

27	22	31
18	20	25
21	28	24

(i) Find the mean and standard deviation of *setting times* of the ceramic tile glue.

(ii) How consistent are the *setting times* across the different batches? Compute the *coefficient of variation* as a consistency index measure.
(iii) If the consistency index must be less than 10% for the consignment to be passed by the quality controller, will this consignment be approved for dispatch? Explain your answer.

6.4 X6.4 – wage increases

A labour consultant analysed the agreed *percentage wage increases* in 16 wage negotiations conducted between labour unions and employers. They were:

5,6	7,3	4,8	6,3	8,4	3,4	7,2	5,8
8,8	6,2	7,2	5,8	7,6	7,4	5,3	5,8

(i) Find the mean and median negotiated *percentage wage increases.*
(ii) Find the variance and standard deviation of the percentage wage increases.
(iii) Compute two standard deviation limits about the mean. Interpret.
(iv) How consistent are the *percentage wage increases* agreements? Compute the *coefficient of variation* as a consistency index measure.

6.5 Two groups of bank trainees each wrote a banking exam with the following *percentage* results:

	Mean	Variance	Sample Size
Group 1	76	110	34
Group 2	64	88	26

(i) Compute the coefficient of variation of *exam scores* for each trainee group.
(ii) Which group showed greater consistency in *exam score* results? Why?

6.6 X6.6 – fuel bills

The *monthly fuel bills* of a random sample of 75 Cape Town motorists who commute to work daily by car was recorded in a recent survey.

(i) Use the **Tools/Data Analysis/Descriptive Statistics** option in *Excel* to find the mean, median, variance, standard deviation, and skewness coefficient of the *monthly fuel bill* of the sample of car commuters.
(ii) Interpret the meaning of the standard deviation.
(iii) Find the coefficient of variation for *monthly fuel bills.* Is the *relative variability* between the sampled motorists' *monthly fuel bills* low?
(iv) Use the *Excel* function key (QUARTILE) operation to find the *inter quartile range* of *monthly fuel bills* of motorists. Interpret its meaning.
(v) Compile the five-number summary table for *monthly fuel bills.*
(vi) Construct *a box plot* of *monthly fuel bills.*
(vii) Describe the profile of the *monthly fuel bills* of Cape Town motorists who use their cars to commute daily to work and back.
(viii) Assume that the cost of fuel is R6 per litre and that there are 25 000 motorists who commute to work daily in Cape Town by car. Estimate the *most likely total amount of fuel used* (in litres) by all car commuters in Cape Town in a month.

6.7 X6.7 – service periods

The Association of Professional Engineers recently surveyed a sample of 100 of its members to identify their *length of service* with their company. The length of service (in *years*) for each surveyed member is shown in the database.

(i) Use *Excel's* **Tools/Data Analysis/Descriptive Statistics** option to find the mean, median, standard deviation and skewness measure of the *length of service* for the sample of professional engineers.

(ii) Interpret the meaning of each descriptive statistical measure in (i).

(iii) Use *Excel's* **Tools/Data Analysis/Histogram** option to compute a frequency table and a histogram of the *length of service* for the sample of professional engineers. Hint: Use the bin range given in the database.

(iv) Compute an interval for the *length of service* of professional engineers which covers one standard deviation either side of the mean length of service.
What percentage of professional engineers' length of service does this represent?
What assumption is made about the distribution of the lengths of service? Is this assumption satisfied?

(v) The Association of Professional Engineers would like to see a mix of 'experience' and 'new blood' amongst its members. Ideally they would like to have at least 20% of their members with less than 4 years of service (i.e. 'new blood' members); and at least 20% of their members with more than 12 years of service (i.e. 'experienced' members).
Use *Excel's* function key operations (PERCENTILE, PERCENTRANK) to determine whether their guideline for the mix of length of service is satisfied.

6.8 X6.8 – dividend yields

A survey of 44 JSE-listed companies recorded their dividend yields (as a %) for last year as shown in the following table.

5,3	4,8	3,1	4,1
6,1	4,1	3,2	4,6
7,6	1,6	4,6	1,9
4,8	2,9	1,5	5,1
2,8	3,6	3,3	5,5
2,8	4,2	3,6	3,1
5,9	2,9	3,6	4,1
4,9	2,7	3,7	7,1
6,2	2,8	5,1	3,8
3,4	3,9	5,8	6,3
6,8	4,3	5,1	5,4

(i) Define the *random variable* and its *data type*.
(ii) Use *Excel's* **Tools/Data Analysis/Descriptive Statistics** option to find the mean, median, mode, standard deviation and skewness measure of the *dividend yields* of the JSE-listed companies.
(iii) Interpret the meaning of each descriptive statistical measure in (ii).
(iv) Which central location measure would you use to report on the *dividend yields* of companies? Why?
(v) Use *Excel's* **Tools/Data Analysis/Histogram** option to compute a frequency table and a histogram of the *dividend yields* of the sampled JSE companies.
Hint: Use the bin range given in the database.
(vi) Use *Excel's* function key operations (MIN, MAX, MEDIAN, and QUARTILE) to compute the five-number summary table.
(vii) Construct a box plot of the *dividend yields* of the JSE-listed companies and interpret the profile of the *dividend yields* declared by JSE companies last year.
(viii) What was the minimum *dividend yield* declared by the top 10% of JSE companies? Hint: Use the PERCENTILE function key.
(ix) What percentage of JSE companies did not declare more than a 3% *dividend yield* last year? Hint: Use the PERCENTRANK function key.

6.9 **X5.15 – rose buds**
Refer to **Exercise 5.15** (chapter 5) and its database of the unit selling price (in cents) of rose buds.

(i) Use *Excel's* **Tools/Data Analysis/Descriptive Statistics** option to find the mean, standard deviation and skewness coefficient measures of the *unit selling price of rose buds*.
(ii) Compute and interpret the coefficient of variation of the unit selling price of rose buds.
(iii) Use *Excel's* function key operation (QUARTILE) to compute the upper and lower quartiles of the *unit selling price of rose buds*.
(iv) Identify if there are any outliers in the dataset of *unit selling prices*.
(v) Remove any outliers from the data set and re-compute the mean, standard deviation, skewness coefficient and the coefficient of variation measures.
(vi) Compare the results of (i), (ii) and (v). Comment on what effect, if any, the removal of outlier(s) has had on each of the descriptive statistics of the *unit selling price of rose buds*?
(vii) Construct a box plot based on the original data set. Fully interpret the profile of the *unit selling price* of rose buds for the flower grower.

PART 3

The Foundation of Statistical Inference: Probability and Sampling

Chapter
7

Basic Probability Concepts

Objectives

In order to generalise sample findings from a survey to estimate population parameters, the reliability and certainty of such estimates must be determined. This is done through probability theory. Probability theory describes ways in which uncertainty can be quantified and measured. The chapter provides a brief overview of the basic concepts of probability, to help a manager to understand and use probabilities in decision making.

After studying this chapter, you should be able to:

- understand the importance of probability in statistical analysis
- define the different types of probabilities
- describe the properties and concepts of probabilities
- apply the rules of probability to empirical data
- construct and interpret probabilities from two-way pivot tables
- understand the use of counting rules (permutations and combinations).

7.1 Introduction

Uncertainty surrounds every aspect of business. Many business decisions are made under conditions of uncertainty. Probability theory provides the foundation for quantifying and measuring uncertainty. It is used to estimate the reliability in making inferences from samples to populations, as well as to quantify the uncertainty of future events in practice. It is therefore necessary to review basic concepts and laws of probability to fully understand how to manage uncertainty.

Probability is the chance, or likelihood, of a particular outcome out of a number of possible outcomes occurring for a given event.

Examples of typical probability-type questions are:
- What is the likelihood that a new travel magazine will achieve a 10% market share within a year?
- How likely is it that a new bottling machine will not break down within the first six months?
- What is the chance of a telesales consultant making a sale on a call?

7.2 Types of Probabilities

Probabilities are broadly of two types:
- subjective
- objective.

Subjective Probabilities

Where the probability of an event is based on an *educated guess*, *expert opinion* or just plain *intuition*, it is referred to as a **subjective probability**. Subjective probabilities cannot be statistically verified and are not used extensively in statistical analysis.

Objective Probabilities

When the probability of an event can be *verified* statistically through surveys or empirical observations, it is referred to as an **objective probability**. This is the type of probability used extensively in statistical analysis.

Formula

Mathematically, a probability is defined as the ratio of two numbers, i.e.:

$$P(A) = \frac{r}{n}$$

where

A = *event* of a specific type (or with specific properties)

r = number of *outcomes* of event A

n = total number of all possible outcomes (called the **sample space**)

P(A) = *probability* of event A occurring

Example 7.1 Ford Car Owners – Brand Loyalty study

Assume that 360 Ford car owners (n = 360) were randomly selected and asked the following question:
"When you buy your next car, will you buy another Ford product?" (event A).
Assume that 74 respondents answered "Yes". (r = 74)

Then $\quad P(A) = \frac{74}{360} = 0{,}2056$

Management interpretation

There is a 20,56% chance that a current Ford car owner will remain loyal to the Ford brand name and purchase another Ford car on his or her next car purchase. Alternatively, one in five Ford car owners are brand loyal.

Deriving objective probabilities

There are three ways in which objective probabilities can be derived:

- *a priori:* i.e. when the outcomes are known in advance – such as tossing a coin, or selecting cards from a deck;
- *empirically:* i.e. when the values of r and n are not known in advance and have to be observed empirically through data collection (i.e. using surveys to collect the relevant data); or
- *theoretically:* i.e. through the use of theoretical distribution functions where mathematical formulae can be used to compute probabilities for certain event types.

This chapter focuses on computing and interpreting *empirically* derived objective probabilities, while chapter 8 shows how objective probabilities can be found using *theoretical distributions.*

7.3 Properties of a Probability

There are five basic properties that apply to every derived probability:

(i) A probability value lies only between 0 and 1 $\quad 0 < P(A) < 1$

(ii) If an event A cannot occur (i.e. an impossible event), then $\quad P(A) = 0$

(iii) If an event A is certain to occur, then $\quad P(A) = 1$

(iv) Probabilities for a collectively exhaustive set of n events sum to one:

$$P(A_1) + P(A_2) + P(A_3) + \ldots. + P(A_n) = 1$$

For example, if *cash*, *cheque*, *debit card* or *credit card* are the only possible payment methods (outcomes) for groceries, then for a randomly selected grocery purchase:
P(cash) + P(cheque) + P(debit card) + P(credit card) = 1

(v) *Complementary probability*: If P(A) is the probability of event A occurring, then the probability of event A *not occurring* is defined as: $\quad P(\bar{A}) = 1 - P(A)$
Note: $P(\bar{A})$ is also written as P(A').
For example, if the event being observed is *choosing the Kelloggs brand of cornflakes*, and if there is a 30% chance of a cereal consumer choosing Kelloggs, as opposed to other cornflake brands, we can write:
P(choosing Kelloggs) = 0,30 and
P(*not* choosing Kelloggs) = 1 – P(choosing Kelloggs) = 1 – 0,30 = 0,70

Example 7.2 Petrol Brand Preference study

Table 7.1 shows the frequency count and percentage table for the *petrol brand most preferred* by 50 motorists who live in George.

Table 7.1 Petrol Brand Preference – frequency counts and percentages

Petrol Brand	Count	%
BP	13	26
Caltex	9	18
Engen	6	12
Shell	22	44
Total	**50**	**100**

Management question (1)

What is the **likelihood** that a selected motorist prefers the *Engen* brand of petrol?

Solution (1)

Let A = *event* of a motorist who prefers *Engen* petrol

Then

$$P(A) = \frac{6}{50} = 0{,}12$$

Management interpretation (1)

There is only a 12% chance of finding a motorist who prefers *Engen*.

Management question (2)

What is the **chance** of finding a motorist who does ***not prefer*** *Shell*?

Solution (2)

Let A = *event* of a motorist who *prefers Shell* petrol

Let $\overline{A}$ = *event* of a motorist who does ***not prefer*** Shell petrol

Since

$$P(A) = \frac{22}{50} = 0{,}44$$

Then

$$P(\overline{A}) = 1 - P(A) = 1 - 0{,}44 = 0{,}56$$

Management interpretation (2)

There is a 56% chance of finding a motorist who does not prefer Shell petrol. This means that more than half the motorists surveyed (56%) prefer another brand of petrol.

Management question (3)

What is the **likelihood** of finding a motorist who *prefers* either *BP, Caltex, Engen* or the *Shell* brand of petrol?

Solution (3)

Let A_1 = event: motorist who prefers the *BP* brand of petrol
Let A_2 = event: motorist who prefers the *Caltex* brand of petrol
Let A_3 = event: motorist who prefers the *Engen* brand of petrol
Let A_4 = event: motorist who prefers the *Shell* brand of petrol
These four events represent the *collectively exhaustive* set of events for the variable *petrol brand preferred.*

Then $P(A_1) + P(A_2) + P(A_3) + P(A_4) = \frac{13}{50} + \frac{9}{50} + \frac{6}{50} + \frac{22}{50} = 1$

Management interpretation (3)

There is *complete certainty* that a randomly chosen motorist will prefer one of these four petrol brands.

These probabilities illustrate how managers can quantify uncertain events and use them as a basis for decision making.

7.4 Basic Probability Concepts

The basic probability concepts are derived and illustrated using the following example:

Example 7.3 JSE Companies – Sector and Size study

One hundred and fifty companies from the Johannesburg Securities Exchange (JSE) were randomly selected and classified by *sector* and *size.*

Table 7.2 shows the two-way pivot table (also called a **cross-tabulation table**), which summarises the values of the two categorical random variables – *sector* and *company size* – into frequency counts.

Table 7.2 Two-way pivot table – JSE companies by Sector and Size

Sector	Company Size			Row Total
	Small	Medium	Large	
Mining	0	5	30	35
Financial	9	21	42	72
Service	6	3	1	10
Retail	14	13	6	33
Column Total	29	42	79	150

These frequency counts are used to derive various probabilities – called **empirical probabilities** – as the data necessary for their construction first has to be gathered from surveys and organised into summary table form.

Concept 1 Intersection of Two Events ($A \cap B$)

The *intersection* of events A and B is the set of outcomes that belongs to *both* A *and* B *simultaneously.* It is written as ($A \cap B$) (i.e. A and B), and the keyword is "and".

Figure 7.1 shows the intersection of events graphically, using a Venn diagram. The intersection of two simple events in a Venn diagram is called a **joint event**.

Figure 7.1 Venn diagram of the **intersection** of two events (A ∩ B)

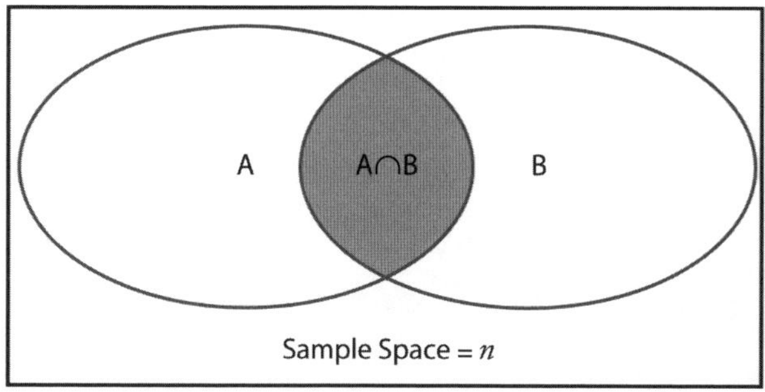

Management question (1)

What is the *probability* that a randomly selected JSE company will be a *small service* company?

Solution (1)

Let A = event *(small* company), and
Let B = event *(service* company)

Then

(A ∩ B) is the set of all *small* ***and*** *service* companies.

From Table 7.2, there are six companies that are both *small* and *service* companies, out of 150 JSE companies surveyed. This is shown graphically in the Venn diagram in Figure 7.2 below.

Thus $P(A \cap B) = P(small \cap service) = \frac{6}{150} = 0{,}04$

There is only a 4% chance of selecting a small service JSE company.

Figure 7.2 Venn diagram of **Small** and **Service** JSE companies (intersection)

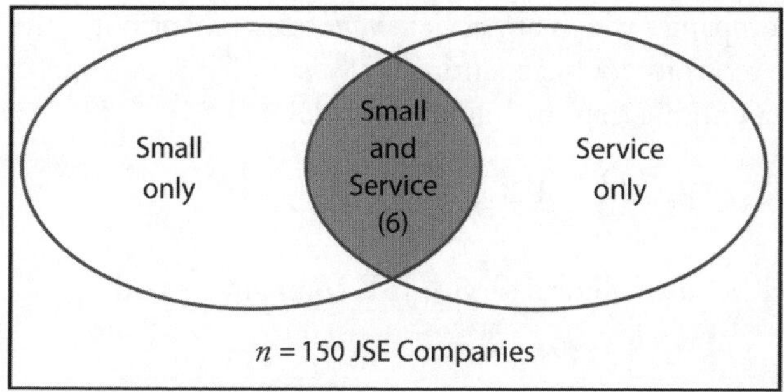

Concept 2 Union of Two Events (A ∪ B)

The *union* of events A and B is the set of outcomes that belongs to *either* event A *or* B *or both*. It is written as (A ∪ B) (i.e. either A or B or both) and the key word is "or".

Figure 7.3 shows the union of events graphically using a Venn diagram.

Figure 7.3 Venn diagram of the **union** of events (A ∪ B)

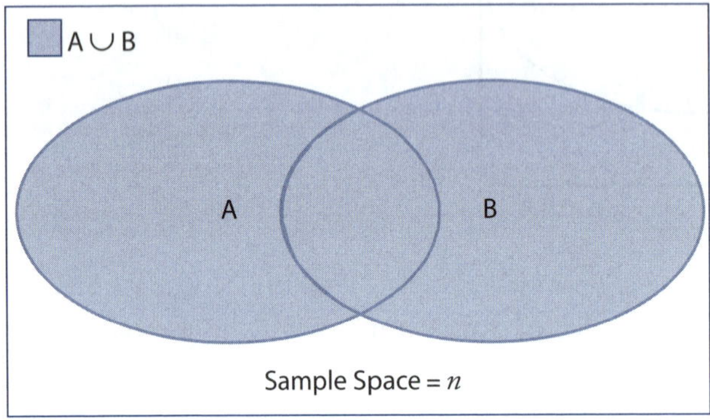

Management question (2)

What is the *probability* that a randomly selected JSE company will be either a *small* company or a *service* company or *both*?

Solution (2)

Let A = event (*small* company), and
Let B = event (*service* company)

Then

(A ∪ B) is the set of all *small* ***or*** *service* ***or both*** (*small* and *service*) companies.

As seen in Table 7.2, there are 29 *small* companies (includes six *service* companies); 10 *service* companies (includes six *small* companies), and six *small* and *service* companies. Therefore, there are 33 separate companies (29 + 10 – 6) which are either *small* or *service* or both. In the calculation of the number of companies which are either *small* or *service* or both, the intersection event is subtracted once to avoid double counting.

This is shown graphically in the Venn diagram in Figure 7.4 below.

Thus: $P(A \cup B) = P(small \cup service) = \frac{(29 + 10 - 6)}{150} = \frac{33}{150} = 0{,}22$

There is a 22% chance of selecting either a small or a service JSE company or both.

Figure 7.4 Venn diagram of **Small** or **Service** JSE companies (union)

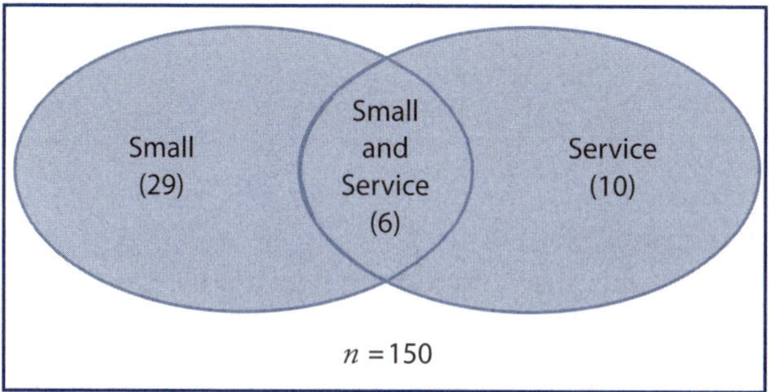

Concept 3 Mutually Exclusive Events

Events are *mutually exclusive* if they *cannot occur together* on a single trial of a random experiment, (i.e. not at the same point in time). Figure 7.5 graphically shows events that are mutually exclusive (i.e. there is no intersection) using a Venn diagram.

Figure 7.5 Venn diagram of **mutually exclusive** events $(A \cap B) = 0$

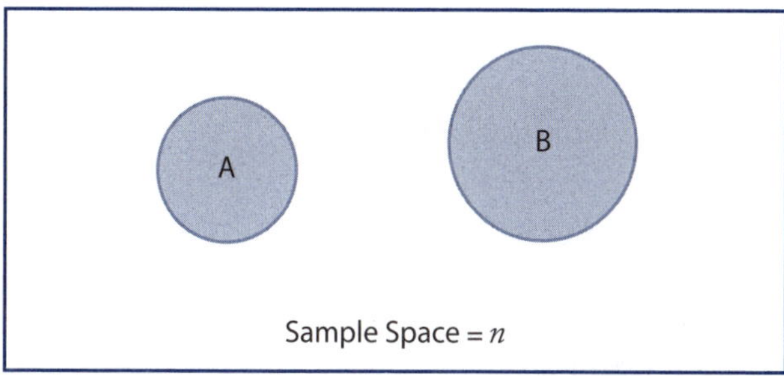

Management question (3)

What is the *probability* of a randomly selected JSE company being both a *small* and a *medium* company?

Solution (3)

Let A = event *(small* company), and
Let B = event *(medium* company)

Events A and B are mutually exclusive, because a randomly selected company from the JSE sample *cannot* be both *small* and *medium* at the same time.

Thus $P(A \cap B) = P(small \cap medium) = 0$

There is no chance of selecting a small and medium JSE company. It is an impossible event.

Management question (4)

What is the *probability* of a randomly selected JSE company being both a *small* and a *financial* company?

Solution (4)

Let A = event (*small* company), and
Let B = event (*financial* company)

Events A and B are **not** mutually exclusive, because a randomly selected company from the JSE sample *can* be both *small* and *financial* at the same time.

Thus $P(A \cap B) = P(small \cap financial) = \frac{9}{150} = 0{,}06$

There is a 6% chance of selecting a small, financial JSE company.

Concept 4 Collectively Exhaustive Events

Events are *collectively exhaustive* when the *union* of all possible events is *equal* to the *sample space.* This means that at least one of these events is certain to occur in a randomly drawn object (or element) from the sample space.

Management question (5)

What is the *probability* of a selecting either a *small*, *medium* or *large* JSE company from the sample of 150 companies surveyed?

Solution (5)

Let A = event (*small* company)
Let B = event (*medium* company), and
Let C = event (*large* company)

If $(A \cup B \cup C)$ = (sample space of all *small*, *medium*, and *large* JSE companies),

Then $P(A \cup B \cup C) = P(small) + P(medium) + P(large)$

$$= \frac{29}{150} + \frac{42}{150} + \frac{79}{150} = 0{,}193 + 0{,}28 + 0{,}527 = 1$$

Since the events comprise the *collectively exhaustive* set for all company sizes, the event of selecting either a *small*, or a *medium* or a *large* JSE company is *certain* to occur.

Concept 5 Statistically Independent Events

Two events, A and B, are *statistically independent* if the *occurrence* of event A has *no effect* on the *outcome* of *event B* and *vice versa.*

Management question (6)

Are male customers equally as likely as female customers to pay for their transactions at Woolworths by credit card? (i.e. is *payment by credit card* statistically independent of *gender*?)

Solution (6)

Let A = event (pay by *credit card*), and
Let B = event (*male* [or *female*] customer of Woolworths)

If it can be shown empirically that a randomly selected customer of Woolworths, who *pays for transactions by credit card* (event A), is **equally likely** to be a *male* or a *female* customer (event B), then the two events A and B are statistically independent.

A word of caution

The terms "statistically independent" events and "mutually exclusive" events are often confused. These are two very different concepts: When two events are "mutually exclusive", they cannot occur together; while events that are statistically independent, can occur together, but not have an influence on each other.

7.5 Computation of Objective Probabilities

Empirically derived objective probabilities can be classified into three categories:

- marginal probability
- joint probability
- conditional probability.

Example 7.4 JSE Companies – Sector and Size study

Refer to the two-way pivot table in Table 7.2, on page 150, to compute marginal, joint and conditional probabilities.

The definition and computation of each type follows.

7.5.1 Marginal Probability P(A)

A **marginal probability** is the probability of *only a single event* A occurring. It is written as P(A).

A **single event** refers to the outcomes of only one random variable.

A *frequency table* describes the occurrence of only one characteristic of interest at a time and hence is used to estimate *marginal probabilities*.

Management question (1)

What is the *likelihood* that a randomly selected JSE company is *large*?

Solution (1)

The random variable *company size* is described by the frequency distribution (one-way pivot table) in the "Column Total" row of Table 7.2. It can be used to find marginal probabilities for the variable *company size*.

$$\text{Let A} = \text{event (}\textit{large}\text{ company)}$$

Then

$$P(A) = \frac{79}{150} = 0{,}5266\ (52{,}66\%)$$

There is a 52,66% chance that a randomly selected JSE company will be large.

Management question (2)

What is the *likelihood* that a JSE-listed *mining* company is randomly selected?

Solution (2)

The random variable *sector* is described by the frequency distribution (one-way pivot table) in the "Row Total" column of Table 7.2. It can be used to find marginal probabilities for the variable *sector*.

$$\text{Let A} = \text{event (}\textit{mining}\text{ company)}$$

Then

$$P(A) = \frac{35}{150} = 0{,}2333\ (23{,}33\%)$$

There is a 23,33% chance of randomly selecting a mining JSE company.

7.5.2 Joint Probability $P(A \cap B)$

A **joint probability** is the probability of *both* event A *and* event B occurring simultaneously on a given trial of a random experiment.

A **joint event** simultaneously describes the behaviour of two or more random variables (i.e. the characteristics of interest). A joint event was defined earlier as the *intersection of two simple events* in a Venn diagram. It is written as $P(A \cap B)$.

A **two-way pivot table** shows the behaviour of two random variables simultaneously. Two-way pivot tables are used to find *joint probabilities*.

Management question (3)

What is the *likelihood* that a randomly selected JSE company is a *medium*-sized *financial* company?

Solution (3)

$$\text{Let A} = \text{event (}\textit{medium}\text{ company)}$$
$$\text{Let B} = \text{event (}\textit{financial}\text{ company)}$$

From Table 7.2 we know that 21 companies, out of the 150 JSE companies surveyed, are both *medium*-sized and *financial* companies.

Then $$P(A \cap B) = \frac{21}{150} = 0{,}14\ (14\%)$$

There is a 14% chance that a randomly selected JSE company is both medium- sized and a financial company.

7.5.3 Conditional Probability **P(A/B)**

A **conditional probability** is the probability of one event A occurring, *given* information about the occurrence of a prior event B.

A conditional event (A) is an event that depends upon the outcome of a prior event (B).

Formula

A **conditional probability** is defined as:

$$P(A/B) = \frac{P(A \cap B)}{P(B)}$$

The essential feature of the conditional probability is that the *sample space* is *reduced* from all possible outcomes (as for marginal and joint probabilities) to *only* that subset of outcomes describing event B (the *given* prior event).

Management question (4)

What is the *likelihood* that a randomly selected *medium*-sized company from the JSE sample is a *retail* company?

Solution (4)

Let A = event (*retail* company)
Let B = event (*medium* company)

Then P(A/B) is the probability of randomly selecting a *retail* company will be randomly selected from the JSE sample *given* that the company is known to be *medium-sized.*

From Table 7.3 (a repeat of Table 7.2), the frequency distribution of *medium*-sized companies (highlighted) represents the reduced sample space (of only 42 companies) from which the *retail* company is randomly selected.

Table 7.3 Two-way pivot table – JSE companies by Sector and Size

Sector	Company Size			Row Total
	Small	Medium	Large	
Mining	0	5	30	35
Financial	9	21	42	72
Service	6	3	1	10
Retail	14	**13**	6	33
Column Total	29	**42**	79	150

There are 13 *retail* companies out of a total of 42 *medium*-sized companies.

Therefore $P(A/B) = P(retail/medium) = \frac{13}{42} = 0{,}3095(30{,}95\%)$

Using the formula

$$P(B) = P(\textit{medium}) = \frac{42}{150} = 0{,}28 \quad (\textit{marginal}\text{ probability})$$

$$P(A \cap B) = P(\textit{retail} \cap \textit{medium}) = \frac{13}{150} = 0{,}0866 \quad (\textit{joint}\text{ probability})$$

Then

$$P(A/B) = \frac{\frac{13}{150}}{\frac{42}{150}} = \frac{13}{42} = 0{,}3095 \quad (\textit{conditional}\text{ probability})$$

There is a 30,95% chance that a randomly selected *medium*-sized company from the JSE sample is a *retail* company.

7.6 Probability Rules

Probability rules have been developed to compute probabilities of compound or multiple events. There are two basic probability rules:

- *Addition rule:*
  - for non-mutually exclusive events, and
  - for mutually exclusive events.
- *Multiplication rule:*
  - for statistically dependent events, and
  - for statistically independent events.

7.6.1 Addition Rule: Non-mutually Exclusive Events

Formula

If two events are *not* mutually exclusive, then the probability of *either* event A *or* event B *or both* occurring in a single trial of a random experiment is defined as:

$$\mathbf{P(A \cup B) = P(A) + P(B) - P(A \cap B)}$$

In Venn diagram terms, the union of two non-mutually exclusive events is the *combined outcomes* of the two overlapping events A, B. (See Figure 7.6.)

Figure 7.6 Venn diagram for the **addition rule** – for **non-mutually exclusive** events

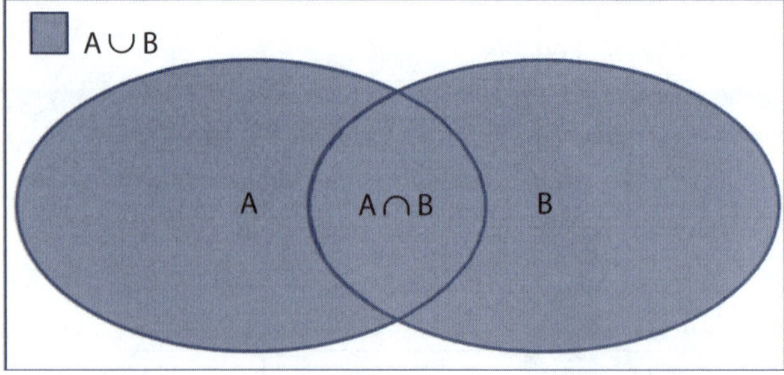

Management question (5)

What is the *probability* that a randomly selected JSE-listed company is either a *large* company or a *financial* company or both?

Solution (5)

Let A = event (*large* company)
Let B = event (*financial* company)

Events A and B are *not* mutually exclusive as they can occur simultaneously (i.e. a company can be both *large* and *financial*).

From Table 7.3, the following marginal and joint probabilities can be derived:

$$P(A) = P(\textit{large}) = \frac{79}{150} = 0{,}5267$$

$$P(B) = P(\textit{financial}) = \frac{72}{150} = 0{,}48$$

$$P(A \cap B) = P(\textit{large} \text{ and } \textit{financial}) = \frac{42}{150} = 0{,}28$$

Then

$$P(A \cup B) = P\text{ (either } \textit{large} \text{ or } \textit{financial} \text{ or both)}$$

$$= P(\textit{large}) + P(\textit{financial}) - P(\textit{large} \text{ and } \textit{financial})$$

$$= \frac{79}{150} + \frac{72}{150} - \frac{42}{150} = \frac{109}{150} = 0{,}7266 = 72{,}66\%$$

There is a 72,66% chance that a randomly selected JSE-listed company will be either a *large* company or a *financial* company or both (i.e. a *large financial* company).

7.6.2 Addition Rule: Mutually Exclusive Events

Formula

If two events A and B are mutually exclusive (i.e. they cannot occur together), then the probability of *either* event A *or* event B occurring in a single trial of a random experiment is defined as:

$$\mathbf{P(A \cup B) = P(A) + P(B)}$$

i.e. the sum of the two marginal probabilities.

In Venn diagram terms, the union of two mutually exclusive events is the *combined outcomes* of each of the two events A, B *separately*, as shown in Figure 7.5 on page 153. For mutually exclusive events, there is *no intersectional* event.

Thus $P(A \cap B) = 0$

Management question (6)

What is the **probability** that a randomly selected JSE-listed company is either a *mining* company or a *service* company?

Solution (6)

Let A = event (*mining* company)
Let B = event (*service* company)

Events A and B are *mutually exclusive* as they cannot occur simultaneously (i.e. a company **cannot** be both *mining* and *service*).

From Table 7.3, on page 157, the following marginal probabilities can be derived:

$$P(A) = P(\textit{mining}) = \frac{35}{150} = 0{,}2333\ (23{,}33\%)$$

$$P(B) = P(\textit{service}) = \frac{10}{150} = 0{,}0667\ (6{,}67\%)$$

$$P(A \cap B) = 0$$

Then

$$P(A \cup B) = P\ (\text{either } \textit{mining} \text{ or } \textit{service})$$

$$= P\ (\textit{mining}) + P(\textit{service})$$

$$= \frac{35}{150} + \frac{10}{150} = \frac{45}{150} = 0{,}30\ (30\%)$$

There is a 30% chance that a randomly selected JSE-listed company will be either a *mining* company or a *service* company but not both.

7.6.3 Multiplication Rule: Statistically Dependent Events

The multiplication rule is used to find the *joint probability* of events A and B occurring together on a single trial of random experiment. The two events have common outcomes as represented by the *intersection* of the two events.

This rule also assumes that the event B influences the outcomes of the other event A (i.e. they are dependent events).

Formula

By rearranging the conditional probability formula, the *multiplication rule* is defined as:

$$\mathbf{P(A \cap B) = P(A/B) \times P(B)}$$

Where $P(A \cap B)$ = joint probability of A and B
$P(A/B)$ = conditional probability of A given B
$P(B)$ = marginal probability of B only

Management question (7)

What is the **probability** of selecting a *small*, *retail* company from the JSE-listed sample of companies?

Solution (7)

Let A = event (*small* company)
Let B = event (*retail* company)

Intuitively from Table 7.3:

$$P(A \cap B) = P(\textit{small} \text{ and } \textit{retail}) = \frac{14}{150} = 0{,}0933$$

Applying the *multiplication rule* formula:

$$P(B) = P(\textit{retail}) = \frac{33}{150} = 0{,}22$$

$$P(A/B) = P(\textit{small/retail}) = \frac{14}{33} = 0{,}4242$$

Then

$$P(A \cap B) = P(A/B) \times P(B) = P(\mathit{small/retail}) \times P(\mathit{retail})$$
$$= \frac{14}{33} \times \frac{33}{150} = \frac{14}{150} = 0{,}0933\ (9{,}33\%)$$

There is only a 9,33% chance that a randomly selected JSE-listed company will be a *small, retail* company.

7.6.4 Multiplication Rule: Statistically Independent Events

Formula

If two events, A and B, are *statistically independent* (i.e. there is ***no influence*** of one event on the other event) then the *multiplication rule* reduces to:

$$\mathbf{P(A \cap B) = P(A) \times P(B)}$$

i.e. it reduces to the product of the two marginal probabilities only.

Where $P(A \cap B)$ = joint probability of A and B
$P(A)$ = marginal probability of A only
$P(B)$ = marginal probability of B only

HOW TO

To test for statistical independence of events

Two events are statistically independent if the following relationship can be shown to be true:

$$P(A/B) = P(A) \quad \text{or} \quad P(B/A) = P(B)$$

This means that if the *marginal probability* of, say, event A *equals* the *conditional probability* of event A *given* that event B has occurred, then the two events are statistically independent.

This relationship implies that the prior occurrence of event B – i.e. (A/B) – in *no way influences* the outcome of the single (marginal) event A.

Management question (8)

Is company *size* ***statistically independent*** of *sector* in the JSE-listed sample of companies? Stated differently: Is the likelihood of finding a company of a particular *size*, say *medium*-sized, the ***same*** across all *sectors*?

Solution (8)

To test for statistical independence, select one event from each measure and apply the decision rule.

Let A = event (*medium* company)
Let B = event (*mining* company)

Then $P(A) = P(\mathit{medium}) = \frac{42}{150} = 0{,}28\ (28\%)$

and $P(A/B) = P(\mathit{medium/mining}) = \frac{5}{35} = 0{,}1428\ (14{,}28\%)$

Since the two probabilities are not equal (i.e. P(A/B) ≠ P(A)) there is sufficient empirical evidence to conclude that the two events are statistically dependent (i.e. company *size* and *sector* are related). The difference in probabilities of selecting a medium-sized company is due to a relationship between size and sector – the size profile of companies differs across sectors.

7.7 Counting Rules

Probability computations involve *counting* the number of event outcomes (r) and the total number of possible outcomes (n) and expressing these as a ratio.

Often the values for r and n cannot be counted, because of the large number of possible outcomes involved. Counting rules assist in finding values for r and n.

There are three basic counting rules:

- multiplication rule
- permutations
- combinations.

7.7.1 The Multiplication Rule of Counting

The multiplication rule is applied in two ways:

(i) For single events

To find the total number of different ways in which n objects of a single event can be arranged (ordered)

$$n! = n \text{ factorial}$$
$$= n(n-1)(n-2)(n-3) \ldots 3.2.1 \qquad \text{Note: } 0! = 1$$

Example 7.5 Car Showroom Display study

Management question

In how many different (unique) ways can six new cars be displayed on a showroom floor?

Solution

The event = *displaying new cars*. The number of different (unique) ways in which six cars can be arranged on a showroom floor for display purposes is given by:

$$6! = 6.5.4.3.2.1$$
$$= 720 \text{ different car arrangements.}$$

(ii) For combined events

If a particular random process has:

- n_1 possible outcomes for event 1,
- n_2 possible outcomes for event 2, ...
- n_j possible outcomes for the jth event,

then

> the total number of possible outcomes for the j events is:
>
> $$n_1 \times n_2 \times n_3 \times \ldots \times n_j$$

Example 7.6 Investment Portfolio Selection study

Management question

How many possible combinations of three equities can an investment portfolio consist of if there is a choice of four *property* equities, ten *financial* equities and six *mining* equities? Each equity in the portfolio must come from a different sector.

Solution

There are 3 events: *choosing an equity from each of 3 different sectors*. The total number of possible combinations of three equities, each from a different sector, is:

$4 \times 10 \times 6 = 240$ different portfolio combinations

7.7.2 Permutations

> A **permutation** is the number of *distinct ways* of arranging a subset of r objects, selected from a group of n objects where *order is important.*

Each possible arrangement (ordering) is called a **permutation** and can be computed from the following formula.

Formula

The number of distinct ways of arranging r objects selecting from n objects, where *order is important*, is given by:

$$_nP_r = \frac{n!}{(n-r)!}$$

where $n! = n$ factorial $= n(n-1)(n-2)(n-3) \ldots 3.2.1$
r = number of objects selected at a time
n = total number of objects from which to select

Example 7.7 Worker Assignment study

A production supervisor has to assign one worker to each of *three* tasks.

Management questions

(1) How many distinct assignments (orderings) of workers to tasks are possible if the supervisor has eight workers to choose from?

(2) What is the probability that the supervisor will select a particular *ordering* of workers to assign to the three tasks?

Solutions

(1) Given $n = 8$ and $r = 3$

Then $${}_8P_3 = \frac{8!}{(8-3)!} = \frac{(8.7.6.5.4.3.2.1)}{(5.4.3.2.1)} = 336 \text{ permutations}$$

There are 336 distinct ways in which the supervisor can select three workers and assign them individually to each of three tasks.

(2) The probability of selecting a particular grouping of three workers in a particular order is:
P(*particular order* of 3 workers) $= \frac{1}{336} = 0{,}00297$ (0,297%)
There is a very small probability (only 0,297% chance) that a particular ordering of three workers will be selected by the supervisor to perform each of the three tasks.

7.7.3 Combinations

A **combination** is the number of *different ways* of arranging a subset of r objects selected from a group of n objects *where the order is not important.*

Each separate grouping of r objects out of n objects is called a **combination**.

Formula

The number of ways of arranging r objects selected from n objects, *not considering order*, is given by the formula:

$${}_nC_r = \frac{n!}{r!(n-r)!}$$

where $n! = n$ factorial $= n(n-1)(n-2)(n-3) \ldots 3.2.1$
$r! = r(r-1)(r-2)(r-3) \ldots 3.2.1$
r = number of objects selected at a time
n = total number of objects from which to select

Example 7.8 Fruit Juice Shelf Display study

A fruit juice company produces fruit juice in 10 different flavours. A local supermarket sells the product, but has only sufficient shelf space to display three of the company's 10 fruit juice flavours.

Management questions

(1) How many possible *groupings* (*combinations*) of three flavours can the fruit juice company display on the local supermarket shelf?

(2) What is the probability that a *particular* combination of three fruit juice flavours will be selected by the juice company for display?

Solutions

(1) The *order* in which the three fruit juices flavours are chosen for display is *not important*, hence apply the combination formula.

Given n = 10 fruit flavours, and $r = 3$ flavours for display

Then

$$_{10}C_3 = \frac{10!}{[3!\,(10-3)!]}$$

$$= \frac{(10.9.8.7.6.5.4.3.2.1)}{[(3.2.1)(7.6.5.4.3.2.1)]}$$

= 120 combinations

There are 120 different groupings of three fruit juice flavours that can be selected from a possible 10 flavours, without regard to order.

(2) The probability of selecting a particular combination of three fruit juice flavours out of a possible 10 flavours is:

$$\text{P(combination of 3 flavours out of 10 flavours)} = \frac{1}{120} = 0{,}0083.$$

There is only a 0,83% chance that a particular combination of three fruit juice flavours will be selected.

7.8 Summary

This chapter introduced the concept of probabilities as the foundation for inferential statistics, which is covered in later chapters. The term "probability", as a measure of the *uncertainty* associated with the outcome of a specific event, and the *properties* of probabilities were defined. Also examined, were the *concepts* of probabilities, such as the *union* and *intersection* of events, *mutually exclusive* events, *collectively exhaustive* sets of events and *statistically independent* events.

The basic probability types, namely *marginal, joint* and *conditional probabilities,* were computed from two-way pivot tables. Probability computations for more complex, related events were also derived by using the *addition rule* and the *multiplication rule.* Finally, the counting rules for *permutations* and *combinations* were introduced as a way of finding the number of outcomes associated with specific events.

The next chapter will compute probabilities for random variables that follow certain defined theoretical patterns, called **probability distributions**.

Exercises

7.1 In a survey of companies, it was found that 45 were in the mining sector, 72 were in the financial sector, 32 were in the IT sector and 101 were in the production sector.

(i) Show the data as a percentage frequency table.
(ii) What is the probability that a randomly selected company is in the financial sector?
(iii) If a company is selected at random, what is the probability that this company is *not* in the production sector?
(iv) What is the likelihood that a randomly selected company is *either* a mining company *or* an IT company?
(v) Name the probability rules used in questions (iii) and (iv).

7.2 An apple cooperative in Elgin, Cape receives and groups apples into A, B, C and D grades for packaging and export. In a batch of 1 500 apples, 795 were found to be grade A, 410 were of grade B, 106 were of grade C and the rest grade D.

(i) Construct a percentage frequency distribution of apple grades.
(ii) What is the probability that a randomly selected apple from the batch will belong to grade A?
(iii) If an apple is selected at random from the batch, what is the likelihood that it is *either* of grades B *or* D?
(iv) Grade C and D apples are not exported. What is the probability that a randomly selected apple is export quality?
(v) Name the probability rules used in questions (iii) and (iv).

7.3 Statistics South Africa reported the number of persons employed by sector in a given year as follows (in thousands of persons): 6 678 in the formal business sector (excluding agriculture); 1 492 in the commercial agricultural sector; 653 in subsistence agriculture; 2 865 in the informal business sector; and 914 in the domestic service sector.

(i) Construct a percentage frequency distribution of employment by sector.
(ii) What is the probability that a randomly selected employed person works in the domestic service sector?
(iii) If an employed person is selected at random from the workforce, what is the likelihood that the person earns a living through agriculture?
(iv) If a person is known to work in the business sector (both formal and informal), what is the likelihood that the person is an informal trader?
(v) Name the probability rules used in questions (iii) and (iv).

7.4 X7.4 – **qualification levels**
The human resources department of an insurance company analysed the *qualifications* profile of their 129 managers in terms of their highest qualification achieved. The findings are shown in the two-way pivot table.

	Managerial Level		
Qualification	Section Head	Dept Head	Division Head
Matric	28	14	?
Diploma	20	24	6
Degree	?	10	14
Total	53	?	28

(i) Define the two random variables, their measurement scale and data type.
(ii) Complete the above two-way pivot table (joint frequency table).
(iii) What is the probability that a manager selected at random:
  (a) has only a matric?
  (b) is a section head and has a degree?
  (c) is a department head given that the manager has a diploma?
  (d) is a division head?
  (e) is either a division head or a section head?
  (f) has either a matric, or a diploma, or a degree?
  (g) has a degree given that the person is a department head?
  (h) is either a division head or has a diploma or both?
(iv) For each probability computed in (iii), state:
  (a) the type of probability (i.e. marginal; joint; conditional)
  (b) which probability rule, if any, was applied (i.e. addition rule; multiplication rule)
(v) Are the events in (iii)(e) and (iii)(f) mutually exclusive?

7.5 X7.5 – bonus options

A company offered each of its employees a choice of three performance bonus options: a cash bonus option; a profit sharing option; and a share option. The number of employees who selected each bonus option together with their work function (administration or production) is shown in the following two-way pivot table.

	Cash bonus	**Profit-sharing**	**Share options**
Admin	28	44	68
Production	56	75	29

(i) What is the probability that an employee selected a cash bonus?
(ii) If income tax must only be paid on the cash bonus or the profit sharing option, what is the probability that an employee selected a tax-free bonus option?
(iii) What is the likelihood that an employee works in production and chose the cash bonus option?
(iv) If an employee is in administration, what is the likelihood that the employee chose the share option?

(v) If a cash bonus was chosen, what is the probability that it was chosen by a production worker?
(vi) If event A = *share option* and event B = an *administration employee*, test whether the choice of bonus option is statistically independent of the work function of the employee.
(vii) State the probability type (marginal; joint or conditional) or probability rule that applied in each of (i) to (v).

7.6 X7.6 – age profile
The following table shows the 300 employees of a glass manufacturing company cross-classified on the basis of *age* and *department.*

	Department			
Age	Production	Sales	Administration	**Total**
<30	60	25	18	103
30–50	70	29	25	124
>50	30	8	35	73
Total	160	62	78	300

(i) An employee is selected at random from this company. Calculate the probability that the employee is:
(a) under 30 years of age;
(b) a production worker;
(c) a sales person and between 30 and 50 years of age;
(d) over 50, given that he or she is in administration;
(e) a production worker or under 30 years, or both.
(ii) Are the two events, age and department mutually exclusive? Justify.
(iii) Are age and department statistically independent? Justify your answer.
(iv) State the probability type and probability rule, if appropriate, used in each of (i) (a) – (e).

7.7 X7.7 – digital cameras
Consider the following two-way pivot table of *brand preference* for digital cameras and their *primary usage* (professional or personal).

	Digital Camera Brand Preference			
Usage	Canon	Nikon	Pentax	Total
Professional	48	15	27	90
Personal	30	95	65	190
Total	78	110	92	280

(i) What is the probability of randomly selecting a *professional* user?
(ii) What is the probability of selecting a user who prefers the *Nikon brand*?

(iii) Find the probability that a user prefers the *Pentax brand* given that their usage is primarily for *personal* use.
(iv) Is *brand preference* statistically independent of *primary usage*? Justify your answer with a statistical illustration and explain the meaning of your finding.
(v) What is the likelihood that a randomly selected user prefers the *Canon brand* and is a *professional* user?
(vi) Find the probability of randomly selecting either a *professional* user or a user who prefers the *Nikon brand* of digital camera.
(vii) Are the two events, *primary usage* and *brand preference* mutually exclusive? Justify statistically.

7.8 An electronic device consists of two components, A and B. The probability that component A will fail within the guarantee period is 0,20. There is also a 15% chance that component B will fail within the guarantee period. Assume the components operate entirely independently of each other.
(i) What is the probability that both components will fail within the guarantee period?
(ii) If either or both components fail within the guarantee period, the company will replace the electronic device free of charge. What is the probability that the electronic device will *not* need to be replaced during the guarantee period?

7.9 Find the value of

(i) 6!	(ii) 3! 5!	(iii) 4! 2! 3!
(iv) ${}_7C_4$	(v) ${}_9C_6$	(vi) ${}_8P_3$
(vii) ${}_5P_2$	(viii) ${}_7C_7$	(ix) ${}_7P_4$

Explain the meaning of each of these calculations in terms of a practical scenario.

7.10 A company has 12 products in its product range. It wishes to advertise in the local newspaper, but due to space constraints, it is allowed to display only 7 of its products at a time. How many different ways can this company compose a display in the local newspaper?

7.11 There are 5 levels of shelving in a supermarket. If 3 brands of soup must each be placed on a separate shelf, how many different ways can a packer arrange the soup brands?

7.12 For a balanced investment portfolio consisting of 4 equities, an investor must select only one equity from each of 9 economic sectors (labelled 1 to 9).
(i) How many different portfolios consisting of 4 equities can be selected?
(ii) What is the probability that the portfolio will consist of one equity each from economic sectors 3, 5, 7 and 8?

7.13 What is the probability that each of five identical screws that are removed from the back cover of stove will be replaced in exactly the same holes from which they were removed?

7.14 A selection of 10 tourist attractions is available in Cape Town.

(i) How many separate selections are there of 3 attractions, not considering the order in which the 3 attractions are visited?

(ii) What is the probability of selecting a particular day tour package of three attractions, regardless of the order in which they are visited?

7.15 A planning committee for a major development project such as 2010 Soccer World Cup, must consist of 2 architects and 4 engineers. There are 4 architects and 7 engineers available from which to choose.

(i) How many different combinations of committee members can be formed?

(ii) If the committee must also include an environmental lawyer of which there are 2 available, how many different committee compositions are now possible?

Chapter

8

Probability Distributions

Objectives

Probabilities can also be derived using mathematical functions known as **probability distributions**. Probability distributions describe the uncertain behaviour of many variables in management practice. They indicate patterns of outcomes for discrete events and for continuous events. This chapter introduces a few important probability distributions common to management situations.

After studying this chapter, you should be able to:

- understand the concept of a probability distribution
- describe four common probability distributions used in management practice
- recognise when to apply each probability distribution in management
- compute and interpret probabilities associated with each distribution.

8.1 Introduction

Chapter 7 showed that probabilities can be derived *empirically* through data collection and analysis of sample data. By summarising empirically gathered data into a frequency count (or pivot) table, it is possible to estimate the probability that specific events will occur. This chapter describes alternative methods of deriving probabilities, namely by using *mathematical functions* known as **probability distributions**.

A **probability distribution** is a list of all the possible outcomes of a random variable and their associated probabilities of occurrence.

There are numerous problem situations in practice where the outcomes of a specific random variable follow *known probability patterns*. If the behaviour of a random variable under study can be matched to one of these known probability patterns, then probabilities associated with specific outcomes of the random variable can be found directly by applying an appropriate theoretical probability distribution function. This eliminates the need to capture and analyse empirical data in order to derive the probabilities.

The following examples *illustrate* patterns of random variable behaviour for which probabilities can be derived using a mathematical function:

- What is the probability that three out of 10 *new product* concepts will be *accepted* by the market?
- What is the likelihood that, for a consignment of 20 Apple Macintosh computers received by a computer retailer, no more than two will be *returned for repairs* during the one-year warranty period?
- What is the probability that a car dealer in Bellville will *sell* no more than four *Opel Corsa cars per week*?
- What is the probability that fewer than 10 *companies* will be forced into *liquidation* within the *next month*?
- What is the probability that a particular branch of Edgars will achieve a *turnover* of R500 000 or more per day?
- What is the probability that Mastercard clients *settle outstanding balances* before due date?

Types of Probability Distributions

The choice of a particular probability distribution function depends primarily on the nature of the random variable (i.e. whether it is *discrete* or *continuous*) under study.

Probability distribution functions can be classified as:

- *discrete* probability distributions, or
- *continuous* probability distributions.

This chapter will describe two discrete probability distribution functions (the **binomial** and the **Poisson processes**) and two continuous probability functions (the **normal distribution** and the **Student t distribution**).

8.2 Discrete Probability Distributions

Discrete probability distributions assume that the *outcomes* of a random variable under study can take on *only specific* (usually *integer*) values.

The following examples *illustrate* discrete probability distributions:

- a car can have only 0, 1, 2, 3 or 4 flat tyres
- a bookshop has only 0, 1, 2, 3, 4 or 5 copies of a particular title in stock
- a machine can produce 0, 1, 2, 3, etc., defective products in a given production run
- the number of employees absent on a given day is 0, 1, 2, 3, etc.

In discrete probability distributions, a non-zero probability is associated with each possible outcome of the random variable. The probability is zero for values of the random variable that are not valid (i.e. fractional values when only integers are permissable).

Two common discrete probability distribution functions are the:

- *binomial* probability distribution, and
- *Poisson* probability distribution.

For a discrete random variable to follow either a *binomial* or a *Poisson* process, it must possess a number of specific characteristics. In sections 8.3 and 8.4, these features are identified for each of the probability distribution functions.

8.3 Binomial Probability Distribution

A *discrete* random variable can be described by the *binomial* distribution if it satisfies the following *four conditions*:

(i) There are only *two*, mutually exclusive and collectively exhaustive, *outcomes* of the random variable. Generally, these two outcomes are referred to as *success* and *failure*.

(ii) Each outcome has an associated *probability*:
   - The probability for the *success* outcome is denoted by p.
   - The probability for the *failure* outcome is denoted by q.

   Note: $p + q = 1$ *Hence*: $q = (1 - p)$.

(iii) The random variable is observed n times. Each observation of the random variable in its problem setting is called a *trial*.
   Each trial generates either a *success* or a *failure* outcome. Thus, n outcomes are observed.

(iv) The trials are assumed to be *independent* of each other. This means that p and q remain constant for each trial of the process under study (i.e. the outcome on any trial is in no way influenced by the outcome on any previous trial).
   If these four conditions are satisfied, then the following binomial question can be addressed:

The **binomial question**:
"What is the probability that r *successes* will occur in n trials of the process under study?"

Formula

The formula for the **binomial probability distribution** is:

$$P(r) = {}_nC_r\, p^r\, q^{(n-r)} \qquad \text{for} \qquad r = 0, 1, 2, 3, \ldots, n$$

where n = the sample size, i.e. the number of independent trials (observations)
r = the number of *success* outcomes in the n independent trials
p = probability of a *success* outcome on a single independent trial
q = probability of a *failure* outcome on a single independent trial

Note: The r values are the set of all possible occurrences of the *success* outcome ($r \leq n$). It is called the **domain**.

The *domain* is the set of success outcomes (r) for which probabilities can be derived. In the case of the binomial probability distribution, only integer values (including zero) up to the number of trials, n (sample size), can occur (i.e. $r = 0, 1, 2, 3, \ldots, n$).

The rationale of the *binomial* process is illustrated by the following problem.

Example 8.1 Zeplin Car Hire study

The Zeplin car hire firm rents out only Opel and Ford cars. Experience has shown that *one in four* clients request to hire an Opel car.

Management question

If five reservations are received on a given day, what is the ***probability*** that *two clients* will have *requested an Opel car*?

Solution (with justification)

To use the *binomial probability distribution* to find the required probability, the random variable must be shown to follow the **binomial process**. For a random variable to follow the binomial process, it must satisfy the four conditions identified above.

In this example the *random variable* is *discrete*. It is defined as the *number of Opel car hire requests* which can be 0, 1, 2, 3, 4, ... etc. up to n on any given day.

Condition (i) There are only two possible outcomes

- The *hire request* for an Opel car (the *success* outcome).

  or
- The *hire request* is *not* for an Opel car (the *failure* outcome).

Condition (ii) Each outcome has an associated probability

The probability of each outcome occurring whenever a *reservation call* is received (i.e. a *single trial* of the random experiment), can be found from the statement:

"Experience has shown that *one in four* clients request to hire an Opel car."

Translated, this gives:

p (= probability of *hiring* an Opel car) = 0,25

q (= probability of ***not*** *hiring* an Opel car) = 0,75

Condition (iii) The random variable is observed *n* times

Five reservations by clients were sampled, hence $n = 5$. Each of the five reservation requests is a single trial in the study of *car hire request* patterns.

Condition (iv) The trials are independent

Each client's car preference (Opel or Ford) is independent of every other client's preference. This implies that p and q will not change from trial to trial (i.e. from client to client).

The binomial question:

In the car hire study, the *binomial question* requires finding the probability that *two* out of *five* reservations will request an Opel car.

In *probability notation,* find P(r = 2) when $n = 5$ and $p = 0{,}25$

The random variable and problem description satisfies the *binomial process*. Hence the *binomial probability distribution* formula can be used to find the required probabilities.

In Example 8.1, the following values apply:

$n = 5 \quad p = 0{,}25 \quad \text{and} \quad q = 0{,}75$

Find P(r = 2)

Then P(r = 2) $= {}_5C_2\,(0{,}25)^2\,(0{,}75)^{(5-2)}$

$= (10)(0{,}0625)(0{,}4219) \quad = 0{,}2637$ (26,37% chance)

Solution using *Excel*

The function operation BINOMDIST can be used to compute both marginal and cumulative binomial probabilities for values of r (*success* outcomes).
The function and its arguments are:

= **BINOMDIST(*r*, *n*, *p*, cumulative)**

where

- r, n, p are defined as for the binomial formula above.
- the *cumulative* argument is a logical value, which is either *true* or *false*, with the following meanings:
  true = find cumulative probability *false* = find marginal probability.
  In Example 8.1, P(r = 2) is a marginal probability, hence set *cumulative* = *false*.

Thus, to find P(r = 2)

use = **BINOMDIST(2,5,0.25,false)**

giving a result = **0,26367**

Management interpretation

There is a 26,37% chance that two out of five reservation calls to Zeplin Car Hire on a randomly selected day will request to hire an Opel car.

HOW TO

To select p – a valuable hint

The *success* outcome is always associated with the probability, p. The outcome, which must be labelled as the *success* outcome, is determined by the *binomial question*. Care must be exercised in selecting the *success* outcome and its corresponding p, since erroneous identification will result in incorrect probabilities.

To *illustrate:* In the *Zeplin Car Hire* example, the *binomial question* is related to finding probabilities associated with a *hire request for an Opel car*. Thus the *success* outcome is "receiving a hire request *for an Opel car*". On the other hand, the *failure* outcome, which is q, represents the probability of "receiving a hire request *not* for an Opel car".

Example 8.2 Life Assurance Policy Surrender study

Global Insurance has found that 20% (*one in five*) of all insurance policies are surrendered (cashed in) before their maturity date. Assume that 10 policies are randomly selected from the company's policy database.

Management question (1)

What is the ***probability*** that four of these *insurance policies* will have been *surrendered* before maturity date?

Solution (1) (with justification)

The random variable, *number of policies surrendered*, is discrete since there can be 0, 1, 2, 3, . . . 9, 10 surrendered policies in the sample of 10 policies drawn. This random variable "fits" the binomial probability distribution for the following four reasons:

(i) There are only two possible outcomes for each policy

- a policy is *surrendered* before maturity (the *success* outcome), and
- a policy is *not surrendered* before maturity (the *failure* outcome).

(ii) A probability can be assigned to each outcome for a policy

p (= probability of a policy *being surrendered)* = 0,20
q (= probability of a policy ***not*** *being surrendered)* = 0,80
Note: The *success* outcome refers to a *surrendered* policy, since the *binomial question* relates to finding probabilities for *surrendered policies.*

(iii) The random variable is observed 10 times

Since 10 policies are randomly selected, n = 10.
Each of the 10 policies is a single trial of this study.

(iv) The trials are independent

Each policy's status (surrendered or not) is independent of any other policy's status.

Therefore the required probability can be found using the *binomial probability distribution* with the following values:

$n = 10 \qquad p = 0{,}20 \qquad q = 0{,}80$

The domain, r, of all possible *success* outcomes = 0, 1, 2, 3 ,4, 5, 6, 7, 8, 9, 10.

Thus, find P(r = 4 *surrendered policies* out of 10 observed policies)

$$P(r = 4) = {}_{10}C_4\,(0{,}20)^4\,(0{,}80)^{(10-4)}$$
$$= (210)(0{,}0016)(0{,}2621) = 0{,}088 \text{ (8,8\% chance)}$$

Solution (1) using *Excel*

Since P(r = 4) is a *marginal* probability set cumulative = *false* in the function key operation.

Thus, to find P(r = 4)
use = **BINOMDIST (4, 10, 0.20, false)**
giving a result = **0,08808**

Management interpretation (1)

There is only a 8,8% chance that four out of ten policy holders will surrender their policies before maturity date.

Management question (2)

What is the probability that *no more than three* of these ten *insurance policies* will have been surrendered before maturity date?

Solution (2)

The binomial approach is still appropriate. This translates mathematically into finding P($r \le 3$).

This implies that either 0 or 1 or 2 or 3 of the *policies* will be *surrendered* before maturity.

Using the *addition rule* of probability for *mutually exclusive* events, the combined probability is:

$$P(r \le 3) = P(r = 0) + P(r = 1) + P(r = 2) + P(r = 3)$$

The three binomial probabilities must now be computed separately and summed:

$$P(r = 0) = {}_{10}C_0\,(0{,}20)^0\,(0{,}80)^{(10-0)} = 0{,}107$$
$$P(r = 1) = {}_{10}C_1\,(0{,}20)^1\,(0{,}80)^{(10-1)} = 0{,}269$$
$$P(r = 2) = {}_{10}C_2\,(0{,}20)^2\,(0{,}80)^{(10-2)} = 0{,}302$$
$$P(r = 3) = {}_{10}C_3\,(0{,}20)^3\,(0{,}80)^{(10-3)} = 0{,}201$$

Then $P(r \le 3) = 0{,}107 + 0{,}269 + 0{,}302 + 0{,}201 = 0{,}879$ (87,9%)

Solution (2) using *Excel*

Since P($r \le 3$) is a *cumulative* probability, set cumulative = *true*. The cumulative probability is the sum of all the marginal probabilities, from $r = 0$ to $r = 3$.

Thus,	to find $P(r \leq 3)$
use	**= BINOMDIST (3,10,0.20,true)**
giving a result	**= 0,879126**

Management interpretation (2)

There is an 87,9% chance that *no more than three* of the 10 policies selected will be surrendered before maturity date.

Management question (3)

What is the probability that *at least two* out of the 10 randomly selected *policies* will be *surrendered* before maturity date?

Solution (3)

Expressed mathematically, the question translates into finding:
$P(r \geq 2) = P(r = 2) + P(r = 3) + P(r = 4) + \ldots + P(r = 10)$

This requires that nine binomial calculations be performed. However, to avoid onerous calculations, the *complementary law* of probability can be used. This is applied as follows:

$$
\begin{aligned}
P(r \geq 2) &= 1 - P(r \leq 1) \\
&= 1 - [P(r = 0) + P(r = 1)] \\
&= 1 - [\,0{,}107 + 0{,}269] && \text{(from question 2 above)} \\
&= 1 - 0{,}376 = 0{,}624 && (62{,}4\%)
\end{aligned}
$$

Solution (3) using *Excel*

To find $P(r \geq 2) = 1 - P(r \leq 1)$, apply both the complementary rule of probability and the cumulative function (i.e. set cumulative = *true*). The cumulative probability is the sum of all the marginal probabilities from $r = 0$ to $r = 1$.

Excel's BINOMDIST function can only compute *less than* cumulative probabilities. Therefore, use *Excel* to find $P(r \leq 1)$ and then subtract this result from 1 to give the required answer (using the complementary rule).

Thus,	to find $P(r \geq 2)$
use	**= 1 – BINOMDIST (1,10,0.20,true)**
giving a result	**= 0,62419**

Management interpretation (3)

There is a 62,4% chance that *at least two* of the 10 randomly selected policies will be *surrendered* before maturity date.

Computational issues

- Key words such as *at least*, *no more than*, *at most*, *no less than*, *smaller than*, *larger than*, *greater than*, *no greater than*, etc., imply the summing of marginal probabilities (i.e. computing cumulative probabilities).
- The *complementary rule* should be considered whenever practical, to reduce the number of calculations.

Descriptive Statistical Measures of the Binomial Distribution

Formula

A measure of *central location* and a measure of *dispersion* can be computed for any random variable that follows a binomial distribution, using the following formulae:

Mean: $\mu = np$
Standard deviation: $\sigma = \sqrt{npq}$ where $q = 1 - p$

In Example 8.2 (**Life Assurance Policy Surrender study**), where $p = 0{,}20$:

- the *mean* (average) number of policies that can be expected to be surrendered, based on a sample of 10 randomly selected policies, is:
  (10)(0,2) = ***2 policies*, on *average***, out of 10 policies.
- the *standard deviation* for this sample of 10 policies would be:
  $\sqrt{(10)(0{,}2)(0{,}8)} = 1{,}265$ policies.

8.4 Poisson Probability Distribution

A *Poisson* process is also a *discrete* process.

The **Poisson process** measures the *number of occurrences* of a particular event of a discrete random variable in a *predetermined time, space* or *volume interval*, for which an *average number of occurrences* of the event is known or can be determined.

The following *illustrate* instances in which a discrete random variable can be described by the Poisson process:

- the *number of peak caps* sold by a store in a *week*
- the *number of customers arriving* at a supermarket checkout counter in a *one-hour* time interval
- the *number of telephone calls* made by a telesales person in a *10-minute* interval
- the *number of cars sold* by a dealer in a given *month*
- the *number of defective garments* (e.g. jeans) per *consignment*
- the *number of particles of chlorine* in *one litre of pool water*.

In each case, the number of occurrences of a given event of the random variable, x, can take on any one of the integer values 0, 1, 2, 3 . . . up to infinity (in theory).

The Poisson Question

"What is the *probability* of x occurrences of a given event being observed in a predetermined time, space or volume interval?"

Formula

The Poisson question can be answered by applying the *Poisson probability distribution* function, which is defined as follows:

$$P(x) = \frac{e^{-a}\,a^{x}}{x!} \qquad \text{for } x = 0, 1, 2, 3 \ldots$$

where a = the *mean number of occurrences* of a given event of the random variable for a predetermined time, space or volume interval

e = a mathematical constant approximately equal to 2,71828

(*Note:* e^x is a function on all scientific calculators and in *Excel* (=EXP(x)).

x = *number of occurrences* of a given event for which a probability is required. The value, x, is given in the Poisson question. Thus x can be any discrete value 0, 1, 2, 3, 4 . . . and is called the **domain**.

The Poisson Domain

Note that the *domain* of a *Poisson* process – which identifies all the possible outcomes for x – is the set of all integer values from *zero to infinity*. There is no theoretical upper limit to the number of occurrences of a given event of the random variable.

Two examples to *illustrate* the idea of domain as infinite or finite:

- If, in the *Poisson model*, x is the number of customers arriving at a supermarket checkout counter in a one-hour period, then x can be any positive integer value starting with zero (i.e. $x = 0, 1, 2, 3, 4, 5 \ldots$ with no theoretical upper limit (although in reality a limit does exist, in this case because of physical capacity).
- In contrast, the domain of the *binomial process* – the number of r success outcomes out of n trials – has a finite length. The domain of a binomial process is only the set of positive integers from zero to n (sample size), because the number of success outcomes (r) observed cannot exceed the number of trials. To *illustrate* further*:* if $n = 12$ car sales at an Opel dealer, then r, which could be defined as the number of Opels sold, can be only one of the following values: 0, 1, 2, 3, 4 . . . or 12.

Shape of the Poisson Probability Distribution

The general shape of the Poisson probability distribution is shown in Figure 8.1. The distribution always peaks at the mean number of occurrences of a given event. This corresponds with the most likely probability.

Figure 8.1 Illustration of a **Poisson distribution** with a = 5

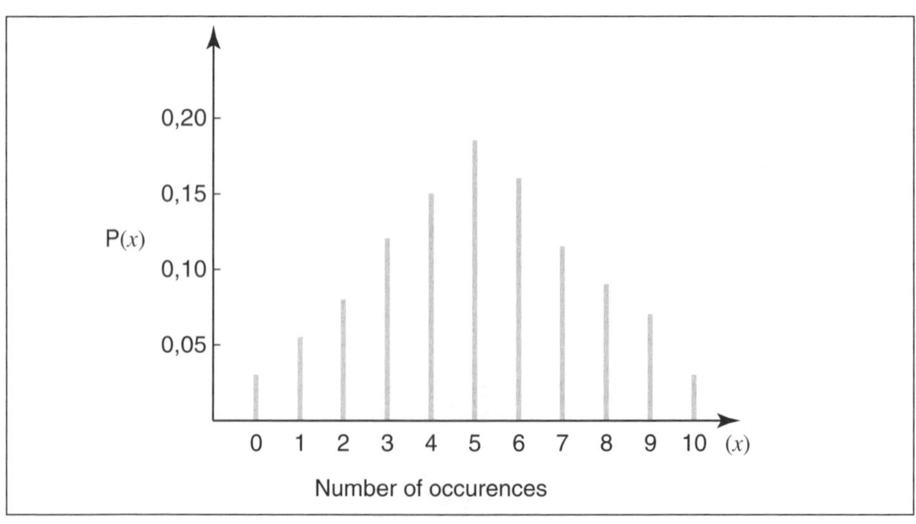

Example 8.3 Heritage Properties – Office Lease study

Heritage Properties is a national company specialising in rental office accommodation. An analysis of lease records at their Durban branch has established that, on average, five lease agreements are signed per day for office space in the Durban metropolitan area.

Management question (1)

What is the probability that, on a given day, the Durban branch will sign only *three lease agreements* for office space?

Solution (1)

The random variable, x = *number of signed lease agreements*, "fits" the Poisson process for the following reasons:

(i) The random variable is discrete

It measures the *number* of *lease agreements signed* per day. Theoretically, any number of lease agreements, from zero to infinity, can be signed on any given day.

(ii) The outcomes of the random variable occur in a predetermined time interval

The problem is a Poisson process as it describes the number of occurrences (*signed lease agreements*) in a predetermined time interval (*one day*).

(iii) The average number of occurrences is given (or can be determined)

The average number of occurrences (i.e. signed lease agreements per day, a) is given. In this instance, $a = 5$.

Given a = average number of lease agreements signed per day
= 5 per day

Required to find P(x = 3 lease agreements signed on a given day)

$$P(x = 3) = \frac{e^{-3}\,5^3}{3!} = 0{,}006738 \times 20{,}833$$
$$= 0{,}1404$$

Solution (1) using *Excel*

The function operation POISSON can be used to compute both marginal and cumulative Poisson probabilities for values of x (number of occurrences of an observed event).

The function and its arguments are: **= POISSON (*x*, *mean*, *cumulative*)**

where x = the number of occurrences of an observed event (given in the Poisson question)
mean = a (the expected value of the Poisson process), and
cumulative = *true* or *false*
(*true* = find cumulative probability; *false* = find marginal probability)

Thus, to find P(x = 3): = **POISSON(3,5,false)**
gives the result = **0,14037**

Management interpretation (1)

There is only a 14,04% chance that exactly three lease agreements will be signed on a given day, when the average number of lease agreements signed per day is five. This event therefore has a low probability of occurring.

Management question (2)

What is the probability that, on a given day, the Durban branch will sign *at most two lease agreements* for office space?

Solution (2)

Expressed mathematically, *at most two* signed lease agreements imply either 0 or 1 or 2 *signed lease agreements per day.*
These possible outcomes (0, 1, 2) are *mutually exclusive* and the combined probability can be found using the *addition rule* of probability for mutually exclusive events.

Thus $P(x \leq 2) = P(x = 0) + P(x = 1) + P(x = 2)$

Each probability is separately computed before being summed.

P(*0 lease agreements signed*): $P(x = 0) = \frac{e^{-5}5^0}{0!} = 0{,}00674$ Recall: 0! = 1

P(*1 lease agreement signed*): $P(x = 1) = \frac{e^{-5}5^1}{1!} = 0{,}0337$

P(*2 lease agreements signed*): $P(x = 2) = \frac{e^{-5}5^2}{2!} = 0{,}0842$

Then $P(x \leq 2) = 0{,}00674 + 0{,}0337 + 0{,}0842 = 0{,}12464$

Solution (2) using *Excel*

Since the cumulative probability is required, set *cumulative* = *true*.

Thus, to find P(x ≤ 2): = **POISSON (2,5,true)**
gives the result = **0,12465**

Management interpretation (2)

There is only a 12,46% chance that at most two lease agreements will be signed on a given day, when the average number of lease agreements signed per day is five. Again, this low probability implies that this event is unlikely to occur.

Management question (3)

What is the probability that the Durban branch will sign *more than four lease agreements* for office space on a given day?

Solution (3)

Expressed mathematically, the question requires us to find P(x > 4). Since x is a discrete random variable, the first integer value of x above 4 is x = 5. Hence the problem becomes one of finding:

$$P(x \geq 5) = P(x = 5) + P(x = 6) + P(x = 7) + \ldots$$

The values of x, for which probabilities must be found, continue to infinity. To solve this problem, the *complementary rule of probability* must be used. The complement of $x \geq 5$ is $x \leq 4$.

Thus
$$\begin{aligned} P(x \geq 5) &= 1 - P(x \leq 4) \\ &= 1 - [P(x = 0) + P(x = 1) + P(x = 2) + P(x = 3) + P(x = 4)] \\ &= 1 - [0{,}0067 + 0{,}0337 + 0{,}0842 + 0{,}1404 + 0{,}1755] \\ &= 1 - 0{,}4405 \\ &= 0{,}5595 \end{aligned}$$

Solution (3) using *Excel*

To find P($x \geq 5$) = 1 – P($x \leq 4$), apply both the complementary rule of probability and the cumulative function (i.e. set *cumulative* = *true*), as follows:

= 1–POISSON(4,5,true)

which gives the result **= 0,559507**

Management interpretation (3)

There is a 55,95% chance that the Durban branch will sign more than four lease agreements for office space on a given day, when the average number of lease agreements signed per day is five. This moderately high probability implies that such an event is reasonably likely to occur on any given day.

Management question (4)

What is the probability that the Durban branch will sign *more than four lease agreements* for office space in any *two-day period*?

Solution (4)

Note: The *time interval* over which a lease agreement can be signed has changed from one day to *two* days. Thus the *average value*, *a*, must now be adjusted to refer to the average number of lease agreements signed *over two* days (instead of one day), before the Poisson process can be applied.

Thus, *a* equals an average of *10* lease agreements signed *per two days* (i.e. 5 per day × 2-day interval).

For the above question, using a = 10, the problem is to find:

$$P(x > 4) = P(x \geq 5) = [P(x = 5) + P(x = 6) + P(x = 7) + \ldots]$$

This can be solved using the *complementary rule,* as follows:

$$\begin{aligned} P(x > 4) &= 1 - P(x \leq 4) \\ &= 1 - [P(x = 0) + P(x = 1) + P(x = 2) + P(x = 3) + P(x = 4)] \end{aligned}$$

Each Poisson probability is computed separately using $a = 10$.

Thus $P(x > 4) = 1 - [P(x = 0) + P(x = 1) + P(x = 2) + P(x = 3) + P(x = 4)]$
$= 1 - [0{,}0000454 + 0{,}000454 + 0{,}00227 + 0{,}00757 + 0{,}01892] = 1 - 0{,}02925$
$= 0{,}97075$

Solution (4) using *Excel*

To find $P(x > 4) = 1 - P(x \leq 4)$, apply both the complementary rule of probability and the cumulative function (i.e. set *cumulative = true*), but with $a = 10$, as follows:

=1–POISSON(4,10,true)

which gives the result = **0,970747**

Management interpretation (4)

There is a 97,075% chance that the Durban branch will sign more than four lease agreements for office space in any two-day period. It is an almost complete certainty that at least four agreements will be signed, when the average number of lease agreements signed per two days is 10.

Descriptive statistical measures of the Poisson distribution

Formulae

A measure of *central location* and a measure of *dispersion* can be computed for any random variable that follows a Poisson process, using the following formulae:

Mean	$\mu = a$
Standard deviation	$\sigma = \sqrt{a}$

8.5 Continuous Probability Distributions

A *continuous* random variable can take on *any value* (as opposed to only discrete values) in an *interval*. *Examples* of continuous random variables include sales volumes, equity prices, store floor area, length of time to complete a task, policy claim values, etc.

Since there is an infinite number of possible outcomes associated with a continuous random variable, probabilities are found for *ranges of x-values* only, rather than for individual x-values, as is the case in discrete probability distributions. *Continuous probability distribution functions* are used to find probabilities associated with *intervals of x-values.*

The distribution (or probability) of outcomes of a large majority of *continuous* random variables can be described by the *normal probability distribution* function.

8.6 Normal Probability Distribution

The **normal probability distribution** has the following properties:

- It is a smooth *bell-shaped* curve.
- It is *symmetrical* about a central mean value, μ.
- The tails of the curve are asymptotic (meaning there is always a non-zero probability associated with every value in the problem domain).

- The distribution is always described by two parameters: a *mean* (μ), and a *standard deviation* (σ).
- The total *area under the curve* will always *equal one,* since it represents the total sample space of collectively exhaustive events (i.e. all possible *x-values*).
- Due to symmetry, the area under the curve that is *above* μ is 0,5 (or 50%). The area under the curve *below* μ is also 0,5 (or 50%).
- The *probability* associated with a particular range of x-values is described by the area under the curve between the limits of the given x range ($x_1 < x < x_2$).

Figure 8.2 illustrates the shape of the *normal probability distribution* and highlights the area under the curve between the x-limits of x_1 and x_2. This *area* represents the *probability* that x lies between the limits of x_1 and x_2 for a normally distributed random variable with a mean of μ and a standard deviation of σ.

Figure 8.2 The **normal probability distribution** showing $P(x_1 < x < x_2)$

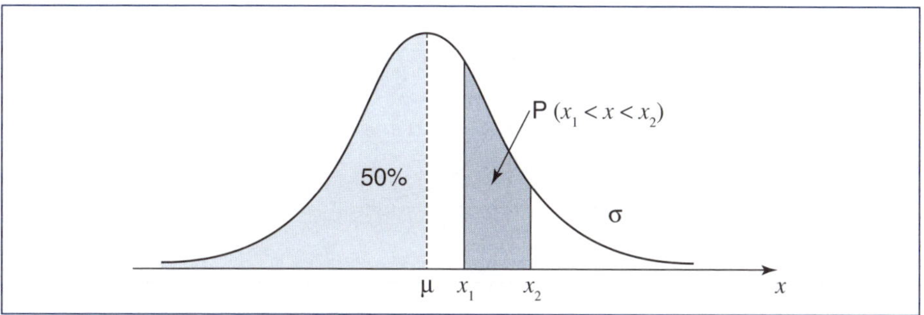

Finding Probabilities using the Normal Distribution

To find a probability for the outcomes of a random variable, x, which is *normally distributed*, it is necessary to find the appropriate *area under the bell-shaped curve* between the x-limits for which the probability is required.

Either a *manual approach* or a *computer-based approach,* using *Excel* functions, can be used to find a probability associated with a normally distributed random variable, x. The manual approach uses a set of statistical tables for which probabilities (or areas) have already been worked out. Both approaches are illustrated in this next section.

8.7 Standard Normal (z) Probability Distribution

A **statistical table** (refer to the **z-table** in Appendix 1) is used to manually compute areas (probabilities) under a normal curve. The areas read off from the statistical table are associated with only *one particular* normal probability distribution, called the **standard normal distribution** (or the ***z*-distribution**).

The **standard normal distribution**, with random variable z, has the following properties:

a mean equal to 0 $(\mu_z = 0)$
and a standard deviation equal to 1 $(\sigma_z = 1)$

8.7.1 Finding probabilities using the z-distribution

The statistical table in Appendix 1 gives the probability of z lying between its mean $(\mu_z = 0)$ and a given upper z-limit, say k [i.e. $P(0 < z < k)$] as shown in Figure 8.3.

Figure 8.3 Standard normal distribution showing $P(0 < z < k)$

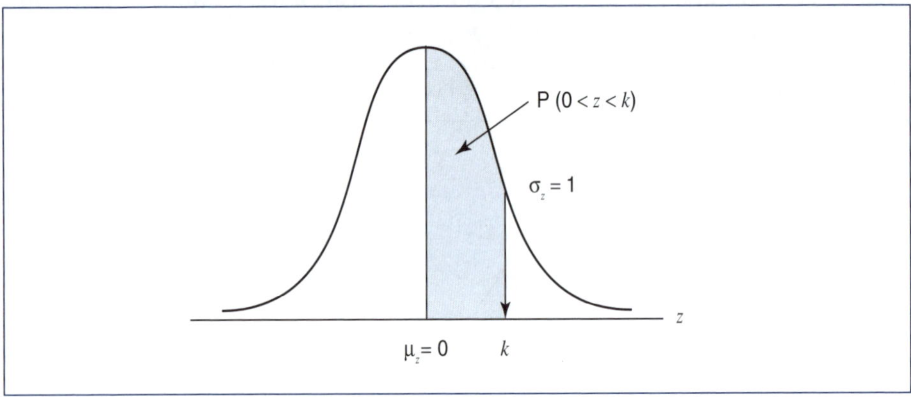

When reading values (areas) off the **z-table**, it should be noted that:

- The z-values are located down the left column (to one decimal place), and the second decimal positions of z are shown across the top row.
- The value read off at the *intersection* of the z-value, to two decimal places, is the *area under the standard normal curve* (i.e. probability) between $(0 < z < k)$.

The following *examples, solutions and interpretations* illustrate the use of the **standard normal (z) table** to find probabilities (areas) for different ranges of z-limits.

Example 8.4 Using the *z*-table to find Normal Probabilities

Refer to the ***z*-table** in Appendix 1 for questions (1) to (5) below.

Management question (1)

Find $P(0 < z < 1{,}46) = ?$

Refer to Figure 8.4 overleaf, which shows the required area.

Figure 8.4 Standard normal area between $z = 0$ and $z = 1{,}46$

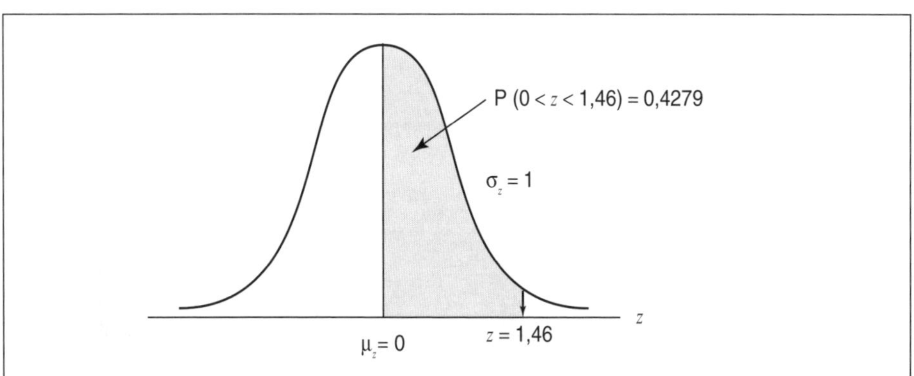

Using the *standard normal* table (Appendix 1), read down the left column of z until $z = 1{,}4$. Then read across the $z = 1{,}4$ row until $z = 0{,}06$
The area found at this intersection is 0,4279
Then $\quad P(0 < z < 1{,}46) = 0{,}4279$

Management interpretation (1)

There is a 42,79% chance that a z-value (associated with a normal distribution with a mean of 0 and a standard deviation of 1) will lie between 0 and 1,46.

Solution (1) using *Excel*

The function key operation NORMSDIST can be used to compute probabilities for an interval of z-values from the standard normal distribution, as follows:

The function is **=NORMSDIST(z)** where z is the z-limit specified in the question.

Note: This function computes the *cumulative probability* from $-\infty$ to the *z-limit.*

For management question (1), the *Excel* function operation is as follows:

=NORMSDIST(1.46) with a result = **0,927855**

To find the required probability of $P(0 < z < 1{,}46)$,
subtract 0,5 (the area below $z = 0$) from this result, to give 0,427855.

Management question (2)

Find $\quad P(-2{,}3 < z < 0) = ?$
Refer to Figure 8.5 below, which shows the required area.

Figure 8.5 Standard normal area between $z = -2,3$ and $z = 0$

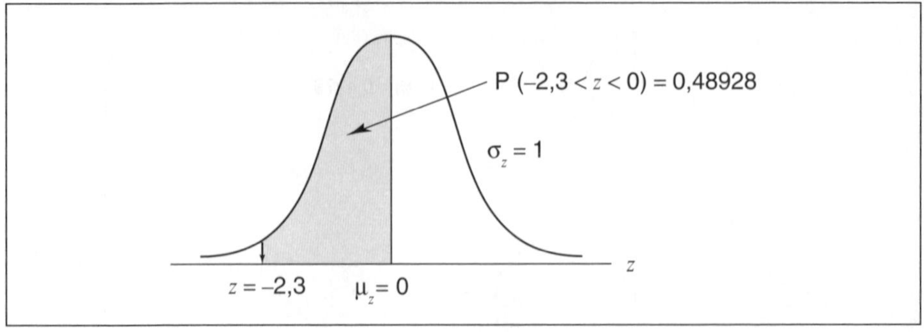

Due to symmetry, this area (probability) is equivalent to finding the area of $P(0 < z < 2,30)$ on the positive z side.

Reading from the **z-table** (left column) at $z = 2,3$, this area equals 0,48928.
Then $\quad P(-2,3 < z < 0) = 0,48928$

Management interpretation (2)

There is a 48,928% chance that a z-value (associated with a normal distribution with a mean of 0 and a standard deviation of 1) will lie between –2,3 and 0.

Solution (2) using *Excel*

To find $P(-2,3 < z < 0)$, the cumulative probability (area) from $-\infty$ up to $z = -2,3$ is subtracted from 0,5, i.e:

=0.5-NORMSDIST(–2.3) with a result = (0,5 – 0,010724) = **0,489276**

Management question (3)

Find $\quad P(z > 1,82) = ?$
Refer to Figure 8.6, which shows the required area.

Figure 8.6 Standard normal area above $z = 1,82$

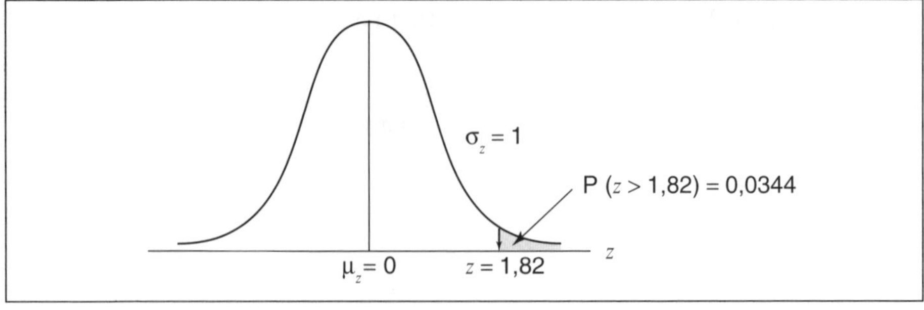

The total area under the normal curve to the right of the midpoint (mean of z) at $z = 0$ is 0,5. The standard normal (z) table only computes areas between the limits of ($0 < z < k$). The area **above** k is found by the **complementary rule of probability** – by subtracting the area between ($0 < z < k$) from 0,5.

Thus, from ***z*-table** $P(0 < z < 1{,}82) = 0{,}4656$

Then $P(z > 1{,}82) = 0{,}5000 - 0{,}4656 = 0{,}0344$

Management interpretation (3)

There is only a 3,44% chance that a z-value (associated with a normal distribution with a mean of 0 and a standard deviation of 1) will lie above 1,82.

Solution (3) using *Excel*

To find $P(z > 1{,}82)$, the cumulative probability (area) from $-\infty$ up to $z = 1{,}82$ must be subtracted from 1,0, i.e.:

=1.0–NORMSDIST(1.82) with a result = (1.0 – 0.96562) = **0,03438**

Management question (4)

Find $P(-2{,}1 < z < 1{,}32) = ?$

Refer to Figure 8.7, which shows the required area.

Figure 8.7 Standard normal area between $z = -2{,}1$ and $z = 1{,}32$

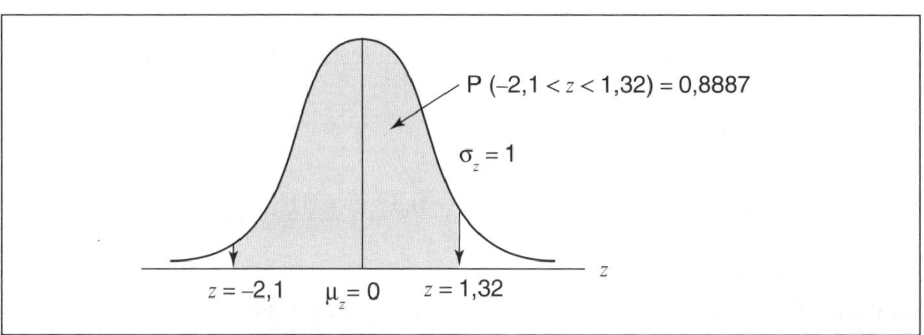

$P(-2{,}1 < z < 1{,}32)$ is equal to the *sum* of two mutually exclusive areas, each of which can be looked up separately in the z-table.

Thus $P(-2{,}1 < z < 1{,}32) = P(-2{,}1 < z < 0) + P(0 < z < 1{,}32)$

From ***z*-table** $P(-2{,}1 < z < 0) = 0{,}4821$ (using the property of *symmetry*), and

$P(0 < z < 1{,}32) = 0{,}4066$

Giving $P(-2{,}1 < z < 1{,}32) = 0{,}4821 + 0{,}4066 = 0{,}8887$

Management interpretation (4)

There is an 88,87% chance that a z-value (associated with a normal distribution with a mean of 0 and a standard deviation of 1) will lie between –2,1 and 1,32.

Solution (4) using *Excel*

The area can be found by subtracting the two *cumulative probabilities,* i.e.:
$P(-\infty < z < 1{,}32) - P(-\infty < z < -2{,}1)$ i.e.:

=NORMSDIST(1.32) – NORMSDIST(–2.1) = 0,906582 – 0,017864 = **0,8887**

Management question (5)

Find $P(1{,}24 < z < 2{,}075) = ?$
Refer to Figure 8.8, which shows the required area.

Figure 8.8 Standard normal area between z = 1,24 and z = 2,075

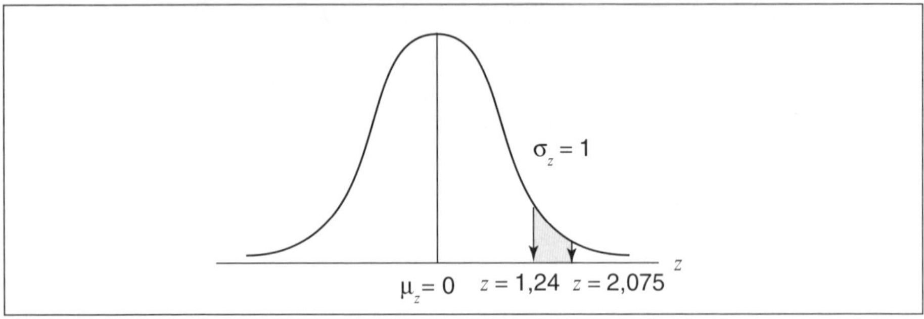

To compute the probability using the ***z*-table** (in Appendix 1), the required area can be split into two parts, i.e.:
$P(0 < z < 1{,}24)$ and $P(0 < z < 2{,}075)$
The *difference* between these two areas isolates the required probability.

From ***z*-table**	$P(0 < z < 2{,}075)$	= 0,4812	*Note:* 2,075 is rounded to 2,08.
	$P(0 < z < 1{,}24)$	= 0,3925	
Giving	$P(1{,}24 < z < 2{,}075)$	= 0,4812 – 0,3925 = 0,0887	

Management interpretation (5)

There is only an 8,87% chance that a z-value (associated with a normal distribution with a mean of 0 and a standard deviation of 1) will lie between 1,24 and 2,075.

Solution (5) using *Excel*

The area can be found by subtracting the two *cumulative probabilities,* i.e.:
$P(-\infty < z < 2{,}075) - P(-\infty < z < 1{,}24)$ i.e.:

=NORMSDIST(2.075) – NORMSDIST(1.24) = 0,9810 – 0,8925 = **0,08849**

Note: *Excel* uses z = 2,075 (not rounded to 2,08) to find $P(-\infty < z < 2{,}075)$. This accounts for the small difference in results from *Excel* compared to the z-table.

8.7.2 Finding probabilities for *x*-limits using the *z*-distribution

Many numeric random variables x (e.g. monthly household grocery expenditure, delivery time, product weight, etc.) follow a normal probability distribution, each with their own mean (μ) and standard deviation (σ) values. To use the *standard normal* table (the z-

table) to find probabilities associated with outcomes of any normally distributed random variable x, each x-value must be converted into a corresponding standard normal (z) value, which can then be used to read off probabilities from the z-table.

Formula

The formula to transform any x-value of a normally distributed random variable x to a corresponding z-value on the *standard normal* distribution is:

$$z = \frac{x - \mu}{\sigma}$$

Figure 8.9 below shows the correspondence between the area under a normal distribution for a random variable x between $x = 14$ and $x = 20$, with a mean (μ) = 20 and a standard deviation (σ) = 4, and the *standardised* (z) normal probability distribution. The equivalent z-values for the given x-values are found by using the above z-transformation formula.

For $x = 14$ the equivalent z-value is $z = \frac{(14–20)}{4} = –1,5$

Similarly, for $x = 20$ the equivalent z-value is $z = \frac{(20–20)}{4} = 0$

Thus finding $P(14 < x < 20)$ is equivalent to finding $P(–1,5 < z < 0)$

Using **z-table** $P(–1,5 < z < 0) = 0,4332$

Figure 8.9 Equivalence between ***x*-values** and ***z*-values** under a normal distribution

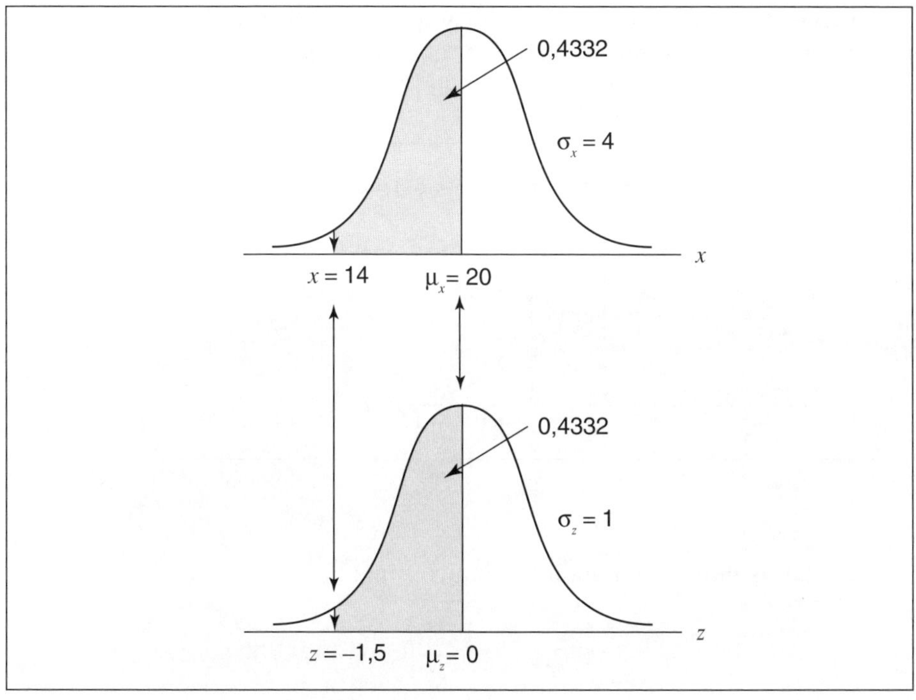

Note on the meaning of the *z*-value

A z-value measures how far (in standard deviation terms) a corresponding *x-value lies from its mean*, μ. In the above illustration, where $\mu = 20$ and $\sigma = 4$, the $z = -1{,}5$ implies that $x = 14$ lies 1,5 standard deviations *below* the mean of 20. Similarly, where $z = 0$, this implies that $x = 20$ lies at its mean of 20 (i.e. zero deviation from its mean).

Example 8.5 Sun Couriers – Delivery Time study

Sun Couriers – a parcel delivery company – has found that the *delivery time* of parcels to clients in the Durban metropolitan area after airport collection is normally distributed with a *mean delivery time* equal to 45 minutes ($\mu = 45$) and a *standard deviation* of 8 minutes ($\sigma = 8$).

Management questions

For a newly arrived consignment at Durban airport, what is the probability that a randomly selected parcel will take:

(1) *between 45 and 51 minutes* to deliver to the client?

(2) *less than 48 minutes* to deliver?

Solution (1)

Find $P(45 < x < 51)$

Step 1

Always sketch a normal probability distribution and indicate the area (probability) to be found, as shown in Figure 8.10 for Management question (1).

Figure 8.10 Area under normal curve between $x = 45$ and $x = 51$

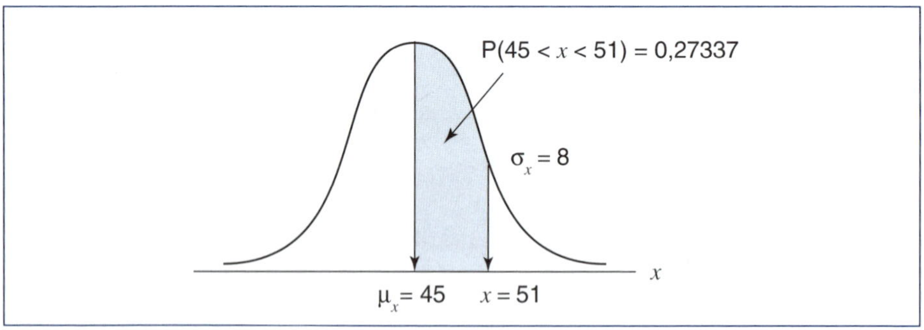

Step 2

Transform the x-limits into corresponding z-limits using:

$$z = \frac{x - \mu}{\sigma}$$

In this example:

$x = 45$ corresponds to $z = \dfrac{45 - 45}{8} = 0$

and $x = 51$ corresponds to $z = \dfrac{51 - 45}{8} = 0{,}75$

Thus P(45 < x < 51) is equivalent to finding P(0 < z < 0,75)

Step 3

Compute the required probability P(45 < x < 51).
Three approaches are possible:

Approach 1: *Reading off the z-table* (use the **z-table** in Appendix 1)
The area between P(0 < z < 0,75) = 0,2734

Approach 2: Using *Excel's* function for the *z-distribution*
=NORMSDIST(0.75) – 0.5 = (0,77337 – 0,5) = **0,27337**

Approach 3: Using *Excel's* function for a *normal* distribution with x-limits.

Refering to approach 3, *Excel* offers another function operation to compute the cumulative normal probabilities directly for the x-limits of the management question.
The function operation is:

=NORMDIST(*x-limit*, *μ*, σ, *true*)

This function computes the *cumulative normal* probability P(–∞ < x < *x-limit*).

The values *x-limit*, μ, σ are specified in the management problem. The argument *true* identifies that *cumulative normal* probabilities are computed.

Thus P(45 < x < 51) = P(–∞ < x < 51) – P(–∞ < x < 45)
=NORMDIST(51,45,8,true) – NORMDIST(45,45,8,true)
= (0,77337 – 0,5) = **0,27337**

Management interpretation (1)

There is a 27,337% chance that it will take between 45 minutes and 51 minutes for a randomly selected parcel to be delivered to a client (only a one in four chance, approximately) of delivering within the time interval of 45 and 51 minutes.

Solution (2)

Find P(x < 48)

Step 1

Sketch a normal probability distribution and indicate the area (probability) to be found, as shown in Figure 8.11, overleaf, for management question (2).

Figure 8.11 Area under normal curve below $x = 48$

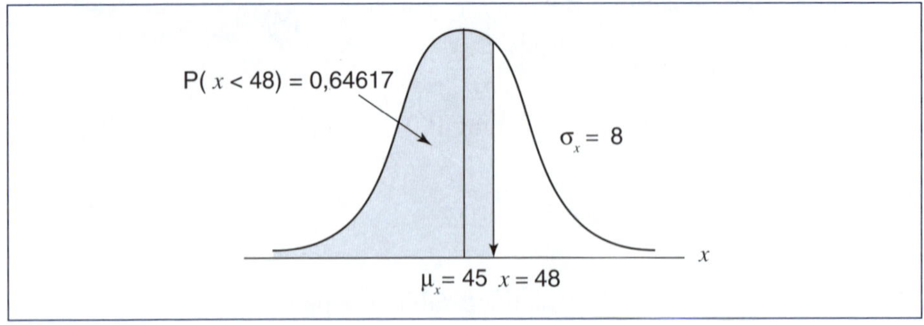

Step 2

Transform the x-limits into corresponding z-limits using:

$$z = \frac{x - \mu}{\sigma}$$

In this example:

$x = 48$ corresponds to $z = \frac{48 - 45}{8} = 0{,}375$

Thus $\quad$ $P(x < 48)$ is equivalent to finding $P(z < 0{,}375)$

Step 3

Compute the required probability $P(x < 48)$.

Approach 1: *Reading off the z-table* (see **z-table** in Appendix 1)
The area between $P(0 < z < 0{,}375) = 0{,}1480$ (use $z = 0{,}38$)

Thus $P(x < 48) = P(z < 0{,}375) = (0{,}5 + 0{,}1480) = 0{,}6480$

Approach 2: Using *Excel's* function for the *z-distribution*
=NORMSDIST(0.375) with a result = **0,64617**

Approach 3: Using *Excel's* function for the *normal* distribution with x-limits.
=NORMDIST(*x-limit*, *μ*, σ, true)
=NORMDIST(48,45,8,true) with a result = **0,64617**

Management interpretation (2)

There is a 64,617% chance (approximately a two-thirds chance) that a randomly selected parcel will be delivered to the client within 48 minutes.

8.7.3 Find *x*-limits associated with given probabilities for a Normal Distribution

Often the value of a normally distributed random variable x, that corresponds to a given probability, is required.

To *illustrate* this, assume the marketing manager at Edgars stores would like to answer the following question:

"What is the minimum *purchase value of transactions*, x, for the *highest-spending* 15% of Edgars' customers?"

The 15% represents the *probability* of being a high-spending Edgars' customer.

A two-step approach is used to identify the required ***x*-value**.

Step 1

First, find the z-value corresponding to the given area under the normal curve. The z-value is found by reversing the procedure for finding (probability) areas for given *z-limits* (as shown in the previous section).

Step 2

Then use the z-transformation formula to convert the derived z-value (from step 1) into the corresponding x-value.

The following example illustrates how to find z-values from given areas (or probabilities) under the *standard normal* distribution (i.e. *step 1* only).

Example 8.6 Find *z*-values Corresponding to Given Areas (Probabilities)

Find the z-values for questions (1) to (3) below.

Management question (1)

Find k such that $P(0 < z < k) = 0{,}3461$

This probability (area) is shown in Figure 8.12.

Figure 8.12 z-distribution showing $P(0 < z < k) = 0{,}3461$

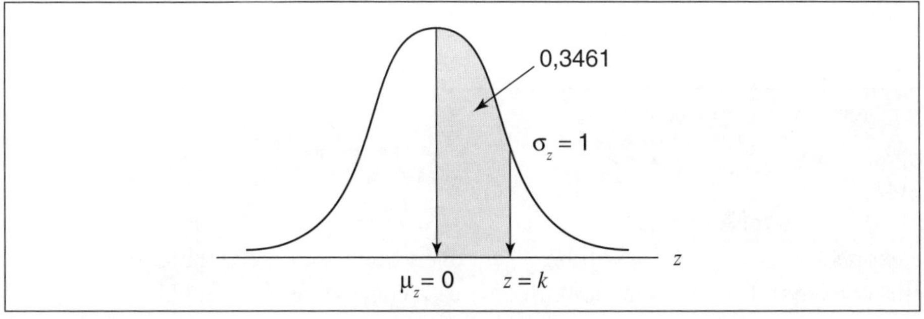

Solution (1)

Approach 1: Using **z-tables**

To find k such that $P(0 < z < k) = 0{,}3461$, the body of the **z-table** (in Appendix 1) is scanned for this exact area (probability) or its closest approximation. Then the z-value corresponding to this area is read off.

Thus $k = 1,02$ since $P(0 < z < 1,02) = 0,3461$

Approach 2: Using *Excel* **=NORMSINV(cumulative probability)**

The NORMSINV (i.e. standard normal inverse) function finds the *z-limit* associated with the *cumulative probability* up to z where the mean of $z = 0$ and the standard deviation of $z = 1$.

Thus, to find k such that $P(0 < z < k) = 0,3461$, the *cumulative area* from $-\infty$ up to k must be used in the *Excel* function. The cumulative area is $(0,5 + 0,3461) = 0,8461$.

Then k = **=NORMSINV(0.8461) = 1,019849**

Thus $k = 1,019849$

Management interpretation (1)

34,61% of all z-values lie between $z = 0$ and $z = 1,019849$.

Management question (2)

Find k such that $P(k < z < 0) = 0,1628$

Refer to Figure 8.13, which shows the appropriate area (probability).

Figure 8.13 z-distribution showing $P(k < z < 0) = 0,1628$

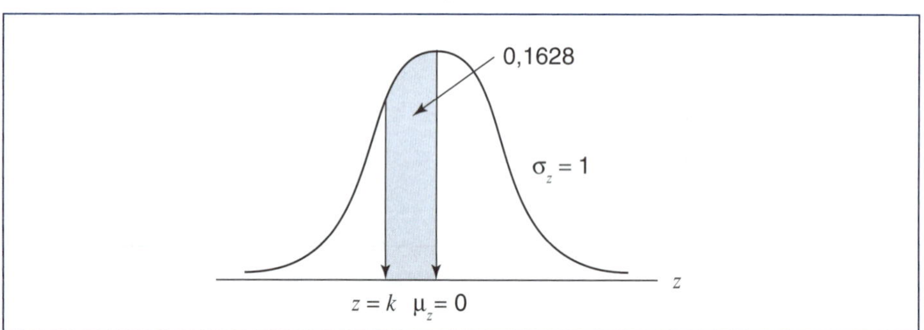

Solution (2)

Approach 1: Using **z-tables**

From the expression ($k < z < 0$), k will be a negative value. Scan the **z-table** for an area of 0,1628. This corresponds to a z-value of 0,42. Since k is negative, $k = -0,42$.

Thus $k = -0,42$ satisfies $P(-0,42 < z < 0) = 0,1628$.

Approach 2: Using *Excel* **=NORMSINV(cumulative probability)**

To find k such that $P(k < z < 0) = 0,1628$, the *cumulative area* up to k must be used in the *Excel* function. The cumulative area up to $k = (0,5 - 0,1628) = 0,3372$.

Then k = **=NORMSINV(0.3372) = –0,42012**

Thus k = –0,42012

Management interpretation (2)

16,28% of all z-values lie between $z = -0,42012$ and $z = 0$.

Management question (3)

Find k such that P ($z > k$) = 0,8051.
Refer to Figure 8.14 for the appropriate area (probability).

Figure 8.14 z-distribution showing $P(z > k) = 0,8051$

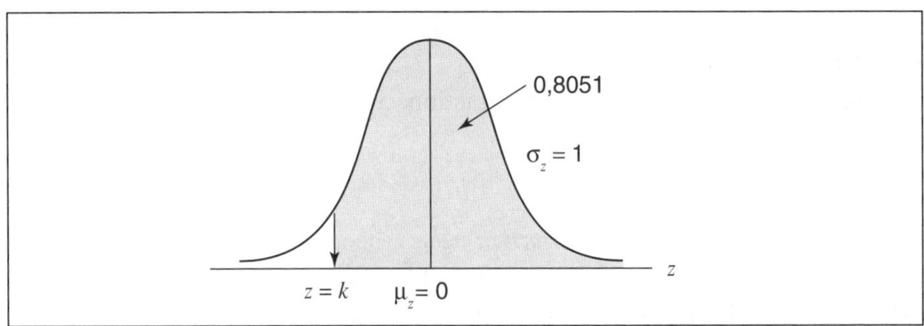

Solution (3)

Approach 1: Using **z-tables**

For the area above k to be 0,8051, which is greater than 0,5000, k must lie below $z = 0$ (the central mean value of the *z-distribution*). Thus, k will again have a negative sign; and the area that must be found in the z-table is not 0,8051, but 0,3051 (i.e. 0,8051 – 0,5000), as the z-table shows areas for only half the z-distribution.

The area of 0,3051 corresponds to a z-value of 0,86.

Since k is negative, $k = -0,86$

Thus P($z > -0,86$) = 0,8051

Approach 2: Using *Excel* **=NORMSINV(cumulative probability)**

To find k such that P(z > k) = 0,8051, the *cumulative area* up to k must be used in the *Excel* function. The cumulative area up to k = (1,0 – 0,8051) = 0,1949.

Then k = **=NORMSINV(0.1949) = –0,85998**

Thus k = –0,85998

Management interpretation (3)

80,51% of all z-values lie above $z = -0,85998$ (rounded to –0,86).

Once z-values corresponding to given areas (probabilities) under the normal curve have been found, *step 2* can be applied. This requires converting z-values into their corresponding x-*values* using the z-transformation formula:

$$z = \frac{x - \mu}{\sigma}$$

Example 8.7 Edgars Purchase Value of Transactions study

Assume that the *purchase value of transactions*, x, at Edgars stores are normally distributed with a mean of R244 and a standard deviation of R68.

Management question (1)

What is the *minimum purchase value* of transactions for the *highest spending* 15% of Edgars' customers?

Solution (1)

This question requires that a specific *transaction value* x be identified such that, above this value, the top 15% of high-spending customers are found.
The problem can be graphically displayed, as shown in Figure 8.15.

Figure 8.15 Edgars **Purchase Value of Transactions**: highest 15% of customers

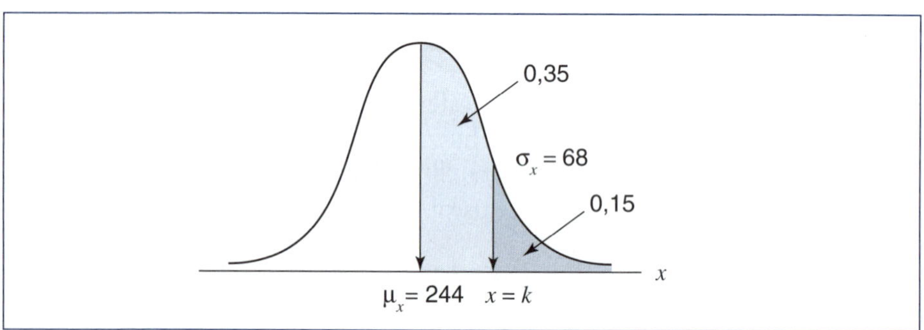

Approach 1: Using **z-tables**

Step 1

Find the z-value which corresponds to an area of 0,15 in the top tail of a normal distribution.

To use the z-table, the area which must be found is $(0,5 - 0,15) = 0,35$ (i.e. the middle area). The closest z-value is 1,04. The area between $[0 < z < 1,04]$ is 0,3508, which is a close enough approximation to 0,3500.

Step 2

Find the x-value associated with the identified z-value in *step 1*.

Substitute z = 1,04; μ = 244; and σ = 68 into the z-transformation formula, and solve for x.

Using $z = \frac{x - \mu}{\sigma}$ i.e. $1{,}04 = \frac{x - 244}{68}$

Solve for x $x = \mu + z\sigma$ $= 244 + (1{,}04 \times 68)$

$x = 244 + 70{,}72$

$x =$ R314,72

Approach 2: Using *Excel* **=NORMINV(cumulative probability, mean, std dev)**

The NORMINV (i.e. normal inverse) function finds the *x-limit* associated with a normal *cumulative probability* distribution with a specified *mean* μ and *standard deviation* σ.

To find k such that $P(x > k) = 0{,}15$, the *cumulative area* up to k must be used in the *Excel* function.

The cumulative area up to $k = (1{,}0 - 0{,}15) = 0{,}85$.

Then k = **=NORMINV(0.85,244,68) = 314,4775**

Thus k = 314,48 (rounded)

Management interpretation (1)

The highest spending 15% of Edgars customers spend at least R314,48 on each purchase occasion.

Note: The NORMSINV function could also be used to find the z-value associated with the given probability (step 1 of approach 1). Then the z-transformation formula can be applied to compute the required x-value. (step 2 of approach 1)

Management question (2)

What *purchase value of transactions* separates the *lowest spending* 20% of Edgars customers from the remaining customers?

Solution (2)

This question requires that a specific *transaction value x* be identified such that the area under the normal curve below this value is 20%, which represents the lowest spending 20% of Edgars customers.

The problem can be viewed graphically, as shown in Figure 8.16 overleaf.

Figure 8.16 Edgars **Purchase Value of Transactions**: lowest 20% of customers

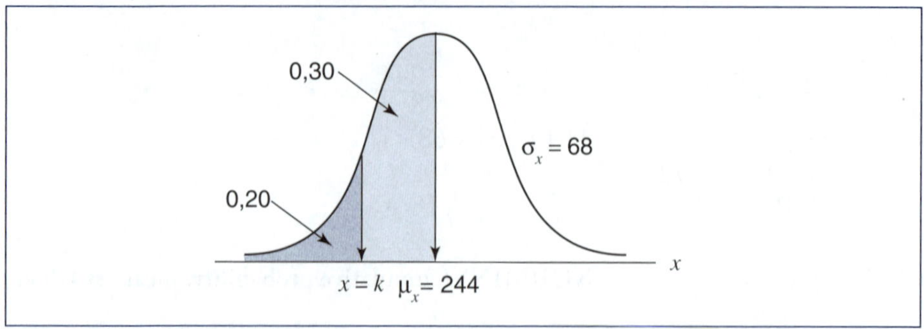

Approach 1: Using **z-tables**

Step 1

Find the z-value which corresponds to an area of 0,20 in the bottom tail of a normal distribution.

To use the z-table, the area that must be found is (0,5 – 0,20) = 0,30 (i.e. the middle area). The closest z-value is 0,84. The area between $[0 < z < 0{,}84]$ is 0,2995, which is close enough an approximation to 0,30.
Since the required z-value is below its mean, the z-value will be negative.

Hence $\quad z = -0{,}84$

Step 2

Find the x-value associated with the identified z-value in *step 1*.
Substitute $z = -0{,}84$; $\mu = 244$; and $\sigma = 68$ into the z-transformation formula, and solve for x.

Using $\quad z = \dfrac{x - \mu}{\sigma} \quad$ i.e. $-0{,}84 = \dfrac{x - 244}{68}$

Solve for x: $\quad x = \mu + z\,\sigma \quad = 244 - (0{,}84 \times 68)$
$x = 244 - 57{,}12$
$x = \text{R}186{,}88$

Approach 2: Using *Excel* **=NORMINV(cumulative probability, mean, std dev)**
The lower tail area is given as 20%, which corresponds to the *cumulative area* up to k.

Then $\quad k$ = **=NORMINV(0.20,244,68)** = **186,7698**
Thus $\quad k$ = 186,77 (rounded)

Management interpretation (2)

The lowest spending 20% of Edgars customers spend at most R186,77 on each purchase occasion.

8.8 Student *t* Probability Distribution

When the normal distribution is used, it is assumed that the population standard deviation, σ, is known. However, this is often not the case. Invariably σ is unknown and only the **sample statistic**, ***s***, is known.

When the sample standard deviation (s) is used in place of σ, probabilities based on the bell-shaped distribution are derived, not from the z-distribution, but from another distribution called the **Student *t*-distribution** (shortened to the ***t*-distribution**).

The ***t*-distribution** has similar properties to the standard normal probability distribution (z). It is also bell-shaped and symmetrical about its mean of zero, but it *does **not** have* a ***constant*** *standard deviation* (which the z-distribution does have). The *t-distribution*'s standard deviation is derived from the sample standard deviation and hence its value varies inversely with the size of the sample used.

Thus, the *t-distribution* is actually a family of distributions about the same mean of zero. These distributions vary only in width (i.e. their standard deviations). For small samples, the distribution tends to have a large standard deviation, while for large samples, the distribution tends to have a small standard deviation.

Therefore, when computing probabilities associated with the t-distribution, the sample size (known as **degrees of freedom**) must be known, as this influences the outcome.

See Figure 8.17 to illustrate the family of t distributions.

Figure 8.17 t-distribution

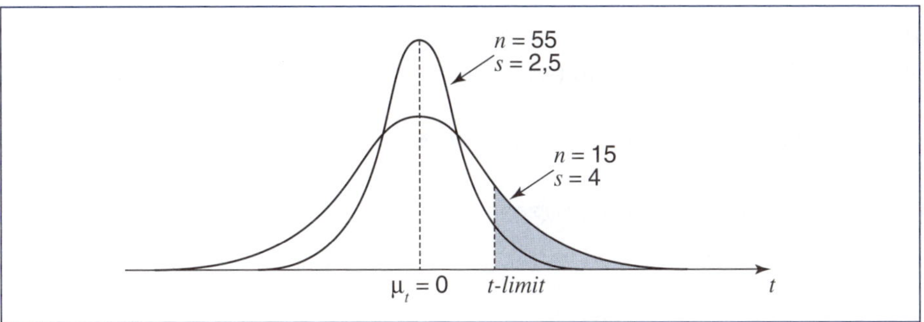

Formula

The formula to transform any x-limit to a corresponding *t-limit*, when the ***population standard deviation is not known***, is as follows:

$$t = \frac{x - \mu}{s}$$

where s = sample standard deviation

HOW TO

To find probabilities using the t-distribution

Using *Excel*

=TDIST(*t*, *degrees of freedom*, *tails*)

Where t = t-limit
degrees of freedom = $n - 1$, and
tails = 1 or 2, for which the *tail* probabilities must be found
If tails = 1 only the probability in either the upper (or lower) tail is computed.
If tails = 2 the combined tail probabilities are computed.

Note: Manual calculations to compute probabilities using the t-distribution are not performed. The formula is too complicated.

Example 8.8 Find Probabilities using the *t*-distribution

Management question

Find P(t > 0,2446) when n = 28
This implies that only the probability in the *upper tail* of the *t-distribution* must be found.

Thus =TDIST(0.2446,27,1) = 0,4043077

Management interpretation

40,43% of data values lie above 0,2446 (with mean = 0 and standard deviation = 1).

HOW TO

To find t-limits associated with given probabilities

=TINV(*combined tail probability*, *degrees of freedom*)

This finds the *t-limit* associated with a given *combined* tail probability.

Example 8.9 Find *t*-values corresponding to given Probabilities

Management question

Find P(t > t-limit) = 0,05 when n = 28
This t-limit corresponds to an *upper tail area* of 0,05 only. Since the *Excel* function requires the combined tail probability, this must be set to 0,1 (i.e. 0,05 × 2). Also, for a single sample, the appropriate degrees of freedom = $n - 1 = 28 - 1 = 27$.

Hence,
to find the t-limit: use **=TINV(0.10,27)**
giving a result of t-limit = **+1,70329**

Thus P(t > 1,70329) = 0,05
The t-distribution is used extensively in statistical inference, covered from chapter 9 onwards.

8.9 Summary

This chapter covered four theoretical probability distributions: The **binomial** and the **Poisson** probability distributions are used to find probabilities for *discrete numeric* random variables, while the **normal** and the **Student *t*** probability distributions compute probabilities for *continuous numeric* random variables.

The particular properties of each probability distribution were described, with the emphasis that these must be matched to a problem situation before the distribution can be validly applied to finding probabilities. The *standard normal* (z) probability distribution was introduced as a way of computing probabilities for any normally distributed random variable x. The chapter illustrated the use of both the z statistical tables and the function operations in *Excel* to derive probabilities for the *normal* and the *Student t-distributions* (NORMSDIST; NORMDIST and TDIST). *Excel's* functions can also be used compute binomial and Poisson probabilities (BINOMDIST and POISSON).

Finally, the chapter showed how values of x for normally distributed random variables associated with given probabilities can be found, using either the z-tables or an appropriate *Excel* function (NORMSINV; NORMINV or TINV).

The z- and t-distributions will be used in inferential statistics, when the topics of confidence intervals (chapter 10) and hypothesis testing (chapters 11–14) are discussed.

Exercises

8.1 (i) Use the binomial formula to find each of the following probabilities:

(i) $n = 7$ $p = 0{,}2$ and $r = 3$
(ii) $n = 10$ $p = 0{,}2$ and $r = 4$
(iii) $n = 12$ $p = 0{,}3$ and $r \leq 4$
(iv) $n = 10$ $p = 0{,}05$ and $r = 2$ or 3
(v) $n = 8$ $p = 0{,}25$ and $r \geq 3$

(ii) Use the *Excel* function **BINOMDIST** to find the binomial probabilities.

8.2 Once a week a merchandiser replenishes the stocks of a particular product brand in 6 stores for which she is responsible. Experience has shown that there is a *one in five* chance that a given store will have run out of stock before the merchandiser's weekly visit.

(i) Which probability distribution is appropriate in this problem? Why?
(ii) What is the probability that, on a given weekly round, the merchandiser will find exactly one store out of stock?
(iii) What is the probability that at most two stores will be out of stock?
(iv) What is the probability that no stores will be out of stock?
(v) What is the *mean number* of stores out of stock each week?

Note: Compute the probabilities in (ii)–(iv) both manually and using the *Excel* function **BINOMDIST**.

8.3 A tele-marketing company that sells house-owner insurance has found that 15% of all calls made to households lead to a sale of a house-owner insurance policy. Assume that each call is independent of all other calls.

(i) Find the probability that exactly no sales result from 12 calls.
(ii) What is the likelihood that fewer than 3 house-owner policies are sold in 15 calls.

Note: Compute the probabilities both manually and using the *Excel* function **BINOMDIST**.

8.4 A marketing manager makes the statement that the long-run probability that a customer would prefer the deluxe model to the standard model is 30 per cent.

(i) What is the probability that exactly 3 in a random sample of 10 customers will prefer the deluxe model?
(ii) What is the probability that more than 2 in a random sample of 10 customers will prefer the standard model?

Note: Compute the probabilities both manually and using the *Excel* function **BINOMDIST**.

8.5 A Tata truck dealer has established that 5% of new Tata trucks sold are returned for defective assembly repairs within their 12-month warranty period. Assume that the dealer has recently sold 8 new Tata trucks.

(i) What is the probability that only one of the 8 recently sold Tata trucks will be returned for defective assembly repairs within their 12-month warranty period?
(ii) What is the probability that at most 2 of the 8 recently sold Tata trucks will be returned for defective assembly repairs within their 12-month warranty period?
(iii) What is the probability that all 8 Tata trucks sold are fault-free and will not need repairs due to defective assembly within their 12-month warranty period?
(iv) If the Tata truck dealer sells 64 new trucks per year, what is the *average number* of new Tata trucks sold which will need assembly defective repairs under their 12-month warranty agreement?

Note: Compute the probabilities in (i)–(iii) both manually and using the *Excel* function **BINOMDIST**.

8.6 Micropal SA is a research organisation which monitors unit trust performances in South Africa. They have found that there is a four in five chance that a general equity unit trust fund will *perform better* than the overall JSE share index over any one year period. If six general equity unit trust funds are randomly selected from all general equity unit trust funds, what is the probability that:
(i) *all* of these general equity unit trust funds *performed better* than the overall JSE share index over the past year?
(ii) only 2 or 3 of these general equity unit trust funds *performed better* than the overall JSE share index over the past year?
(iii) *at most two* performed *worse* than the overall JSE share index over the past year?

Note: Compute the probabilities in (i)–(iii) both manually and using the *Excel* function **BINOMDIST**.

8.7 Markinor, which is a market research company, has found from experience that *one in five* people are willing to participate in focus group interviews. The company has been commissioned to conduct a focus group interview on the consumption patterns of bread for a bakery client.
(i) If 12 people are approached, what is the probability that only two are willing to participate in the focus group interview?
(ii) Five people are required for the focus group interview. What is the probability that Markinor will find sufficient consumers to participate in the focus group interview session if they randomly approached 12 people?
(iii) What is the probability that Markinor will recruit more than the required 5 consumers for the focus group interview session if they randomly approached 12 people?

Note: Compute all the probabilities both manually and using the *Excel* function **BINOMDIST**.

8.8 A market research study into reading habits of magazine readers found that 10% of the general population of magazine readers are "heavy readers" (i.e. read more than 6 different magazines per week). They also found that 35% of pensioners who read magazines are "heavy" readers of magazines.

(i) Find the probability of there being fewer than two "heavy readers" of magazines in any 10 randomly selected sample from the following groups:
the general population of magazine readers
the pensioner sub-population of magazine readers.

(ii) If a random sample of 280 pensioners who read magazines were interviewed, how many of them are not likely to be "heavy readers" of magazines?

8.9 A telephone help-line receives calls that can be described by the Poisson process. The average rate at which calls come in is 3 calls per minute.

(i) Find the probability that the help-line will receive exactly 5 calls in a given minute.

(ii) What is the likelihood that the help-line will receive 4 of more calls in a given minute?

(iii) What chance is there that no calls will be received in a given minute?

Note: Compute the probabilities in (i), (ii) and (iii) both manually and using *Excel's* **POISSON** function.

8.10 A motor spares dealer sells, on average, 4 car batteries per week.

(i) What is the probability that the dealer will sell no more than 2 batteries in a given week?

(ii) If the dealer has 3 batteries in stock at the beginning of a given week, what is the probability that the dealer will run out of stock in that week?

Note: Compute the probabilities above both manually and using *Excel's* **POISSON** function.

8.11 A company which supplies ready-mix concrete receives, on average, 6 orders per day.

(i) What is the probability that, on given day:

(a) only one order will be received?

(b) no more than 3 orders will be received?

(c) at least 3 orders will be received?

(ii) What is the probability that, on a given half-day, only one order will be received?

(iii) What is the mean and standard deviation of orders received per day?

8.12 The number of tubes of toothpaste purchased by a typical family is a random variable having a Poisson distribution with an average of 1,8 tubes per month.

(i) What is the probability that a typical family will purchase at least 3 tubes of toothpaste in any given month?

(ii) What is the likelihood that a typical family will purchase less than 4 tubes of toothpaste in any given month?

Note: Compute the probabilities above both manually and using *Excel's* **POISSON** function.

8.13 A short-term insurance company receives 7 motor vehicle claims, on average, per day. Assume that the daily claims rate follows a Poisson process.

(i) What is the probability that on a given day no more than 5 motor vehicle claims will be received?

(ii) How likely is it that either 6 or 9 motor vehicle claims will be received on a given day?

(iii) What is the chance that more than 20 motor vehicle claims will be received by the company over any two day period?

Note: Compute the probabilities above both manually and using *Excel's* **POISSON** function.

8.14 (i) Find the following probabilities using the standard normal z tables. Give a sketch with the appropriate area shaded in.

(a) $P(0 < z < 1{,}83)$
(b) $P(z > -0{,}48)$
(c) $P(-2{,}25 < z < 0)$
(d) $P(1{,}22 < z)$
(e) $P(-2{,}08 < z < 0{,}63)$
(f) $P(z < -0{,}68)$
(g) $P(0{,}33 < z < 1{,}5)$

(ii) Find the probabilities in (i) using *Excel's* **NORMSDIST** function.

8.15 (i) Find the missing values for the following probabilities for the standard normal distribution, z using the z tables.

(a) $P(z < ?) = 0{,}9147$
(b) $P(z > ?) = 0{,}5319$
(c) $P(0 < z < ?) = 0{,}4015$
(d) $P(? < z < 0) = 0{,}4803$
(e) $P(? < z) = 0{,}0985$
(f) $P(z < ?) = 0{,}2517$
(g) $P(? < z) = 0{,}6331$

(ii) Find the values in (i) using *Excel's* **NORMSINV** function.

8.16 (i) Given that x (where x = flight times between cities A and B) follows a normal distribution with a mean (μ) of 64 minutes and a standard deviation (σ) of 2,5 minutes, use the standard normal z table to find:

(a) $P(x < 62)$
(b) $P(x > 67{,}4)$
(c) $P(59{,}6 < x < 62{,}8)$
(d) $P(x > ?) = 0{,}1026$
(e) $P(x > ?) = 0{,}9772$

(f) P(60,2 < x < ?) = 0.6652

(ii) Interpret the meaning of each probability in (i).

(iii) Use the *Excel* functions, **NORMDIST** and **NORMINV** to solve for the values in (i).

8.17 The manager of a local gym has determined that the *length of time* patrons spend at the gym is a normally distributed variable with a mean of 80 minutes and a standard deviation of 20 minutes.

(i) What proportion of patrons spend more than two hours at the gym?

(ii) What proportion of patrons spend less than one hour at the gym?

(iii) What is the least amount of time spent by 60% of patrons at the gym?

Note: Compute the results both manually and using the appropriate *Excel* function (i.e. **NORMDIST** or **NORMINV**).

8.18 The *lifetime* of a certain type of automatic washing machine is normally distributed with mean and standard deviation equal to 3,1 and 1,1 years respectively.

(i) If this type of washing machine is guaranteed for one year, what percentage of original sales will require replacement if they fail within the guarantee period?

(ii) What percentage of these washing machines is likely to be operating after 4 years? After 5,5 years?

(iii) If the manufacturer of these washing machines wants to ensure that no more than 5% of these washers will be replaced within a guarantee period, what new guarantee period should they choose?

Note: Compute the results both manually and using the appropriate *Excel* function (i.e. **NORMDIST** or **NORMINV**).

8.19 A recent survey by a local municipality established that *daily water usage* by its households is *normally distributed* with a mean of 220 litres and a standard deviation of 45 litres.

(i) Use standard normal z tables to answer the following questions.

(a) What percentage of households are likely to use more than 300 litres of water per day?

(b) What is the probability of finding a household that uses less than 100 litres of water per day?

(c) What is the most amount of water likely to be used per day by the lowest consuming 15% of households?

(d) The municipality plans to implement a differential rates policy to charge households who use more than a certain volume of water per day a higher rate per litre. If the municipality wants no more than 20% of households to pay this higher rate per litre, how much water per day must a household use before they will pay the higher rate per litre?

(ii) Use *Excel's* **NORMDIST** function to solve (i)(a) and (i)(b).

(iii) Use *Excel's* **NORMINV** function to solve (i)(c) and (i)(d).

8.20 A study was recently conducted on the *reaction time* of long-distance truck drivers (after 2 hours of non-stop driving). Assume *reaction times* (after two hours of non-stop driving) are known to be normally distributed with a mean of 1,4 seconds and a variance of 0,0625 seconds. Reaction times would be recorded (in seconds between the presentation of a stimulus and braking) by subjecting a truck driver to a simulated environment.

(i) What is the probability that a particular truck driver who has been driving for 2 hours non-stop has a reaction time of:

(a) more than 2 seconds

(b) between 1,2 and 1,4 seconds

(c) less than 0,9 second

(d) between 0,5 and 1 second.

(ii) If a random sample of 120 truck drivers is drawn on the Golden Highway Plaza (Nl near Johannesburg), what percentage are likely to have a reaction time slower than 1,8 seconds? How many truck drivers does this represent?

(iii) The National Transport Department is implementing a policy which requires truck drivers to undergo further training if their reaction time is slower than 1,7 seconds. How many drivers out of a random sample of 360 are likely to need further training?

Note: Use both the *z*-tables and *Excel's* **NORMDIST** function to answer the questions.

8.21 A machine filling 18 gram containers of a hair dye is set so that the average fill is 18,2 grams with a variance of 0,49 grams. Assume that the filling of containers by this machine is normally distributed.

(i) What percentage of the containers are not likely to meet the producer's specification of at least 18 grams per container?

(ii) What is the minimum weight of the heaviest 15% of containers?

Note: Compute the results both manually and using appropriate *Excel* functions.

8.22 The service time of the first service of a BMW car is found to be normally distributed with a mean of 70 minutes and a variance of 81 minutes.

(i) If a customer brings her BMW car in for its first service, what is the probability that the car will be ready within one hour?

(ii) What is the probability that the job will take more than an hour and a half?

(iii) What percentage of first services will be completed between 50 and 60 minutes?

(iv) The BMW dealer has a policy to give its customers a 15% discount on the cost if the first service if the service is not complete within 80 minutes. From a sample of 80 customers who brought their BMW cars in for its first service, how many are likely to receive the 15% discount?

(v) If the BMW dealer wants to ensure that no more than 5% of all first services will take longer than 80 minutes, what should the mean service time be?

Note: Compute the results both manually and using appropriate *Excel* functions.

8.23 A coffee dispensing machine used in cafeterias is set to dispense coffee with an average fill of 230 ml and a standard deviation of 10 ml per cup. Assume that the volume dispensed is normally distributed.

(i) For a randomly selected cup dispensed by the machine, what is the probability that:

(a) the cup is filled to more than 235 ml?

(b) the cup is filled to between 235 and 245 ml?

(c) the cup is less than 220 ml full?

(ii) If the company supplying the coffee machines would want only 15% of cups to exceed a given fill level, what level of fill (in ml) does this correspond to?

(iii) What must the mean fill level (in ml) be set to in order to ensure that no more than 10% of cups are filled to less than 220 ml?

8.24 Assume that the mean life of a particular brand of car battery is normally distributed with a mean of 28 months and a standard deviation of 4 months.

(i) For a randomly selected battery of this make, what is the probability that it will last between 30 and 34 months?

(ii) What is the probability that a randomly selected battery of this make will fail within 2 years of the date of purchase?

(iii) After what time period will 60% of all batteries of this make fail?

(iv) If a guarantee period is to be set, how many months would it have to be to replace no more than 5% of batteries of this make?

Note: Compute the results both manually and using appropriate *Excel* functions.

Chapter

9

Sampling and Sampling Distributions

Objectives

Inferential statistics generalises sample findings (i.e. descriptive statistics) to the broader population from which the sample was drawn. To produce valid population estimates from sample findings, a number of conditions with respect to the sample and the tools for inferential analysis must be satisfied. This chapter provides the foundation for satisfying these conditions.

After studying this chapter, you should be able to:

- describe the purpose of inferential statistics
- distinguish between a sample and a population
- explain the reasons for sampling
- explain the different types of sampling methods
- explain when it is appropriate to use each sampling method
- understand the concept of the sampling distribution
- explain the role of the sampling distribution in inferential statistics.

9.1 Introduction

Inferential statistics is the basis of statistical management decision making. It uses sample findings (covered in chapters 4 to 8) to statistically estimate the likely population values of random variables under study.

For *example,* a quality controller in a cooldrink bottling process needs to know the actual *population mean volume* of all bottles filled, rather than the *sample mean volume* of a few filled bottles drawn at random from the production line and tested. *Inferential statistics* will statistically estimate the true mean fill of *all* bottles based on the sample mean fill statistics.

There are three pillars of inferential statistics. Without them, inferential statistics is neither feasible nor valid. The pillars of inferential statistics are:

- the concept of probabilities, especially the normal probability distribution
- sampling and sampling error, and
- the concept of the sampling distribution.

The concept of probabilities and the normal probability distribution were covered in chapters 7 and 8. This chapter covers the importance of, and different types of *sampling methods,* explains the meaning of *sampling error,* and derives and explains the significance of the *sampling distribution*. Thereafter, the next four chapters will draw on these principles and concepts to describe the inferential methods used to estimate actual population measures.

9.2 Sampling

To understand inferential statistics, it is essential to distinguish between a *population* and a *sample.*

A **population** is *every object* which possesses data on the random variable under study.

Examples of populations are:

- *all ratepayers* in Johannesburg
- *all car owners* in South Africa
- *all companies* listed on the JSE
- *all foreign tourists* in South Africa in January
- *all students* registered for a Management course at Unisa this year
- *all Standard Bank employees*
- *all sectional title owners* in a townhouse complex, and
- *all members* of a sports club.

A **census** involves the gathering of data on a random variable from *every member* of the target population.

Two *examples* of a census are: (1) Stats SA conducts a population census every 10 years (the most recent was in 2001) to establish the size and demographic profile of the country's citizens; and (2) all registered unit trust funds report their closing price daily to I-Net Bridge.

Census data is intended to provide complete information, as all the possible data on the random variable under study are gathered and analysed. However, a census is only practical if the *population size* is relatively *small* and/or *geographically concentrated* and the members are easily accessible. There must also be no significant cost or time constraints on gathering the complete data set.

Instances in which a census could be conducted if the management problem focused on these easily identifiable and accessible target populations include:

- *all employees* of Woolworths stores in Port Elizabeth
- *all timeshare owners* at Bakubung Resort in the North West Province
- *all Shell service station franchises* in KwaZulu-Natal.

A **sample** is a *subset* of all members of a target population.

It is not always practical to gather data from every possible member in a population. In such cases, a *subset of all members,* called a **sample**, is drawn and data gathered from these selected members on the random variable under study. Only the recorded sample observations are analysed and used as the basis for decision making. Ideally, the selected sample is *representative* of all the members of the target population.

Sampling is generally preferred to a census for the following reasons:

- *Cost* — It is generally *less expensive* to gather sample data.
- *Timeliness* — Sample data can be gathered *quicker* than census data to meet decision deadlines.
- *Destructive testing* — Data on certain random variables can only be generated by consuming or destroying the sampling unit, for *example*, testing *tread life* of car tyres; measuring the *shelf life* of milk; measuring the *sulphur level in wine*. A census is not appropriate under such data gathering requirements.
- *Accuracy* — Better control can usually be exercised over the data collection process in a sample than in a census. This results in cleaner, more accurate data being produced from a sample.

Sampling is the only practical alternative for the gathering of data for large and/or geographically dispersed populations and where resources (time and/or money) are significant constraints.

9.3 Sampling Methods

A sample must be *representative* of all the members of the target population if it is to produce *valid* and *precise* statistical inferences of population parameters based on sample evidence. There are two basic *methods of sampling*. Each has its own advantages and disadvantages in terms of population representativeness.

The two methods of sampling are:

- *non-probability* sampling methods, and
- *probability* sampling methods.

9.3.1 Non-probability (Non-Random) Sampling

Any sampling method where the sample members are *not selected randomly* is called **non-probability sampling**. Criteria *other than random selection* are used as the basis for choosing the sample members from the population. The main non-random selection criteria are the *personal judgement* of the researcher and/or *convenience*.

There are four types of non-probability based sampling methods:

(i) convenience sampling
(ii) judgement sampling
(iii) quota sampling, and
(iv) snowball sampling.

(i) Convenience sampling

When the sampling units are selected to suit the convenience of the researcher, convenience sampling has been applied. Respondents are included in the sample if they happen to be in the right place at the right time.

- In a study on employment practices in the textile industry, a researcher may find it more convenient to interview *employees within only one clothing manufacturing company*, instead of employees from a number of clothing manufacturing companies.
- In a study on shopping habits, a researcher may select shoppers *from only one shopping mall*, or interview shoppers *only on a Saturday morning.*
- In a student survey on study habits, students in a *given class only* are selected for reasons of convenience.

Convenience sampling is the least expensive and least time consuming of all sampling techniques. Furthermore, respondents are easily accessible and generally cooperative. However, convenience sampling is generally *not representative* of the target population and therefore the findings cannot be validly generalised to the broader target population. *Statistical inference* is *not valid* on convenience sample findings.

(ii) Judgement sampling

When a researcher uses *personal judgement* alone to select whom he or she considers to be the most appropriate sampling units to include in the sample in order to provide data to address the management problem under study, then judgement sampling has been applied.

- Only beauticians, instead of all female users of cosmetics, may be selected to provide information on skin care practices.
- A researcher conducting a study into labour practices may select only labour consultants instead of selecting from employees in general, in the belief that the former are more knowledgeable about labour practices.

(iii) Quota sampling

The population is divided into segments (or strata) and a quota of sampling units is selected from each segment. Quotas for various strata of the target population are set and an interviewer samples until the quota is met.

It is not the design of the quota sample that is non-random, instead it is the process of respondent selection. This selection usually takes place in a non-random manner, thus introducing *selection bias.* While the advantage of quota sampling is lower cost, its main drawback is that the data is unsuitable for inferential analysis.

(iv) Snowball sampling

Snowball sampling is used to reach target populations where the sampling units are difficult to identify. Under snowball sampling, each identified member of the target population is asked to identify other sampling units who belong to the same target population. Snowball sampling would be used to identify successive sampling units, for *example,* in a study on *Aids sufferers,* or a study into *drug addiction,* or a study into *illegal immigrants.* The issues under investigation are usually confidential or sensitive in nature.

The following are *disadvantages* of non-probability sampling:

- It can introduce *bias* into the statistical findings due to the *unrepresentative nature* of the sample with respect to the population from which it is drawn. Bias occurs when significant sections of a population are excluded from being considered for selection to the sample. Unless a sample can be regarded as representative of the population from which it is drawn, the inferences based on this sample evidence are likely to be misleading and erroneous.
- The *sampling error* cannot be *validly* measured from data drawn from a non-probability-based sample. **Sampling error** is the difference between the actual population parameter value and its corresponding sample statistic.

Consequently it is not valid to apply inferential techniques to non-probability sample data, as the results will be invalid. Thus only *descriptive statistical analysis* can be performed on non-probability derived sample data.

However, descriptive statistical findings derived from non-probability samples can be useful in *exploratory research* situations or in *less scientific opinion surveys* to provide initial, non-rigorous estimates or profiles of random variables under study.

9.3.2 Probability Sampling (Random-based Sampling)

Probability-based sampling includes any selection method where the sample members (sampling units) are *selected* from the target population on a *purely random* (chance) basis. Under random sampling, every member of the target population has a chance of being selected for the sample.

There are four probability-based sampling methods:

(i) *simple* random sampling
(ii) *systematic* random sampling
(iii) *stratified* random sampling
(iv) *cluster* random sampling.

(i) Simple random sampling

Every member in the target population has an *equal chance* of being selected. This method of sampling is used when it is assumed that the population is relatively *homogeneous* with respect to the random variable under study. This means that different sub-groups within the population are likely to provide similar responses.

The following are illustrative examples:

- A simple random sample of students is selected if it can be assumed that their responses to a question – such as "*Should a university degree focus more on theory than on practice*?" – are not likely to be influenced by factors such as a student's year of study, degree for which he or she is registered, gender, nationality, etc.
- The target population of Johannesburg motorists is to be surveyed for their views on *road safety*. It is assumed, by drawing a *simple random sample* of Johannesburg motorists, that their views are not likely to differ significantly across gender, age, car type driven or use of vehicle (i.e. private or business).
- The target population of recent commerce graduates from Stellenbosch University is to be surveyed for their perceptions of the *employment market*. Again, by selecting a *simple random sample* of recent Stellenbosch commerce graduates, it is assumed there are no biographical factors (such as age, gender, language, pass grade, etc.) that are likely to result in significantly different response profiles (i.e. perceptions of the employment market) from all the respondents.
- The target population of tourists to Cape Town is to be surveyed for their views on *standards of service* (quality and price) from the Cape Town leisure industry (i.e. with respect to accommodation, transport, attractions, restaurants). A *simple random sample* assumes that neither age, nationality, nor any other biographical factor will produce significantly different response profiles (i.e. their attitudes towards service standards) from all tourists interviewed.

To generate a *simple random sample* using *Excel* if a sampling frame or database of contact details of the target population is available, use either:

- the function operation =**RAND()** to generate random numbers to identify records, or
- the **Data Analysis** option from the **Tools** menu which allows **simple random sampling** to take place from a data list. The data preparation dialog box for the **Sampling** process is shown in Figure 9.1 overleaf.

Figure 9.1 Data preparation dialog box for **sampling** from a **data list**

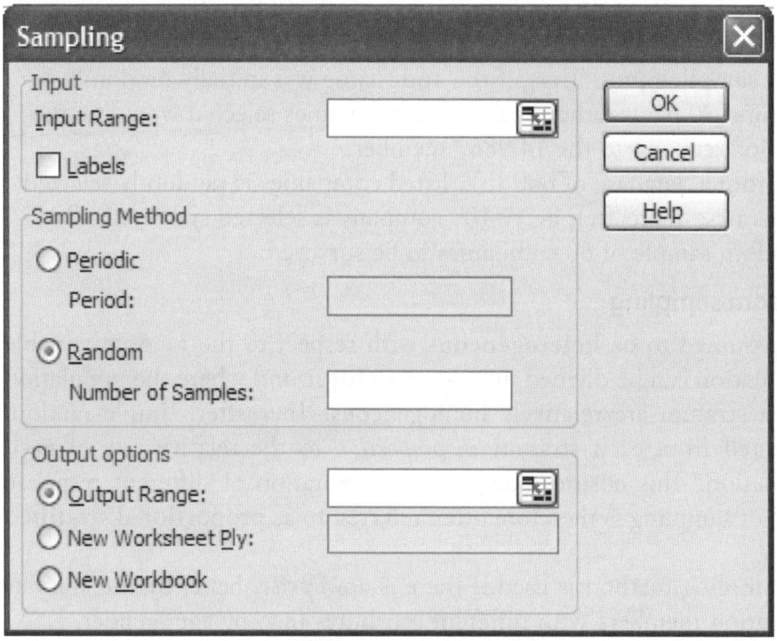

Sampling
Input
Input Range:
Labels
Sampling Method
Periodic
Period:
Random
Number of Samples:
Output options
Output Range:
New Worksheet Ply:
New Workbook
OK
Cancel
Help

(ii) Systematic random sampling

Systematic random sampling is similar to simple random sampling, but differs only in the way the sampling units are selected.

The sampling approach uses a *sampling frame* (i.e. an address list or database of population members) to select the respondents in a quasi-random manner. Sampling begins by *randomly selecting* the *first sampling unit* from the sampling frame. Thereafter, subsequent sampling units are selected at a *uniform interval* relative to the first sampling unit.

Since only the first sampling unit is randomly selected, some randomness is sacrificed.

HOW TO

To draw a systematic random sampling

First divide the sampling frame by the sample size to determine the size of a sampling block. Now *randomly* select the first sample member from within the first sampling block; and one sample member from each of the remaining sampling blocks, choosing that sample member at a *constant interval* from the previous sampled member.

The following two *examples* illustrate this process.

- Assume the sampling frame of, say, 15 000 registered property owners in Paarl (from the Municipal Rates Schedule) is available. From this, a systematic random sample of 500 owners is to be drawn to canvass opinions on revising residential land use legislation to allow for greater densification of erven. There will be 500 sampling blocks each consisting of 30 $\left(\frac{15\,000}{500}\right)$ property owners. Using systematic random

sampling, the first sampled property owner would be selected randomly from the first 30 names on the list. Thereafter, one property owner will be selected from each of the remaining 499 sampling blocks at a uniform interval (every 30th person) relative to the first sampling unit. Thus, if the 16th name was initially randomly selected from the first 30 names, then the subsequent names selected would be the 46th, 76th, 106th, 136th, etc., up to the 14 986th member.
- The fourth name from a database of 600 JSE-listed companies is randomly selected from the first 10 names. Thereafter, every 10th company is selected systematically to draw a simple random sample of 60 companies to be surveyed.

(iii) Stratified random sampling

If the population is assumed to be **heterogeneous** with respect to the random variable under study, the population can be divided into *segments* (or *strata*) where the population members within each stratum are relatively homogeneous. Thereafter, simple random sub-samples are selected from each stratum *in proportion* to the relative size of each stratum in the population. This ensures adequate representation of different response profiles. This method of sampling is therefore often referred to as **proportional stratified random sampling**.

This probability sampling method is used if there is an *a priori* belief by the analyst/ researcher that population members with different attributes (e.g. by age, gender, LSM (socio-economic status); political affiliation; residence; marital status; economic sector; country of origin, etc.) will produce significantly different response profiles to the random variables under study.

The stratified random sampling method is commonly used in marketing research studies. It generally ensures *greater representativeness* across the entire target population and also results in a *smaller sampling error*, giving *greater precision* in estimation.

However, stratified random sampling requires *larger samples* than simple random sampling to ensure adequate representation from each stratum. This *increases costs* of data collection.

The following two *examples* illustrate this approach:
- If *age* and *gender* of the motoring public are assumed, *a priori*, to influence their responses to questions on *car type preferred* and *features sought* in a car, then stratifying this population by these two characteristics and drawing a simple random sample from each strata of *age/gender* combination is likely to ensure a more representative sample of observations.
- Cape Town ratepayers could be stratified by the criteria *property value per square metre*. All "low-valued" suburbs would form one stratum; all "medium-valued"' suburbs would form a second stratum, and all "high-valued" suburbs would form a third stratum. A simple random sample of households within each strata would be selected and interviewed. Their responses to questions on *rates increases* would be assumed to represent the responses of all ratepayers across all strata of property values.

(iv) Cluster random sampling

Certain target populations form *natural* clusters which make for easier sampling.

- Labour forces cluster within factories.
- Accountants cluster within accounting firms.
- Lawyers cluster within law firms.
- Shoppers cluster at shopping malls.
- Students cluster at educational institutions.
- Outputs from different production runs (e.g. margarine tubs) are batched and labelled separately, forming clusters.

Cluster sampling is used where the target population can be naturally divided into clusters, where each cluster is *similar in profile* to every other cluster. A subset of clusters is then randomly selected for sampling.

Cluster sampling tends to be used when the population is large and geographically dispersed. In such cases, smaller regions or clusters (with similar profiles) can be more easily sampled.

The sampling units within these sampled clusters may themselves be randomly selected to provide a representative sample from the population. For this reason, it is also called **two-stage cluster sampling**. For *example*: select schools (stage 1) as clusters, then pupils within schools (stage 2); select companies (stage 1) as clusters, then employees within companies (stage 2).

The *primary benefit* of cluster random sampling is that it usually *reduces* the *per unit cost* of sampling. For a fixed sampling expenditure, it is nearly always possible to get a larger sample than with simple random sampling methods.

However, cluster sampling tends to produce *larger sampling errors* than sampling errors resulting from simple random sampling.

The following three *examples* illustrate the cluster sampling approach:

- In a study on *mine safety awareness* amongst miners, each gold mine could be considered to be a separate cluster. Assume there are 27 such mine clusters in the Gauteng area. A randomly drawn sample of, say, eight mine clusters would first be selected. Then a simple random sample of miners within each of the randomly chosen mines would be identified and interviewed. The responses of interviewed miners within each mine cluster are then assumed to be representative of all miners (including those in mine clusters which were not sampled).
- Each of the major shopping malls in the Western Cape can be classified as a cluster. A researcher may randomly choose, say, three of these shopping malls, and randomly select customers within each of these selected clusters for interviews on, for example, *clothing purchase behaviour* patterns.
- Assume the population under study is teachers at secondary schools in the Cape Town area. Their views on outcomes-based education are sought. Since all secondary schools follow the same curricula, *geographical clusters* of secondary schools can be formed by *suburbs*. A random sample of suburbs would be selected first, followed by a simple random sample of secondary schools within the randomly chosen

suburbs. A further simple random sample of teachers within the sampled secondary schools can be drawn and interviewed to gather responses to curriculum design. The responses from teachers within these sampled clusters (by suburb) can be seen as representative of all secondary school teachers' views on outcomes-based education, including those in clusters that were not sampled.

Advantages of random sampling methods

(i) Random sampling reduces the likelihood of *selection bias*, hence the sample statistics are likely to be unbiased estimates of their population parameters.

(ii) Random sampling methods make it possible to measure the *sampling error*, which is the difference between the calculated sample statistic and the population parameter it is attempting to estimate. Being able to measure the sampling error makes it feasible and valid to apply inferential statistical methods to the randomly drawn sample data as it is used to quantify the precision of estimates.

Table 9.1 summarises the different sampling methods and highlights valid statistical analysis that can be performed on data derived from each sampling method.

Table 9.1 Summary of sampling methods and valid statistical analysis

Sampling Methods	Sample Types	Valid Statistical Analyses
Non-probability (Non-random Selection)	Convenience Judgement Quota Snowball	Exploratory Descriptive Statistics only
Probability (Random Selection)	Simple Random Systematic Random Stratified Random Cluster Random	Descriptive Statistics Inferential Statistics

9.4 The Sampling Distribution

When conducting statistical inference, an *important statistical question* is:
"How *reliable* and *precise* is a single sample statistic (such as the sample mean) as a representative measure of its associated population measure (i.e. the population mean)?" In other words: "How close does a sample statistic lie to its population parameter?" The sampling distribution provides the answer to this question.

A **sampling distribution** shows the relationship between a sample statistic (e.g. sample mean) and its corresponding population parameter (e.g. population mean).

A sampling distribution describes how a sample statistic varies about its true population parameter. From this relationship, the *level of confidence* in estimating the population parameter from a single sample statistic can be established.

The behaviour of four sample statistics with respect to their corresponding population parameters are described in this chapter and then used as the basis for inferential methods in chapters 10 to 15. These sample statistics and the population parameters to which they relate are given in Table 9.2. The parameters are all measures of central location.

Only the sampling distribution of the sample mean, $\bar{x}$, will be described and discussed in this chapter. The rationale and interpretation of the sampling distributions for the other three sample statistics are identical to that for the sample mean.

Table 9.2 Selected population parameters and their associated sample statistics

Central Location Measure	Population Parameter	Sample Statistic
Single Mean	μ	$\bar{x}$
Single Proportion	π	p
Difference between two Means	$\mu_1 - \mu_2$	$\bar{x}_1 - \bar{x}_2$
Difference between two Proportions	$\pi_1 - \pi_2$	$p_1 - p_2$

9.5 Sampling Distribution of the Sample Mean

This section will describe how the sample mean, $\bar{x}$, is related to the population mean μ for any random variable, x. The following explanation is given to provide an understanding of how a sample mean relates to the population mean that it attempts to estimate.

Rationale of a Sampling Distribution

Consider the problem of determining the average *years of experience* of all 2 814 engineers in South Africa. For this population, consider the hypothetical situation of drawing every possible sample of size n (say $n = 100$) from this population. Assume that there are k such samples. If the sample mean is computed for each of these k samples, then there will be k sample means produced.

If a *frequency distribution* of these k sample means is now constructed and the mean and standard deviation of this distribution of k sample means is found, the following properties will emerge:

(i) The sample means are themselves random variables, since their values will vary from sample to sample. Each separate sample of 100 engineers will have a different sample value for their mean average *years of experience.*

(ii) The mean of all these k sample means will equal the true population mean, μ, i.e:

$$\mu = \frac{\bar{x}_1 + \bar{x}_2 + \bar{x}_3 + \dots\dots\dots + \bar{x}_k}{k} = \frac{\Sigma \bar{x}_i}{k}$$

(iii) The standard deviation of these k sample means will be equal to:

$$\sigma_{\bar{x}} = \frac{\sigma}{\sqrt{n}}$$

$\sigma_{\bar{x}}$ is called the **standard error (SE)** of the sample means. It measures the average deviation of sample means about the true population mean.

The standard error assumes that the population from which the sample is drawn is large, and that the population standard deviation, σ, is known.

(iv) The histogram of these k sample means will have the shape of a *normal distribution.*

This *distribution of the sample means* is called the **sampling distribution** of $\bar{x}$.

To summarise, the *sample mean* is a random variable with the following properties:
- It is **normally distributed**
- with a **mean** equal to the **population mean,** μ, and
- a standard deviation, called the **standard error,** $\sigma_{\bar{x}}$, equal to $\frac{\sigma}{\sqrt{n}}$.

Based on these three properties, and using *normal* probability distribution theory, it is possible to conclude the following about how *sample means* behave in relation to their *population mean*:
- 68,26% of all sample means will lie *within one standard error* of their true population mean.
- 95,44% of all sample means will lie *within two standard errors* of their true population mean.
- 99,73% of all sample means will lie *within three standard errors* of their true population mean.

Alternatively, it can be stated that:
- there is a 68,26% chance that a single sample mean will lie *no further than* **one** *standard error* away from its true population mean
- there is a 95,44% chance that a single sample mean will lie *no further than* **two** *standard errors* away from its true population mean, and
- there is a 99,73% chance that a single sample mean will lie *no further than* **three** *standard errors* away from its true population mean.

This implies that *any* sample mean which is computed from a *randomly* drawn *sample*, has a high probability (99,73%) of being no more than three standard errors away from its true, but unknown, population mean value.

These probabilities can be found by relating the sampling distribution of $\bar{x}$ to the standard normal, z-distribution.

Formula

The sampling distribution of the *sample mean* is related to the standard normal probability distribution (the z-distribution) through the following z-transformation formula:

$$z = \frac{\bar{x} - \mu}{\sigma_{\bar{x}}} \quad \text{or} \quad z = \frac{\bar{x} - \mu}{\frac{\sigma}{\sqrt{n}}}$$

The sampling distribution of the sample mean is shown graphically in Figure 9.2 below.

Figure 9.2 Sampling distribution of the sample mean ($\bar{x}$)

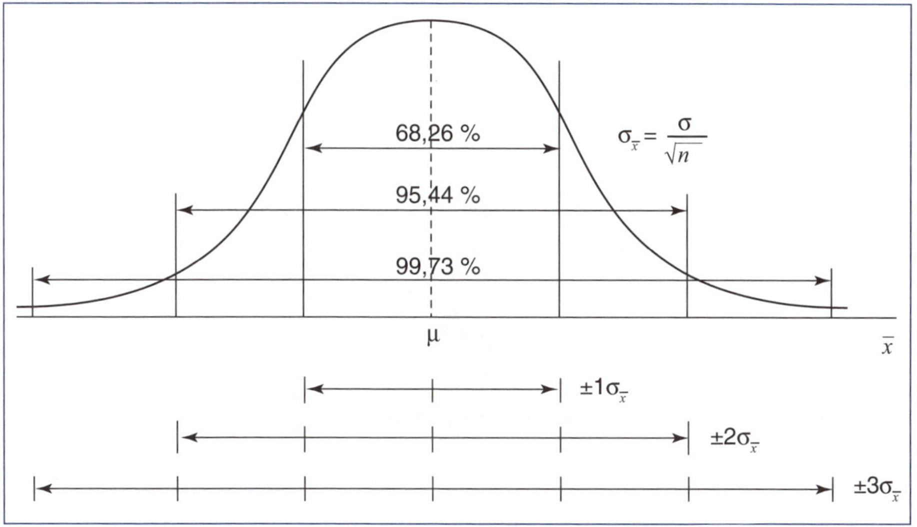

This relationship between the sample mean and its population mean can be used to:

(i) find probabilities that a single sample mean will lie within a specified distance of its true, but unknown population mean

(ii) compute probability-based interval estimates of the population mean, and

(iii) test claims/statistical hypotheses about a value for the true population mean.

The sampling distribution is the basis for the two inferential techniques of *confidence intervals* and *hypotheses tests,* which are covered in the following chapters.

9.6 Sampling Distribution of the Sample Proportion

The sample proportion, p, is the measure of central location when the random variable under study is *qualitative*. In such cases, the data collected is *categorical* (i.e. nominal/ ordinal) and sample statistics are found through a counting process only, as illustrated in Table 9.3.

Table 9.3 Illustrations of sample proportions for categorical variables

Qualitative Random Variable	Sample Statistic
Gender	Proportion of females in a sample of students
Trade Union Membership	Proportion of employees who are trade union members
Mobile Phone Brand Preference	Proportion of mobile phone users who prefer Nokia

This section will show how the sample proportion, p, is related to the true, but unknown population proportion, π, for any *categorical* random variable, x.

In the same way that the relationship between sample means and their population mean was described by the sampling distribution of the sample mean, the relationship between a sample proportion p and its population proportion π can be described by the **sampling distribution of the single sample proportion**.

This relationship can be summarised as follows for a given *categorical* random variable, x:

(i) The sample proportion, p, is itself a random variable, as each sample proportion will vary from sample to sample.

(ii) The **mean** of all sample proportions is equal to the true population proportion, π.

(iii) The **standard deviation** of all sample proportions is equal to:

$$\sigma_p = \sqrt{\frac{\pi(1-\pi)}{n}}$$

σ_p is called the **standard error of sample proportions**.

(iv) The histogram of all these *sample proportions* will be **normally distributed**.

Based on these properties and using *normal* probability distribution theory, it is possible to conclude the following about how *sample proportions* behave in relation to their *population proportions*:

- 68,26% of all sample proportions will lie *within one standard error* of their true population proportion
- 95,44% of all sample proportions will lie *within two standard errors* of their true population proportion
- 99,73% of all sample proportions will lie *within three standard error* of their true population proportion.

These probabilities can be found by relating the sampling distribution of p to the standard normal, z-distribution.

Formula

The sampling distribution of the *sample proportion* is related to the z-distribution through the following z-transformation formula:

$$z = \frac{p-\pi}{\sigma_p} \qquad \text{or} \qquad z = \frac{p-\pi}{\sqrt{\frac{\pi(1-\pi)}{n}}}$$

Figure 9.3 overleaf shows the sampling distribution of sample proportions graphically.

This relationship can now be used to derive probabilities; develop probability-based estimates; and test hypotheses of the population proportion in statistical inference.

Figure 9.3 Sampling distribution of sample proportions (p)

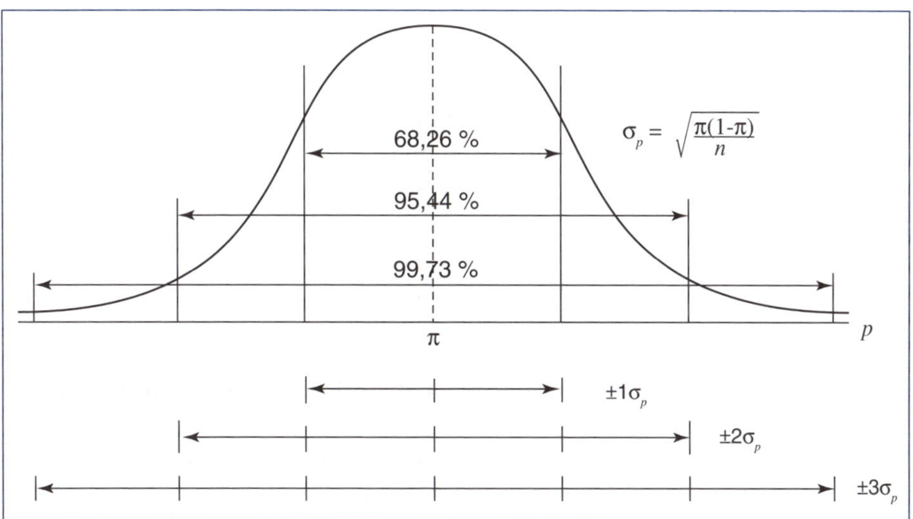

9.7 Sampling Distribution of the Difference Between Two Sample Means

Often the means of two samples are compared to establish if any differences exist between their corresponding population means, as illustrated in Table 9.4.

Table 9.4 Illustrations of the sample statistic – differences between two sample means

Random Variable	Two Independent Samples (derive sample means)	Sample Statistic
Age (in years)	Sample 1: Male shoppers Sample 2: Female shoppers	Is there a difference between the mean ages of *male* and *female* shoppers? $(\bar{x}_{male} - \bar{x}_{female}) = 0$**?**
Turnover (in Rands)	Sample 1: Branch 1 monthly turnover Sample 2: Branch 2 monthly turnover	Is *branch 1's* mean monthly turnover greater than *branch 2's* mean monthly turnover? $(\bar{x}_{branch1} - \bar{x}_{branch2}) > 0$**?**
Erf Sizes (in m^2)	Sample 1: Erf sizes in Durban Sample 2: Erf sizes in Pretoria	Are average erf sizes in Durban smaller than those in Pretoria? $(\bar{x}_{Durban} - \bar{x}_{Pretoria}) < 0$**?**

In inferential statistics, the need is to know whether differences exist between two unknown population means. It is therefore necessary to know how the sample statistic – the *difference between two sample means* – is related to its true, but unknown population parameter – *the difference between two population means* – for any random variable under study. The relationship can be described by the **sampling distribution of the difference between two sample means**.

The appropriate sample statistic is $(\bar{x}_1 - \bar{x}_2)$ and the corresponding population parameter is $(\mu_1 - \mu_2)$.

Using a similar rationale to that developed for the sampling distribution of a single mean, the following can be stated:

(i) The sample statistic, $(\bar{x}_1 - \bar{x}_2)$ is a random variable, as its value is likely to vary from sample to sample.

(ii) The **mean** of all the sample statistics made up of differences in two sample means is equal to the difference between the two population means $(\mu_1 - \mu_2)$.

(iii) The **standard deviation** of all differences in two sample means is defined as follows:

$$\sigma_{\bar{x}_1-\bar{x}_2} = \sqrt{\frac{\sigma_1^2}{n_1} + \frac{\sigma_2^2}{n_2}}$$

- It is referred to as the **standard error** of the **difference between two sample means.**
- It is assumed that the populations from which the two samples are drawn are large and that each population's standard deviation is known.

(iv) The histogram of all these *differences in two sample means* will be **normally distributed**.

Consequently, similar probability statements as applied to sampling distributions for single sample means and proportions can be made about the behaviour of differences in two sample means relative to the true differences in their population means, namely that 68,26%; 95,44% and 99,73% respectively of sample mean differences $(\bar{x}_1 - \bar{x}_2)$ are likely to fall within one, two and three standard errors about its population parameter $(\mu_1 - \mu_2)$.

Formula

In probability computations, the sample statistic – the *difference between two sample means* – is related to the *z*-distribution through the following *z*-transformation formulae:

$$z = \frac{(\bar{x}_1-\bar{x}_2) - (\mu_1 - \mu_2)}{\sigma_{\bar{x}_1-\bar{x}_2}} \quad \text{or} \quad z = \frac{(\bar{x}_1-\bar{x}_2) - (\mu_1 - \mu_2)}{\sqrt{\frac{\sigma_1^2}{n_1} + \frac{\sigma_2^2}{n_2}}}$$

9.8 Sampling Distribution of the Difference Between Two Sample Proportions

If the proportions of a qualitative random variable between two samples are compared to establish if any differences exist between them, the appropriate sample statistic to compute is the *difference in two sample proportions* as illustrated in Table 9.5 below.

Table 9.5 Illustrations of the sample statistic – difference between two sample proportions

Random Variable	Two Independent Samples (derive sample proportions)	Sample Statistic
Gender of customers who purchase groceries on credit	Sample 1: Male customers Sample 2: Female customers	Is the proportion of male customers who purchase groceries on credit *different from* the proportion of female customers who purchase groceries on credit? i.e. $(p_m - p_f) = 0$**?**
Advertising recall rate	Sample 1: Single persons Sample 2: Married persons	Is the proportion of single persons who recalled a car advertisement *greater than* the proportion of married persons who recalled the same advertisement? i.e. $(p_s - p_m) > 0$**?**

The relationship between this sample statistic (the *difference between two sample proportions*) and its true, but unknown population parameter (the difference between two population proportions) is described by the **sampling distribution of the difference between two sample proportions**.

The appropriate sample statistic is $(p_1 - p_2)$, and the corresponding population parameter is $(\pi_1 - \pi_2)$.

Using a similar rationale to that developed for the sampling distribution of a single mean, the following can be stated:

(i) The sample statistic $(p_1 - p_2)$ is a random variable, as its value is likely to vary from sample to sample.

(ii) The **mean** of all the sample statistics made up of differences in two sample proportions is equal to the difference between the two population proportions $(\pi_1 - \pi_2)$.

(iii) The **standard deviation** of all differences in two sample proportions is defined as follows:

$$\sigma_{p_1-p_2} = \sqrt{\hat{\pi}(1-\hat{\pi})\left(\frac{1}{n_1} + \frac{1}{n_2}\right)}$$

$$\text{where} \quad \hat{\pi} = \frac{x_1 + x_2}{n_1 + n_2}$$

It is called the **standard error of the difference between two sample proportions.**

(iv) The histogram of all these *differences in two sample proportions* is **normally distributed.**

Consequently, similar probability statements as applied to sampling distributions for single sample means and proportions can be made about the behaviour of differences in two sample proportions relative to the true differences between their two population proportions, namely that 68,26%, 95,44% and 99,73% respectively of sample values

$(p_t - p_2)$ are likely to fall within one, two and three standard errors about its population parameter $(\pi_1 - \pi_2)$.

Formula

In probability computations, the sample statistic – the *difference between two sample proportions* – is related to the z-distribution through the following z-transformation formula:

$$z = \frac{(p_1 - p_2) - (\pi_1 - \pi_2)}{\sigma_{p_1 - p_2}} \quad \text{or} \quad z = \frac{(p_1 - p_2) - (\pi_1 - \pi_2)}{\sqrt{\hat{\pi}(1-\hat{\pi})\left(\frac{1}{n_1} + \frac{1}{n_2}\right)}}$$

$$\text{where} \quad \hat{\pi} = \frac{x_1 + x_2}{n_1 + n_2} \quad p_1 = \frac{x_1}{n_1} \quad p_2 = \frac{x_2}{n_2}$$

In conclusion, Table 9.6 summarises each sample statistic and the properties of its sampling distribution.

Table 9.6 Summary of each sample statistic and its sampling distribution properties

Sample Statistic		Population Parameter to be estimated	Standard Normal (z) distribution formula required in Inferential Statistics
Sample mean $\bar{x}$	→	Population mean μ	$z = \frac{\bar{x} - \mu}{\frac{\sigma}{\sqrt{n}}}$
Sample proportion p	→	Population proportion π	$z = \frac{p - \pi}{\sqrt{\frac{\pi(1-\pi)}{n}}}$
Difference between two sample means $(\bar{x}_1 - \bar{x}_2)$	→	Difference between two population means $(\mu_1 - \mu_2)$	$z = \frac{(\bar{x}_1 - \bar{x}_2) - (\mu_1 - \mu_2)}{\sqrt{\frac{\sigma_1^2}{n_1} + \frac{\sigma_2^2}{n_2}}}$
Difference between two sample proportions $(p_1 - p_2)$	→	Difference between two population proportions $(\pi_1 - \pi_2)$	$z = \frac{(p_1 - p_2) - (\pi_1 - \pi_2)}{\sqrt{\hat{\pi}(1-\hat{\pi})\left(\frac{1}{n_1} + \frac{1}{n_2}\right)}}$ where $\hat{\pi} = \frac{x_1 + x_2}{n_1 + n_2}$ $p_1 = \frac{x_1}{n_1}$ $p_2 = \frac{x_2}{n_2}$

The *z-formulae* are used in *inferential statistics* to:

- derive probabilities of closeness to the population parameter
- set up confidence intervals to estimate the population parameter, and
- test hypotheses about values of the population parameters.

9.8 Summary

This chapter introduced the building blocks of *inferential statistics,* which are covered further in chapters 10 to 15. The need for inferential statistical methods arises because most statistical data is gathered from a sample instead of from the population as a whole.

The reasons an analyst would choose *sampling,* instead of conducting a *census,* were explained. The different types of *non-probability* and *probability* sampling methods were also examined.

An understanding of the different sampling procedures facilitates the decision whether inferential statistical methods may be validly applied to sample data.

The concept of the *sampling distribution* was introduced and described for four sample statistics, namely the *single sample mean,* the *single sample proportion,* the *difference between two sample means,* and the *difference between two sample proportions.* The sampling distribution describes, in probability terms, how close a *sample statistic* can lie to its corresponding *population parameter.* This relationship provides the basis for *inferential statistics.*

PART 4

Making Statistical Inferences

Chapter

10

Confidence Interval Estimation

Objectives

A useful and reliable method of estimating a population parameter is to define an interval of values around a sample statistic. This chapter explains how to do this and how much confidence a manager can have in methods identifying the most likely value of population parameters.

After studying this chapter, you should be able to:

- understand and explain the concept of a confidence interval
- compute a confidence interval for a population mean and a population proportion
- correctly interpret a confidence interval in a management context
- identify factors that affect the precision and reliability of confidence intervals.

10.1 Introduction

The role of inferential statistics is to describe the properties of a random variable in the population from which it came, based on sample evidence. Thus the *sample statistic* is always used to estimate the most likely value of its *population parameter*.

This chapter considers *two estimation methods* to arrive at the most likely value of the true population parameter. These methods are:

- *point estimation*, and
- *confidence interval* estimation.

The most common population parameter for which an estimate is required is a central location measure. Therefore this chapter considers the estimation of the following population central location measures:

- the population *mean*, μ, and
- the population *proportion*, π.

The chapter shows how each population parameter can be estimated, using its corresponding sample statistic.

10.2 Point Estimation

A **point estimate** is the value of a single *sample statistic*, which is used to represent the true, but unknown value of a *population parameter*.

Thus, the value of a single *sample mean*, $\bar{x}$, is used as an unbiased point estimate of the actual *population mean*, μ. Similarly, the single *sample proportion*, p, is used as an unbiased point estimate of the single *population proportion*, π.

The following two examples serve to *illustrate* point estimation:

(i) A recent survey found that the mean *travelling time to work* of a random sample of 100 car commuters in Cape Town was 35,8 minutes ($\bar{x}$ = 35,8). Then an unbiased point estimate of the actual mean travelling time to work of all Cape Town car commuters, μ, is assumed to be 35,8 minutes (i.e. μ = 35,8).

(ii) A random sample of 340 consumers was observed purchasing cornflakes at the Ottery hypermarket. 102 of these consumers selected the Bokomo brand of cornflakes. This represents a sample proportion, p of 0,30 (or 30%), who selected the Bokomo brand of cornflakes. Then an unbiased point estimate of the actual proportion of all cornflake consumers who would select the Bokomo brand of cornflakes is assumed to be 0,30 (i.e. π = 0,3).

The *drawback* of a point estimate is that there is *no knowledge of the sampling error* which measures the *reliability* of the point estimate in terms of its closeness to its population parameter. The probability that a single sample statistic actually equals the population parameter is extremely small.

For this reason, point estimates are seldom used alone to estimate population parameters. It is better to offer a range of values within which the population parameter is expected to fall, so that the reliability (sampling error) of the estimate can be measured. This is the purpose of *interval estimation.*

10.3 Confidence Interval Estimation

A **confidence interval estimate** is a range of values defined around a sample statistic within which the population parameter is expected to lie with a specified level of confidence. It is therefore called a **confidence interval**.

The specified *confidence level* is the probability that the interval constructed around the sample point estimate will include (cover) the true population parameter.

Confidence intervals will be constructed for the single population mean, μ, and the single population proportion, π, based on their respective sample statistics.

10.4 Confidence Interval Estimate for a Population Mean (μ) when the Population Standard Deviation is Known

The population parameter to be estimated is μ. The appropriate sample statistic to estimate μ is the sample mean, $\bar{x}$.

Typical questions that imply the use of confidence intervals include:

- Find 95% confidence limits for the actual average *years of experience* of all financial advisors.
- Estimate, with 99% confidence, the true average *amount spent* by all motorists on fuel per month.
- What is the average *daily television viewing time* of children between five and 10 years of age? Estimate with 90% confidence.

The following example *illustrates* the construction of a confidence interval.

Example 10.1 Kimberley Convenience Stores – Purchase Value study

A recent survey of 236 customers who frequent convenience stores in Kimberley found that the mean value of purchases was R48,45. Assume that the population standard deviation of purchase values at convenience stores is R18,58 and that purchase values are normally distributed.

Management question

Find the 95% confidence limits for the *actual mean value* of all purchases at convenience stores in Kimberley.

Solution (with explanation)

Setting confidence limits around a single sample mean to estimate the population mean, with a specified confidence level, requires the following statistical measures:

- the sample mean, $\bar{x}$ $\quad\quad \bar{x} = \text{R}48{,}45$
- the sample size, n $\quad\quad n = 236$
- the *standard error* of the sample mean $\sigma_{\bar{x}} = \frac{\sigma}{\sqrt{n}}$ $\quad\quad \sigma_{\bar{x}} = \frac{18{,}58}{\sqrt{236}} = 1{,}2095$

  Note: $\sigma_{\bar{x}}$ requires that the population standard deviation, σ, is known.
- the z-*limits* corresponding to a specified 95% *confidence level.*

The first three statistical measures required, namely the *sample mean,* the *sample size* and the *standard error* of the sample mean, are derived from sample findings and an assumed or known value of the population standard deviation.

The fourth measure, namely the z-*limits*, which correspond to the specified 95% confidence level, are found from the standard normal (z) distribution. These are the z-*limits* which bound a symmetrical area of 0,95around the mean z-value of zero.

Using the **z-table** in Appendix 1, a 95% confidence level corresponds to z-*limits* of ±1,96. The z-table shows that a symmetrical area of 0,95 is found under the standard normal distribution between $z = -1{,}96$ and $z = +1{,}96$.

These z-*limits* represent the *95% confidence interval in z terms.* To express the confidence limits in $\bar{x}$ terms, the z-limits must be converted into $\bar{x}$-*limits* using the z-transformation formula relevant to the *sampling distributions of the sample mean*. This is given by the following formula.

Formula

The z-transformation formula for the sampling distribution of the sample mean is: (*also see page 222*)

$$z = \frac{\bar{x} - \mu}{\frac{\sigma}{\sqrt{n}}}$$

Thus $\quad z = \frac{\bar{x} - \mu}{\frac{\sigma}{\sqrt{n}}}$ becomes $\pm 1{,}96 = \frac{(48{,}45 - \mu)}{\frac{18{,}58}{\sqrt{236}}} = \frac{(48{,}45 - \mu)}{1{,}2095}$

To solve for μ, multiply both sides by $\frac{\sigma}{\sqrt{n}}$

to give $\quad \pm z \frac{\sigma}{\sqrt{n}} = \bar{x} - \mu \quad\quad \pm 1{,}96\ (1{,}2095) = 48{,}45 - \mu$

Then re-arrange to isolate μ. This results in

$$\mu = \bar{x} \pm z \frac{\sigma}{\sqrt{n}} \quad\quad \mu = 48{,}45 \pm 1{,}96\ (1{,}2095)$$

$$\mu = 48{,}45 \pm 2{,}3706$$

which gives a *lower* confidence limit and an *upper* confidence limit about μ.

- The *lower* 95% confidence limit is 48,45 – 2,3706 = 46,079 (R46,08), and
- The *upper* 95% confidence limit is 48,45 + 2,3706 = 50,821 (R50,82).

Formula

Thus, in general, the *confidence interval for a single population mean*, μ, is given as:

$$\bar{x} - z\frac{\sigma}{\sqrt{n}} \leq \mu \leq \bar{x} + z\frac{\sigma}{\sqrt{n}}$$

(lower limit) (upper limit)

In Example 10.1, the 95% confidence interval for the *mean value of all purchases* at Kimberley convenience stores can be written as: [R46,08 ≤ μ ≤ R50,82].

Solution using *Excel*

The function key **=CONFIDENCE(alpha, std deviation, size)** will compute a range which corresponds to the specified confidence level. This range must be subtracted from, and also added to, the sample mean to derive the *lower* and *upper confidence limits*.

The following values must be provided:

- *alpha* = 1 – the specified confidence level (i.e. α = (1 – 0,95) = 0,05 for a 95% confidence level)
- population *standard deviation* (σ = 18,58)
- *sample size* (n = 236).

Then **=CONFIDENCE(0.05, 18.58, 236)** produces the result of **2,3705**

To find the *lower 95% confidence limit,* compute: 48,45 – 2,3705 = R46,08
To find the *upper 95% confidence limit,* compute: 48,45 + 2,3705 = R50,82

Management interpretation

There is a 95% chance that the interval from R46,08 to R50,82 will cover the actual mean value of all purchases at convenience stores in Kimberley.

Assumptions for valid results

The following *assumptions* are made about this confidence interval. It assumes that:

- the population standard deviation σ is known
- the sample size is large *(n > 40)*
- the population of the random variable x is normally distributed.

These assumptions must be satisfied to produce valid and reliable confidence interval estimates.

10.5 The Precision of Confidence Intervals

The *precision* with which a specified confidence interval estimates the true population parameter is determined by the *width* of the confidence interval. The *narrower* the confidence interval, the *more precise* the interval estimate and vice versa.

The width is influenced by:

- the specified *confidence level*
- the *sample size*, and
- the population *standard deviation.*

10.5.1 The Specified Level of Confidence

The *confidence level* is expressed by the *z-limits* derived from a standard normal probability distribution. The *z-limits* identify the number of standard errors on either side of the sample mean point estimate. The confidence level specifies the probability that the derived confidence limits will cover the true population mean.

Table 10.1 shows the commonly used confidence levels of 90%, 95% and 99% and their associated *z-limits*. The higher the desired confidence level, the larger the *z-limits* become and consequently, the wider will be the resulting confidence interval. This indicates that there is a trade-off between precision and confidence. Greater confidence is associated with lower precision and vice versa.

Table 10.1 Typical confidence limits and associated *z*-limits

Confidence level	*z*-limits
90%	±1,645
95%	±1,96
99%	±2,58

These critical *z*-limits can be found either from the *standard normal* (*z*) table (see **z-table** in Appendix 1), or by using the *Excel* function **=NORMSINV(cumulative probability)**.

To *illustrate*:

For a 90% confidence level **=NORMSINV(0.95)** gives $z = 1{,}6448$

For a 99% confidence level **=NORMSINV(0.995)** gives $z = 2{,}5758$

Note: A 90% confidence limit means that 5% lies in each tail of a normal distribution. Thus to find the corresponding *z*-limits using NORMSINV, a cumulative probability of 0,95 must be specified.

Table 10.2 shows how the confidence interval width (and hence the precision of the estimation) varies according to the chosen confidence level for Example 10.1.

Table 10.2 Influence of confidence levels on confidence interval width

Confidence level	Formula	Illustration (applied to Example 10.1)
90%	$\mu = \bar{x} \pm 1{,}645 \frac{\sigma}{\sqrt{n}}$	$\mu = 48{,}45 \pm 1{,}645\ (1{,}2095)$ $[46{,}46 \le \mu \le 50{,}44]$
95%	$\mu = \bar{x} \pm 1{,}96 \frac{\sigma}{\sqrt{n}}$	$\mu = 48{,}45 \pm 1{,}96\ (1{,}2095)$ $[46{,}08 \le \mu \le 50{,}82]$
99%	$\mu = \bar{x} \pm 2{,}58 \frac{\sigma}{\sqrt{n}}$	$\mu = 48{,}45 \pm 2{,}58\ (1{,}2095)$ $[45{,}33 \le \mu \le 51{,}57]$

10.5.2 Sample Size

Large sample sizes decrease the value of the *standard error*, resulting in narrower confidence intervals (for the same standard deviation and level of significance), and *more precise estimates* of the population parameter.

Small sample sizes, on the other hand, *increase* the *standard error* and result in wider confidence (for the same standard deviation and level of significance), and *less precise estimates* of the population parameter.

This effect of sample size is illustrated in Table 10.3.

Table 10.3 Effect of sample size on confidence interval precision

Population parameter	Standard error	Illustrations for two different sample sizes		
μ	$\frac{\sigma}{\sqrt{n}}$	$\sigma = 10$	$n = 50$	$\frac{\sigma}{\sqrt{n}} = 1{,}4140$
		$\sigma = 10$	$n = 250$	$\frac{\sigma}{\sqrt{n}} = 0{,}6325$
π	$\sqrt{\frac{\pi(1-\pi)}{n}}$	$\pi = 0{,}4$	$n = 50$	$\sqrt{\frac{\pi(1-\pi)}{n}} = 0{,}0693$
		$\pi = 0{,}4$	$n = 250$	$\sqrt{\frac{\pi(1-\pi)}{n}} = 0{,}0310$

Using Example 10.1, the 95% confidence interval limits are illustrated for two different sample sizes (based on *z-limits* = ± 1,96 and population standard deviation, σ = 18,58).

(1) $n = 236$ $\quad \mu = \bar{x} \pm z\frac{\sigma}{\sqrt{n}}$ $\quad \mu = 48{,}45 \pm 1{,}96\ (1{,}2095)$
$[R46{,}08 \leq \mu \leq R50{,}82]$

(2) $n = 96$ $\quad \mu = \bar{x} \pm z\frac{\sigma}{\sqrt{n}}$ $\quad \mu = 48{,}45 \pm 1{,}96\ (1{,}8963)$
$[R44{,}73 \leq \mu \leq R52{,}17]$

The *decrease in sample size* from 236 customers to only 96 customers has significantly *reduced the precision* of the confidence interval estimate for the true mean value of purchases at convenience stores by *widening the range* which is likely to cover μ.

10.5.3 Standard Deviation

If the population standard deviation (σ) is *small* in relation to its mean, variability in the data is low, hence the confidence interval will be *narrower*. This results in a *more precise estimate* of the population mean.

If, on the other hand, the population standard deviation (σ) is *large* relative to its mean, the confidence interval will be *wider*, which results in a *less precise estimate* of the population mean.

Note: Whenever the population standard deviation (σ) is unknown, it is usually estimated by the sample standard deviation (s). The sample standard deviation has the same effect on the estimated standard error as the actual population standard deviation.

Example 10.2 Car Commuter Time study

From a sample of 100 Cape Town car commuters, the sample mean time to commute to work daily was found to be 35,8 minutes. Assume that the population standard deviation is 11 minutes and that commuting times are normally distributed.

Management question (1)

Set *95% confidence limits* for the actual mean time taken by all car commuters in Cape Town to travel to work daily.

Solution (1)

Given $\bar{x}$ = 35,8 minutes
σ = 11 minutes
n = 100 commuters

Compute the *standard error* of the sample mean: $= \frac{\sigma}{\sqrt{n}} = \frac{11}{\sqrt{100}}$
= 1,1 minutes

Using either the **z-table** in Appendix 1, or the ***Excel* function** **=NORMSINV(0.975)**

the *95% confidence level* corresponds to *z-limits* = ±1,96

Then the *lower limit* is [35,8 – 1,96(1,1)] = [35,8 – 2,156] = 33,64 minutes, and
the *upper limit* is [35,8 + 1,96(1,1)] = [35,8 + 2,156] = 37,96 minutes

Thus, the *95% confidence interval* is defined as [33,64 ≤ μ ≤ 37,96] minutes.

Solution using *Excel*

=CONFIDENCE(0.05, 11, 100) gives a 95% confidence interval width = **2,156**

This value of 2,156 must be subtracted from – and then added to – the sample mean of 35,8 minutes to give the respective *lower* and *upper* confidence limits (as shown above).

Management interpretation (1)

There is a 95% chance that the interval from 33,64 minutes to 37,96 minutes will cover the actual mean time taken by *all* car commuters in Cape Town to travel to work daily.

Management question (2)

Set *90% confidence limits* for the actual mean time taken by all car commuters in Cape Town to travel to work daily.

Solution (2)

The measures of $\bar{x}$ = 35,8 minutes; σ = 11 minutes; n = 100 commuters; and the standard error = 1,1 all remain unchanged. Only the values of the *z-limits* will change.

Using either the **z-table** in Appendix 1, or the ***Excel* function**: =NORMSINV(0.95)
the *90% confidence level* corresponds to *z-limits* = ±1,645

Then, the *lower limit* is [35,8 – 1,645 (1,1)] = [35,8 – 1,81] = 33,99 minutes, and
the *upper limit* is [35,8 + 1,645 (1,1)] = [35,8 + 1,81] = 37,61 minutes

Thus the *90% confidence interval* is defined as [33,99 ≤ μ ≤ 37,61] minutes.

Solution using *Excel*

=CONFIDENCE(0.10, 11, 100) gives a 90% confidence interval width = **1,81**

This value of 1,81 must be subtracted from – and then added to – the sample mean of 35,8 minutes to give the respective *lower* and *upper* confidence limits (as shown above).

Management interpretation (2)

There is a 90% chance that the interval from 33,99 minutes to 37,61 minutes will cover the actual mean time taken by *all* car commuters in Cape Town to travel to work daily.

If the widths of the two confidence intervals computed for the *Car Commuter Time study* are compared, it will be noted that, for the same sample mean, sample size and standard error, the confidence limits are further apart at the 95% confidence level than at the 90% confidence level.

Logically, the more confident a decision maker wishes to be that the true mean is within the derived interval, the wider the limits must be set. The trade-off is between setting too high a confidence level and creating too wide an interval to be of any practical use.

Example 10.3 Coal Miners–Employment Period study

A human resources consultant to the Chamber of Mines has been asked to *estimate* the *true mean employment period* of coal miners employed by *all coal mines* over the past five years.

From a random sample of the records of 144 coal miners, the sample mean employment period was found to be 88,4 months. The population standard deviation is assumed to be 21,5 months with employment periods being normally distributed.

Management question

Find the 95% *confidence interval* estimate for the *actual mean employment period* (in months) for all coal miners employed in South African mines.

Solution

Given $\bar{x}$ = 88,4 months
σ = 21,5 months
n = 144 coal miners

Using either the **z-table** in Appendix 1, or the ***Excel* function** =NORMSINV(0.975) the *95% confidence level* corresponds to *z-limits* = ±1,96

Also, the *standard error* of $\bar{x}$ is $\sigma_{\bar{x}} = \frac{\sigma}{\sqrt{n}} = \frac{21,5}{\sqrt{144}} = 1,792$

Thus, the *95% confidence interval estimate* is given by:

$$[88,4 - (1,96(1,792)) \leq \mu \leq 88,4 + (1,96(1,792))]$$
$$= [88,4 - 3,51 \leq \mu \leq 88,4 + 3,51]$$
$$= [84,89 \leq \mu \leq 91,91] \text{ months}$$

Solution using *Excel*

=CONFIDENCE(0.05, 21.5, 144) gives a 95% confidence interval width = **3,51**

This value of 3,51 must be subtracted from – and then added to – the sample mean of 88,4 months to give the respective *lower* and *upper* confidence limits (as shown above).

Management interpretation

There is a 95% chance that the interval from 84,89 months to 91,91 months will cover the true mean employment period of all South African coal miners.

Example 10.4 Radial Tyres–Tread Life study

The Automobile Association (AA) found that the sample mean tread life of 81 SWP4 radial tyres tested is 52 345 km. It is also known that the population standard deviation is 6 144 km and that the tread life of SWP4 radial tyres is normally distributed.

Management question

Estimate, with *99% confidence*, the true mean tread life of all SWP4 radial tyres manufactured. Also interpret the results.

Solution

Given $\bar{x}$ = 52 345 km
σ = 6 144 km
n = 81 tyres

Using either the ***z*-table** in Appendix 1, or the ***Excel* function** **=NORMSINV(0.995)**

the *99% confidence level* corresponds to *z-limits* = ± 2,58 (actually = 2,5758)

Further, the *standard error* of $\bar{x}$ is $\sigma_{\bar{x}} = \frac{\sigma}{\sqrt{n}} = \frac{6\,144}{\sqrt{81}} = 682,67$

Thus, the *99% confidence interval estimate* is given by:

$$[52\,345 - (2,58(682,67)) \leq \mu \leq 52\,345 + (2,58(682,67))]$$
$$= [52\,345 - 1\,761,29 \leq \mu \leq 52\,345 + 1\,761,29]$$
$$= [50\,583,7 \leq \mu \leq 54\,106,3] \text{ km}$$

Solution using *Excel*

=CONFIDENCE(0.01, 6144, 81) gives a 99% confidence interval width = **1758,43**

This value of 1758,43 must be subtracted from – and then added to – the sample mean of 52 345 km to give the respective *lower* and *upper* confidence limits (as shown above).

Note: *Excel* uses z = 2,5758 (instead of z = 2,58), resulting in minor discrepancies in the limits.

Management interpretation

The AA can be 99% confident that the interval from 50 583,7 km to 54 106,3 km covers the true mean tread life of all SWP4 radial tyres manufactured.

10.6 The Rationale of a Confidence Interval

The following explanation indicates why a given confidence interval estimate will cover the true population parameter at the specified level of confidence. The *Car Commuter Time study* data (refer to Example 10.2) is used to illustrate this rationale.

(1) Assume that the population mean, μ, is known. If 95% confidence limits were set around this true mean, these limits would be:

$$\left(\mu - 1{,}96\frac{\sigma}{\sqrt{n}}\right) \quad \text{and} \quad \left(\mu + 1{,}96\frac{\sigma}{\sqrt{n}}\right)$$

(lower limit) and (upper limit)

Using Example 10.2, assume that the true *mean time to commute daily* to work by car in Cape Town is 32 minutes (μ = 32). Then the 95% confidence limits become:

$$[\mathbf{32} - 1{,}96(1{,}1) \le \mu \le \mathbf{32} + 1{,}96(1{,}1)]$$
$$= [\mathbf{32} - 2{,}156 \le \mu \le \mathbf{32} + 2{,}156]$$
$$= [29{,}84 \le \mu \le 34{,}16] \text{ minutes}$$

(2) Now, construct a series of 95% confidence intervals on the basis of:
$[\bar{x} - 1{,}96(1{,}1) \le \mu \le \bar{x} + 1{,}96(1{,}1)]$

using a random selection of *sample mean commuting times,* some of which:

(i) fall within the confidence limits of 29,84 and 34,16 minutes and others which

(ii) fall outside the confidence limits of 29,84 and 34,16 minutes.

Refer to Table 10.4 overleaf for a selection of *sample mean commuting times* and their respective 95% confidence intervals.

Table 10.4 Car Commuter Times: sample means and their 95% confidence intervals

Sample means *within* the interval [29,84 ≤ μ ≤ 34,16] minutes		Associated 95% confidence interval (using *z*-limits = ±1,96)
29,84	(lower limit)	27,6 ≤ μ ≤ **32**
	30,6	28,44 ≤ μ ≤ 32,76
	31,4	29,24 ≤ μ ≤ 33,56
	32,9	30,74 ≤ μ ≤ 35,06
	33,5	31,34 ≤ μ ≤ 35,66
34,16	(upper limit)	**32** ≤ μ ≤ 36,32
Sample means *outside* the interval [29,84 ≤ μ ≤ 34,16] minutes		**Associated 95% confidence interval (using *z*-limits = ±1,96)**
	28,4	26,24 ≤ μ ≤ 30,56
	35,5	33,34 ≤ μ ≤ 37,66

(3) From Table 10.4, the following will be observed:

(i) Each 95% confidence interval derived from a sample mean that falls *within* or *at the limits* of the interval [29,84 ≤ μ ≤ 34,16] will *cover* the *actual mean* commuting time of 32 minutes. The sample means which are equal to the confidence interval limits of 29,84 and 34,16 minutes also cover the population mean, but at their upper and lower limits respectively.

Since there is a 95% chance of a single sample mean falling within the limits of [29,84 ≤ μ ≤ 34,16] minutes as shown in (2) above, there is a 95% chance that a single confidence interval will cover the true population mean.

(ii) Each 95% confidence interval derived from a sample mean that falls outside the interval [29,84 ≤ μ ≤ 34,16] will *not cover* the *actual mean* commuting time of 32 minutes.

This is likely to happen only 5% of the time that sample means are computed.

Figure 10.1 below illustrates this rationale with numerous intervals based on sample means for a given sample size, n, falling both inside and outside of the 95% confidence limits around the sampling distribution of $\bar{x}$.

Figure 10.1 Illustration of the **Confidence Interval concept** (using a 95% confidence level)

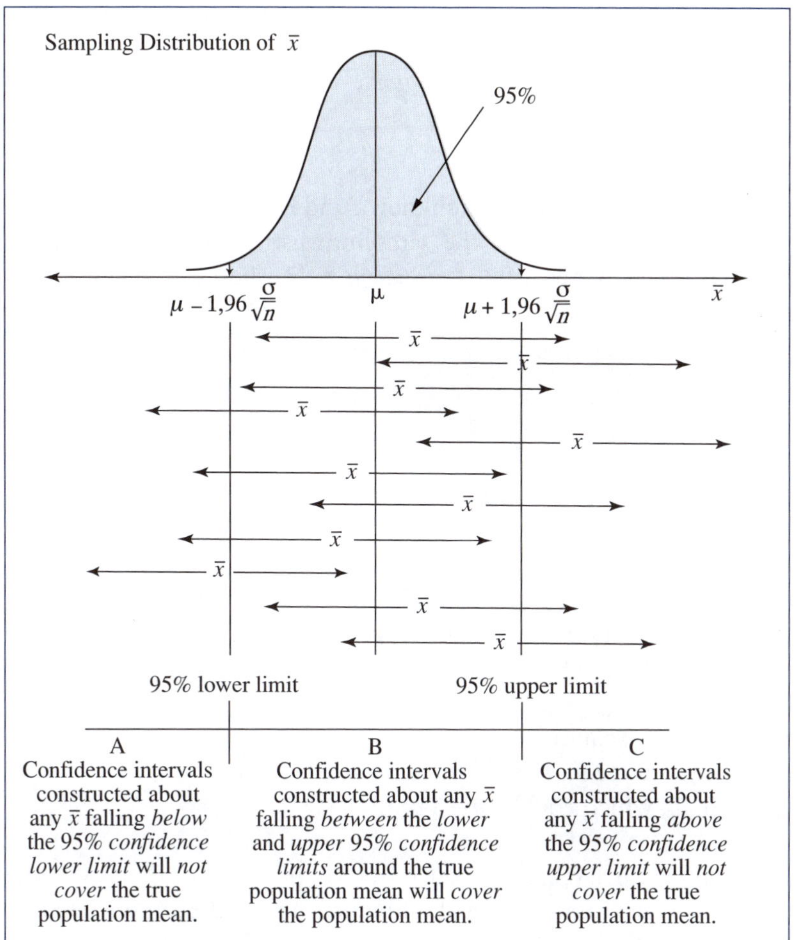

Thus, a single confidence interval at, say, a 95% confidence level, can be interpreted as follows:

"There is a 95% chance that the limits of this single confidence interval *will cover* the true population mean."

10.7 The Student *t*-Distribution

The confidence intervals constructed in section 10.4 assumed that the population standard deviation was known. The population standard deviation is needed to compute the standard error of the sample mean. However, it is often the case that the population standard deviation is unknown and needs to be estimated from the *sample standard deviation, s*.

When this is the case, probabilities associated with the sampling distribution of the sample mean (and used in the construction of confidence limits) are derived, not from the *z*-distribution, but from a distribution called the **Student *t*-distribution**.

The *Student t-distribution* (or *t*-distribution) is similar to the *z*-distribution. The *t*-distribution is also bell-shaped and symmetrical about its mean of zero. However, it does not have a constant standard deviation (which the *z*-distribution does have). The *t*-distribution's standard deviation is based on a *sample standard deviation* and varies inversely with the size of the sample used.

Formula

Thus, when the population standard deviation is unknown and is estimated by the sample standard deviation, the relationship between the sampling distribution of the sample mean and its standardised values is given by the *Student t*-distribution transformation formula:

$$t_{(n-1)} = \frac{\bar{x} - \mu}{\frac{s}{\sqrt{n}}}$$

where $(n - 1)$ is called **degrees of freedom.**

This transformation formula converts sample mean values, $\bar{x}$, into standardised *t*-values. For confidence interval estimation, *t-limits* corresponding to a specified level of confidence, are found either from the ***t*-table** (see Table 2 in Appendix 1), or by using the ***Excel* function** =TINV.

To find a *t*-value, the following is required:

(i) a specified *level of confidence* (e.g. 90%, 95%, or 99%).

(ii) the *degrees of freedom*, *df*, which equals $(n - 1)$.

In general, for a given confidence level, the smaller the sample size, *n*, the larger the *t-limits* become, to reflect the greater uncertainty of estimating σ from the sample standard deviation, *s*. This is illustrated in Table 10.5 of *t-limits*, assuming a 95% confidence level.

Table 10.5 The influence of sample size, *n*, on t-limits

Sample size n	Degrees of freedom $(n - 1)$	t-limits (read off *t*-table)
6	5	±2,571
11	10	±2,228
26	25	±2,060
41	40	±2,021
61	60	±2,000
121	120	±1,980
∞	∞	±1,960

Note: As *n* increases towards infinity, the *t-limits* approach ±1,96 which are the *z-limits* corresponding to a 95% confidence level.

Example 10.5 Finding *t*-limits for given Confidence Levels

Find the *t-limits* associated with a 95% confidence level and a sample size $n = 26$.

HOW TO

To find t-limits

(i) Using the ***t*-table** (refer to Table 2 in Appendix 1.)
The ***t*-table** requires the *degrees of freedom* ($df = n-1$) and the *upper tail area* (labelled α) of the *t*-distribution, which is determined by the specified confidence level.
In this example, the $df = n - 1 = 25$; and the upper tail area = 2,5% (hence $\alpha = 0{,}025$). From the ***t*-table**, for $df = 25$ (row) and $\alpha = 0{,}025$ (column), the *t-limit* = 2,060.

(ii) **Using *Excel*** **=TINV(probability, degrees of freedom)**

In this example, *probability* = the *combined* (lower and upper) *tail areas* = 5%; and *degrees of freedom* (*df*) = 25.
Then **=TINV(0.05,25)**
gives the *t-limit* = 2,059539 (rounded to 2,060 in the ***t*-table**)

General Rule: When to use *z* or *t*

- As a general rule, whenever the population standard deviation σ is *unknown*, the *t*-distribution should be *used*, instead of the *z*-distribution, to define the standard limits associated with a specified confidence level.
- However, if the *sample size is greater than 40*, the *t*-distribution values are "close enough" to the *z*-distribution values that for practical purposes, *z-limits* can be used in place of *t-limits*.

10.8 Confidence Interval Estimate for μ (when *σ* is unknown)

Formula

When σ is unknown, a confidence interval estimate for μ with a specified *confidence level* and *sample size*, *n*, is given by the following formula:

$$\bar{x} - t_{(\alpha)(n-1)}\frac{s}{\sqrt{n}} \leq \mu \leq \bar{x} + t_{(\alpha)(n-1)}\frac{s}{\sqrt{n}}$$

(lower limit) (upper limit)

Where
$\bar{x}$ = sample mean
s = sample standard deviation
n = sample size
$(1-\alpha)\%$ = specified confidence level where α = combined tail area *outside* the *t-limits*
$\pm t_{(\alpha)(n-1)}$ = *t-limits* for a specified confidence level $(1-\alpha)\%$
df = $(n - 1)$

Note: The standard error of $\bar{x}$, *which is* $\sigma_{\bar{x}}$ $(= \frac{\sigma}{\sqrt{n}})$ is now *estimated* by $\frac{s}{\sqrt{n}}$

Example 10.6 Jed Home Stores – Credit Card Purchases study

Refer to the *Excel* file: **C10.1 – credit customers**

Jed Home Stores (Pty) Ltd analysed the *value of purchases* made on credit card by a sample of 25 credit card customers. The sample mean was found to be R170,08 with a sample standard deviation of R21,90. Assume purchase values are normally distributed.

Management question (1)

Estimate, with 95% confidence, the actual *mean value* of *credit card purchases* at this store.

Solution (1)

Given $\bar{x}$ = R170,08
s = R21,90
n = 25 credit card customers

The standard error of $\bar{x}$ is *estimated* by $\sigma_{\bar{x}} \approx \frac{s}{\sqrt{n}} = \frac{21,9}{\sqrt{25}} = 4,38$

Since σ is *unknown* and the *sample size* is *small* ($n = 25$), the *t*-distribution must be used to find the *t-limits* based on the 95% confidence level ($\alpha = 0,05$) and degrees of freedom equal to $(n - 1) = (25 - 1) = 24$.

- From the ***t*-table**
  The *t-limits* associated with $\frac{\alpha}{2} = 0,025$ and $df = 24$ are $\pm$ 2,064
- **Using *Excel***
  =TINV(0.05,24) gives a *t-limit* equal to 2,063899

Thus, the *95% confidence interval estimate* for μ is given by:

$$[170,08 - 2,064(4,38) \leq \mu \leq 170,08 + 2,064(4,38)]$$
$$= [R161,04 \leq \mu \leq R179,12]$$

Management interpretation (1)

The probability is 0,95 that the interval R161,04 to R179,12 covers the *actual mean value* of *credit card purchases* at Jed Home Stores.

Management question (2)

Assume that 46 credit card purchases were sampled. Set 95% confidence limits for the actual *mean value* of *credit card purchases* at this home store. (σ is unknown)

Solution (2)

The increase in sample size to 46 will change the values of both:

- the *t-limits*, which will become $\pm$ 2,014 since $\frac{\alpha}{2} = 0,025$ and $df = (n - 1) = 45$ (use the ***t*-table** in Appendix 1), and

- the *estimated* standard error of $\bar{x}$, which becomes $\sigma_{\bar{x}} \approx \frac{s}{\sqrt{n}} = \frac{21,9}{\sqrt{46}} = 3,23$

Thus, the *95% confidence interval estimate* for μ (the actual mean credit card value of purchases) is given by:

$$[170,08 - 2,014(3,23) \le \mu \le 170,08 + 2,014(3,23)]$$
$$= [R163,57 \le \mu \le R176,59]$$

Management interpretation (2)

There is a 95% chance that the interval R163,57 to R176,59 will cover the actual mean value of *credit card purchases* at Jed Home Stores.

It can be seen from the above two examples that the larger sample size has resulted in narrower (more precise) confidence limits for the same confidence level. This reflects the greater certainty as seen in both (i) the smaller *t-limits* (for the same confidence level), and (ii) the lower value of the *estimated standard error* as a result of the larger sample size.

Note: Since $n = 46 > 40$, the *z-limits* of ± 1,96 (associated with the 95% confidence level) could have been used as an approximation to the *t-limits* of ± 2,014.

Deriving Confidence Intervals using *Excel's* Data Analysis

HOW TO

To use Excel's Data Analysis

If a database of data values is available, it is possible to use Data Analysis in *Excel* to compute the confidence limits for a population mean (refer to chapter 3). The *confidence limits* for a population mean for a given numeric random variable are computed in the Descriptive Statistics option of Data Analysis, as illustrated by Example 10.7.

Example 10.7 Jed Home Stores – Credit Card Purchases study

Refer to the *Excel* file: C10.1 – credit customers

Management question

Estimate, with 95% confidence, the actual *mean value* of *credit card purchases* at this store.

Solution using *Excel*

Select the Descriptive Statistics option of Data Analysis and tick the box labelled Confidence Level for Mean. The results produced are given in Table 10.6 overleaf.

Table 10.6 Data, descriptive statistics and confidence interval estimate for the mean value of Credit Card Purchases

Purchase Value		
179,4	Purchase Value	
143,6	**Mean**	**170,076**
164,3	**Standard Error**	**4,380023**
182,6	Median	174,8
192,3	Mode	#N/A
174,8	Standard Deviation	21,9001
148,4	Sample Variance	479,6152
178,3	Kurtosis	−1,0078
190,7	Skewness	−0,0268
202,1	Range	75,4
165,2	Minimum	135,1
179,5	Maximum	210,5
210,5	Sum	4251,9
148,5	Count	25
180,4	**Confidence Level (95,0%)**	**9,0399**
135,1	**95% Confidence Interval is given by:**	
146,7	**Lower 95% limit**	**161,04**
182,3	**Upper 95% limit**	**179,12**
146,5		
166,3		
138,9		
184,2		
138,6		
202,6		
170,1		

Note 1: The lower and upper 95% confidence limits are derived from the sample mean (R170,08) and the Confidence Level (95%) value (R9,04) as follows:

- *lower* 95% confidence limit = 170,08 – 9,04 = R161,04
- *upper* 95% confidence limit = 170,08 + 9,04 = R179,12.

Note 2: The Data Analysis option always uses the *t-limits* to compute the confidence interval as it assumes that the population standard deviation, σ, is unknown.

10.9 Confidence Interval for the Population Proportion (π)

If the data of a random variable is categorical, the appropriate measure of central location is a *proportion*. In the same way that the population mean can be estimated from a sample mean, a population proportion, π, can be estimated based on the point estimate of its sample proportion, p.

The following statistical measures are required to construct *confidence interval estimates* about the true population proportion π:

- a single sample proportion point estimate, p where $p = \frac{x}{n}$
- a given sample size, n
- the *standard error* of a sample proportion, which indicates the closeness of sample proportions to their corresponding population proportion (refer to chapter 9, section 9.5). This is defined as follows:

$$\sigma_p = \sqrt{\frac{\pi(1-\pi)}{n}}$$

However, σ_p is generally unknown, because it depends on π – the population proportion parameter being estimated. Hence the sample point estimate, p, is used to estimate σ_p. As a result, the *estimated* standard error for proportions is:

$$\sigma_p \approx \sqrt{\frac{p(1-p)}{n}}$$

- Standard normal *z-limits* corresponding to a specified level of confidence.

Now, the *confidence interval* for a *single population proportion n* is given by:

$$p - z\sqrt{\frac{p(1-p)}{n}} \leq \pi \leq p + z\sqrt{\frac{p(1-p)}{n}}$$

(lower limit) (upper limit)

Example 10.8 Johannesburg Street Vendor By-law study

A recent survey amongst 240 randomly selected street vendors in Johannesburg showed 84 of them felt that local by-laws hampered their trading.

Management question

Construct a *95% confidence interval* for the true *population proportion*, π, of *street vendors* who believe that local by-laws hamper their trading.

Solution

From the data $x = 84$ (number of "success" outcomes)
$n = 240$ (sample size)

then $p = \frac{84}{240} = 0{,}35$

Using the sample proportion, p, an *estimate* of the standard error is given by:

$$\sigma_p \approx \sqrt{\frac{p(1-p)}{n}} = \sqrt{\frac{(0{,}35)(1-0{,}35)}{240}} = 0{,}0308$$

Based on a 95% confidence level, the *z-limits* = ± 1,96 (use **z-table** in Appendix 1).

Thus, the *95% confidence interval* for the actual proportion of all street vendors who feel that the local by-laws hamper their trading is given by:

$$[0{,}35 - 1{,}96\ (0{,}0308) \le \pi \le 0{,}35 + 1{,}96\ (0{,}0308)]$$
$$= [0{,}2896 \le \pi \le 0{,}4104]$$

Management interpretation

There is a 95% chance that the interval from 29% to 41% will cover the actual percentage of all street vendors who believe that local by-laws hamper their trading.

10.10 Summary

This chapter focused on the estimation of population parameters using *confidence intervals.* Two separate population parameters, namely the population mean μ, and the population proportion π, were estimated. The confidence interval for each of these two population parameters uses the same underlying rationale and construction approach. Each, however, was described by its own *sampling distribution* and *standard error.*

The chapter showed that, in cases where the population standard deviation is known, the *z*-distribution is used to provide the *standardised confidence limits.*

The *t-distribution* was introduced as an alternative standard distribution to the *z*-distribution: the *t*-distribution is used whenever the population standard deviation is unknown and needs to be estimated, using the sample standard deviation. However, the *z*-distribution can be used to approximate the *t*-distribution whenever the sample size is large (i.e. above 40).

Exercises

10.1 The Department of Trade and Industry (DTI) conducted a survey to estimate the average *number of employees* per small and medium-sized enterprises (SME) in Gauteng. A random sample of 144 SME's in Gauteng found that the average number of employees was 24,4 employees. Assume that the population standard deviation is 10,8 employees and that the number of employees per SME is normally distributed.

(i) Estimate, with 95% confidence, the actual average number of employees per SME in Gauteng. Interpret the findings for the DTI.
(ii) Re-compute (i) using *Excel's* NORMSINV function to find the z-value.
(iii) Use *Excel's* CONFIDENCE function to produce the findings in (i).

10.2 The operations manager of a sugar mill in Durban wants to estimate the average *size of an order received*. An order is measured in the number of palettes shipped. A random sample of 87 orders from customers had a sample mean value 131,6 palettes. Assume that the population standard deviation is 25 palettes and that order size is normally distributed.

(i) Estimate, with 90% confidence, the mean size of orders received from all its customers. (Compute manually using the z-tables.)
(ii) Compute (i) using *Excel's* NORMSINV function to find the z-value.
(iii) Use *Excel's* CONFIDENCE function to produce the findings in (i).
(iv) If the sugar mill receives 720 orders this year, compute, with 90% confidence, the total number of palettes of sugar that they will ship during the year.

10.3 For a random sample of 256 owners of medium-sized cars, it was found that their average *monthly car insurance premium* for comprehensive cover was R356. Assume that the population standard deviation is R44 per month and that insurance premiums are normally distributed.

(i) Find the 95% confidence interval for the average monthly comprehensive car insurance premium paid by all owners of medium-sized cars. Interpret the result.
(ii) Find the 90% confidence interval for the same problem. Interpret the result and compare it to (i).
(iii) Re-compute (i) using *Excel's* NORMSINV function to find the z-value.
(iv) Use *Excel's* CONFIDENCE function to re-compute (i).
(v) If 3 000 car owners are comprehensively insured by the Sun Insurance company, estimate, with 95%, the total monthly premium income of the company.

10.4 Suppose that a paint supply shop wanted to estimate the correct amount of paint contained in five-litre cans purchased from a nationally known manufacturer. It is known from the manufacturer's specifications that the standard deviation of the amount of paint is equal to 0,04 litres. A random sample of 50 cans is selected, and the average amount of paint per five-litre can is 4,985 litres. Assume a normal distribution of fill.

(i) Set up a 99% confidence interval estimate of the true population average amount of paint included in a five-litre can.
(ii) Based on your results, do you think that the store owner has a right to complain to the manufacturer? Why?
(iii) Compute (i) using *Excel's* **NORMSINV** function to find the *z*-value.
(iv) Use *Excel's* **CONFIDENCE** function to re-compute (i).

10.5 The mean annual inventory turnover rate of a random sample of 24 convenience stores was found to be 3,8 times per annum. Assume that the population standard deviation is 0,6 and that annual inventory turnover rate amongst convenience stores is normally distributed.

(i) Compute the actual average annual inventory turnover rate, with 90% confidence for all convenience stores. (Compute manually using the *z*-table.)
(ii) Compute (i) using *Excel's* **NORMSINV** function to find the *z*-value.
(iii) Use *Excel's* **CONFIDENCE** function to re-compute (i).

10.6 A travel agency call centre wants to know the average number of calls received per day by its call centre. A random sample of 21 days is selected and the sample mean number of calls received was found to be 166,2 calls with a sample standard deviation of 22,8 calls. Assume that calls received daily are normally distributed.

(i) Find a 95% confidence interval for the mean number of daily calls received by the call centre. Interpret the findings.
(ii) Find a 99% confidence interval for the mean number of daily calls received by the call centre.
(iii) Compare the findings of (i) and (ii) and explain the reason for the difference.
(iv) Re-compute the confidence interval in (i) using *Excel's* **TINV** function.
(v) Estimate, with 95% confidence, the total number of calls received over a 60-day period. Interpret the result.

10.7 The average dividend yield of a random sample of 28 JSE-listed companies last year was found to be 12,5% with a sample standard deviation of 3,4%. Assume that dividend yields are normally distributed.

(i) Compute, with 90% confidence, the actual mean dividend yield of all JSE-listed companies last year. Interpret the finding.
(ii) Re-compute the confidence interval in (i) using *Excel's* **TINV** function.

10.8 Litre cartons of milk are advertised to contain 1-litre of milk. From a random sample of 18 1-litre cartons whose contents were accurately measured by the South African Bureau of Standards (SABS), it was found that the average fill was 0,981 litres with a sample standard deviation of 0,052 litres. Assume that the fill of 1-litre milk cartons is normally distributed.

(i) Using a 99% confidence level, estimate the actual mean fill of all 1-litre milk cartons. Interpret your findings and comment on the question: "Do 1-litre cartons of milk contain one litre of milk on average?"
(ii) Repeat the exercise in (i) above, but use a 95% confidence level. Explain any differences in the conclusions.
(iii) Re-compute the confidence intervals in (i) and (ii) using *Excel's* TINV function.

10.9 Before entering into wage negotiations, the workers' representative of the newly formed farm workers trade union wanted to know the average wage of its union members. The average wage of a random sample of 50 members was found to be R1 420 per month with a sample standard deviation of R160 per month. Assume wages are normally distributed.
(i) What is the 90% confidence interval estimate for the true mean monthly wages paid to farm workers?
(ii) What is the 99% confidence interval estimate for the true mean monthly wages paid to farm workers?
(iii) Compare and comment on the results of (i) and (ii).
(iv) Re-compute the confidence intervals in (i) and (ii) using *Excel's* TINV function.

10.10 The DTI wants to determine the percentage of manufacturing firms that have met the employment equity charter. To assist the department, Statistics SA (Statssa) selected a random sample of 200 manufacturing firms and established that 84 have met the employment equity charter.

Determine, with 95% confidence, the percentage of manufacturing firms that have met the employment equity charter. Prepare a brief report to the DTI detailing your findings.

10.11 A Spar retailer observed a random sample of 160 customers and found that 68 customers paid for their grocery purchases by cash.

Construct a 95% confidence interval for the actual percentage of customers who pay cash for their grocery purchases. Interpret the findings.

10.12 A national bank analysed a random sample of 365 cheque accounts at their Tshwane branch and found that 78 of them were overdrawn.

Estimate, with 90% confidence, the percentage of all bank accounts at the Tshwane branch of the bank that were *not* overdrawn. Interpret the findings.

10.13 A random sample of 300 shoppers in a shopping mall is interviewed to identify their reasons for coming to this particular mall. The factor of store mix was the most important reason for 120 of those interviewed.

Estimate the likely percentage of all shoppers who frequent this shopping mall primarily because of the mix of stores in the mall, using 90% confidence limits.

Use *Excel's* **Data Analysis** for Exercises 10.14 to 10.16.

10.14 X10.14 – cashier absenteeism

A supermarket manager analysed the number of days absent per year for a random sample of 29 cashiers. Assume that *days absent* is normally distributed.

(i) Compute the *descriptive statistics* for *days absent* by cashiers and interpret these findings for the manager.
(ii) Estimate, with a 95% confidence level, the mean number of days absent per year for all supermarket cashiers.
(iii) If its company policy that average absenteeism level should not exceed 10 days per cashier per year, based on a 95% confidence level, is the company's policy being adhered to? Comment.
(iv) Re-compute and confirm the 95% confidence limits using the TINV function in *Excel* to find the *t-limits*.

10.15 X10.15 – parcel weights

Post Net wants to estimate the actual weight of documents placed in their medium-sized plastic envelopes (*parcel weights*) that are couriered to clients throughout the country. A random sample of filled 43 medium-sized plastic envelopes were selected and weighed. Assume that *parcel weights* (in kg) are normally distributed.

(i) Compute the *descriptive statistics* for *parcel weights*. Report these findings to the manager of Post Net.
(ii) Estimate, with a 90% confidence level, the mean parcel weight of their filled medium-sized plastic envelopes.
(iii) These envelopes are designed to carry documents that do not exceed 3 kg on average, based on a 90% confidence level. Is Post Net adhering to this requirement? Comment.
(iv) Re-compute and confirm the 90% confidence limits using the TINV function in *Excel* to find the *t-limits*.

10.16 X10.16 – cost-to-income

A company's *cost-to-income ratio* is a measure of its ability to control its costs. The lower the ratio (expressed as a percentage), the better the cost management within the company. An analyst recorded the cost-to-income ratio (as percentage) of 50 randomly selected public companies to study their ability to control their operating cost. Assume that *cost-to-income ratios* across public companies are normally distributed.

(i) Compute the *descriptive statistics* for the *cost-to-income ratio*. Interpret the profile of this measure across the sample of public companies surveyed.
(ii) Find the 95% confidence interval for the mean cost-to-income ratio for all public companies.
(iii) Re-compute and confirm the 95% confidence limits using the TINV function in *Excel* to find the *t-limits*.
(iv) As a rule of thumb, a public company's cost-to-income ratio should not exceed 75%. Use *Excel's* TDIST function and the sample evidence from (i) to determine what percentage of all public companies are likely to be in violation of the rule of thumb?

Chapter

11

Hypotheses Tests – Single Population (Means and Proportions)

Objectives

In certain problem situations a manager uses personal judgement or experience to postulate a value for a population parameter. Such statements are called **hypotheses**. This chapter introduces the statistical concept of hypothesis testing. Hypothesis testing is a rigorous process of testing the validity of management claims using sample evidence. The result of this statistical process is either to support or refute the management claims, based on an analysis of the sample evidence.

The chapter covers hypothesis testing for a single population mean and a single population proportion. In later chapters, hypothesis testing is extended to include multiple population scenarios. The use of *Excel* to test hypothesis will also be demonstrated.

After studying this chapter, you should be able to:

- understand the concept of hypothesis testing
- perform hypothesis tests for single population means
- perform hypothesis tests for single population proportions
- distinguish when to use the *z-test statistic* or the *t-test statistic*
- correctly interpret the results of a hypothesis test
- correctly translate the statistical results into management conclusions.

11.1 Introduction

Chapter 10 considered one important approach of inferential statistics, namely, the setting of *confidence intervals* around sample statistics to estimate the true value of the population parameter from which the sample was drawn.

Another approach of inferential statistics is to test, using sample evidence, whether a claim made about the true value of a population parameter is valid. This inferential approach is known as **hypothesis testing**.

The following examples illustrate *claims* made about population parameters:

- an investment company *claims* that their average return across all their portfolios is 19% p.a.
- a detergent manufacturer *states* that one in four households use their product
- a tyre manufacturer *believes* that the average tread life of their tyres is 75 000 km
- a tax auditor is *convinced* that more than 15% of all company tax returns are incorrectly completed
- an economist *believes* that there is no difference in the mean starting salaries earned between civil engineers and electrical engineers
- the factory manager of an exhaust manufacturer *believes* that the average worker output is higher during the day shift than during the night shift.

To test these claims statistically, sample data is gathered and analysed. On the basis of the sample findings, the hypothesised value of the population parameter is either accepted as *probably true* or rejected as *probably false*. This statistical process of testing the validity of a claim about the true value of any population parameter is known as **hypothesis testing**.

Hypothesis tests are conducted, in chapters 11 and 12, on the following four population parameters, all of which are measures of central location:

- the single population mean μ
- the single population proportion π
- the difference between two population means $(\mu_1 - \mu_2)$
- the difference between two population proportions $(\pi_1 - \pi_2)$.

This chapter examines hypothesis testing for a *single population parameter*, namely a *single mean* and a *single proportion*; while chapter 12 conducts hypotheses on central location parameters *between two populations* (i.e. comparing differences between two means, and differences between two proportions). Conclusions drawn from hypothesis tests provide managers with statistically verified findings on which to base decisions.

11.2 The Process of Hypothesis Testing

Hypothesis testing is a process of testing how "close" a sample statistic lies to a hypothesised value of its population parameter. The sampling distribution of the sample statistic (see chapter 9) is used to test for "closeness". The central location value of a sampling distribution *is* the hypothesised value of the population parameter. The closer the sample statistic lies to the central location value of the sampling distribution, the more likely it is that the hypothesised population parameter is probably true. Similarly, the further away the sample statistic lies from the central location position of the sampling distribution, the more likely it is that the hypothesised population parameter is probably false.

Hypothesis testing is the statistically rigorous process of testing for the "closeness" of a sample statistic to a hypothesised population parameter.

This process is formalised in a four-step procedure, as follows:

Step 1: Formulate the *statistical hypotheses* (null and alternative hypotheses).

Step 2: Compute the *sample test statistic.*

Step 3: Derive a decision rule to accept or reject the null hypothesis, either by a
- (i) traditional approach – using the *region of acceptance/rejection*, or a
- (ii) modern approach – using the *p-value* method.

Step 4: Compare the sample test statistic to the decision rule and draw the *statistical* and *management conclusions.*

Each step will now be explained and illustrated under a variety of problem scenarios.

Step 1 Define the Statistical Hypotheses (Null and Alternative)

Hypothesis testing begins when a value is assumed or claimed for the particular population parameter being investigated. This results in *two* statistical hypotheses or mathematical statements being formulated, as follows:

(1) The **null hypothesis** – written as H_0

The null hypothesis states that the true population parameter value is equivalent to a single hypothesised value. For *example*, if the mean output per worker is claimed to be 146 units per hour, then:

$$H_0: \mu = 146$$

(2) The **alternative hypothesis** – written as H_1

The alternative hypothesis states that the true population parameter is *not* equivalent to the hypothesised population parameter, as stated in the null hypothesis. It is always expressed in a manner which negates the null hypothesis.

For the above *example:* $H_1: \mu \neq 146$

The hypotheses can be formulated in one of *three ways*, depending on how the management claim is stated.

(i) A two-sided hypothesis test

Example

$$H_0: \mu = 146$$
$$H_1: \mu \neq 146$$

When a management claim is made that a population parameter is *equal to* a specific value and the test is to verify that specific value only, then a **two-sided hypothesis test** is formulated.

H_0: population parameter = hypothesised value
H_1: population parameter ≠ hypothesised value

In this instance, the null hypothesis will be rejected in favour of the alternative hypothesis if the statistical evidence points towards the true population parameter being either significantly *less than* ($\mu < 146$) or significantly *greater than* ($\mu > 146$) the null hypothesised value.

The *null hypothesis* must always contain the equality sign (e.g. $\mu = 146$). Hence, in two-sided tests, the *management claim* always *resides* in the *null hypothesis*.

(ii) A one-sided (upper-tailed) hypothesis test

Example

$$H_0: \mu \leq 146$$
$$H_1: \mu > 146$$

When a management claim is made that a population parameter is *more than* a specified value, then the hypotheses are formulated as a **one-sided (upper-tailed) test**.

H_0: population parameter ≤ hypothesised value
H_1: population parameter > hypothesised value

In this instance, the null hypothesis will be rejected in favour of the alternative hypothesis if the statistical evidence points towards the true population parameter being only significantly *greater than* the null hypothesised value.

As indicated above, the *null hypothesis* must always contain the equality sign. Since the *claim* states that the population parameter is *more than* (>) a *specific value*, the *management claim resides* in the *alternative hypothesis*.

The one-sided upper-tailed hypothesis test will also be used if the *management claim* is made as follows: "The population parameter is *equal to or less than* a specified value". Any values less than or equal to (≤) the null hypothesised value will not lead to a rejection of the null hypothesis. Hence, the null hypothesis will only be rejected in favour of the alternative hypothesis if the statistical evidence points towards the true population parameter being significantly *greater than* (>) the claimed value, as stated in the null hypothesis.

(iii) A one-sided (lower-tailed) hypothesis test

$$H_0: \mu \geq 146$$
$$H_1: \mu < 146$$

When a management claim is made that a population parameter is *less than* a specified value, then the hypotheses are formulated as a **one-sided (lower-tailed) test**.

H_0: population parameter ≥ hypothesised value
H_1: population parameter < hypothesised value

The null hypothesis will be rejected in favour of the alternative hypothesis if the statistical evidence points towards the true population parameter being only significantly *smaller than* the null hypothesised value.

Since the *null hypothesis* must always contain the equality sign, any *management claim* that the population parameter is *less than* a *specific value* (<) implies that the *management claim resides* in the *alternative hypothesis*.

This one-sided lower-tailed hypothesis test would also be used if the *management claim* is made as follows: "The population parameter is *equal to or more than* a specified value". Any values greater than or equal to (≥) the null hypothesised value will not lead to a rejection of the null hypothesis. Hence, the null hypothesis will only be rejected in favour of the alternative hypothesis if the statistical evidence points towards the true population parameter being only significantly *smaller than* (<) the claimed value as stated in the null hypothesis.

Note: The null hypothesis must always contain an equality sign, because it refers to a single sampling distribution whose central location value is the null hypothesised value against which an alternative hypothesis is being tested.

The remaining three steps of a hypothesis test seek either to *support* or *reject* the *null hypothesis*.

Step 2 Compute the Sample Test Statistic

Sample data is used to provide the evidence to test the validity of the null hypothesis. A *sample statistic* must therefore be computed. For hypothesis tests of a central location nature and from either one or two populations, the sample statistic is one of the following:

- The single *sample mean* $\bar{x}$
- The single *sample proportion* p
- The *difference* between *two sample means* $(\bar{x}_1 - \bar{x}_2)$
- The *difference* between *two sample proportions* $(p_1 - p_2)$

The sample statistic is usually expressed in standardised terms (i.e. as a *z*-statistic). When the sample statistic is expressed in *z standardised form*, it is called the **sample test statistic** – and written as ***z-stat***.

Formulae

The following *z*-transformation formulae are used to translate a given sample statistic into its corresponding *z*-statistic. The resultant *z*-value is referred to as ***z-stat***. These *z* formulae are derived from the appropriate sampling distribution, which relates a sample statistic to the standardised *z*-statistic.

(1) For the *single sample mean,* $\bar{x}$, the appropriate *z*-transformation formula is:

$$z\text{-}stat = \frac{\bar{x} - \mu}{\frac{\sigma}{\sqrt{n}}}$$

(2) For the *single sample proportion, p,* the appropriate z-transformation formula is:

$$z\text{-}stat = \frac{p - \pi}{\sqrt{\frac{\pi(1-\pi)}{n}}}$$

(3) For the *difference between two sample means,* $(\bar{x}_1 - \bar{x}_2)$, the appropriate z-transformation formula is:

$$z\text{-}stat = \frac{(\bar{x}_1 - \bar{x}_2) - (\mu_1 - \mu_2)}{\sqrt{\frac{\sigma_1^2}{n_1} + \frac{\sigma_2^2}{n_2}}}$$

(4) For the *difference between two sample proportions,* $(p_1 - p_2)$, the appropriate z-transformation formula is:

$$z\text{-}stat = \frac{(p_1 - p_2) - (\pi_1 - \pi_2)}{\sqrt{\hat{\pi}(1-\hat{\pi})\left(\frac{1}{n_1} + \frac{1}{n_2}\right)}}$$

where $\hat{\pi} = \frac{x_1 + x_2}{n_1 + n_2}$ $\quad p_1 = \frac{x_1}{n_1}$ $\quad p_2 = \frac{x_2}{n_2}$

$\hat{\pi}$ is called the **pooled estimate** of the population proportion.

Interpreting *z-stat*

This *z-stat* value measures the number of standard errors that a sample statistic (e.g. sample mean) lies from its null hypothesised population parameter (e.g. the population mean). The smaller the *z-stat* value (i.e. closer to zero), the closer the sample statistic lies to its hypothesised population parameter value, and vice versa.

To make the decision whether the sample statistic, *z-stat*, lies "close enough" to the null hypothesised value to accept H_0 or not, a decision rule is needed in order to define "closeness". This is the purpose of *step 3.*

Step 3 Decision rule to Accept or Reject the Null Hypothesis

This step sets up a *decision rule* to determine when to *reject* or *not reject* the null hypothesis as the likely true value of the population parameter being tested.

The central value of a sampling distribution is assumed to be the null hypothesised population parameter value being tested. Hence the sampling distribution of a sample statistic is used to test the validity of a claim as stated in the null hypothesis.

HOW TO

To test the validity of a claim

Two approaches can be used to conduct the validity test:

- **Approach 1** is called the **region of acceptance/rejection** method. It is a traditional approach that uses an *interval around the null hypothesised value* as the basis for deciding whether to accept or reject the null hypothesis.

- **Approach 2** is called the ***p-value*** method. This is the more modern view on hypothesis testing and uses *probabilities* to decide whether the null hypothesised value is true or false.

Both approaches are covered in this text but, in practice, an analyst would select and apply only one approach. The *p-value* method is used in all statistical software packages, including *Excel.*

Approach 1 The region of acceptance/rejection method

The **region of acceptance** is an interval of sample statistic values *centred about the null hypothesised population parameter.*

The null hypothesis will *not be rejected* if the value of a sample statistic falls *within these limits* about H_0.

The **region of rejection** is an interval of sample statistic values lying outside the region of acceptance.

The null hypothesis *will be rejected* if the value of a sample statistic falls *within its limits.*

Figures 11.1, 11.2, and 11.3 illustrate the regions of acceptance and rejection about a null hypothesised population mean, μ, for the three different formulations of the null hypothesis.

(i) A two-sided hypothesis test

Figure 11.1 Region of **acceptance** and **rejection** for a **two-sided** hypothesis test

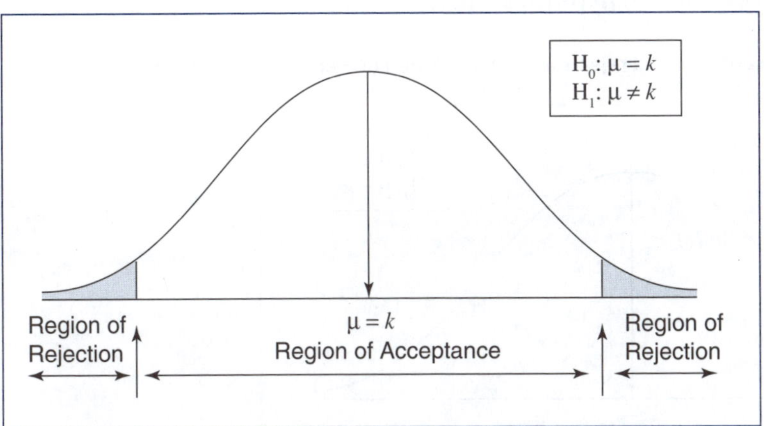

A *two-sided* test has a *region of rejection* both *below* and *above* the null hypothesised value of the population parameter, *k*.

Two-sided tests are always associated with the following hypotheses:

H_0: population parameter = hypothesised value
H_1: population parameter ≠ hypothesised value

(ii) A one-sided (upper-tailed) hypothesis test

Figure 11.2 Region of **acceptance** and **rejection** for a **one-sided (upper-tailed)** hypothesis test

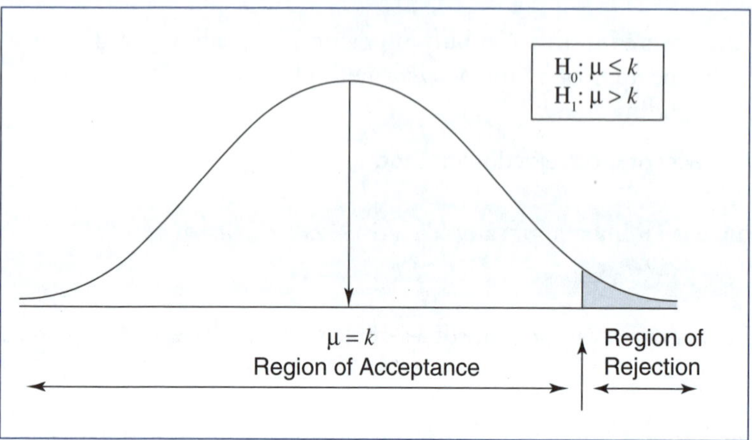

A *one-sided (upper-tailed)* test means that the *region of rejection* lies only *above* the null hypothesised value of the population parameter, *k*.

One-sided (upper-tailed) tests are always associated with the following hypotheses:

H_0 : population parameter ≤ hypothesised value
H_1 : population parameter > hypothesised value

(iii) A one-sided (lower-tailed) hypothesis test

Figure 11.3 Region of **acceptance** and **rejection** for a **one-sided (lower-tailed)** hypothesis test

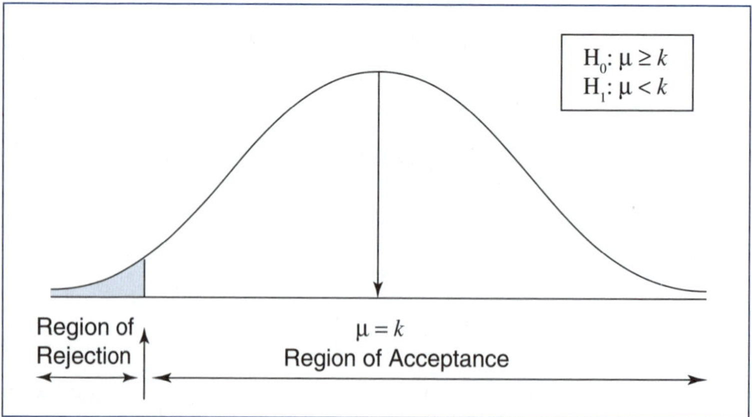

A *one-sided (lower-tailed)* test means that the *region of rejection* lies only *below* the null hypothesised value of the population parameter, *k*.

One-sided (lower-tailed) tests are always associated with the following hypotheses:

H_0: population parameter ≥ hypothesised value
H_1: population parameter < hypothesised value

Factors affecting the choice of the critical limit(s) of the region of acceptance

The *critical limits* that define the regions of acceptance and rejection of the null hypothesised population parameter are determined by the *level of risk* acceptable to the decision maker in drawing an incorrect conclusion. There are two basic risks involved in testing any hypothesis.

They are called the **Type I error**, and the **Type II error**:

- *Type I error* This is the probability of *rejecting a true null hypothesis.* A type I error occurs when the sample evidence indicates that the null hypothesis should be rejected when in fact the null hypothesis is actually true. The likelihood (or probability) of this occuring is represented by the area under the sampling distribution over the *region of rejection.*
- *Type II error* This is the probability of *accepting a false null hypothesis.*

These two error types move inversely to each other. By reducing the Type I error, the chances of incurring a Type II error increase and vice versa.

In hypothesis testing, the practice is to *control the level* of the *Type I error* and set the critical limits of the region of acceptance accordingly.

Level of significance (α)

A Type I error is called the **level of significance**, and is represented by the symbol α (alpha). The level of significance is the area (probability) in the "tails" of a sampling distribution, as this is where the rejection region is located.

The level of significance, α, is used to find the critical limits which separate the region of acceptance from the region of rejection.

The **level of significance**, therefore, defines the likelihood of rejecting the null hypothesis when, in fact, it is true (i.e. Type I error).

This level of risk is usually set at 1%, 5% or 10%, depending on the decision maker's willingness to reject H_0 when it is actually true.

Figure 11.4 overleaf illustrates the relationship between the level of significance and the region of rejection for any sampling distribution for a *two-sided* test.

Figure 11.4 Level of significance and the **region of rejection** (two-sided tests)

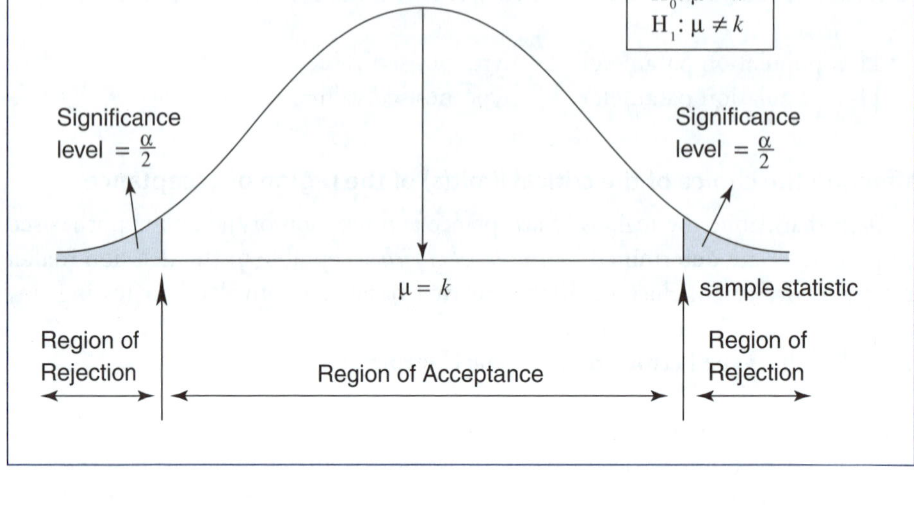

Note: α is split between the lower and the upper regions of rejection. Each tail = $\frac{\alpha}{2}$.

For *one-tailed tests*, the level of significance, α, appears only in the *one tail* of a sampling distribution. For a one-sided (upper-tailed) hypothesis test, the level of significance, α, is contained only in the upper tail area, while for a one-sided (lower-tailed) hypothesis test, the level of significance, α, is contained only in the lower tail of the sampling distribution. The shaded regions of rejection in Figures 11.2 and 11.3 represent the levels of significance, α, for one-sided hypotheses tests.

HOW TO

To find the critical limits between the regions of acceptance and rejection

To determine the critical limits for the region of acceptance, the *level of significance* of a test must be specified. For example, a 5% level of significance (α = 0,05) means that there is a 5% chance of rejecting a true null hypothesis.

From the *z*-distribution, these critical limits are:

- the two *z-limits* (i.e. ± *z-limit*) which bound a combined area (probability) of α in its tails for **two-sided tests** (note that $\frac{\alpha}{2}$ is contained in each tail), or
- a single *z-limit* which bounds an area (probability) of α in only one tail for **one-sided tests**.

The *critical limits*, which define the region of acceptance, are usually expressed in *z* terms and written as ***z*-crit**. These critical *z-limits* are found:

- from the ***z*-table** (refer to **Table 1** in Appendix 1), or
- using *Excel*'s **NORMSINV** function, with the specified level of significance, α.

(i) For a two-sided hypothesis test
Region of acceptance: $[-z\text{-}crit \leq z \leq +z\text{-}crit]$
Example: For $\alpha = 0{,}05$ the $z\text{-}crit = \pm 1{,}96$ and the acceptance region is $[-1{,}96 \leq z \leq +1{,}96]$

(ii) For a one-sided (lower-tailed) hypothesis test
Region of acceptance: $[z \geq -z\text{-}crit]$
Example: For $\alpha = 0{,}05$ the $z\text{-}crit = -1{,}645$ and the acceptance region is $[z \geq -1{,}645]$

(iii) For a one-sided (upper-tailed) hypothesis test
Region of acceptance: $[z \leq +\ z\text{-}crit]$
Example: For $\alpha = 0{,}05$ the $z\text{-}crit = +1{,}645$ and the acceptance region is $[z \leq +1{,}645]$

Table 11.1 shows commonly used significance levels and their associated *z-limits* for both two-tailed and one-tailed hypotheses tests.

Table 11.1 z-Limits for given levels of significance (one-sided and two-sided tests)

Level of significance (α)	Type of hypothesis test	z-limit(s)
0,01 (1%)	two-sided	±2,58
0,05 (5%)	two-sided	±1,96
0,10 (10%)	two-sided	±1,645
0,01	one-sided lower-tailed	−2,33
0,05	one-sided lower-tailed	−1,645
0,10	one-sided lower-tailed	−1,28
0,01	one-sided upper-tailed	+2,33
0,05	one-sided upper-tailed	+1,645
0,10	one-sided upper-tailed	+1,28

This means that the null hypothesis will be accepted as the true state of nature *if* the *z*-statistic, derived from the appropriate sample statistic, falls within the region of acceptance as defined by the appropriate *z-limits*.

It can be seen that a significance level is related to a confidence level as used in chapter 10. If α defines the significance level, then $(1 - \alpha)$ describes the corresponding confidence level. For *example*, a 5% level of significance corresponds to a 95% confidence level.

HOW TO

To formulate a decision rule for accepting the null hypothesis

On the basis of the defined region of acceptance, a decision rule can be formulated to guide the decision at the conclusion phase (i.e. at *step 4*). The *decision rule* will read as follows:

Do Not Reject H_0

If the sample test statistic (***z-stat***) falls *within* the *region of acceptance*, there *is not* sufficient sample evidence at the given level of significance, α, to reject H_0 in favour of H_1.

Reject H_0 in favour of H_1
If the sample test statistic (***z-stat***) falls *outside* the region of acceptance (i.e. *within* the region of *rejection*), then there *is* sufficient sample evidence at the given level of significance, α, to reject H_0 in favour of H_1.

HOW TO

To choose a level of significance

The lower the significance level, the stronger the findings if the null hypothesis is rejected.

Thus, if H_0 is rejected at a low level of significance, say at $\alpha = 0{,}01$ (as opposed to $\alpha = 0{,}05$), this strengthens the conclusion that the null hypothesis is not the true state of nature for the relevant population parameter being tested. Therefore, choosing a lower level of significance leads to more conclusive evidence about the true state of nature of the relevant population parameter being tested, if the null hypothesis is rejected.

Approach 2 The *p-value* method

An alternative decision rule for the region of acceptance/rejection is called the ***p-value*** method.

The ***p-value*** is the *probability* of observing the sample statistic or a more extreme value of it **if** the null hypothesis were true.

The ***p-value*** method therefore reflects how likely it is that the sample statistic (or a more extreme value) will be observed under the null hypothesised population parameter value.

HOW TO

To interpret the p-value

- A small *p-value* (i.e. closer to zero) indicates a low probability of observing the computed sample statistic if the null hypothesis were true. This provides stronger evidence to reject H_0 in favour of H_1.
- Similarly, a large *p-value* (i.e. closer to one) indicates a high chance of observing the computed sample statistic if the null hypothesis were true. The sample evidence therefore tends to supports H_0.

The following decision rules can be used to decide when the *p-value* is small enough to reject H_0 in favour of H_1.

Decision rules for the *p-value* (based on a significance level of 5%)

(i) [*p-value* > 0,10]

If the *p-value* exceeds 10%, there is *not sufficient* sample evidence to infer that the alternative hypothesis is true. The null hypothesised value is therefore accepted as the true state of nature for the population parameter.

(ii) [0,05 < *p-value* ≤ 0,10]

If the *p-value* lies below 10% but above 5%, then there is *weak* sample evidence to infer that the alternative hypothesis is true. The sample evidence is *not statistically significant* and cannot be used to reject the null hypothesis in favour of the alternative hypothesis.

(iii) [0,01 ≤ *p-value* ≤ 0,05]

If the *p-value* lies below 5% but above 1%, then there is *strong* sample evidence to infer that the alternative hypothesis is true. The sample evidence is *statistically significant.* It can therefore be inferred with strong confidence that the alternative hypothesis is true.

(iv) [*p-value* < 0,01]

If the *p-value* lies below 1% , then there is *overwhelmingly strong* sample evidence to infer that the alternative hypothesis is true. The sample evidence is *statistically highly significant.* It can therefore be inferred with overwhelming confidence that the alternative hypothesis is true.

Figure 11.5 shows this decision rule graphically.

Figure 11.5 Decision rule for **p-values** shown on the probability interval [0 to 1]

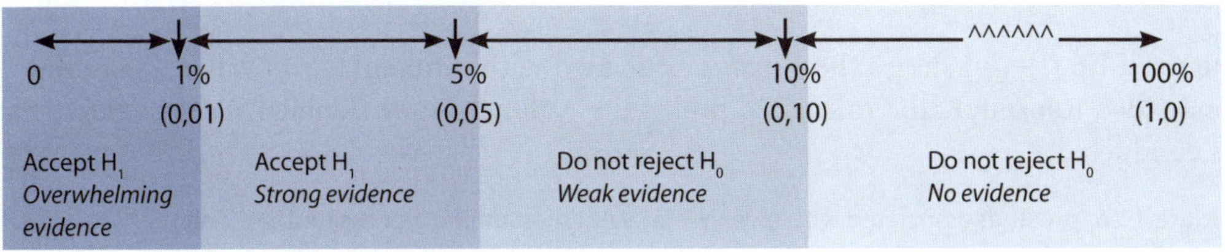

Note (1): The above decision rule applies when the *level of significance is 5%.* Thus any *p-value* above 5% implies *not rejecting* H_0, while a *p-value* below 5% implies rejecting H_0 in favour of H_1.

Note (2): If a different level of significance [e.g. α = 0,10 (10%) or α = 0,01 (1%)] is specified, then the *decision rule* is modified to use this specified significance level as the cut-off point between significant and non-significant results.

To *illustrate*, assume that α = 0,01 (1%) is specified as the significance level for a hypothesis test. Then any *p-value* above 1% implies not rejecting H_0, while a *p-value* below 1% implies rejecting H_0 in favour of H_1. The strength of the rejection (i.e. strongly significant or overwhelmingly significant) depends on how small the *p-value* is below 0,01 (1%).

HOW TO

To calculate the p-value

- The *p-value* is a probability defined by the *tail areas* of a sampling distribution.
- The tail area is determined by the *sample statistic, z-stat*, as computed in *step 2.*

Example

Find the *p-value* for the sample statistic, *z-stat* = 2,16.

Solution

The *p-value* is the *tail area* of a sampling distribution *above* $z = 2{,}16$.

- **Using the *z*-table**

Thus $P(z > 2{,}16) = 0{,}5 - 0{,}4846 = 0{,}0154$ (from **Table 1** in Appendix 1)
Then *p-value* = 0,0154 (1,54%)

- **Using *Excel***

The *Excel* function **=NORMSDIST(2.16)** results in the cumulative probability of

$P(z < 2{,}16) = 0{,}984614$

Thus *p-value* = 1 – 0,984614 = 0,015386

Note:

- In a **one-tailed test** (lower or upper), the *p-value* refers only to the *single area* in *one tail* (lower or upper) of the sampling distribution.
- In a **two-tailed test**, the *p-value* refers to the *combined area* in *both tails* of the distribution. Thus, the probability value, which is computed for one tail, must be doubled to give the *p-value* for a two-tailed test.

Figure 11.6 (i)–(iv) shows the *p-value* associated with different *z-stat* values (assuming a one-sided test only). The calculated probability value must be doubled if a two-sided test is conducted.

Figure 11.6 p-values associated with given **z-stat** values (assuming a one-sided test only)

(i) For *z-stat* = 0,85 *p-value* = 0,1977 Conclusion: Do not reject H_0 – No evidence

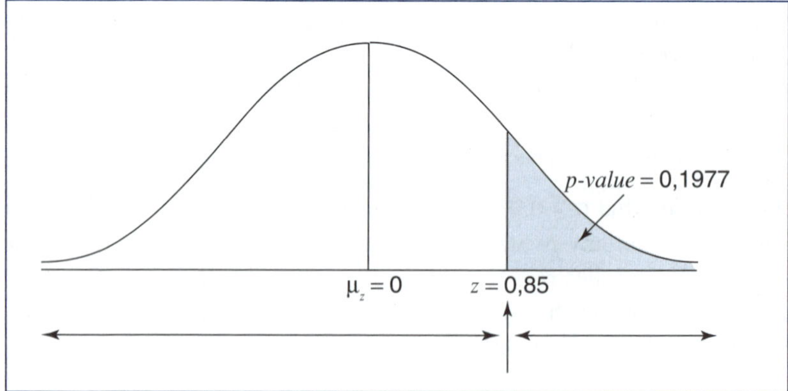

(ii) For *z-stat* = 1,47 *p-value* = 0,0708 Conclusion: Do not reject H_0 – Only weak evidence

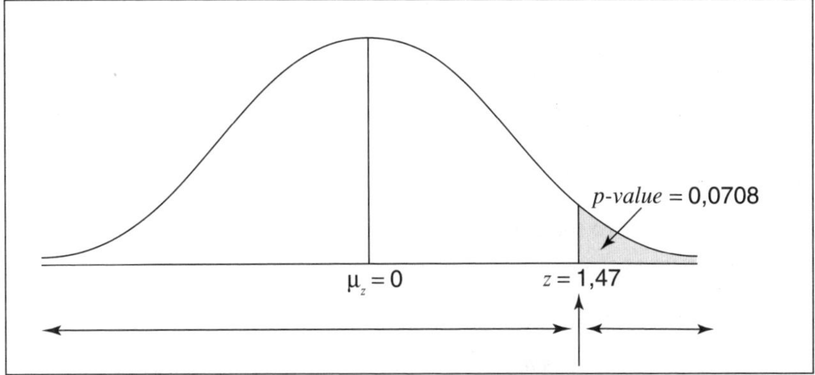

(iii) For *z-stat* = 2,01 *p-value* = 0,0222 Conclusion: Reject H_0 – Strong evidence

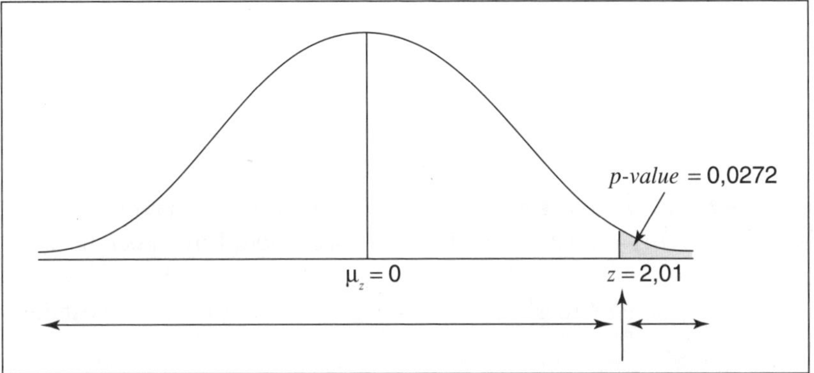

(iv) For *z-stat* = 2,62 *p-value* = 0,0044 Conclusion: Reject H_0 – Overwhelming evidence

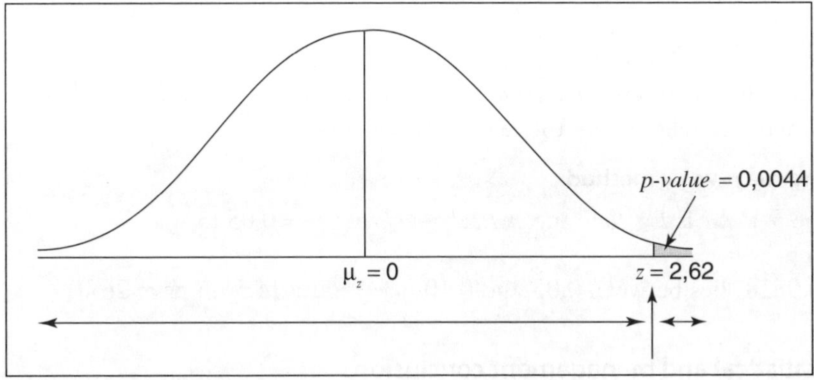

From Figures 11.6 (i)–(iv) it can be seen that the *p-value* is an indication of the "closeness" of the sample statistic to the null hypothesised population parameter.

The *larger* the *p-value*, the *closer* the *sample statistic* is to the *hypothesised population parameter* at the centre position of the null hypothesised sampling distribution and, therefore, the greater the likelihood that this *hypothesised value is true.*

Conversely, the *smaller* the *p-value*, the *further* the *sample statistic* is from the *hypothesised population parameter* at the centre position of the null hypothesised sampling distribution and, in this case therefore, it is highly unlikely that this null hypothesised value is true.

From a management point of view, the *p-value* of a hypothesis test provides a *measure of the intensity* with which the sample evidence (as reflected in the sample test statistic) supports the alternative hypothesis. Low *p-values* (below 5%) show strong to overwhelming support for the alternative hypothesis, H_1, while high *p-values* (above 5% and certainly above 10%) show weak to no support for the alternative hypothesis, H_1.

Step 4 Compare Sample Evidence to the Decision Rule and Draw the Statistical and Management Conclusions

(i) Compare sample evidence to the decision rule

The sample test statistic, ***z-stat*** (or the *p-value*), is now compared to its respective decision rule from *step 3* to allow a statistical conclusion about the validity of the null hypothesis to be drawn. Either approach, namely the *region of acceptance/rejection* approach or the *p-value* approach, can be used.

Example

Assume that: *z-stat* = 1,74 and α = 0,05 (5% significance level) for a two-tailed hypothesis test.

Then *region of acceptance* = [−1,96 ≤ z ≤ 1,96] (see **Table 1** in Appendix 1), and
p-value = P(z > 1,74) = 0,0409 × 2 = 0,0818 (see **Table 1** in Appendix 1)

Note: The actual *p-value* is *doubled* to show the combined tail area for a two-tailed tests.

Approach 1 Using the region of acceptance/rejection method

State whether the sample test statistic, *z-stat*, falls *inside* or *outside* the region of acceptance.

Since ***z-stat*** **(= 1,74)** lies between the *critical z-limits* of ***z-crit*** = **±1,96**, the sample test statistic (*z-stat*) therefore falls *within* the *region of acceptance.*

Approach 2 Using the *p-value* method

State whether the *p-value* is *less than* the *critical p-value* of α = 0,05 (5%).

The *p-value* (= 0,0818) lies between 0,05 and 0,10 (see Figure 11.5 on page 267).

(ii) Draw the statistical and management conclusions

Depending on the outcome of the comparison above, the course of action, as identified by the *decision rule* in *step 3,* is taken.

First, a *statistical conclusion* should be drawn, followed by the *management interpretation* and conclusion. This ensures that the statistical conclusion is correctly translated into valid and consistent management conclusions. The following two points are important:

- accepting the null hypothesis does not necessarily mean accepting the management claim; and

- the *statistical conclusion* refers to whether the *null hypothesis* is *accepted or rejected* on the basis of the sample evidence, and not necessarily to whether the management claim is true or not.

Statistical conclusion

Approach 1 Using the region of acceptance/rejection method

If the sample test statistic (***z-stat***) falls *within* the limits of the *region of acceptance*, the statistical conclusion is that there is *insufficient sample evidence*, at the specified level of significance (α), to infer that H_1 is true. The *null hypothesis* H_0 is *probably true.*

If, on the other hand, the sample test statistic (***z-stat***) falls *outside* the limits of the *region of acceptance* (i.e. within the region of rejection), the statistical conclusion is that there is *sufficient sample evidence*, at the specified level of significance (α), to infer that H_1 is true. The *alternative hypothesis* H_1 is *probably true.*

For the above *example*, the following statistical conclusion is drawn:
"Since *z-stat* (= 1,74) lies within the region of acceptance (i.e. $-1{,}96 \leq 1{,}74 \leq 1{,}96$), there is *insufficient sample evidence*, at the 5% significance level, to reject the null hypothesis H_0 in favour of H_1. The null hypothesis is therefore *probably true.*"

Every statistical conclusion, using the region of acceptance/rejection method, must always be qualified to reflect the lack of complete certainty that the correct decision was made *based on sample evidence only*. The level of significance for the test (e.g. $\alpha = 0{,}05$) is used to qualify the statistical conclusion.

Approach 2 Using the *p-value* method

(Refer to Figure 11.5 on page 267.)
For the above *example*, the decision rule in Figure 11.5 is interpreted as follows:

"Since the *p-value* (= 0,0818) is greater than 0,05 but less than 0,10, (i.e. $0{,}10 < 0{,}0818 < 0{,}05$), there is *weak sample evidence* to reject the null hypothesis H_0 in favour of H_1. The null hypothesis is therefore *probably true.*"

Management conclusion

The *management conclusion* considers the claim in relation to the statistical conclusion.

(i) If the management claim resides in the null hypothesis, then:

- by not rejecting the null hypothesis, the claim is probably true.
- by rejecting the null hypothesis in favour of the alternative hypothesis, the claim is probably false.

(ii) If the management claim resides in the alternative hypothesis, then:

- by not rejecting the null hypothesis, the claim is probably false.
- by rejecting the null hypothesis in favour of the alternative hypothesis, the claim is probably true.

This decision rule is summarised in Figure 11.7 overleaf.

Figure 11.7 Statistical conclusion in relation to the management claim

Location of Claim	Statistical Conclusion	
	Accept Ho	Reject Ho
Claim in H_0	Claim probably true	Claim probably false
Claim in H_1	Claim probably false	Claim probably true

This hypothesis testing procedure, for management claims made about the population parameters of a *single mean* and a *single proportion,* will be illustrated in the remaining sections of the chapter. Chapter 12 considers hypotheses tests for comparing the difference in two means and the difference in two proportions.

11.3 Hypothesis Test for a Single Population Mean (μ) – (σ is known)

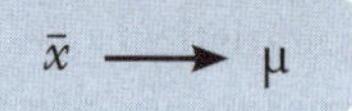

Whenever a management claim or statement is made about the likely value of a *single population mean*, the assertion can be tested using the *sampling distribution of* $\bar{x}$.

Example

Illustrative claims:

- "The *mean employment period* of call-centre employees is claimed to be 16 months."
- "The Life Office Association (LOA) believes *the average value of endowment policies* sold by all financial advisors last year was above R125 000."

The following information is required to conduct a hypothesis test for a single mean:

- a single *sample mean* $\bar{x}$
- a *population standard deviation* σ
- a *sample size* n
- a specified *level of significance* α
- the appropriate *z-transformation formula*, which is:

Formula

$$z\text{-}stat = \frac{\bar{x} - \mu}{\frac{\sigma}{\sqrt{n}}}$$

Note: For the purposes of explanation, worked examples 11.1 to 11.4, will show both approaches to hypothesis testing (namely, *the region of acceptance/rejection* method, and the *p-value* method). However, an analyst would normally only choose one of the two approaches to conduct a hypothesis test.

Example 11.1 Purchase Value of Grocery Baskets study

The Grocery Retailers Association (GRA) believes that grocery shoppers in Cape Town spend on average R175 during each visit to a supermarket. To test this belief, the Association commissioned Market Research e-Afrika (MR e-A) to conduct a survey among a random sample of 360 grocery shoppers at supermarkets in Cape Town.

The survey found that the average value of grocery purchases was R182,4. Assume that the population of grocery *purchase values* is normally distributed and that the standard deviation of the *value of grocery purchase* is R67,5.

Management question

Can the GRA conclude that grocery shoppers spend R175, on average, on each visit to a supermarket? Test statistically, at the 5% level of significance, that the mean value for grocery purchases in Cape Town is R175.

Solution

A two-tailed hypothesis test

Step 1: Define the null and alternative hypotheses

Since the Management question (claim) is to test whether the mean value of grocery purchases by all Cape Town shoppers is equal to R175 only, this is a *two-sided hypothesis test.*

Thus $H_0: \mu = 175$ This represents the *management claim* to be tested.
$H_1: \mu \neq 175$

The *null hypothesis* will be *rejected* in favour of the alternative hypothesis if the sample evidence shows that the actual *mean value of grocery purchases* is either *significantly less* or *significantly more* than the null hypothesised value.

Step 2: Compute the sample test statistic (z-stat)

The sample mean $\bar{x}$ = R182,40 and the sample size, n = 360 shoppers are used to compute the sample test statistic, *z-stat.*

Since the population standard deviation, σ, is known (i.e. given σ = 67,5), the standardised z-distribution test statistic is produced from the formula:

$$z\text{-}stat = \frac{\bar{x} - \mu}{\sigma/\sqrt{n}} = \frac{182{,}4 - 175}{67{,}5/\sqrt{360}} = \frac{7{,}4}{3{,}558} = 2{,}08$$

This *z-stat* value measures the number of standard errors that the sample mean of R182,4 lies from the null hypothesised population mean (μ = R175). In this case, the sample mean lies 2,08 standard errors above the hypothesised mean value.

This sample statistic must now be compared to a decision rule, which is computed in *step 3*, in order to decide if it is "close enough" to the null hypothesised population mean to accept H_0.

Step 3: Decision rule to guide the acceptance/rejection of the null hypothesis

Approach 1 Using the region of acceptance/rejection method

A specified level of significance is needed to find the *critical z-limits* between the regions of acceptance and rejection. In this *example*, $\alpha = 0{,}05$ (5% level of significance).

- **Using the *z*-table**

The appropriate *critical z-limits* are those that identify a *combined area* of $\alpha = 0{,}05$ in the two tails of the z-distribution.
From the **z-table**, the *critical z-limit* is *z-crit* = 1,96 (**Table 1** in Appendix 1)

- **Using *Excel***

The *Excel* function =NORMSINV(0.975) gives the same *z-crit* = 1,96

Since this is a two-tailed test, the *critical z-limits* are given by *z-crit* = ±1,96

Thus the *region of acceptance* for H_0 is $[-1{,}96 \leq z \leq +1{,}96]$

The *decision rule* is then stated as follows:
Do not reject H_0 if *z-stat* falls within the limits of −1,96 and +1,96.
Reject H_0 in favour of H_1 if *z-stat* falls either below −1,96 or above +1,96.

Approach 2 Using the *p-value* method

Given *z-stat* = 2,08 (from *step 2*), the *combined tail area* above *z* = 2,08 and below *z* = −2,08 (because this is a two-tailed test) is found as follows:

- **Using the *z*-table**

$P(z > 2{,}08) = (0{,}5 - 0{,}4812) = 0{,}0188$ (from **Table 1** in Appendix 1)

Thus *p-value* = 0,0188 × 2 = 0,0376 (combined tail areas)

- **Using *Excel***

From *Excel's* function = NORMSDIST(2.08), the cumulative probability = 0,9812

Thus *p-value* = (1,0 − 0,9812) × 2 = 0,0188 × 2 = 0,0376

The *decision rule* is derived from Figure 11.5 on page 267.

Step 4: Compare the sample evidence to the decision rule and draw the statistical and management conclusions

Statistical conclusion

The *statistical conclusion* refers to whether the *null hypothesis* is *accepted or rejected* on the basis of the sample evidence.

Since

- the *p-value* (= 0,0376) lies below 0,05 but above 0,01 (see Figure 11.5), or
- *z-stat* (= 2,08) > *z-crit* (= +1,96) and hence lies *outside* the region of acceptance, there is *strong sample evidence* to support the alternative hypothesis H_1. The alternative hypothesis is therefore probably true.

Figure 11.8 shows the sample test statistic (*z-stat*) and its associated *p-value* in relation to the region of acceptance/rejection (*z-crit*).

Figure 11.8 Purchase Value of Grocery Baskets study – *p*-value, *z*-stat, and region of acceptance

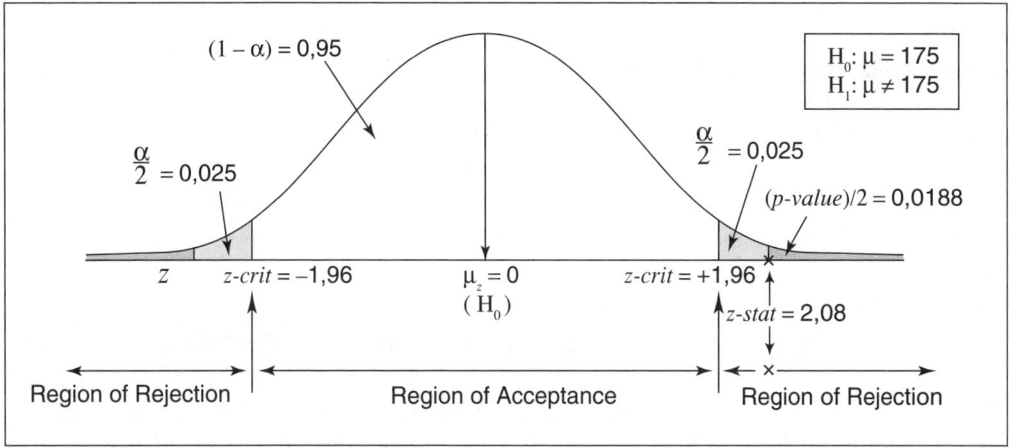

Management conclusion

Since the management claim resided in the null hypothesis (i.e. H_0: μ = 175), which was rejected at the 5% significance level in favour of the alternative hypothesis (i.e. H_1: $\mu \neq 175$), the following management conclusion can be drawn:

"There is strong statistical evidence that the actual mean value of grocery purchases is *not* R175."

Note: Since a two-sided test was conducted, it can only be validly concluded that the mean value is not the null hypothesised value. If it is the analyst's intention to establish whether the mean value is either *less than* or *more than* R175, a *one-sided* (either upper-tailed or lower-tailed) *test* must be conducted. Only then can the conclusions about the direction (either *smaller than* or *larger than*) of the hypothesis value be regarded as valid.

Example 11.2 Executive Weekly Hours Worked study

An international study on executive working hours reported that company CEOs (chief executive officers) worked *more than 60 hours* per week *on average*. The South African

Institute of Management (SAIM) wanted to test whether this norm applied to South African CEOs as well.

A random sample of 90 CEOs from SA companies was drawn and each executive was asked to record his or her number of hours worked during a given week. The sample mean number of *hours worked per week* was found to be 61,3 hours.

Assume a normal distribution for *weekly hours worked* and a population standard deviation of 8,8 hours.

Management question

Do South African CEOs work *more than* 60 hours per week, on average? Test this claim at the 5% level of significance.

Solution

A one-sided (upper-tailed) hypothesis test

Step 1: Define the null and alternative hypotheses

Since the Management question (claim) is to test whether the mean number of hours worked per week by all South African CEOs is *more than* 60 hours, this is a one-sided (upper-tailed) hypothesis test.

Thus $H_0: \mu \leq 60$

$H_1: \mu > 60$ This represents the *management claim* to be tested.

The *null hypothesis* will only be *rejected* in favour of the alternative hypothesis if the sample evidence shows that the actual *mean number of hours worked per week* is *significantly higher* than 60 hours (i.e. the null hypothesised value).

Note: Since the Management question (claim) is a strict inequality (i.e. *more than* 60 hours), the claim must reside in the alternative hypothesis. The null hypothesis must always (and only) contain the equality sign.

Step 2: Compute the sample test statistic (z-stat)

The sample mean $\bar{x}$ = R61,3 hours and the sample size, n = 90 CEOs are used to compute the sample test statistic, *z-stat.*

Since the population standard deviation, σ, is known (i.e. given σ = 8,8 hours), the standardised *z*-distribution test statistic is used. It is produced from the following formula:

$$z\text{-stat} = \frac{\bar{x} - \mu}{\sigma/\sqrt{n}} = \frac{(61{,}3 - 60)}{8{,}8/\sqrt{90}} = \frac{1{,}3}{0{,}9276} = 1{,}4015$$

The *z-stat* value means that the sample mean ($\bar{x}$) of 61,3 hours lies 1,4015 standard errors *above* the null hypothesised population mean μ of 60 hours.

This sample statistic must now be compared to a decision rule, which is computed in *step 3,* to decide if it is "close enough" to the null hypothesised population mean to accept H_0.

Step 3: Decision rule to guide the acceptance/rejection of the null hypothesis

Approach 1 Using the region of acceptance/rejection method

Since this is a one-sided (upper-tailed) test, the level of significance $\alpha = 0{,}05$ is found only in the upper tail of the sampling distribution for the sample mean.

- **Using the *z-table***

The *critical z-limit* is *z-crit* = 1,645 (from **Table 1** in Appendix 1)

- **Using *Excel***

The function **=NORMSINV(0.95)** gives the same *z-crit* = 1,645

Thus the *region of acceptance* for H_0 is $[z \leq +1{,}645]$

The *decision rule* is then stated as follows:

Do not reject H_0 if *z-stat* falls at or below the *z-crit* limit of +1,645.
Reject H_0 in favour of H_1 if *z-stat* falls above +1,645.

Approach 2 Using the *p-value* method

Given *z-stat* = 1,4015 (from *step 2*), the associated *upper tail area* above $z = 1{,}4015$ is found as follows:

- **Using the *z-table***

$P(z > 1{,}4015) \approx P(z > 1{,}40) = (0{,}5 - 0{,}4192) = 0{,}0808$
(**Table 1** in Appendix 1)

Thus *p-value* = 0,0808 (requires only the upper tail area)

- **Using *Excel***

From *Excel's* function **=NORMSDIST(1.4015)** gives a cumulative probability = 0,9195

Thus *p-value* = (1,0 – 0,9195) = 0,0805 (greater precision, using *Excel*)

The *decision rule* is derived from Figure 11.5 on page 267.

Step 4: Compare the sample evidence to the decision rule and draw the statistical and management conclusions

Statistical conclusion

The *statistical conclusion* refers to whether the *null hypothesis* is *accepted or rejected* on the basis of the sample evidence.

Since:

- the *p-value* (= 0,0805) lies above 0,05 but below 0,10 (see Figure 11.5), or
- *z-stat* (= 1,4015) < *z-crit* (= 1,645), and hence lies *within* the region of acceptance of H_0

there is only *weak sample evidence* to support the alternative hypothesis H_1. The null hypothesis is therefore probably true.

Figure 11.9 shows the sample test statistic (*z-stat*) and its associated *p-value* in relation to the region of acceptance/rejection (+*z-crit*).

Figure 11.9 Executive Weekly Hours Worked study – *p*-value, *z*-stat, and region of acceptance

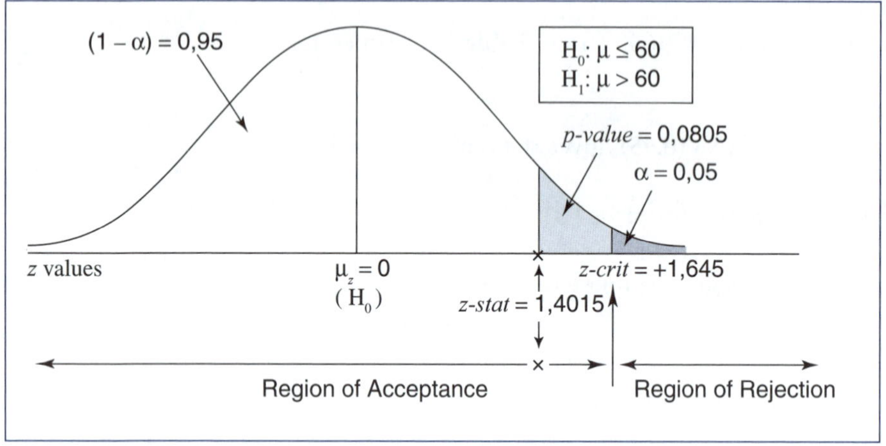

Management conclusion

Recall that the management claim resides in the alternative hypothesis (i.e. H_1: $\mu > 60$). Since the null hypothesis was not rejected at the 5% significance level, the following management conclusion can be drawn:

"There is no *significant statistical evidence* to confirm that South African CEOs work more than 60 hours a week." The SA Institute of Management (SAIM) can therefore be advised that SA CEOs do not appear to be following the norm of the international CEOs of working, on average, more than 60 hours per week.

11.4 Hypothesis Test for a Single Population Mean (μ) – (σ is unknown)

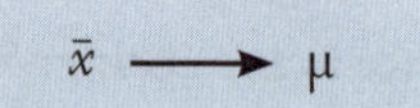

In chapter 10 it was seen that if the population standard deviation, σ, is unknown, it can be estimated by its sample standard deviation, *s*. Under these circumstances, the *Student t* (or *t)* distribution (instead of the standard normal (or *z*) distribution) is used to compute the sample test statistic. The sample test statistic is now called ***t-stat***.

In hypothesis testing for a *single population mean*, the *critical z-limits* (*z-crit*) (which identify the region of acceptance) and the *z-stat* statistic (which is computed from sample data) are replaced by corresponding *critical t-limits* (called ***t-crit***) and ***t-stat*** whenever the **population standard deviation is unknown**.

The *critical t-limits* (***t-crit***) can be found from the ***t*-table** (see **Table 2** in Appendix 1) or by using the *Excel* function

=**TINV(combined two tails probability, degrees of freedom).**

Formula

The ***t-stat*** sample test statistic is derived from the following transformation formula:

$$t\text{-}stat = \frac{\bar{x} - \mu}{\frac{s}{\sqrt{n}}}$$

These adjustments occur in *steps 2* and *3* of the hypothesis testing procedure, as illustrated in the following example.

Example 11.3 Music ipod Market Test study

A large national discount chain is considering whether to extend the range of electronic goods sold at its outlets to include music ipods. To test market response, 20 branches were randomly selected, out of the 410 branches the company operates nationwide, to sell music ipods on a one-month trial basis. A one-week advertising campaign was launched prior to the month-long trial period and sales were monitored during the trial month.

The number of music ipods sold per store during the trial month was:

6	10	2	6	9	10	6	7	4	5	8	5	11	10	4	6	10	5	8	7

Management would only consider introducing the music ipods product range into all stores if *average sales* per store were *at least eight* per month.

Management question

Should management introduce the music ipods into the range of electronic goods at all outlets? Test, at the 5% level of significance, the hypothesis that average music ipod sales per month are likely to be *at least eight* units.

Solution

Refer to the *Excel* file: **C11.1 – ipod sales**, and Table 11.2 overleaf for the data set, the relevant descriptive statistics, and the *t-stat*, *t-crit* and *p-value* for the hypothesis test.

Table 11.2 ipod Test Market sales – data and hypothesis test calculations using *Excel*

Data	Descriptive Statistics – Ipod Sales	
	ipod Sales (Trial Month)	
Ipod Sales		
6	Mean	6,95
10	Standard Error	–0,554764056
2	Median	6,5
6	Mode	6
9	Standard Deviation	2,480980282
10	Sample Variance	6,155263158
6	Kurtosis	–0,805484266
7	Skewness	–0,028548389
4	Range	9
5	Minimum	2
8	Maximum	11
5	Sum	139
11	Count	20
10		
4		
6	**Step 2 - Compute test statistic**	
10	***t-stat***	**–1,893**
5		
8		
7	**Step 3 - Define critical *t*-limits**	
	t-crit (α = 0,05; *df* = 19)	**–1,729**
	p-value	**0,0369**

A one-sided (lower-tailed) test

The numeric random variable is the *number* of *music ipods sold per store.*

This is a hypothesis test for a single mean. However, since the population standard deviation of *music ipod sales per store* is unknown, and the *sample size* is *small* ($n = 20$), the t-statistic must be used to test the hypothesis.

Step 1: Define the null and alternative hypotheses

The management question to be answered (claim to be tested) is whether management can assume that the actual average number of music ipods sold per store is likely to be *at least* 8 units ($\mu \geq 8$).

Since the Management question – expressed in a mathematical form ($\mu \geq 8$) – contains the equality sign within it, this must reside in the null hypothesis. The alternative hypothesis will therefore reflect that music ipod sales per store, on average, are significantly less than (<) 8 units per store. This mathematical expression of the management question means that this is a ***one-sided lower-tailed test***.

Thus $H_0: \mu \geq 8$ This represents the *management claim* to be tested.
$H_1: \mu < 8$

Step 2: Compute the sample test statistic (t-stat)

From the sample data, the sample mean $\bar{x}$ = 6,95 units per store, with a sample standard deviation s = 2,481 units, and sample size n = 20.

Since the population standard deviation, σ, is unknown, the *student t-test statistic* (***t-stat***) is appropriate to use and is computed as follows:

$$t\text{-}stat = \frac{\bar{x} - \mu}{\frac{s}{\sqrt{n}}} = \frac{(6{,}95 - 8)}{\frac{2{,}481}{\sqrt{20}}} = \frac{-1{,}05}{0{,}5548} = -1{,}8926$$

The *t-stat* value means that the sample mean ($\bar{x}$) of 6,95 units lies 1,8926 standard errors *below* the null hypothesised population mean μ of 8 units.

Step 3: Decision rule to guide the acceptance/rejection of the null hypothesis

Approach 1 Using the region of acceptance/rejection method

Since this is a one-sided (lower-tailed) test, the level of significance α = 0,05 is found only in the *lower tail* of the sampling distribution of $\bar{x}$.

The degrees of freedom = n – 1 = 20 – 1 = 19.

- **Using the *t*-table**
  The *critical t-limit* (***t-crit***) is $t_{(0.05,\ 19)} = -1{,}729$ (from **Table 2** in Appendix 1)

- **Using *Excel***
  The function **=–TINV(0.10,19)** gives the same ***t-crit*** = –1,729

Thus the *region of acceptance* for H_0 is $[t \geq -1{,}729]$

The *decision rule* is then stated as follows:

Do not reject H_0 if *t-stat* falls at or above the *t-crit* limit of –1,729.
Reject H_0 in favour of H_1 if *t-stat* falls below –1,729.

Approach 2 Using the *p-value* method

The ***t*-table** is not structured to allow the *p-value* to be read off from it. Therefore it is not possible to derive *p-values* from the *t*-tables.

- **Using *Excel***

The *p-value* can be found using the *Excel* function **=TDIST(x, df, tail)**

This function gives the probability in the tail area(s) of the *t*-distribution above x = *t-stat*. Note that only positive *t-stat* values can be used in the function. The *tail* value indicates whether the test is one-tailed (*tail* = 1) or two-tailed (*tail* = 2).

Thus **=TDIST(1.8926, 19, 1)** gives a result = 0,0369

Hence the *p-value* = 0,0369

The *decision rule* is derived from Figure 11.5 on page 267.

Step 4: Compare the sample evidence to the decision rule and draw the statistical and management conclusions

Statistical conclusion

Since

- the *p-value* (= 0,0369) lies below 0,05 but above 0,01 (see Figure 11.5), or
- *t-stat* (= –1,8926) < *t-crit* (= –1,729), and hence lies *outside* (*below*) the region of acceptance of H_0

there is *strong sample evidence* to support the alternative hypothesis H_1. The alternative hypothesis is therefore probably true.

Figure 11.10 shows the sample test statistic (*t-stat*) and its associated *p-value* in relation to the region of acceptance/rejection (-*t-crit*).

Figure 11.10 Music ipod Test Market study – *p*-value, *t*-stat, and region of acceptance

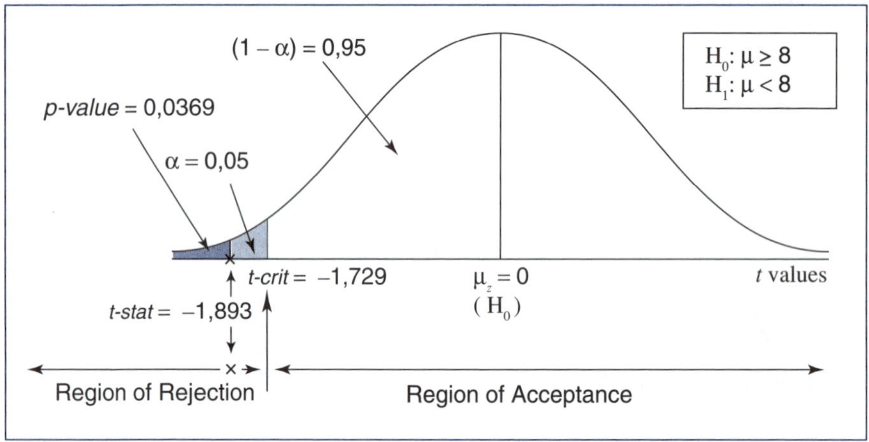

Management conclusion

Recall that the management claim resides in the null hypothesis (i.e. $H_0 : \mu = 8$). Since the null hypothesis was rejected at the 5% significance level, in favour of the alternative hypothesis (i.e. $H_1 : \mu < 8$), the following management conclusion can be drawn:

"There is *strong statistical evidence* to support the view that the monthly mean number of music ipods sold per store is likely to be *less than* eight units."

Based on the company guideline, management would be advised *not to introduce* the new music ipods into their stores nationwide.

HOW TO

When to use the Student t statistic: Review

The t-distribution, theoretically, is the correct standardised distribution to use in place of the z-distribution whenever the *population standard deviation,* σ, is unknown.

However, it can be seen from the ***t-table*** that the t-value depends on the sample size, n, as shown in the degrees of freedom. As n increases, the t-value approaches the z-value, for the same level of significance.

Thus, in practice, if the *sample size exceeds 40* for any hypothesis test of means, the z-statistic can be used as a *good approximation* to the t-statistic. If, however, the *sample size is less than 40,* the *t-statistic must be used.*

To summarise:

- If the population standard deviation, σ, is unknown, and the *sample size* is *small* (i.e. $n \leq 40$), then *always use* the *t-statistic* (with appropriate degrees of freedom) instead of the z-statistic.
- If the population standard deviation, σ, is unknown, and the *sample size* is *large* (i.e. $n > 40$), then the *z-statistic* can be *used* as a *good approximation* to the *t-statistic*, with the sample standard deviation, s, used as an estimate for the unknown population standard deviation, σ.

11.5 Hypothesis Test for a Single Population Proportion (π)

In management, many attributes of consumers, products, employees, etc., are expressed in proportions (or percentages).

Examples

- What percentage of cinema goers are pensioners?
- What proportion of golf balls are undersized?
- What percentage of employees are union members?

Each question above measures a qualitative attribute of a categorical random variable. Thus, when a claim or assertion is made about the central value of a categorical random variable, the claim can be tested by examining the value of a *sample proportion* in relation to a null hypothesised population proportion. Such a hypothesis test is referred to as a test for a *single population proportion.*

The *sampling distribution of the single sample proportion*, as described in chapter 10, is used as the basis for this hypothesis test.

The following information is required:

- the single *sample proportion* p
- the *sample size* n
- a specified *level of significance* α
- the appropriate *z-transformation formula*, which is:

Formula

$$z\text{-}stat = \frac{(p - \pi)}{\sqrt{\dfrac{\pi(1 - \pi)}{n}}}$$

Example 11.4 The Skincare Market Share study

The Auro cosmetics company believes that it holds a 35% share of the market in skincare products in the country. This claim was questioned by a competitor, the Betta cosmetic house. Betta consequently commissioned a market research company to undertake a survey of females who use skincare products. The market research company sampled 360 females who use skincare products. Of the respondents, 108 indicated that they used Auro products exclusively.

Management question (1)

Is the claim made by Auro cosmetics true? Test, at the 1% level of significance, the hypothesis that the market share for Auro skincare products is 35%.

Solution (1)

A two-tailed single proportion hypothesis test

The type of hypothesis test is identified by the following properties:

- The random variable is categorical (qualitative) since it measures the *proportion* of females who use Auro skincare products exclusively.
- It is also a *two-sided (two-tailed)* hypothesis test because the population proportion is being tested for a *specified value only* (i.e. market share = 35%).

Step 1: Define the null and alternative hypotheses

$H_0: \pi = 0{,}35$ This represents the 35% market share claim by Auro cosmetics.
$H_1: \pi \neq 0{,}35$

In this formulation the management claim of a market share of 35% resides in the null hypothesis.

Step 2: Compute the sample test statistic (z-stat)

The appropriate sample statistic is the single sample proportion, p, which is defined as the proportion of females who use Auro skincare products exclusively. This sample statistic must now be expressed in z terms.

Given $x = 108$ (number of respondents who use Auro products exclusively)
$n = 360$

then $p = \frac{108}{360} = 0{,}30$

The sample test statistic relevant to the single sample proportion (*z-stat*) is computed as follows:

$$z\text{-}stat = \frac{(0{,}30 - 0{,}35)}{\sqrt{\frac{(0{,}35(1 - 0{,}35)}{360}}} = -1{,}989$$

Note: The hypothesised population proportion value (π = 0,35) is used to compute the standard error for a single population proportion (i.e. the denominator of *z-stat*).

Step 3: Decision rule to guide the acceptance/rejection of the null hypothesis

Approach 1 Using the region of acceptance/rejection method

The significance level of this hypothesis test is 1% (α = 0,01).

Since this is a *two-tailed* test, the region of acceptance is defined by a *lower* and an *upper z-limit* (± ***z-crit***). The *critical z-limits* are those that identify a combined area of α = 0,01 in the two tails of the z-distribution (i.e. $\frac{\alpha}{2}$ = 0,005 in each tail).

- **Using the *z*-table**
  The *critical z-limit* is *z-crit* = 2,58 (from **Table 1** in Appendix 1)

- **Using *Excel***
  The function **=NORMSINV(0.995)** gives the same *z-crit* = 2,5758 (or 2,58)

Since this is a *two-tailed* test, these *z-limits* are ***z-crit*** = ±2,58

Thus the *region of acceptance* for H_0 is [−2,58 ≤ *z* ≤ +2,58]

The appropriate *decision rule* is then:
Do not reject H_0 if *z-stat* falls between −2,58 and +2,58 inclusive.
Reject H_0 in favour of H_1 if *z-stat* falls below −2,58 or above +2,58.

Approach 2 Using the *p-value* method

Given *z-stat* = −1,989 (from *step 2*), the associated combined tail area below *z* = −1,989 and also above *z* = +1,989 (because this is a two-tailed test) is found as follows:

- **Using the *z*-table**
  P(*z* < −1,989) ≈ P(*z* < −1,99) = (0,5 – 0,4767) = 0,0233 (**Table 1** in Appendix 1)

  Thus *p-value* = 0,0233 × 2 = 0,0466 (require combined tail areas)

- **Using *Excel***
  The *Excel* function = **NORMSDIST(−1.989)** gives a cumulative probability = 0,0233

  Thus *p-value* = 0,0233 × 2 = 0,0466

The *decision rule* is derived from Figure 11.5 on page 267.

Step 4: Compare the sample evidence to the decision rule and draw the statistical and management conclusions

Statistical conclusion

Since

- the *p-value* (0,0466) lies above 0,01 (which was specified as the significance level of the test) (refer to *Note 2* of Figure 11.5 for the interpretation), or
- $-2{,}58 < z\text{-}stat\ (-1{,}989) < +2{,}58$, and hence lies *inside* the region of acceptance of H_0

there is only *weak sample evidence* to support the alternative hypothesis H_1. The null hypothesis is therefore probably true.

Figure 11.11 shows the sample test statistic (*z-stat*) and its associated *p-value* in relation to the region of acceptance/rejection (±*z-crit*).

Figure 11.11 The Skincare Market Share study – *p*-value, *z*-stat, and region of acceptance

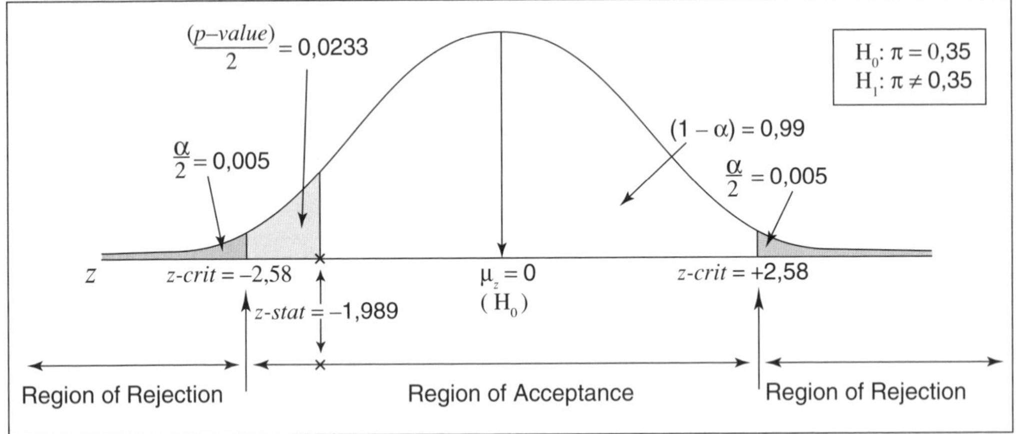

Management conclusion

Recall that the management claim resides in the null hypothesis (i.e. H_0: $\pi = 0{,}35$). Since the null hypothesis was not rejected at the 1% significance level, the following management conclusion can be drawn:

"The Betta cosmetic company has no significant sample evidence to refute Auro's claim that their market share is 35%."

Management question (2)

Assume that the Betta cosmetic company wants to establish whether Auro's market share of skincare products is significantly *less than* 35%.

Use the same marketing research data to test, at the 1% level of significance, whether Auro's market share of skincare products is *less than* 35%.

Solution (2)

One-sided lower-tailed hypothesis test for a single proportion

Step 1: Define the null and alternative hypotheses

The management question requires that a strict inequality relationship be tested (i.e. that $\pi < 0{,}35$). This mathematical expression is therefore reflected in the alternative hypothesis.

The hypotheses are then stated as follows:

H_0: $\pi \geq 0{,}35$

H_1: $\pi < 0{,}35$ This represents the *management question* to be tested.

Step 2: Compute the sample test statistic (z-stat)

The sample test statistic (*z-stat*) is derived from the same sample data as in management question (1) above. The nature of the test (a one-sided or two-sided test) does not affect the *z-stat* value.

Thus **z-stat** = –1,989 [same as for question (1) above]

Step 3: Decision rule to guide the acceptance/rejection of the null hypothesis

Approach 1 Using the region of acceptance/rejection method

The significance level of this hypothesis test is 1% ($\alpha = 0{,}01$).

Since this is a *one-sided lower-tailed* test, the region of acceptance is defined by a *lower z-limit* only. Thus, the *critical z-limit* identifies an area of $\alpha = 0{,}01$ only in the lower tail of the *z*-distribution.

- **Using the *z*-table**
  The *critical z-limit* is *z-crit* = –2,33 (from **Table 1** in Appendix 1)

- **Using *Excel***
  The function **=NORMSINV(0.01)** gives the same *z-crit* = –2,326

Since this is a *one-sided lower-tailed* test, the *z-limit* is **z-crit** = –2,33

Thus the *region of acceptance* for H_0 is [$z \geq -2{,}33$]

The appropriate *decision rule* is then:

Do not reject H_0 if *z-stat* falls at or above –2,33.

Reject H_0 in favour of H_1 if *z-stat* falls below –2,33.

Approach 2 Using the *p-value* method

The *p-value* must reflect only the lower tail area below the **z-stat** = –1,989.

- **Using the *z*-table**
  $P(z < -1{,}989) \approx P(z < -1{,}99) = (0{,}5 - 0{,}4767) = 0{,}0233$ (**Table 1** in Appendix 1)

  Thus *p-value* = 0,0233 (require only lower tail area)

- **Using *Excel***

  The function **=NORMSDIST(–1.989)** gives a cumulative probability = 0,023351

  Thus *p-value* = 0,0233

The *decision rule* is derived from Figure 11.5 on page 267.

Step 4: Compare the sample evidence to the decision rule and draw the statistical and management conclusions

Statistical conclusion

Since

- the *p-value* (0,0233) lies above 0,01 (which was specified as the significance level of the test) (refer to *Note 2* of Figure 11.5 for the interpretation), or
- *z-crit* (–2,33) < *z-stat* (–1,989), and hence lies *inside* the region of acceptance of H_0

there is only *weak sample evidence* to support the alternative hypothesis H_1. The null hypothesis is therefore probably true.

Figure 11.12 shows the sample test statistic (*z-stat*) and its associated *p-value* in relation to the region of acceptance/rejection (-*z-crit*).

Figure 11.12 The Skin Care Market Share study – *p*-value, *z*-stat, and region of acceptance

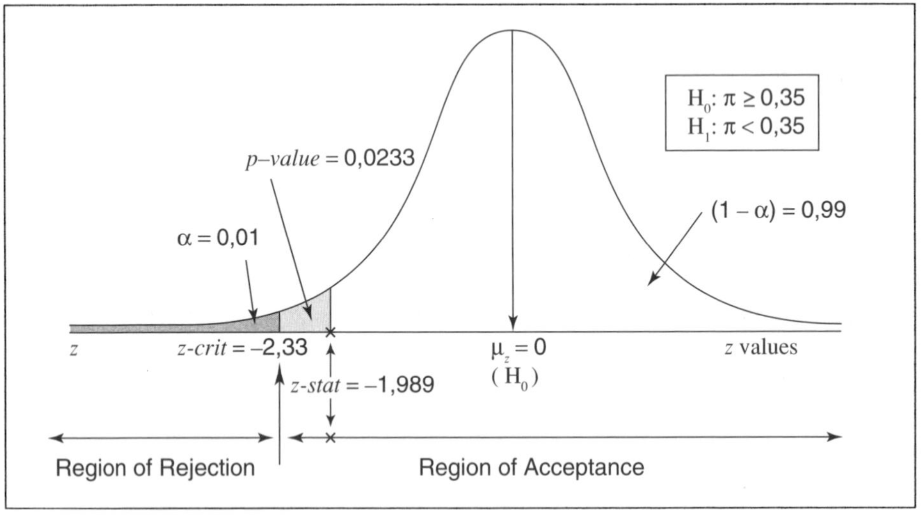

Management conclusion

Recall that the management claim resides in the alternative hypothesis (i.e. H_1: π < 0,35). Since the *null hypothesis* was *not rejected* at the 1% significance level, the following management conclusion can be drawn:

"There is *no significant sample evidence* to conclude that Auro's market share is less than 35%."

Chapter 12 will illustrate the hypothesis testing process for the comparison of population parameters between *two populations*. The population parameters covered are both central location measures, namely, the difference between population means, and the difference between two population proportions.

11.6 Summary

This chapter introduced the concept of *hypothesis testing* as a process by which claims/assertions are made about population parameter central location values. Such claims or assertions are supported or refuted on the basis of sample evidence.

The four steps of hypothesis testing were identified and explained. Two methods of conducting hypothesis tests – the *region of acceptance/rejection* method and the *p-value* method – were introduced.

The full hypothesis testing procedure was illustrated on population parameters for a single population: the single *population mean* and the single *population proportion*. (Chapter 12 will consider inferences when comparing central location measures between two population parameters, namely, the difference between two population means and the difference between two population proportions.)

The process of identifying the correct nature of the hypothesis test – whether the test is two tailed, one-sided lower-tailed or one-sided upper-tailed – was emphasised. In addition, the chapter covered the appropriate formulation of the *null hypothesis* (which must always contain the equality sign) and the *alternative hypotheses*, based on the wording of the management question. Incorrect formulations lead to invalid management conclusions at the end of the test procedure.

The chapter showed that the selection of the appropriate *sample test statistic* for hypothesis tests for a single population mean depends on knowing the *population standard deviation*. If it is known, the z-distribution is used to derive the sample test statistic. Alternatively, if the population standard deviation is unknown but estimated using the sample standard deviation, then the t-distribution must be used to derive the sample test statistic.

Exercises

11.1 For each of the following hypothesis tests, state whether the test is *two-tailed*, one-sided *upper tailed*, or one-sided *lower tailed*, and find the appropriate *area of acceptance*. Also compute the appropriate sample test statistic from the given sample information and decide whether there is sufficient sample evidence to reject the null hypothesis in favour of the alternative hypothesis.

1. $H_0: \mu \leq 560$ $H_1: \mu > 560$
$\bar{x} = 577$ $\sigma = 86$ $n = 120$ $\alpha = 0{,}05$

2. $H_0: \pi \geq 0{,}72$ $H_1: \pi < 0{,}72$
$x = 216$ $n = 330$ $\alpha = 0{,}10$

3. $H_0: \mu = 8{,}2$ $H_1: \mu \neq 8{,}2$
$\bar{x} = 9{,}6$ $s = 2{,}9$ $n = 30$ $\alpha = 0{,}01$

4. $H_0: \mu \geq 18$ $H_1: \mu < 18$
$\bar{x} = 14{,}6$ $s = 3{,}4$ $n = 12$ $\alpha = 0{,}01$

5. $H_0: \pi = 0{,}32$ $H_1: \pi \neq 0{,}32$
$x = 68$ $n = 250$ $\alpha = 0{,}05$

Also compute the *p-value* for each of the test statistics using either the NORMSDIST, the NORMDIST, or the TDIST function in *Excel*. Interpret the meaning of each *p-value*.

11.2 The manager of large shopping mall in George believes that visitors to the mall spend, on average, 85 minutes in the mall on any one occasion. To test this belief, the manager commissioned a study which found that, from a random sample of 132 visitors to the mall, the average *visiting time* in the mall was 80,5 minutes. Assume a population standard deviation of 25 minutes and that *visiting time* is approximately normally distributed.

(i) Formulate a suitable null and alternative hypothesis for this test situation.

(ii) Which test statistic (z or t) is appropriate for this test? Why?

(iii) Conduct the appropriate statistical test at the 5% significance level to support or refute the manager's belief. What management conclusion would be drawn from the findings?

(iv) Use *Excel's* NORMDIST function to compute the *p-value* for the test. What statistical and management conclusion could be drawn from the derived *p-value*?

11.3 A supermarket chain believes that customers to its stores spend half-an-hour or more, on average, doing their purchases. A consumer body wants to verify this claim. They observed the entry and departure times from supermarkets in the chain of 86 randomly selected customers. The sample average time in the store was

27,9 minutes. Assume a population standard deviation of 10,5 minutes and that *shopping time* is approximately normally distributed.

(i) Formulate a suitable null and alternative hypothesis for this test situation.
(ii) Which test statistic (z or t) is appropriate for this test? Why?
(iii) Test the validity of the supermarket's belief. Use α = 0,01.
(iv) Use *Excel's* NORMDIST function to compute the *p-value* for the test and draw the appropriate management conclusion.

11.4 Cape Town harbour is facing congestion resulting from the increase in international trade routed through Cape Town. The Port and Customs authorities at Cape Town harbour claim that imported textile consignments are cleared within an average of 72 hours of the goods being offloaded from a vessel. A local textile importer is not convinced of this and believes that the average clearance time is much longer. He analysed documents of 46 recent consignments and found that the average *clearance time* was 75,9 hours. Assume a population standard deviation of 18 hours and that *clearance time* is approximately normally distributed.

Are the harbour authorities working to their stated clearance times?

(i) Formulate a suitable null and alternative hypothesis to test whether the local importer's claim is justified. Use α = 0,10.
(ii) Also compute the *p-value* using *Excel's* NORMDIST function and draw the appropriate management conclusion.

11.5 The Department of Health is concerned that the average *percentage mark-up* on a particular vitamin product is more than 40%. To test their concern, they sampled 76 pharmacies that sell the product and found that the mean percentage mark-up was 44,1%. Assumed that the population standard deviation of the *percentage mark-up* is 14,7%.

(i) What is the appropriate *test statistic* to statistically determine whether their concern is justified. Why?
(ii) What statistical assumption is made to ensure valid statistical findings?
(iii) Conduct an appropriate statistical test at the 1% level of significance to determine whether the Department of Health's concern is justified. What conclusion can be drawn from the findings?
(iv) Use *Excel's* NORMDIST function to compute the *p-value* for the test and draw the appropriate management conclusion.

11.6 The weight of a standard loaf of white bread is, by law, meant to be 700 gms. The Ryeband Bakery which supplies outlets throughout the Eastern Cape regularly checks the weights of its standard loaf of white bread. If their bread is underweight, on average, they are liable to a fine by the Provincial Department of Health whose inspectors undertake random checks; if they are overweight, on average, the bakery is wasting its ingredients.

On a given day a random sample of 64 loaves is selected and weighed. The sample mean weight was found to be 695 gms with a sample standard deviation of 21 gms. Assume that the weight of bread is approximately normally distributed.

(i) Is Ryeband Bakery complying with provincial government regulations while also not wasting its own resources? Formulate a suitable null and alternative hypothesis and perform the hypothesis test at the 5% level of significance.

(ii) Use *Excel's* TDIST function to compute the *p-value* for the test. Interpret the findings for the Eastern Cape's Provincial Department of Health.

(iii) Reformulate the hypothesis test if it is more important for the bakery to comply with government regulations (i.e. ensure that the average weight of a standard loaf of white bread is not less than 700 gms). Conduct the test at the 5% level of significance and state the conclusion.

11.7 Mores Desserts launched a new flavoured pudding recently. The marketing manager now wants to assess the product's success in the market place. If average *sales per week* were less than R5 500 per outlet, the product would be withdrawn. The results from a sample of 18 supermarket outlets countrywide showed that average *sales per week* were R5 275 with a sample standard deviation of R788.

(i) What statistical assumption should be made about weekly sales to produce reliable results from a hypothesis test?

(ii) Should the new pudding flavour be withdrawn? Advise the marketing manager by performing an appropriate hypothesis test at the 10% level of significance. Also formulate a suitable null and alternative hypothesis.

(iii) Use *Excel's* TDIST function to find the *p-value* of the hypothesis test. Interpret the findings for the marketing manager.

11.8 A company, Marathon Products, has purchased a large quantity of steel wire from Gate and Fence (Pty) Ltd. The supplier, Gate and Fence (Pty) Ltd. claims that the wire has a mean *tensile strength* (i.e. breaking strength) of more than 80 kg. Marathon Products will only accept the consignment of wire if this claim can be supported.

Their quality controller sampled 26 pieces of this wire and found that the sample mean *tensile strength* was 81,3 kg with a standard deviation of 3,6 kg. Assume that tensile strength is approximately normally distributed.

Should Marathon Products accept this steel wire consignment?

(i) Conduct a suitable statistical test at the 5% significant level and advise the management of Marathon Products accordingly.

(ii) Also compute the *p-value* using an appropriate *Excel* function and interpret the findings in the management context.

11.9 Litre cartons of milk are advertised to contain 1 litre of milk. To test this claim, the Consumer Council of SA measured a random selection of 20 cartons from supermarket shelves. They found that the average fill was 0,982 litres with a sample standard deviation of 0,068 litres. Assume that carton fills is approximately normally distributed.

(i) Formulate a suitable null and alternative hypothesis to test the claim that 1 litre cartons of milk are being *under-filled.* Use $\alpha = 0{,}05$.

(ii) Use *Excel's* TDIST function to find the *p-value* of the hypothesis test. Interpret the findings for the Consumer Council of SA.

11.10 A local radio station advertises that *at least* 30% of listeners in its reception area tune into its daily news broadcasts. A company that is considering advertising on this radio station in its news slot wants to test the validity of this statement. They will place adverts in the news timeslots if the radio station's statement can be verified.

The company conducted a telephone survey of 400 randomly selected listeners to test the radio station's statement. If 106 listeners in the survey indicated that they tuned into the local radio's news broadcasts, should the company place adverts in the radio station's news timeslots?

(i) Recommend a course of action the management of the company based on the results of an appropriate hypothesis test conducted at the 5% level of significance.

(ii) Compute the *p-value* of the test statistic using *Excel's* NORMSDIST function. Interpret the *p-value* for the management of the company.

(iii) Confirm the *p-value* in (ii) using *Excel's* NORMDIST function.

11.11 An motor vehicle insurance advisor stated recently in a newspaper report that *more than* 60% of Cape Town motorists *do not have* motor vehicle insurance. A random survey amongst 150 motorists found that 54 *do have* motor vehicle insurance.

(i) Is the motor vehicle insurance advisor's claim valid. Formulate a suitable null and alternative hypothesis and conduct the test using $\alpha = 0{,}05$.

(ii) Use the NORMSDIST function in *Excel* to compute the *p-value* of the test statistic. Interpret its findings in terms of the insurance advisor's claim.

11.12 "Churn" is a term used to describe the rate at which a company looses customers to its competitors. In the telecommunications industry it is believed that the churn rate between cellphone service providers (e.g. Vodacom, MTN, Virgin Mobile and Cell C) is *not more than* 15%.

A telecommunications analyst surveyed a random sample of 560 cellphone subscribers and established that 96 of them had changed service provider within the past year.

(i) Is there sufficient statistical evidence at the 10% significance level to conclude that the churn rate in the telecommunications industry is in excess of 15%? Conduct a suitable hypothesis test and report the findings.

(ii) Use the NORMSDIST function in *Excel* to compute the *p-value* for the test. Interpret the findings for the telecommunications analyst.

(iii) Confirm the *p-value* in (ii) using *Excel's* NORMDIST function.

11.13 A farming cooperative in the Free State buys barley seeds for its farmer members from seed merchants. A particular seed merchant claims that their barley seeds have *at least* a 90% germination rate. Before the farming cooperative will buy from this seed merchant, they want to verify this claim.

A random sample of 300 barley seeds supplied by this seed merchant was tested and it was found that only 260 seeds germinated.

(i) Is there sufficient statistical evidence at the 1% significance level to justify the purchase of barley seeds from this seed merchant? Conduct a suitable hypothesis test and report the findings to the Free State farming cooperative.

(ii) Use the NORMSDIST function in *Excel* to compute the *p-value* for the test. Interpret the findings for the Free State farming cooperative.

(iii) Confirm the *p-value* in (ii) using *Excel's* NORMDIST function.

For the following *Excel*-based exercises, use the **Descriptive Statistics** option in *Excel's* **Data Analysis** to compute appropriate *descriptive measures* to derive the *test statistic, t-stat.* Compute both the *t-crit* values (using TINV) based on the given level of significance of each test; and the *p-value* of the test (using TDIST).

11.14 X10.16 – cost-to-income

A company's *cost-to-income ratio* is a measure of its ability to control its costs. The lower the ratio (expressed as a percentage), the better the cost management within the company. For a company to remain profitable and attract investment, a rule of thumb exists that states that the company's cost-to-income ratio should be *less than* 75%.

An investment analyst wished to test this rule of thumb amongst JSE companies.

Refer to the *Excel* file **X10.16** for the cost-to-income ratios for a sample of 50 JSE companies.

Test, at the 5% significance level, whether the average cost-to-income ratio amongst all JSE companies adheres to the rule of thumb. Interpret the findings.

11.15 X11.15 – kitchenware

The management of a kitchenware company is evaluating the financial viability of one of its stores located in Claremont, Cape Town. One measure they would like to estimate is the mean value of purchases at this store. If the mean value of purchases (in Rands) is likely to be *less than* R150, the management would consider closing the branch.

The management selected a random sample of 50 invoices of recent sales and recorded each transaction value (in Rands). Refer to the *Excel* file **X11.15**.

(i) Use the **Histogram** option in **Data Analysis** to check the assumption of normality. Comment on the findings.

(ii) What recommendation would you make to the management about the continued trading of this Claremont store? Base your recommendation derived from a suitable hypothesis test conducted at the 5% significance level, assuming normality for the distribution of transaction values.

11.16 X11.16 – flight delays

The Airports Company of South Africa (ACSA) is investigating the length of flight delays on departure. It is acceptable to have flight delays due to various environmental and operational factors, provided these delays do not exceed 10 minutes on average. ACSA management would conduct an investigation into the causes of lengthy flight delays if the average delay *significantly exceeds* 10 minutes.

To test whether flight delays do not exceed 10 minutes on average, a random sample of 80 delayed flights over the past month were drawn from airport records. Refer to the *Excel* file **X11.16**.

(i) Use the **Histogram** option in **Data Analysis** to check the assumption of normality. Comment on the findings.

(ii) What recommendation would you make to ACSA management about the average length of flight delays? Should they conduct a detailed investigation in the causes of flight delays? Base your recommendation derived from a suitable hypothesis test conducted at a 10% level of significance. Assume flight delay times are approximately normally distributed.

11.17 X11.17 – medical claims

The manager of the claims department of a medical scheme can motivate to employ additional staff if she can show that the average number of claims being received for processing per day is more than 180. To motivate her need for additional staff, the manager selected a random sample of 100 days over the past year and recorded the number of claims received on each of these days. The data is recorded in the *Excel* file **X11.17**.

(i) Use the **Histogram option** in **Data Analysis** to check the assumption of normality. Comment on the findings.

(ii) Does the claims manager have good statistical evidence to support her request for additional staff? Conduct an appropriate hypothesis test at the 1% level of significance.

11.18 X11.18 – tabloid readership

The *Guardian* tabloid newspaper claims that it has at least 40% of the tabloid readership market. To test this claim, a print-media analyst conducted a survey amongst tabloid readers. Each of the 120 randomly sampled tabloid readers was asked to identify which tabloid newspaper (i.e. *Voice*, *Sun*, *Mail*, or *Guardian*) they buy and read most often. Their responses are recorded in the *Excel* file **X11.18**.

(i) Use the **PivotTable and PivotChart Report** from the **Data** option to produce a pivot table and bar chart of *tabloid readership preferences*. Interpret the summary statistics.

(ii) Test the *Guardian* tabloid's claim by conducting a suitable hypothesis test at the 5% level of significance. Is the *Guardian's* claim overstated? Justify.

11.19 X11.19 - citrus products

Fruitco is an organisation that distributes and markets citrus products throughout the country. It believes that the general awareness of the nutritional value of citrus products is low amongst consumers. Fruitco's current view is that no more than 15% of consumers have a high level of awareness and understanding of the health benefits of consuming citrus products regularly.

Before conducting a national awareness campaign, Fruitco ran a pilot study amongst a random sample of 170 consumers to gauge their level of awareness of the nutritional value of citrus products. Their awareness responses were classified as *low*, *moderate* or *high* and are recorded in the *Excel* file **X11.19**.

(i) Use the **PivotTable and PivotChart Report** from the **Data** option to produce a pivot table and bar chart of the *awareness levels* of the nutritional value of citrus products. Interpret the summary statistics findings.

(ii) Fruitco will launch a national awareness campaign if there is sufficient sample evidence that the level of *high* consumer awareness is *no more than* 15% amongst all consumers. Should Fruitco launch a national awareness campaign? Base your recommendation on a suitable hypothesis test conducted at the 1% level of significance.

Chapter

12

Hypotheses Tests – Comparison between Two Populations (Means and Proportions)

Objectives

When two samples of a random variable are drawn, the question most commonly asked is whether they come from the same population. This chapter uses hypothesis testing procedures to determine whether two samples represent one population or two distinct populations.

The chapter covers hypotheses tests for the difference between two population means, as well as tests for the difference between two population proportions. Both the *z-statistic* and the *t-statistic* are used to conduct these two sample hypotheses tests.

In the case of the two-sample means tests, different hypothesis test procedures are illustrated for the following sampling conditions: independent samples; dependent samples (matched pairs samples); and unknown population variances.

The chapter also illustrates how to set up null and alternative hypotheses for directional tests between two samples.

After studying this chapter, you should be able to:

- distinguish between *difference in means* tests and *difference in proportions* tests
- distinguish between independent means tests and matched pairs tests of means

- recognise when to apply the *z*-test statistic or the *t*-test statistic for two sample tests
- understand the assumptions for each two-sample hypothesis test procedure
- correctly formulate the null and alternative hypotheses from the management question
- perform the hypothesis test for two-sample tests between population means
- perform the hypothesis test for matched pairs samples
- perform the hypothesis test for differences between two population proportions
- correctly interpret the statistical findings in the context of the management question.

12.1 Introduction

Chapter 11 conducted hypotheses tests for a single population parameter, namely a single population mean, if the random variable is numeric (e.g. age, distance, price), or a single population proportion, if the random variable is categorical (e.g. preferred brand, gender, transport mode).

This chapter now *compares* differences of central location parameters between two populations. The hypothesis testing procedure establishes statistically whether two *samples of data* for a random variable have the same central location measure or not.

Statistically, the question being asked is whether the samples are drawn from different populations or the same population. If the populations are different (i.e. central location measures differ), then the factor that distinguishes the samples is assumed to explain the differences in the results. If the populations are the same (i.e. central location measures are equal), then there is no influence from the factor that distinguishes the two samples. This insight could result in managers adopting different courses of action, depending on whether differences are shown to exist or not.

Hypothesis testing will be applied to the following measures of central location:

- a difference between two population *means* ($\mu_1 - \mu_2$) (for numeric measures), and
- a difference between two population *proportions* ($\pi_1 - \pi_2$) (for categorical measures).

Managers can apply hypothesis testing methods to a wide range of management issues to statistically confirm or refute claims.

Examples

- In marketing, a manager can test the belief that "proportionately more females than males prefer rooibos tea".
- In finance, portfolio managers believe that "an equity-weighted portfolio produces higher returns on average than a bond-weighted portfolio".
- In manufacturing, a production manager would like to know whether "on-the-job training leads to higher worker output, on average, than classroom training".

Conclusions drawn from hypothesis tests that compare differences between the central location measures of two populations provide managers with statistically verified findings on which to base their decisions.

12.2 Hypothesis Tests for the Difference Between Two Population Means ($\mu_1 - \mu_2$) Assuming Independent Samples and Known Population Standard Deviations

$$(\bar{x}_1 - \bar{x}_2) \longrightarrow (\mu_1 - \mu_2)$$

Claims or assertions made about differences between the likely values of two population means for the *same* random variable can be tested using the *sampling distribution* of the *difference between two sample means* (as covered in chapter 9).

The following two assumptions are made:
(i) The two population standard deviations are known.
(ii) The two samples are independent of each other.

Illustrative *examples* of differences between the values of two population means for the same random variable are:
- Is the mean *monthly turnover* of the Vodacom outlet at Tygervalley Centre the same as that of the Cavendish Square outlet?
- Is the average *age of female shoppers* at Truworths lower (i.e. are they younger?) than the average age of female shoppers at Foschini?
- Is the mean *level of absenteeism* at Eskom different to that at Telkom?

The following information is required to perform a hypothesis test for the difference between two population means:
- The *sample means* for each independent sample — $\bar{x}_1$ and $\bar{x}_2$
- Each *population's standard deviation* — σ_1 and σ_2
- The *sample size* for each sample — n_1 and n_2
- A specified *level of significance* — α
- The appropriate *z-transformation formula*, which is:

Formula

$$z\text{-}stat = \frac{(\bar{x}_1 - \bar{x}_2) - (\mu_1 - \mu_2)}{\sqrt{\frac{\sigma_1^2}{n_1} + \frac{\sigma_2^2}{n_2}}}$$

where $(\bar{x}_1 - \bar{x}_2)$ = the sample statistic, and
$(\mu_1 - \mu_2)$ = the associated population parameter.

The numerator measures the difference between the sample statistic $(\bar{x}_1 - \bar{x}_2)$ and the hypothesised population parameter $(\mu_1 - \mu_2)$. The denominator measures the standard error of the sample statistic (difference between two sample means). The *z-stat* value then measures the number of standard errors (the denominator) that the sample statistic $(\bar{x}_1 - \bar{x}_2)$ lies from the hypothesised population parameter $(\mu_1 - \mu_2)$ (the numerator).

Example 12.1 Courier Service study

An airfreight company, Doc-Speed cc, is evaluating the delivery time of two motorcycle courier delivery services in Johannesburg to speed up its service of document delivery to clients. The initial belief of Doc-Speed cc is that there is *no difference* between the *average local delivery times* of the two courier services.

Doc-Speed cc used both courier services daily on a random basis over a period of three months for deliveries to similar destinations. *Delivery times* were recorded by a dispatch clerk in the marketing department. Courier service A was used 60 times over this period and the sample mean delivery time was computed to be 42 minutes. Courier service B was used 48 times over the same period and the sample mean delivery time was computed to be 38 minutes.

Assume that the population standard deviation of delivery times for courier service A is 14 minutes; for courier service B assume that it is 10 minutes. Also assume that delivery times are normally distributed.

Management question (1)

Doc-Speed cc wishes to sign a one-year contract with one of the motorcycle courier services after this trial period. They would like to use the services of the more efficient (i.e. quicker) delivery service.

Test the hypothesis, at the 5% level of significance, that there is *no difference* between the mean delivery times of the two courier services.

Solution (1)

Refer to the *Excel* file: **C12.1 – courier service**, shown in Figure 12.1 below for the data set (only the first 33 cases are shown), the relevant descriptive statistics, the *z-stat, z-crit,* and *p-value* for the hypothesis test.

By inspecting the sample means, it would appear that courier A takes longer, on average, to deliver documents to clients than courier B. The question that needs to be addressed statistically, is whether this observed difference in sample means is statistically significant (i.e. a genuine difference), or only due to sampling error (i.e. random sampling or chance sampling). Rigorous hypothesis testing is now used to answer this question.

A two-sided difference between two means hypothesis test

This hypothesis test can be classified as:

- a *difference between two means test*, because the random variable is numeric (i.e. *delivery time*), which is measured between two similar, but independent, populations;
- a *two-sided hypothesis test*, because the difference between the mean delivery times of the two courier services is being tested for only a specified value (i.e. no difference implies that the specified value of the population parameter is zero i.e. $(\mu_1 - \mu_2) = 0$).

Figure 12.1 Courier Service – data and hypothesis test calculations using *Excel*

Microsoft Excel - C12.1 - courier service.xls

	Courier A	Courier B
2	48	20
3	44	23
4	47	50
5	49	42
6	55	48
7	32	50
8	35	15
9	50	40
10	51	60
11	62	44
12	26	45
13	22	35
14	10	50
15	23	38
16	50	50
17	42	55
18	48	26
19	59	50
20	15	42
21	52	40
22	65	38
23	48	44
24	46	50
25	11	38
26	78	42
27	38	21
28	55	38
29	72	24
30	56	36
31	51	30
32	42	31
33	41	48

Table 1 Descriptive statistics - Courier A

	Courier A
Mean	42
Standard Error	1.8077
Median	44
Mode	44
Standard Deviation	14.0024
Sample Variance	196.0678
Kurtosis	0.2767
Skewness	-0.1441
Range	68
Minimum	10
Maximum	78
Sum	2520
Count	60

Table 2 Descriptive statistics - Courier B

	Courier B
Mean	38
Standard Error	1.443989745
Median	39
Mode	50
Standard Deviation	10.0043
Sample Variance	100.0851
Kurtosis	-0.4476
Skewness	-0.1872
Range	45
Minimum	15
Maximum	60
Sum	1824
Count	48

Table 3 z-Test: Two Sample for Means

	Courier A	*Courier B*	Hypothesis Test steps
Mean	42	38	
Known Variance	196	100	
Observations	60	48	
Hypothesized Mean Difference	0		← Step 1
z	1.7294		← Step 2
P(Z<=z) one-tail	0.0419		← Step 3 (One sided test)
z Critical one-tail	1.6449		
P(Z<=z) two-tail	0.0837		← Step 3 (Two sided test)
z Critical two-tail	1.9600		

delivery times data + analysis / Sheet3

Step 1: Define the null and alternative hypotheses

Let population 1 refer to *courier service A.*
Let population 2 refer to *courier service B.*

The management claim is to test for *no difference* between the mean *delivery times* of the two courier services. Hence the null and alternative hypotheses are formulated as a two-sided test, as follows:

$H_0: \mu_1 - \mu_2 = 0$ This represents the *management claim* to be tested.

$H_1: \mu_1 - \mu_2 \neq 0$

Step 2: Compute the sample test statistic (z-stat)

The ***z-stat*** test statistic is derived from the following two samples of data:

Sample 1 (Courier A)	Sample 2 (Courier B)
$n_1 = 60$	$n_2 = 48$
$\bar{x}_1 = 42$ *minutes*	$\bar{x}_2 = 38$ *minutes*
$\sigma_1 = 14$ *minutes*	$\sigma_2 = 10$ *minutes*

The appropriate *z-stat* sample statistic is computed as follows:

$$z\text{-}stat = \frac{(\bar{x}_1 - \bar{x}_2) - (\mu_1 - \mu_2)}{\sqrt{\frac{\sigma_1^2}{n_1} + \frac{\sigma_2^2}{n_2}}} = \frac{(42 - 38) - (0)}{\sqrt{\frac{14^2}{60} + \frac{10^2}{48}}} = 1{,}73$$

Thus $\quad$ ***z-stat*** = 1,73

This result means the sample statistic ($\bar{x}_1 - \bar{x}_2$) is 1,73 standard errors away from the population parameter ($\mu_1 - \mu_2$) that it is attempting to estimate. *Step 3* identifies the decision rule that determines whether this is close enough to accept H_0.

Step 3: Decision rule to guide the acceptance/rejection of the null hypothesis

Both the region of acceptance/rejection method and the *p-value* method will be considered here.

Approach 1 Using the region of acceptance/rejection method

A specified level of significance is needed to find the *critical z-limits* between the regions of acceptance and rejection. In this example $\alpha = 0{,}05$ (5% level of significance).

Since this is a two-tailed test, the *critical z-limits* are given by ***z-crit*** = ±1,96
From *Excel*, the function **=NORMSINV(0.975)** gives the same ***z-crit*** = 1,96.

Thus, the *region of acceptance* for H_0 is $[-1{,}96 \leq z \leq +1{,}96]$

The *decision rule* is then stated as follows:

Do not reject H_0 $\quad$ if *z-stat* falls within the limits of –1,96 and +1,96.
Reject H_0 in favour of H_1 $\quad$ if *z-stat* falls either below –1,96 or above +1,96.

Approach 2 Using the *p-value* method

Given *z-stat* = 1,73 (from *step 2*), the *p-value* is derived from the *combined tail areas* both above $z = 1{,}73$ and below $z = -1{,}73$ (because this is a two-tailed test).

- **Using the *z*-table**
  $P(z > 1{,}73) = (0{,}5 - 0{,}4582) = 0{,}0418$ (**Table 1** in Appendix 1)
  Thus $\quad$ *p-value* = 0,0418 × 2 = 0,0836 (require combined tail areas)

- **Using *Excel***
  Excel's function **=NORMSDIST(1.73)** gives a cumulative probability = 0,9582

  Thus *p-value* = (1,0 – 0,9582) × 2 = 0,0418 × 2 = 0,0836

The *decision rule* is derived from Figure 11.5 in chapter 11 on page 267.

Step 4: Statistical conclusion and Management interpretation

Statistical conclusion

The *statistical conclusion* refers to whether the *null hypothesis* is *accepted or rejected* on the basis of the sample evidence.
Since

- the *p-value* (= 0,0836) is above 0,05 but below 0,10 (see Figure 11.5), or
- –1,96 < *z-stat* (= 1,73) < 1,96 and hence lies *within* the region of acceptance of H_0

there is *weak sample evidence* to support the alternative hypothesis H_1. The null hypothesis is therefore probably true.

Figure 12.2 shows the sample test statistic (*z-stat*), its associated *p-value* and the region of acceptance/rejection (*z-crit*).

Figure 12.2 Courier Service study – *p*-value, *z*-stat, and region of acceptance

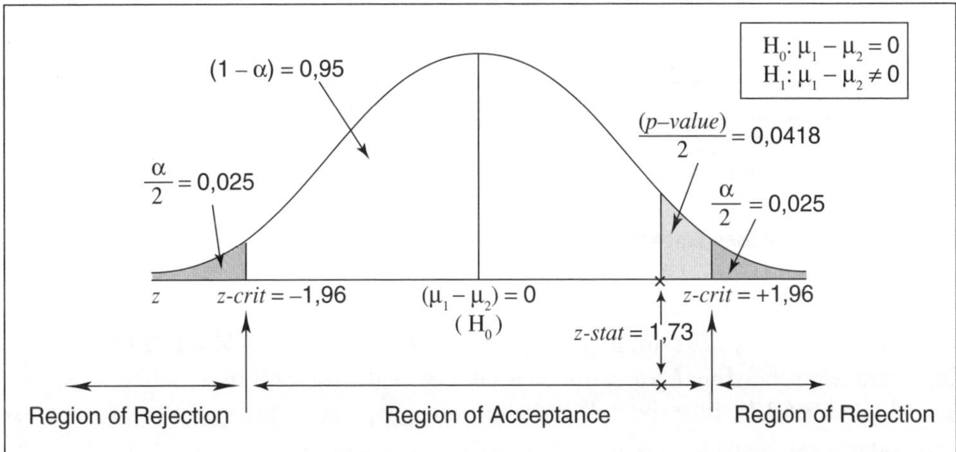

Management interpretation

Since the management claim resided in the null hypothesis (i.e. $H_0: \mu_1 - \mu_2 = 0$), which was not rejected at the 5% significance level, the following *management interpretation* (or conclusion) applies:

"There is *no significant difference* in the mean delivery times between the two courier companies."

As a *management recommendation*, Doc-Speed cc can enter into a contract with either courier service, as each company's delivery time, on average, is no better and no worse than its competitor's.

Solution using *Excel's* Data Analysis

The **Data Analysis** facility in *Excel* can be used to derive all of the above statistical findings, which are needed to draw the appropriate conclusion for the two sample tests of means. The option used is **z-Test: Two Sample for Means.**

Table 12.1 (extracted from **Table 3** of **Figure 12.1**) shows the findings from **Data Analysis** for the Courier Service study. Refer to the *Excel* data file: **C12.1 – courier service.**

Table 12.1 Two sample test of means for the Courier Service study (*Excel*)

z-Test: Two Sample for Means		
	Courier A	**Courier B**
Mean	42	38
Known Variance	196	100
Observations	60	48
Hypothesized Mean Difference	0	
Z	**1,7294**	
P(Z < = *z*) one-tail	0,0419	
Z Critical one-tail	1,6449	
P(Z < = *z*) two-tail	**0,0837**	
Z Critical two-tail	**1,9600**	

The four steps of the hypothesis testing procedure must always be followed.

The *Excel* output provides statistical findings for:

Step 1 that shows the *null hypothesised mean difference* = 0. (i.e. H_0: $\mu_1 - \mu_2 = 0$)

Step 2 that computes the *sample test statistic.*
In Table 12.1, the sample test statistic (***z-stat***) is given by **Z = 1,7294.**

Step 3 that identifies the *decision rule* to accept or reject the null hypothesis.
In Table 12.1, since the null and alternative hypothesis are formulated as a two-tailed test:

- the region of acceptance/rejection is given by: **Z Critical two-tail = 1,96** and
- the *p-value* which is given by: **P(Z < z) two-tail = 0,0837**

The statistical conclusion and management interpretation (*step 4*) are the same as described above.

Management question (2)

Assume, instead, that the management of Doc-Speed cc would like to know whether courier service A *is slower*, on average, than courier service B in its delivery times to clients.

Statistically, this translates into conducting a hypothesis test to establish whether courier service A's mean delivery time is *greater than* courier service B's mean delivery time. Test this hypothesis at the 5% level of significance.

Solution (2)

Use the **Data Analysis** output in Table 12.1 (extracted from **Table 3** of **Figure 12.1**).

The appropriate hypothesis test can now be redefined as:

- a *difference between two means* test (as before), and
- a *one-sided upper-tailed* hypothesis test, because it is required to show that courier service A's mean delivery time is *more than* (*slower*) courier service B's mean delivery time, ($\mu_1 - \mu_2 > 0$).

Step 1: Define the null and alternative hypotheses

Let population 1 refer to *courier service A.*
Let population 2 refer to *courier service B.*

Then H_0: $\mu_1 - \mu_2 \leq 0$
H_1: $\mu_1 - \mu_2 > 0$ This represents the *management question.*

Step 2: Compute the sample test statistic (z-stat)

The same ***z-stat*** test statistic, as computed in (1) above applies to this management question.

i.e. ***z-stat*** = 1,73 or from **Table 12.1, Z = 1,7294**

Step 3: Decision rule to guide the acceptance/rejection of the null hypothesis

Approach 1 Using the region of acceptance/rejection method

Given α = 0,05 (5% significance level) and that this is a one-sided (upper-tailed) test, the *critical z-limit* is given by:

- **Using the *z*-table** *z-crit* = +1,645 (from **Table 1** in Appendix 1)

  or
- **Using the *Excel* function** **=NORMSINV(0.95)** giving *z-crit* = 1,6448 (or 1,645)

  or
- **Z Critical one-tail = 1,6449** from *Excel's* **Data Analysis** (refer to Table 12.1)

Thus, the *region of acceptance* for H_0 is [$z \leq +1{,}645$]

The *decision rule* is then stated as follows:

Do not reject H_0 if *z-stat* falls at or below the upper limit of 1,645
Reject H_0 in favour of H_1 if *z-stat* falls above 1,645

Approach 2 Using the *p-value* method

Given ***z-stat*** = 1,73 (from *step 2*), the *p-value* refers only to the upper tail area above *z* = 1,73 (because this is a **one-sided upper-tailed** test).

- **Using the *z*-table**
  $P(z > 1{,}73) = (0{,}5 - 0{,}4582) = 0{,}0418$ (see **Table 1** in Appendix 1)

  Thus *p-value* = 0,0418

- **Using *Excel***
  = NORMSDIST(1.73) gives a cumulative probability = 0,9582

  Thus *p-value* = (1,0 – 0,9582) = 0,0418

- **Using Data Analysis** (Refer to Table 12.1.)
  The *p-value* for this one-sided test is computed to be: **P(Z < = z) one-tail = 0,0419**

The *decision rule* is derived from **Figure 11.5** on page 267.

Step 4: Statistical conclusion and Management interpretation

Statistical conclusion

The *statistical conclusion* refers to whether the *null hypothesis* is *accepted or rejected* on the basis of the sample evidence.

Since

- the *p-value* (= 0,0418) lies between 0,05 and 0,01 (see Figure 11.5), or
- *z-stat* (= 1,73) > *z-crit* (= 1,645) and hence lies *outside* the region of acceptance of H_0

there is *strong sample evidence* to support the alternative hypothesis H_1. The alternative hypothesis is therefore probably true.

Figure 12.3 below shows the sample test statistic (*z-stat*) and its associated *p-value* in relation to the region of acceptance/rejection (*z-crit*).

Figure 12.3 The Courier Service study – *p*-value, *z*-stat, and region of acceptance

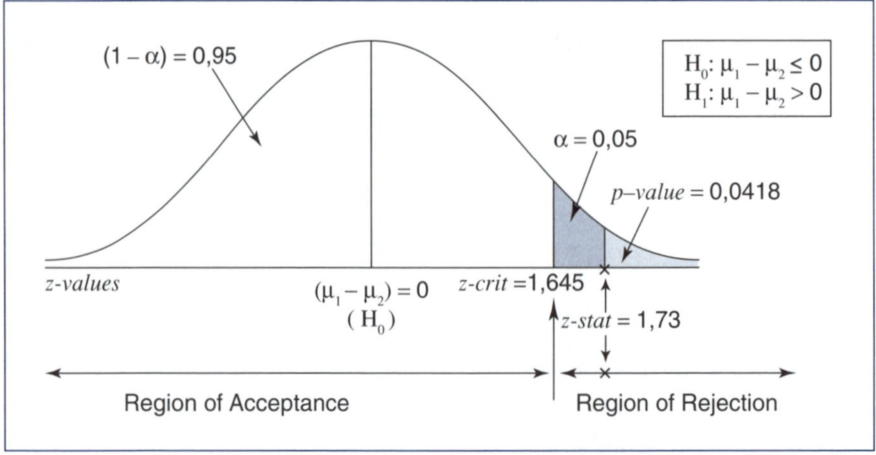

Management interpretation

Since the null hypothesis is rejected at the 5% significance level, and the management claim resides in the alternative hypothesis (i.e. H_0: $\mu_1 - \mu_2 > 0$), the following *management interpretation* applies:

"There is *strong sample evidence* to conclude that, on average, courier A is *significantly slower* than courier B in delivering to the clients of Doc-Speed cc." (Alternatively, "Courier A's mean delivery time is significantly greater than courier B's mean delivery time".)

As a *management recommendation,* Doc-Speed cc should contract with Courier B, because, on average, it delivers documents faster to Doc-Speed's clients than Courier A.

Note: When the findings to Management question (1) and Management question (2) of Example 12.1 are compared, it will be seen that the two-sided test indicated no significant difference, while the one-sided (upper-tailed) test showed that courier service A's mean delivery time is significantly longer (slower) than courier service B's mean delivery time.

This shows that a one-sided hypothesis test is more discriminating (sensitive), as all the Type I error is contained in only one tail, instead of being divided between the two tails. This increases the likelihood of rejecting the null hypothesis when it is false. Also, it will be seen in the two-sided test that ***z-stat*** lay close to the limits of the region of rejection. A higher level of significance, say $\alpha = 0{,}10$ (i.e. 10%) would have resulted in the null hypothesis being rejected in favour of the alternative hypothesis.

12.3 Hypothesis Tests – Difference Between Two Means ($\mu_1 - \mu_2$) Assuming Independent Samples and Unknown Population Standard Deviations

$$(\bar{x}_1 - \bar{x}_2) \longrightarrow (\mu_1 - \mu_2)$$

When the population standard deviations (σ_1 and σ_2) are *unknown*, but assumed to be equal (i.e. $\sigma_1 = \sigma_2$), the appropriate sample test statistic is the *Student t* statistic.

The rationale, as explained in chapter 11 (**section 11.3**), for the use of the *t-test statistic* is the same for the two sample means tests of hypotheses.

Thus, in hypotheses tests for the *difference between two population means*, whenever the **population standard deviations** are **unknown** (but assumed to be equal), then:

- the *t-stat* statistic replaces the *z-stat* statistic as the test statistic for the hypothesis.
- the *t-stat transformation* formula (required at step 2) is:

$$t\text{-}stat = \frac{(\bar{x}_1 - \bar{x}_2) - (\mu_1 - \mu_2)}{\sqrt{s^2\left(\frac{1}{n_1} + \frac{1}{n_2}\right)}}$$

$$\text{where } s^2 = \frac{(n_1 - 1)s_1^2 + (n_2 - 1)s_2^2}{n_1 + n_2 - 2}$$

Note: The s^2 statistic is called a **pooled variance**. It is computed from the two sample standard deviations and is used as an estimate of the common population variance, σ^2, when the two population variances, σ_1^2 and σ_2^2, are unknown, but are assumed to be equal.

- the *degrees of freedom* (*df*) for two independent sample tests equals $(n_1 + n_2 - 2)$. These *degrees of freedom* are required at *step 3* of the hypothesis testing procedure to identify the *critical t-limits* of the regions of acceptance/rejection.
- the effect of *sample sizes:* the *z* statistic (***z-stat***) can be used to approximate the *t* statistic (***t-stat***) when the two *sample sizes* are both *large* (i.e. $n_1 > 40$ and $n_2 > 40$).

Example 12.2 Corporate Financial Performance study

Refer to the *Excel* file: **C12.2 – roi performance**

A financial analyst at Investica wished to establish whether the mean ROI% of *financial companies* is *greater than* the mean ROI% of *manufacturing companies.*

An answer to this question may influence the investment strategy of Investica's portfolio managers. To address this question, the financial analyst selected a random sample of 28 financial companies and found the sample mean ROI% to be 18,714% with a sample standard deviation of 9,645%. For a random sample of 24 manufacturing companies, the sample mean ROI% was found to be 15,125% with a sample standard deviation of 8,823%.

Management question

Test, at the 5% level of significance, whether the financial analyst can conclude that *financial* companies have a *higher* mean ROI% than *manufacturing* companies.

Solution

Figure 12.4 overleaf shows the ROI% data for the two sectors and the *t-test* findings for the hypothesis test between the mean ROI% of the two sectors.

Figure 12.4 Hypothesis test – ROI% between financial and manufacturing companies

Microsoft Excel - C12.2 - roi performance.xls

Finance	Manuf
24	3
5	35
21	20
16	26
15	31
34	29
28	3
33	4
23	12
38	2
4	17
18	21
27	20
22	10
24	12
6	16
14	14
7	13
21	12
32	18
15	8
17	12
7	10
5	15
18	
9	
27	
14	

Table 1 *t*-Test: Two-Sample Assuming Equal Variances

	Finance	*Manuf*	
Mean	18.714	15.125	
Variance	93.026	77.853	
Observations	28	24	
Pooled Variance	86.0468		
Hypothesized Mean Differenc	0		Step 1
df	50		
t Stat	1.3910		Step 2
P(T<=t) one-tail	0.0852		Step 3 (One sided test)
t Critical one-tail	1.6759		
P(T<=t) two-tail	0.1704		Step 3 (Two sided test)
t Critical two-tail	2.0086		

Exploratory data analysis

An inspection of the *sample means* shows that financial companies do appear to have a higher mean ROI% than manufacturing companies. To establish whether this difference is statistically significant in the two populations, a two-sample hypothesis test is conducted.

A one-sided upper-tailed hypothesis test for the difference between two means

This hypothesis test can be classified as:

- a *difference between two means* test (financial and manufacturing ROI%); and
- a *one-sided upper-tailed* hypothesis test, because it is required to show that the mean ROI% of financial companies is *greater* than the mean ROI% of manufacturing companies, $(\mu_f - \mu_m > 0)$.

Step 1: Define the null and alternative hypotheses

Let *f* refer to the population of *financial companies.*
Let *m* refer to the population of *manufacturing companies.*

Then H_0: $\mu_f - \mu_m \leq 0$
H_1: $\mu_f - \mu_m > 0$ This represents the *management question.*

Step 2: Compute the sample test statistic (t-stat)

Table 12.2 (extracted from **Figure 12.4**) shows the ***t-stat*** sample test statistic computed using **Data Analysis**. The option used is **T-Test: Two-sample Assuming Equal Variances**

Table 12.2 t-test hypothesis test results (financial versus manufacturing) (*Excel*)

t-Test: Two-sample Assuming Equal Variances		
	Financial	**Manufacturing**
Mean	18,714	15,125
Variance	93,026	77,853
Observations	28	24
Pooled Variance	86,0468	
Hypothesised Mean Difference	**0**	
df	50	
***t*-Stat**	**1,391**	
P(T<=t) one-tail	**0,0852**	
t Critical one-tail	**1,6759**	
P(T<=t) two-tail	0,1704	
t Critical two-tail	2,0086	

i.e. $t\text{-}stat = 1{,}391$

This result is also computed from the ***t-stat*** transformation formula given on page 308:

$$t\text{-}stat = \frac{(18{,}714 - 15{,}125) - (0)}{\sqrt{(86{,}046)\left(\frac{1}{28} + \frac{1}{24}\right)}} = 1{,}391$$

$$\text{where} \quad s^2 = \frac{[(28-1)(93{,}026) + (24-1)(77{,}853)]}{(28 + 24 - 2)} = 86{,}0468$$

Step 3: Decision rule to guide the acceptance/rejection of the null hypothesis

Approach 1 Using the region of acceptance/rejection method

Given $\alpha = 0{,}05$ (5% significance level) and degrees of freedom = (28 + 24 – 2) = 50, then the *critical t-limit* for this *one-sided* (*upper-tailed*) test, is given by:

- **Using the *t*-table** $t\text{-}crit = t_{(0,05)(50)} = +1{,}676$ (from **Table 2** in Appendix 1)
  or
- using *Excel's* **function =TINV(0.10,50)** which gives the *t-crit* = **1,6759** (or 1,676)
  or
- **t Critical one-tail = 1,6759** from *Excel's* **Data Analysis** (refer to Table 12.2)

Thus the *region of acceptance* for H_0 is $[t \leq +1{,}676]$

The *decision rule* is then stated as follows:

Do not reject H_0 if *t-stat* falls at or below the upper limit of 1,676.
Reject H_0 in favour of H_1 if *t-stat* falls above 1,676.

Approach 2 Using the *p-value* method

Given ***t-stat*** = 1,391 (from *step 2*), the *p-value* refers only to the *upper tail area* above t = 1,391 (because this is a **one-sided upper-tailed** test).

Recall that it is not possible to compute the *p-value* from the ***t*-table**. It can only be computed using *Excel.*

- **Using the *Excel* function TDIST(x, df, tails)**
  With x = 1,391; *degrees of freedom* = 50 and *tails* = 1 (one-tailed test), the function **=TDIST(1.391,50,1)** gives a tail area = 0,0852.

- **Using *Excel's* Data Analysis** (Refer to Table 12.2.)

  The *p-value* for this *one-sided* test is: **P(T < = t) one-tail = 0,0852**
  Thus *p-value* = 0,0852

The *decision rule* is derived from **Figure 11.5** on page 267.

Step 4: Statistical conclusion and Management interpretation

Statistical conclusion

The *statistical conclusion* refers to whether the *null hypothesis* is *accepted or rejected* on the basis of the sample evidence.
Since

- the *p-value* (= 0,0852) lies between 0,05 and 0,10 (see Figure 11.5), or
- *t-stat* (= 1,391) < *t-crit* (= 1,676) and hence lies *inside* the region of acceptance of H_0

there is *weak sample evidence* to support the alternative hypothesis H_1. The null hypothesis is therefore probably true.

Figure 12.5 overleaf shows the sample test statistic (*t-stat*) and its associated *p-value* in relation to the region of acceptance/rejection (*t-crit*).

Figure 12.5 Corporate Financial Performance study – *p*-value, *z*-stat, and region of acceptance

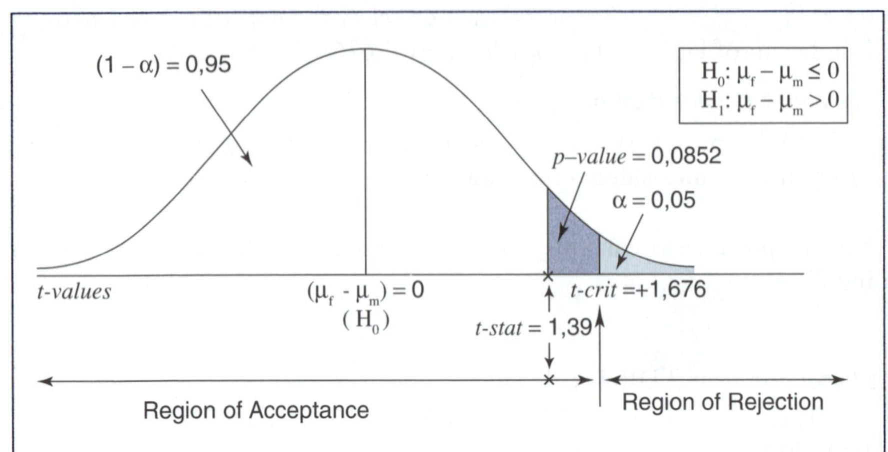

Management interpretation

Since the null hypothesis is supported at the 5% significance level, and the management claim resides in the alternative hypothesis (i.e. H_0: $\mu_f - \mu_m > 0$), the following *management interpretation* applies:

"The statistical evidence *does not support* the view that the mean ROI% of financial companies is greater than the mean ROI% of manufacturing companies".

12.4 Hypothesis Tests – Difference Between Two Means for Dependent Samples – The Matched Pairs Test (μ_D)

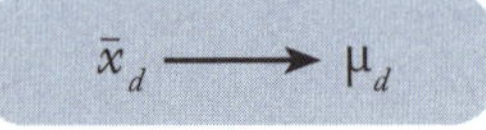

In certain management areas, data is recorded on the *same object* (i.e. consumer, employee, product, company) for a given numeric random variable at two different points in time. In such instances, the two samples of numeric data are *not independent* of each other.

Examples

- An employee's job performance is recorded *before* a training programme and then again *after* the training programme to observe whether any differences occurred.
- A patient's blood pressure is recorded *before* a drug is administered and then again *after* the treatment, to see whether the treatment had any effect on blood pressure.
- Internet usage of subscribers *last year* is compared to the same subscribers' Internet usage *this year*, to determine whether there is any change in usage.

Since the same respondents (i.e. employees, patients, subscribers) are measured twice over time on the same attribute, the two samples are *not independent* and are referred to as **matched pair samples**.

The hypothesis testing procedure that is applied to *matched pairs samples* (dependent samples) is called the **paired *t*-test**.

The purpose of the matched pairs hypothesis tests is to determine whether there has been *any significant change* in the mean level of activity of a numeric random variable under study between the *before* and the *after* measurements.

The Student *t* statistic for Matched Pairs Samples

When the samples are matched, the sample data for each record (respondent) consists of the *difference between paired observations.*

$$x_d = (x_1 - x_2) \qquad \text{(i.e. differences between pairs)}$$

where x_1 = first observation for a respondent
x_2 = second observation for the *same* respondent

This results in a new random sample, x_d, which consists of *differences in paired data.*

The descriptive statistics for this random sample of *paired difference* data are:

Sample mean $\bar{x}_d = \dfrac{\Sigma x_d}{n}$

n = sample size and is equal to the number of paired difference observations

Sample standard deviation $s_d = \sqrt{\dfrac{(x_d - \bar{x}_d)}{(n-1)}}$

In inferential analysis (confidence intervals and hypothesis testing), the sample test statistic is the *student t* statistic, since the population standard deviation of the matched pairs difference (x_d) is unknown. The **Student *t*-test** statistic is always used, regardless of the sample size (n).

Formula

For hypothesis tests and confidence interval estimation, the *Student t* transformation formula is:

$$t\text{-}stat = \frac{(\bar{x}_d - \mu_d)}{\frac{s_d}{\sqrt{n}}}$$

The *population parameter* being tested is the **population mean,** derived from *all differences in matched pair* data. It is stated as follows:

$$\mu_d = (\mu_1 - \mu_2)$$

Example 12.3 Internet Usage study

Refer to the *Excel* file: **C12.3 – internet usage**

A random sample of 12 home Internet users were selected from Telkom's database and their *average monthly Internet usage* (in hours) was identified for the last three months of last year (period 1) and the first three months of this year (period 2).

The period 1 and period 2 *Internet usage* data, extracted from Telkom's technical reports of the 12 randomly selected subscribers, are shown in Table 12.3. The new random sample of *difference in matched pairs* data (x_d) is shown in the **Difference** column.

Table 12.3 Internet Usage data (period 1 and period 2) and the difference measure (in *hours*)

Subscriber	Period 1	Period 2	Difference
A	70	72	–2
B	85	84	1
C	64	68	–4
D	83	88	–5
E	68	68	0
F	91	95	–4
G	65	64	1
H	78	76	2
I	96	102	–6
J	92	94	–2
K	86	89	–3
L	73	75	–2

Management question

Telkom's marketing manager asked the question: "Is Internet usage *increasing*?"

Statistically this translates into testing, at the 5% significance level, whether the average monthly Internet usage has shown a significant increase from period 1 to period 2.

Solution

Figure 12.6 overleaf shows the *Internet Usage* data for the two periods and the *t-test* findings for the *matched pairs* hypothesis test (in **Table 1**).

The *random variable* under study is *Internet usage* (in hours per month) of each subscriber. Since the two samples of Internet usage data (period 1 and period 2) are *related (dependent),* the matched pairs sample design is appropriate. This means computing the *difference statistic* as shown in Table 12.3 (or cells [E2:E14] in Figure 12.6).

This single sample of "*difference data*" is now used in a hypothesis test for a single sample mean (of differences in matched pairs).

The *four steps* of the *hypothesis testing* procedure also apply to matched pairs test data.

Figure 12.6 Hypothesis test – **Internet usage** between period 1 and period 2

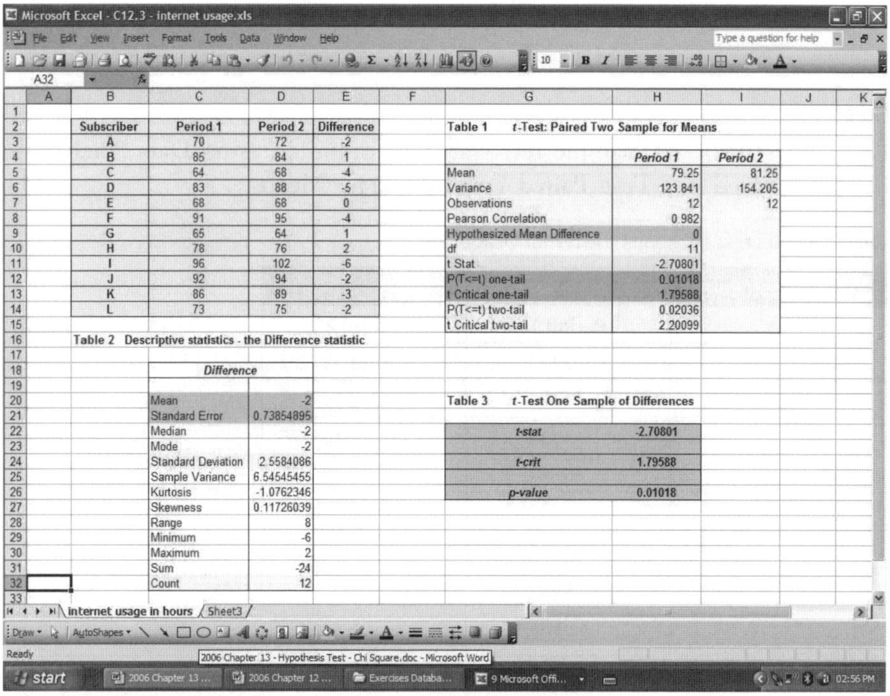

Microsoft Excel - C12.3 - internet usage.xls

Subscriber	Period 1	Period 2	Difference
A	70	72	-2
B	85	84	1
C	64	68	-4
D	83	88	-5
E	68	68	0
F	91	95	-4
G	65	64	1
H	78	76	2
I	96	102	-6
J	92	94	-2
K	86	89	-3
L	73	75	-2

Table 1 *t*-Test: Paired Two Sample for Means

	Period 1	Period 2
Mean	79.25	81.25
Variance	123.841	154.205
Observations	12	12
Pearson Correlation	0.982	
Hypothesized Mean Difference	0	
df	11	
t Stat	-2.70801	
P(T<=t) one-tail	0.01018	
t Critical one-tail	1.79588	
P(T<=t) two-tail	0.02036	
t Critical two-tail	2.20099	

Table 2 Descriptive statistics - the Difference statistic

Difference	
Mean	-2
Standard Error	0.73854895
Median	-2
Mode	-2
Standard Deviation	2.5584086
Sample Variance	6.54545455
Kurtosis	-1.0762346
Skewness	0.11726039
Range	8
Minimum	-6
Maximum	2
Sum	-24
Count	12

Table 3 *t*-Test One Sample of Differences

t-stat	-2.70801
t-crit	1.79588
p-value	0.01018

internet usage in hours / Sheet3

Step 1: Define the null and alternative hypotheses

Since the difference statistic $x_d = (x_1 - x_2)$ is computed by subtracting period 2's Internet usage from period 1's Internet usage, a significant increase in Internet usage (to be tested through the hypothesis test) would be represented by a *negative difference* in the paired data.

Statistically, therefore, the Management question is to show that $\mu_d < 0$. Since this is a strict inequality relationship, the Management question (claim) resides in the alternative hypothesis.

The statistical test is defined as a *one-sided lower-tailed* hypothesis test, as follows:

H_0: $\mu_d \geq 0$

H_1: $\mu_d < 0$ This represents the *management question.*

Step 2: Compute the sample test statistic

- **Using the *t-stat* formula**

The *t-stat* test statistic can be computed using the *t*-formula on page 313, which uses *descriptive statistics* derived from the *difference data* as shown in **Table 2** and **Table 3** of **Figure 12.6.**

$\bar{x}_d$ = (79,25 – 81,25) = 22,00 (period 1 sample mean – period 2 sample mean)

s_d = 2,5584 (using the standard deviation formula on the difference data)

n = 12 (12 subscribers were observed)

Then $$t\text{-}stat = \frac{(-2{,}00 - 0)}{\frac{2{,}5584}{\sqrt{12}}} = \frac{-2{,}00}{0{,}73855} = -2{,}70801$$

- **Using *Excel***

  Table 12.4 shows the ***t-stat*** sample test statistic, computed using **Data Analysis** in *Excel*. The option used is: ***t*-Test: Paired Two Sample for Means.**

Table 12.4 Matched pairs test of means – Internet Usage study

***t*-Test: Paired Two Sample for Means**		
	Period 1	**Period 2**
Mean	79,25	81,25
Variance	123,841	154,205
Observations	12	12
Pearson Correlation	0,982	
Hypothesised Mean Difference	0	
df	11	
***t*-Stat**	**-2,70801**	
P(T<=*t*) one-tail	**0,01018**	
***t* Critical one-tail**	**1,79588**	
P(T<=*t*) two-tail	0,02036	
t Critical two-tail	2,20099	

i.e. $t\text{-}stat = -2{,}708$

Step 3: Decision rule to guide the acceptance/rejection of the null hypothesis

Approach 1 Using the region of acceptance/rejection method

To identify the *critical t-limits*, a level of significance (α), and degrees of freedom are required. The *degrees of freedom* for *matched pairs samples* is:

$$\begin{aligned} \textit{Degrees of freedom } (df) &= \text{number of pairs of data} - 1 \\ &= \text{sample size} - 1 \end{aligned}$$

Given $\alpha = 0{,}05$ (5% significance level) and *degrees of freedom* = (12 – 1) = 11, then the *critical t-limit* for this one-sided (lower-tailed) test, is given by:

- **Using the *t*-table** $t\text{-}crit = t_{(0{,}05)(11)} = -1{,}796$ (from **Table 2** in Appendix 1)

  or

- **Using the *Excel* function** **=–TINV(0.10,11)** which gives the *t*-crit = **–1,79588**

  or

  t Critical one-tail = 1,79588 from *Excel's* **Data Analysis** (refer to Table 12.4)

Note: In *Excel*, the *t-crit* is always given as positive. However, it must be interpreted as −1,79558 (a *negative* value), since this is a *lower-tailed* test.

Thus, the *region of acceptance* for H_0 is $[t \geq -1{,}796]$

The *decision rule* is then stated as follows:

Do not reject H_0 — if *t-stat* falls at or above the lower limit of −1,796.
Reject H_0 in favour of H_1 — if *t-stat* falls below −1,796.

Approach 2 Using the *p-value* method

Given ***t-stat*** = −2,708 (from *step 2*), the *p-value* refers only to the *lower tail area* below *t* = −2,708 (because this is a **one-sided lower-tailed** test).

Note that it is not possible to compute the *p-value* from the ***t*-table**. It can only be computed through the *Excel* function.

- **Using the *Excel* function** TDIST(x, df, tails)
  With *x* = 2,708 (use positive *x* because of symmetry); *degrees of freedom* = 11 and *tails* = 1 (one-tailed test), the function = **TDIST(2.708,11,1)** gives a tail area = 0,0101818 (see **Table 3** of **Figure 12.6**).

- **Using *Excel's* Data Analysis** (Refer to Table 12.4.)
  The *p-value* for this *one-sided* test is **P(T< = t) one-tail = 0,01018**

Thus the *p-value* = 0,0101818.

The *decision rule* is derived from **Figure 11.5** on page 267.

Step 4: Statistical conclusion and Management interpretation

Statistical conclusion

The *statistical conclusion* refers to whether the *null hypothesis* is *accepted or rejected* on the basis of the sample evidence.
Since

- the *p-value* (= 0,01018) lies well below 0,05 (see Figure 11.5), or
- *t-stat* (= −2,708) < *t*-crit (= −1,796) and hence lies *outside* (*below*) the region of acceptance of H_0

there is *strong to overwhelming sample evidence* to reject the null hypothesis H_0 in favour of H_1. The alternative hypothesis is therefore probably true.

Figure 12.7 overleaf shows the sample test statistic (*t-stat*) and its associated *p-value* in relation to the region of acceptance/rejection (*t-crit*).

Figure 12.7 Internet Usage study – *p*-value, *z*-stat, and region of acceptance

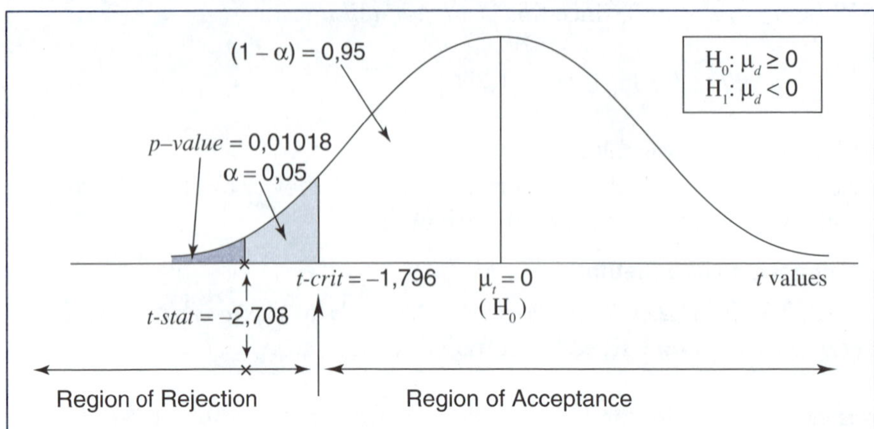

Management conclusion

Since the null hypothesis is rejected at the 5% significance level, and the management claim resides in the alternative hypothesis (i.e. H_0: $\mu_d < 0$), the following *management conclusion* applies:

"The statistical evidence *overwhelmingly supports* the view that the mean Internet usage has *increased significantly* from period 1 to period 2."

Note: The effect of defining the difference statistic (x_d)

The formulation of the null and alternative hypothesis depends on how x_d is defined. If, for *example*, $x_d = x_2 - x_1$ (i.e. period 2's usage – period 1's usage) in the *Internet Usage* study, then a *significant increase* in Internet usage (to be tested through the hypothesis test) would be represented by a *positive difference* in the paired data. This would result in the alternative hypothesis being formulated as: H_1 : $\mu_d > 0$. The hypothesis test is then conducted as a one-sided *upper-tailed* test. Either definition of x_d is acceptable. Both will result in the same statistical and management conclusions.

12.5 Hypothesis Tests – Difference Between Two Proportions

$$(p_1 - p_2) \longrightarrow (\pi_1 - \pi_2)$$

Similarities or differences between two population proportions can be tested using the *sampling distribution* of the *difference between two sample proportions.*

Examples

- In marketing: "Is there a difference in market share between Olé and Flora brands of margarine?"
- In finance/insurance: "For all household insurance policyholders, is the claims ratio higher in Gauteng than it is in KwaZulu-Natal?"

- In production: "Does stamping machine 1 produce a lower defective rate of motor vehicle bumpers than stamping machine 2?"

All three random variables (market share; claims ratio; defective rate) are categorical in nature, since they involve counting the rate of occurrence of each outcome under different scenarios. Hence each Management question can be tested statistically, using a *difference in two proportions* hypothesis test.

To conduct a *hypothesis test* for the *difference between two proportions*, the following information is required:

- the *sample proportions* for each of the two independent samples — p_1 and p_2
- the *sample size* for each sample — n_1 and n_2
- a specified *level of significance* — α
- the appropriate *z-transformation formula*, which is:

Formula

$$z\text{-}stat = \frac{(p_1 - p_2) - (\pi_1 - \pi_2)}{\sqrt{\hat{\pi}(1-\hat{\pi})\left(\frac{1}{n_1} + \frac{1}{n_2}\right)}}$$

where $\hat{\pi} = \frac{x_1 + x_2}{n_1 + n_2}$ $\quad p_1 = \frac{x_1}{n_1}$ $\quad p_1 = \frac{x_2}{n_2}$

$(p_1 - p_2)$ = the sample statistic, and

$(\pi_1 - \pi_2)$ = the associated population parameter

$\hat{\pi}$ = pooled sample proportion

This *z*-distribution assumes that the null hypothesised difference in population proportions $(\pi_1 - \pi_2)$ is zero (i.e. that there is no difference between the two proportions). This assumption is valid for most hypotheses tests of this nature.

Example 12.4 Aids Awareness Campaign study

After a recent national Aids Awareness campaign, a market research company conducted a countrywide survey on behalf of the Department of National Health. The brief was to establish whether the *recall rate* of *teenagers* differed from that of *young adults* between 20 and 30 years of age.

The market research company interviewed 640 teenagers and 420 young adults countrywide. Three hundred and sixty-two teenagers recalled the Aids Awareness slogan used during the campaign, and 260 young adults were able to recall the same Aids Awareness slogan of "Aids: don't let it happen".

Management question (1)

Test, at the 5% level of significance, the hypothesis that there is an *equal recall rate* between teenagers and young adults (i.e. that the campaign was equally effective for both groups).

Solution (1)

Exploratory data analysis

The sample data and sample proportions for each group is given in Table 12.5

Table 12.5 Sample data for the Aids Awareness Campaign study

Sample 1 (Teenagers)	Sample 2 (Young Adults)
$n_1 = 640$	$n_2 = 420$
$x_1 = 362$	$x_2 = 260$
$p_1 = \frac{362}{640} = 0{,}5656$	$P_2 = \frac{260}{420} = 0{,}6190$

From the sample survey data:

- the *recall rate* of *teenagers* is 56,56% and
- the *recall rate* of *young adults* is 61,9%.

By inspection of the sample proportions, it would appear that teenagers have a lower recall rate than young adults. But is this difference statistically significant?

A statistical test for the difference between two proportions will establish, at the 5% significance level, whether this difference is insignificant (i.e. due to chance sampling), or whether it is significant (i.e. a genuine difference).

A two-sided difference between two proportions hypothesis test

This hypothesis test can be classified as follows:

- A *difference between two population proportions* test, because the random variable measures the *proportion of respondents* between two similar populations who could recall the Aids Awareness campaign slogan (i.e. the *recall rate*).
- A *two-tailed* (*two-sided*) hypothesis test, because the difference between two proportions is being tested for a value of zero only. No difference (or equal recall rate) implies that the population parameter value is zero ($\pi_1 - \pi_2 = 0$).

Step 1: Define the null and alternative hypotheses

The claim (or assertion) requires the hypothesis test to show that there is no difference between the proportions of each population (teenagers and young adults) who could recall the campaign slogan. Thus the null hypothesis, which assumes equal proportions, represents the Management question (or claim).

Let population 1 refer to *teenagers.*
Let population 2 refer to *young adults.*

Then $H_0: \pi_1 - \pi_2 = 0$ This represents the *management question* that no difference exists in recall rates.

$H_1: \pi_1 - \pi_2 \neq 0$ This indicates that a *difference exists* between the recall rates of the two population groups.

Step 2: Compute the sample test statistic

Based on the sample data given in Table 12.5, the ***z-stat*** transformation formula, as given on page 319, is computed in two stages, as follows:

(i) The *pooled sample proportion* of p_1 and p_2 is computed:

$$\hat{\pi} = \frac{362 + 260}{640 + 420} = 0{,}5868$$

(ii) This result is then substituted into the *z-stat* formula:

$$z\text{-}stat = \frac{(0{,}5656 - 0{,}6190) - (0)}{\sqrt{(0{,}5868)(0{,}4132)(\frac{1}{640} + \frac{1}{420})}} = -1{,}7277$$

Step 3: Decision rule to guide the acceptance/rejection of the null hypothesis

Approach 1 Using the region of acceptance/rejection method

Given α = 0,05 (5% significance level), then the *critical z-limits* for this two-sided hypothesis test is given by:

- **Using the *z*-table** ***z*-crit** = ± 1,96 (from **Table 1** from Appendix 1)
  or

- **Using the *Excel* function** **=NORMSINV(0.975)** = 1,959964

  Thus, the *region of acceptance* for H_0 is [$-1{,}96 \le z \le +1{,}96$]

The *decision rule* is then stated as follows:

Do not reject H_0 if *z-stat* falls within the interval from –1,96 to +1,96.
Reject H_0 in favour of H_1 if *z-stat* falls below –1,96 or above +1,96.

Approach 2 Using the *p-value* method

Given ***z-stat*** = –1,7277 (from *step 2*), the *p-value* refers to both the *lower and upper tail areas* below *z* = –1,7277 and above *z* = +1,7277 (because this is a **two-tailed** test).

- **Using the *z*-table**
  z = 1,73 (rounded), find P(*z* > 1,73) = (0,5 – 0,4582) = 0,0418 (see **Table 1** in Appendix 1)

  Since this is a two-tailed test, this probability is doubled i.e. 0,0418 × 2 = 0,0836
  Thus *p-value* = 0,0836

or

- **Using *Excel's*** **=NORMSDIST(1.7277)** gives a cumulative probability of 0,9580.
  Then the upper tail probability = (1 – 0,958) = 0,042
  Again, since this is a two-tailed test, this upper tail probability is doubled.

  Thus *p-value* = 0,084

The *decision rule* is derived from **Figure 11.5** on page 267.

Step 4: Statistical conclusion and Management interpretation

Statistical conclusion (1)

The *statistical conclusion* refers to whether the *null hypothesis* is *accepted or rejected* on the basis of the sample evidence.

Since

- the *p-value* (= 0,084) lies between 0,05 and 0,10 (see Figure 11.5), or
- −1,96 < *z-stat* (= −1,7277) < 1,96 and hence *z-stat* lies *within* the acceptance region of H_0

there is *weak sample evidence* to support the alternative hypothesis H_1. The null hypothesis is therefore probably true.

Figure 12.8 shows the sample test statistic (*z-stat*) and its associated *p-value* in relation to the region of acceptance/rejection (*z-crit*).

Figure 12.8 Aids Awareness Campaign study – *p*-value, *z*-stat, and region of acceptance

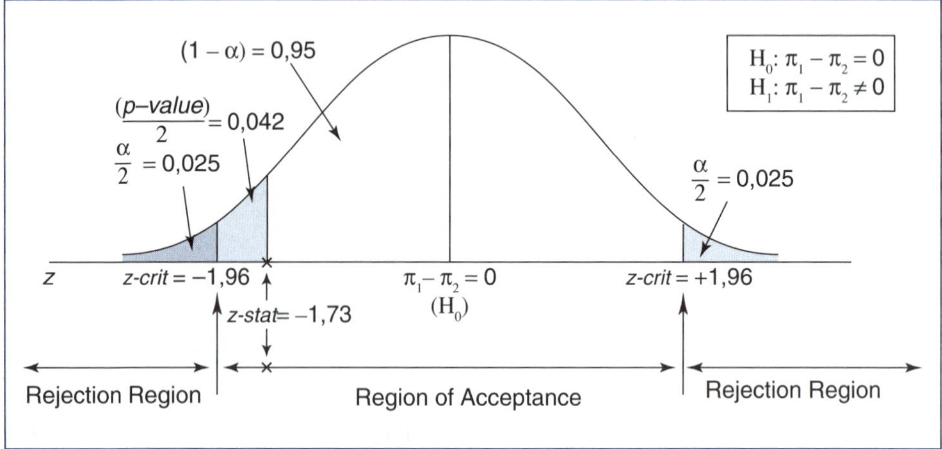

Management conclusion (1)

Since the null hypothesis cannot be rejected at the 5% significance level, and the management claim resides in the null hypothesis (i.e. $H_0: \pi_1 - \pi_2 = 0$), the following *management interpretation* applies:

"There is *no difference* in *recall rate* of the Aids Awareness slogan "*Aids, don't let it happen*" between *teenagers* and *young adults*".

Note: Again, this hypothesis test did not specifically test which population group (*teenagers* or *young adults*) showed the greater rate of recall. A *one-sided hypothesis test* must be formulated and conducted to enable a statistically validated conclusion to be reached as to which population group showed a *higher rate of recall.* This is illustrated in the next question.

Management question (2)

Using the same market research findings as in Management question (1), test at the 5% level of significance, the hypothesis that *teenagers* have a *lower recall rate* for the Aids Awareness campaign slogan than *young adults*.

Solution (2)

Difference between two population proportions – one-sided lower tailed

Again, the nature of the hypothesis test can be identified as follows:

- A *difference between two proportions* test (as above), because the categorical random variable measures the proportion of persons between two independent populations (teenagers and young adults) who could recall the Aids Awareness campaign slogan.
- A *one-sided lower-tailed* hypothesis test, because it is being claimed that population l's proportion (*teenagers*) is strictly smaller (lower) than population 2's proportion (*young adults*). This would be expressed mathematically as $(\pi_1 - \pi_2) < 0$.

Step 1: Define the null and alternative hypotheses

The Management question requires the hypothesis test to establish whether the *proportion of teenagers* who can recall the Aids Awareness slogan is *strictly less* than the *proportion of young adults* who can recall the Aids Awareness slogan. Thus, the alternative hypothesis, which contains the strict inequality (<), represents the Management question (or claim).

Let population 1 refer to *teenagers.*
Let population 2 refer to *young adults.*

Then $H_0: \pi_1 - \pi_2 \geq 0$
$H_1: \pi_1 - \pi_2 < 0$ This represents the *management question.*

Step 2: Compute the sample test statistic

The *z-stat* sample test statistic is the same as for Management question (1) above, as it depends only on the data obtained from the two samples.

i.e. $z\text{-}stat = -1{,}7277$

Step 3: Decision rule to guide the acceptance/rejection of the null hypothesis

Approach 1 Using the region of acceptance/rejection method

Given $\alpha = 0{,}05$ (5% significance level), then the *critical z-limit* for this *one-sided lower-tailed* hypothesis test is given by:

- **Using the *z*-table** $z\text{-}crit = -1{,}645$ (from **Table 1** in Appendix 1)

  or

- **Using *Excel's* function**
  =NORMSINV(0.05) = −1,6448 (from *Excel's* **NORMSINV(cum probab)**)
  The cumulative probability = 5% (i.e. 5% in the lower tail only of this one-tailed test).

Thus, the *region of acceptance* for H_0 is $[z \geq -1{,}645]$

The *decision rule* is then stated as follows:

Do not reject H_0 if *z-stat* falls at or above −1,645.
Reject H_0 in favour of H_1 if *z-stat* falls below −1,645.

Approach 2 Using the *p-value* method

Given ***z-stat*** = −1,7277 (from *step 2*), the *p-value* refers only to the *lower-tail area* below $z = -1{,}7277$ (because this is a **one-sided lower-tailed** test).

- **Using the *z*-table**
  With $z = -1{,}73$ (rounded), find $P(z < -1{,}73) = (0{,}5 - 0{,}4582) = 0{,}0418$

  Thus *p-value* = 0,0418

or

- **Using *Excel***

=NORMSDIST(x) with $x = -1{,}7277$ gives a cumulative probability of 0,04202

Thus *p-value* = 0,04202 (minor differences due to using rounded *z-stat*)

The *decision rule* is derived from **Figure 11.5** on page 267.

Step 4: Statistical conclusion and Management interpretation

Statistical conclusion (2)

The *statistical conclusion* refers to whether the *null hypothesis* is *accepted or rejected* on the basis of the sample evidence.

Since

- the *p-value* (= 0,042) lies between 0,05 and 0,01 (see Figure 11.5), or
- *z-stat* (= −1,7277) < *z-crit* (= −1,645) and hence z-stat lies *outside* the region of acceptance of H_0

there is *strong sample evidence* to support the alternative hypothesis H_1. The alternative hypothesis is therefore probably true.

Figure 12.9 below shows the sample test statistic (*z-stat*) and its associated *p-value* in relation to the region of acceptance/rejection (*z-crit*).

Figure 12.9 Aids Awareness Campaign study – *p*-value, *z*-stat, and acceptance region

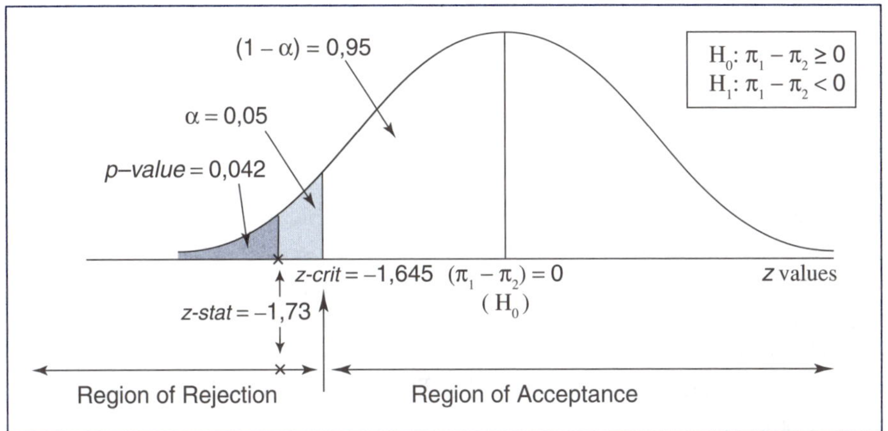

Management conclusion (2)

Since the sample evidence rejects the null hypothesis at the 5% significance level, and the management claim resides in the alternative hypothesis (i.e. $H_1 : \pi_1 - \pi_2 < 0$), the following *management interpretation* applies:

"Teenagers have a significant *lower recall rate* than young adults of the Aids Awareness slogan "Aids, don't let it happen".

Note: The findings between the Management questions differ. The reason for the different conclusions results from the nature of each hypothesis test. A two-tailed hypothesis test (as used in Management question 1) splits the level of significance between two tails and is more likely to lead to a non-rejection of the null hypothesis (because of the wider limits of the region of acceptance). In a one-sided test (as used in Management question 2) the level of significance resides only in one tail. This produces a smaller region of acceptance and is therefore more likely to lead to a rejection of the null hypothesis – especially if the sample test statistic, *z-stat*, lies close to this limit (as is the case in this example).

12.6 Summary

This chapter extended the *hypothesis testing process* to examine for significant differences between two *population parameters*. The same four steps of hypothesis testing were applied to each of these two-sample test situations.

The population parameters tested were the *difference between two population means* and the *difference between two population proportions*. For each population parameter, the chapter emphasised that the appropriate hypothesis testing procedure must be selected. This involves deciding whether the test is two-tailed, one-tailed upper or one-tailed lower, and this is determined by the nature of the claim or assertion made in the Management question.

In addition to choosing the appropriate tailed test, this chapter also distinguished between cases where the population standard deviation is either known or unknown. If known, the *z-test statistic* is the appropriate test statistic to compute at steps 2 and 3 of the hypothesis testing procedure. Alternatively, the *t-test statistic* would be selected. However, for large samples (exceeding 40), the *t*-test statistic is reasonably well approximated by the *z-test statistic* and may thus be used in place of the *t*-test statistic.

This chapter also introduced the concept of the *matched pairs* hypothesis test, which is appropriate when two samples of data for a random variable are taken from the *same respondents*. In such instances, the two samples are *not independent* of each other and a *difference statistic (paired t*-statistic) hypothesis test must then be employed. This test is suitable for many marketing situations where *before/after* measurements are taken on a given numeric random variable.

The use of *Excel's function operations* and the *Data Analysis* option was extensively illustrated for all examples.

Exercises

12.1 A financial analyst asked the following question: "Is the average *earnings yield* of *manufacturing* companies the same as the average *earnings yield* of *retailing* companies?" To examine this question, the analyst randomly sampled 19 manufacturing companies and 24 retailing companies. The descriptive statistics from each sample of companies are as follows:

	Manufacturers	**Retailers**
Sample mean (%)	8,45	10,22
Sample standard deviation	3,32	4,14
Sample size	19	24

(i) What statistical assumptions must the financial analyst make before applying an appropriate hypothesis test between two means?

(ii) Can the financial analyst conclude that there is *no difference* in the average *earnings yield* between companies in the manufacturing and retailing sectors? Provide statistical evidence by conducting a hypothesis test at the 5% level of significance. Also formulate appropriate null and alternative hypotheses.

12.2 The do-it-yourself (DIY) consumer movement has had a profound impact on the retailing business. A recent study conducted by the Centre for Consumer Research examined various traits of persons classified as *do-it-yourselfers* and *non do-it-yourselfers*. One factor considered was a person's *age*. Because younger people are generally healthier, but less affluent, it is reasonable to expect do-it-yourselfers to be younger.

The *ages* (in years) of the persons in the two groups from the study are summarised as follows:

	DIY Consumers	**Non-DIY Consumers**
Mean (years)	41,8	47,4
Standard deviation	15,9	16,2
Sample size	29	34

Do these data support the hypothesis that *do-it-yourselfers* are younger, on average, than *non do-it-yourselfers*?

(i) Draw a conclusion based on a hypothesis test at a 10% level of significance.
Formulate appropriate null and alternative hypothesis for the test.

(ii) Use the TDIST function in *Excel* to find the *p-value* for the test statistic in (i). Interpret the *p-value* in the context of the management scenario.

(iii) Will the conclusion differ if the hypothesis test was conducted at the 5% level of significance? Justify your answer statistically.

12.3 A transport sub-committee of the Cape Town City Council wanted to know if there is any difference in the mean *commuting time* to work between *bus* and *train* commuters. They therefore conducted a small-scale survey amongst bus and train commuters and computed the following descriptive statistics for each sample of commuters.

	Bus Commuters	**Train Commuters**
Sample mean (minutes)	35,3	31,8
Sample standard deviation	7,8	4,6
Sample size	22	36

(i) Test a hypothesis at the 1% significance level that it takes bus commuters longer, on average, to get to work than train commuters. Show appropriate null and alternative hypotheses for the test.

(ii) Based on the statistical findings in (i), which of the two public transport facilities (bus or train) should the City Council prioritise for upgrading to reduce the average commuting time of workers?

12.4 A large multibranch bank is affiliated with both *Mastercard* and *Visa credit cards*. A random sample of 45 Mastercard clients found that their average *month-end credit card balance* was R922. For a random sample of 66 Visa card clients, their average month-end credit card balance was found to be R828.

Assume that the population of month-end credit card balances for Mastercard and Visa card clients is normally distributed, with population standard deviations of R294 for Mastercard clients and R336 for Visa card clients respectively.
Establish at the 5% level of significance, whether there is *any significant difference* in the average month-end credit card balances between Mastercard and Visa card clients.

12.5 A national car dealer has been running job enrichment workshops for its sales consultants over the past three years. To establish if these programmes have been effective, the human resource manager conducted a study amongst the sales consultants to measure their *degree of job satisfaction* on a 10-point rating scale (1 = low job satisfaction, 10 = high job satisfaction).

A random sample of 22 sales consultants who *had not attended* a job enrichment workshop had a mean rating score on job satisfaction of 6,9. The mean rating score on job satisfaction for 25 randomly selected sales consultants who *had attended* a job enrichment workshop was 7,5.

Assume that the population of rating scores for each groups of sales consultants is normally distributed. Also assume a population standard deviation of rating scores for non-attendees of 1,1 and for attendees of job enrichment workshops, assume a population standard deviation of rating scores of 0,8.

Can the human resource manager conclude, at the 5% significance level, that the job enrichment workshops *increase* sales consultants' *job satisfaction levels*? Present your findings to the human resource manager.

12.6 The Medical Aid Board wanted to find out if the mean *time to settle medical claims* of members differs between two major medical schemes – the Green-Aid Fund and the Explorer Fund.

Fourteen Green-Aid Fund medical claims received were randomly selected and monitored and the sample mean time to settlement was 10,8 days. Assume a population standard deviation of 3,2 days. For a random sample of 15 Explorer Fund medical claims received, the average time to settlement 12,4 days. Assume a population standard deviation of 2,3 days. Assume settlement times are normally distributed.

(i) Estimate, with 95% confidence, the actual average settlement time (in days) for claims received by the Explorer Fund only. Interpret the result.

(ii) Can the Medical Aid Board conclude that the Green-Aid medical fund settles claims *sooner*, on average, than the Explorer medical fund? Test this hypothesis at the 5% significance level.

(iii) Use the NORMSDIST function in *Excel* to compute the *p-value* for this test statistic. Interpret the *p-value* in the context of this scenario.

12.7 A consumer testing service compared gas ovens to electric ovens by baking one type of bread in five separate ovens of each type. Assume the baking times are normally distributed. The electric ovens had an average baking time of 0,89 hours with a standard deviation of 0,09 hours and the gas ovens had an average baking time of 0,75 hours with a standard deviation of 0,16 hours.

Test the hypothesis, at the 5% significance level, that gas ovens have a faster baking time, on average, than electric ovens. Assume identical population variances. Show suitable null and alternative hypotheses for the test.

12.8 The operations manager of a computer accessories firm with branches in Cape Town and Durban wants to establish whether their *Cape Town branch* is *performing better* than their *Durban branch* in terms of the average *size of orders* received. Both branches have been operating for only one year.

A random sample of 18 orders from the Cape Town branch had a average order value of R335,2 with a standard deviation equal to R121,5. Orders received by the Durban branch of the firm were also randomly sampled. The average of the 15 orders sampled was R265,6 with a sample standard deviation of R152,2.

(i) Name two assumptions that must be satisfied to produce valid findings from a two sample hypothesis test. How would you examine each of these assumptions statistically? Comment.

(ii) Assume that the above two assumptions are satisfied. Can the operations manager conclude, at the 10% significance level, that the Cape Town branch is performing better than the Durban branch? Justify your answer. Show appropriate null and alternative hypotheses for the test.

(iii) Use the TDIST function in *Excel* to find the *p-value* for the test statistic in (ii). Interpret the *p-value* in the context of the management scenario.

(iv) Will the management conclusion to (ii) change if the level of significance of the hypothesis test was changed to 5%? Justify your answer.
(v) In which conclusion (i.e. either (ii) or (iv)) would the operations manager have greater confidence? Comment.

12.9 X12.9 – package designs

A fruit juice producer conducted a study at a large supermarket to determine the possible influence of different *package designs* on the sales volume of their one-litre cartons of pure apple juice. The apple juice was sold in *pyramid-shaped* cartons for the first 8 weeks, after which the same product packaged in *barrel-shaped* cartons was sold for a further 8 weeks. The data is given in the *Excel* file **X12.9**.
Weekly sales (in cases) were recorded over each period of 8 weeks.

	Carton Shape	
	Pyramid	**Barrel**
	27	25
	16	28
	25	34
	32	28
	20	22
	22	35
	26	18
	22	29
Mean	23,750	27,375
Std dev	4,862	5,706

Assume weekly sales are normally distributed for each carton design and that population variances are equal.

If the marketer's decision is to choose the package design that is likely to lead to larger national sales, on average, should they use the barrel-shaped carton design?

Conduct a suitable one-sided hypothesis tests at the 5% level of significance to determine if the mean weekly sales of pure apple juice in the *barrel-shaped carton* design is *greater than* the mean *weekly sales* in the *pyramid-shaped* carton.

12.10 X12.10 – aluminium scrap

The plant manager at an aluminium processing plant in KZN recorded the *percentage of scrap produced daily* by each of two sheet rolling machines. Scrap is measured as a percentage of daily machine output. The data are recorded in the *Excel* file **X12.10**.

(i) Use the **Histogram** option from **Data Analysis** to examine whether the assumption of normality for the daily percentage scrap of *machine 1* is satisfied. Comment on the findings.

(ii) Use the **Descriptive Statistics** option from **Data Analysis** to derive the 95% confidence interval estimate for the actual mean percentage of scrap produced daily by *machine 2*. Interpret the findings.

(iii) It is company policy that a machine must be stopped and fully serviced if its average daily percentage scrap is 3,75% or more. Test, at the 5% significance level whether *machine 2* is due for a full service. Use the TINV and TDIST functions in *Excel* to find the *critical test statistic* and the *p-value* of the test statistic.

(iv) Can the plant manager conclude that *machine 1*, on average, produces *less scrap* – as a percentage of its daily output – than *machine 2*? Test this hypothesis at the 5% level of significance and advise the plant manager accordingly. Assume population variances are equal.

(v) Identify the *p-value* for the test statistic derived in (iv) and interpret its value in the context of the management question.

12.11 X12.11 – water purification

The quality of drinking water is measured by the number of impurities per million particles of water. If the *average* number of impurities *exceeds* 27 parts per million, water is considered impure and needs further purification before being piped to households for domestic consumption.

The department of health recently conducted a study at two separate water purification plants – one in the Free State, and the other in KZN. Impurity readings were recorded for a random sample of 24 days at the Free State plant and for a separate random sample of 29 days at the KZN plant. The daily impurity readings at each water purification plant are given in the *Excel* file **X12.11**.

(i) Examine the *assumption of normality* for the impurity readings for each of the two purification plants separately. Use the **Histogram** option from **Data Analysis**. Comment on the findings.

(ii) Compute the *descriptive statistics* of the impurity readings from each of the two purification plants separately. Use the **Descriptive Statistics** option from **Data Analysis**. Comment on the assumption of equal variances. Also consider the coefficient of skewness measures for each plant and comment on the assumption of normality of impurity readings for each of the plants.

(iii) Can the health department conclude that the purification process at the Free State plant is producing drinking water of an acceptable standard (i.e. that the average number of impurities does not exceed 27 parts per million). Conduct a suitable hypothesis test at the 1% level of significance to advise the health department. Use the TINV and TDIST functions in *Excel* to find the *critical test statistic* and the *p-value* of the test statistic.

(iv) The manager of the KZN water purification plant claims that their plant produces drinking water which has an average of only 25,5 parts per million of impurities. Examine the validity of this statement by constructing and interpreting a 99% confidence interval estimate of the actual average impurity level of drinking water from the KZN plant. Use the Descriptive Statistics option from Data Analysis to derive the confidence limits.

(v) Is the drinking water produced by the KZN purification plant of a *higher quality* (i.e. fewer impurities, on average) than that of the Free State purification plant? Substantiate your answer by conducting a suitable hypothesis test at the 1% significance level. Assume population variances are equal.

(vi) Identify the *p-value* for the test statistic derived in (v) and interpret its value in the context of the management question.

12.12 X12.12 – herbal tea

The rooibos herbal tea contains the vitamin quercetin which is known to improve blood circulation. To determine whether two brands of the rooibos herbal tea have equal amounts of this vitamin, a chemist conducted a study in which she examined random samples from two rooibos brands of tea – Freshpak and Yellow Label – and recorded the quercetin content of each tea. The data in mg/kg is recorded in the *Excel* file **X12.12**.

Assume that quercetin levels are normally distributed and that their population variances are equal between the two brands of rooibos tea.

(i) Provide statistical evidence at the 5% significance level that there is no difference in the mean quercetin levels between the two brands of rooibos tea tested. Show appropriate null and alternative hypotheses for the test.

(ii) If the producers of the Freshpak brand claim that their brand of rooibos tea contains more quercetin, on average, than the Yellow Label brand, test, at the 5% significance level, whether their claim can be supported by the sample evidence.

12.13 X12.13 – meat fat

The fat content (in grammes per kilogram) of two large consignments of meat received from different regions (one from Namibia and other from the Little Karoo) were analysed by the quality controller of a local meat distributor. Random samples of portions were selected from each consignment and tested. Assume that the data on fat content for the two consignments are normally distributed and that population variances are equal. The data are shown in the *Excel* file **X12.13**.

(i) The meat distributor's policy on fat content is as follows: "Any consignment with an average fat content of *more than* 28 gms per kg will be refused and returned to the producer." Consequently any acceptance/rejection decision must be statistically justified.

Provide statistical evidence, by conducting a suitable hypothesis test at the 5% significance level, as to whether the consignment received from the *Little Karoo* producer only meets the distributor's fat content specifications. What action would you recommend to the meat distributor?

(ii) The distributor is considering signing an exclusive supply contract with the Namibian meat producer. However, they will only sign the contract if it can be shown statistically that the mean fat content is *significant lower* for meat supplied by the Namibian producer compared to the Little Karoo meat producer.

Provide statistical evidence, at the 1% significance level, as to whether the distributor should sign the exclusive supply contract with the Namibian producer. Consider both the *critical test statistic* and the *p-value* in your conclusion.

12.14 Two test products of a new fruit flavoured wheat cereal were market tested recently. Fifty-four of a consumer test panel of 175 households said that they would buy their test product cereal labelled "Fruit Puffs" if offered on the market. Also, 36 of a separate consumer test panel of 150 households said that they would buy their test product cereal labelled "Fruity Wheat". Based on these test market responses of product acceptance, the cereal company will decide which one of the two cereals to launch.

After an inspection of the test market data, the marketing manager concluded that Fruit Puffs are preferred by a larger percentage of households than Fruity Wheat. He therefore believes that they should launch the Fruit Puff cereal.
Provide statistical evidence at the 5% significance level to examine the marketing manager's claim. What recommendation would you make? Show appropriate null and alternative hypotheses for the test.

12.15 A survey amongst a random sample of 250 male and female respondents was conducted into their music listening preferences. Each respondent was asked whether they enjoy listening to jazz.

Of the 140 males surveyed, 46 answered "Yes". Of the 110 female respondents, 21 answered "Yes".

(i) Is there statistical evidence at the 5% level of significance that males and females equally enjoy listening to jazz? What conclusion do you reach?

(ii) Compute the *p-value* for the test statistic in (i) using the **NORMSDIST** function in *Excel*. Interpret its value in the context of the management question.

12.16 A random sample of 300 Status cheque accounts at Capital Bank showed that 48 were overdrawn. When 250 Elite cheque accounts at the same bank were randomly checked, it was found that 55 were overdrawn.

(i) Can the bank manager conclude that more Elite cheque account clients, *proportionately*, are likely to be overdrawn than Status cheque account clients? Test this hypothesis at the 5% level of significance. What conclusion can be drawn?

(ii) Compute the *p-value* for the test statistic in (i) using the **NORMSDIST** function in *Excel*. Interpret its value in the context of the management question.

12.17 X12.17 – disinfectant sales

A supplier of a household disinfectant liquid launched a promotional campaign to increase sales of its 500 ml bottles. Before the campaign, the average weekly sales (in cases sold) were recorded at 12 randomly chosen retail outlets throughout KwaZulu-Natal. Three weeks after the campaign, average weekly sales were again recorded at the same 12 outlets. The average weekly sales (in cases sold) are shown for each of the 12 retail outlets as follows:

	Sales (in cases)	
Outlet	**Before**	**After**
1	12	12
2	8	11
3	14	14
4	9	9
5	13	11
6	15	16
7	10	11
8	12	13
9	10	11
10	13	13
11	12	14
12	10	11

The data is given in the *Excel* file **X12.17**.

Can the suppliers of the household disinfectant conclude that the promotional campaign has been a success? Test at the 5% significance level. What is your conclusion? Show suitable null and alternative hypotheses for the test.

12.18 X12.18 – performance ratings

The human resources department of Escom – an national electricity supplier – ran a series of workshops and seminars for its field employees aimed at increasing their motivation and productivity. To test the effectiveness of this programme, the training manager randomly selected 18 field employees and recorded their most recent performance ratings (conducted after the workshop programme) and their ratings prior to attending the workshops. Performance ratings are scored from 1 to 20. The results are available in the *Excel* file **X12.18**. Assume performance rating scores are normally distributed.

	Performance Rating	
Employee	**Before**	**After**
1	12,8	13,1
2	8,5	9,2
3	10,2	12,6
4	8,3	7,8
5	13,1	14
6	11,2	12,1
7	9,3	9,7
8	6,6	7,5
9	14,8	15,2
10	11,2	11,9
11	14,1	13,8
12	7,8	8,1
13	10,6	10,2
14	12,7	12,9
15	9,8	10,2
16	14,3	13,8
17	13,8	13,9
18	10,1	9,6

(i) Are the two samples of performance rating scores independent or not? Why or why not?

(ii) Has the workshop programme been effective for Escom field workers in general? Provide statistical evidence by conducting a suitable hypothesis test at the 5% level of significance. Also formulate appropriate null and alternative hypotheses for the test.

12.19 X12.19 – household debt

The debt ratio of 10 households was monitored from a year ago when the prime interest rate was 6% to the current period where the prime interest rate has risen to 11%. The analyst wanted to find out if the increase in prime interest rate has had a significant impact on reducing the average level of household debt. Assume that the household debt ratio is normally distributed. The data on household debt from a year ago and currently is given in the *Excel* file **X12.19**.

	Household debt ratio	
Household	**Year ago**	**Current**
H1	45	43
H2	39	37
H3	46	46
H4	51	48
H5	38	40
H6	31	29
H7	37	36
H8	43	44
H9	41	37
H10	34	33

(i) At the 5% level of significance, can the analyst conclude that the increase in prime interest rate from 6% a year ago to 11% currently has lead to a significant reduction in the average level of household debt? Formulate a suitable null and alternative hypothesis for the test.

(ii) What assumption is necessary to perform the hypothesis test in (i).

(iii) Identify the *p-value* for the test statistic and interpret its meaning in the context of the analyst's question.

12.20 X12.20 – jeans purchase

A survey was conducted recently amongst young adults (under 35 years) to examine their jeans purchasing behaviour. A random sample of 45 young adults who indicated that they wear jeans often were interviewed and asked to respond to the following questions:

Question 1	Age (in years)
Question 2	Gender
Question 3	How much did you spend on your last clothing purchase occasion?
Question 4	What brand of jeans do you prefer to wear? Choices: Lee, Wrangler, Levis
Question 5	How much did you pay for your most recent purchase of jeans?
Question 6	Which word best describes why you wear jeans often? Choices: Comfortable, Stylish, Convenient

The response data is given in the *Excel* file **X12.20**.

Assume that the purchase value of jeans is normally distributed. Also assume that population variances are equal. For each hypothesis test, show appropriate null and alternative hypotheses.

(i) Refer to the responses to Question 5. Can the researcher conclude that females tend to pay more, on average, for their jeans than males? Justify your answer statistically at the 5% level of significance. See worksheet **data (i)**.

(ii) Refer to the responses to Question 4 and Question 5. Is there a difference in the *average price of jeans* between the Wrangler and Levis brands? Test at the 5% level of significance. See worksheet **data (ii)**.

(iii) Refer to the responses to Question 1 and Question 4. The researcher is of the opinion that those respondents who prefer the Levi brand of jeans are younger, on average, than respondents who prefer the Lee brand. Provide statistical evidence at the 5% level of significance to support or refute the researcher's belief. What is your conclusion? See worksheet **data (iii)**.

(iv) Construct a two-way pivot table between *gender* (question 2) and *jeans brand preference* (question 4). Show brand preferences as a percentage of each gender. What percentage of the sampled females prefer Levis? What percentage of the sampled males prefer Levis?

(v) Conduct a suitable statistical test at the 5% significance level to determine if the percentage of males and females who prefer the Levi brand is the same. What is your management conclusion?

Chapter 13

Chi-Squared Hypotheses Tests

Objectives

Hypothesis tests have also been developed to examine associations between two different variables. When the two random variables are both *categorical*, the relationship can be summarised using a pivot table (also called a **cross-tabulation table**). Any association between the two categorical variables, as displayed in a pivot table, can be tested using the *chi-squared statistic.*

This chapter focuses on the setting up of pivot tables between two categorical attributes and then *testing the association for statistical significance.* Pivot tables are used extensively in marketing to identify market segments based on consumer demographic measures.

Other types of hypothesis tests using the chi-squared statistic – such as *goodness-of-fit tests* and *equality of multiple proportions tests* – are also discussed and illustrated.

After studying this chapter, you should be able to:

- understand the concept and rationale of the chi-squared statistic
- understand the use of the chi-squared statistic in market research
- perform *independence of association* hypothesis tests using the chi-squared statistic
- perform *equality of multiple proportions* hypothesis tests using the chi-squared statistic
- perform *goodness-of-fit* hypothesis tests, using the chi-squared statistic and
- interpret the results of the various chi-squared tests.

13.1 Introduction and Rationale

The *chi-squared* statistic, written as χ^2, is a statistical measure used to test hypotheses on *patterns of outcomes* of a random variable in a population. The patterns of outcomes are based on *frequency counts* of categorical random variables.

It differs from the *z*-statistic and the *Student t*-statistic that test for measures of central location of population parameters. In chi-squared tests, the emphasis is on establishing whether a *single categorical random variable* exhibits a certain *pattern of outcomes*. It is also commonly used to test whether *two categorical random variables are associated by* examining *their joint pattern of outcomes*.

Examples

- Is machine downtime per day at a car manufacturer normally distributed?
- Is daily absenteeism at a large insurance company uniformly distributed across the days of the week?
- Is the choice of savings plans offered by a bank related to the marital status of the client?
- Is the choice of magazine read associated with the reader's gender?

There are three scenarios in inferential statistics in which the chi-squared test for significance is commonly applied. They are the:
- test for *independence of association*
- test for *equality of proportions in two or more populations*, and
- *goodness-of-fit* test.

In all three test scenarios, the four steps of the hypothesis testing procedure apply. When formulating the hypotheses (*step 1*), the population measure being tested is a *pattern of outcomes*, not a central location parameter. Also, the test statistic used in *steps 2* and *3* is the *chi-squared statistic*, χ^2, instead of the *z* or the *t*-statistic.

The Rationale of the Chi-squared Statistic

The data required for all three hypotheses test situations is *frequency counts*. The chi-squared statistic tests a null hypothesis by comparing a set of *observed frequencies* (the *pattern* of *observed* responses), obtained from a random sample, to a set of *expected frequencies* (the *pattern* of *expected* responses) that describes the null situation.

The *chi-squared statistic* measures the extent to which the *observed* and *expected frequencies differ*. If this difference is small, the null hypothesis is likely to be accepted. Conversely, a large difference is likely to result in the null hypothesis being rejected.

Formula

The **chi-squared statistic** that transforms *sample frequencies* into a *test statistic* is given by:

$$\chi^2 = \sum \frac{(f_o - f_e)^2}{f_e}$$

where f_o = *observed frequency* of a category of a categorical random variable
f_e = *expected frequency* of a category of a categorical random variable

13.2 The Chi-Squared Test for Independence of Association

In many management situations, the chi-squared statistic is used mostly to test for *independence of association.* This test establishes whether the response profiles between two categorical random variables are statistically related. The statistical test will establish whether the observed association is purely a chance occurrence or reflects a genuine association between the variables in the population from which the sample was drawn.

This hypothesis test establishes whether or not two categorical random variables are statistically related (dependent or independent). *Independence* means that the outcome of one random variable in no way influences (or is influenced by) the outcome of a second random variable.

Knowing whether two random variables are associated can influence many a decision process. For *example,* if market research establishes that consumer *brand choices* of *fruit juices* are influenced by the type of *packaging* or the *shelf position* in a supermarket, decisions about which packaging to use or which shelf level to select are important. If, however, *brand choice* is found to be independent of packaging or shelf level, these factors need not be considered in the promotion of fruit juices.

The *test for independence of association* follows the same four steps of hypothesis testing. The general nature of this test is explained by an example.

Example 13.1 Teenage Magazine Preferences study

Refer to the *Excel* file: **C13.1–teenager magazines**

The Abacus Media Company publishes four magazines for the teenage market (readers between 13 and 17 years of age). The Management question, which the executive editor of Abacus would like to answer, is the following:

"Are *readership preferences* for the three magazines similar or different across *gender*?"

A survey was carried out amongst 200 teenagers (of both genders and between the ages of 13 and 17 years) in various book stores. Randomly selected teenagers who bought at least one of the three magazines were interviewed and asked the following two questions:

Question 1: "Which one of these three magazines do you most prefer to read?

Beat		*Youth*		*Grow*	

Question 2: Gender?

Boy		*Girl*	

The survey response data is available in the *Excel* data file.

The cross-tabulation table (two-way pivot-table) shown in Table 13.1 below was constructed on the basis of the *magazine preference* responses and identified *gender*.

Table 13.1 Pivot table of Gender with Magazine Preference

Gender		Magazine Preference		
	Beat	***Youth***	***Grow***	**Total**
Girl	13	28	39	80
Boy	33	45	42	120
Total	46	73	81	200

Management question

"Are *readership preferences* for the three magazines similar or different across *gender*?"

Statistically, this translates into conducting a hypothesis test, at the 5% level of significance, on whether there is a statistical association between *gender* and *magazine preference* (i.e. whether or not they are statistically related).

Solution (with explanation)

The two categorical random variables are *gender* and *magazine preference.*
Each cell in the pivot table (Table 13.1) shows the *observed joint frequency count* for each category combination of the two random variables being tested (e.g. 33 *boys* prefer the *Beat* magazine, and 28 *girls* prefer the *Youth* magazine).

Figure 13.1 overleaf shows the *observed frequencies* (**Table 1**); the *row percentages* of the observed frequencies (**Table 2**); *expected frequencies* (**Table 3**) and the computed *chi-squared test statistics* using *Excel* (**Table 4**) for the *test for independence of association* between *magazine preferences* and *gender*. A *stacked bar chart* of preferences by gender is also shown in **Chart 1**. Refer to the *Excel* file: **C13.1–teenager magazines**

(i) Exploratory data analysis

The sample profile is as follows: 80 girls and 120 boys were interviewed. 46 teenagers prefer *Beat*; 73 prefer *Youth* and 81 prefer *Grow*.

An inspection of the *row percentages* gives an indication of the likely association between these two measures. See Table 13.2 (and **Table 2** of **Figure 13.1**) for the row percentages table.

Table 13.2 Row percentage pivot table of Gender with Magazine Preference

Gender		Magazine Preference		
	Beat	***Youth***	***Grow***	**Total column**
Girl	16,25%	35%	48,75%	100%
Boy	27,50%	37,50%	35%	100%
Total row	23%	36,50%	40,50%	100%

Figure 13.1 Teenage Magazine Preferences – chi-squared computations using *Excel*

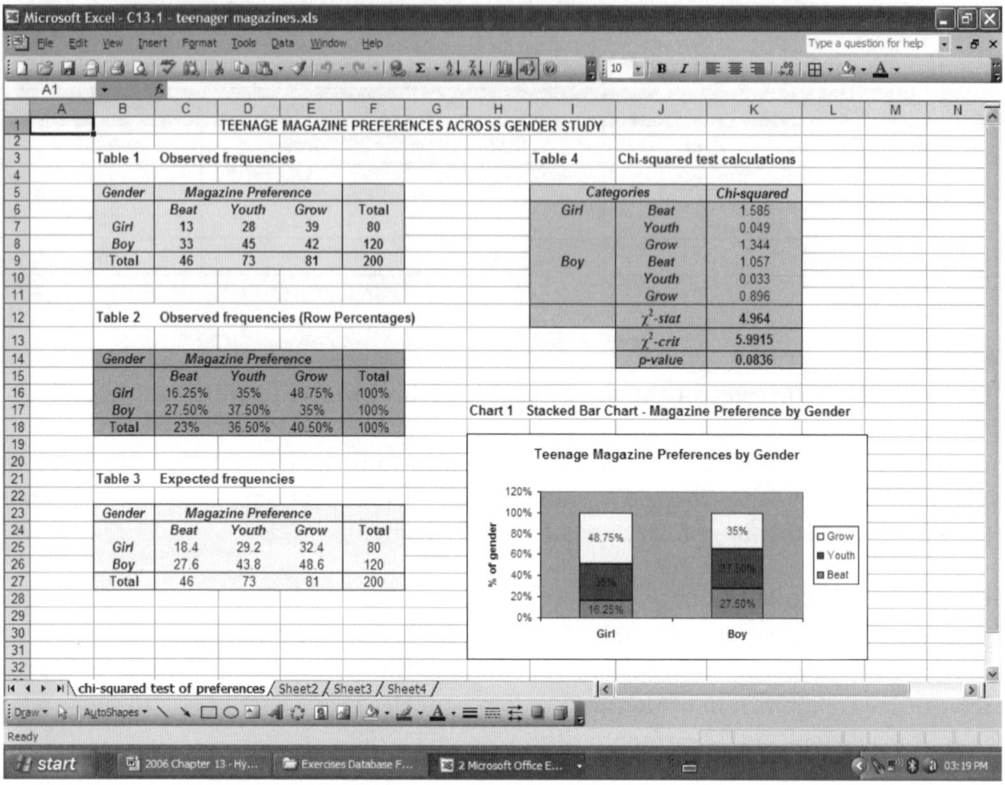

Microsoft Excel - C13.1 - teenager magazines.xls

TEENAGE MAGAZINE PREFERENCES ACROSS GENDER STUDY

Table 1 Observed frequencies

Gender	Magazine Preference			
	Beat	Youth	Grow	Total
Girl	13	28	39	80
Boy	33	45	42	120
Total	46	73	81	200

Table 2 Observed frequencies (Row Percentages)

Gender	Magazine Preference			
	Beat	Youth	Grow	Total
Girl	16.25%	35%	48.75%	100%
Boy	27.50%	37.50%	35%	100%
Total	23%	36.50%	40.50%	100%

Table 3 Expected frequencies

Gender	Magazine Preference			
	Beat	Youth	Grow	Total
Girl	18.4	29.2	32.4	80
Boy	27.6	43.8	48.6	120
Total	46	73	81	200

Table 4 Chi-squared test calculations

Categories		Chi-squared
Girl	Beat	1.585
	Youth	0.049
	Grow	1.344
Boy	Beat	1.057
	Youth	0.033
	Grow	0.896
	χ^2-stat	4.964
	χ^2-crit	5.9915
	p-value	0.0836

Chart 1 Stacked Bar Chart - Magazine Preference by Gender

From Table 13.2, it would appear that almost half of the *girls* prefer *Grow* (48,75%), and only 16,25% prefer *Beat.* In contrast, more than a quarter of the boys prefer *Beat* (27,5%), and the rest equally prefer *Youth* (37,5%) and *Grow* (35%). The percentage profiles by gender – based on the sample data – therefore appear to be different for girls and boys.

The statistical question that hypothesis testing will address is whether this observed *difference in patterns of outcomes* is due to chance (i.e. sampling error) or due to a genuine difference in readership profiles between girls and boys across the three teenage magazines.

(ii) Hypothesis test for independence of association

Step 1: Define the null and alternative hypotheses

H_0: There is *no association* between *gender* and *magazine preference* (i.e. they are independent).

H_1: There *is* an *association* (i.e. they are not independent).

The *null hypothesis* always states that the two categorical random variables are *independent* of (or *not associated* with) each other.

If the null hypothesis were true, this would mean that:

- the profile of magazine preferences will be the same for both boys and girls (based on row percentages); and
- the gender profile for each magazine will be the same (based on column percentages).

Stated mathematically, the row percentage profile for each gender would be equal to the total row percentage profile, and the column percentage profile for each magazine would be equal to the total column percentage profile.

If, on the other hand, the null hypothesis were not true, *different magazine preference profiles* between girls and boys would emerge. The implication for management is that, for each gender group, different promotional strategies for each magazine would have to be considered.

Step 2: Compute the sample test statistic

The appropriate sample *test statistic* is ***χ^2-stat***. As shown in the formula in section 13.1 above, the ***χ^2-stat*** is a measure of the *squared differences* between a set of *observed* (actual) frequencies (f_0) and a set of *expected* (theoretical) frequencies (f_e).

The *observed* frequencies are given in the two-way pivot table (see Table 13.1, or **Table 1** of **Figure 13.1**), which is compiled from sample data.

The *expected* frequencies are based on the *assumption* that the *null hypothesis* is *true* (i.e. that the two measures are independent of each other) and must be computed.

Deriving the expected frequency table

The expected frequency table is a separate two-way pivot table that has the same row totals and column totals as the sample table (Table 13.1). However, the joint frequen-cies are constructed in a way that reflects *no statistical association* between the two categorical random variables. This shows what the observed sample frequency table would look like if the two categorical random variables are *independent*.

Formula

The following formula is used to compute the *expected frequency* for each cell (i,j) of the pivot table:

$$\text{Expected frequency}_{i,j} = f_e = \frac{i^{th} \text{ row total} \times j^{th} \text{ column total}}{\text{sample size } (n)}$$

Table 13.3 (and **Table 3** of **Figure 13.1**) shows the computed *expected frequencies* for the *teenager magazine readership* study.

Table 13.3 Expected Frequencies for Teenage Magazine Preferences study

Gender	Magazine Preference			
	Beat	***Youth***	***Grow***	**Total**
Girl	18,4	29,2	32,4	80
Boy	27,6	43,8	48,6	120
Total	46	73	81	200

To illustrate (refer to Table 13.3), consider the cell of "*boys* who most prefer the *Beat* magazine":

$$\text{Expected frequency} = \frac{(\textit{Boy} \text{ row total} \times \textit{Beat} \text{ column total})}{\text{sample size}}$$

$$= \frac{120 \times 46}{200} = 27{,}6$$

Similarly, consider the cell of "*girls* who most prefer the *Grow* magazine":

$$\text{Expected frequency} = \frac{(\textit{Girl} \text{ row total} \times \textit{Grow} \text{ column total})}{\text{sample size}}$$

$$= \frac{80 \times 81}{200} = 32{,}4$$

Each expected frequency cell represents the *theoretical number* of teenagers within each gender that would prefer each type of magazine **if** the two measures are **independent.** For *example*, out of the sample of 200 teenagers surveyed, 18,4 *girls* and 27,6 *boys* would each be expected to prefer the *Beat* magazine, **if** there were **no association** between *gender* and *magazine preference.*

To confirm that these expected frequencies reflect the null hypothesis of *no association* (or *independence)*, compute the *row (or column) percentages* for the expected table as shown in Table 13.4.

Table13.4 Row percentages for expected frequency pivot table of the Teenage Magazine Preferences study

Gender	Magazine Preference			
	Beat	***Youth***	***Grow***	**Total**
Girl	23%	36,5%	40,5%	100%
Boy	23%	36,5%	40,5%	100%
Total	23%	36,5%	40,5%	100%

From Table 13.4 it can be seen that the readership profile (in percentage terms) is the same for both boys and girls, which is the same as the overall gender profile. This shows that it does not matter whether the reader is a boy or a girl in terms of preference for a particular magazine. These equal readership profiles across genders imply that *magazine preference* is independent of (not related to) *gender.*

Deriving the χ^2-*stat* sample test statistic

Table 13.5 (and **Table 4** of **Figure 13.1**) shows the calculation of the chi-squared statistic, based on the formula shown in section 13.1 on page 339.

Table 13.5 χ^2-stat for the Teenage Magazine Preferences study

Joint Categories		f_o	f_e	$(f_o - f_e)^2$	$(f_o - f_e)^2/f_e$
Girls	*Beat*	13	18,4	29,16	1,585
	Youth	28	29,2	1,44	0,049
	Grow	39	32,4	43,56	1,344
Boys	*Beat*	33	27,6	29,16	1,057
	Youth	45	43,8	1,44	0,033
	Grow	42	48,6	43,56	0,896
				χ^2-***stat***	**4,964**

Thus χ^2-***stat*** = 4,964

Step 3: Decision rule to guide the acceptance/rejection of the null hypothesis

Approach 1 Using the region of acceptance/rejection method

The chi-squared hypothesis test is only an *upper-tailed test*. Hence, only a single *critical* χ^2-*limit* is required. To find the *critical* χ^2-*limit*, both a *level of significance*, α, and *degrees of freedom* must be known.

The *level of significance*, α, is given as $\alpha = 0{,}05$ (5% significance level).

The value for the *degrees of freedom* is related to the size (dimensions) of the cross-tabulation table. The general rule for degrees of freedom for a cross-tabulation is:

degrees of freedom (df) = $(r - 1)(c - 1)$
where r = number of rows
c = number of columns

In the example, the *degrees of freedom* is $df = 2$ [i.e. $(2 - 1)(3 - 1)$]

Then the *critical* χ^2-*limit* is given by:

- **Using the χ^2-table**

  $\chi^2_{(\alpha = 0{,}05)(df = 2)} = 5{,}991$ (from **Table 3** in Appendix 1)

or

- **Using the *Excel* function**
  =CHIINV(upper tail probability, degrees of freedom)

  where the *upper-tail probability* = the level of significance, α.

  Then the critical χ^2-limit is χ^2-crit =CHIINV(0.05,2) = 5,991465

Figure 13.2 shows the shape of the *chi-squared distribution* and the *upper-tailed region of rejection.*

Thus, the *region of acceptance* for H_0 is [$\chi^2 \leq 5{,}991$]

The *decision rule* is then stated as follows:

Do not reject H_0 if χ^2-*stat* falls at or below the upper limit of 5,991.
Reject H_0 in favour of H_1 if χ^2-*stat* falls above 5,991.

Approach 2 Using the *p-value* method

Given χ^2-*stat* = 4,964 (from *step 2*), the *p-value* refers to the *upper-tail area* only of the chi-squared distribution above χ^2 = 4,964

The *p-value* cannot be found from the chi-squared tables. It can only be computed using an *Excel* function, as follows:

Using Excel's function

=CHIDIST(x, df) where $x = \chi^2$-*stat* = 4,964 and *df* = 2

i.e. =CHIDIST(4.964,2) gives an upper tail area = 0,083576

Thus *p-value* = 0,0836

The *decision rule* is derived from **Figure 11.5** on page 267.

Step 4: Statistical conclusion and Management interpretation

Statistical conclusion

The *statistical conclusion* refers to whether the *null hypothesis* is *accepted or rejected* on the basis of the sample evidence.

Since

- the *p-value* (= 0,0836) lies between 0,05 (5%) and 0,10 (10%) or
- χ^2-*stat* (= 4,964) < χ^2-*crit* (5,991) and therefore lies *within* the region of acceptance of H_0

there is *weak sample evidence* to support the alternative hypothesis H_1. The null hypothesis is therefore probably true.

Figure 13.2 below shows the sample test statistic (χ^2-*stat*) in comparison to the region of acceptance/rejection (χ^2-*crit*) and the *p-value* of the test.

Figure 13.2 Chi-squared distribution: Teenage Magazine Preferences study

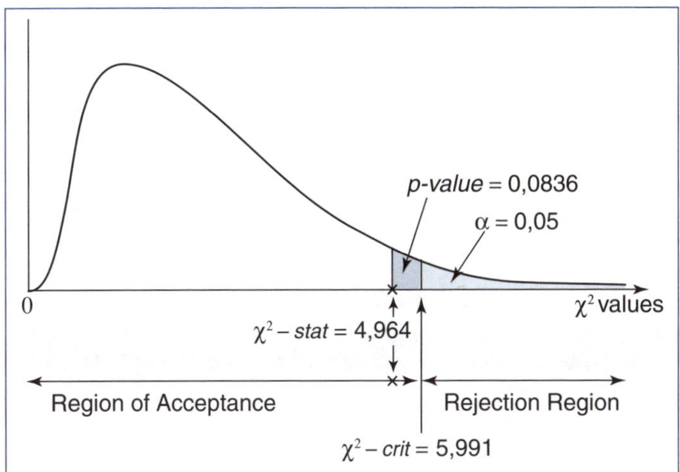

Management interpretation

Since the null hypothesis cannot be rejected at the 5% significance level, the following *management interpretation* can be given:

"*Magazine preference / readership* and *gender* are independent of each other", or
"There is no association between magazine preference and gender."

The stacked bar chart in Figure 13.3 (and **Chart 1** of **Figure 13.1**) highlights the similarity of profiles of *magazine preferences* between girls and boys. Any observed differences in profiles is not statistically significant, and can only be attributed to chance.

Figure 13.3 Stacked bar chart – Teenage Magazine Preferences by Gender

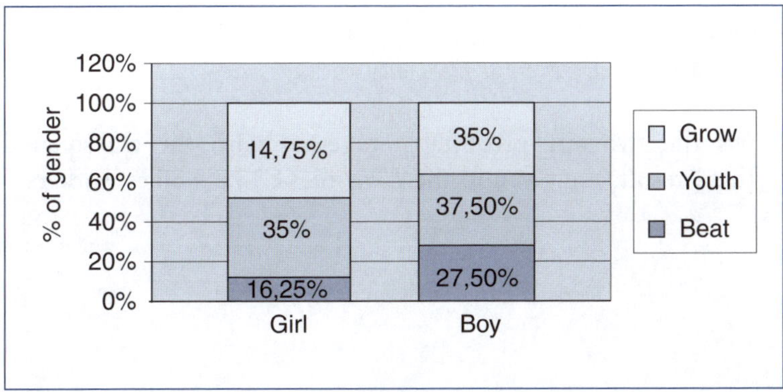

Therefore a *common* promotional strategy for both genders can be adopted by each of the three magazines. These findings suggest that there is no perceived product differentiation between the three magazines by the teenage target population, nor is there any evidence of market segmentation by gender.

Example 13.2 Office Workers – Healthy Exercise study

Refer to the *Excel* file: **C13.2–office workers**

The Department of Health conducted a study amongst office workers to establish the extent to which office workers exercise on a regular basis.

A survey of 250 randomly selected office workers was conducted. Each selected office worker was asked his or her *age category* and how often he or she *exercised*. The sample findings are shown in Table 13.6.

Table 13.6 Pivot table of survey data for office workers' Healthy Exercise study

Age	Frequency of Exercise			
	Often	**Seldom**	**Never**	**Total**
Under 30	42	26	22	90
30-45	35	18	30	83
46-60	22	35	20	77
Total	99	79	72	250

Management question

The director in charge of the study asked the following question:

"Does *exercise frequency* decrease with *age*?"

Stated statistically, can it be concluded at the 5% significance level, that there is an association between the *age category* of an office worker and the frequency with which he or she *exercises*?

Solution (with explanation)

The two categorical random variables are *exercise frequency* and *age category*.

Figure 13.4 overleaf shows the two-way pivot table together with the chi-squared hypothesis test findings. These results are given in the *Excel* file: **C13.2 – office workers**.

Figure 13.4 Office workers' Age and Exercise Frequency: Chi-squared computations using *Excel*

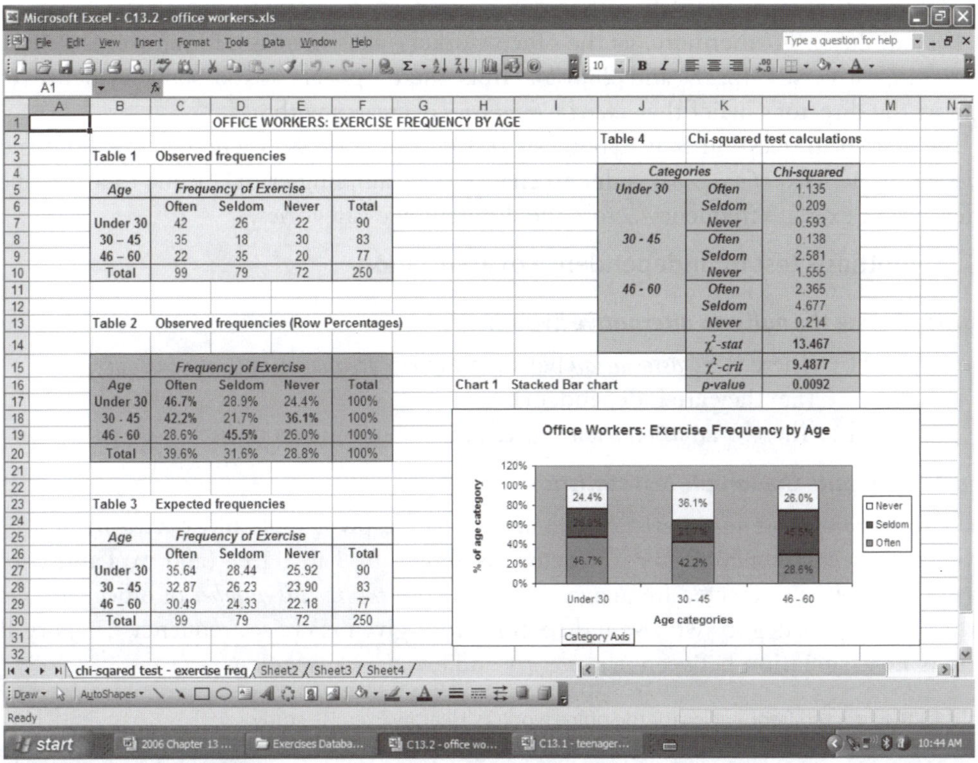

OFFICE WORKERS: EXERCISE FREQUENCY BY AGE

Table 1 Observed frequencies

Age	Frequency of Exercise			
	Often	Seldom	Never	Total
Under 30	42	26	22	90
30 – 45	35	18	30	83
46 – 60	22	35	20	77
Total	99	79	72	250

Table 2 Observed frequencies (Row Percentages)

Age	Frequency of Exercise			
	Often	Seldom	Never	Total
Under 30	46.7%	28.9%	24.4%	100%
30 - 45	42.2%	21.7%	36.1%	100%
46 - 60	28.6%	45.5%	26.0%	100%
Total	39.6%	31.6%	28.8%	100%

Table 3 Expected frequencies

Age	Frequency of Exercise			
	Often	Seldom	Never	Total
Under 30	35.64	28.44	25.92	90
30 – 45	32.87	26.23	23.90	83
46 – 60	30.49	24.33	22.18	77
Total	99	79	72	250

Table 4 Chi-squared test calculations

Categories		Chi-squared
Under 30	Often	1.135
	Seldom	0.209
	Never	0.593
30 - 45	Often	0.138
	Seldom	2.581
	Never	1.555
46 - 60	Often	2.365
	Seldom	4.677
	Never	0.214
	χ^2-stat	13.467
	χ^2-crit	9.4877
	p-value	0.0092

Chart 1 Stacked Bar chart

(i) Exploratory data analysis

The sample profile is as follows: 90 office workers are under the age of 30; 83 office workers are between 30 and 45 years of age; and 77 office workers are over 45 years of age. In addition, the study found that 99 office workers *often* exercised; 79 *seldom* exercised; and 72 *never* exercised.

An inspection of the row percentages gives an indication of the likely association between these two measures. See Table 13.7 (and **Table 2** of **Figure 13.4**) for the row percentages table.

Table 13.7 Row percentage pivot table of Age and Exercise Frequency of office workers

	Frequency of Exercise			
Age	**Often**	**Seldom**	**Never**	**Total**
Under 30	46,7%	28,9%	24,4%	100%
30–45	42,2%	21,7%	36,1%	100%
46–60	28,6%	45,5%	26,0%	100%
Total	39,6%	31,6%	28,8%	100%

From Table 13.7, it would appear that more office workers in the middle age category (30–45 years), compared to the other two age categories, *never exercise* (36,1% versus 24,4% and 26%). Furthermore, as the office workers' ages increase, fewer exercise more often (46,7% versus 42,2% and 28,6%). Thus there appears to be some evidence to support the director's belief that *exercise frequency* decreases with *age*.

The statistical question that hypothesis testing can address is whether this observed *difference in patterns of outcomes* is due to chance (i.e. sampling error) or due to a genuine difference in exercise frequency across the different age categories.

(ii) Hypothesis test for independence of association

Step 1: Define the null and alternative hypotheses

H_0: There is *no association* between *exercise frequency* and *age category* (i.e. they are independent).

H_1: There *is* an *association* (i.e. they are not independent).

Step 2: Compute the sample test statistic

To derive the sample test statistic, χ^2*-stat*, a separate pivot table of *expected frequencies* (representing *no association*) is constructed, as shown in Table 13.8 (and in **Table 3** of **Figure 13.4**). Each expected frequency represents the *theoretical number* of office workers within each age category who would respond to a given exercise frequency category **if** there is **no association** between *age category* and *exercise frequency*.

Table 13.8 Expected frequencies for the office workers' Healthy Exercise study

Age	Frequency of Exercise			
	Often	**Seldom**	**Never**	**Total**
Under 30	35,64	28,44	25,92	90
30–45	32,87	26,23	23,90	83
46–60	30,49	24,33	22,18	77
Total	99	79	72	250

Using the chi-squared test statistic based on the formula shown in section 13.1 above, the χ^2*-stat* computation is shown in Table 13.9 (and **Table 4** of **Figure 13.3**).

Table 13.9 χ^2-stat for the office workers' Healthy Exercise study

Joint Categories		f_o	f_e	$(f_o - f_e)^2$	$(f_o - f_e)^2/f_e$
Under 30	Often	42	35,64	40,45	1,135
	Seldom	26	28,44	5,954	0,209
	Never	22	25,92	15,366	0,593
30–45	Often	35	32,87	4,545	0,138
	Seldom	18	26,23	67,7	2,581
	Never	30	23,9	37,161	1,555
46–60	Often	22	30,49	72,114	2,365
	Seldom	35	24,33	113,806	4,677
	Never	20	22,18	4,735	0,214
				χ^2***-stat***	**13,467**

Thus χ^2-***stat*** = 13,467

Step 3: Decision rule to guide the acceptance / rejection of the null hypothesis

Approach 1 Using the region of acceptance/rejection method

The *level of significance* is specified at 5%. Hence $\alpha = 0{,}05$

The *degrees of freedom,* where $r = 3$ and $c = 3$, in this problem is 4 [i.e. $(3-1) \times (3-1)$]

Then the *critical* χ^2*-limit* is given by:

- **Using the χ^2 table**

  $\chi^2_{(\alpha = 0,05)(df = 4)}$ = 9,488 (from **Table 3** in Appendix 1)

or

- **Using the *Excel* function**

  =CHIINV(α , df)

Then the ctitical χ^2*-limit* is χ^2*-crit* =CHIINV(0.05,4) = 9,487729

Thus, the *region of acceptance* for H_0 is $[\chi^2 \leq 9{,}488]$

The *decision rule* is then stated as follows:

Do not reject H_0 if χ^2*-stat* falls at or below the upper limit of 9,488
Reject H_0 in favour of H_1 if χ^2*-stat* falls above 9,488

Approach 2 Using the *p-value* method

Given χ^2*-stat* = 13,467 (from *step 2*), the *p-value* refers to the *upper-tail area* of the chi-squared distribution above $\chi^2 = 13{,}467$.

- **Using *Excel's* function**

  =CHIDIST(x, df) where $x = \chi^2$*-stat* = 13,467 and *df* = 4
  i.e.
  =CHIDIST(13.467,4) gives an upper tail area = 0,0092

Thus *p-value* = 0,0092

The *decision rule* is derived from **Figure 11.5** on page 267.

Step 4: Statistical conclusion and Management interpretation

Statistical conclusion

The *statistical conclusion* refers to whether the *null hypothesis* is *accepted or rejected* on the basis of the sample evidence.

Since

- the *p-value* (= 0,0092) lies well below 0,01 (1%)
- χ^2*-stat* (= 13,467) > χ^2*-crit* (= 9,488), and therefore lies well *outside* the region of acceptance of H_0,

there is *overwhelming sample evidence* to support the alternative hypothesis H_1. The alternative hypothesis is therefore probably true.

Figure 13.5 below shows the sample test statistic (χ^2-*stat*) in comparison to the region of acceptance/rejection (χ^2-*crit*) and the *p-value* of the test.

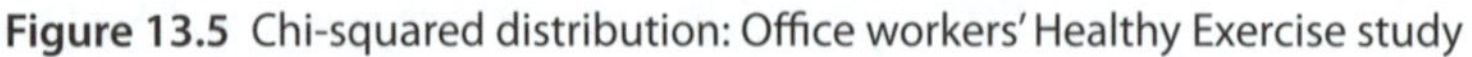

Figure 13.5 Chi-squared distribution: Office workers' Healthy Exercise study

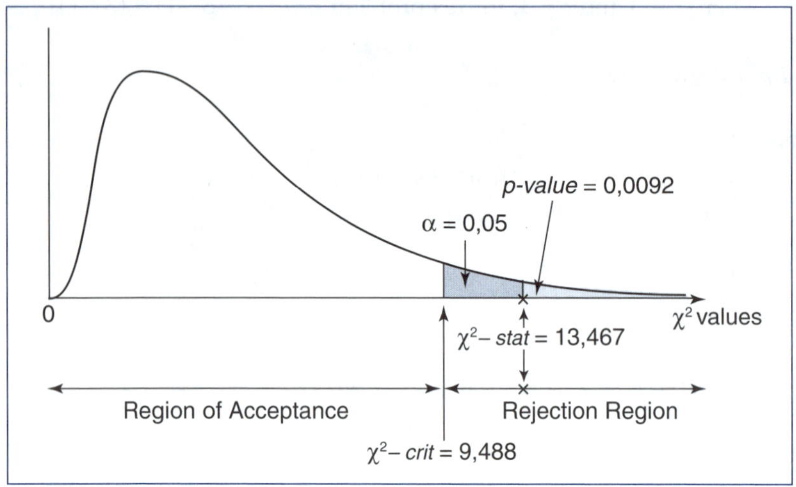

Management interpretation

Since the null hypothesis is rejected at the 5% significance level, the following *management interpretation* can be given:

"There is *overwhelming sample evidence* to conclude that *exercise frequency* is associated with the *age category* of office workers."

Describe the nature of the identified association

The identified association can be interpreted by examining the row (or column) percentage pivot table. Table 13.7 (repeated in **Table 13.10**) shows the *row percentages* per age category of office workers, while Figure 13.6 (and **Chart 1** in **Figure 13.3**) shows the stacked bar chart of these row percentages, for easier interpretation.

High percentages per column relative to other percentages within the column identifies the nature of the association.

Table 13.10 Row percentage pivot table of Age and Exercise frequency of office workers

Age	Frequency of Exercise			
	Often	**Seldom**	**Never**	**Total**
Under 30	46,7%	28,9%	24,4%	100%
30–45	42,2%	21,7%	36,1%	100%
46–60	28,6%	45,5%	26,0%	100%
Total	39,6%	31,6%	28,8%	100%

Figure 13.6 Stacked bar chart of row percentages – office workers' Healthy Exercise study

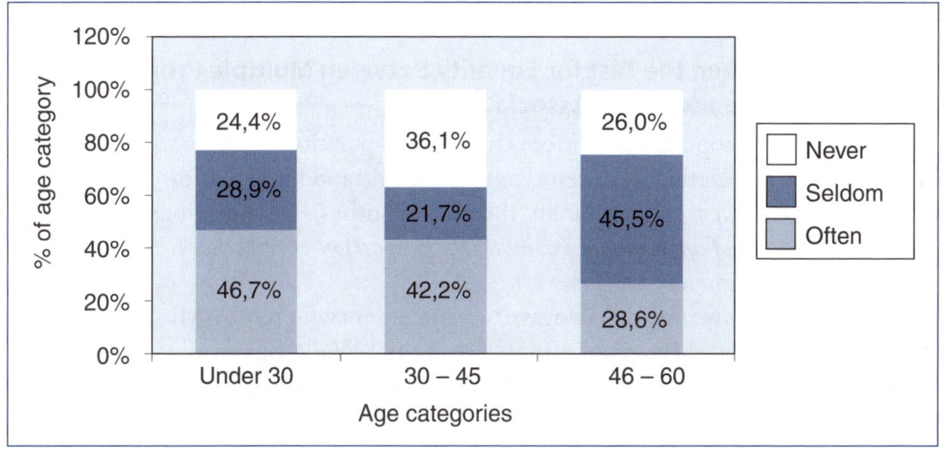

Thus, office workers under 45 years (46,7% and 42,2%) tend to exercise more *often* than older office workers (only 28,6%). Occasional (*seldom*) exercise is undertaken more by older office workers (46–60 years) (45,5%) than younger office workers (28,9% and 21,7%). Finally, the office workers in the middle age group (30–45 years) are more likely *never* to exercise (36,1%), compared to the younger office workers (24,4%) and older office workers (26%).

The Department of Health may wish to formulate a policy to incentivise older office workers to undertake more regular exercise. In addition, the reasons for the proportionately greater percentage of the middle-aged office workers (36% versus 24% and 26%) who do not exercise should be investigated further.

13.3 Test for Equality of Proportions in Two or More Populations

Consider the following Management question:

Is the *percentage of Woolworths' customers* who pay for their purchases *by Mastercard* credit card, the *same* at three of the store's major retail outlets (*Canal Walk*, *Sandton Mall* and *Somerset Mall*)?

To answer this question, the *population proportions* of Woolworths' customers at the three retail outlets who pay for their purchases by Mastercard credit card must be *tested for equality* across all stores.

In chapter 12, hypotheses were tested for equality between *two population proportions* using the *z*-distribution. However, if *more than two* population proportions are to be compared, the *z*-distribution is no longer the appropriate test statistic. Instead, the *chi-squared statistic* is used to test the null hypothesis for *equality of proportions* in *more than two populations*.

In fact, the chi-squared statistical test can also be used as an alternative testing procedure to the z statistics in two population proportion cases.

The Equivalence Between the Test for Equality Between Multiple Proportions and the Test for Independence Of Association

The test for equality of proportions in more than two populations is *equivalent* to the test for independence of association between two categorical random variables.

In the *test for independence of association*, the null hypothesis of "no association" means that *for a specific category of one random variable, the proportion of responses is the same across all categories of the second random variable.*

To *illustrate*: If the *proportion* of Woolworths' customers who pay by Mastercard credit card is the *same* across the three retail outlets (i.e. Canal Walk, Sandton Mall, Somerset Mall), then this is equivalent to stating that there is *no association* between *type of credit card* and *retail outlet.*

Thus "no association" implies *equality of proportions across multiple populations.*

As a result, the **same hypothesis test procedure** is followed when either a test of *independence of association* or a *test for equality of multiple proportions* is required. The only difference is in the way in which the null hypothesis *(step 1)* is phrased - and in the manner in which the conclusion *(step 5)* is drawn.

Example 13.3 Mastercard Payment study

Refer to the *Excel* file: C13.3–mastercard

Management at Woolworths' head office wanted to know whether the proportion of their credit card customers who pay for their purchases by *Mastercard credit card* varies across three of their major retail outlets (i.e. Canal Walk, Sandton Mall, Somerset Mall).

A random sample of 180 credit card purchases across the three retail outlets was selected and the number of Mastercard credit card transactions per store was recorded. The sample findings are shown in Table 13.11.

Table 13.11 Pivot table of credit card transaction by store and credit card

Card Type	Retail Outlet			
	Canal Walk	**Sandton Mall**	**Somerset Mall**	**Total**
Mastercard	36	44	26	106
Other Card	16	40	18	74
Total	52	84	44	180

Management question

Can Woolworths' management conclude that the proportion of Mastercard credit card payments for transactions is the same across the three retail outlets?

Stated statistically, can it be concluded, at the 10% significance level, that the proportion of credit card customers who pay for their purchases by Mastercard is equal across the three populations of credit card customers at Canal Walk, Sandton Mall and Somerset Mall?

Solution (with explanation)

The two categorical random variables are *credit card type* and *retail outlet.*

Figure 13.7 shows the two-way pivot table together with the chi-squared hypothesis test findings. These results are given in the *Excel* file: **C13.3 – mastercard**.

Figure 13.7 Mastercard Payment Preference: Chi-squared computations using *Excel*

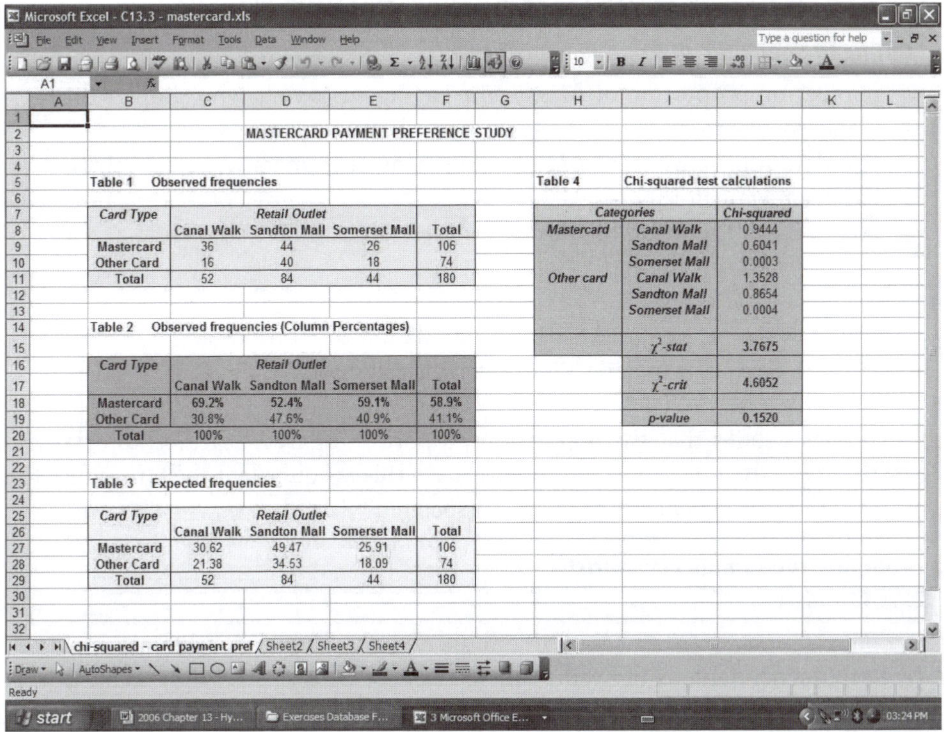

MASTERCARD PAYMENT PREFERENCE STUDY

Table 1 Observed frequencies

Card Type	Retail Outlet			
	Canal Walk	Sandton Mall	Somerset Mall	Total
Mastercard	36	44	26	106
Other Card	16	40	18	74
Total	52	84	44	180

Table 2 Observed frequencies (Column Percentages)

Card Type	Retail Outlet			
	Canal Walk	Sandton Mall	Somerset Mall	Total
Mastercard	69.2%	52.4%	59.1%	58.9%
Other Card	30.8%	47.6%	40.9%	41.1%
Total	100%	100%	100%	100%

Table 3 Expected frequencies

Card Type	Retail Outlet			
	Canal Walk	Sandton Mall	Somerset Mall	Total
Mastercard	30.62	49.47	25.91	106
Other Card	21.38	34.53	18.09	74
Total	52	84	44	180

Table 4 Chi-squared test calculations

Categories		Chi-squared
Mastercard	Canal Walk	0.9444
	Sandton Mall	0.6041
	Somerset Mall	0.0003
Other card	Canal Walk	1.3528
	Sandton Mall	0.8654
	Somerset Mall	0.0004
	χ^2-stat	3.7675
	χ^2-crit	4.6052
	p-value	0.1520

(i) Exploratory data analysis

The sample profile is as follows: Of the 180 credit card transactions sampled, 52 were sampled from Canal Walk, 84 from Sandton Mall, and 44 from Somerset Mall. Also, 106 of the customers sampled paid by Mastercard, and the balance (74 customers) paid for their purchasing using other brands of credit cards (e.g. Visa card, American Express, etc.).

Table 13.12 shows the column percentages per store for each type of credit card used.

Table 13.12 Column percentage analysis of the proportion of Mastercard payments by Store

Card Type	Retail Outlet			
	Canal Walk	**Sandton Mall**	**Somerset Mall**	**Total**
Mastercard	69,2%	52,4%	59,1%	58,9%
Other Card	30,8%	47,6%	40,9%	41,1%
Total	100%	100%	100%	100%

The sample data shows that 69,2% of credit card customers at Canal Walk paid for their purchases by Mastercard, while 52,4% of Sandton Mall customers and 59,1% of Somerset Mall customers used their Mastercard credit card to pay for their purchases.

The statistical question is whether these observed *sample differences in proportions* are significant or whether they are due purely to *chance* sampling. Hence a hypothesis test for equality of proportion in three populations is conducted.

(ii) Hypothesis test for equality of proportions in three populations

Step 1: Define the null and alternative hypotheses

Let π_1 = population proportion of *Mastercard*-paying customers who shop at the Canal Walk store

Let π_2 = population proportion of *Mastercard*-paying customers who shop at the Sandton Mall store

Let π_3 = population proportion of *Mastercard*-paying customers who shop at the Somerset Mall store.

Then H_0: $\pi_1 = \pi_2 = \pi_3$ (equality of population proportions across stores)
H_1: At *least one* population proportion is different.

The null hypothesis states that the population proportion of credit card customers who pay by Mastercard is the *same across* the three stores. This is equivalent to stating that the *credit card type* used is independent of (or not associated with) the *retail store*.

Step 2: Compute the sample test statistic

The sample test statistic is χ^2-*stat*.

To compute χ^2-*stat*, both an *observed* and an *expected* frequency table are required. The *observed* frequency table is derived from the sample data as shown in Table 13.11, while the *expected* frequency table is constructed in the same way as for the *independence of association* test (i.e. $\frac{\text{a row total} \times \text{a column total}}{\text{sample size}}$) and is shown in Table 13.13 (and **Table 3** of **Figure 13.7**).

Table 13.13 Expected frequency table for the Mastercard Payment study

Card Type	Retail Outlet			
	Canal Walk	Sandton Mall	Somerset Mall	Total
Mastercard	30,62	49,47	25,91	106
Other Card	21,38	34,53	18,09	74
Total	52	84	44	180

Table 13.14 below (and **Table 4** of **Figure 13.7**) shows the calculation of χ^2-*stat* using the formula given in section 13.1.

Table 13.14 χ^2-stat for the Mastercard Payment study

Joint Categories		f_o	f_e	$(f_o - f_e)^2$	$(f_o - f_e)^2/f_e$
Mastercard	Canal Walk	36	30,62	28,9444	0,945278
	Sandton Mall	44	49,47	29,9209	0,604829
	Somerset Mall	26	25,91	0,0081	0,000313
Other Card	Canal Walk	16	21,38	28,9444	1,353807
	Sandton Mall	40	34,53	29,9209	0,866519
	Somerset Mall	18	18,09	0,0081	0,000448
		180	180	χ^2***-stat***	**3,771193**

Thus χ^2*-stat* = 3,771193

(The difference with χ^2*-stat* = 3,7675 from **Table 4** of **Figure 13.7** is due to intermediate rounding errors.)

Step 3: Decision rule to guide the acceptance/rejection of the null hypothesis

Approach 1 Using the region of acceptance/rejection method

The *level of significance* is specified at 10%. Hence $\alpha = 0{,}10$

The *degrees of freedom* where $r = 2$ and $c = 3$ in this problem is 2 [i.e. $(2-1) \times (3-1)$]

Then the *critical* χ^2*-limit* is given by:

- **Using the χ^2-table**
  $\chi^2_{(\alpha = 0{,}10)(df = 2)} = 4{,}605$ (from **Table 3** in Appendix 1)

or

- **Using the *Excel* function**
  =CHIINV(α , df)

Then the *critical* χ^2*-limit* is χ^2*-crit* =CHIINV(0.10,2) = 4,60517

Thus, the *region of acceptance* for H_0 is $[\chi^2 \leq +4{,}605]$

The *decision rule* is then stated as follows:

Do not reject H_0 if χ^2*-stat* falls at or below the upper limit of 4,605.
Reject H_0 in favour of H_1 if χ^2*-stat* falls above 4,605.

Approach 2 Using the *p-value* method

Given χ^2*-stat* = 3,771 (from *step 2*), the *p-value* refers to the *upper-tail area* of the chi-squared distribution above $\chi^2 = 3{,}771$

- **Using *Excel's* function**
  =CHIDIST(x, df) where $x = \chi^2$*-stat* = 3,771 and $df = 2$

i.e.

=CHIDIST(3.771,2) gives an upper tail area = 0,15175

Thus $\quad p\text{-}value = 0{,}15175$

Given $\alpha = 0{,}10$, this critical value will override the *decision rule* from **Figure 11.5** of chapter 11 where $\alpha = 0{,}05$ is the cut-off point. In this instance:

Do not reject H_0	if $p\text{-}value \geq 0{,}10$.
Reject H_0 in favour of H_1	if $p\text{-}value < 0{,}10$.

Step 4: Statistical conclusion and Management interpretation

Statistical conclusion

The *statistical conclusion* refers to whether the *null hypothesis* is *accepted or rejected* on the basis of the sample evidence.
Since

- the *p-value* (= 0,15175) lies well above 0,10 (10%) or
- χ^2-*stat* (= 3,771) < χ^2-*crit* (= 4,605) and therefore lies well *inside* the region of acceptance of H_0

there is *no sample evidence* to support the alternative hypothesis H_1. The null hypothesis is therefore probably true.

Figure 13.8 shows the sample test statistic (χ^2-*stat*) in comparison to the region of acceptance/rejection (χ^2-*crit*) and the *p-value* of the test.

Figure 13.8 Chi-squared distribution: Mastercard Payment study

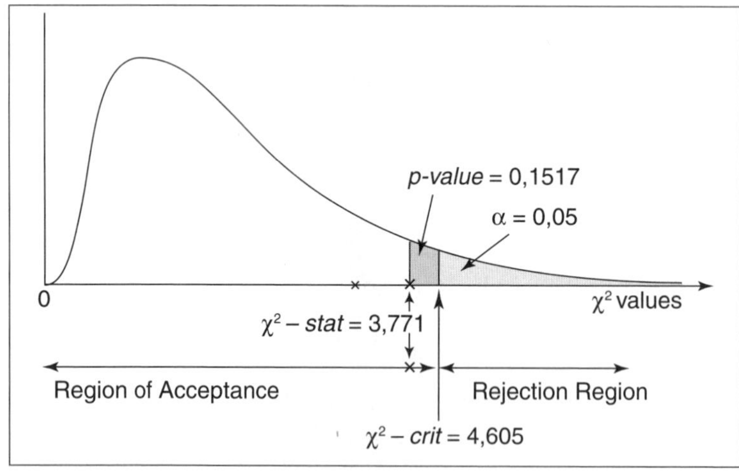

Management interpretation

Since the null hypothesis cannot be rejected at the 10% significance level, the following *management interpretation* can be given:

"The proportion (percentage) of Woolworths' credit card customers who pay for their purchases with a *Mastercard* is most likely the *same* between the three stores (Canal Walk, Sandton Mall, and Somerset Mall)."

13.4 The Chi-Squared Goodness-of-Fit Test

The chi-squared statistic can also be used to describe the *pattern of responses* for a *single categorical random variable.* If a random variable's response profile can be matched to a theoretical probability distribution, such as the *normal*, the *binomial*, the *Poisson* or some *other* user-defined probability distribution, then this theoretical distribution can be used to explain the behaviour of the random variable in general.

The chi-squared statistic can provide a measure of the *goodness-of-fit* between an *observed frequency* distribution of a random variable derived from sample data, and an *expected frequency* distribution. The expected frequencies would be based on a particular theoretical or an empirical (user-defined) distribution, which the random variable is hypothesised to follow.

If the chi-squared measure shows that there is a significant difference between the observed and the expected frequency distributions, the random variable cannot be assumed to follow the given theoretical or empirical distribution.

The hypothesis testing procedure is identical to the procedure followed in the independence of association hypothesis test.

Fitting Sample Data to User-defined Probability Distributions

The following *example* illustrates how to test the fit of sample data to a *user-defined probability* distribution.

Example 13.4 Commuter Transport Patterns study

***Excel* datafile:** C13.4 – commuters

An economist employed by the Metro Rail Commuter Service is studying the daily *commuting patterns of workers* into the central business district (CBD) of Cape Town. A study conducted five years ago found that 40% of commuters used trains, 25% used cars, 20% used taxis and 15% used buses. The economist's own *recent survey* of 400 randomly selected commuters found that 135 commuters used trains, 115 used cars, 96 used taxis and the remainder traveled by bus.

Management question

Can the economist conclude that *commuting patterns* into the CBD of Cape Town have changed since the study five years ago? Test the hypothesis at the 5% level of significance.

Solution

Step 1: Define the null and alternative hypotheses

The *null hypothesis* always states that the *observed data* of the categorical random variable *fits* the proposed theoretical or user-defined probability pattern of outcomes. In this example, the user-defined probability distribution is represented by the commuting patterns of five years ago.

Thus H_0: The commuting patterns are the *same* today as they were five years ago (i.e. the commuting pattern is still 40% trains; 25% cars: 20% taxis; and 15% buses).

H_1: The commuting patterns today *differ* from those of five years ago (i.e. the commuting pattern *is not* 40% trains; 25% cars; 20% taxis; and 15% buses).

Step 2: Compute the sample test statistic

The sample test statistic is χ^2-*stat*.

To compute χ^2-*stat*, both an *observed* and an *expected* frequency table are required. The *observed* frequencies (f_o) are derived from the economist's sample survey data of 400 commuters, as shown in the column labeled $\mathbf{f_o}$ in Table 13.15.

The *expected* frequencies ($\mathbf{f_e}$) are derived from the study of five years ago on the distribution of *transport modes used.* The distribution of percentages ($\mathbf{\%f_e}$) given, from the previous study, needs to be expressed as *actual expected frequencies* to be consistent with the sample observed frequencies. The percentages are converted to actual expected frequencies by multiplying each transport mode percentage by the sample size of 400 (i.e. $f_e = n \times$ *transport mode %*).

Table 13.15 shows the calculation of χ^2-*stat* using the formula given in section 13.1 above.

Table 13.15 χ^2-stat for the Commuter Transport Patterns study

Transport Mode	Observed frequencies		Expected frequencies		$(f_o - f_e)^2/f_e$
	$\% f_o$	f_o	$\% f_e$	f_e	
Train	34%	135	40%	160	3,906
Car	29%	115	25%	100	2,25
Taxi	24%	96	20%	80	3,2
Bus	14%	54	15%	60	0,6
	100%	400	100%	400	**9,956**

Thus $\quad \chi^2$-***stat*** $= 9{,}956$

Step 3: Decision rule to guide the acceptance/rejection of the null hypothesis

Approach 1 Using the region of acceptance/rejection method

The *level of significance* is specified at 5%. Hence $\alpha = 0{,}05$

The *degrees of freedom* for goodness-of-fit tests is: $df = (k - m - 1)$

where k = number of classes (categories); and
m = number of population parameters to estimate from the sample data

In this example, there are four *transport modes* ($k = 4$) and no parameters to estimate ($m = 0$).

Note: The m term is only appropriate if the sample data is being fitted to one of the theoretical probability distributions such as the *binomial*, *Poisson* or the *normal*. If the sample data is being fitted to a user-defined empirical distribution, there are no population parameters to estimate, hence $m = 0$.

Thus, the degrees of freedom $df = (4 - 0 - 1) = 3$

Then the *critical* χ^2*-limit* is given by:

- **Using the χ^2-table**
  $\chi^2_{(\alpha = 0{,}05)(df = 3)} = 7{,}815$ (from **Table 3** in Appendix 1)

or

- **Using the *Excel* function**
  =CHIINV(α , df)
  Then the *critical* χ^2*-limit* is χ^2*-crit* =CHIINV(0.05,3) = 7,8147

Thus, the *region of acceptance* for H_0 is $[\chi^2 \leq +7{,}815]$

The *decision rule* is then stated as follows:

Do not reject H_0 if χ^2*-stat* falls at or below the upper limit of 7,815.
Reject H_0 in favour of H_1 if χ^2*-stat* falls above 7,815.

Approach 2 Using the *p-value* method

Given χ^2*-stat* = 9,956 (from *step 2*), the *p-value* refers to the *upper-tail area* of the chi-squared distribution above $\chi^2 = 9{,}956$.

Using *Excel's* function

=CHIDIST(x, df) where $x = \chi^2$*-stat* = 9,956 and $df = 3$.

i.e.

=CHIDIST(9.956, 3) gives an upper-tail area = 0,0189

Thus *p-value* = 0,0189

The *decision rule* is derived from **Figure 11.5** on page 267.

Step 4: Statistical conclusion and Management interpretation

Statistical conclusion

The *statistical conclusion* refers to whether the *null hypothesis* is *accepted or rejected* on the basis of the sample evidence.
Since

- the *p-value* (= 0,0189) lies well below 0,05 (5%) but just above 0,01 (1%)
- χ^2*-stat* (= 9,956) > χ^2*-crit* (= 7,815), and therefore lies well *outside* the region of acceptance of H_0

there is *strong (to overwhelming) sample evidence* to support the alternative hypothesis H_1. The alternative hypothesis is therefore probably true.

Figure 13.9 below shows the sample test statistic (χ^2*-stat*) in comparison to the region of acceptance/rejection (χ^2*-crit*) and the *p-value* of the test.

Figure 13.9 Chi-squared distribution: Commuter Transport Patterns study

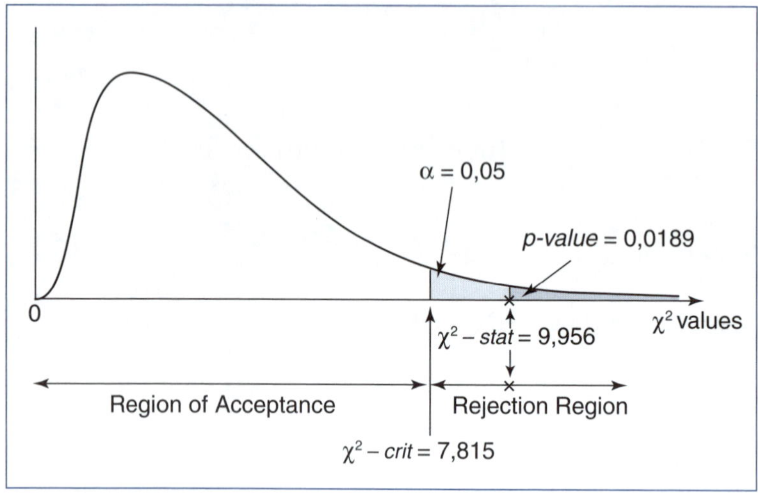

Management interpretation

Since the null hypothesis is rejected at the 5% significance level, the following *management interpretation* can be given:

"The commuting patterns into the CBD of Cape Town today *are significantly different* from the commuting patterns of five years ago".

To determine the nature of the changed pattern of commuting, the current pattern (i.e. the observed frequency percentages) can be compared to the previous pattern (i.e. five years ago survey) as shown in Table 13.16 and the multiple bar chart of Figure 13.10 below.

Table 13.16 Current and previous percentages of Commuting Patterns

Transport Mode	Previous Pattern (% f_e)	Current Pattern (% f_0)
Train	40%	33,75%
Car	25%	28,75%
Taxi	20%	24%
Bus	15%	13,50%
	100%	100%

Figure 13.10 Multiple bar chart of current and previous Commuting Patterns

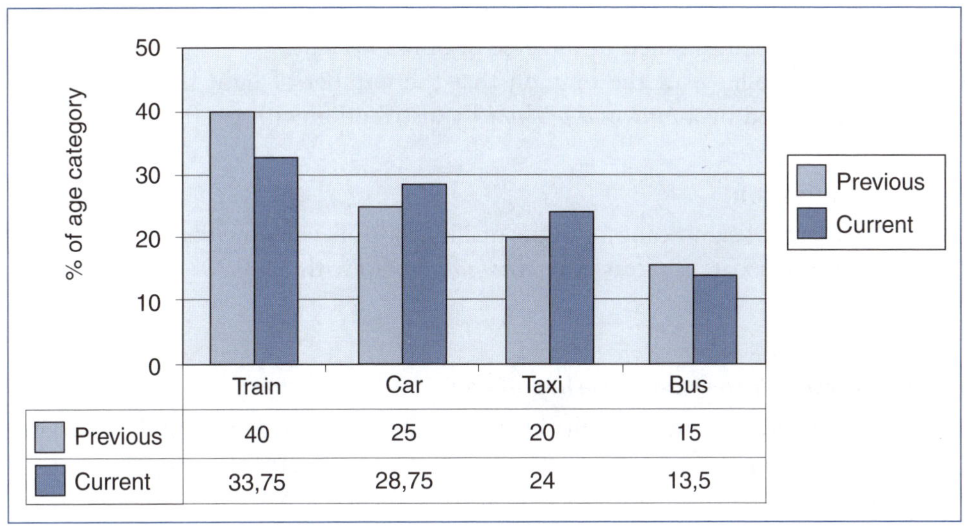

From Table 13.16 and Figure 13.10, it can be seen that *train* and *bus usage* have both *decreased* over the past five years (train usage more significantly so than buses). *Car* and *taxi* usage, on the other hand, have both shown about a 20% increase over the past five years.

13.5 Fitting Sample Data to Theoretical Probability Distributions

The following two examples (Example 13.5 and 13.6) test whether observed sample data fits a theoretical probability distribution; such as the *normal, Poisson* or *binomial* distributions.

If a good fit is found to exist, the central location and dispersion parameters of the given theoretical distribution can then be applied to the empirical sample data and used:

(i) to describe the profile of the random variable from which the data was derived, and
(ii) to compute probabilities of outcomes of the random variable occurring.

A. Fitting the BINOMIAL Probability Distribution

Example 13.5 Light Bulb Testing study

Excel **datafile:** C13.5 – light bulbs

The quality control procedure used by a factory which manufactures light bulbs is to randomly select a batch of three bulbs every hour and subject these bulbs to a testing process. The quality control department has estimated that each light bulb has a 20% chance of failing the test.

From records kept, a sample of findings from each of 200 batches of three bulbs examined showed that 90 batches had no failures, 80 had one failure, 26 had two failures, and all three bulbs failed in the case of only four batches.

The quality controller is of the opinion that the number of light bulb failures per batch can be described by a *binomial probability* distribution with $p = 0{,}20$.

Management question

At the $\alpha = 0{,}01$ level of significance, can the quality controller assume that the number of light bulb failures per batch follows the *binomial process* with $p = 0{,}20$?

Solution

Step 1: Define the null and alternative hypotheses

The *null hypothesis* always states that the *observed data* of the categorical random variable *fits* the proposed *theoretical probability distribution.* In this example, the theoretical probability distribution is the *binomial distribution* with $p = 0{,}20$.

Thus H_0: The number of bulb failures per batch of 3 is *described* by (or fits) the *binomial* distribution with $p = 0{,}20$.

H_1: The number of bulb failures per batch of 3 *does not fit* the *binomial* distribution with $p = 0{,}20$.

Step 2: Compute the sample test statistic

The sample test statistic is χ^2-*stat.*

To compute χ^2-*stat,* both an *observed* and an *expected* frequency table are required. The *observed* frequencies (f_o) are derived from the sample profile of 200 randomly selected batches of light bulbs off the production line.

The *expected* frequencies (f_e) are derived from the *binomial distribution* for the random variable, *failures per batch*, with $p = 0{,}20$ as follows:

HOW TO

To compute the expected frequencies

- Find the binomial probabilities for each value of the random variable x (failures per batch) with $n = 3$ and $p = 0{,}20$ (refer to chapter 10).

  The binomial probabilities can be computed by:
  - using the *binomial formula* given in chapter 10; or
  - using binomial Tables (not supplied in this text); or
  - using the *Excel* function =BINOMDIST(x, n, p, false)
    e.g. for $x = 0$, $n = 3$, $p = 0{,}2$ then =BINOMDIST(0,3,0.2,false) = 0,512.
- Compute the expected frequencies from the binomial probabilities by multiplying each binomial probability by the number of trials (= 200).

The calculations are shown in Table 13.17 below.

Table 13.17 Expected frequencies for the binomial distribution – Light Bulb Testing study

No. of failures per batch (x)	Binomial distribution	Probability $P(x = k)$	Expected Frequency ($f_e = n \times$ Probability)
0	${}_3C_0\,(0.20)^0\,(0.80)^3$	0,512	102,4
1	${}_3C_1\,(0.20)^1\,(0.80)^2$	0,384	76,8
2	${}_3C_2\,(0.20)^2\,(0.80)^1$	0,096	19,2
3	${}_3C_3\,(0.20)^3\,(0.80)^0$	0,008	1,6
		1	**200**

Table 13.18 shows the calculation of χ^2-*stat* using the formula given in section 13.1.

Table 13.18 Chi-squared sample test statistic calculation for the Light Bulb Testing study

No. of failures per batch (x)	Observed Frequencies (f_o)	Expected Frequencies (f_e)	$(f_o - f_e)^2/f_e$
0	90	102,4	1,502
1	80	76,8	0,133
2	26	19,2	2,408
3	4	1,6	3,6
	200	**200**	**7,643**

Thus χ^2-***stat*** = 7,643

Step 3: Decision rule to guide the acceptance/rejection of the null hypothesis

Approach 1 Using the region of acceptance/rejection method

The *level of significance* is specified at 1%. Hence $\alpha = 0{,}01$

The *degrees of freedom* for goodness-of-fit tests is $df = (k - m - 1)$, as indicated earlier,

where k = number of classes (categories), and
m = number of population parameters to estimate from the sample data

Table 13.19 shows the number of population parameters (m) that need to be estimated from sample data when fitting a theoretical probability distribution such as the binomial, Poisson or the normal distribution.

Table 13.19 Population parameters to be estimated (m) for degrees of freedom

Probability distribution	Population parameters to be estimated	m
Normal	μ and σ^2	2
Binomial	π	1
Poisson	a	1
Uniform	–	0

In this example, since a binomial distribution is hypothesised, the appropriate degrees of freedom equal 2 (i.e. 4−1−1) as $k = 4$ categories (0, 1, 2, 3 failures per batch) and $m = 1$ parameter (i.e. π) to estimate.

Then the *critical* χ^2*-limit* is given by:

- **Using the χ^2-table**
  $\chi^2_{(\alpha = 0,01)(df = 2)} = 9,21$ (from **Table 3** in Appendix 1)

or

- **Using the *Excel* function**
  =CHIINV(α , df)
  Then the *critical* χ^2*-limit* is χ^2*-crit* =CHIINV(0.01,2) = 9,2103

Thus, the *region of acceptance* for H_0 is $[\chi^2 \leq +9,21]$

The *decision rule* is then stated as follows:

Do not reject H_0 if χ^2*-stat* falls at or below the upper limit of 9,21.
Reject H_0 in favour of H_1 if χ^2*-stat* falls above 9,21.

Approach 2 Using the *p-value* method

Given χ^2*-stat* = 7,643 (from *step 2*), the *p-value* refers to the *upper-tail area* of the chi-squared distribution above $\chi^2 = 7,643$

Using *Excel's* function

=CHIDIST(x, df) where $x = \chi^2$*-stat* = 7,643 and $df = 2$

i.e.

=CHIDIST(7.643, 2) gives an upper-tail area = 0,02189

Thus *p-value* = 0,02189

Decision rule:
Since the significance level of this test is set at 1% (α = 0,01), a significant result to reject H_0 in favour of H_1 occurs when the computed *p-value* for the test statistic is *less than* 0,01.

Step 4: Statistical conclusion and Management interpretation

Statistical conclusion

The *statistical conclusion* refers to whether the *null hypothesis* is *accepted or rejected* on the basis of the sample evidence.
Since

- the *p-value* (= 0,02189) lies marginally above 0,01 (1%)
- χ^2*-stat* (= 7,643) < χ^2*-crit* (= 9,2103) and therefore lies *inside* the region of acceptance of H_0

there is *weak sample evidence* at the 1% significance level to support the alternative hypothesis H_1. The null hypothesis is therefore probably true.

Figure 13.11 below shows the sample test statistic (χ^2-*stat*) in comparison to the region of acceptance/rejection (χ^2-*crit*) and the *p-value* of the test.

Figure 13.11 Chi-squared test statistic and decision rules for Light Bulb Testing study

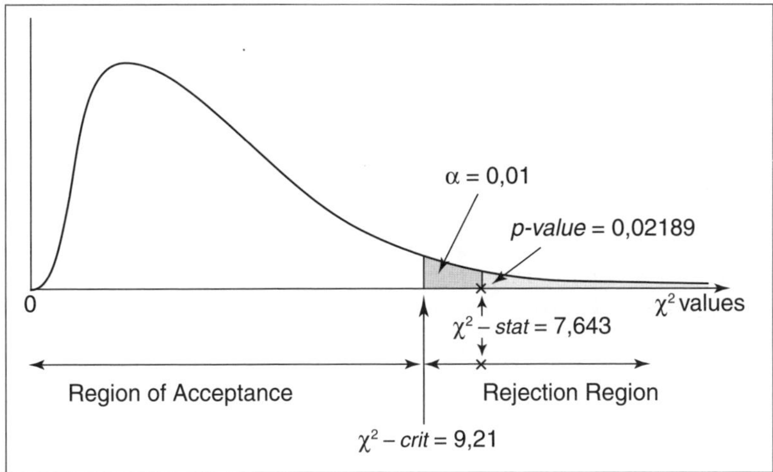

Management interpretation

Since the null hypothesis cannot be rejected at the 1% significance level, the following *management interpretation* can be given:

"The pattern of *light bulb failures* when tested in batches of 3 (n = 3) with p = 0,20, follows the binomial probability distribution."

Note: If the null hypothesis were rejected, it would mean that the sample data did not fit the binomial distribution with p = 0,20. It may well fit a binomial pattern, but with a different value for p (probability of failure of a light bulb), say, p = 0,10.

B. Fitting the NORMAL Probability Distribution

Many continuous numeric random variables are assumed to follow the normal distribution pattern of outcome (as seen in chapter 10). It may be necessary on occasions to test this assumption. The **chi-squared goodness-of-fit test** can be used to conduct the test to show that a sample of data of a numeric continuous random variable is normally distributed.

Example 13.6 Electricity Usage study

***Excel* datafile:** C13.6 – electricity usage

The manager of a Formula One Hotel recorded the *daily usage* of *electricity* – in kilowatts (kw) – by the hotel for a period of 160 days. The data are summarised into the following frequency table (**see Table 13.20** overleaf).

Table 13.20 Frequency table of daily Electricity Usage by a Formula 1 Hotel

Usage Intervals (kw/day)	Number of Days (f_o)
Below 20	7
20–35	24
36–50	69
51–65	52
Above 65	8
	160

Management question

Can the manager conclude that *daily electricity usage* is *normally distributed* with a *mean* of 45 kw and a *standard deviation* of 14 kw?

Conduct a chi-squared goodness-of-fit test at the 1% significance level (α = 0,01) to confirm or refute the manager's belief.

Solution

(i) Exploratory data analysis

A histogram of the frequency data (as shown in Figure 13.12) shows that the data are uni-modal and also moderately skewed to the left.

A goodness-of-fit test – at the 1% significance level – will establish whether the shape of the histogram is sufficiently normally distributed with a mean = 45 and a standard deviation 5 14.

Figure 13.12 Histogram of daily Electricity Usage by Formula One Hotel

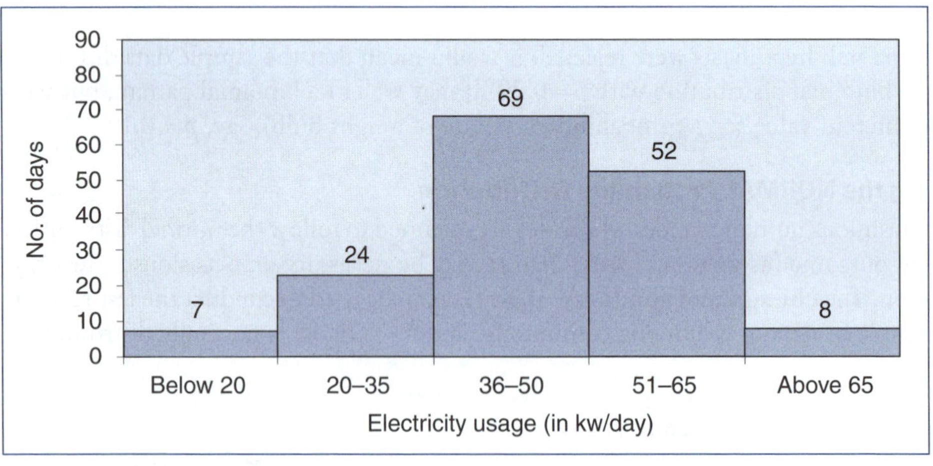

(ii) Goodness-of-fit test for normal distribution (with $\mu = 45$ and $\sigma = 14$).

Step 1: Define the null and alternative hypotheses

The *null hypothesis* states that the *observed data* of the continuous numeric random variable (x = *daily electricity usage*) *fits* the *normal probability distribution* with $\mu = 45$ kw and $\sigma = 14$ kw.

Thus H_0: *Daily electricity usage* fits the *normal* distribution with $\mu = 45$ kw and $\sigma = 14$ kw

H_1: *Daily electricity usage* does not fit the *normal* distribution with $\mu = 45$ kw and $\sigma = 14$ kw

Step 2: Compute the sample test statistic

The sample test statistic is χ^2-*stat*.

To compute χ^2-*stat*, both an *observed* and an *expected* frequency table are required. The *observed* frequencies (f_o) are derived from the sample profile of 160 days of *electricity usage* recorded by the manager of the Formula One Hotel.

The *expected* frequencies (f_e) are derived from the *normal distribution* for the random variable, *daily electricity usage* with $\mu = 45$ kw and $\sigma = 14$ kw, as follows:

HOW TO

To compute the expected frequencies

- Find the normal probabilities for each interval of electricity usage (as given in Table 13.20) with $\mu = 45$ kw and $\sigma = 14$ kw.
  The normal probabilities can be computed by:
  - using the standard normal (z) tables (refer to **Table 1** in Appendix 1), or
  - using the *Excel* function **=NORMDIST(x, μ, s, true)** which gives the cumulative probability from $-\infty$ to x.
    e.g. for $x = 20$, $\mu = 45$; $\sigma = 14$
    then $P(x < 20)$ is **=NORMDIST(20,45,14,true) = 0,0370**
- Compute the expected frequencies for each usage interval from the normal probabilities by multiplying each normal probability by the sample size, $n = 160$.

Table 13.21 shows the calculation of the *expected frequencies* that follow a *normal* distribution (with $\mu = 45$ kw and $\sigma = 14$ kw) and the χ^2-*stat* using the formula given in section 13.1.

Table 13.21 Normal expected frequencies and χ^2-stat calculations for Electricity Usage study

Usage Intervals (kw/day)	Observed frequency (f_o)	Normal Probability $P(k_1 < x < k_2)$	Normal Probability value	Expected frequency (f_e) = Probability ×160	Chi-squared $(f_o - f_e)^2/f_e$
Below 20	7	$P(x < 20)$	0,037	5,93	0,192
20–35	24	$P(20 < x < 35)$	0,122	19,45	1,063
36–50	69	$P(35 < x < 50)$	0,533	85,25	3,097
51–65	52	$P(50 < x < 65)$	0,286	45,73	0,861
Above 65	8	$P(x > 65)$	0,023	3,6	5,367
	160		**1**	**160**	**10,58**

Thus χ^2-*stat* = 10,58

Step 3: Decision rule to guide the acceptance / rejection of the null hypothesis

Approach 1 Using the region of acceptance/rejection method

The *level of significance* is specified at 1%. Hence $\alpha = 0{,}01$
The *degrees of freedom* for this *normal* distribution *goodness-of-fit* test is $df = (k - m - 1)$

where k = 5 *usage* intervals, and
m = 2 (see Table 13.19)

Thus df = 2 (= – 2 – 1)

Then the *critical* χ^2-*limit* is given by:

- **Using the χ^2-table**
  $\chi^2_{(\alpha = 0{,}01)(df = 2)} = 9{,}21$ (from **Table 3** in Appendix 1)

or

- **Using the Excel function** =CHIINV(α, df)
  Then the *critical* χ^2-*limit* is χ^2-*crit* =CHIINV(0.01,2) = 9,2103

Thus, the *region of acceptance* for H_0 is $[\chi^2 \leq 9{,}21]$

The *decision rule* is then stated as follows:

Do not reject H_0 if χ^2-*stat* falls at or below the upper limit of 9,21.
Reject H_0 in favour of H_1 if χ^2-*stat* falls above 9,21.

Approach 2 Using the *p-value* method

Given χ^2-*stat* = 10,58 (from *step 2*), the *p-value* refers to the *upper-tail area* of the chi-squared distribution above $\chi^2 = 10{,}58$.

- **Using *Excel's* function**
  =CHIDIST(x, df) where $x = \chi^2$-*stat* = 10,58 and $df = 2$

i.e.

=CHIDIST(10.58, 2) gives an upper tail area = 0,00504

Thus *p-value* = 0,00504

Decision rule:
Since the significance level of this test is set at 1% ($\alpha = 0{,}01$), a significant result to reject H_0 in favour of H_1 occurs when the computed *p-value* for the test statistic is *less than* 0,01.

Step 4: Statistical conclusion and Management interpretation

Statistical conclusion

The *statistical conclusion* refers to whether the *null hypothesis* is *accepted or rejected* on the basis of the sample evidence.

Since

- the *p-value* (= 0,00504) lies well below 0,01 (1%)
- χ^2-*stat* (= 10,58) > χ^2-*crit* (= 9,21) and therefore lies *outside* the region of acceptance of H_0

there is *overwhelming sample evidence* to support the alternative hypothesis H_1. The alternative hypothesis is therefore probably true.

Figure 13.13 shows the sample test statistic (χ^2-*stat*) in comparison to the region of acceptance/rejection (χ^2-*crit*) and the *p-value* of the test.

Figure 13.13 Chi-squared test statistic and decision rules for Electricity Usage study

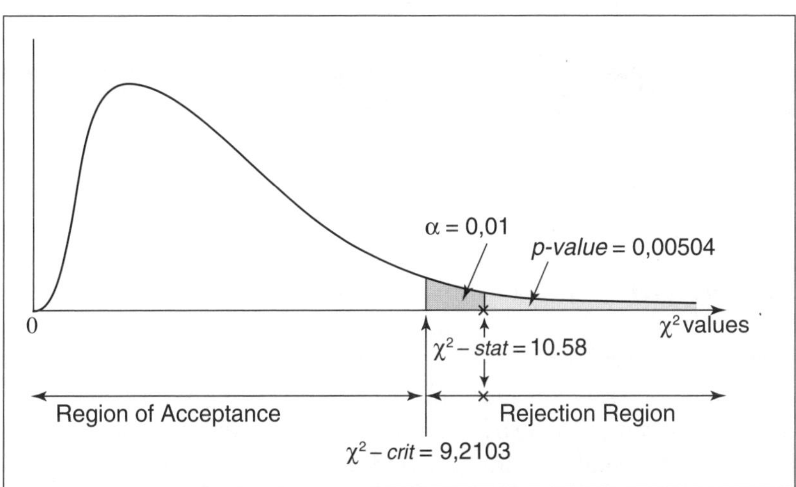

Management interpretation

Since the null hypothesis is rejected at the 1% significance level, the following *management interpretation* can be given:

"The pattern of *daily electricity usage* **does not follow** a normal probability distribution (with μ = 45 kw and σ = 14 kw)."

Note: By rejecting the null hypothesis, it could either mean that:

- the data are sufficiently skewed as to be genuinely non-normal, or
- that the pattern of daily electricity usage does actually follow a normal distribution, but with different parameter values for the mean μ and the standard deviation σ. Different μ and σ values can then be tested in further goodness-of-fit tests.

Fitting other theoretical distributions

Any theoretical probability distribution can be tested against a set of observed frequencies of a random variable using the chi-squared goodness-of-fit test. Two further distributions include the *Poisson distribution* and the *Uniform distribution*, the latter assuming that equal proportions of observations fall into each category.

The statistical procedure for deriving the expected frequencies for any other probability distributions is similar to that for the binomial and normal distributions.

The Rule of Five

When fitting any observed sample-derived frequencies to a set of expected frequencies, the only *condition that must be satisfied* is that each **expected frequency** should be **at least 5**. This condition is necessary to ensure that the χ^2-*stat* test statistic is stable and that reliable conclusions can be drawn.

This condition is applicable whenever the χ^2 statistic is used in hypothesis testing.

To ensure this condition is met, it may be necessary to *combine adjacent classes* or *categories* (if meaningful) for both the observed and expected frequency tables.

13.6 Summary

This chapter introduced the *chi-squared* test statistic, which is used to test hypotheses that the outcomes of a random variable follow specific patterns. The chi-squared statistic is applied to three hypothesis test situations, namely the test for *independence of association* between two categorical random variables; the test for *equality of proportions* in two or more populations; and the *goodness-of-fit* test.

The first two tests are equivalent tests and establish a relationship between two categorical variables. Goodness-of-fit tests, on the other hand, are used when it is necessary to examine whether the response patterns of a random variable follow a given theoretical or user-defined empirical distribution.

In management situations, especially marketing and marketing research, *chi-squared tests for association* are regularly applied to cross-tabulated data. In most instances the manager is seeking associations between various categorical *demographic measures* and *consumer behaviour attributes* (e.g. usage, attitudes towards brands, perceptions, buying intentions, etc.) which are of value for market segmentation purposes.

In all these chi-squared test situations, the four steps of the hypothesis testing procedure are applicable. *Excel* can be used to derive the sample test statistic, χ^2-*stat*, the *critical* χ^2-*limit*, which defines the regions of acceptance and rejection; and the *p-value* for the test statistic on which a statistical conclusion and management interpretation can be based.

Exercises

13.1 X13.1 – **motivation status**

A company conducted a study on motivation levels amongst its clerical employees recently. The HR manager wished to establish if there is any association between the *gender* of the employee and their *level of motivation*. The following cross-tabulation (two-way pivot table) was compiled from the survey data. Refer to the *Excel* file **X13.1**.

Gender	**Motivation Level**		
	High	Moderate	Low
Male	8	8	14
Female	19	12	9

(i) Compute a *row percentage* cross-tabulation table to show the motivation level profile for each gender. Interpret each gender's profile. By inspection, would you conclude that an association exists between an employee's gender and their motivation level?

(ii) Now conduct a suitable hypothesis test to identify statistically whether there is an association between employees' gender and their motivation level. Use $\alpha = 0{,}10$. State your management conclusion.

(iii) Use the CHIDIST function in *Excel* to compute the *p-value* for the test statistic. Interpret its meaning in the context of the management question.

13.2 X13.2 – **internet shopping**

A large supermarket offers an internet shopping service to its customers. They recently conducted a survey amongst their customers to find out if *full-time employed* customers are more likely to use the internet shopping facility than *at-home* customers. Their survey findings are summarised in the following two-way pivot table. Refer to the *Excel* file **X13.2**.

Employment Status	**Use Internet Shopping**	
	Yes	No
Full-time	35	109
At-home	40	176

(i) Show the joint frequency counts in the two-way pivot table as row percentages. Interpret these percentages.

(ii) At the 5% significance level, is there sufficient statistical evidence to conclude that full-time employed customers are *more likely* to use the internet shopping service than at-home customers? (i.e. is employment status and the use of Internet shopping statistically dependent?) What conclusion can be drawn?

(iii) Use the CHIDIST function in *Excel* to compute the *p-value* for the test statistic. Interpret its meaning in the context of the management question.

13.3 X13.3 – car size

A national motor vehicle distributor wishes to find out if the size of car bought is related to the age of a buyer. From sales transactions over the past two years, a random sample of 300 buyers were classified by size of car bought and buyer's age. The following two-way pivot table was constructed. Refer to the *Excel* file **X13.3**.

Buyer's Age	Car size bought		
	Small	Medium	Large
Under 30	10	22	34
30–45	24	42	48
Over 45	45	35	40

(i) Construct a row percentage table. Interpret the percentages.

(ii) Test, at the 1% level of significance, whether car size bought and buyer's age are statistically independent. Interpret your findings and make a recommendation to the marketing manager of the national motor vehicle distributor.

(iii) Use the CHIDIST function in *Excel* to compute the *p-value* for the test statistic. Interpret its meaning in the context of the management question.

13.4 X13.4 – sports readership

An advertising agency wanted to establish if the proportion of people who read a particular magazine, *Sports News*, was the same across three geographical regions. A total of 300 readers of magazines were randomly sampled from the three regions and their readership of *Sports News* was recorded in the following two-way pivot table. Refer to the *Excel* file **X13.4**.

Read Sports News	Region		
	E Cape	W Cape	KZN
No	84	86	78
Yes	16	10	26

(i) Formulate a null and alternative hypothesis to test whether the advertising agency can assume *equal proportions* of readership of *Sports News* across the three regions.

(ii) Conduct the hypothesis test formulated in (i). Use α = 0,01. What conclusion can be drawn.

(iii) Rephrase the null hypothesis as a test for independence of association between readership of *Sport News* and geographical region.

(iv) Use the CHIDIST function in *Excel* to compute the *p-value* for the test statistic in (ii). Interpret its meaning in the context of the management question.

13.5 X13.5 – gym activity

In a recent health and racquet club survey, 140 members were randomly interviewed at a gym and asked to indicate their most preferred gym activity. The choices were *spinning, swimming* or *'doing the circuit'*. The gender of the member was also noted. Their summarized responses are shown in the two-way pivot table. Refer to the *Excel* file **X13.5**.

Gender	**Most preferred activity**		
	Spinning	Swimming	Circuit
Male	36	19	30
Female	29	16	10

(i) Compute row percentages from the joint frequency counts. Interpret the preferred gym activity profile of each gender.

(ii) Is their a statistical association between *most preferred gym activity* and *gender?* Test at the 10% level of significance.

(iii) Use the CHIDIST function in *Excel* to compute the *p-value* for the test statistic in (ii). Interpret its meaning in the context of the management question.

(iv) Formulate the hypothesis in an alternative way as a test of equality of proportions.

(v) If the hypothesis test was conducted at the 5% significance level, would the conclusion change? Justify your answer.

13.6 X13.6 – supermarket visits

The manager of a large supermarket in Nelspruit believes that 25% of their customers shop for groceries daily, 35% shop at least 3 or 4 times per week; 30% shop twice weekly; and the balance shop only once a week.

In a survey conducted amongst a random sample of 180 customers, the following shopping frequencies were identified. Refer to the *Excel* file **X13.6** for the one-way pivot table.

Visits per Week	**Customers**
Daily	36
3–4 times	55
Twice	62
Once only	27

(i) Based on the survey findings, what is the percentage profile of shopping frequencies by customers? Interpret.

(ii) Does the survey data support the manager's belief about the frequency of store visits by customers? Use $\alpha = 0{,}05$. In what way, if any, does the current shopping profile of customers differ from the manager's belief? Comment.

(iii) Use the CHIDIST function in *Excel* to compute the *p-value* for the test statistic in (ii). Interpret its meaning in the context of the management question.

13.7 An investor on the JSE held a 2 : 3 : 1 : 4 ratio of equities between the mining, industrial, retail and financial sectors in 2004. In 2007, of the 4 500 shares which she currently holds, 900 shares are in mining companies, 1 400 shares are in industrial companies, 400 shares are in retail companies, and the rest in financial companies.

Has this investor changed her portfolio mix substantially since 2004?

(i) Test the hypothesis, at the 5% significance level, that there has been no change in portfolio mix since 2004.

(ii) Use the CHIDIST function in *Excel* to compute the *p-value* for the test statistic in (i). Interpret its meaning in the context of the management question.

13.8 X13.8 – payment method

The financial officer of an electronics goods company which sells TVs, sound systems, DVDs, VCRs, etc., knows from past experience that 23% of the store's customers pay cash for their purchases, 35% issue cheques, and the remaining 42% use credit cards. He wants to confirm that this is still the payment method for electronic goods purchases.

Based on a random sample of 200 recent sales receipts, a pivot table showing the breakdown of payment methods was constructed. Refer to the *Excel* file **X13.8**.

Payment method	Customers
Cash	41
Cheque	49
Credit card	110

(i) Use the chi-square goodness-of-fit test to determine whether the payment patterns of the past are still relevant today. Use $\alpha = 0{,}05$. What should the financial officer conclude about customers' current payment methods for electronic goods?

(ii) Use the CHIDIST function in *Excel* to compute the *p-value* for the test statistic in (i). Interpret its meaning in the context of the management question.

13.9 Bokomo Breakfast Cereal is sold in three package sizes: large, midsize and small. National sales figures have shown that these sell in the ratio of 3 : 5 : 2. Sales returns for the Limpopo region show that 190 cases, 250 cases and 100 cases respectively of the different package sizes have been sold recently.

(i) Is the Limpopo region's pattern of sales significantly different from the national sales pattern? Test at the 5% level of significance. If so, in what way does it differ from the national sales profile?

(ii) Use the CHIDIST function in *Excel* to compute the *p-value* for the test statistic in (i). Interpret its meaning in the context of the management question.

13.10 X13.10 – flight delays

Refer to problem 11.16 which investigates the flight delay times of scheduled commercial aircraft.

(i) Use the **Histogram** option in **Data Analysis** to check the assumption of normality by inspection. Comment on the findings.

(ii) Use the **Descriptive Statistics** option in **Data Analysis** to compute the mean and standard deviation of the sample flight delay times (in minutes).

(iii) Use the chi-square goodness-of-fit test to test, at the 1% level of significance, that the data on flight delays follows a *normal distribution* with a mean of 10,324 minutes and a standard deviation of 2,333 minutes. What conclusion can be drawn?

Hint:

(a) Use the interval limits as given in the bin range of *Excel* file **X13.10**.

(b) Compute the expected normal probabilities using the standard normal statistical tables; then use *Excel's* NORMDIST function to confirm the results.

(iv) Use the CHIDIST function in *Excel* to compute the *p-value* for the test statistic in (iii). Interpret its meaning in the context of the management question.

13.11 A sales representative for a pharmaceutical firm visits three clients each day. The company has calculated that a sales representative has a 40% chance of making a sale to each of the three clients visited daily. An analysis of the results for 2007 for 200 days of visits by the sales representative showed that the number of sales per day, namely 0, 1, 2 or 3 were concluded on 46 days, 73 days, 58 days and 23 days respectively.

(i) Test, using $\alpha = 0{,}05$, if the sales per day for this sales representative can be described by a Binomial distribution with $p = 0{,}40$.

Hint:

Compute the expected binomial probabilities using the binomial formula; then use *Excel's* BINOMDIST function to confirm the results.

(ii) Use the CHIDIST function in *Excel* to compute the *p-value* for the test statistic in (i). Interpret its meaning in the context of the management question.

13.12 X13.12 – **plant absenteeism**

The human resources department of a large manufacturer examined the rate of absenteeism in their major plant. Over a 240-day period, the number of employees absent was recorded. The summarised data are shown in the pivot table below. Refer to the *Excel* file **X13.12**.

Employees absent	Number of days
0	18
1	56
2	72
3	45
4	29
5 or more	20

(i) Does it follow the Poisson process with $a = 2$? Test at the 5% level of significance. Interpret your answer.
Hint:
Compute the expected Poisson probabilities using the Poisson formula; then use *Excel's* POISSON function to confirm the results.

(ii) Use the CHIDIST function in *Excel* to compute the *p-value* for the test statistic in (i). Interpret its meaning in the context of the management question.

13.13 X13.13 – **compensation plan**

An insurance organisation sampled its field sales staff in four provinces concerning their preference for compensation. Employees were given the choice between the present compensation method (*fixed salary plus year-end bonus*) and a proposed new method (*straight commission*).

The responses of the randomly sampled field sales staff are summarised in the following two-way pivot table. Refer to the *Excel* file **X13.13**.

Compensation plan	Province			
	Cape	Gauteng	Free State	KZN
Present payment plan	62	140	47	80
New payment plan	38	45	23	30

(i) Compute the column percentage pivot table. Interpret the findings.

(ii) Formulate a suitable null and alternative hypothesis to test whether there is any *difference across the four provinces* in the *proportion* of field sales staff who *prefer the present compensation method*?

(iii) Test the hypotheses formulated in (ii). Use $\alpha = 0{,}10$. Interpret your findings in a brief report to the HR manager of the insurance company.

(iv) What is an alternative way to formulate the null and alternative hypotheses in (ii) above? Show the re-formulated null and alternative hypotheses.
(v) Use the CHIDIST function in *Excel* to compute the *p-value* for the test statistic in (iii). Interpret its meaning in the context of the management question.
(vi) If the hypothesis test was conducted at the 5% significance level, would the management conclusion change? Justify your answer with reference to the *p-value* computed in (v).

13.14 X13.14 – tyre defects

The quality control manager in a tyre manufacturing plant in Port Elizabeth wants to test a belief that the nature of defects found in manufactured tyres depends upon the shift during which the defective tyre is produced. He therefore compiled the following two-way pivot table showing the number of defective tyres identified by *shift* and by *nature of defect* (i.e. *technical* (operator induced), *mechanical* (machine fault), *material* (raw material quality)).

Shift	Nature of tyre defect		
	technical	mechanical	material
Morning	15	42	11
Afternoon	26	40	20
Night	29	25	14

(i) Compute a *row percentage* pivot table. Interpret the findings.
(ii) Is there evidence to substantiate a claim that there is a statistical association between the nature of defective tyres and the shift on which they are produced? Perform a statistical test at the 5% significance level to establish if these two criteria are statistically independent or not.
(iii) What conclusion will the quality control manager communicate to the production manager concerning this issue?
(iv) Use the CHIDIST function in *Excel* to compute the *p-value* for the test statistic in (ii). Interpret its meaning in the context of the management question.
(v) Re-formulate the null and alternative hypotheses to test whether the *proportion of defective tyres* caused by mechanical factors is the same across all shifts. Conduct this revised hypothesis test (use α = 0,05). What conclusion can be drawn?

13.15 X13.15 – newspaper sections

A *Daily Mail* newspaper conducted a survey amongst a random sample of 185 of its readers to determine which of the three sections (namely sport, social, and business) they most prefer to read. The gender of the respondents was also recorded. The individual readers' responses are given in the *Excel* file **X13.15**.

(i) Use the **PivotTable and PivotChart Report** option in the **Data** command to construct a two-way pivot table to show the association between *gender* (row variable) and *section preference* (column variable). Show both the frequency counts and row percentages. Interpret the percentage pivot table.

(ii) Use the **Chart Wizard** option in *Excel* to display the percentage pivot table graphically using a stacked bar chart.

(iii) Are *gender* and *section preference* statistically independent? Test the hypothesis at the 10% level of significance. What conclusion can be drawn?

(iv) Re-formulate the hypothesis as a *test for equality of proportions* of female preferences across the different newspaper sections. What statistical conclusion can be drawn (use α = 0,10).

(v) Use the CHIDIST function in *Excel* to compute the *p-value* for the test statistic in (iii). Interpret its meaning in the context of the management question.

13.16 X13.16 – vehicle financing

Wesbank is a motor vehicle financing company. The financial director wants to know if the pattern of loan amounts that car buyers applied for have changed over the past 4 years. Four years ago, 10% of car loan applications were for amounts of less than R100 000; 20% of applications were for car loans of between R100 000 and R150 000; 40% of car loan applications were for amounts of between R150 000 and R200 000; 20% were for amounts of between R200 000 and R250 000 and 10% of applications were for amounts above R250 000.

An analysis was undertaken recently. A random sample of 300 car financing applications were selected and their loan sizes were recorded. The data are given in the *Excel* file **X13.16**.

(i) Use the **PivotTable and PivotChart Report** option in the Data command to construct a one-way pivot table to show the sample profile of vehicle financing applications received by Wesbank. Show both the frequency counts and percentages. Interpret the percentage pivot table.

(ii) Use the **Chart Wizard** option in *Excel* to show the percentage pivot table as a bar chart.

(iii) Formulate a suitable null and alternative hypothesis to test whether the pattern of vehicle loan amounts applied for has changed from four years ago.

(iv) Test, at the 5% significance level, whether the financial director of Wesbank can conclude that there has been no change to the pattern of vehicle loan amounts requested from four years ago.

(v) Use the CHIDIST function in *Excel* to compute the *p-value* for the test statistic in (iv). Interpret its meaning in the context of the management question.

13.17 X13.17 – milk products

In a survey amongst a random sample of 76 customers at the dairy products section of a supermarket, consumers were asked the following two questions:

Question 1: Do you purchase mainly fat-free milk, low fat milk, or full cream milk?

Question 2: Do you consider yourself to be a health-conscious consumer? (Yes, No)

The customers' responses are given in the *Excel* file **X13.17**.

(i) Use the **PivotTable and PivotChart Report** option in the Data command to construct a two-way pivot table to show the association between *milk type purchased* (row variable) and the *health-conscious status* of a consumer (column variable). Show both the frequency counts and column percentages. Interpret the percentage pivot table.

(ii) Use the **Chart Wizard** option in *Excel* to display the percentage pivot table graphically using a stacked bar chart.

(iii) Can it be concluded that consumers who are more health-conscious are more likely to purchase milk with a lower fat content? Or are they statistically independent? Test the hypothesis at the 5% level of significance. What conclusion can be drawn?

(iv) Re-formulate the hypothesis as a *test for equality of proportions* of milk type purchased by the health-conscious consumers. What statistical conclusion can be drawn (use $\alpha = 0{,}05$).

(v) Use the CHIDIST function in *Excel* to compute the *p-value* for the test statistic in (iii). Interpret its meaning in the context of the management question.

Chapter 14

Analysis of Variance: Comparing Multiple Population Means

Objectives

Analysis of variance (ANOVA) is an inferential statistical technique used to test hypotheses about *multiple population means*. It is an extension of the z-test or t-test, which test equality between only two population means.

Analysis of variance asks the question whether different sample means of a numeric random variable come from the same population, or whether at least one sample mean comes from a different population. The test statistic used to test this hypothesis is called the ***F-statistic***.

If significant differences between sample means are found to exist, it is assumed to be the result of an influencing factor rather than chance. This chapter will consider the case that only one factor influences the differences in sample means. Hence the method known as **One-factor ANOVA** will be used to test for differences in means.

After studying this chapter, you should be able to:

- identify when to apply analysis of variance as a hypothesis testing technique
- understand the rationale of ANOVA and how it tests for equality of means
- compute the *F-statistic* for a One-factor ANOVA problem, and
- interpret the findings of an ANOVA application.

14.1 Introduction and Concepts

In Chapter 12, the *z* or the *t*-test statistic was used to compare the means between two populations (i.e. H_0: $\mu_1 = \mu_2$), using data drawn from two independent samples.

However, when *more than two* population *means* are compared for equality, data drawn from multiple random samples are tested for equality using a test statistic that is based on the *F*-distribution (i.e. *F-stat*). The method used to compute the *F* test statistic (*F-stat*) is called **Analysis of Variance (ANOVA)**. Thus, Anova is an extension of the two-sample test of means to *test for equality of means* across multiple (more than two) populations.

In many management areas there is a need to compare the means of a *numeric* random variable across two or more populations. Each population represents a different influence (called **levels** of a **treatment variable**) on the numeric random variable.

Examples

- A car magazine editor would be interested to compare the fuel consumption (the numeric measure) of 1 800 cc *motor vehicles* of five different makes of car (the *treatment measure* with *five levels*).
- A financial analyst would like to know whether the yield on equities (the numeric measure) between *companies* from four different economic sectors (the *treatment measure* with *four levels*) is the same or different.
- A human resources manager would like to know whether three different *training methods* (the *treatment measure* with *three levels*) have a different effect on worker performance (the numeric measure).

In all cases, a relevant statistical question would be:
"Are the means of the numeric variable the same across the different levels of the treatment measure?"
Stated alternatively: *Is there at least one treatment level mean of the numeric variable that differs from the different treatment level means?*

ANOVA is a hypothesis testing technique that tests for any differences in population means. Its aim is to identify any *influence* of the *treatment measure* on the outcome of the *numeric measure* based on sample evidence.

Figure 14.1(a) overleaf pictorially shows the data values and their respective means for three sets of samples, each corresponding to a different treatment level. The statistical question is whether these three sample means come from different populations [as illustrated in Figure 14.1(b) overleaf], caused by the influence of the treatment variable, or whether they belong to one population [as illustrated in Figure 14.1(c) overleaf].

If there are *significant differences in means* across treatment levels, then a statistical relationship exists between the treatment variable and the response variable (i.e. the two measures are statistically *dependent*). This implies that at least one sample mean comes from a different population to the other samples. This is illustrated in Figure 14.1(b).

If, on the other hand, the *mean outcomes* of the numeric response variable are the *same*, regardless of the condition under which it is observed, then these two measures are *independent* of each other (i.e. no statistical relationship). The implication is that observed sample mean differences are due purely to chance and that all sample data was actually drawn from one homogeneous population. This is illustrated in Figure 14.1(c).

Figure 14.1(a) Sample data and sample means representing three treatment levels

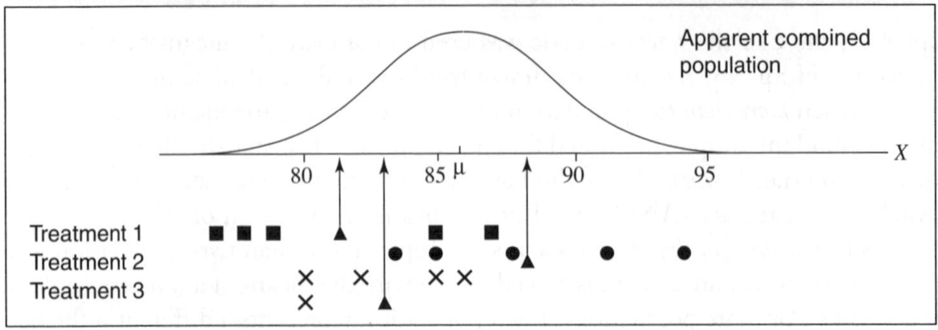

Figure 14.1(b) Sample means belonging to different populations

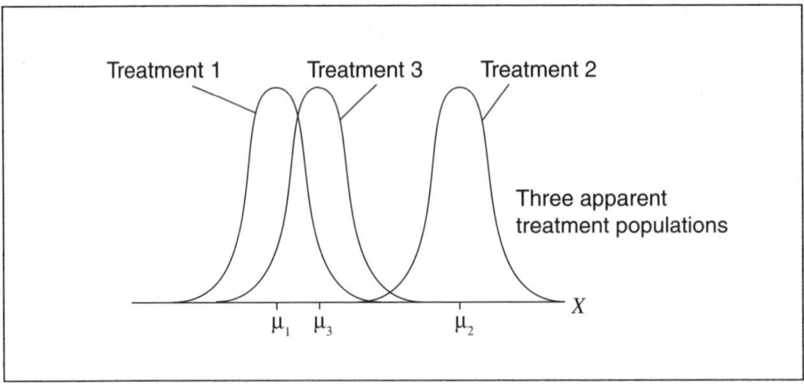

Figure 14.1(c) Sample means belonging to one population

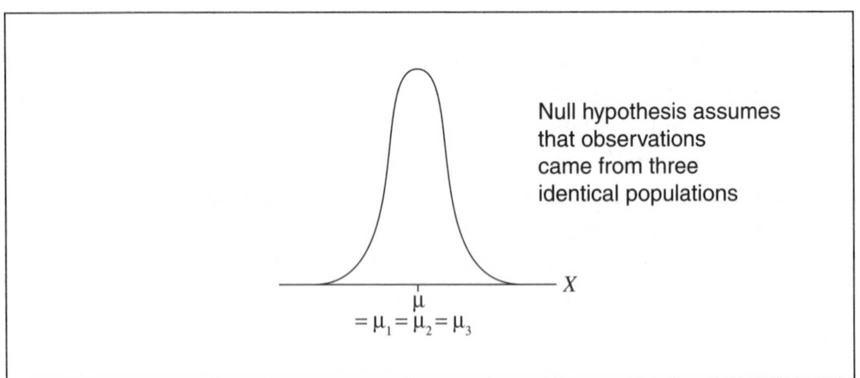

This chapter will cover One-factor ANOVA. One-factor Anova examines the influence of a *single treatment variable* on the outcome of the *numeric response variable*. To conduct One-factor Anova, data from multiple samples must be drawn and compared.

14.2 One-Factor Analysis of Variance (One-factor Anova)

The rationale of One-factor Anova is explained by way of an example.

Example 14.1 Car Battery Rejects study

Excel data file: **C14.1 – car batteries**

The production manager of Raylite Batteries, a car battery manufacturer, wants to know whether the three machines used for this process (labelled A, B and C) produce equal amounts of rejects. A random sample of shifts for each machine was selected and the number of rejects produced per shift was recorded. The data are shown in Table 14.1.

Table 14.1 Sample data of Battery Rejects by machine

Machine A	Machine B	Machine C
11	7	14
9	10	13
6	8	11
12	13	16
14		16
11		

Management question

Can the production manager of Raylite Batteries conclude that the three machines used to manufacture car batteries produce rejects at the *same average rate* per shift?

Statistically, this translates into testing, at the 5% significance level, whether the *mean reject rate* is the *same* across the *three machines*.

Solution (with explanation)

ANOVA is an **inferential hypothesis testing** technique to test for equality of means across multiple samples. As such it follows the same *four steps of hypothesis testing* as outlined in earlier hypotheses tests.

However, before performing a rigorous statistical test for significant differences, it is useful to inspect the sample data (using *exploratory data analysis* methods) and draw an observational conclusion about any possible differences in mean reject rates by machine type.

(i) Naming the variables in the study

- The *numeric* random variable (*response variable*) is the *reject rate per shift*.
- The *treatment variable* – which is categorical – is *machine type*.
- The *treatment level* is the *different types of machines* (A, B and C).
- The treatment variable is categorical and it identifies the different samples of data to be compared.

Figure 14.2 shows the descriptive statistics and ANOVA hypothesis test findings for the *car battery* study. This analysis is also given in the *Excel* file: **C14.1 – car batteries.**

Figure 14.2 Car Battery Rejects - ANOVA findings using *Excel*'s Data Analysis tool

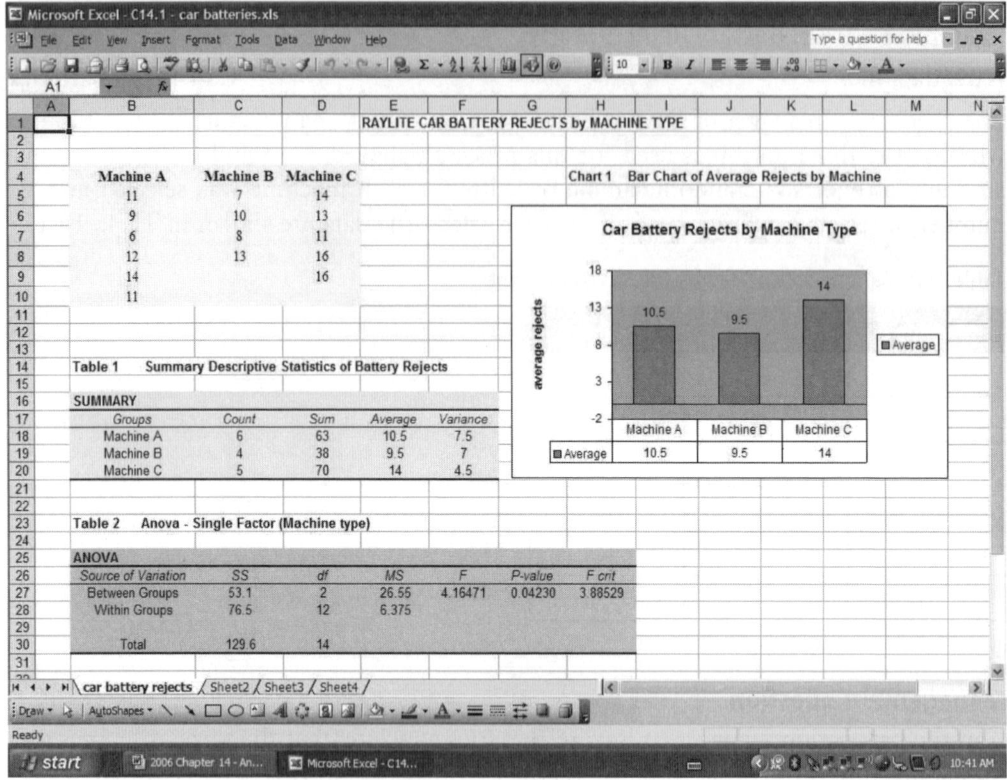

RAYLITE CAR BATTERY REJECTS by MACHINE TYPE

Machine A	Machine B	Machine C
11	7	14
9	10	13
6	8	11
12	13	16
14		16
11		

Table 1 Summary Descriptive Statistics of Battery Rejects

SUMMARY

Groups	Count	Sum	Average	Variance
Machine A	6	63	10.5	7.5
Machine B	4	38	9.5	7
Machine C	5	70	14	4.5

Table 2 Anova - Single Factor (Machine type)

ANOVA

Source of Variation	SS	df	MS	F	P-value	F crit
Between Groups	53.1	2	26.55	4.16471	0.04230	3.88529
Within Groups	76.5	12	6.375			
Total	129.6	14				

(ii) Exploratory data analysis

(See **Table 1** and **Chart 1** of **Figure 14.2.**)

An inspection of the *sample mean* reject rate per machine type shows that machine B produces the lowest average rate of reject batteries per shift (9,5 batteries), while machine C produces the highest average rate of reject batteries per shift (14 batteries).

The Management question is whether these observed sample mean differences are statistically significant. Are the observed differences in sample means "small enough" to be attributed to pure sampling error only (in which case H_0 is accepted), or are these observed differences "large enough" to be due to the influence of the treatment variable (in which case reject H_0 in favour of H_1)?

Thus, a rigorous hypothesis test of equality of means, using the **Anova** approach, is required. The Anova method applies the same four steps of hypothesis testing, but uses the *F-stat* test statistic in place of either the *z-stat* or the *t-stat* test statistic.

(iii) Hypothesis test for equality of three means – the Anova approach

(See **Table 2** of **Figure 14.2.**)

Step 1: Define the null and alternative hypotheses

The null hypothesis always states that *all* the *population means* are *equal* (this is identical to the null hypothesis for the *two sample* test of means).

Thus H_0: $\mu_1 = \mu_2 = \mu_3$
(i.e. the *mean reject rate* is the *same* for all machine types)
H_1: At least one μ_i differs ($i = 1, 2, 3$)
(i.e. at least one machine produces a *different* mean reject rate to the rest)

Note: The alternative hypothesis only states that *at least one* (and not all) of the population means must be different. It **does not imply** that they *must all differ* from one another.

Accepting H_0 implies that the mean reject rate of batteries is not influenced by the type of machine on which they are produced. This means that each machine produces the same average rate of reject batteries per shift and that any sample mean differences are due to chance sampling.

Alternatively, if *at least one sample mean* is significantly different to the rest, then it can be concluded that the treatment variable (i.e. machine type) has influenced the reject rate.

The Anova test will determine whether the three (3) sample means of *battery reject rates* are sufficiently close to each other for any observed differences in means to be attributed to chance (i.e. pure sampling error) only. If so, it can be concluded that the three samples all come from the same population with a common mean value and the *null hypothesis* cannot therefore be rejected in favour of the alternative hypothesis.

Step 2: Compute the sample test statistic

The appropriate sample test statistic is ***F-stat***.

Unlike the two-sample means test, which compares the two sample means directly, the Anova test computes its test statistic (***F-stat)***, by *comparing variances* **within** and **between** the different samples.

The following explanation and derivation of the ***F-stat*** test statistic is given to develop an understanding of the rationale of the Anova approach. In addition, *Excel* is used to perform the *one-factor Anova* computations using the **Anova: Single Factor Data Analysis.** The computations are given in Table 14.2 overleaf and will be referred to in subsequent explanations.

Table 14.2 One-factor Anova output for Battery Rejects study

Summary				
Groups	**Count**	**Sum**	**Average**	**Variance**
Machine A	6	63	10,5	7,5
Machine B	4	38	9,5	7
Machine C	5	70	14	4,5

Anova						
Source of Variation	**SS**	**Df**	**MS**	**F stat**	**P-value**	**F crit**
Between Groups	53,1	2	26,55	**4,16471**	**0,04230**	**3,88529**
Within Groups	76,5	12	6,375			
Total	129,6	15				

Rationale of One-Factor Anova and the Derivation of the Test Statistic *F-stat*

Anova identifies *three measures of variability* in the total sample data:

- total sample variability
- between-sample variability, and
- within-sample variability.

Variability is measured by the *sum of squared deviations* (as used in the calculation of a variance (see chapter 6)). It is called **sum of squares** or **SS**.

(i) Total sample variability

If all the samples were combined into one overall sample, then *total sample variability* is a measure of variability of the combined data values about an overall *grand mean* computed from the combined samples data.

It is called the **Total Sum of Squares (SST)**.

$$SST = \sum_i \sum_j (x_{ij} - \bar{\bar{x}}_{..})^2 \quad = 129{,}6 \qquad \text{(see **Table 14.2**)}$$

where x_{ij} = the ith observation of the jth sample
$\bar{\bar{x}}_{..}$ = the overall grand mean ($= \sum_i \sum_j x_{ij} / N$)
(*Note:* $N = n_1 + n_2 + n_3 + \ldots + n_k$)

Applying the formula:

$\sum\sum x_{ij}$ = (11 + 9 + 6 + 12 + 14 + 11 + 7 + 10 + 8 + 13 + 14 + 13 + 11 + 16 + 16)
= 171

N = 6 + 4 + 5 = 15

$\bar{\bar{x}}_{..} = \frac{171}{15} = 11{,}4$

Then

SST $= (11 - 11{,}4)^2 + (9 - 11{,}4)^2 + (6 - 11{,}4)^2 + \ldots + (16 - 11{,}4)^2 + (16 - 11{,}4)^2$
= 129,6

This measure of *total variability* (SST) is now divided into two components: *between*-sample variability and *within*-sample variability.

(ii) Between-sample variability

This measures the variability *between* the sample means and the overall grand mean. The extent to which the sample means deviate about the overall *grand mean* explains the influence of the different sample treatment levels (i.e. the *different machine types*).

It is called the **Between Samples Sum of Squares (SSB)** and is calculated as follows:

$$SSB = \sum_{j}^{k} n_j(\bar{x}_j - \bar{x}..)^2 = 53{,}1$$ (see **Table 14.2**)

where n = sample size of the the jth sample
$\bar{x}_j$ = j^{th} sample mean
k = number of different samples (or treatment levels)

Applying the formula

$$SSB = 6(10{,}5 - 11{,}4)^2 + 4(9{,}5 - 11{,}4)^2 + 5(14 - 11{,}4)^2 = 53{,}1$$

It can now be seen that 53,1 units (i.e. SSB) out of the *total variability* (SST) of 129,6 units from the combined samples is **explained** by the different *machine types* (i.e. different treatment levels). This variation is called **explained variation** or variation *due to the treatment effect*.

(iii) Within-sample variability

This is the variability that occurs between data values *within* each sample. It represents the *error* (or chance) variation, since it *cannot be explained* by the different levels of the treatment variable.

It is called the **Within Samples Sum of Squares (SSW)** and is calculated as follows:

$$SSW = \sum_{j}\sum_{i} (x_{ij} - \bar{x}_j)^2 = 76{,}5$$ (see **Table 14.2**)

Applying the formula

$$SSW = [(11 - 10{,}5)^2 + (9 - 10{,}5)^2 + \ldots + (11 - 10{,}5)^2] + [(7 - 9{,}5)^2 + \ldots + (10 - 9{,}5)^2] + [(14 - 14)^2 + (13 - 14)^2 + \ldots + (16 - 14)^2] = 76{,}5$$

This SSW value of 76,5 measures the amount of variation *within* each sample (and summed across all samples) that cannot be "explained" by the treatment variable. Theoretically, SSW should be zero if the treatment variable can explain *all* the variation in the overall sample data.

It is therefore also called the **unexplained variation** or the **error sum of squares** or the **residual sum of squares**. (Some texts will use the notation SSE – error sum of squares – to identify it.)

These three measures of variability are related as follows:

Total sample variation = *Between* sample variation + *Within* sample variation.

or, using alternative wording

Total sum of squares = *Explained* sum of squares + *Unexplained* sum of squares

or

Total sum of squares = *Treatment* sum of squares + *Residual* (*Error*) sum of squares.

In statistical notation form:

SST = SS Between (SSB) + SS Within (SSW)

i.e. 129,1 = 53,1 + 76,5 (see **Table 14.2**)

Computing Variances from Sum of Squares

All these terms (i.e. SST, SSB and SSW) are the *numerator values* for a *variance* (see the variance formula in chapter 6). Thus, when each *Sum of Squares* term is divided by its respective *degrees of freedom* (based on its sample size), the resultant measure is a *variance*. Recall that the degrees of freedom for a variance is always its sample size minus one (i.e. $(n - 1)$).

Another name used to describe a *variance* is a **mean square error** – standing for the *mean* of the *sum of squares*. It shows that a variance is an *average* of the *squared deviations*. This term – mean square error – is used extensively in Anova.

Computing Variances from Sum of Squares

(i) Total sample variance = SST/$(N - 1)$

The combined sample size is $N = n_1 + n_2 + n_3 = 6 + 4 + 5 = 15$

Hence its degrees of freedom = $N - 1 = 15 - 1 = 14$

Given SST = 129,6 and degrees of freedom = 14

Then Mean Square Total (MST) = $\frac{129,1}{14} = 9,22$

This is the total (combined) sample variance (i.e. also written as σ^2_{Total}).

Note: MST is not shown in the Anova table in Table 14.2, as it is not used to compute *F-stat*, but is an important intermediate calculation.

(ii) Between Groups Variance = SSB/$(k - 1)$

Since k sample means (i.e. $k = 3$) are used to compute SSB,

the degrees of freedom = $k - 1$

The resultant variance estimate is called the **Mean Square Between Groups (MSB)**.

Thus $$\text{MSB} = \frac{\text{SSB}}{(k-1)}$$

i.e. $\text{MSB} = \frac{53,1}{2} = 26,55$ (see **Table 14.2**)

(iii) Within Groups Variance = SSW/$(N - k)$

For each sample, the degrees of freedom are $(n - 1)$. Since SSW is found by summing squared deviations per sample over all samples, the total degrees of freedom is:

$(n_1 - 1) + (n_2 - 1) + (n_3 - 1) + \ldots + (n_k - 1) = (N - k)$ for k samples

The resultant variance estimate is called the **Mean Square Within Groups (MSW)**.

Thus $$\text{MSW} = \frac{\text{SSW}}{(N-k)}$$ where $N = 15$ and $k = 3$

i.e. $$\text{MSW} = \frac{76{,}5}{(15-3)} = \frac{76{,}5}{12} = 6{,}375$$ (see **Table 14.2**)

Finally, the two variance estimates (MSB and MSW) are used to compute the *F-statistic* relevant to the specific sample data.

The ***F*-statistic**, which is derived from an analysis of sample variances (hence the name Anova), is defined as a **ratio of two variances**.

Hence $$F\text{-}stat = \frac{\text{MSB}}{\text{MSW}}$$

i.e. $$F\text{-}stat = \frac{26{,}55}{6{,}375} = 4{,}16471$$ (see *F-stat* in cell [F27] **Table 14.2**)

For ease of reference, the above computations are usually set out in an ANOVA table, as shown in Table 14.2. The general layout for an Anova Table is shown in Figure 14.3 below.

Figure 14.3 The One-factor Anova table

Source of Variation	Sums of Squares SS	Degrees of Freedom df	Mean Square MS	F
Between Groups (Explained variation)	SSB	$(k - 1)$	$\text{MSB} = \frac{\text{SSB}}{(k-1)}$	$\frac{\text{MSB}}{\text{MSW}}$
Within Groups (Unexplained variation)	SSW	$(N - k)$	$\text{MSW} = \frac{\text{SSW}}{(N-k)}$	
Total Sample Variation	SST	$(N - 1)$		

Note: The *sums of squares* measures and *degrees of freedom* are additive, but *not* the mean square measures.

Step 3: Decision rule to guide the acceptance / rejection of the null hypothesis

Approach 1 Using the region of acceptance/rejection method

Since two variances are used to construct F, this statistic can never be negative. Hence the Anova hypothesis test is only an *upper-tailed test* with a single *critical F-limit* (*F-crit*). To find *F-crit*, both a *level of significance*, α, and *degrees of freedom* must be known.

- **Level of significance**

  The *level of significance*, α, is given as α = 0,05 (5% significance level).

- **Degrees of freedom**

  There are two values for the *degrees of freedom* of an *F*-statistic. They are called the *numerator* degrees of freedom and the *denominator* degrees of freedom. These are the values that are divided into each sum of squares (i.e. SSB and SSW) respectively.

  For SSB, the *numerator* degrees of freedom, $df_1 = k - 1$
  For SSW, the *denominator* degrees of freedom, $df_2 = N - k$. where k = number of samples, N = total (combined) sample size.

  In the example, the *degrees of freedom* are: $df = [(3 - 1),(15 - 3)] = (2, 12)$

  In general the *critical F-value* is defined as $\textbf{F-crit} = F_{(\alpha)((k-1);(N-k))}$

To find the critical *F*-limit (*F-crit*)

F-crit could either be read off a statistical table (see **Table 4(a)** and **4(b)** in Appendix 1) for the *F*-distribution; or found by using the **=FINV** function in *Excel.*

- **Using the *F*-table**

  $F_{(\alpha = 0,05)(df = 2, 12)} = 3,8853$ (from **Table 4(a)** in Appendix 1).

To read the F-table

Select the table for α = 0,05; then identify the *column* for the *numerator* degrees of freedom, and the *row* for the *denominator* degrees of freedom. The value read off at the intersection of the row and column is the *F-crit* statistic.

or

- **Using the *Excel* function =FINV(probability=α , numerator df, denominator df)**

  i.e. **=FINV(0.05,2,12)** = 3,885294

Thus, the *region of acceptance* for H_0 is $[F \leq 3,8853]$

The *decision rule* is then stated as follows:

Do not reject H_0 if *F-stat* falls at or below the upper limit of 3,8853.
Reject H_0 in favour of H_1 if *F-stat* falls above 3,8853.

Approach 2 Using the *p-value* method

Given *F-stat* = 4,1647 (from *step 2*), the *p-value* refers to the *upper tail area* of the *F*-distribution above *F* = 4,16471

The *p-value* cannot be found from the *F*-tables. It can only be computed using an *Excel* function as follows:

- **Using *Excel's* function**
  =FDIST(x, df_1, df_2) where x = *F-stat* = 4,16471 $df_1 = 2$ $df_2 = 12$

i.e.

=FDIST(4.16471,2,12) gives an upper tail area = 0,0423

Thus *p-value* = 0,0423

The *decision rule* is derived from **Figure 11.5** of chapter 11.

Step 4: Statistical conclusion and Management interpretation

Statistical conclusion

The *statistical conclusion* refers to whether the *null hypothesis* is *accepted or rejected* on the basis of the sample evidence.

Since

- the *p-value* (= 0,0423) lies between 0,05 (5%) and 0,01 (1%)
- *F-stat* (= 4,1647) > *F-crit* (= 3,8853), and therefore lies *outside* the region of acceptance of H_0

there is *strong sample evidence* to support the alternative hypothesis H_1. Therefore, the alternative hypothesis is probably true.

Figure 14.4 shows the sample test statistic (*F-stat*) in comparison to the region of acceptance/rejection (*F-crit*) and the *p-value* of the test.

Figure 14.4 F-distribution: test statistic and decision rules for Car Battery Rejects study

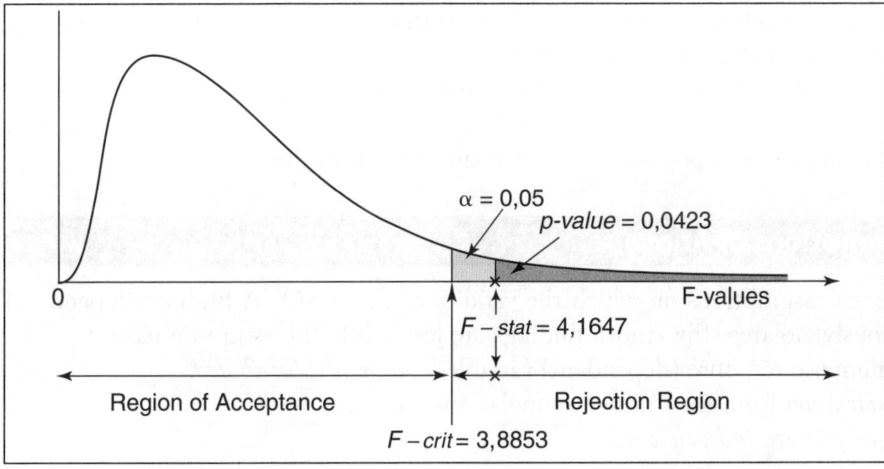

Management interpretation

Since there is strong sample evidence to reject the null hypothesis at the 5% significance level, the following *management conclusion* can be drawn:

"At least one machine's *mean reject rate* differs from that of the remaining machines."

To identify the nature of the differences, the sample means can be inspected and an observational conclusion drawn (see **Table 1** of **Figure 14.2**).

Machine C produces a significantly higher average rate of reject batteries per shift (14 batteries) than machines A and B. There appears to be no significant difference, however, in the average rate of reject batteries produced by machines A and B.

Therefore, management attention should focus on Machine C and the reasons for its high reject rate.

14.3 How the Anova Method Tests for Equality of Means

The test statistic *F-stat* is the *ratio of two variances – between samples* variance and *within samples* variance.

$$F = \frac{\text{Between Samples Variance}}{\text{Within Samples Variance}} = \frac{\frac{SSB}{(k-1)}}{\frac{SSW}{(N-k)}} = \frac{MSB}{MSW}$$

Recall that SSB + SSW = SST. For a given set of data across multiple samples, SST will be a fixed value, while SSB and SSW will vary, depending on these data values within each sample.

If *SSB is large* in relation to SSW, this implies that there are some *large differences* in *sample means*. This will result in a *large F-stat* value.

If *SSB is small* in relation to SSW, this implies that the *sample means are close* to each other. This will result in a *small F-stat* value.

Thus small *F-stat* values (i.e. close to zero) imply that H_0 is probably true and that all the population means are equal. Conversely, large *F-stat* values imply that H_0 is probably false, and that at least one population mean is different from the rest.

14.4 Assumptions of Anova

There are three assumptions on which the validity of the ANOVA findings depends. If any are seriously violated, the Anova findings are less valid. The assumptions are:

(i) The numeric response (dependent) variable is *normally distributed.*
(ii) The *variances* from the different populations are *equal.*
(iii) The *samples* are *independent.*

These assumptions can be examined by inspection of the data.

- The normality assumption can be examined by inspecting a histogram.
- The following rule of thumb can be used to test the assumption of equal variances:

"Divide the *largest sample variance* by the *smallest sample variance*. If this ratio is less than 3, accept H_0 of equal variances, otherwise reject H_0".

14.5 Summary

Analysis of variance (ANOVA) was introduced as the method to compare means across multiple populations. Each population represents a different level of a categorical treatment variable.

ANOVA follows the same four-step hypothesis testing procedure as outlined in earlier chapters. It computes a test statistic called *F-stat,* which is the ratio of two variances.

The *numerator variance* measures variability *between* the sample means of the different treatment levels. As such, it is termed the "explained variance" since any observed differences could be "explained" by the different treatment levels applied to each sample separately. The *denominator variance*, on the other hand, measures the variability *within* the different samples, and averaged across all samples. It is termed the "unexplained" variance, since variability within samples cannot be explained by the different treatment levels.

ANOVA works on the principle that large *F-stat* values imply significant differences between at least two population means and hence is sufficient evidence to reject H_0 in favour of H_1. Alternatively, small *F-stat* values imply no significant differences between population means and hence the sample evidence indicates that H_0 – i.e. that all the population means are equal – is probably true.

Finally, the assumptions of ANOVA were identified. While formal statistical tests exist to test each of these assumptions, it is generally adequate to examine them by inspection of the sample data and the application of basic rules of thumb.

Exercises

14.1 X14.1 – car fuel efficiency

A car magazine tested the fuel efficiency of three makes of 1 600 cc motor vehicles (Peugot, VW, Ford). A sample of 1 600 cc motor vehicles from each make were road tested under identical driving conditions and their consumption in l/100 km were recorded. The consumption data is given in the *Excel* file **X14.1**.

Peugot	VW	Ford
7	6,8	7,6
6,3	7,4	6,8
6	7,9	6,4
6,4	7,2	7
6,7		6,6

(i) Compute the average fuel consumption for each make of motor vehicle. Display them graphically as a bar chart, using the **Chart Wizard** in *Excel.*

(ii) Can the car magazine editor conclude that the *average fuel consumption* across the three makes of 1 600 cc motor vehicles are the same? Test an appropriate hypothesis at the 5% level of significance assuming that the three populations are normally distributed with equal variances. Which make of motor vehicle, if any, is the most fuel efficient?

(iii) Find the *p-value* for the test statistic in (ii) using the FDIST function in *Excel.* Interpret the meaning of the *p-value* in the context of the management question.

(iv) If the significance level of the test was 1%, would this change the conclusion reached in (ii)? Support your answer with statistical evidence.

14.2 X14.2 – package design

A cereal manufacturer evaluated three different package designs (A, B and C) to test market their new muesli breakfast cereal. Each design was tested in separate samples of randomly selected convenience grocery stores in locations with similar customer profiles. The number of cartons (where each carton contains 50 packs of cereal) was recorded for a one-month trial period in each store. The data are given in the *Excel* file **X14.2**.

Sales of cereal packs		
design A	**design B**	**design C**
35	35	38
37	34	34
39	30	32
36	31	34
30	34	34
39	32	33
36	34	
34		

(i) Name two statistical assumptions that must be satisfied to produce valid results for an Anova hypothesis test.

(ii) Is any package design more effective in generating higher sales of packs of the Muesli cereal? Test this assertion at the 5% significance level using One-Factor Anova. Formulate the null and alternative hypotheses and show the Anova table. Which one package design should the cereal producer use to market their product?

(iii) Find the *p-value* for the test statistic in (ii) using the FDIST function in *Excel.* Interpret the meaning of the *p-value* in the context of the management question.

14.3 X14.3 – bank service

Random samples of customers from each of three banks were asked to rate the level of service of their bank on a 10-point rating scale (1 = extremely poor; 10 = extremely good). Assume that the three populations of rating scores are normally distributed with equal variances. The rating scale responses are given in the *Excel* file **X14.3.**

Bank service levels ratings		
Bank X	**Bank Y**	**Bank Z**
8	5	8
6	6	7
6	7	6
7	5	7
6	5	6
6	5	6
7	7	5
9	5	6
	7	5
		6

(i) Test the hypothesis that the mean service level rating scores are the same across all three banks. Use α = 0,10. Show the null and alternative hypotheses and the Anova table. Interpret the findings.
(ii) Find the *p-value* for the test statistic in (ii) using the FDIST function in *Excel.* Interpret the meaning of the *p-value* in the context of the management question.
(iii) If the significance level of the test was 5%, would this change the conclusion reached in (ii)? Support your answer with statistical evidence.

14.4 X14.4 – shelf height

The manager of a grocery retail chain wished to find out if shelf height played a role in influencing a product's sales. A drinking chocolate product was displayed at four different shelf heights for equal periods of time and the volume of sale (units sold) was recorded. The sales data are given in the *Excel* file **X14.4**.

Shelf Height			
Bottom	**Waist**	**Shoulder**	**Top**
78	78	83	69
84	85	86	76
74	76	75	74
75	82	78	72
68	81	80	83
80	75	88	75
74	94	90	
	80	78	
		84	

(i) Can the manager of the grocery retail chain conclude that mean product sales are independent of shelf height? Test at the 5% significance level. Assume the populations are normally distributed with equal variances. What conclusion can the manager draw from the findings?
(ii) Find the *p-value* for the test statistic in (ii) using the FDIST function in *Excel.* Interpret the meaning of the *p-value* in the context of the management question.

14.5 X14.5 – earnings yields

A business analyst recorded the earnings yields of a random sample of public companies from each of four economic sectors (financial, retail, industrial, and mining). She wanted to know if the average earnings yields are different across sectors. The earnings yield data are given in the *Excel* file **X14.5**.

Earnings yields by Sector			
Industrial	**Retail**	**Financial**	**Mining**
3.4	6,4	4,6	7,2
5	3,6	6,2	5,4
4	4,4	3,8	5,8
4	4,4	4,6	6
4,2	3,8	4,2	7,6
5,2	4	6,6	6,8
5	5,8	4,4	4
3,8	6	5	3,6
5,7	7,6	3,8	4,2
6,2	3,8	4,8	6,6
3.8	5	7,2	4,4
4,2	4	5,4	5
5,2	3,6	5,8	3,8
4	4,2	6	5
4	5,2	7,6	3,6
6,8	6,8	7,6	6
7,2	3,4	7,2	7,6
5,2	5	5,4	6,8
5	4	5,8	4
4,2	3,4	7,2	7,6

(i) Formulate a suitable null and alternative hypothesis to test whether there is any difference in the mean earnings yields across the four economic sectors.

(ii) Use the **Anova: Single Factor** option in **Data Analysis** to perform the hypothesis test at the 5% level of significance. Interpret the findings for the business analyst.

(iii) Are the two assumptions of (a) equal variances and (b) independent samples satisfied in the example? Explain.

(iv) Find the *p-value* for the test statistic in (ii) using the FDIST function in *Excel*. Interpret the meaning of the *p-value* in the context of the management question.

14.6 X14.6 – advertising strategy

A deodorant manufacturer test marketed a new ladies deodorant under three different advertising strategies. The same deodorant was marketed over three consecutive periods of 20 weeks each as "sophisticated", then as "athletic", and finally as "trendy". The level of sales achieved each week under each advertising strategy was recorded and is given in the *Excel* file **X14.6**.

Deodorant sales by Advertising strategy		
Sophisticated	**Athletic**	**Trendy**
428	424	444
259	280	310
394	349	340
435	362	379
517	342	447
302	253	298
463	407	413
338	417	362
428	430	434
437	401	445
477	475	458
441	429	405
503	392	408
415	234	419
356	296	438
553	527	532
373	314	364
454	308	444
426	252	280
381	349	410

(i) Formulate a suitable null and alternative hypothesis to test whether mean deodorant sales differs according to advertising strategy used.

(ii) Use the **Anova: Single Factor** option in **Data Analysis** to perform the hypothesis test at the 5% level of significance. Which advertising strategy should the company adopt for maximum sales impact?

(iii) Find the *p-value* for the test statistic in (ii) using the FDIST function in *Excel*. Interpret the meaning of the *p-value* in the context of the management question.

(iv) Use the **t-Test: Two-Sample Assuming Equal Variances** option in **Data Analysis** to test for equality of mean sales between the two advertising strategies that generated the two highest sample average sales volumes of deodorant. Use α = 0,05. What conclusion can be drawn?

(v) Find the *p-value* for the test statistic in (iv) using the TDIST function in *Excel.* Interpret the meaning of the *p-value* in the context of the management question.

(vi) Based on the statistical findings in (ii)–(v), which advertising strategy would you recommend that the deodorant manufacturer adopt to achieve maximum sales impact?

14.7 X14.7 – machine evaluation

A company which produces labelled packaging (e.g. cereal boxes) plans to buy a new shaping and labelling machine. They are considering three different machines. Each machine's method of operation differs and therefore so does its processing time to complete tasks. The company subjected each machine to five randomly selected shaping and labelling tasks and recorded the processing time of each machine (in minutes). The data are given in the *Excel* file **X14.7.**

Processing time by Machine		
Machine A	**Machine B**	**Machine C**
11	10	15
13	11	13
12	13	15
9	8	17
14	14	12

(i) Can it be concluded that there is no difference in the mean processing time between the three different machines? Use $\alpha = 0{,}10$. Formulate the null and alternative hypotheses and compute the Anova table. Interpret the findings for the company.

(ii) Use the *t*-test for equal means (assuming equal population variances) to test the hypothesis that there is no difference in the processing speeds between the *two fastest* processing machines. Use $\alpha = 0{,}10$. Interpret the findings.

(iii) Based on the findings of the two hypotheses tests in (i) and (ii), which shaping and labelling machine would you recommend that the company purchase? Why?

(iv) Compute the *p-values* for each hypothesis test (in (i) and (ii)) using FDIST and TDIST respectively. Interpret the meaning of each in the context of their respective null and alternative hypotheses.

14.8 X14.8- leverage ratio

A financial investor recorded the leverage ratios of a random selection of companies from four different economic sectors (technology, construction, banking, and manufacturing). The leverage ratio is the ratio of company debt to the value of shareholder equity and is a measure of financial risk. The higher the leverage ratio, the greater the risk is to shareholders. The investor wants to invest in a low risk economic sector.

The leverage ratio data are given in the *Excel* file **X14.8**.

Leverage ratios by Economic sector			
Technology	**Construction**	**Banking**	**Manufacturing**
83	70	66	44
62	75	87	59
61	72	55	47
85	68	41	60
60	72	68	79
78	92	49	62
68	70	52	73
66	71	57	64
83	74	66	69
81	80	62	81
63	71	78	70
67	88	75	80
88	90	68	78
60	85	75	72
71	78	57	71
86	69	68	75
71	60	84	80
60	80	69	81
88	61	55	87
68	89	78	84
82	97	99	85
85	98	87	83
86	79	57	94
71	80	84	89
72	84	93	77
77	58	64	94
73	79	70	92
68	86	80	82
75	91	64	93
77	75	84	86

(i) Compute the descriptive statistics of leverage ratio for each sector using the **Descriptive Statistics** option in **Data Analysis**. By inspection, what conclusions can the financial investor draw about differences in mean leverage ratios between the four economic sectors?

(ii) Are the assumptions of normality and equal population variances likely to be satisfied for an Anova test? Use the descriptive statistics findings (skewness and sample variances) to justify your answer.

(iii) What statistical and management conclusions can the financial investor draw about differences in the mean leverage ratios between the different economic sectors? Use the **Anova: Single Factor** option in **Data Analysis** to perform the hypothesis test at the 5% level of significance. In which economic sector should the financial investor invest his funds? Provide statistical evidence.

(iv) Use the **t-Test: Two-Sample Assuming Equal Variances** option in **Data Analysis** to test the hypothesis that there is no difference in the mean leverage ratios between the *two sectors* with the *lowest risk* in terms of sample mean leverage ratios. Use α = 0,05. Interpret the findings.

(v) Based on the findings of the two hypotheses tests in (iii) and (iv), into which economic sector would you recommend that the financial investor invests his funds? Why?

(vi) Compute the *p-values* for each hypothesis test (in (iii) and (iv)) using FDIST and TDIST respectively. Interpret the meaning of each in the context of their respective null and alternative hypotheses.

14.9 X14.9 – training methods

The HR department of a telecommunications organisation (such as MTN or Vodacom) want to find the most effective training method for their employees in dealing with their customers. A random sample of 56 employees was selected from their various client services departments and randomly assigned to one of *four training methods* (on-the-job training; lectures; role play; and audio-visual).

After receiving the appropriate training method, a measure of performance was recorded for each employee as a score on a 10 point scale (assessed by a training evaluator). The *performance scores* on each of the sampled employees are given in the *Excel* file **X14.9**.

Method of Employee Training			
On-the-Job	**Lecture**	**Role Play**	**Audio-Visual**
9,3	9,1	9,6	8,7
8,9	8,3	9	9
8,7	8,2	9,2	8,4
9,1	9	9,7	7,7
8,6	9,2	9,6	9,2
9,1	8,5	8,9	8,8
9,5	8,7	8,8	8,9
9,7	8,5	9,3	9,4
9	9	9,4	8,9
8,6	8,5	8,8	9,3
9	8,6	8,9	8,6
9	8,9	9,2	9
8,5	9,7		9,1
8,8	8,3		8,9
9			
9,2			

(i) Compute the descriptive statistics of *performance scores* for each training method using the **Descriptive Statistics** option in **Data Analysis**. By inspection, what conclusions can the HR manager draw about differences in mean performance scores between the different training methods?

(ii) What statistical and management conclusions can the HR manager draw about differences in the mean performance scores between the different training methods? **Use the Anova: Single Factor** option in **Data Analysis** to test the hypothesis at the 5% significance level.

Is there any one training method that is more effective than the rest in producing superior employee performance levels when dealing with the company's customers? Provide statistical evidence.

Formulate appropriate null and alternative hypotheses for this hypothesis test.

(iii) Use the **t-Test: Two-Sample Assuming Equal Variances** option in **Data Analysis** to test the hypothesis that there is no difference in the mean performance scores between the two training methods with the highest sample mean performance scores. Use $\alpha = 0{,}05$. Interpret the findings.

(iv) Based on the findings of the two hypotheses tests in (ii) and (iii), which single training method, if any, would you recommend that the HR manager adopts for all company employees? Why?

(v) Compute the *p-values* for each hypothesis test (in (ii) and (iii)) using FDIST and TDIST respectively. Interpret the meaning of each in the context of their respective null and alternative hypotheses.

PART
5

Statistical Models for Forecasting and Planning

Chapter

15

Linear Regression and Correlation Analysis

Objectives

In many business decisions it is necessary to predict the unknown values of a numeric variable using other numeric variables for which values are known.

Regression analysis is a statistical technique that builds a model of the relationship between the unknown variable and the set of known variables. This model is used for prediction purposes. Correlation analysis, on the other hand, identifies the strength of the relationships and determines which variables are useful in predicting the unknown variable.

After studying this chapter, you should be able to:

- explain the meaning of regression analysis
- identify practical examples where regression analysis can be used
- construct both a simple and a multiple linear regression model
- prepare estimates of the unknown variable using the regression model
- compute and interpret the correlation coefficient
- compute and interpret the coefficient of determination
- test the overall regression model for statistical significance, and
- test the individual regression variables for statistical significance.

15.1 Introduction

In management, many numeric measures are related (either closely or loosely) to one another.

Examples

- Advertising expenditure is assumed to have an influence on sales volumes.
- Share price is influenced mainly by a company's return on investment.
- Hours of operator training is likely to impact positively on productivity.
- Operating speed of a bottling machine affects the reject rate of under-filled bottles.

A **scatter plot** of pairs of data between two *numeric* random variables, x and y, visually displays the likely relationship between them, as illustrated graphically in Figure 15.1.

Figure 15.1 A Scatter plot between pairs of x and y data values

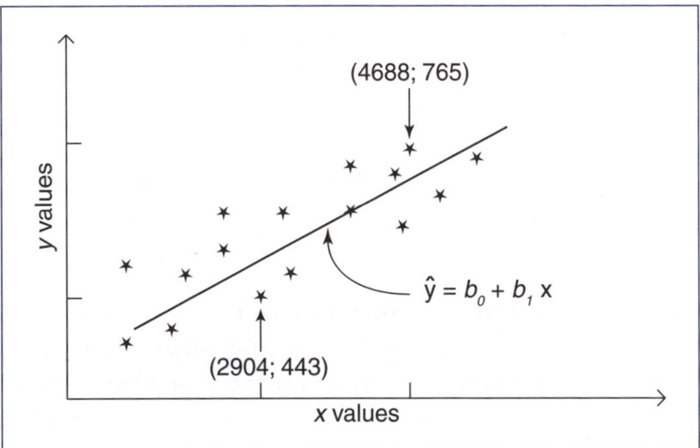

If a structural relationship exists between two *numeric* random variables – and can be measured and quantified – then knowing the values of one of the variables, x, can be used to predict (or estimate) the outcome of the other variable, y, for which values are generally unknown. This is the primary purpose of regression and correlation analysis. These techniques can provide managers with a powerful tool for prediction purposes.

> **Regression analysis** defines the structural *relationship* between two numeric random variables as a mathematical equation (usually a straight-line equation), while **correlation analysis** measures the *strength* of this identified *association* between the variables.

In Figure 15.1, the straight-line equation is fitted using regression analysis. The degree of closeness of the plots to the straight line is measured by correlation analysis. The straight-line equation can be used to estimate the y-values based on known x-values. Correlation analysis provides a measure of the confidence a manager can have in the estimated y-values.

Regression and correlation analysis require that the *data type* for all variables (e.g. marketing, economic, financial, production, human resources, etc.) must be *numeric.*

This chapter examines the following topics in regression analysis:

- Simple linear regression analysis, which examines the relationship between two numeric variables only;
- Correlation analysis, which computes the strength of a relationship; and
- Multiple linear regression analysis, where numerous numeric measures are used to influence the outcome of a single numeric measure.

15.2 Simple Linear Regression Analysis

Simple linear regression analysis finds a *straight-line equation* between the values of *two numeric* random variables only. The one variable is called the **independent** or **predictor variable**, *x*, and the other is termed the **dependent** or **response variable**, *y*.

Independent variable (x)

The *independent variable* is represented by the symbol *x*. It is the variable *influencing* the *outcome* of the other variable. For this reason it is also called the predictor variable. Its values are usually known or easily determined. In certain instances, the independent variable's values can be controlled or manipulated. In the *examples* in section 15.1 above, the independent variables would be: *advertising expenditure*; *company return on investment*; *hours of operator training*; and *bottling machine speed.*

Dependent variable (y)

The other numeric random variable is called the **dependent variable** and is represented by the symbol *y*. The dependent variable is *influenced by* (or responds to) *the independent variable.* Hence it is also called the **response variable**. Values for the dependent variable are not readily known and need to be estimated from values of the independent variable (*x*). In the *examples* in section 15.1 above, the dependent variables are: *sales volumes*; *share price*; *productivity*; and *reject rate.*

In simple linear regression, only one independent variable, *x*, is used to estimate or predict values of the dependent variable, *y*. Multiple regression, which is covered in section 15.3, uses two or more independent variables to estimate the value of the dependent variable.

To build a simple linear regression model, a number of steps are followed, as illustrated below.

5.2.1 Identify the Dependent and Independent Variables

An essential prerequisite is to correctly identify the independent and dependent variables. This is necessary to ensure that a valid relationship is established. A useful rule of thumb is to ask the following question: "Which variable is to be estimated?"

The answer to this question will identify the dependent variable, *y*. Thus the logic of the relationship must be checked before proceeding with regression analysis.

5.2.2 Use a Scatter Plot to Graphically Examine the Relationship Between the Dependent and Independent Variables

The *first step* towards identifying a possible relationship between two numeric random variables is to prepare a visual plot of their data values. This is done through a *scatter plot*.

A **scatter plot** (or *scatter graph*) graphically displays all pairs of data values of the independent and dependent variables on an *x*–*y* axis. The *x* values are recorded along the horizontal axis and the *y* values along the vertical axis, as was shown in Figure 15.1.

A visual inspection of the scatter plot will show whether there is a relationship between the two variables, *x* and *y*, and how strong it is likely to be. These initial insights are likely to be reflected in the regression and correlation analysis findings. If, for *example*, the data points are widely scattered, then a linear regression equation will be of little value in estimating the *y*-variable. The correlation measure will also show almost no association.

Figures 15.2 to 15.6 show various possible *patterns of relationships* between a dependent numeric variable, *y*, and an independent numeric random variable, *x*.

Figure 15.2 Direct linear relationship with small dispersion (i.e. for any given *x* value, the range in *y* values is small)

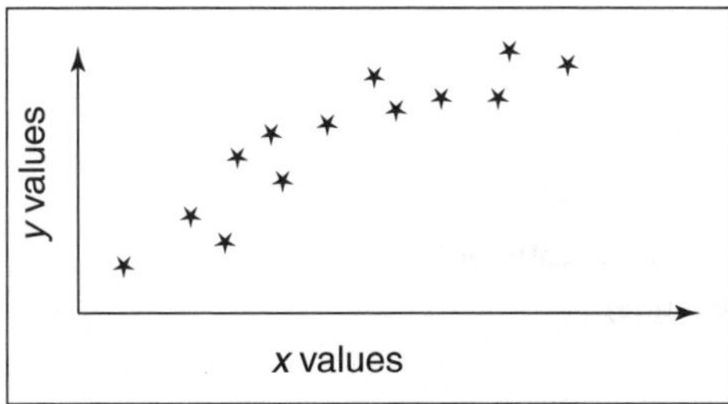

Figure 15.3 Inverse linear relationship with small dispersion (i.e. for any given *x* value, the range in *y* values is small)

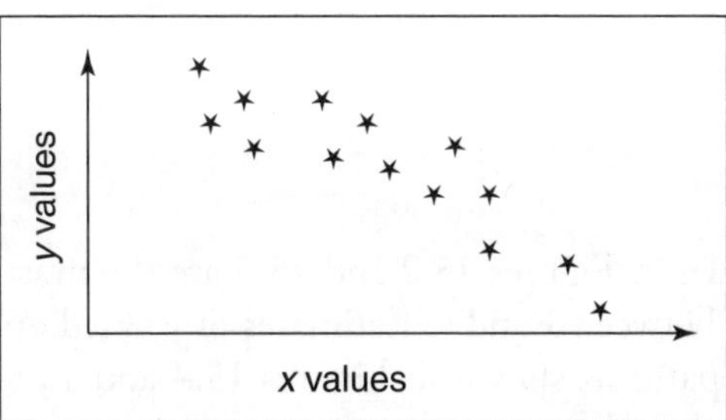

Figure 15.4 Direct linear relationship with greater dispersion (i.e. for any given x value, the range in y values is larger)

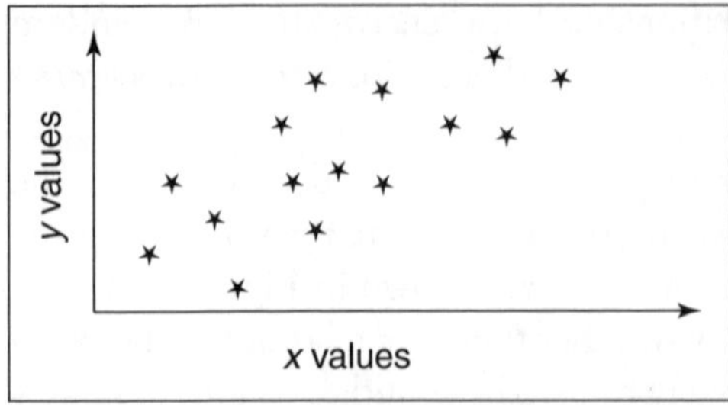

Figure 15.5 Inverse linear relationships with greater dispersion (i.e. for any given x value, the range in y values is larger)

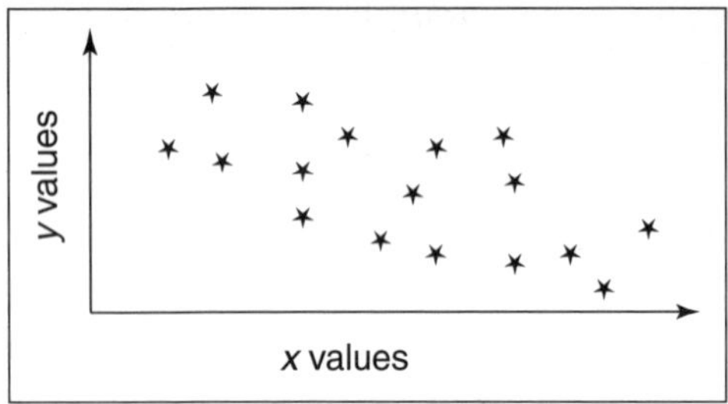

Figure 15.6 No linear relationship (values of x and y are randomly scattered) (i.e. for any given x value, y can have any value over a wide range)

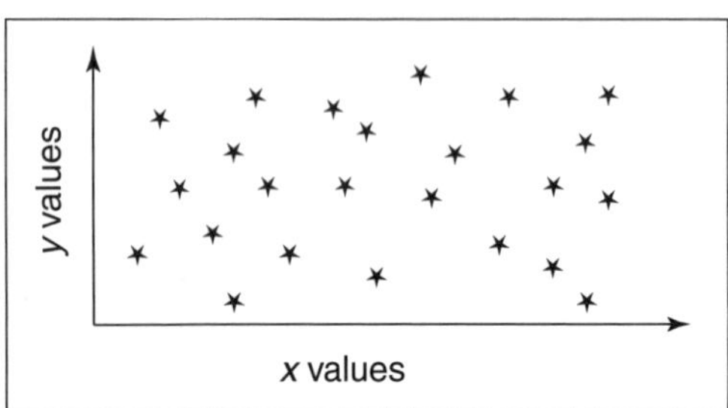

From a *manager's* perspective, the patterns shown in Figures 15.2 and 15.3 are the most desirable as they show *strong linear relationships* between *x* and y. Estimates of *y* based on these relationships will be highly reliable. The patterns shown in Figures 15.4 and 15.5 are evidence of *moderate to weak linear relationships* that are of less value for estimation purposes. Nevertheless, some benefit is derived from even moderate relationships, but managers must exercise caution in using these linear regression relationships to predict *y*-values from *x*-values. Finally, the pattern shown in Figure 15.6 is evidence of *no statistical relationship* between the two numeric measures. In such cases, there is no value in using regression analysis to estimate *y* based on *x* values. The estimates will be unreliable.

15.2.3 Calculating the Linear Regression Equation

Regression analysis finds the equation of the *best-fitting* straight line to represent the actual data points.

Formula

A straight line graph is defined as follows:

$$\hat{y} = b_0 + b_1 x$$

where
- x = values of the independent variable
- $\hat{y}$ = estimated values of the dependent variable
- b_0 = the *y intercept* coefficient (where the regression line cuts the y axis)
- b_1 = the *slope (gradient)* coefficient of the regression line (i.e. for every one unit change in x, y will change by b_1)

The method of least squares (MLS)

Regression analysis uses the *method of least squares* to find the *best-fitting* straight-line equation to the plotted data points. The method of least squares is a mathematical technique which finds values for the coefficients, b_0 and b_1, such that:

"the sum of the squared deviations of the data points from the fitted line is minimised."

A brief explanation of the rationale is given and is illustrated using the three data points shown as asterisks in Figure 15.7 overleaf.

(i) A deviation (error) (written as e_i), which is a measure of the vertical distance from an actual y-value to the fitted line, is first computed for each y_i-value.

$$e_i = (y_i - \hat{y}_i)$$

(ii) Each deviation is now squared to avoid positive and negative deviations cancelling each other out when summed.

$$e^2_i = (y_i - \hat{y}_i)^2$$

(iii) A measure of total squared deviations is then found by summing the individual squared deviations.

$$\Sigma e^2_i = \Sigma(y_i - \hat{y}_i)^2$$

(iv) Values for b_0 and b_1 are now found, which will minimise the sum of these squared deviations in (iii). The mathematical calculation that will minimise the sum of these squared deviations, is called the method of least squares.

Figure 15.7 Graphical illustration of the method of least squares (MLS)

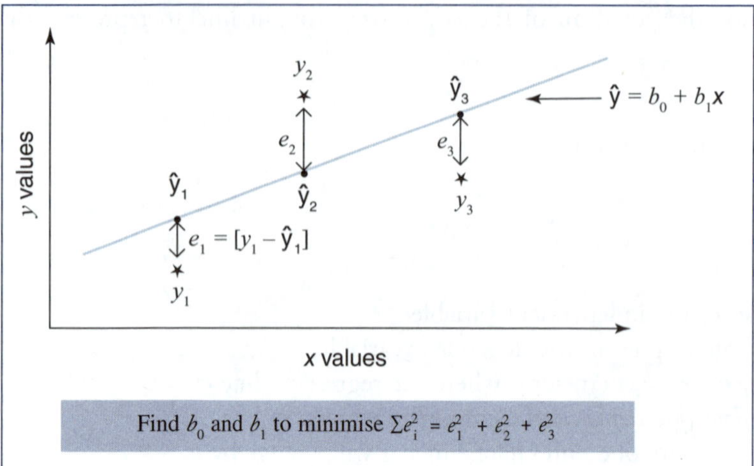

Without showing the mathematical calculations, the coefficients b_0 and b_1 that result from the *method of least squares* are given as follows.

$$b_1 = \frac{n\Sigma xy - \Sigma x\Sigma y}{n\Sigma x^2 - (\Sigma x)^2}$$

$$b_0 = \frac{\Sigma y - b_1\Sigma x}{n}$$

The values of b_0 and b_1 that are found from the above formulae define the *best-fitting* linear regression line. This means that no other straight-line equation can be found that will give a better fit (i.e. a smaller sum of squared deviations) than the regression line. The calculation of these regression coefficients can also be found using the **Regression** option in **Data Analysis**, as will be illustrated in Example 15.1.

15.2.4 Estimating y-values using the Regression Equation

The regression equation can now be used to estimate values of y from (known) x-values. Estimates of y are found by substituting a given x-value into the regression equation. The values of x that can be substituted in the regression equation should lie only within the *domain* of the x variable. The *domain* of the x variable is defined as the range of x-values from the data set that were used to calculate the regression line.

The dangers of extrapolation

Extrapolation occurs when y-values are estimated using *x-values* that *lie outside the domain* of the x-values. Valid estimates of y are produced only from x-values that lie within its domain. If the values of y are estimated for x-values *outside the limits of the domain* (i.e. extrapolation has taken place), the *estimates* may be *invalid*, as the relationship between x and y beyond these limits is unknown (or has not been defined). The relationship may in fact be quite different from that which is defined between x and y within the x-domain. Extrapolation can sometimes lead to absurd and meaningless estimates of y.

The following example illustrates the above process of building a simple linear regression model.

Example 15.1 ipod Sales study

***Excel* file:** **C15.1 – ipods**

Music Technologies, an electronics retail company in Durban, has kept records of the number of ipods sold within a week of placing advertisements in the *Mercury*. Table 15.1 shows the *number of ipods sold* and the corresponding *number of advertisements placed* in the *Mercury* for 12 randomly selected weeks over the past year.

Table 15.1 Database of ipod sales and newspaper advertisements placed

Ads	Sales
4	26
4	28
3	24
2	18
5	35
2	24
4	36
3	25
5	31
5	37
3	30
4	32

Management questions

(1) Find the straight-line regression equation to estimate the *number of ipods* that Music Centre can *expect to sell* within a week, based on the *number of advertisements* placed.

(2) Estimate the likely *mean sales of ipods* when three *advertisements* are placed.

Solution

Figure 15.8 overleaf shows the linear regression computations using the **Regression** option from **Data Analysis**.

Figure 15.8 ipod Sales and Advertisements – Regression Analysis using *Excel*

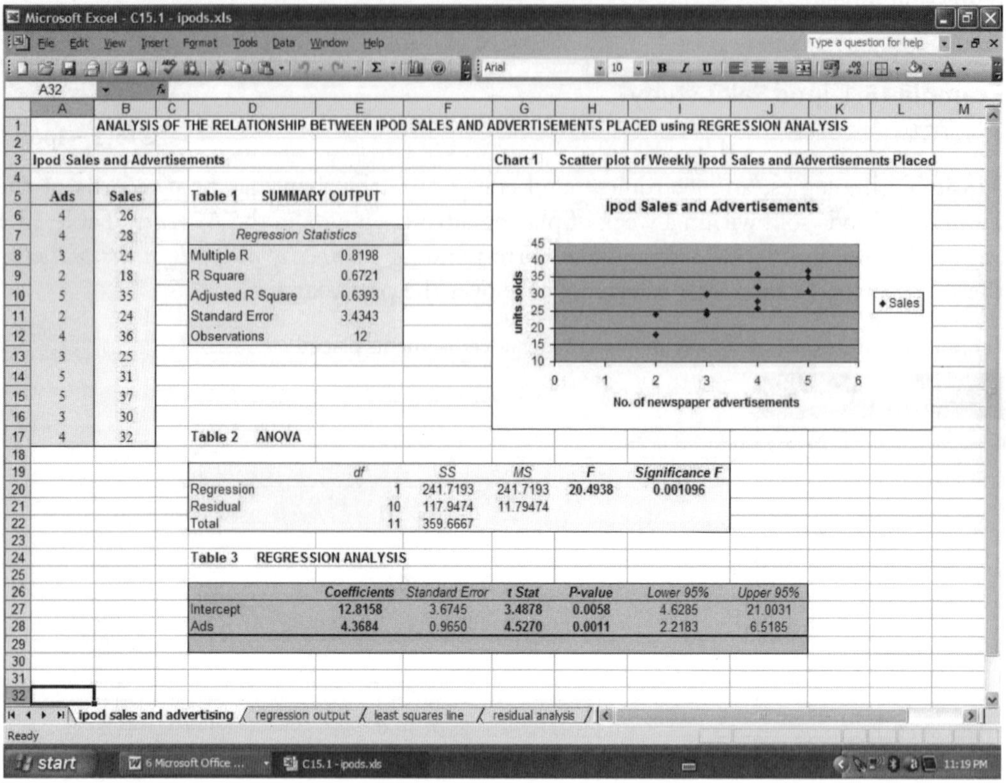

Microsoft Excel - C15.1 - ipods.xls

ANALYSIS OF THE RELATIONSHIP BETWEEN IPOD SALES AND ADVERTISEMENTS PLACED using REGRESSION ANALYSIS

Ipod Sales and Advertisements

Ads	Sales
4	26
4	28
3	24
2	18
5	35
2	24
4	36
3	25
5	31
5	37
3	30
4	32

Table 1 SUMMARY OUTPUT

Regression Statistics	
Multiple R	0.8198
R Square	0.6721
Adjusted R Square	0.6393
Standard Error	3.4343
Observations	12

Chart 1 Scatter plot of Weekly Ipod Sales and Advertisements Placed

Table 2 ANOVA

	df	*SS*	*MS*	*F*	*Significance F*
Regression	1	241.7193	241.7193	**20.4938**	**0.001096**
Residual	10	117.9474	11.79474		
Total	11	359.6667			

Table 3 REGRESSION ANALYSIS

	Coefficients	*Standard Error*	*t Stat*	*P-value*	*Lower 95%*	*Upper 95%*
Intercept	**12.8158**	3.6745	**3.4878**	**0.0058**	4.6285	21.0031
Ads	**4.3684**	0.9650	**4.5270**	**0.0011**	2.2183	6.5185

ipod sales and advertising / regression output / least squares line / residual analysis

(i) Identify the dependent and independent variables

The *dependent* variable y = number of *ipods sold*
The *independent* variable x = number of newspaper *advertisements placed.*

(ii) Scatter plot of the dependent variable against the independent variable

Chart 1 of **Figure 15.8** shows the scatter plot between *ipod sales* and *advertisements* placed, produced by the XY (Scatter) graph option of *Excel's* Chart Wizard.

By inspection of the scatter plot, it appears that there is a reasonably good positive relationship between sales of ipods and the number of newspaper advertisements placed. The relationship also appears to be linear (i.e. a straight-line equation would best represent the relationship).

(iii) Calculate the linear regression equation:

The regression coefficients, b_0 and b_1, can be found either:

- manually, by evaluating the two formulae derived from the method of least squares,

or

- by using the **Regression** option from the **Data Analysis** add-in in *Excel.*
  Both approaches will be demonstrated.

Solution (manual)

Table 15.2 shows the intermediate calculations required for use in the formulae.

Table 15.2 Computing the regression coefficients, b_0 and b_1, for the ipod Sales study

Ads (x)	ipods (y)	x^2	xy
4	26	16	104
4	28	16	112
3	24	9	72
2	18	4	36
5	35	25	175
2	24	4	48
4	36	16	144
3	25	9	75
5	31	25	155
5	37	25	185
3	30	9	90
4	32	16	128
44	**346**	**174**	**1 324**

Thus $\Sigma x = 44$ $\Sigma y = 346$ $\Sigma x^2 = 174$ $\Sigma xy = 1324$ and $n = 12$

Then $$b_1 = \frac{12(1324) - (44)(346)}{12(174) - (44)^2} = \frac{664}{152} = 4{,}368$$

and $$b_0 = \frac{346 - 4{,}368(44)}{12} = 12{,}817$$

Thus the estimated linear regression equation is defined as:

$\hat{y} = 12{,}817 + 4{,}368x$ for $2 \le x \le 5$ (i.e. the *domain* of x values)

Solution using *Excel*

This equation can also be computed using the **Regression** option in *Excel's* **Data Analysis**. The detailed regression output is shown in Table 15.3 (and **Tables 1, 2** and **3** of **Figure 15.8**) with the regression equation coefficients, b_0 (Intercept) and b_1 (Ads), shown in bold in the "Coefficients" column.

Table 15.3 *Excel's* regression analysis output for the ipod Sales study

Summary Ouput	
Regression Statistics	
Multiple R	0,8198
R Square	0,6721
Adjusted R Square	0,6393
Standard Error	3,4343
Observations	12

Anova					
	df	***SS***	***MS***	***F***	**Significance F**
Regression	1	241,7193	241,719298	**20,4938**	**0,001096**
Residual	10	117,9474	11,7947368		
Total	11	359,6667			

	Coefficients	Standard Error	*t* Stat	p-value	Lower 95%	Upper 95%
Intercept	**12,8158**	3,6745	3,4878	0,0058	4,6285	21,0031
Ads	**4,3684**	0,9650	4,5270	0,0011	2,2183	6,5185

Note: The minor differences in coefficient values are due to rounding error in the manual approach.

The regression line and its equation can be superimposed on the scatter plot data as shown in Figure 15.9 below.

HOW TO

To fit the regression line in Excel

- right-click on any data point in the scatter plot
- select **Add Trendline**
- select **Linear** from the **Type** tab; and
- from the **Option** tab – tick both boxes **Display equation on chart**; and **Display R-squared value on chart**, and click **OK**.

Figure 15.9 Regression Line on Scatter plot of ipod Sales Data

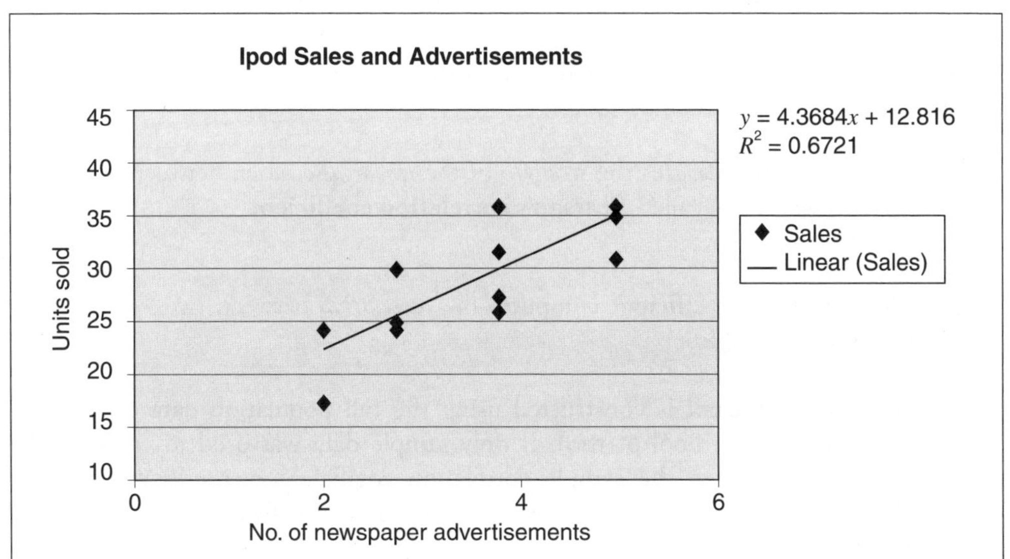

(iv) Estimating *y*-values using the regression equation

The Management question (2) asks for an estimate of mean ipod sales when three newspaper advertisements are placed. This requires that $x = 3$ is substituted into the regression equation.

i.e. $\hat{y} = 12{,}817 + 4{,}368\,(\mathbf{3})$
$= 12{,}817 + 13{,}104 = 25{,}921 = 26$ (rounded)

The management of Music Technologies can therefore expect to sell, on average, 26 ipods weekly when three newspaper advertisements are placed.

Note (1): Since $x = 3$ is within the domain of x (i.e. $2 \leq x \leq 5$), the y-estimate is valid.

Graphically, the estimated y value of 26 units is the y-value that lies on the regression line that corresponds to $x = 3$.

Note (2): It should also be noted that the estimated (or expected) value of the dependent variable, y, is an *average* (or *likely value*) for the given value of the x variable. The actual value of *ipod sales* will not necessarily be 26 units when three advertisements have been placed. It only reflects the most likely value for y ($\hat{y} = 26$) for the given x-value ($x = 3$). If the regression equation is reliable, as will be examined in the next section dealing with correlation analysis, the *actual* y-value which will result in practice (i.e. actual units of ipods sold), should not be far off the estimated y-value from the regression line.

15.3 Correlation Analysis

The reliability of the estimate of y is determined by the *strength* of the *relationship* between the x and the y variables. A strong relationship will result in a more accurate and reliable estimate of y.

Correlation analysis measures the *strength* of the *linear association* between x and y. The statistical measure is called **Pearson's correlation coefficient**.

Pearson's correlation coefficient computes the *correlation* between two *ratio-scaled (numeric)* random variables.

If the correlation coefficient is constructed using the full population data of x and y, it is represented by the symbol ρ (rho). If only sample data was used to compute the correlation coefficient, then the sample correlation coefficient is represented by the symbol r. In practice, only a sample correlation coefficient is usually computed, hence the term r is commonly used.

Interpretation of correlation coefficient

A correlation coefficient is a *proportion* that takes on values *between -1 and +1 only.*

$$-1 \leq r \leq +1$$

Figure 15.10 shows how the strength of the association between two numeric random variables is represented by the correlation coefficient.

Figure 15.10 Graphical display of interpretation of a correlation coefficient

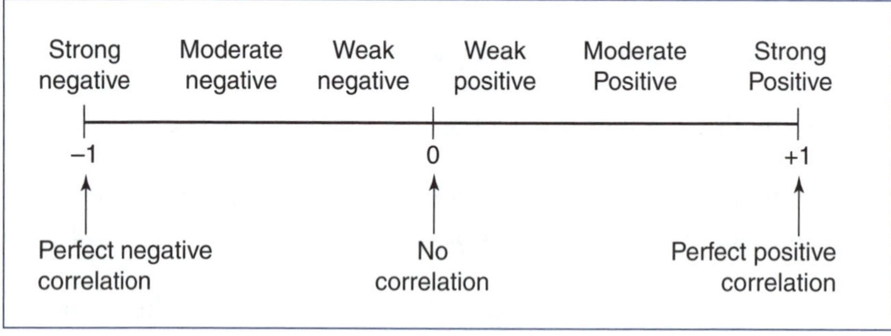

Any interpretation should take the following two points into account.

(i) A low correlation does not necessarily imply that the variables are unrelated, but simply that the relationship is poorly described by a straight line. A non-linear relationship may well exist. Pearson's correlation coefficient does not measure non-linear relationships.

(ii) A correlation does not imply a cause and effect relationship. It is merely an observed statistical association.

Figures 15.11 to 15.17 visually illustrate both the *direction* and *magnitude* of a correlation coefficient associated with various scatter plots of two numeric random variables.

Perfect associations

Figure 15.11 Perfect positive linear correlation (r = + 1)

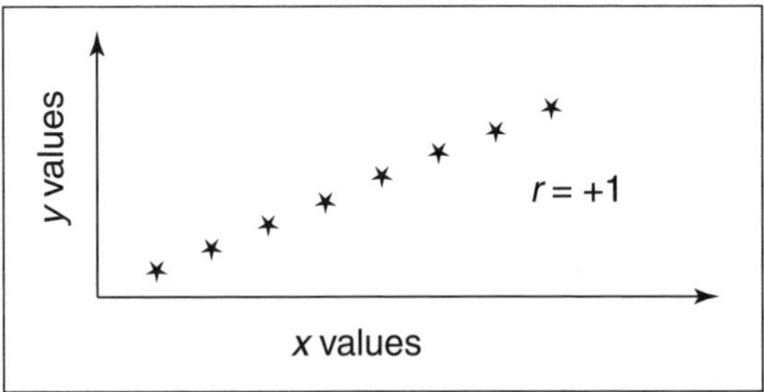

All the data points of a scatter plot will lie on a positively sloped straight line.

Figure 15.12 Perfect negative linear correlation (r = −1)

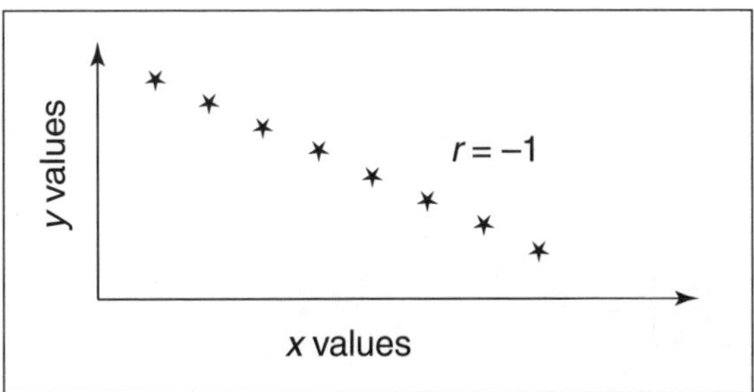

All the data points will again lie on a straight line, but in an inverse direction (i.e. as x increases, y decreases and vice versa). It is thus a negatively sloped straight line.

In both cases, the values of x *exactly predict* values of y. All the actual y-values lie on the regression line. Such a perfect relationship between two economic/business variables is highly unlikely to occur in practice. The following diagrams are more realistic management scenarios.

Strong associations

Figure 15.13 Positive linear correlation ($0 < r < +1$) with r being closer to +1

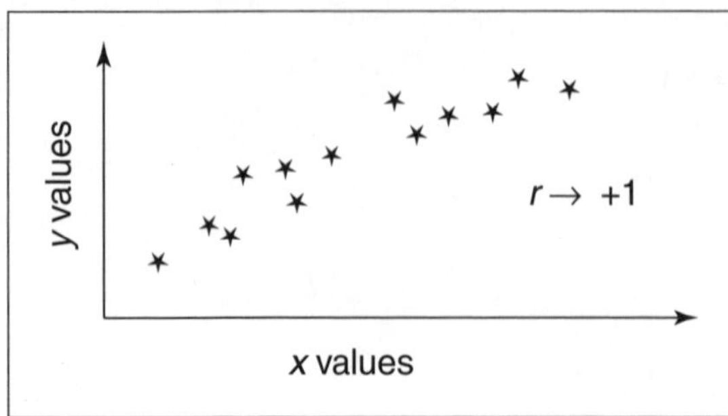

This is a direct relationship, since an increase (decrease) in x results in an increase (decrease) in y.

Figure 15.14 Negative linear correlation ($-1 < r < 0$) with r being closer to –1

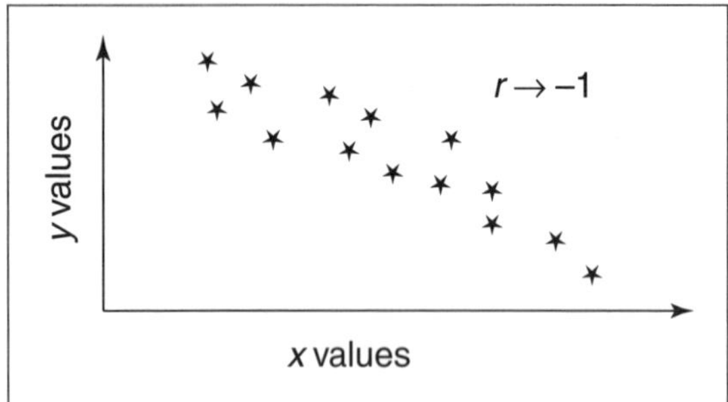

This is an indirect relationship, since an increase (decrease) in x results in a decrease (increase) in y.

The *close grouping* of the scatter points in both diagrams implies a *strong linear relationship*, with the correlation coefficient r being close to +1 if the relationship is positive (or direct), or close to –1 if the relationship is negative (or inverse).

Moderate to weak associations

Figure 15.15 Positive linear correlation (0 < r < +1) with r being closer to 0

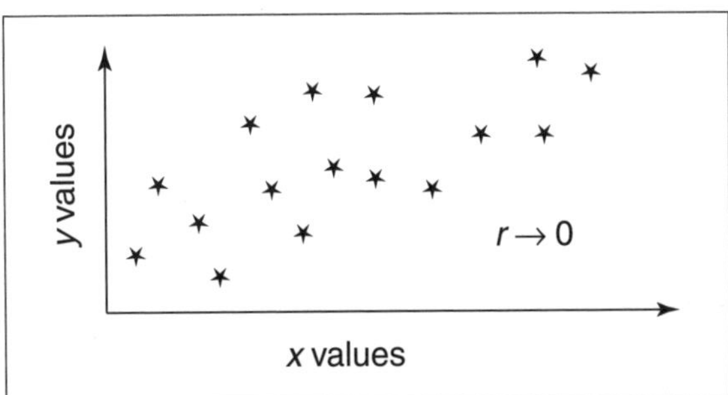

This is also a direct relationship, since an increase (decrease) in x results in an increase (decrease) in y.

Figure 15.16 Negative linear correlation (–1 < r < 0) with r being closer to 0

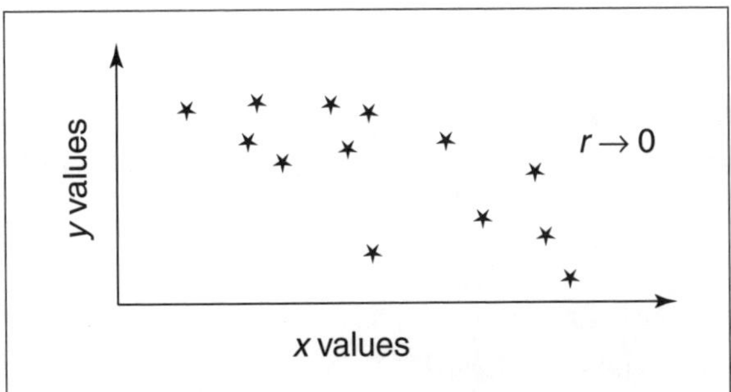

This is also an inverse (or indirect) relationship, since an increase (decrease) in x results in a decrease (increase) in y.

The *loose grouping* of the scatter points in both cases show a *moderate to weak linear relationship*, with the correlation coefficient, r lying closer to 0.

No association

Figure 15.17 No linear correlation (r = 0)

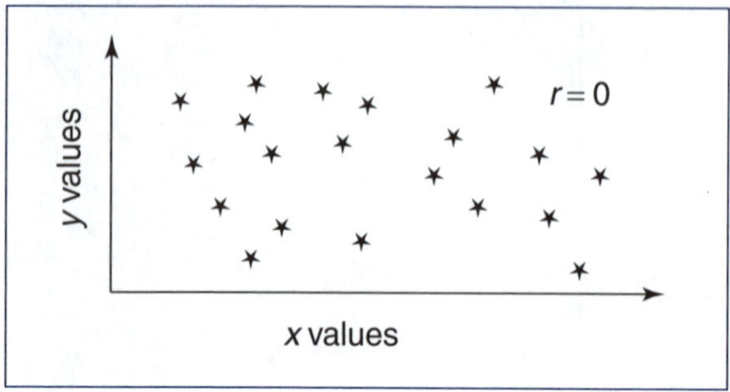

The values of x are of *no value* in estimating values of y. The data points are randomly scattered.

From the above illustrations, it can be seen that the closer r is to −1 or +1, the stronger the association. Similarly, the closer r is to zero, the weaker the linear relationship between x and y.

Computation of Pearson's Correlation Coefficient

Pearson's coefficient represents the correlation between *two numerical* random variables only and is computed as follows:

Formula

$$r = \frac{n\Sigma xy - \Sigma x \Sigma y}{\sqrt{[n\Sigma x^2 - (\Sigma x)^2] \times [n\Sigma y^2 - (\Sigma y)^2]}}$$

where r = the sample Pearson's correlation coefficient
x = the values of the independent variable
y = the values of the dependent variable
n = the number of paired data points in the sample

Pearson's correlation coefficient formula is derived from the least squares regression approach, hence its formula has similar terms to the regression coefficients. The calculation of Pearson's correlation coefficient and its interpretation is illustrated for the *ipod Sales* study in Example 15.1.

Example 15.2 ipod Sales study

Refer to the management scenario of Example 15.1 and the *Excel* file: C15.1 – ipods.

Management question

Compute the *sample correlation coefficient*, r, to measure the strength of the linear relationship between the *number of newspaper advertisements placed* and the *number of ipods sold* in the week after the advertisements appeared. Comment on the relationship.

Solution

Table 15.4 shows the calculations for Pearson's correlation coefficient for the *ipod Sales study*. The computational data is the same as in Table 15.2, but with an additional column to compute $\sum y^2$.

Table 15.4 Pearson's correlation coefficient for the ipod Sales study

Ads (x)	Ipods (y)	x^2	xy	y^2
4	26	16	104	676
4	28	16	112	784
3	24	9	72	576
2	18	4	36	324
5	35	25	175	1225
2	24	4	48	576
4	36	16	144	1296
3	25	9	75	625
5	31	25	155	961
5	37	25	185	1369
3	30	9	90	900
4	32	16	128	1024
44	**346**	**174**	**1 324**	**10 336**

Thus $\quad \sum x = 44 \quad \sum y = 346 \quad \sum x^2 = 174 \quad \sum xy = 1324 \quad \sum y^2 = 10\,336$ and $n = 12$

Then

$$r = \frac{12(1324) - (44)(346)}{\sqrt{[12(174) - (44)^2]\,[12(10336) - (346)^2]}} = \frac{664}{\sqrt{(152)\,(4316)}}$$

$$= 0{,}8198$$

Note: In the *Excel* output shown in Table 15.3 (and in cell [E8] of **Table 1** of **Figure 15.8**), Pearson's correlation coefficient is called **Multiple R** with a value of 0,8198.

Management interpretation

The sample correlation coefficient of r = 0,8198 is relatively close to +1, hence the statistical association between x (number of newspaper advertisements placed) and y (sale of ipods) is *strong* and *positive*. Thus the number of newspaper advertisements placed is a *good estimator* of the actual number of ipods that Music Technologies can expect to sell in the following week.

In more general terms, if the correlation is *moderate to good* (say, either above +0,70 or below –0,70), then values of x can be used with reasonable confidence to estimate y-values.

15.4 Coefficient of Determination

When the sample correlation coefficient, r, is *squared* (r^2), the resultant statistical measure is called the *coefficient of determination.*

The coefficient of determination, r^2, is defined as the proportion (or percentage) of variation in the dependent variable, y, that is explained by the independent variable, x.

The coefficient of determination *ranges between 0 and 1 (or 0% and 100%)*

i.e. $$0 \le r^2 \le 1$$

HOW TO

To interpret the coefficient of determination

The proportion (or percentage) of variation in y that x can *explain* is a measure of how strongly x and y are associated. If x can explain a high proportion (or percentage) of the variation in y, then x and y are strongly associated and vice versa.

Figure 15.18 below graphically illustrates the meaning of the coefficient of determination.

When $r^2 = 0$ *no variation* in y can be explained by the x variable.
This corresponds to the scatter plot shown in Figure 15.17, where x is of no value in estimating y. There is no association between x and y.

When $r^2 = 1$ the values of y are *completely explained* by the x-values.
There is *perfect association* between x and y. This corresponds to the scatter plots shown in Figures 15.11 and 15.12 respectively, where x-values *exactly estimate* the y-values.

When $0 < r < 1$

- Values of r^2 that lie *closer to zero* (or 0%) indicate a *low percentage* of variation in y explained by the x variable (refer to Figures 15.15 and 15.16). This represents a *weak association* between x and y.
- Alternatively, values of r^2 that lie *closer to 1* (or 100%) show that the x variable is of real value in estimating the actual values of the y variable (refer to Figures 15.13 and 15.14). This represents a *strong association* between x and y.

Figure 15.18 Interpretation of the coefficient of determination

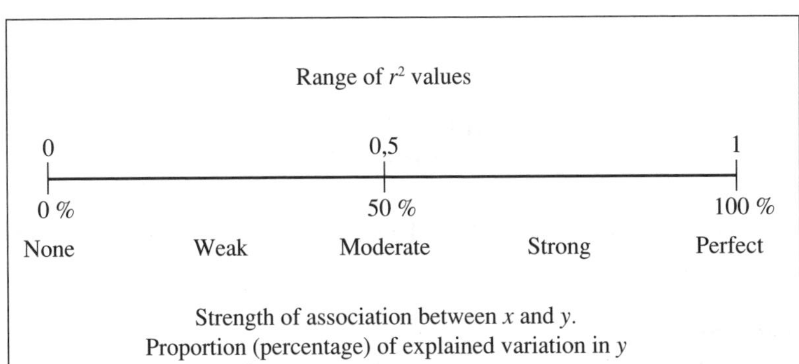

Examples

To *illustrate:*
If r^2 = 0,82 (or 82 %), then 82 % of the variation in the *y* variable is explained by the *x* variable. This implies that *x* and y are *strongly associated.* Therefore *x* is a *good predictor* of *y*. Only 18% of the variation in *y* is unexplained by the *x* variable. In such cases, a manager can have high confidence in the accuracy of the estimated *y*-value based on a given *x*-value.

If, on the other hand, r^2 = 0,14 (or 14%), then only 14% of the variation in the *y* variable is explained by the *x* variable. The *association* between *x* and *y* is *weak,* meaning that *x* is a *poor predictor* of *y*. More than eighty percent (86%) of the variation in *y* is unexplained by the *x* variable.

The coefficient of determination is more useful than the correlation coefficient when interpreting the strength of association between two random variables, because it measures the *exact strength* of *the association* – since it lies between 0% and 100%.

Example 15.3 ipod Sales study

Refer to the management scenario of Example 15.1 and the *Excel* file: **C15.1 – ipods.**

Management question

"How well does the *number of newspaper advertisements* placed **explain** *ipod sales?*"

This translates into the following statistical question:
"What *percentage of variation* in *ipod sales* is ***explained*** by the *number of newspaper advertisements* placed?" Comment on the strength of the relationship.

Solution

This problem requires the computation and interpretation of the *coefficient of determination*, r^2.

Given the correlation coefficient $r = 0{,}8198$
then, the coefficient of determination $r^2 = (0{,}8198)^2 = 0{,}6721$ (67,21%)

In the *Excel* output in Table 15.3 (and in cell [E9] of **Table 1** of **Figure 15.8**), it is shown as *R Square* with a value of 0,6721.

Management interpretation

The number of newspaper advertisements placed, *x*, explains 67,21% of the variation in the number of ipods sold, *y*. This is a *moderate to strong level* of explained variation in *ipod sales*. Thus, estimates of *ipod sales,* based on the number of newspaper advertisements placed, can be viewed with a moderately high degree of confidence, as only 32,79 % of the variation in *ipod sales* is unexplained by the number of advertisements placed.

The next section *statistically tests the significance* of this sample-derived association between *x* and *y*.

15.4 Testing the Significance of the Overall Regression Model

Once the regression equation (also called the **regression model**), the correlation coefficient, and the coefficient of determination have been derived from *sample data,* it is necessary to determine whether this overall model is statistically significant. This requires testing whether the relationship found in the sample is a genuine measure of association between the two numeric random variables in the population.

To establish whether this relationship is meaningful and, hence, whether it is valid to use the regression equation to estimate *y*-values from the *x* variable, a *hypothesis test* is conducted.

It should be noted that the correlation coefficient, *r*, is closely linked to the regression equation's gradient (slope) coefficient, b_1, which measures the influence of the *x* variable on the *y* variable. If, for *example*, the correlation coefficient between *x* and *y* is low (i.e. *r* will be close to zero), then b_1 will be close to zero, implying a minimal influence of *x* on *y*.

Therefore, the hypothesis test for significance of the regression model can be performed on either the population correlation coefficient, ρ, or the population gradient coefficient, β_1, for the *x* variable. Both statistical tests will produce the same statistical conclusion.

The test procedure is identical for each population parameter. They differ only in *step 1* (define the null and alternative hypothesis) and *step 2* (formula for deriving the *t-stat* sample test statistic). The four-step hypothesis testing procedure is illustrated using the *ipod Sales study.*

Example 15.4 ipod Sales study

Refer to the management scenario of Example 15.1. *Excel* file: **C15.1 – ipods.**

Management question

"Is the *relationship* between the number of *newspaper advertisements* placed and *ipod sales* meaningful (or significant)?"

Statistically, this translates into the following question:

Test, at the 5% significance level, whether a *statistically significant relationship* exists between the *number of newspaper advertisements* placed and *ipod sales,* i.e. whether the overall regression model (between *ipod sales, y,* and number of *advertisements* placed, *x*) is statistically significant at the 5% level of significance.

Solution (two-tailed hypothesis test)

Step 1: Define the null and alternative hypotheses

The null hypothesis always states that there is *no relationship* between the two variables, *x* and *y*. This is equivalent to saying either that the population correlation coefficient is zero (i.e. $\rho_1 = 0$), or that the population slope coefficient is zero (no slope) (i.e. $\beta_1 = 0$).

Thus H_0: $\rho =$ 0 (i.e. newspaper *advertisements* and *ipod sales are not* related)
H_1: $\rho \neq$ 0 (i.e. newspaper a*dvertisements* and *ipod sales are* related)

The closer *r* is to zero, the more likely it is that the null hypothesis will be accepted.

Alternatively, it can be expressed as follows:
H_0: $\beta_1 =$ 0 (i.e. there is no gradient, implying *no relationship* between newspaper *advertisements* and *ipod sales*)
H_1: $\beta_1 \neq$ 0 (i.e. there is a significant gradient)

The closer b_1 is to zero, the more likely it is that the null hypothesis will be accepted.

Note: This is a two-tailed hypothesis test since both the *correlation coefficient* and the *slope coefficient* could be either negative or positive.

Step 2: Compute the sample test statistic

The appropriate sample test statistic for both population parameters is ***t-stat***.

Formula – for the correlation coefficient

The *t-stat* test statistic is computed from the following formula:

$$t\text{-}stat = r\sqrt{\frac{(n-2)}{1-r^2}}$$

with r = sample correlation coefficient (= 0,8198)
n = sample size (n = 12)

Then $\quad t\text{-}stat = 0{,}8198\sqrt{\dfrac{(12-2)}{(1-0{,}8198^2)}} = 0{,}8198 \times \sqrt{\dfrac{10}{0{,}3279}} = 4{,}527$

Formula – for the slope (gradient) coefficient

The *t-stat* test statistic is computed from the following formula:

$$t\text{-}stat = \frac{b_1 - \beta_1}{\text{SE}(b_1)}$$

where b_1 = sample coefficient of x (the *number of advertisements placed*)
β_1 = population coefficient of x
$\text{SE}(b_1)$ = standard error of b_1

Note: The formula for the standard error of b_1 is not given here, as it is complex to compute manually.

From the *Excel* output in Table 15.3, the slope coefficient b_1 (Ads) = 4,3684 and the *standard error* of b_1 = 0,9650.

Then $\quad t\text{-}stat = \dfrac{(4{,}3684-0)}{0{,}9650} = 4{,}5270$

Note: $\beta_1 = 0$ since it represents H_0
(see the *Ads* row and *t-Stat* column in Table 15.3)

Step 3: Decision rule to guide the acceptance/rejection of the null hypothesis

Approach 1 Using the region of acceptance/rejection method

To determine the *critical t-limits*, both a *level of significance* and *degrees of freedom* are required.

The *level of significance* is given as 5% (i.e. α = ,05)

The *degrees of freedom* are given by the formula $\boldsymbol{df = (n - p - 1)}$

where n = sample size and p = number of independent variables.

In this example, there is only one independent variable, *Ads*

hence $\quad p = 1$ and $df = (12 - 1 - 1) = 10$

In general, the *critical t-value* is defined as: $\boldsymbol{t\text{-}crit = t_{(\alpha)(n-p-1)}}$

Then the *critical t-limits* (*t-crit*) are given by either:

- **Using the *t*-table**
  $t_{(\alpha/2=0{,}025)(df=10)} = \pm 2{,}228$ (from the **Table 2** with $\frac{\alpha}{2} = 0{,}025$ – see Appendix 1)

or

- **Using *Excel's* function =TINV(probability=α, df)**

i.e.

=TINV(0.05,10) = ±2,22814

Thus, the *region of acceptance* for H_0 is $[-2{,}228 \le t \le +2{,}228]$

The *decision rule* is then stated as follows:

Do not reject H_0 if *t-stat* falls between –2,228 and +2,228 inclusive.
Reject H_0 in favour of H_1 if *t-stat* falls below –2,228 or above +2,228.

Approach 2: Using the *p-value* method

Given *t-stat* = 4,527 (from *step 2*), the *p-value* refers to the *combined upper and lower tail areas* of the *t*-distribution.

The *p-value* cannot be found from the *t*-tables. It can only be derived using an *Excel* function, as follows:

- **Using *Excel's* function**
  =TDIST(x, df, tails) where x = *t-stat* = 4,527 *df* = 10 and *tails* = 2

i.e. **=TDIST(4.527,10,2)** gives a combined tail area = 0,0010964

Thus *p-value* = 0,0011

This *p-value* is shown in the *Excel* output in Table 15.3 in the *Ads* row and *p-value* column.

The *decision rule* is derived from **Figure 11.5** of chapter 11.

Step 4: Statistical conclusion and Management interpretation

Statistical conclusion

Since the *p-value* of 0,0011 lies well below 0,01 (1%) (or since *t-stat* = 4,527 > *t-crit* = 2,228), there is *overwhelming strong sample evidence* to support the alternative hypothesis H_1.

Management interpretation

It can therefore be concluded that a *strong positive relationship* exists between the *number of newspaper advertisements placed* and the level of *ipod sales* in the week following the appearance of the advertisements.

Hence, the regression model is *highly significant*. Useful and valid estimates of *ipod sales* can therefore be made, based on the *number of newspaper advertisements placed.*

Figure 15.19 shows the sample test statistic (*t-stat*) in comparison to the region of acceptance/rejection (*t-crit*) and the *p-value* of the test.

Figure 15.19 *t*-distribution; regions of acceptance/rejection; *p*-value for the Ipod Sales study

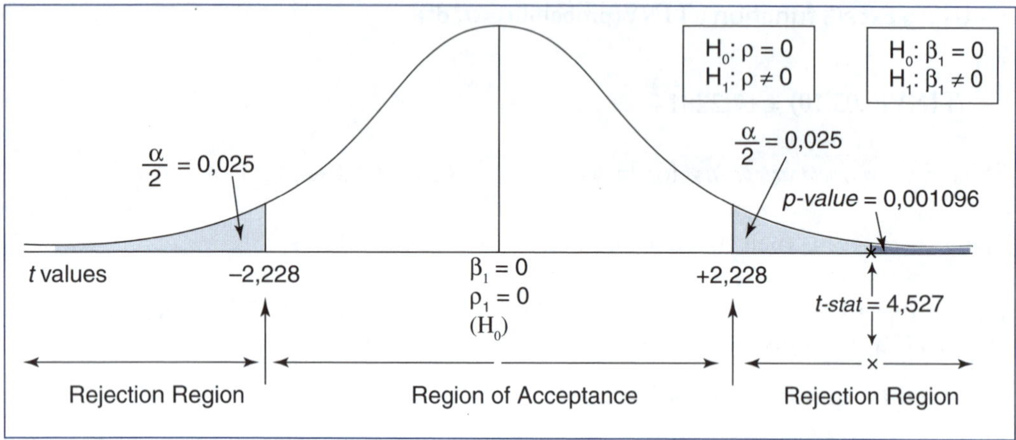

The effect of sample size on the significance of a simple linear regression model

The level at which a sample correlation coefficient (or the slope coefficient) becomes statistically significant decreases as the sample increases (and vice versa). The rationale for this is that larger samples are more representative of a target population than smaller samples, hence lower correlations (for larger *n)* can still indicate significant associations in the population.

Table 15.5 shows the minimum correlation coefficient required to be statistically significant at the 5% level of significance for different sample sizes.

Table 15.5 Sample size influence on the significance of sample correlation coefficients

n	*r*
10	0,619
20	0,441
30	0,36
40	0,312
60	0,254
120	0,179
200	0,138

Examples

To *illustrate*:
If a random sample of size 30 was used in a study, a minimum correlation coefficient of 0,36 must exist before two numeric random variables are statistically associated.
On the other hand, if the sample size was 120, the sample correlation coefficient only has to be at least 0,179 for x and y to be significantly related.

15.5 Multiple Linear Regression Analysis

Multiple linear regression analysis is an extension of simple linear regression analysis. In simple linear regression there is only one independent variable, x, that is assumed to influence the outcome of the dependent y variable. Multiple Linear Regression, on the other hand, assumes that *more than one* independent variable can influence the outcome of y.

Multiple linear regression analysis is arguably the most widely used statistical modelling technique in practice.

Examples

Multiple linear regression is used in areas such as:
- econometrics (i.e. building mathematical equations to estimate economic activity)
- financial modelling to estimate investment risks and returns, and
- as a general forecasting tool in business (finance, marketing, human resource management, and production management).

The Form of a Multiple Regression Model

If the relationships between a set of numeric variables (called **regressors**) and a dependent variable are reasonably linear (i.e. a straight-line relationship), then a regression equation consisting of all of these independent variables could be more useful in estimating the values of the dependent y variable than any independent variable separately.

Formula

The form of the sample-based *multiple regression equation* is:

$$\hat{y} = b_0 + b_1x_1 + b_2x_2 + b_3x_3 + \ldots + b_px_p$$

where $x_1, x_2, x_3, \ldots, x_p$ = the p independent variables
$\hat{y}$ = *estimated* value of the dependent variable
b_0 = the y *intercept* coefficient
$b_1, b_2, b_3, \ldots, b_p$ = the sample coefficients for the p independent variables

The data for both the set of *independent variables* (x_1, x_2, x_3, .. ,x_p) and the *dependent variable, y*, must be *numeric*.

The regression coefficients and their interpretation

The regression coefficients (b_i for i = 1, 2, 3, ..., p) are *weights* that measure the relative importance of each independent variable in estimating the dependent variable, y.

Each coefficient is *interpreted* as follows:

Holding all other variables constant, for every one unit change in x associated with the coefficient, y will change by the value of this coefficient.

For *example*, if b_1 = 7,85 in a multiple regression equation, then if x_1 changes by 1 unit, while holding all other variables constant, the value of y in the regression equation will change by 7,85 units.

Computing the multiple regression equation

The same mathematical principle of the *method of least squares* is used to derive the coefficients of the multiple regression equation. The computational procedures and formulae of multiple regression analysis are more complex. As a result, all multiple regression analysis is produced by *Excel's* **Regression** option in **Data Analysis**.

The emphasis here is on the interpretation of findings. The process and interpretation of multiple linear regression are illustrated for a *two-independent variables* management problem.

Example 15.5 Knitting Machine Operator study

***Excel* file:** **C15.2 – machinist output**

The production manager of BBB knitting mills, with a few hundred machinists, wanted to know what factors influence worker output. He therefore randomly selected 15 machinists and recorded for each, their level of *work experience* (in months) x_1, their *training score* (out of 25) x_2, and their *daily output* y. The data is shown in Table 15.6.

Table 15.6 Data for Knitting Machine Operator study

Experience	Training Score	Output
40	9	217
56	18	241
49	16	258
33	10	175
39	24	247
34	21	191
45	21	223
37	12	173
38	10	234
35	12	221
29	6	156
34	12	183
53	9	224
34	18	197
42	15	180

Management questions

(1) Construct a multiple linear regression equation to show the relationship between the knitting machine operators' *daily output* and the independent variables, *work experience* and *training score*.

(2) Is the overall multiple regression equation statistically significant? Test at the 5% significance level.

(3) Identify which independent variables, if any, are statistically significant at the 5% level of significance.

(4) Estimate the likely *average daily output* for all knitting machinists who have 40 months of relevant *work experience* and have a *training score* of 20.

Solution

Refer to Table 15.7 for *Excel's* **Regression** output, using **Data Analysis.**

(i) Identify the dependent and independent variables

The dependent variable is: y = *daily output* of a knitting machine operator
The independent variables are: x_1 = work *experience* (in months)
x_2 = *training score* (out of 25)

(ii) Exploratory data analysis using scatter plots

Before constructing a multiple regression model, it is good practice to inspect the data visually, using *scatter plots*, to determine its suitability for regression analysis. A scatter plot will identify whether the relationship between each x_i and y is reasonably linear (do they lie in a straight line?), and how strong the relationship is likely to be.

An initial inspection of the scatter plots between the dependent variable, *daily output*, and each independent variable, *experience* and *training score* respectively, shows that there is a moderate positive linear correlation between *daily output* and *experience* (Figure 15.20(a) overleaf), and a slightly weaker positive linear correlation between *daily output* and *training score* (Figure 15.20(b) overleaf).

This initial inspection of the data set shows that there is value in setting up a multiple regression equation between y and the two independent variables, x_1 and x_2.

Figure 15.20 Scatter plots of (a) Output vs Experience and (b) Output vs Training Score

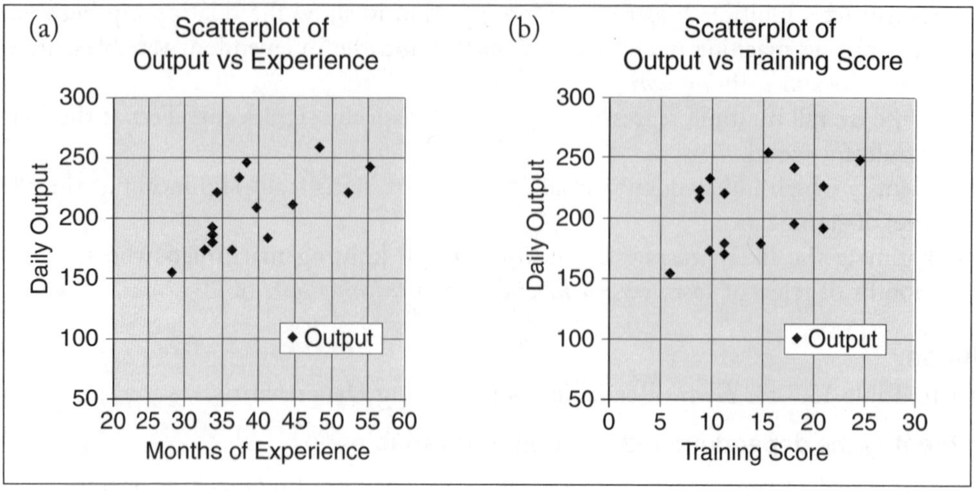

(iii) Construction and evaluation of the Multiple Regression Model

Question (1) The multiple regression equation (called the regression model)

The form of the sample multiple regression equation is: $y = b_0 + b_1x_1 + b_2x_2$

The method of least squares is used to derive the intercept, $b_{0,}$ and the coefficients, b_1 and $b_{2,}$ of the two independent variables. Table 15.7 below gives the derived regression coefficients using *Excel's* **Data Analysis** tool, as follows:

y-intercept	b_0	=	88,457
work experience variable	b_1	=	2,424
training score variable	b_2	=	1,613

Thus the multiple regression model is: $\hat{y} = 88{,}457 + 2{,}424\ x_1 + 1{,}613\ x_2$

This equation represents the *best-fitting linear relationship* between all the *x*'s and *y*.

Each *regression coefficient* (b_i) shows the amount by which *daily output*, *y*, will change for a unit change in each independent variable separately. For *example*, if the *training scores* of knitting machinists are held constant, then a ***one-month*** increase (or decrease) in *work experience* will increase (decrease) the average *daily output* of a machinist by 2,424 units. Similarly, holding the *work experience* of machinists constant, then a ***one-point*** increase (or decrease) in *training score* will increase (or decrease) the average *daily output* of a machinist by 1,613 units.

Table 15.7 Multiple regression analysis for the Knitting Machine Operators study

Regression Statistics	
Multiple R	0,7264
R Square	0,5276
Adjusted R Square	0,4489
Standard Error	22,9284
Observations	15

Anova					
	df	***SS***	***MS***	***F***	***Significance F***
Regression	2	7045,4405	3522,7203	6,70084	0,011115
Residual	12	6308,5595	525,7133		
Total	14	13354			

	Coefficients	Standard Error	*t* Stat	*p*-value	Lower 95%	Upper 95%
Intercept	88,457	33,29518	2,65674	0,02092	15,912	161
Experience	2,424	0,80642	3,00599	0,01094	0,667	4,181
Training Score	1,613	1,188088	1,3576	0,19959	–0,976	4,202

Once the multiple regression equation has been derived, various statistical tests are conducted on the equation to assess how useful it is to produce reliable estimates of the dependent variable. The first hypothesis test will evaluate the overall regression model for statistical significance. Thereafter, if there is some value in the overall regression model, a further set of hypotheses tests will separately test each regressor (independent variable) for statistical significance. The purpose of these hypotheses tests is to identify the most useful subset of independent variables to estimate the dependent variable, *y*.

Question (2) Testing the overall regression model for statistical significance

An important regression descriptive statistic that should always be inspected and interpreted once the regression equation has been constructed, is the *coefficient of multiple determination*, R^2 (**R Square**). From Table 15.8 (extracted from Table 15.7):

$$\text{R Square} = 0{,}5276$$

This means that the two independent variables, *experience* and *training score*, collectively explain 52,76% of the total variation in the dependent variable, *daily output*. This is a moderately high percentage of explained variation in *y*.

Table 15.8 Summary descriptive statistics for the multiple regression model

Regression Statistics	
Multiple R	0,7264
R Square	0,5276
Adjusted R Square	0,4489
Standard Error	22,9284
Observations	15

However, this observed percentage of explained variation of y must still be tested statistically to establish whether it is evidence of a genuine statistical relationship between the two independent variables on the one hand, and the dependent variable on the other hand, or whether the explained variation is merely due to chance. The following hypothesis test will establish if these observed relationships are statistically significant.

Hypothesis test

The *hypothesis test* for the *significance of the overall regression equation* can be seen either as a test of the significance of R^2 (i.e. is it zero or not?), or as a test of significance of the independent variables (i.e. is there is at least one independent variable that is useful in explaining y?). The tests are equivalent.
The general practice is to test the coefficients of the independent variables for statistical significance.

Step 1: Define the null and alternative hypotheses

The test is conducted on the regression coefficients. If the *population* regression coefficients (β_1 and β_2) are both zero, then the multiple regression model is of no value in estimating the y variable. Alternatively, if there is a least one regression coefficient that is not zero, then there is value in the regression model.

Hence H_0: $\beta_1 = \beta_2 = 0$ (i.e. the regression model is of *no* value)
H_1: At least one $\beta_i \neq 0$ $(i = 1, 2)$ (i.e. there *is* value in the regression model)

The closer the sample regression coefficients, b_1 and b_2, are to zero, the more likely it is that the null hypothesis will be accepted.

Step 2: Compute the sample test statistic

The F statistic, *F-stat*, is the appropriate *test statistic* to test the significance of the overall regression model. Table 15.9 shows the ANOVA table extracted from Table 15.7.

Table 15.9 ANOVA table – test for the overall significance of the regression model

ANOVA					
	df	***SS***	***MS***	***F***	***Significance F***
Regression	2	7045,4405	3522,7203	6,70084	0,011115
Residual	12	6308,5595	525,7133		
Total	14	13354			

The F statistic (*F-stat*) is derived in the same way as used in chapter 14 for one-factor *analysis of variance.*

Of the total sum of squares (SS Total = 13354), an amount of 7045,44 is "explained" by the regression equation (called SS Regression). This leaves an amount of 6308,56 which is "unexplained" by the regression equation (called SS Residual).

These sum of squares (*SS*) are *divided* by their respective *degrees of freedom* (*df*) to compute variances (or mean sum of squares = *MS*).

- For the SS Regression, its degrees of freedom is the *number of independent variables* (*p*) in the model. Thus $df_1 = 2$.
- For the SS Residual, its degrees of freedom is (*sample size – number of independent variables* – 1) (i.e. $n - p - 1$). Thus $df_2 = (15 - 2 - 1) = 12$.

This results in:

$$\text{MS Regression} = \frac{7045{,}4405}{2} = 3522{,}7203$$

$$\text{MS Residual} = \frac{6308{,}5595}{12} = 525{,}7133$$

Finally

$$\textbf{\textit{F}-stat} = \frac{\text{Regression variance}}{\text{Residual variance}} = \frac{\text{MS Regression}}{\text{MS Residual}} = \frac{3522{,}7203}{525{,}7133} = \mathbf{6{,}70084}$$

Note: R^2 is closely related to *F-stat*. When R^2 is high (close to 1), then *F-stat* will be large; and vice versa.
R^2 is the proportion of total sum of squares (total variation) that is "explained" by the regression equation.

Thus

$$\mathbf{R^2} = \frac{\text{SS Regression}}{\text{SS Total}} = \frac{7045{,}4405}{13354} = 0{,}5276$$

Step 3: Decision rule to guide the acceptance/rejection of the null hypothesis

Table 15.9 shows the *p-value* for *F-stat* = 0,011115 (called ***Significance F***)

It is also found from *Excel* using: **=FDIST(6.70084,2,12)** giving **0,011115**

The *decision rule* is derived from **Figure 11.5** of chapter 11.

Step 4: Statistical conclusion and Management interpretation

Statistical conclusion

Since the *p-value* of 0,011115 lies well below 0,05 (5%), but slightly above 0,01 (1%), there is *very strong sample evidence* to support the alternative hypothesis H_1.

Management interpretation

The sample evidence is very strong that *at least one* of the two independent variables, *work experience* and *training score*, is of value in estimating the knitting machinists' *average daily output*.

Note: This hypothesis test of the overall regression model has not identified which of the two independent variables is statistically significant. It could be either *work experience*, or *training score*, or both.

To establish which are the significant independent variables, each independent variable must be tested separately for statistical significance.

Question (3) Testing individual regressors (independent variables) for statistical significance

The t-test statistic, *t-stat*, is used to test each individual independent variable for statistical significance.

For the experience variable x_1

Step 1: Define the null and alternative hypotheses

The hypothesis tests whether the *population* regression coefficient of the *experience* variable (i.e. β_1) is zero or not. If β_1 is zero, then the *experience* variable is of no value in estimating the y variable. Alternatively, if β_1 is not zero, then the *experience* variable is significant.

Hence H_0: $\beta_1 = 0$ (i.e. *experience* is of no value in estimating y)
H_1: $\beta_1 \neq 0$ (i.e. *experience* is useful in estimating y)

The closer the sample regression coefficient, b_1 is to zero, the more likely it is that the null hypothesis will be accepted.

Step 2: Compute the sample test statistic

The t-test statistic, *t-stat*, is the appropriate *test statistic* to test the significance of individual regressors.

Formula

The *t-stat* test statistic is computed from the following formula:

$$t\text{-}stat = \frac{b_1 - \beta_1}{SE(b_1)}$$

where b_1 = *sample* coefficient of the *experience* variable, x_1
β_1 = *population* coefficient of the *experience* variable, x_1
$SE(b_1)$ = standard error of b_1

Table 15.10 shows the *t-test* statistic calculations extracted from Table 15.7.

Table 15.10 t-test statistic calculations for Experience and Training Score

	Coefficients	Standard Error	t-stat	P-value
Intercept	88,457	33,29518	2,65674	0,02092
Experience	2,424	0,80642	**3,00599**	0,01094
Training Score	1,613	1,188088	**1,3576**	0,19959

Then $t\text{-}stat = \frac{(2,424 - 0)}{0,80642} = 3,00599$ Note: $\beta_1 = 0$ since it represents H_0

(see the *Experience* row and *t-stat* column in Table 15.10)

Step 3: Decision rule to guide the acceptance/rejection of the null hypothesis

Table 15.10 shows the *p-value* for *t-stat* = 0,01094

Recall that for *t-stat* = 3,00599 (from *step 2*), the *p-value* refers to the combined upper and lower tail areas of the *t*-distribution.

The *p-value* cannot be found from the *t*-tables. It can only be computed through the *Excel* function, as follows:

- **Using Excel**
  =TDIST(x, df, tails)
  where x = *t-stat* = 3,00599
  df = (sample size – number of independent variables – 1)
  = $(n - p - 1) = (15 - 2 - 1) = 12$
  tails = 2

i.e. =TDIST(3.00599,12,2) gives a combined tail area = 0,0109442.

Thus *p-value* = 0,0109442 (or 0,01094 rounded)

The *decision rule* is derived from **Figure 11.5** of chapter 11.

Step 4: Statistical conclusion and Management interpretation

Statistical conclusion

Since the *p-value* (= 0,01094) lies well below 0,05 (5%), but slightly above 0,01 (1%) (see Figure 11.5), there is *very strong sample evidence* to support the alternative hypothesis H_1.

Management interpretation

There is very strong sample evidence to conclude that *work experience* is of great value (highly significant) in estimating the knitting machinists' *average daily output*.

For the *training score* variable x_2

Step 1: Define the null and alternative hypotheses

The *population* regression coefficient of the *training score* variable is β_2.
If β_2 is zero, then the *training score* variable is of no value in estimating the y variable. Alternatively, if β_2 is not zero, then the *training score* variable is significant.

Hence H_0: $\beta_2 = 0$ (i.e. *training score* is of no value in estimating y)
H_1: $\beta_2 \neq 0$ (i.e. *training score* is useful in estimating y)

The closer the sample regression coefficient, b_2 is to zero, the more likely it is that the null hypothesis will be accepted.

Step 2: Compute the sample test statistic

The *t-test* statistic, *t-stat*, for the *training score* variable is constructed in an identical way to that of the *experience* variable, namely:

$$t\text{-}stat = \frac{b_2 - \beta_2}{SE(b_2)}$$

where b_2 = *sample* coefficient of the *training score* variable, x_2
β_2 = *population* coefficient of the *training score* variable, x_2
$SE(b_2)$ = standard error of b_2

Table 15.10 shows the *t-test* statistic calculations extracted from Table 15.7.

i.e. $t\text{-}stat = \frac{(1{,}613 - 0)}{1{,}188088} = 1{,}3576$ Note: $\beta_2 = 0$ since it represents H_0

(see the *Training Score* row and *t-Stat* column in Table 15.10)

Step 3: Decision rule to guide the acceptance/rejection of the null hypothesis

Table 15.10 shows the *p-value* for *t-stat* = 0,19959

This *p-value* can be derived using the following *Excel* function:

=TDIST(x, df, tails)
where *x* = *t-stat* = 1,3576
df = $(n - p - 1) = (15 - 2 - 1) = 12$
tails = 2

i.e. =TDIST(1.3576,12,2) gives a combined tail area = 0,19959

Thus *p-value* = 0,19959

The *decision rule* is derived from **Figure 11.5** of chapter 11.

Step 4: Statistical conclusion and Management interpretation

Statistical conclusion

Since the *p-value* of 0,19959 lies well above 0,10 (10%), there is *no sample evidence* to support the alternative hypothesis H_1. Therefore, the null hypothesis is probably true.

Management interpretation

The *training score* measure is of no value (insignificant) in estimating average *daily worker output*.

Overall, it has been established statistically that *only* the *experience* variable is of value in estimating *average daily worker output*. Thus, any estimates of *daily worker output* should only be based on their level of *work experience*.

Question 4 – Using the multiple regression model for y-estimation purposes

Finally, it is required to estimate the likely average daily output for all machinists who have 40 months of relevant work experience and have a training score of 20.

Only the *significant* independent variables must be included in the multiple regression equation model to estimate values of y. Since only the level of *work experience* is significant in estimating average *daily output*, the multiple linear regression equation used to estimate y is as follows:

i.e. $\mathbf{\hat{y} = 88{,}457 + 2{,}424\,x_1}$ where x_1 = months of *work experience*

Thus for $x_1 = 40$ $\hat{y} = 88{,}457 + 2{,}424(\mathbf{40}) = 185{,}42$ units

Management interpretation

Machinists who have 40 months of *work experience* (regardless of their *training score*), are likely to produce an average of 185 units of *output daily.*

15.6 Summary

Regression analysis is shown in this chapter to be a technique which quantifies the relationship between a set of independent variables, x, and a dependent variable, y. The purpose of building a regression model is to estimate values of y from known, or assumed, values of x by substituting the x-value(s) into a regression equation. If there is only one independent variable, x, then a simple linear regression analysis is performed, which uses a straight-line equation to show the relationship between x and y. If there is more than one independent variable, say, p variables (i.e. $x_1, x_2, ..., x_p$), then a multiple linear regression equation consisting of many variables is constructed.

The data of all the independent variables and the dependent variable must be *numeric*.

The *method of least squares* is used to find the *best-fit* equation to express this relationship. The coefficients of the regression equations are weights that measure the importance of each of the independent variables in estimating the y-variable.

The linear regression equation, which is always based on sample data, must be tested for statistical significance before it can be used to produce valid and reliable estimates of the true mean value of the dependent variable.

- In simple linear regression, a test of significance of the simple correlation coefficient, ρ, between x and y; or a test of the slope coefficient, β_1, for significance, will establish whether x is of any significant value in estimating y.
- In multiple regression analysis, two levels of hypothesis tests are required to identify a useful multiple regression model. First, a significance test of the overall model – to establish whether there is any value in the overall regression equation, using the *F-stat* test statistic – is conducted. If value is found statistically, then a second set of hypotheses tests – using the *t-stat* test statistic – is conducted on each independent variable separately, to identify the subset of significant regressors.

  Only the significant independent variables are used in an equation to estimate y.

This regression analysis technique is of real value to managers, because it is used as a forecasting and planning tool.

Exercises

Part A: Simple Linear Regression and Correlation Analysis

15.1 X15.1 – **training effectiveness**

The training manager of a company that assembles and exports pool pumps wants to know if there is a link between the number of hours spent by assembly workers in training and their productivity on the job. A random sample of 10 assembly workers was selected and their performances evaluated. The data is given in the *Excel* file **X15.1**.

Training hours	Output
20	40
36	70
20	44
38	56
40	60
33	48
32	62
28	54
40	63
24	38

(i) Construct a *scatter plot* of the sample data and comment on the likely relationship between the two measures (i.e. hours of training and output).

(ii) Compute a *simple regression line* using the method of least squares to identify a linear relationship between the hours of training received by assembly workers and their productivity (in terms of units assembled per day).

(iii) Derive the *coefficient of determination* between training hours received and worker productivity. Interpret its meaning and advise the training manager.

(iv) *Estimate* the average daily output of an assembly worker who has received only 25 hours of training.

15.2 X15.2 – **capital utilisation**

A business analyst believes that capital utilization (as measured by inventory turnover) has a direct effect on a company's earnings yield. To examine this belief, the analyst randomly surveyed 9 JSE listed companies and recorded their inventory turnover and their earning yield. The data are given in the *Excel* file **X15.2**.

Inventory turnover	Earnings yield
3	10
5	12
4	8
7	13
6	15
4	10
8	16
6	13
5	10

(i) *Graphically display* the relationship between inventory turnover and earnings yield for the sample of 9 companies. What relationship can be observed?

(ii) Compute a linear regression equation to express the relationship between the inventory turnover and earnings yields of companies.

(iii) Construct the *correlation coefficient* between inventory turnover and earnings yield. Does this value support the business analyst's view? Comment.

(iv) What percentage of variation in earnings yield is explained by the inventory turnover level of a company? Based on this measure, can the regression equation be used with confidence to estimate a company's earnings yield based on their expected level of inventory turnover? Explain.

(v) What earnings yield can a company expect to achieve if they have an inventory turnover of 6 next year?

15.3 X15.3 – loan applications

A bank wanted to find out whether *loan applications received* are influenced by the current loan *interest rate*. The manager selected 11 monthly periods where different interest rates applied and recorded the number of loan applications received. The data are given in the *Excel* file **X15.3**.

Loan applications received	
Interest rate %	**Loan applications**
7	18
6,5	22
5,5	30
6	24
8	16
8,5	18
6	28
6,5	27
7,5	20
8	17
6	21

(i) Identify the independent variable and the dependent variable. Explain.

(ii) Show the data graphically in a scatter plot. What relationship is observed?

(iii) Compute the correlation coefficient between the *rate of interest* and number of *loan applications received*. Comment on the strength of the association.

(iv) Test the association between the *rate of interest* and number of *loan applications received* for statistical significance. Use α = 0,05. Show the null and alternative hypotheses and interpret the findings of the hypothesis test.

(v) Use the TDIST function in *Excel* to find the *p-value* for the test statistic computed in (iv). Interpret its meaning in the context of the hypothesis test in (iv).

(vi) Derive the least squares regression line between the *rate of interest* and number of *loan applications received*.

(vii) Interpret the meaning of the regression coefficient (b_1) of the independent variable.

(viii) How many loan applications can the bank expect to receive when the interest rate is 6%?

15.4 X15.4 – **maintenance costs**

A company that manufacturers wooden products (e.g. garden furniture, ladders, benches) regularly maintains its lathe machines which are used for cutting and shaping components. The manager would like to know whether the *cost of machine maintenance* is related to the *age* of the machines. For a random sample of 12 lathe machines in the company's factory, the annual maintenance cost and age of each machine was recorded. The data are given in the *Excel* file **X15.4**.

Maintenance Costs Analysis		
Machine	**Age (yrs)**	**Annual Cost (R)**
1	4	45
2	3	20
3	3	38
4	8	65
5	6	58
6	7	50
7	1	16
8	1	22
9	5	38
10	2	26
11	4	30
12	6	35

(i) Identify the independent variable and the dependent variable. Explain.
(ii) Show the data graphically in a scatter plot. What relationship is observed?
(iii) Compute the correlation coefficient between the *age of lathe machines* and their *annual maintenance costs*. Comment on the strength of the association.
(iv) Is the correlation statistically significant? Test at the 5% significance level. What conclusion can be drawn?
(v) Use the TDIST function in *Excel* to find the *p-value* for the test statistic computed in (iv). Interpret its meaning in the context of the hypothesis test in (iv).
(vi) Use the method of least squares to find the best fitting line between the *age of lathe machines* and their annual maintenance costs.
(vii) Interpret the meaning of the regression coefficient (b_1) of the independent variable.
(viii) What is the expected average maintenance cost of a lathe machine that is 5 years old?

15.5 X15.5 – employee performance

A call centre requires that each new employee undertakes an aptitude test when hired. A year later, their job performance is evaluated. The call-centre manager would like to know if aptitude test scores can be used to predict job performance. The aptitude scores (measured out of 10) and job performance scores (measured out of 100) of 12 randomly selected employees is recorded in the *Excel* file **X15.5**.

Employee Performance Ratings		
Employee	**Aptitude score**	**Performance rating**
1	7	82
2	6	74
3	5	82
4	4	68
5	5	75
6	8	92
7	7	86
8	8	69
9	9	85
10	6	76
11	4	72
12	6	64

(i) Show the relationship between *aptitude score* (x) and *performance rating* (y) graphically. What relationship is observed?

(ii) Measure the strength of the statistical relationship by computing the correlation coefficient between the aptitude score and performance ratings of call centre employees.

(iii) Test the sample correlation for statistical significance. Use $\alpha = 0{,}05$. Interpret the findings for the call-centre manager.

(iv) Use the TDIST function in *Excel* to find the *p-value* for the test statistic computed in (iii). Interpret its meaning in the context of the hypothesis test in (iii).

(v) Compute the simple linear regression equation and estimate the likely average performance rating score for call-centre employees with an aptitude score of 8. How much confidence can the call-centre manager have in this estimate? Comment.

15.6 X15.6 – opinion polls

Opinion polls are often criticised for their lack of predictive validity (i.e. the ability to reliably estimate the actual election results). In a recent election in each of 11 regions, the percentage of votes predicted by opinion polls for the winning political party are recorded together with the actual percentage of votes received by this political party during the election. The data are given in the *Excel* file **X15.6**.

Region	Opinion poll (%)	Actual election (%)
1	42	51
2	34	31
3	59	56
4	41	49
5	53	68
6	40	35
7	65	54
8	48	52
9	59	54
10	38	43
11	62	60

(i) Determine the degree of association between the opinion poll results and the results of the actual election by computing Pearson's correlation coefficient.

(ii) Test the sample correlation for statistical significance at the 5% level. Discuss the findings in the context of this study.

(iii) Set up a least squares regression equation to estimate actual election results based on opinion poll results.

(iv) Compute the coefficient of determination for this model. Interpret its value.

(v) If an opinion poll showed a 58% support for the winning party, what is the actual election result likely to be?

(vi) If an opinion poll showed a 82% support for the winning party, what is the actual election result likely to be? Is this a valid and reliable result? Comment.

Use *Excel* to generate the statistical results for Exercises 15.7 and 15.8.

15.7 X15.7 – capital investment

Companies regularly need to invest capital into their business operations to continue to grow and generate profits. A business analyst examined the relationship within companies between their level of *capital investment* (expressed as a percentage of turnover) and their *return on investment* (recorded in the financial period after the capital investment). A random sample of 45 companies was included in the study. The data is given in the *Excel* file **X15.7**.

(i) Define the independent and dependent variables in this study. Explain.

(ii) Use the **XY (Scatter)** option from the **Chart Wizard** to graphically display the relationship between *capital investment* and *ROI.*

(iii) Use the **Regression** option in **Data Analysis** to derive the correlation coefficient and regression line between a company's level of *capital investment* and its *return on investment.*

(iv) Identify the coefficient of determination and interpret its value.

(v) Test the regression equation for statistical significance. Use $\alpha = 0{,}05$. State the null and alternative hypotheses, the appropriate test statistic, and the *p-value* for the test. Interpret the findings of the hypothesis test for the business analyst.

(vi) Interpret the meaning of the regression coefficient (b_1) of the independent variable.

(vii) Interpret the meaning of the *95% confidence interval* for the regression coefficient (b_1) of the dependent variable.

(viii) Estimate the expected *return on investment* for a company that is planning a 55% level of capital investment.

15.8 X15.8 – property valuations

A property analyst wished to examine the relationship between the town council's valuation of residential property in Bloemfontein and the market value (selling price) of the properties. A random sample of 40 recent property transactions was examined.

All data values are expressed in R1 000s. The data are given in the *Excel* file **X15.8**.

Property market analysis		
Property	**Council valuations**	**Market values**
1	54	156
2	144	189
3	96	110
4	150	198
5	84	144
6	132	226
7	62	106
8	120	182
9	114	147
10	98	198
11	138	198
12	94	178
13	102	145
14	123	231
15	131	255
16	54	126
17	76	118
18	48	98
19	102	175
20	129	214
21	154	225
22	68	147
23	95	162
24	77	139
25	133	244
26	108	228
27	82	185
28	56	115
29	129	158
30	144	216
31	88	188
32	64	158
33	154	242
34	74	128
35	85	165
36	135	204
37	93	164
38	125	186
39	152	226
40	68	178

(i) Define the independent and dependent variables in this study. Explain.
(ii) Use the **XY (Scatter)** option from the **Chart Wizard** to graphically display the relationship between *council valuations* and *market values.*
(iii) Use the **Regression** option in **Data Analysis** to derive the correlation coefficient and regression line between *council valuations* and *market values.*
(iv) Identify the coefficient of determination and interpret its value.
(v) Test the regression equation for statistical significance. Use α = 0,05. State the null and alternative hypotheses, the appropriate test statistic, and the *p-value* for the test. Interpret the findings of the hypothesis test for the business analyst.
(vi) Interpret the meaning of the regression coefficient (b_1) of the independent variable.
(vii) Interpret the meaning of the *95% confidence interval* for the regression coefficient (b_1) of the dependent variable.
(viii) Estimate the average expected *market value* of properties in Bloemfontein that have a council valuation of R100?

Part B: Multiple Regression Exercises

Use *Excel* to generate all the statistical results for Exercises 15.9–15.12.

15.9 X15.9 – mutual funds

An investment analyst wishes to examine the possible influence on the annualised *returns* of mutual funds of their *risk factor* and *management expense ratio.* A fund's risk factor is scored from 1 (low-risk investments) to 10 (high-risk investments) and its management expense ratio (as a percentage) is a measure of cost to investors of investing in the fund. The data for a random sample of 15 mutual funds are given in the *Excel* file **X15.9**.

Mutual Fund Analysis			
Mutual Fund	**Risk factor**	**Expense ratio**	**Fund return**
1	6	3	23
2	2	6	9
3	7	5	19
4	8	3	20
5	3	8	7
6	3	8	16
7	3	7	13
8	7	2	22
9	9	3	22
10	6	5	17
11	5	2	20
12	5	4	14
13	4	8	12
14	4	6	19
15	5	4	22

(i) Identify the dependent variable and the independent variables.

(ii) On separate graphs, plot the *risk factor* scores against *fund returns*; and then *expense ratios* against *fund returns*. Use the **XY (Scatter)** option from the **Chart Wizard** for each plot. Comment on the pattern of the observed relationship for each scatter plot.

(iii) Use the **Regression** option in **Data Analysis** to derive the multiple regression model to predict *fund returns* using a fund's *risk factor* and its management *expense ratio* as predictors.

(iv) Write out the equation of the multiple regression model.

(v) Identify the *coefficient of determination* and interpret its value.

(vi) Test the significance of the coefficient of determination using the Anova table. Use α = 0,05. State the null and alternative hypotheses, the appropriate test statistic, and the *p-value* for the test. Interpret the findings of the hypothesis test for the investment analyst.

(vii) Interpret the meaning of each of the regression coefficients (b_1 and b_2) of the independent variables (i.e. *risk factor* and *expense ratio*).

(viii) Is each independent variable (i.e. *risk factor* and *expense ratio*) statistically significant in predicting a mutual fund's annualised returns? Use the *t-stat* and the *p-value* for each independent variable to conduct the appropriate hypotheses tests. For each hypothesis test, state the null and alternative hypothesis. What conclusions can be drawn about the statistical significance of each independent variable?

(viii) Use the multiple regression model (from (iv)) to *estimate* the average annualised *return* for mutual funds that have a *risk factor* of 7 and a management *expense ratio* of 4.

15.10 X15.10 – **hotel occupancy**

Hotel occupancy levels are an important indicator of a healthy tourism industry. A large metropolitan city in South Africa asked a statistical analyst to identify possible predictors of *hotel occupancy levels* for the city. The analyst selected a 24-month period and recorded three measures for each month:

- the number of *visitors* arriving through the city's airport (in 10 000's);
- the number of registered *conferences* taking place in the city; and
- the average *occupancy level* across all of the city's hotels.

The data are given in the *Excel* file **X15.10**.

City Hotel Occupancy Rates			
Period	**Visitors**	**Conferences**	**Occupancy**
1	35	10	65
2	40	6	78
3	38	4	60
4	48	3	74
5	44	4	63
6	33	6	78
7	32	8	75
8	44	12	80
9	29	5	64
10	41	6	66
11	46	9	79
12	44	3	71
13	38	8	64
14	36	6	74
15	28	5	56
16	36	10	84
17	32	5	56
18	42	9	76
19	48	10	75
20	40	3	56
21	34	5	62
22	42	4	69
23	40	12	82
24	36	6	60

(i) Construct separate *scatter plots* between the dependent variable, *occupancy level*, and each of the independent variables, *visitors* and *conferences*. Interpret the pattern of the relationship within each plot. Use the XY (Scatter) option from the **Chart Wizard** for each plot.

(ii) Derive the multiple regression model to predict the city's *hotel occupancy levels* based on the number of *visitors* and number of *conferences*. Use the **Regression** option in **Data Analysis**.

(iii) Write out the equation of the multiple regression model.

(iv) Identify the *coefficient of determination* and interpret its value.

(v) Is the overall multiple regression model statistically significant? Test at the 5% significance level. State the null and alternative hypotheses; and identify the appropriate test statistic and its *p-value* from the Anova table. Interpret the findings of the hypothesis test for the city's management.

(vi) Interpret the meaning of each of the regression coefficients (b_1 and b_2) of the independent variables (i.e. *visitors* and *conferences*).

(vii) Test each independent variable (i.e. *visitors* and *conferences*) for statistical significant. Use α = 0,05. Use the *t-stat* and the *p-value* for each independent variable to conduct the appropriate hypotheses tests. For each hypothesis test, state the null and alternative hypothesis. What conclusions can be drawn about the statistical significance of each independent variable?

(viii) Which independent variable (i.e. *visitors* or *conferences*) is more important in estimating average hotel occupancy levels? Why? Refer to their respective *p-values* to explain your answer.

(ix) Using the multiple regression model (from (iii)), *estimate* the likely average hotel occupancy level in the city for next month when 36 *visitors* (in 10 000's) are expected to arrive through the city's airport, and 9 *conferences* are scheduled to take place.

15.11 X15.11 – **employee absenteeism**

The human resources manager for SA Knitting Mills (SAKM) is concerned about the level of *employee absenteeism*. She identified three factors which she believes are the most significant contributors to employee absenteeism at the knitting mill. They are:

- the length of *job tenure* of an employee (measured in months),
- the level of *job satisfaction* (measured by an index from 0 to 75); and
- the level of an employee's *organisational commitment* (also measured by an index from 0 to 70).

Higher scores for the indexes are associated with greater job satisfaction or greater degrees of organisational commitment and should therefore lead to lower levels of absenteeism.

A random sample of 20 employee records was selected and their *number of days absent* over the past year was recorded together with the duration of their *job tenure* (in months); an index of *job satisfaction*; and an index of *organisational commitment*. The data is given in the *Excel* file **X15.11**.

(i) Produce three separate *scatter plots*: (a) between *tenure* and *days absent*; (b) between *job satisfaction* and *days absent*; and (c) between *organisational commitment* and *days absent*. Interpret the pattern of each relationship from the scatter plots. Use the **XY (Scatter)** option from the **Chart Wizard** for each plot.

(ii) Use the **Regression** option in **Data Analysis** to derive the multiple regression model to estimate *absenteeism levels* at the knitting mill based on measures of job tenure, job satisfaction and organisational commitment.

(iii) Write out the equation of the multiple regression model.

(iv) Identify the *coefficient of determination* and interpret its value.

Employee Absenteeism			
Tenure	**Satisfaction**	**Commitment**	**Days absent**
55	46	42	18
79	43	35	21
45	46	24	24
60	42	54	13
88	50	44	22
73	62	48	14
79	40	45	18
54	50	63	7
55	42	41	20
63	57	41	18
33	64	56	6
58	55	49	12
52	48	31	19
75	48	52	15
66	59	46	12
39	50	37	10
88	53	55	20
64	59	53	7
45	52	50	23
42	55	39	14

(v) Is the overall multiple regression model statistically significant? Test at the 5% significance level. State the null and alternative hypotheses; and identify the the appropriate test statistic and its *p-value* from the Anova table. Interpret the findings of the hypothesis test for the knitting mill's HR manager.

(vi) Interpret the meaning of each of the regression coefficients (b_1, b_2 and b_3) of the three independent variables (i.e. *tenure, satisfaction*, and *commitment*).

(vii) Is each independent variable (i.e. *tenure, satisfaction*, and *commitment*) statistically significant? Test each independent variable separately using $\alpha = 0{,}05$. For each hypothesis test, state the null and alternative hypothesis. Identify the *t-stat* and the *p-value* for each test and interpret these findings.

(viii) Which of the three independent variables (i.e. *tenure, satisfaction*, and *commitment*) explains the most variation in absenteeism levels at the knitting mill? Justify your answer by referring to the respective *p-values* of each test in (vii) above.

(ix) Use the multiple regression model (from (iii)) to *estimate* the likely average *number of days absent* by knitting mill employees who have a *job tenure* of 60 months; a job satisfaction index of 65; and an organisational commitment index of 55.

15.12 X15.12 – lock sales

Safeguard Security cc manufactures and markets the *sure-safe* security locks for external doors. The marketing manager would like to identify any significant factors that could influence the sales level of their brand of security lock. Sales and other marketing data was recorded for 26 stores selling the Sure-Safe locks throughout the country.

The sample data set consists of one dependent variable, *sales* (in 1 000's units) and four potential predictor (independent) variables, namely *adspend* (in R10 000's), the number of regional *representatives*, the number of *competing brands* and a *crime index*. The data are given in the *Excel* file **X15.12**.

The primary question that management want answered is: "Can any of the four factors be used to estimate the level of sales of *sure-safe* security locks?

Sure-Safe Lock Sales					
Store id	**Adspend**	**Reps**	**Brands**	**Crimedex**	**Sales**
1	5.5	31	10	8	79,3
2	2.5	45	8	9	200,1
3	8	67	12	9	163,2
4	3	42	7	16	200,1
5	3	38	8	15	146
6	2.9	71	12	17	177,7
7	8	30	12	8	30,9
8	9	48	5	10	291,9
9	4	42	8	4	160
10	6.5	63	5	16	339,4
11	5.5	60	8	7	159,6
12	5	44	12	12	86,3
13	6	50	6	6	237,5
14	5	39	10	4	107,2
15	3.5	55	10	4	155
16	8	52	6	7	291,4
17	6	40	8	6	100,2
18	4	50	11	8	135,8
19	7.5	60	9	13	223,3
20	7	59	9	11	195
21	6.7	58	7	5	72,4
22	6.1	46	10	10	47,7
23	3.6	43	9	8	104,7
24	4.2	26	8	3	93,5
25	4.5	75	8	19	259
26	5.6	68	4	9	331,2

(i) Produce four separate *scatter plots* showing the pattern of *sales* (dependent variable) against each of the independent variables separately. Use the **XY (Scatter)** option from the **Chart Wizard** for each scatter plot.

(ii) Use the **Regression** option in **Data Analysis** to derive the multiple regression model to estimate *sales of sure-safe locks* from the four independent variables.

(iii) Write out the equation of the multiple regression model.

(iv) Identify the *coefficient of determination* and interpret its value.

(v) Is the overall multiple regression model statistically significant? Test at the 5% significance level. State the null and alternative hypotheses; and identify the the appropriate test statistic and its *p-value* from the Anova table. Interpret the findings of the hypothesis test for the management of Safeguard Security cc.

(vi) Interpret the meaning of each of the regression coefficients (b_1, b_2, b_3 and b_4) of the four independent variables.

(vii) Is each independent variable (i.e. *adspend, reps, brands,* and *crimedex*) statistically significant? Test each independent variable separately using $\alpha = 0{,}05$. For each hypothesis test, state the null and alternative hypothesis. Identify the t-stat and the *p-value* for each test and interpret these findings.

(viii) Which of the four independent variables explains the most variation in sure-safe lock sales? Justify your answer by referring to the respective *p-values* of each test in (vii) above.

(ix) Use the multiple regression model (from (iii)) to *estimate* the likely average *number of sure-safe lock sales* for the following values of the independent variables: *adspend* = 4; *reps* = 60; *brands* = 10 and *crimedex* = 9.

Chapter 16

Index Numbers: Measuring Business Activity

Objectives

An index is a summary value that reflects how business or economic activity has changed over time. The CPI is the most commonly understood economic index. Index numbers are used to measure either price or quantity changes over time.

They play an important role in the monitoring of business performance, as well as in the preparation of business forecasts.

After studying this chapter, you should be able to:

- define and explain the purpose of index numbers
- describe applications of index numbers in management practice
- develop and interpret indexes to measure price changes over time
- develop and interpret indexes to measure quantity changes over time
- explain the Laspeyres approach to weighting in a composite index
- distinguish between the *weighted aggregates* method and the *weighted average of relatives* method in composite index construction
- identify pitfalls of index number construction
- relocate the base index of a time series to a different time period
- construct and interpret link relatives
- compute the average rate of change of link relatives over a period of time
- distinguish between price/quantity relatives and link relatives, and
- transform monetary values into constant values, using index numbers.

16.1 Introduction

An **index number** is a *single summary value* which measures the overall change in the level of activity of a *single item* or a *basket of related items* from one time period to another.

An index number summarises into a single numeric value, how any activity of a business, economic or social nature changes over time.

In an economic and business context, index numbers are most commonly used to monitor *price* and *quantity* changes over time, as well as changes in *business performance* on an economic sector and macro-economic level. Index numbers are used both for planning purposes and control purposes.

The best-known and most used index number in any country is the *Consumer Price Index*, or *inflation* indicator (*CPI*). This index measures the general changes of retail prices from month to month and from year to year.

Examples

Examples of important index numbers used in South Africa are:

- a wide range of *financial performance indicators* (over 60 indicators), supplied by I-Net Bridge from JSE data (http://www.inet.co.za) (e.g. JSE All Share index; JSE Gold index; JSE Industrial index; JSE Technologies index; JSE Mining index; JSE Bond index, etc.);
- a number of *economic indicators* made available monthly, quarterly and annually by Stats SA – the central government statistical service (http://www.statssa.gov.za) (e.g. CPI, CPIX [CPI excluding mortgage payments]; PPI Production Price index; Manufacturing Output Index);
- a Business Confidence Index (BCI) (produced monthly by the South African Chamber of Business – SACOB) (http://www.sacob.co.za) as a measure of the level of business confidence within the South African economy.

16.2 Definition and Interpretation of an Index Number

An **index number** is *constructed* by expressing the value of an item (or a basket of items) in the *current period* as a *ratio* of its value in a *base period*.

This ratio is expressed in percentage terms as follows:

$$\text{Index Number} = \frac{\text{Current period value}}{\text{Base period value}} \times 100\%$$

Interpretation of an index number

An index number measures percentage changes from a base period, which has an index value = 100. An index number with a value *above 100* indicates an *increase* in the level of activity being monitored, while an index number *below 100* reflects a *decrease* in activity relative to the base period. The magnitude of the change is shown by the difference between the index number and the base index of 100.

Example

If the index for Electronic Goods sold (TVs, sound systems, VCRs, DVDs, MP3s, Ipods, etc.) stands at 94 in January 2007 relative to January 2006 (base = 100), then this means that the overall prices of Electronic Goods sold in South Africa had fallen by 6% *on average* over the past year. However, if the index was 104 in January 2007, then the overall prices of Electronic Goods sold in South Africa had risen by 4% *on average* over the past year.

16.3 Classification of Index Numbers

There are two major categories of index numbers. Within each category an index can be computed for either a single item or a basket of related items. These categories are:

- *price indexes*
  - single price index, and
  - composite price index.
- *quantity indexes*
  - single quantity index, and
  - composite quantity index.

The *CPI* is an example of a composite price index, while the *Manufacturing Output index* is an example of a composite quantity index.

16.4 Computing Price Indexes

The following *symbolic notation* is used in the construction of index numbers (both price and quantity indexes):

p_0 = base period price
q_0 = base period quantity
p_1 = current period price
q_1 = current period quantity

Price Indexes

A **price index** measures the *percentage change* in price between any *two time periods.*

A price index can be computed for either a single item (e.g. car tyres), or for a basket of items (e.g. car accessories).

(i) Simple Price Index for a single item (called a Price Relative)

For a single item, the relative price change from a base period to another time period is found by computing its *price relative.*

$$\text{Price relative} = \frac{p_1}{p_0} \times 100\%$$

This relative price change is multiplied by 100 to express it in percentage terms.

Example 16.1 95-octane Fuel Price study

***Excel* file:** **C16.1 – fuel price**

In January 2004, the pump price of 95-octane fuel in Cape Town was R3,87 per litre. In January 2005 it cost R4,22 per litre; in January 2006 it cost R4,68 per litre; and in January 2007 it cost R5,29 per litre.

Management question

Using 2004 as the base period, find the *price relatives* for 95-octane fuel in Cape Town for 2005, 2006 and 2007 respectively. Interpret the results.

Solution

Since 2004 is chosen as the base period, p_0 = R3,87, with the base price relative = 100. Table 16.1 shows the calculation of price relatives for 95-octane fuel in Cape Town for each year from 2005 to 2007. To illustrate, the price relative for 2006 is calculated as follows:

$$\frac{4{,}68}{3{,}87} \times 100 = 120{,}9$$

Table 16.1 Price relatives for 95-octane Fuel Price per litre

Year	Price/litre	Price Relative
2004	p_0 = R3,87	100
2005	p_1 = R4,22	109
2006	p_1 = R4,68	120,9
2007	p_1 = R5,29	136,7

Management interpretation

The simple price index (price relative) of 95-octane fuel in Cape Town was 109 in 2005. This means that the price of a litre of 95-octane fuel increased by 9% between January 2004 (with base index = 100) and January 2005. The increase from January 2004 to January 2006 was 20,9%, while the price of a litre of 95-octane fuel increased by 36,7% over the 3-year-period from January 2004 to January 2007.

(ii) Composite Price Index for a basket of items

A **composite price index** measures the *average price change* for a basket of related items (activities) from one time period (the base period) to another period (the current period).

To *illustrate*:
A basket of groceries consists of milk, bread, cheese, margarine, eggs and chicken. The *price* of each item *varies over time*. A composite price index will summarise and report the average "price" change for the same basket of groceries over a given time period.

"Weighting the basket"

To compute a composite index, each item must be *weighted* according to its importance in the basket. *Importance* is determined by the *value of each item* in the basket (i.e. unit price × quantity consumed).

A *composite price index* is intended to measure only *price changes* in a basket of related items over time. Since the quantities consumed can also change over time, it is necessary to *hold all quantities consumed constant*. This allows price changes to be monitored without the confounding effect of simultaneous quantity changes.

The common practice in composite index number construction is to *hold quantities constant* at *base period consumption levels*. This is referred to as the *Laspeyres* approach to *weighting* items in a composite index.

Constructing a composite price index

There are two methods which can be employed to compute a **Laspeyres composite price index**. Both methods produce the same composite price index value, but differ only in their reasoning. The two construction methods are:

- the method of *weighted aggregates*, and
- the method of *weighted average* of *price relatives*.

The construction of a composite price index is illustrated for each method, using the data shown in Table 16.2.

Example 16.2 Toiletries Usage study

***Excel* file:** C16.2 – toiletries

The data in Table 16.2 show the average annual consumption in a two-member household in Tshwane in March 2006 and March 2007 respectively. An economist, who collected the data from a household survey, wants to know the change in the average price of the basket of toiletries from March 2006 to March 2007.

Table 16.2 Annual household consumption of a basket of toiletries (2006–2007)

Toiletry Items	Base Year (2006)		Current Year (2007)	
	Unit Price p_0	Quantity q_0	Unit Price p_1	Quantity q_1
Soap (125 g)	1,95	37	2,1	40
Deodorant (50 ml)	14,65	24	15,95	18
Toothpaste (100 ml)	6,29	14	6,74	16

Solution

Method 1: Laspeyres weighted aggregates method

This method highlights the fact that the composite price index is derived in a similar way to the price relative, but with the *value of the basket* replacing the individual prices in each period.

Since the *Laspeyres* weighting approach is used, only *base period quantities* (consumption levels) are used for these calculations. A three-step approach is now applied.

Step 1 Find the base period value for the basket of items

This means finding out what the basket of items would have cost in the base period (2006) when base period prices (p_0) applied and base period quantities (q_0) were consumed.

Formula

The *base period value* for a basket is found by *multiplying* the *base period prices* with *base period quantities* ($p_0 \times q_0$) for each item, and summing over all items in the basket, i.e.:

$$\text{Base period value} = \Sigma(p_0 \times q_0)$$

The calculations are shown in Table 16.3.

Table 16.3 Value of the toiletries basket in the base period (2006)

Item	Unit Price p_0	Quantity q_0	*Base Period Value* $p \times q_0$
Soap (125 g)	1,95	37	72,15
Deodorant (50 ml)	14,65	24	351,6
Toothpaste (100 ml)	6,29	14	88,06
			511,81

Thus, the *base period value* for the basket of toiletries is:

$$\Sigma(p_0 \times q_0) = \text{R}511{,}81$$

Thus, in 2006, a two-member household in Tshwane spent R511,81 on average on the three toiletry items (soap, deodorant and toothpaste).

Step 2 Find the current period value for the basket of items

This means finding what the basket of items would cost in the current period (2007), when current prices (p_1) were paid for base period quantities (q_0) consumed.

Formula

The *current period value* for a basket is found by *multiplying* the *current period prices* with *base period quantities* ($p_1 \times q_0$) for each item, and summing over all items in the basket, i.e.:

$$\text{Current period value} = \Sigma(p_1 \times q_0)$$

The calculations are shown in Table 16.4 overleaf.

Table 16.4 Value of the toiletries basket in the current period (2007)

Item	Unit Price p_1	Quantity q_0	*Current Period Value* $p_1 \times q_0$
Soap (125 g)	2,1	37	77,7
Deodorant (50 ml)	15,95	24	382,8
Toothpaste (100 ml)	6,74	14	94,36
			554,86

Thus, the *current period value* for the basket of toiletries is:

$$\Sigma(p_1 \times q_0) = \text{R}554{,}86$$

Thus, in 2007, a two-member household in Tshwane spent R554,86 on average on the three toiletry items (soap, deodorant and toothpaste), assuming they consumed the same quantities as in the base period (2006).

Step 3 Find the ratio of these two values (i.e. composite price index)

The ratio is the *current period value divided* by the *base period value.* This is the composite price index.

This ratio will measure the combined *average relative price changes* from the base time period to the current time period for all the items in the basket. This ratio can be seen as an *aggregated price relative.*

$$\text{Laspeyres price index} = \frac{\Sigma(p_1 \times q_0)}{\Sigma(p_0 \times q_0)} \times 100\%$$

For the toiletries usage example:

the *Laspeyres composite price index* $= \dfrac{554{,}86}{511{,}81} \times 100 = \mathbf{108{,}4}$

Management interpretation

If quantities (consumption levels) of the basket of toiletries purchased are held constant at 2006 (*base period*) levels, then this basket of toiletries in 2007 has increased in price by 8,4%, on average, since 2006.

The *computations* for these three steps can be combined into a single table, as illustrated in Table 16.5.

Table 16.5 Laspeyres composite price index for the toiletries basket

Toiletry Items	Base Year (2006)		Current Year (2007)		Value in Period	
	Unit Price p_0	Quantity q_0	Unit Price p_1	Quantity q_1	Base Value $p_0 \times q_0$	Current Value $p_1 \times q_0$
Soap (125 g)	1,95	37	2,1	40	72,15	77,7
Deodorant (50 ml)	14,65	24	15,95	18	351,6	382,8
Toothpaste (100 ml)	6,29	14	6,74	16	88,06	94,36
					511,81	**554,86**
Laspeyres (weighted aggregates) price index =					**108,4**	

Method 2: Laspeyres weighted average of price relatives method

This method highlights the fact that the composite price index is a *weighted average* of the individual items' *price relatives.*

The averaging process takes into account the *relative importance* of each item in the basket. An item's relative value is a percentage showing its contribution to the total basket's value. High-valued items will weight (or influence) the composite price index more than low-valued items.

The *benefit* of this *weighted average of price relatives* method over the weighted aggregates method is the *added insight* that it provides into the *price changes of individual items.*

Since the *Laspeyres* weighting approach is used, only *base period quantities* (consumption levels) are used for these calculations. A three-step approach applies.

Step 1 Find the price relative for each item in the basket

Table 16.6 shows the *price relative* for *each* of the *toiletry items* in the basket.

Table 16.6 Price relatives for each item in the toiletries basket

Toiletry items	Base Year (2006)		Current Year (2007)		
	Unit Price p_0	Quantity q_0	Unit Price p_1	Quantity q_1	Price Relatives $(p_1/p_0) \times 100$
Soap (125 g)	1,95	37	2,1	40	107,7
Deodorant (50 ml)	14,65	24	15,95	18	108,9
Toothpaste (100 ml)	6,29	14	6,74	16	107,2

Management interpretation

Table 16.6 shows that a 125 g bar of soap has increased in price by 7,7% from 2006 to 2007. Similarly, a 50 ml can of deodorant has increased in price by 8,9% over this same period, while a 100 ml tube of toothpaste has increased in price by 7,2% over the past year.

Step 2 Find the base period value of each item in the basket

Using the Laspeyres approach, *base period prices* (p_0) are multiplied by *base period quantities* consumed (q_0), to give the *value* (*weight*) *of each item* in the toiletry basket. The results are shown in Table 16.7 overleaf.

Table 16.7 Value of each item in the toiletries basket, using Laspeyres approach

Toiletry items	Base Year (2006)		Current Year (2007)		Price Relatives $(p_1/p_0) \times 100$	*Base Value* $p_0 \times q_0$
	Unit Price p_0	Quantity q_0	Unit Price p_1	Quantity q_1		
Soap (125 g)	1,95	37	2,1	40	107,7	72,15
Deodorant (50 ml)	14,65	24	15,95	18	108,9	351,6
Toothpaste (100 ml)	6,29	14	6,74	16	107,2	88,06
						511,81

The base period value of each item represents its value (weight or importance) in the basket. As seen from the base period values in Table 16.7, deodorant is the most important (valued) item in the toiletries basket (i.e. R351,6 out of R511,81 = 68,7%). Soap is the least valued item (i.e. only R72,15 out of R511,81 = 14,1%).

Step 3 Weight the price relative for each item by its importance in the basket

To weight each price relative, multiply the price relative by its base period value. Then sum over all items and finally divide by the total value of the basket.
This calculation is shown in the following formula:

$$\textbf{Laspeyres composite price index} = \frac{\Sigma\left[\left(\frac{p_1}{p_0}\right) \times 100 \times (p_0 \times q_0)\right]}{\Sigma\,(p_0 \times q_0)}$$

Table 16.8 shows the weighting of the toiletries' *price relatives* by their respective base period (Laspeyres) weights.

Table 16.8 Weighted average of price relatives (Laspeyres) of toiletries items

Toiletry items	Base Year (2006)		Current Year (2007)		Price Relatives $(p_1/p_0) \times 100$	*Base Value* $p_0 \times q_0$	Weighted Price Relatives
	Unit Price p_0	Quantity q_0	Unit Price p_1	Quantity q_1			
Soap (125 g)	1,95	37	2,1	40	107,7	72,15	7770,56
Deodorant (50 ml)	14,65	24	15,95	18	108,9	351,6	38289,24
Toothpaste (100 ml)	6,29	14	6,74	16	107,2	88,06	9440,03
						511,81	**55499,83**
Laspeyres (weighted average of price relatives) (price index) =						**108,4**	

Finally, the composite price index is computed by dividing the sum of the weighted price relatives (= 55499,83) by the base value of the basket (= 511,81).

Thus: Laspeyres composite price index (based on the *weighted average of price relatives*) $= \frac{55\,499{,}83}{511{,}81} = \mathbf{108{,}4}$

This is the same result as was computed using the method of weighted aggregates.

Note: This calculation is equivalent to working out the *percentage value of each item* in the basket (i.e. the weight of *soap* = $\frac{R72,15}{R511,81}$ % = 14,097%; the weight of *deodorant* = $\frac{R351,6}{R511,81}$ % = 68,697%; and the weight of *toothpaste* = $\frac{R88,06}{R511,81}$ % = 17,206%), and then multiplying the price relative of each item by its respective percentage weight and, finally, summing over all items in the basket.

i.e. weighted average index =
$(107,7 \times 0,14097) + (108,9 \times 0,68697) + (107,2 \times 0,17206) = 108,4$

Unweighted composite index

An *unweighted composite price index* can also be computed. However, an unweighted composite price index ignores the relative importance of each item's quantity consumed. It assumes *equal weights* for each item in a basket. If the quantity consumed is considered to be one unit for each item, an unweighted composite price index formula can be stated as:

$$\text{Unweighted price index} = \frac{\Sigma p_1}{\Sigma p_0} \times 100$$

This method of composite index number construction is only valid if equal quantities of each item in the basket are consumed. Generally this is not the case.

16.5 Computing Quantity Indexes

A **quantity index** measures the *percentage change* in *consumption* level of either an individual item or a basket of items from *one time period to another.*

These changes in consumption patterns can be quantified in similar ways to those for price indexes. When constructing quantity indexes, it is necessary to hold *price levels constant* over time, in order to isolate the effect of quantity (consumption level) changes only.

(i) Simple Quantity Index for a Single Item (called a Quantity Relative)

For a single item, the relative consumption change from a base period to another time period is found by computing its *quantity relative.*

$$\text{Quantity relative} = \frac{q_1}{q_0} \times 100\%$$

where q_1 = the quantity consumed (purchased) in the *current period*
q_0 = the quantity consumed (purchased) in the *base period*

This relative quantity change is multiplied by 100 to express it in percentage terms.

Example 16.3 Toiletries Usage study

***Excel* file:** **C16.2 – toiletries**

For each of the three toiletry items (soap, deodorant and toothpaste) separately, find the relative change in consumption (usage) levels between 2006 and 2007, using the consumption data shown in Table 16.2 above.

Solution

Table 16.9 shows the *quantity relatives* computed for each toiletry item (soap, deodorant and toothpaste).

Table 16.9 Quantity relatives for each toiletries item

Toiletry Items	Base Year (2006)		Current Year (2007)		Quantity Relatives
	Unit Price p_0	Quantity q_0	Unit Price p_1	Quantity q_1	$(q_1/q_0 \times 100)$
Soap (125 g)	1,95	37	2,1	40	108,1
Deodorant (50 ml)	14,65	24	15,95	18	75
Toothpaste (100 ml)	6,29	14	6,74	16	114,3

Management interpretation

The quantity of soap consumed by two-member households in Tshwane has increased by 8,1% from 2006 to 2007. The usage of deodorant, however, has decreased from 2006 to 2007 by 25%. Toothpaste usage, on the other hand, has shown the largest increase of 14,3% over the year from 2006 to 2007.

(ii) Composite Quantity Index for a basket of items

A **composite quantity index** measures the *average consumption (quantity used or purchased) change for a basket of related items* from one time period (the base period) to another period (the current period).

To *illustrate:*
A basket of groceries consists of milk, bread, cheese, margarine, eggs and chicken. The *quantities* of each item purchased *varies over time.* A composite quantity index will summarise and report the average "consumption" change for the same basket of groceries over a given time period.

A quantity index must only reflect changes in consumption, without the confounding effect of simultaneous price changes. As a result, *price levels* must be *held constant* to monitor quantity changes only. The *Laspeyres* approach computes the weights for each item in the basket by *holding prices constant* in the *base period.*

The construction of a composite quantity index is similar to that of a composite price index. The following two examples based on the *toiletries usage* data set (see Table 16.2) illustrate the two methods, namely the *weighted aggregates* and the *weighted average of quantity relatives* using the Laspeyres weighting approach.

Example 16.4 Toiletries Usage study

***Excel* file:** **C16.2 – toiletries**

Construct a *composite quantity index* to find the average change in *usage* (*consumption*) of the three toiletry items (soap, deodorant and toothpaste) between 2006 and 2007, using the *Laspeyres weighted aggregates* method.

Solution – Laspeyres weighted aggregates method

This method compares the *value of the basket* between the base period and the current period, where the basket value is derived by changing quantities while holding price levels constant.

Table 16.10 summarises the three-step approach as follows.

Step 1 Find the base period value for the basket of items

This is what the basket of items cost in the base period (2006) when base period prices (p_0) applied and base period quantities (q_0) were consumed. This *base period value* for the basket is found by *multiplying* the *base period prices* with *base period quantities* ($p_0 \times q_0$) for each item, and summing over all items in the basket (see column labelled *Base Value* in Table 16.10).

Thus, the *base period value* for the basket of toiletries is: $\Sigma(p_0 \times q_0) =$ R511,81

Thus, in 2006, a two-member household in Tshwane spent R511,81, on average, on the three toiletry items (soap, deodorant and toothpaste).

Step 2 Find the current period value for the basket of items

This is what the basket of items would cost in the current period (2007) when current period quantities (q_1) are consumed, but paying base period prices (p_0). The *current period value* for the basket is found by *multiplying* the *base period prices* with *current period quantities* ($p_0 \times q_1$) for each item, and summing over all items in the basket (see column labelled *Current value* in Table 16.10).

Thus, the *current period value* for the basket of toiletries is: $\Sigma(p_0 \times q_1) =$ R442,34

Thus, in 2007, a two-member household in Tshwane spent R442,34, on average, on the three toiletry items (soap, deodorant and toothpaste), assuming they paid the same prices for these items as in the base period (2006).

Step 3 Find the ratio of these two values (i.e. composite quantity index)

The ratio is the *current period value divided* by the *base period value.* This is the composite quantity index.

This ratio will measure the combined *average relative change in consumption* from the base time period to the current time period for all the items in the basket. This ratio can be seen as an *aggregated quantity relative.*

These three steps are summarised in the following *Laspeyres quantity index:*

$$\text{Laspeyres quantity index} = \frac{\Sigma(p_0 \times q_1)}{\Sigma(p_0 \times q_0)} \times 100\%$$

Table 16.10 Composite quantity index for the toiletries basket

Toiletry Items	Base Year (2006)		Current Year (2007)		Value in Period	
	Unit Price p_0	Quantity q_0	Unit Price p_1	Quantity q_1	Base Value $p_0 \times q_0$	Current Value $p_0 \times q_1$
Soap (125 g)	1,95	37	2,1	40	72,15	78
Deodorant (50 ml)	14,65	24	15,95	18	351,6	263,7
Toothpaste (100 ml)	6,29	14	6,74	16	88,06	100,64
					511,81	**442,34**
Laspeyres (weighted aggregates) quantity index =					**86,4**	

For the toiletries usage example:

the *Laspeyres composite quantity index* $= \left(\frac{442,34}{511,81}\right) \times 100 = \mathbf{86,4}$

Management interpretation

If prices are held constant at 2006 (base period) levels, the composite quantity index stands at 86,4 in 2007. This means that the consumption levels of toiletries declined by an average of 13,6% (= 100 – 86,4) between 2006 and 2007. The marginal increases in soap usage (from 37 to 40 per annum) and toothpaste usage (from 14 to 16 per annum) were more than offset by the significant decreased usage of deodorant (from 24 to 18 units).

Example 16.5 Toiletries Usage study

***Excel* file:** **C16.2 – toiletries**

Construct a *composite quantity index* to find the average change in *usage* (*consumption*) of the three toiletry items (soap, deodorant and toothpaste) between 2006 and 2007, using the *Laspeyres weighted average of quantity relatives* method.

Solution – Laspeyres weighted average of quantity relatives method

This method highlights the fact that the composite quantity index is a *weighted average* of the individual items' *quantity relatives.* The weights are determined by an item's relative value in the basket, which is a percentage showing its contribution to the total basket's value.

The appropriate *quantity index* formula using the *Laspeyres weighted average of quantity relatives method* of construction is:

$$\text{Laspeyres quantity index} = \frac{\Sigma\left[\left(\frac{q_1}{q_0}\right) \times 100 \times (p_0 \times q_0)\right]}{\Sigma(p_0 \times q_0)}$$

The formula is similar to that of the Laspeyres composite price index, except that quantity relatives replace price relatives. The *weighting* of the *quantity relatives* is still based on base period prices and quantities.

A similar three-step approach as that used for a price index, is applied. The results are summarised in Table 16.11.

Step 1 Find the quantity relative for each item in the basket

This shows the change in consumption for each toiletry item, individually, from 2006 to 2007 (see column labelled *Quantity Relatives* in Table 16.11, and Table 16.9 for their interpretation).

Step 2 Find the base period value of each item in the basket

Using the Laspeyres approach, *base period prices* (p_0) are multiplied by *base period quantities* consumed (q_0) to give the *value (weight) of each item* in the toiletries basket (see column labelled *Base value* in Table 16.11). When each of these item values is expressed as a percentage of the total value of the basket, they represent the *weights* that will be assigned to each quantity relative. Thus, soap represents only 14,1% of the total toiletries basket by value; deodorant represents a large 68,7% by value; and toothpaste represents the remaining 17,2% of the value of the toiletries basket.

Step 3 Weight the quantity relative for each item by its importance in the basket

To weight each quantity relative, multiply the quantity relative by its base period value. Then sum over all items and, finally, divide by the total value of the basket in the base period.

The column labelled *weighted quantity relatives* shows the weighting of each quantity relative by its corresponding item's relative value in the basket of toiletries.

Table 16.11 Laspeyres weighted average of quantity relatives – Toiletries Usage study

Toiletry items	Base Year (2006)		Current Year (2007)		Quantity Relatives $(q_1/q_0) \times 100$	*Base Value* $p_0 \times q_0$	Weighted Quantity Relatives
	Unit Price p_0	Quantity q_0	Unit Price p_1	Quantity q_1			
Soap (125 g)	1,95	37	2,1	40	108,1	72,15	7 799,42
Deodorant (50 ml)	14,65	24	15,95	18	75	351,6	26 370,00
Toothpaste (100 ml)	6,29	14	6,74	16	114,3	88,06	10 065,26
						511,81	**44 234,68**
Laspeyres (weighted average of quantity relatives) quantity index =						**86,43**	

To compute the composite quantity index, the sum of the weighted quantity relatives (= 44 234,68) is divided by the total base period value of the basket (= 511,81).

Thus *Laspeyres composite quantity index* $= \dfrac{44\ 234{,}68}{511{,}81} = \mathbf{86{,}43}$

Management interpretation

The same interpretation applies as for Table 16.10 above.

Note: If the item weights were computed as the *percentage value* of the item in the basket, (see page 465), then a direct *weighted average* of the *quantity relatives* will give the same result.

i.e. Weighted average index =
$(108{,}1 \times 0{,}14097) + (75 \times 0{,}68697) + (114{,}3 \times 0{,}17206) = 86{,}43$

16.6 Problems of Index Number Construction

Five primary factors require careful consideration when planning the construction of index numbers. These are:

(i) the purpose (scope) of the index
(ii) the selection of the items
(iii) to include choice of weights
(iv) choice of a base year, and
(v) substitution rule.

The Purpose (Scope) of the Index

A clear understanding is necessary of the purpose and scope of a proposed index. This determines the choice of items; the frequency of measurement; the degree of accuracy required; the choice of the weights and the choice of the base year.

If the proposed mix of items is not readily measurable in the time frame required, or if it is not possible to achieve the desired accuracy from the data available, it may be necessary to rethink of the purpose of the index.

It must also be established whether the choice of items to be included in the basket will measure that which is desired by the index (i.e. *construct validity*).

The Selection of the Basket (Mix of Items)

It is generally impractical, from a cost and time point of view, to include every relevant item in the construction of the required index. A *sample of items* is generally selected for inclusion. Considerable care must be taken in the *selection of a representative sample* of relevant items. This may not always be an easy task.

Judgement sampling tends to be used in preference to simple random sampling to ensure representativeness for the purpose of the index. In this regard, it must be decided, first, which items best relate to the purpose of the index and, secondly, which set of products best represent a given item (e.g. cereals are included in a consumer price index, but which brand of cereal, and of what quantity?)

Choice of Item Weights

Each item's relative importance must be reflected in the construction of composite indexes. The problem faced in index number construction is to decide on *typical quantities* (consumption levels) and *prices* to compute *values* that measure the relative importance of items. These typical quantities and prices are obtained either through observation or investigation (e.g. 'pantry audits').

Choice of a Base Year

The base period should be a period of relative economic stability. Defining a normal economic period is difficult. If a period of excessive (severely depressed) economic activity is selected, all indexes will appear to indicate good (poor) performance relative to this base period.

The chosen base period should also be fairly recent, so that comparisons are not excessively affected by changing technology, product quality and/or purchasing habits. For example, the base period for the CPI is currently 2005 and is reset every five years.

Substitution Rule

Every index should have substitution rules. These rules define when items become obsolete or new trends emerge (technology changes), resulting either in existing products being removed from the basket, or new products being added to the basket. It is essential to have valid substitution rules to ensure *continuity validity*. The *weighting* of an item in a basket (for items in the current mix), or the need to maintain *construct validity* of the index (for items not in the current basket), are factors that influence the nature of substitution rules.

The following extracts from the CPI statistical release of Stats SA show how the CPI addresses some of the above issues.

Stats SA (http://www.statssa.gov.za) conducts a "Survey of Income and Expenditure of Households" every five years, to "*identify the goods and services bought* by a typical consumer or household and which should be included in the basket of goods and services used to monitor price changes... The current CPI basket covers approximately 1500 goods and services". In addition, this survey "is used to *determine the weights* of the indicator products in the basket". "The CPI is a Laspeyres weighted index, with the weights remaining constant for the five-year period until the next 'Survey of Income and Expenditure of Households' results become available".

16.7 Limitations on the Use and Interpretation of Index Numbers

Index numbers are generally based on samples of items. For *example*, the CPI uses a *sample* of 1 500 products and services, and the FTSE/JSE Overall index is based on only a *sample* of the approximately 390 companies listed on the JSE. Sampling errors can thus be introduced, which could raise questions of *representativeness* and *construct validity*. Furthermore, technological changes, product quality changes and changes in consumer purchasing patterns can individually and collectively make comparisons of index number series over time both unreliable and incompatible.

Index numbers are useful summary measures of the historical performance of items or groups of related items. Index numbers are useful for the tracking (or monitoring) of past performance, but have limited forecasting capabilities due to their inability to "predict" turning points in economic activity.

16.8 Applications of Index Numbers

16.8.1 Changing the Base of an Index Series

The base of a series of index numbers (price or quantity indexes) can be shifted from one time period to another to make the interpretation of recent values of the index number series more meaningful. Since index numbers are expressed relative to the base period (with index = 100), the base period should not be too far removed from the current levels of activity being monitored by the index number series. This may require repositioning the base year to bring it in line with more recent periods.

HOW TO

To re-base an index series

The base of an index number series is repositioned to a new base period, k, by multiplying each index number in the series by the following adjustment factor:

$$\text{Adjustment factor} = \frac{100}{\text{Index in period } k}$$

Example 16.6 Electrical Appliances Composite Price Index Series study

***Excel* file:** C16.3 – electrical appliances

Consider the following price index series for household electrical appliances from 2001 to 2007, with 2003 as base year.

Year	2001	2002	2003	2004	2005	2006	2007
Price index	78	87	**100**	106	125	138	144

Management question

Revise the price index series to show 2005 as the new base year with base index = 100.

Solution

Calculate the adjustment factor $= \frac{100}{\text{2005 index}} = \frac{100}{125} = 0{,}80$

Now multiply each price index in the series by the adjustment factor of 0,80

2001: 78 × 0,8 = 62,4
2002: 87 × 0,8 = 69,6, etc.

This results in the following *revised* price index series, with 2005 as the new base year (with base price index = 100). Refer to Table 16.12 overleaf.

Table 16.12 Re-based price index series (base = 2005): Electrical Appliances

Year	2001	2002	2003	2004	2005	2006	2007
Price index	62,4	69,6	80	84,8	**100**	110,4	115,2

Management interpretation

In the revised price index series, price changes are now interpreted relative to 2005. For *example*, 2004 prices were 84,8% (or 15,2% below those) of 2005 prices, on average. In the previous price index series, 2004 and 2005 prices could not be compared directly.

Note: Revising the base period does not change the relative relationship between the individual indexes.

16.8.2 Link relatives

The indexes computed above reflect only changes from a base period (with index = 100). They do not reflect period-on-period changes.

Link relatives are indexes which reflect price or quantity changes on a *period-by-period* basis.

Thus, *link relative* indexes show how prices (quantities) have changed from period to period, whereas *price (quantity) relative indexes* show how prices (quantities) have changed relative to a given base period only.

Each period's level of activity (price or quantity) is expressed as a percentage of the *immediately preceding period's* level of activity. The Consumer Price Index (CPI) is always computed as a composite price index, but is transformed into a link relative to highlight the year-on-year changes in the general level of prices in the economy.

Link relatives for a single item

For a *single item,* link relatives are computed as follows:

$$\text{Price link relative} = \frac{p_i}{p_{i-1}} \times 100\%$$

$$\text{Quantity link relative} = \frac{q_i}{q_{i-1}} \times 100\%$$

where i is a given period and $(i-1)$ is its preceding period.

Example 16.7 Standard White Bread Loaf study

***Excel* file:** C16.4 – white bread loaf

The price of a standard white loaf of bread is given in Table 16.13 overleaf for the following eight years (2000–2007). An economist wants to identify the annual price changes, as well as price changes relative to the base year of 2000.

Management question

Compute and interpret both the *link relatives* and *price relatives* for this (single item) price index series of a loaf of white bread.

Solution

The *link relatives* and *price relatives* are shown in Table 16.13 below.

Table 16.13 Link relatives and Price relatives for a Standard White Bread Loaf

Year	Bread Price (Rand)	Link Relative	Price Relative (Base 2000 = 100)
2000	3,15	100	100
2001	3,45	109,5	109,5
2002	3,7	107,2	117,5
2003	3,95	106,8	125,4
2004	4,1	103,8	130,2
2005	4,45	108,5	141,3
2006	4,85	109	154
2007	5,05	104,1	160,3

Management interpretation

The *link relative* column shows that the price of a standard loaf of white bread increased by 9,5% from 2000 to 2001; by 7,2% from 2001 to 2002; by 6,8% from 2002 to 2003, etc. The smallest *year-on-year* increase in the price of a standard loaf of white bread was 3,8% from 2003 to 2004.

On the other hand, the *price relative* column shows how the price of a standard loaf of white bread has increased *relative to the base period price* of 2000. Over the period from 2000 to 2003, the price of bread has risen by 25,4%, while by 2006, the increase has been 54% since 2000. In 2007, a standard loaf of white bread cost 60,3% more than in 2000.

For a **basket of items**, a *link relative* is found by dividing each period's *composite index* (price or quantity) by the preceding period's *composite index*. The interpretation is similar to that for a single item's link relative.

Example 16.8 Paint and Accessories Composite Price Index Series study

***Excel* file:** C16.5 – paint prices

Consider the following composite price index series for domestic paint and painting accessories (brushes, cleansing agents, sandpaper, etc.) from 2001 to 2007, with 2004 as base year (composite price index = 100).

Year	2001	2002	2003	2004	2005	2006	2007
Composite Price Index	79	88	91	100	114	138	151

Management question

Determine the *year-on-year* overall average price changes for paint and accessories from 2001 to 2007. Interpret the findings.

Solution

Table 16.14 below shows the *link relatives* for the above composite price index series for paint and accessories.

Table 16.14 Link relatives for the Paint and Accessories Composite Price Index Series study

Year	2001	2002	2003	2004	2005	2006	2007
Composite Price Index	79	88	91	100	114	138	151
Link Relative	–	111,4	103,4	109,9	114	121,1	109,4

To illustrate, the link relative for 2003 = $\frac{91}{88} \times 100 = 103{,}4$

Management interpretation

Paint and accessories prices have increased steadily over the seven-year period (2001 to 2007) *on average* by: 11,4% from 2001 to 2002; 3,4% from 2002 to 2003; 9,9% from 2003 to 2004, etc. The largest *annual* average percentage increase has been 21,1% from 2005 to 2006, while the smallest *annual* average percentage increase was 3,4% from 2002 to 2003.

16.8.3 Averaging Link Relatives

Link relatives are *rates of change values.* Therefore, they can be *averaged* using a *geometric mean* instead of an arithmetic mean. This will produce the *average rate of change* (increase or decrease) over the period of time for which the average was computed.

A **geometric mean** is defined as the nth root of the product of n link relatives.

i.e. $$GM = \sqrt[n]{(lr_1 \times lr_2 \times lr_3 \times \ldots \times lr_n)}$$

where lr_i is the ith period's link relative

Example 16.9 Paint and Accessories Composite Price Index Series study

Refer to **Example 16.8** for the problem description and the annual price index series for *paint and accessories* from 2001 to 2007.

Management question

What is the average *annual percentage change* in paint and accessory items from 2001 to 2007?

Solution

(Refer to chapter 5 for the *geometric mean.*)

$$\text{Geometric mean} = \sqrt[6]{(111{,}4 \times 103{,}4 \times 109{,}9 \times 114 \times 121{,}1 \times 109{,}4)}$$
$$= \mathbf{111{,}41}$$

The *Excel* function **Geomean** can also be used.

i.e. **=Geomean(111.4, 103.4, ..., 109.4)** gives the result – 111,4068.

Management interpretation

The prices of paint and accessory items have increased by *an average* of 11,41% (111,41 – 100) annually from 2001 to 2007.

Note: It is not correct to use the arithmetic average formula as the base value for each *link relative* is different. An arithmetic mean assumes a constant base which is not the case with link relatives.

16.8.4 Transforming Monetary Values into Real (Constant) Values

As the price of products and services change over time, the monetary value of sales (turnover) derived from these products and services also changes. *Index numbers* can be used to *remove* the influence of the *price adjustments* on sales of products and services to reveal the *real change* in turnover.

These *real values* will reflect the *actual growth* (or *decline*) in sales volumes that are free of the confounding influence of price changes.

Real values – also called **constant values** – show the actual level of business activity in a particular period on the assumption that *base period prices* are paid for products and services in this current period. Thus, real (or constant) values express monetary values relative to a base period.

To *remove the influence of price adjustments* from current monetary earnings, *divide* each period's *monetary value* by its *corresponding composite price index number.* This results in real (or constant) values.

These *real values* can then be *compared* to values in the *base period* to establish the extent to which sales volumes have grown or declined, relative to the base period levels. Real values which are *below base period values* show that sales volumes have declined relative to base period volumes, while real values which are *above base period values* show that sales volumes have increased relative to base period volumes.

This conversion to constant prices of monetary prices is also applied to salary adjustments, to reflect whether salary increases have lagged behind or exceed the CPI. Such adjustments to salaries will reveal the *real purchasing power of earnings*. By adjusting *company turnover* in a similar way, a company can determine *real changes* (either real growth or real decline) in turnover due to increased or decreased demand, without the confounding influence of price changes.

The "price inflation indicator" – namely the *Consumer Price Index* (*CPI*) or, in the case of industrial products, the *Producer Price Index* (*PPI*) – which is published monthly by Statistics South Africa, (http://www.statssa.gov.za) is used to deflate monetary values such as salaries and turnover, to generate real (or constant) values which are more comparable over time.

Example 16.10 The Northern Province Gross National Product (GNP) study

***Excel* file:** **C16.6 – northern prov gnp**

The gross national product (GNP) for the Northern Province for the period 2002 to 2006, together with the CPI for that region, as computed by Stats SA, is given in Table 16.15 below.

Table 16.15 GNP and CPI for Northern Province (2002–2006)

Year	CPI	GNP (R millions)
2002	100	778
2003	104,3	806
2004	110,2	889
2005	112,2	930
2006	118,6	974

Management questions

- Calculate the *real growth in GNP* from 2002 to 2006 for the Northern Province.
- Also compute the *price relatives* (using 2002 as base period) and *link relatives* for *real* GNP growth.
- Compare the real percentage growth in GNP to the CPI for each year and comment on the findings.
- Lastly, find the average annual change in *real GNP* from 2002 to 2006.

Solutions

HOW TO

Convert monetary values into constant values

- Divide monetary value by the CPI.
- Multiply the result by 100.

Divide the CPI into the GNP to remove the effect of GNP increases due to price increases. This gives the *real (constant) GNP* values as shown in Table 16.16 together with the price relatives for real GNP and the link relatives for real GNP.

Table 16.16 Real GNP (in R millions) for the Northern Province

Year	CPI 2002 = 100	GNP (R millions)		Price Relative for Real GNP	Link Relative for Real GNP
		Monetary	Real (Constant)		
2002	100	778	778	100	–
2003	104,3	806	**772,77***	99,33	99,33
2004	110,2	889	806,72	**103,69****	104,39
2005	112,2	930	828,88	106,54	**102,75*****
2006	118,6	974	821,25	105,56	99,08

* $(\frac{806}{104,3} \times 100) = 772,77$

** $(\frac{806,72}{778} \times 100) = 103,69$

*** $(\frac{828,88}{806,72} \times 100) = 102,75$

The average annual change in *real* GNP from 2002 to 2006 is found by computing the *geometric mean* of the *link relatives* as follows:

$$\textbf{Geometric mean} = \sqrt[4]{99,33 \times 104,39 \times 102,75 \times 99,08}$$

$$= \mathbf{101,36}$$

Management interpretation

Real GNP decreased marginally in 2003 from 2002 levels (by 0,67%) (see price relative), but showed real growth (year on year) of 4,39% during 2004 and 2,75% growth during 2005 (see link relatives). It declined in real terms again in 2006 (by 0,92%). Overall in 2006, the Northern Province's real GNP is 5,56% higher when compared to 2002.

Percentage wise, the *real GNP growth rate* has been *significantly below average price increases*, as seen from a comparison of corresponding CPI and real percentage growth indexes (see price relatives and CPI).

Finally, the average annual growth in real GNP from 2002 to 2006 is 1,36% per annum.

Example 16.11 The Engineer Earnings study

***Excel* file:** C16.7 – engineer earnings

The monthly earnings of an engineer over a five-year period (2002–2006) and the CPI for the corresponding periods, with 2002 as base period, are shown in Table 16.17.

Management question

Has the engineer's annual salary adjustments kept ahead of annual inflation?

Compute and compare the engineer's real monthly earnings relative to the base year, (i.e. compute price relatives on the real monthly earnings).

Solution

Table 16.17 reflects the *real earnings* of the engineer over this five-year period.

Table 16.17 Real monthly earnings for engineers (2002–2006)

Year	Monthly Earnings (R)	Consumer Price Index Base 2002 = 100	Real Earnings at 2002 Prices (R)	Price Relative
2002	8 400	100	8 400	100
2003	9 300	116	8 017	95,4
2004	10 500	126	8 333	99,2
2005	12 300	130	9 462	112,6
2006	12 900	135	9 556	113,8

Note: The *real earnings* column reflects the *purchasing power* of monthly income for each year in comparison to 2002.

Management interpretation

Monetary income showed an increase for each of the five years. However, *real income* (purchasing power) for 2003 and 2004 actually declined in relation to 2002. For 2005 and 2006, real income showed an increase over the base period income (2002) of 12,6% in 2005 and 13,8% in 2006 respectively.

16.9 Summary

This chapter described the basic concept of an index number as a *summary measure* of the overall *change in the level of activity* of a single item or basket of items from one time period to another. It is always expressed as a ratio relative to a base period. Common South African index numbers were identified.

The chapter focused on the construction and interpretation of both *price* and *quantity indexes.* In each case, an index was calculated for a single item (called **price/quantity relative**) and a basket of related items (called a **composite price/quantity index**). With the construction of a composite index, a set of *weights* for each item in the basket must be determined. This measure of relative importance was identified as the *Laspeyres approach,* where prices/quantities are held constant in base period terms.

Both the method of *weighted aggregates* and the method of *weighted average of relatives* were demonstrated in the construction of composite indexes.

Problems in index number construction, as well as limitations in respect of their interpretation, were discussed, as were three applications of index numbers, namely: (1) *changing the base* of a series of indexes to a different time period to keep an index series manageable in terms of its economic interpretation; (2) computing *period-on-period changes for indexes,* which are called **link relatives**, and finding the average period-on-period change over a number of periods using the *geometric mean*; and (3) *transforming monetary values into real values.* The difference in interpretation of link relatives and price/quantity relative index numbers was highlighted. Finally, practical uses of index numbers were illustrated.

Exercises

16.1 X16.1 – motorcycle sales

A motorcycle dealer has recorded the unit prices and quantities sold of three models of the Suzuki motorcycle for 2005 and 2006. The quantities sold and unit selling prices for both these years are given in the following table and in the *Excel* file **X16.1**.

	2005		2006	
Motorcycle model	**Unit price (R1000)**	**Quantity (units sold)**	**Unit price (R1000)**	**Quantity (units sold)**
A	25	10	30	7
B	15	55	19	58
C	12	32	14	40

(i) Find the price relative for each motorcycle model. Use 2005 as the base period. Interpret.
(ii) Compute the composite price index for 2006 with 2005 as the base period using each of the following methods:
  (a) the Laspeyres weighted aggregates method;
  (b) the Laspeyres weighted average of price relatives method.
(iii) Interpret the composite price index for the motorcycle dealer.

16.2 Refer to the data given in Exercise 16.1 and the *Excel* file X16.1.

(i) Find the quantity relative for each motorcycle model. Interpret.
(ii) Compute the composite quantity index for 2006 with 2005 as the base period using each of the following methods:
  (a) the Laspeyres weighted aggregates method;
  (b) the Laspeyres weighted average of quantity relatives method.
(iii) By how much has the motorcycle dealer's *volume of sales* (i.e. quantities sold) for all three models changed between 2005 and 2006?

16.3 X16.3 – telkom services

Telkom offers a range of telecommunication services to small businesses. A small printing business has used the services of *TalkPlus* (a value-added telephone service); *SmartAccess* (an advertising service) and *ISDN* (an internet connection) for the past three years. Their annual usage and the unit price of each service are given in the following table and in the *Excel* file **X16.3**.

Telkom Services	2004		2005		2006	
	Unit price (cents/call)	**Quantity (100's calls)**	**Unit price (cents/call)**	**Quantity (100's calls)**	**Unit price (cents/call)**	**Quantity (100's calls)**
TalkPlus	65	14	70	18	55	17
SmartAccess	35	27	40	29	45	24
ISDN	50	16	45	22	40	32

(i) Compute the *price relatives* for 2005 and 2006 for the ISDN service. Use 2004 as the base period.Interpret the meaning of each of these indexes.

(ii) Use Laspeyres weighted aggregates method – with 2004 as the base period - to compute the *composite price indexes* for 2005 and 2006. By what percentage, on average, has the cost of telecommunications services for this printing company changed in 2005 and 2006 relative to 2004?

(iii) Has the printing company's overall usage of the different telecommunication services changed significantly in 2005 and 2006 relative to 2004? Compute the composite quantity indexes for 2005 and 2006 using 2004 as the base period to answer this question.

16.4 X16.4 – computer personnel

The average annual salary and staff complements (number of employees) for each of three IT job categories in a large IT consultancy organization based in Johannesburg are shown in the table below and is given in the *Excel* file **X16.4.**

IT Job categories	**Annual salary (in R10 000)**		**No. of employees**	
	2004	**2007**	**2004**	**2007**
Systems analyst	42	50	84	107
Programmer	29	36	96	82
Network manager	24	28	58	64

(i) Calculate a Laspeyres composite index for 2007 to reflect the overall average change in the annual salaries of IT personnel from 2004. Use 2004 as the base period with index = 100. Apply the method of weighted aggregates. What does this composite index mean in terms of the change of overall remuneration paid to these three IT job categories from 2004 to 2007?

(ii) Compute price relatives for each category of IT personnel. Which category has shown the largest increase in annual salary between 2004 and 2007?

16.5 Refer to the data given in Exercise 16.4 and the *Excel* file X16.4.

(i) Find the quantity relative for each IT job category using 2004 as the base period. Define the meaning of each quantity relative and interpret its value.

(ii) Compute the composite quantity index for 2007 with 2004 as the base period using each of the following methods:
 (a) the Laspeyres weighted aggregates method;
 (b) the Laspeyres weighted average of quantity relatives method.

(iii) On average, by how much has the overall staff complement across the three IT job categories changed from 2004 to 2007?

16.6 **X16.6 – printer cartridges**

A printing company which specializes in business stationery (i.e. letterheads, business cards, reports, invitations, etc.) has recorded its usage and cost of printer cartridges for its four different printers. The printer cartridges are identified as HQ21, HQ25, HQ26 and HQ32. The data are given in the *Excel* file **X16.6.**

Printer cartridges	2004		2005		2006	
	Unit price	Quantity used	Unit price	Quantity used	Unit price	Quantity used
HQ21	145	24	155	28	149	36
HQ25	172	37	165	39	160	44
HQ26	236	12	255	12	262	14
HQ32	314	10	306	8	299	11

Use an *Excel* worksheet to perform the following calculations (to one decimal place).

(i) Using 2004 as the base period, compute the price relatives of the HQ26 and HQ32 printer cartridges for 2006 only. Interpret the meaning of these two price relatives.

(ii) Compute the composite price indexes for 2005 and 2006 with 2004 as the base period using each of the following methods:

(a) the Laspeyres weighted aggregates method;

(b) the Laspeyres weighted average of price relatives method.

(iii) What was the overall average *change in the cost* to the printing company of printer cartridges used between 2004 and 2005; and between 2004 and 2006? Explain.

(iv) Use the composite price indexes computed in (ii) to derive the composite *link relatives* from 2004 to 2006 of printer cartridges used.

16.7 **X16.7 – electrical goods**

The composite price index for electrical goods (e.g. kettles, toasters, refrigerators, stoves, microwave ovens, blenders, etc.) for the period 2000 to 2006 is shown in the following table and given in the *Excel* file **X16.7.**

	2000	2001	2002	2003	2004	2005	2006
Composite Price Index (Electrical goods)	88	96	100	109	114	112	115

For all calculations, compute results to one decimal place.

(i) Reset the base period index for electrical goods from 2002 to 2005. Interpret the revised index number series.

(ii) Compute the *link relatives* for electrical goods and interpret.

16.8 X16.8 – insurance claims

Two insurance companies (Federal Insurance and Baltic Insurance) both use the Laspeyres index number approach to represent how the number of claims processed annually have either increased or decreased. In 2005 the two companies merged, but decided to maintain separate records of claims processed annually. To make comparisons possible between the two companies, management agreed that their respective index series should have a common base period of 2005.

The index series of claims processed for each company is given below and in the *Excel* file **X16.8**.

	2001	2002	2003	2004	2005	2006
Federal Insurance (base = 2003)	92,3	95,4	100	102,6	109,4	111,2
Baltic Insurance (base = 2004)	93,7	101,1	98,2	100	104,5	107,6

(i) Calculate the revised index series for both companies with 2005 as the common base period. Calculate to one decimal place.

(ii) Which company showed the bigger increase in claims processed between 2003 and 2005? Use the results of (i) to justify your answer.

(iii) Compute *link relatives* between successive years for each company.

(iv) Which company showed the bigger increase in claims processed between 2005 and 2006? Refer to the link relatives computed in (iii).

(v) Derive the *average annual percentage* change in claims processed for each insurance company using a *geometric mean* (refer to chapter 5, section 5.9).

Hint: Apply the link relative indexes computed in (iii) to calculate each geometric mean.

(vi) Which Insurance company has experienced the larger average annual increase in insurance claims processed between 2001 and 2006?

16.9 X16.9 – micro-market basket

A micro-market basket price index can be computed for a household by including several food items together that are typically consumed by a household. Consider the basic food items in the following table, with their unit price and per capita annual consumption. The data are also given in the *Excel* file **X16.9**.

Food items in micro market basket	Unit prices (in Rand)		Consumption	
	2006	2007	2006	2007
Milk (litres)	7,29	7,89	117	98
Bread (loaves)	4,25	4,45	56	64
Sugar (kg)	2,19	2,45	28	20
Maize meal (kg)	5,59	5,25	58	64

Show all calculations to one decimal place.

(i) Find the *price relative* for each food item. Interpret the results. Which food item showed the largest price change (increase or decrease) from 2006 to 2007? Justify your answer.
(ii) Calculate the Laspeyres *composite price index* for 2007 (2006 = base period). Use the weighted average of price relatives method. What is the average percentage change in 2007 prices over those in 2006?
(iii) Find the *quantity relative* (or *consumption* relative) for each food item. Interpret the results. Which food item showed the largest consumption change (increase or decrease) from 2006 to 2007?
(iv) Compute the Laspeyres *composite consumption index* for 2007 (2006 = base period). Use the weighted average of quantity relatives method. What is the average percentage change in household consumption between 2006 and 2007?

16.10 X16.10 – utilities usage
A random sample of 100 LSM8 households was selected to participate in a study to establish a composite price index for *household utilities usage* (i.e. electricity, sewage, water, telephone). The following average annual figures have been obtained. Also refer to the *Excel* file **X16.10**.

Household utilities	Prices (in Rand/unit)			Consumption (No. of units)		
	2005	2006	2007	2005	2006	2007
Electricity	1,97	2,05	2,09	745	812	977
Sewage	0,62	0,68	0,72	68	56	64
Water	0,29	0,31	0,35	296	318	378
Telephone	1,24	1,18	1,06	1 028	1 226	1 284

Use an *Excel* worksheet to perform the following calculations (to one decimal place).
(i) Find the price relative for each household utility for 2007. Use 2005 as the base period. Interpret the meaning of each price relative value. Which utility showed the smallest change in price from 2005 to 2007? Justify.
(ii) Compute the composite price indexes for 2006 and 2007 with 2005 as the base period. Use each of the following methods:
(a) the Laspeyres weighted aggregates method;
(b) the Laspeyres weighted average of price relatives method
(iii) Interpret the values of these composite price indexes for 2006 and 2007.

16.11 Refer to the data given **Exercise 16.10** and the *Excel* file **X16.10.**
Use an *Excel* worksheet to perform the following calculations (to one decimal place).
(i) Find the quantity relative for each household utility for 2007 with 2005 as the base period. Which utility showed the greatest change in consumption from 2005 to 2007? Justify.

(ii) Compute the composite quantity (consumption) index for 2006 and 2007 with 2005 as the base period. Use each of the following methods:
(a) the Laspeyres weighted aggregates method;
(b) the Laspeyres weighted average of quantity relatives method.

(iii) Refer to the answers in (ii) and explain how overall consumption of utilities in LSM8 households has changed from 2005 to 2007.

16.12 X16.12 – leather goods

A leather goods manufacturer has kept records of the annual costs of inputs used in the manufacture of its leather products (briefcases, satchels, belts, hats, etc.). An annual Laspeyres composite cost index has been developed by the accountant, with 2002 as the base period. The data is given in the *Excel* file **X16.12**.

	2000	2001	2002	2003	2004	2005	2006
Composite cost index	97	92	100	102	107	116	112

(i) The accountant would like to move the base of the index series to 2004. Prepare the revised cost index series with base period = 100 in 2004.

(ii) Plot the revised cost index series in a line graph. Comment on the pattern of overall costs of inputs changes over the seven-year period from 2000 to 2006.

(iii) By how much have overall costs of inputs changed, on average, from 2004 to 2006?

(iv) Using the original cost index series to prepare link relatives for the period 2000 to 2006. Between which two consecutive years has the change in the costs of inputs been the largest?

(v) Use the geometric mean (refer to chapter 5, section 5.9) to compute the average annual percentage change in the overall costs of inputs from 2000 to 2006. Interpret its value.

16.13 X16.13 – accountants salaries

The following table shows the average annual salary package of chartered accountants with 3 year's work experience and the consumer price index (CPI) for the period 2001 to 2007. The base year for CPI is 2002 (i.e. CPI = 100).
The data is given in the *Excel* file **X16.13**.

Accountants' Salaries (Annual)		
Year	**Salary package (in R1000)**	**CPI**
2001	287	95
2002	306	100
2003	322	104
2004	348	111
2005	366	121
2006	396	126
2007	410	133

(i) Use the Consumer Price Index (CPI) to compute the *real* annual salary package of chartered accountants for each of the years.
(ii) Based on (i), discuss whether chartered accountants' salary packages have kept pace with "headline" inflation (CPI) relative to the base period?
(iii) Compute *salary link relatives* and *CPI link relatives* and determine whether salary adjustments have maintained the real purchasing power of accountants' incomes on a year-to-year basis.

16.14 X16.14 – school equipment

Consider the following cost index series for school equipment supplied by the Northern Province Education Department to schools in the province.
The data is given in the *Excel* file **X16.14.**

	1999	2000	2001	2002	2003	2004	2005	2006
Composite cost index	94,8	97,6	100	105,2	108,5	113,9	116,7	121,1

(i) Change the base-year index from 2001 to 2004. Show the revised composite cost index series for school equipment.
(ii) Plot the revised composite cost index series on a line graph using the **Line chart type** from the **Chart Wizard** in *Excel.* Interpret the pattern of overall cost changes in school equipment provided by the Northern Province Education Department.
(iii) Use the original cost index series and compute *link relatives* to identify year-on-year cost changes. Interpret the link relatives index series.
(iv) If the Department budgeted R5 million in 1999 for school equipment for the Province's schools, what should the budgets have been in each year from 2000 to 2006 to provide at least the same level of service to schools?

16.15 X16.15 – coffee imports

The House of Coffee is a coffee wholesaler which imports and distributes ground coffee to over 300 retailers countrywide. The company has kept records of the unit price paid per kilogram and the number of kilograms imported of its four major coffee types (Java, Colombia, Sumatra and Mocha). Only data for 2003 and 2006 are shown in the following table. The data are also given in the *Excel* file **X16.15.**

	2003		2006	
Coffee types	**Unit price (R/kg)**	**Quantity (1 000 kg)**	**Unit price (R/kg)**	**Quantity (1 000 kg)**
Java	85	52	98	46
Colombia	64	75	74	90
Sumatra	115	18	133	20
Mocha	38	144	42	168

(i) Compute the *price relative* for 2006 for each coffee type. Interpret.
(ii) Calculate, to one decimal place, the Laspeyres *composite price index* for coffee imports for 2006 using 2003 as the base year. Interpret is meaning.
(iii) If the economy's PPI (Producers Price Index) which measures raw material cost changes to producers/wholesalers has increased by 15% from 2003 to 2006, has the cost of coffee imports become cheaper or more expensive in real cost terms?
(iv) Compute, to one decimal place, the Laspeyres *composite quantity index* for coffee imports for 2006 using 2003 as the base year. Interpret is meaning.

16.16 X16.16 – medical claims

Hydrogen is a medical aid fund with over 450 000 members. Data on the *number of claims received* and the *average value of these claims* by the different medical categories (general practitioners, specialists, dentists, medicines) is given for 2004 and 2006. The data are also given in the *Excel* file **X16.16**.

	2004		2006	
Claim type	**Claims (1 000's)**	**Ave. Value (R)**	**Claims (1 000's)**	**Ave. Value (R)**
GP's	20	220	30	255
Specialists	30	720	25	822
Dentists	10	580	15	615
Medicines	50	400	70	438

(i) The management of the medical aid fund would like you to provide them with one overall figure to represent how the *number of claims* (i.e. quantities) have increased in the 3 years from 2004 to 2006. Use 2004 as the base year.
(ii) Compute appropriate indexes for *each claim type* to identify which claim type showed the largest increase in the *number of claims* over this 3-year period.
(iii) Determine the change in the overall *value of claims* received from 2004 to 2006. Use 2004 as the base year. Interpret the result for the management of the Hydrogen medical aid fund.

16.17 X16.17 – tennis shoes

A sports equipment company sells three models of tennis shoes (Trainer, Balance and Dura). Company records for 2005 and 2006 show the unit price and quantities sold of each model of tennis shoe. The data are also given in the *Excel* file **X16.17**.

The company's financial plan requires that *sales volumes* (i.e. quantities sold) of all models of tennis shoes must show an increase of at least 12% per annum.

	2005		2006	
Shoe model	**Unit price**	**Pairs sold**	**Unit price**	**Pairs sold**
Trainer	320	96	342	110
Balance	445	135	415	162
Dura	562	54	595	48

(i) Compute *quantity relatives* for each of the three models of tennis shoes. Which model showed the smallest increase in sales volumes?

(ii) Compute a Laspeyres *composite quantity index* for 2006 using 2005 as the base period to establish whether the company has achieved its sales volume target for tennis shoes. What conclusion can be drawn from the index?

16.18 X16.18 – energy fund

The Central Energy Fund (CEF) monitors the price of crude oil imports and uses it as a basis for setting local fuel prices. The fuel-cost index of crude oil imports is given in the table below for the period 1997 to 2006. The data are also given in the *Excel* file **X16.18.**

	1997	1998	1999	2000	2001	2002	2003	2004	2005	2006
Fuel cost index	100	116,2	122,4	132,1	135,7	140,3	142,8	146,9	153,4	160,5

(i) Every ten years the CEF resets the base 5 years on from the current base. Compute the revised fuel-cost index series with 2002 as the new base year.

(ii) Compute the *link relatives* and plot the annual percentage changes on a line graph. Use the **Line chart type** from the **Chart Wizard** in *Excel.* Comment on the trend in price changes of crude oil imports between 1997 and 2006.

16.19 X16.19 – motorcycle distributor

A motorcycle distributor has recorded the average unit selling prices and quantities sold of three models of a particular make of motorcycle in South Africa from 2003 to 2007. The data are given in the *Excel* file **X16.19**.

	Average Selling Prices (Rand)				
Make	**2003**	**2004**	**2005**	**2006**	**2007**
Blitz	18 050	19 235	21 050	21 950	22 400
Cruiser	25 650	26 200	27 350	28 645	31 280
Classic	39 575	42 580	43 575	43 950	46 750

	Units Sold				
Make	**2003**	**2004**	**2005**	**2006**	**2007**
Blitz	205	185	168	215	225
Cruiser	462	386	402	519	538
Classic	88	70	111	146	132

Use an *Excel* worksheet to perform the following calculations (to one decimal place).

(i) Compute a *price relative* index series for the Cruiser Model using 2003 as base period. Interpret the findings.

(ii) Compute a Laspeyres composite price index series from 2003 to 2007 using 2003 as base period. Use *Excel's* **Line chart type** option in the **Chart Wizard** to display this price index series graphically.

(iii) What has been the average price changes in these three models of motorcycles from 2003 to 2007? Interpret the findings for the motor cycle distributor.

(iv) Compute a *link relative* series for the Classic model using 2003 as base period. Interpret the findings.

(v) Compute a Laspeyres *composite quantity index* series from 2003 to 2007 using 2003 as base period. Use *Excel's* **Line chart type** option in the **Chart Wizard** to display this quantity index series graphically.

(vi) By how much have motorcycle *sales volumes* in these three models changed between 2003 and 2007? Assume prices are held constant at base year 2003. Interpret the findings for the motor cycle distributor.

16.20 X16.20 – tyre production

The Uitenhage Plant of Hillstone (SA) has recorded their unit production costs and volumes for the three makes of tyres (passenger, light truck and giant truck) produced and sold on a monthly basis for 2006. The data are given in the *Excel* file **X16.20.**

Use an *Excel* worksheet to perform the following calculations (to one decimal place).

(i) Compute a *cost relative* index series for the passenger tyre data using January 2006 as base period. Interpret the findings.

(ii) Compute a Laspeyres *composite cost index* series from January to December 2006 using January 2006 as base period.
Use *Excel's* **Line chart type** option in the **Chart Wizard** to display this cost index series graphically.
What has been the average cost changes for these three makes of tyres from the beginning to the end of 2006? Interpret the findings for the production manager.

(iii) Compute a *link relative* index series for the light truck tyres using January 2006 as base period. Interpret the findings.

(iv) Compute a Laspeyres *composite production volume index* series from January 2006 to December 2006 using January 2006 as base period.
Use *Excel's* **Line chart type** option in the **Chart Wizard** to display this production volume index series graphically.
By how much have production volumes of tyres in these three makes changed from the beginning of 2006 to the end of 2006? Assume costs are held constant at base period January 2006.
Interpret the findings for the production manager.

Chapter 17

Time Series Analysis: A Forecasting Tool

Objectives

In addition to analysing survey data, managers also need to know how to treat *time series data*. Time series data is invaluable in the plotting and tracking of trends in business performance.

Time Series Analysis is a statistical approach to quantifying the factors that influence and shape time series data. This understanding can then be applied to the preparation of forecasts of future levels of activity of the time series variables.

After studying this chapter, you should be able to:

- explain the difference between cross-sectional and time series data
- explain the purpose of time series analysis
- identify and explain the components in time series analysis
- compute and interpret the trend values in a time series
- compute and interpret the seasonal influence in a time series
- de-seasonalise a time series and explain its value, and
- prepare seasonally adjusted forecasted values of a time series.

17.1 Introduction

Most data used in statistical analysis is **cross-sectional** data, meaning that the data is gathered from *sample surveys* at one point in time. However, data can also be *collected over time*. For *example*, when a company records its turnover, either daily, weekly or monthly, it is compiling a *time series* of sales data.

A **time series** is a set of numeric data of a random variable that is *gathered over time* at *regular intervals* and arranged in chronological (time) order.

Example

The *Fairlady* magazine receives audited circulation figures, reflecting its sales per issue, from the Audit Bureau of Circulation (the ABC) twice a year (for the periods ending June and December). This data, recorded over a number of years, makes up a time series. It can be analysed to examine trends, identify patterns, and prepare forecasts of future circulation levels for the magazine.

Further examples of time series data are:

- daily closing *share price* of Pick 'n Pay quoted on the JSE
- weekly *absenteeism rates* for an organisation
- daily *occupancy rates* at the Holiday Inn, Newlands
- weekly *pedestrian flows* through the Eastgate Shopping Mall
- monthly *company turnover* for Woolworths
- quarterly *value of new car sales*, published by NAAMSA
- annual *net immigration* figures from the Department of Home Affairs.

The analysis of time series data forms the basis for forecasting, which is essential for budgeting and operational planning in all departments of a company (marketing, production, finance, human resources, etc.).

This chapter describes an approach to analyse time series data, called **time series analysis**. The *purpose* of time series analysis is to identify any recurring patterns in a time series; to quantify these patterns through the building of a statistical model; and then to use the statistical model to prepare forecasts to estimate future values of the time series. Some of the limitations of time series analysis are also highlighted in the chapter.

Plotting Time Series Data

A *line graph* plot of the data values of a time series (y) against time (x) will highlight possible patterns and trends inherent in the data over time.

A visual inspection of a time series line graph will indicate the potential value of time series analysis. If reasonably regular patterns and trends are visible over time, the technique of time series analysis will be of great value as a forecasting tool. If, on the other hand, the data fluctuates irregularly over time, then the usefulness of time series analysis as a potential forecasting tool is limited.

Example 17.1 Monsoon Shoes Sales study

***Excel* file:** **C17.1 – shoe sales**

The accounting department of Monsoon Shoes (Pty) Ltd, a retail shoe company with eight branches nationwide, has recorded the quarterly sales volumes (in R10 000s) since they began trading in January 2003. This sales data is shown in Table 17.1.

Table 17.1 Monsoon Shoes quarterly sales data

Quarterly periods	2003	2004	2005	2006
Q1 (Jan–March)	54	55	49	60
Q2 (Apr–June)	58	61	69	72
Q3 (July–Sept)	94	84	95	99
Q4 (Oct–Dec)	70	76	88	80

Management question

Produce a *line graph* of the quarterly sales data for Monsoon Shoes. Visually establish whether any patterns occur over time.

Solution

The line graph is shown in Figure 17.1 (produced using the **Chart Wizard** from the toolbar with the **Line with markers displayed at each data value** sub-chart type in *Excel*).

Figure 17.1 Line graph of Monsoon Shoes' quarterly sales (in R10 000s)

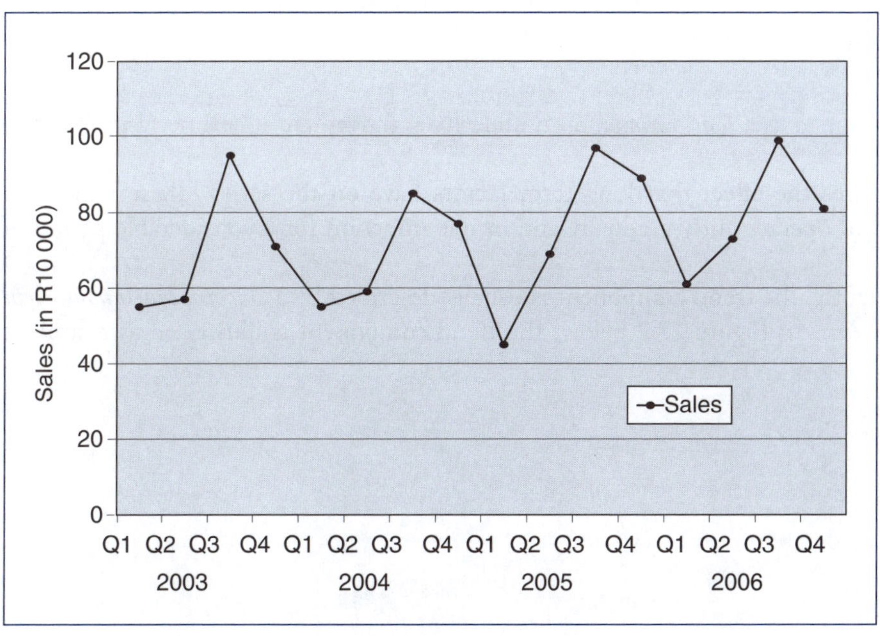

This line graph clearly reveals a fairly regular, fluctuating pattern over time with sales peaking in the third quarter (July to September) and bottoming out in the first quarter (January to March) of each year. There is also a moderate, but steady upward rise in the series.

17.2 The Components of a Time Series

Time series analysis assumes that the actual data values of a random variable in a time series are influenced by a variety of *environmental forces operating over time.*

Time series analysis attempts to isolate and quantify the influence of each of these different environmental forces operating on the time series into a number of different components. This process is known as **decomposition** of the time series.

Once identified and quantified, these components are combined and used to estimate future values of the time series random variable.

An important assumption in time series analysis is the continuation of past patterns into the future (i.e. that the environment in which the time series data occurs is reasonably stable). Under such circumstances, time series analysis is particularly useful as a short to medium-term forecasting tool.

Time series analysis assumes that *four environmental forces*, individually and collectively, determine the value of a time series random variable (such as sales, share price) in any time period. These environmental forces are:

- Trend (T)
- Cycles (C)
- Seasonality (S)
- Irregular (random) influences (I).

(i) Trend (T)

Trend is defined as a *long-term* smooth underlying movement in a time series.

Trend measures the effect that long-term factors have on the series. These long-term factors tend to operate fairly gradually and in one direction for a considerable period of time.

Consequently, the trend component is usually described by a *smooth, continuous curve* or a *straight line*. In Figure 17.2 below, the trend component is illustrated as a straight line.

Figure 17.2 Illustration of a **trend line** to time series data

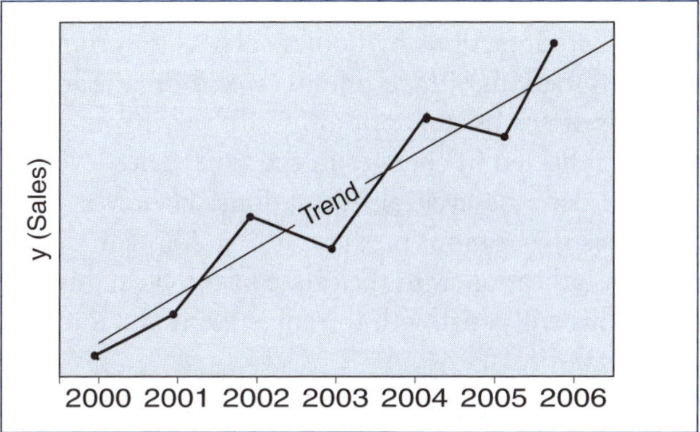

Some of the more important *causes of long-term trend* movements in a time series include: population growth; urbanisation; technological improvements; economic advancements and developments; and consumer shifts in habits and attitudes.

Trend analysis is the *statistical technique* used to isolate underlying long-term movement.

(ii) Cycles (C)

Cycles are *medium to long-term* deviations from the trend.

They reflect alternating periods of *relative expansion* and *contraction* of economic activity.

Cycles are *wave-like movements* in a time series, which can vary greatly in both *duration* and *amplitude*. Consequently, while historical occurrences of cycles can be measured, these past patterns are of little use in forecasting the future patterns of cycles.

Figure 17.3 below illustrates the varying nature of economic cycles.

Figure 17.3 Illustration of **economic cycles** in time series data

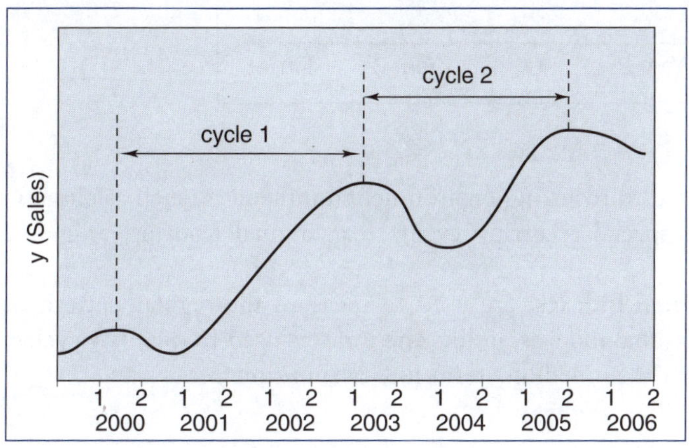

The *causes of cycles* are sometimes difficult to identify and explain, but their impact on a time series is either to stimulate or depress its levels of activity. Generally stated, cycles are caused by "mass psychological hysteria". Certain actions by bodies such as governments (e.g. changes in fiscal, monetary policies, sanctions), trade unions, world organisations, financial institutions, etc., can induce levels of pessimism or optimism of varying intensity and duration into an economy, which are reflected in changes in the time series levels.

Index numbers are used to identify and describe cyclical fluctuations. However, their usefulness as a forecasting tool is limited, as they cannot predict turning points in cycles. Nevertheless, these indexes can provide an indication as to the phase of the cycle through which a particular time series is moving. This will assist with the adjustment of a forecast, to account for the likely influence of cyclical forces.

(iii) Seasonality (S)

Seasonal variations are *fluctuations* in a time series that are *repeated at regular intervals* within a year (e.g. daily, weekly, monthly, quarterly).

These fluctuations tend to occur with a *high degree of regularity* and can be readily isolated through statistical analysis.

Figure 17.4 below illustrates the highly regular nature of seasonal variations.

Figure 17.4 Illustration of **seasonal variations** in time series data

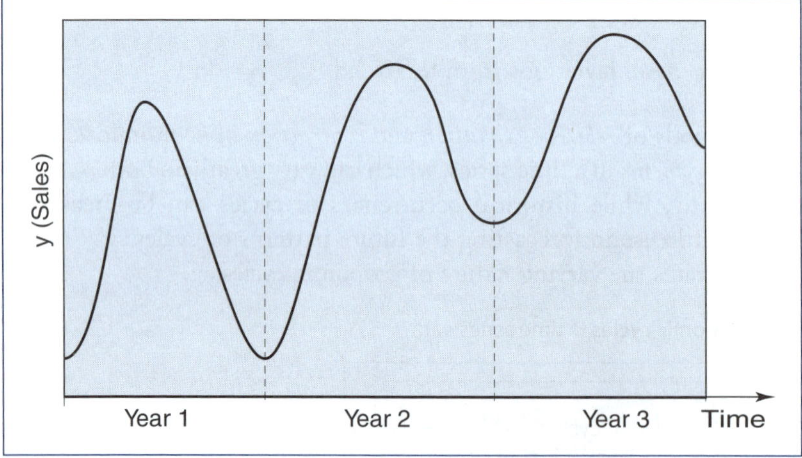

Seasonal variations are attributed to recurring environmental influences, such as climatic conditions (the seasons), and special recurring events (e.g. annual festivals, religious, public and school holidays).

Index numbers, called **seasonal indexes**, are used to measure the regular pattern of seasonal fluctuations. These seasonal indexes, unlike the indexes used to quantify cycles, can be very useful to prepare short to medium-term forecasts in time series data.

(iv) Random Effects (Irregular Fluctuations) (I)

Irregular fluctuations in a time series are attributed to *unpredictable events.*

Their causes are generally *unforeseen one-off events*, such as natural disasters (floods, droughts, fires) or man-made disasters (strikes, boycotts, accidents, acts of violence (e.g. war, riots).

As these occurrences are totally unpredictable and follow no specific pattern, they cannot be harnessed through statistical analysis or incorporated into statistical forecasts.

Irregular behaviour in a time series is illustrated graphically in Figure 17.5 below.

Figure 17.5 Irregular (or **random**) fluctuations in time series data

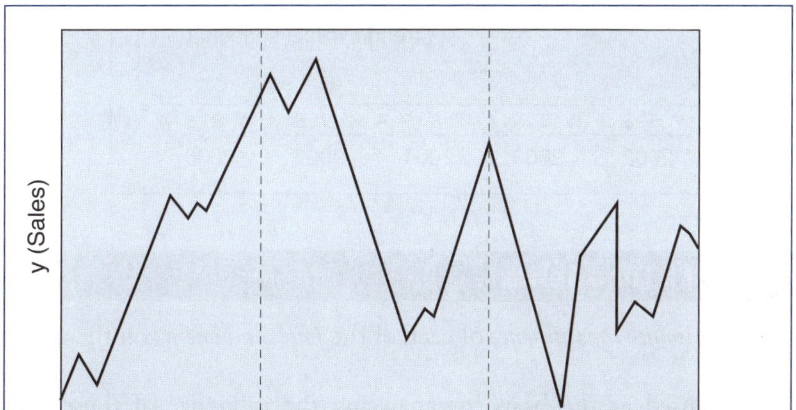

Figure 17.6 overleaf graphically illustrates the three components of a time series that can be statistically isolated, namely trend, cyclical and seasonal variations.

The overall usefulness of statistical time series analysis

The statistical techniques of time series analysis are particularly useful in identifying and quantifying the *trend* and *seasonal* movements in a time series. They are of little use as an identifier of cycles and random occurrences. However, unless cyclical movements are abnormally strong (such as either a depression or a boom), its influence is only marginal and can therefore largely be ignored in preparing forecasts of the time series variable. Thus useful *forecasts using time series* analysis are generally based only on the analysis of *trend* and *seasonal movements.*

Figure 17.6 The combined effect of **trend, cyclical** and **seasonal** components

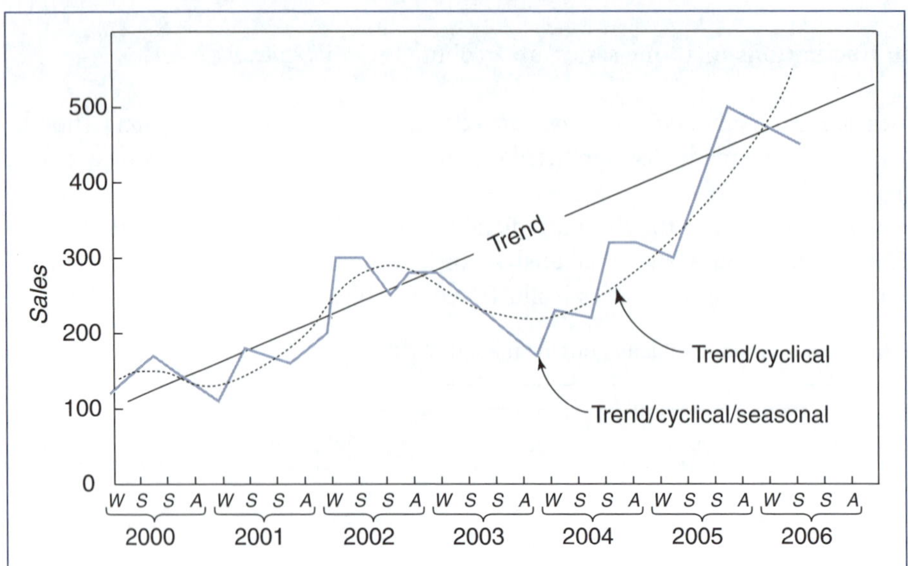

17.3 Decomposition of a Time Series

Time Series Analysis aims to *isolate the influence* of each of the *four components* on the actual time series.

The time series model used as the basis for analysing the influence of these four components assumes a *multiplicative relationship* between the four components.

A **multiplicative time series model** states that:

"The actual values of a time series, represented by ***y***, can be found by *multiplying* the *trend* component, ***T*** (measured in actual units, e.g. money, quantity) by a *cyclical* index, ***C*** (expressed relative to the trend), by a *seasonal* index, ***S*** (expressed relative to *T* and *C*), and by an *irregular* measure, ***I***."

The *multiplicative time series model* is defined, algebraically as:

$$\text{Actual } y = \text{Trend} \times \text{Cyclical} \times \text{Seasonal} \times \text{Irregular}$$

i.e. $$y = T \times C \times S \times I$$

Sections 17.4 and 17.5 will examine statistical approaches to quantify *trend* and *seasonal variations* only. These two components usually account for a significant proportion of an actual value in a time series. By isolating them, most of an actual time series value can be explained.

17.4 Trend Analysis

The long-term *trend* in a time series can be isolated by removing the medium and short-term (i.e. cycles, seasonal and random) fluctuations in the series. This will result in either a smooth curve or a straight line, depending on the method chosen.

Two methods for trend isolation can be used:

- *moving average* method, which produces a smooth curve, or
- *regression analysis,* which results in a straight line trend.

Method 1: The Moving Average Method

A *moving average* removes the short-term fluctuations in a time series by taking successive averages of groups of observations. Each time period's actual value is replaced by the average of observations from time periods that surround it. This results in a *smoothed time series.* Thus, the moving average technique *smoothes* a time series by removing short-term fluctuations.

The number of observations, k, which are summed and averaged in each group, is determined by the number of periods which are believed to span the short-term fluctuations. To *illustrate,* if it is assumed that a time series pattern repeats itself approximately every three consecutive time periods within a year, then a *3-period moving average* is appropriate to remove the short-term fluctuations. Thus, $k = 3$.

HOW TO

To compute a 3-period moving average series

The following four steps are used to compute a 3-period moving average series.

Step 1 Sum the first three periods' observations and position the total opposite the middle (median) time period (i.e. period 2).

Step 2 Repeat the summing of three periods' observations by removing the first period's observation (i.e. period 1) and including the next period's observation (i.e. period 4). This second moving total (using periods 2, 3 and 4) is again positioned opposite the appropriate middle (median) time period which is now period 3.

Step3 Continue producing these moving (or running) totals until the end of the time series is reached.

This process of positioning each moving total opposite the middle (or median) time period of each sum of three observations is called **centering.**

Step 4 The moving average series is now computed by dividing each moving total by $k = 3$ (i.e. the number of observations summed each time).

Note: This procedure is applied whenever the term k of a moving average is odd. (computation of a moving average when k is even is illustrated after the next example.)

Example 17.2 Fire Insurance Claims study

***Excel* file:** **C17.2 – fire insurance claims**

Table 17.2 shows the *number of fire insurance claims* in each *four-month* period, from 2003 to 2006, received by Hollard Insurance.

Table 17.2 Number of Fire Insurance Claims received by Hollard Insurance (2003–2006)

Period		Claims (y)
2003	P1	7
	P2	3
	P3	5
2004	P1	9
	P2	7
	P3	9
2005	P1	12
	P2	4
	P3	10
2006	P1	13
	P2	9
	P3	10

Management question

Compute a *3-period moving average* for the number of *fire insurance claims* received.

Solution

Table 17.3 below shows the four-step approach outlined above and the resulting 3-period moving average of fire insurance claims received.

Note that the *moving average series* is a *smooth curve* which has "ironed out" the short-term fluctuations.

Table 17.3 3-period moving average of the number of fire insurance claims received

Period		Claims (y)	3-period Moving Total (centred)	3-period Moving Average
2003	P1	7	–	–
	P2	3	(7 + 3 + 5) = 15	$\frac{15}{3} = 5$
	P3	5	(3 + 5 + 9) = 17	$\frac{17}{3} = 5{,}67$
2004	P1	9	(5 + 9 + 7) = 21	$\frac{21}{3} = 7$
	P2	7	(9 + 7 + 9) = 25	$\frac{25}{3} = 8{,}33$
	P3	9	(7 + 9 + 12) = 28	$\frac{28}{3} = 9{,}33$
2005	P1	12	(9 + 12 + 4) = 25	$\frac{25}{3} = 8{,}33$
	P2	4	(12 + 4 + 10) = 26	$\frac{26}{3} = 8{,}67$
	P3	10	(4 + 10 + 13) = 27	$\frac{27}{3} = 9$
2006	P1	13	(10 + 13 + 9) = 32	$\frac{32}{3} = 10{,}67$
	P2	9	(13 + 9 + 10) = 32	$\frac{32}{3} = 10{,}67$
	P3	10	–	–

Example 17.3 Fire Insurance Claims study

***Excel* file:** **C17.2 – fire insurance claims**

Management question

Compute and graph the *3-period* and *5-period* moving average series for the *number of fire insurance claims*, as shown in Table 17.2 above. Compare the two moving average series.

Solution

Table 17.4 computes both the *3-period* and *5-period* moving average values of *fire insurance claims* received.

Table 17.4 3-period and 5-period moving averages of fire insurance claims received

Period		Claims (y)	3-period Moving Average	5-period Moving Total	5-period Moving Average
2003	P1	7	–	–	–
	P2	3	5	–	–
	P3	5	5,67	31	6,2
2004	P1	9	7	33	6,6
	P2	7	8,33	42	8,4
	P3	9	9,33	41	8,2
2005	P1	12	8,33	42	8,4
	P2	4	8,67	48	9,6
	P3	10	9	48	9,6
2006	P1	13	10,67	–	–
	P2	9	10,67	–	–
	P3	10	–	–	–

Figure 17.7 is a line plot of the original y-values, and both the *3-period* and *5-period* moving average value of the time series of *fire insurance claims received*. It highlights the effect of different terms (k = 3, and then k = 5) on the smoothing process.

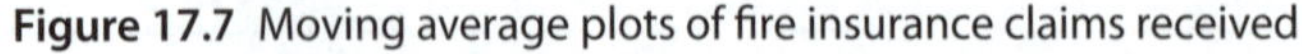

Figure 17.7 Moving average plots of fire insurance claims received

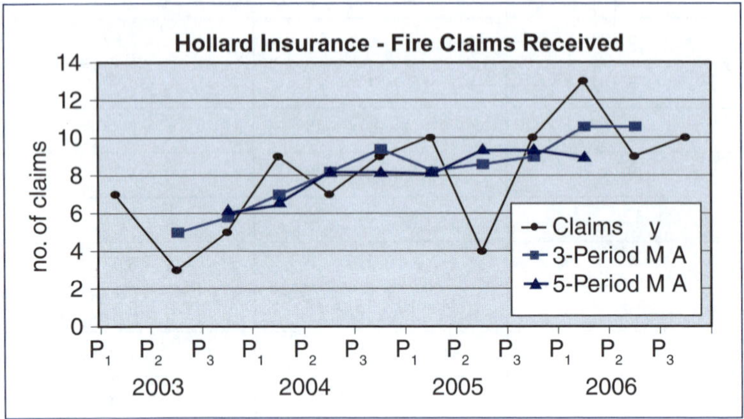

The term, *k*, for the moving average affects the degree of smoothing:

- a shorter term produces a more jagged moving average curve
- a longer term produces a smoother moving average curve.

From a comparison of the 3-period and 5-period moving average values, it can be seen that there is *less fluctuation* (*greater smoothing*) in the 5-period moving average series than in the 3-period moving average series.

Centering an uncentred moving average

A moving average value must always be *centred* on a middle (median) time period.

When the term, *k* (the number of periods to be averaged), is *odd*, centering occurs when the moving average value is placed in the middle time period of a set of *k* observations.

However, when a moving average is computed for an *even* number of time periods (i.e. the term, *k*, is *even*), then the moving totals will be *uncentred* (i.e. the values will lie between two time periods) when attempting to position the value opposite the middle time period. A three-step centering approach is adopted.

To illustrate, in a 4-period moving average calculation:

Step 1 Compute uncentred moving totals

- the first moving total will lie between periods 2 and 3 (i.e. at period 2,5)
- the second moving total will lie between periods 3 and 4 (i.e. at period 3,5)
- the third moving total at period 4,5 and so on.

Step 2 Centre the uncentred moving totals

- To centre these uncentred moving totals opposite an actual middle time period, a second moving total series is computed. To compute this second moving total series, *pairs of the uncentred moving totals* are summed and centred between the two uncentred moving total values. This results in each of these second moving totals being positioned opposite an actual period in the time series.
- The sum of the first pair of uncentred moving totals (in positions 2,5 and 3,5 respectively) will be positioned opposite period 3. The sum of the second pair of uncentred moving totals (in positions 3,5 and 4,5 respectively) will be positioned opposite period 4; the sum of the third pair opposite period 5, and so on.

Step 3 Compute centred moving averages

Finally, a *centred moving average* is computed by dividing the centred moving total values by (2 × *k*) where *k* is the (*even*) term of the moving average. In effect, each centred moving total consists of (2 × *k*) observations.

Example 17.4 Fire Insurance Claims study

Assume that the *fire insurance claims* data in Table 17.2 represent *quarterly* claims for the 2004 to 2006 period as shown in Table 17.5.

Management question

Produce a *4-period* centred moving average for the quarterly *number of fire insurance claims received* by Hollard Insurance during the period 2004 to 2006.

Solution

The resulting calculations are shown in Table 17.5 overleaf.

Table 17.5 Hollard Insurance Quarterly Fire Claims Received (2004–2006)

Period	Claims y	Uncentred 4-period Moving total	Centred 2 × 4-period Moving total	Centred 4-period Moving average
2004 Q1	7		–	–
		–		
Q2	3		–	–
		24		
Q3	5		48	6
		24		
Q4	9		54	6,75
		30		
2005 Q1	7		67	8,375
		37		
Q2	9		69	8,625
		32		
Q3	12		67	8,375
		35		
Q4	4		74	9,25
		39		
2006 Q1	10		75	9,375
		36		
Q2	13		78	9,75
		42		
Q3	9			
Q4	10			

Management interpretation of a moving average

A *moving average time series* is a *smoother series* than the original time series values. A moving average has *removed the effect of short-term fluctuations* (i.e. *seasonal* and *irregular* fluctuations) from the original observations, y (by averaging over these short-term fluctuations).

The moving average value can be seen as reflecting mainly the combined *trend* and *cyclical* movements.

In symbol terms for the multiplicative model:

$$\text{Moving average} = \frac{T.C.S.I}{S.I} = T.C$$

The primary *drawback* of a moving average approach is a *loss of information* (data values) at either end of the original time series. Moving averages cannot be found for the first and last $\frac{k}{2}$ periods. This is caused by the centring process of moving average values. However, this is not a significant drawback if the time series is long, say 50 time periods or more.

The major *benefit* of a moving average is the opportunity it affords a manager to focus more clearly on the long-term trend (and cyclical) movements in a time series without the obscuring effect of short-term "noise" influences.

Method 2: Trend Line using Regression Analysis

A trend line isolates the *trend* (**T**) component only. It shows the general direction (upward, downward, constant) in which the series is moving. It is therefore best represented by a *straight line*.

The *method of least squares* from *regression analysis* is used to find the trend line of *best fit* to a time series of numeric data.

The dependent variable, y, is the actual time series (e.g. sales; breakdowns; output), while the independent variable, x, is *time*. To use *time* as an independent variable in regression analysis, it must be numerically coded. Any *sequential numbering* system can be used, but the most common choice of coding is the set of *natural numbers*, i.e.:

$x = 1, 2, 3, 4, 5, \ldots, , n$

where n = number of time periods in the time series

Two alternative numbering systems include:

- $x = 0, 1, 2, 3, \ldots., ,(n - 1)$, and
- a *zero-sum* approach where the *sum* of the x-values is *zero*.
  - e.g. (if a time series consists of 9 periods, then use $x = -4, -3, -2, -1, 0, 1, 2 , 3, 4$).
  - e.g. (if a time series consists of 8 periods, then use $x = -7, -5, -3, -1, 1, 3, 5, 7$).

If the computations are performed manually, then the zero-sum approach simplifies the calculations. However, such computations are usually performed using *Excel*, in which case, the sequential *natural numbering* system beginning with 1, 2, 3, 4, 5, etc. is the most logical to use.

The choice of the starting value for the time sequence is arbitrary. Each different choice will result in different trend line coefficients, b_0 and b_1, but the *estimated trend values will always be the same*.

The following example will illustrate the *natural* numbering approach.

Approach 1 The Natural Numbering Approach

Example 17.5 Valley Estates Quarterly House Sales study

***Excel* file:** **C17.3 – house sales**

The *number of houses sold* quarterly by Valley Estates in the Cape Peninsula is recorded for the 16 quarters from 2003 to 2006, as shown in Table 17.6 overleaf. The sales director has requested

- a *trend analysis* of this sales data to determine the general direction of quarterly housing sales, and
- an *estimate* of house sales for the first quarter of 2007.

Management questions

(1) Find the *trend line* for the quarterly *house sales* data (2003–2006) for Valley Estates.

(2) Then *estimate* the likely level of *house sales* for the first quarter of 2007.

Solution (Manual)

(1) **Compute trend line equation**

Use the sequential *natural numbering* system: $x = 1, 2, 3, 4, 5, \ldots, 16$

Table 17.6 also shows the intermediate calculations for the trend line coefficients, b_0 and b_1, using the *least squares regression formulae* from chapter 15.

Table 17.6 Intermediate computations for trend line coefficients – House Sales

Period $n = 16$		House sales y	Time x	x^2	xy
2003	Q1	54	1	1	54
	Q2	58	2	4	116
	Q3	94	3	9	282
	Q4	70	4	16	280
2004	Q1	55	5	25	275
	Q2	61	6	36	366
	Q3	87	7	49	609
	Q4	66	8	64	528
2005	Q1	49	9	81	441
	Q2	55	10	100	550
	Q3	95	11	121	1045
	Q4	74	12	144	888
2006	Q1	60	13	169	780
	Q2	64	14	196	896
	Q3	99	15	225	1 485
	Q4	80	16	256	1 280
Totals		**1 121**	**136**	**1 496**	**9 875**

(i) The regression slope (or gradient) (b_1):

$$b_1 = \frac{n\Sigma xy - \Sigma x \Sigma y}{n\Sigma x^2 - (\Sigma x)^2} = \frac{16(9\,875) - (136)(1\,121)}{16(1\,496) - (136)^2} = \frac{5\,544}{5\,440} = \mathbf{1{,}019}$$

(ii) The y-intercept (b_0):

$$b_0 = \frac{\Sigma y - b_1 \Sigma x}{n} = \frac{1121 - 1{,}019(136)}{16} = \frac{982{,}416}{16} = \mathbf{61{,}4}$$

The *regression trend line* (***T***) is now defined by the following straight-line equation:

$T = 61{,}4 + 1{,}019\,x$ where x = 1 in 2003 Q1
= 2 in 2003 Q2
= 3 in 2003 Q3

The *numerical coding scheme* used to code x *must always be shown* together with the trend line equation, otherwise the trend line coefficients are meaningless. They are determined by the choice of x-values. This also assists in determining the appropriate x values to substitute into the trend line when trend projections are performed.

(2) **Estimate trend value(s)**

To estimate the trend value of *house sales* for quarter 1 of 2007, identify the value of x that corresponds to 2007 quarter 1. It is the next sequential value after $x = 16$, corresponding to 2006 quarter 4. Hence $x = 17$.

Now substitute $x = 17$ into the trend line equation as follows:

$$\textbf{Trend } y = 61{,}4 + 1{,}019\ (\mathbf{17}) = 61{,}4 + 17{,}32 = 78{,}72 \text{ (rounded to } \mathbf{79}\text{)}$$

Thus, the sales director of Valley Estates can expect the *trend value* of house sales in quarter 1, 2007 to be 79.

Solution using *Excel*

The trend line coefficients for a given time series of data can be produced and displayed directly from a line plot of the data using *Excel*. (i.e. refer to the *Excel* file: **C17.3 – house sales** and to Figure 17.8 below).

HOW TO

Derive the trend line equation in Excel

- Highlight the time series data range [B5 : C21]
- Produce a *line graph*: Use the **Chart Wizard**, select **Line** chart and sub-chart type **Line with markers displayed at each data value**.
- Right-click on any coordinate of the line graph and select the following options:
  - select **Add Trendline**
  - from the **Trend/Regression Type** tab, select **Linear**
  - from the **Options** tab, tick the box **Display equation on chart** and **OK**.

Figure 17.8 shows the line graph of the Valley Estate *house sales time series data*, and the *trend line* with its *equation* displayed.

Figure 17.8 Trend line analysis for Valley Estates Quarterly House Sales

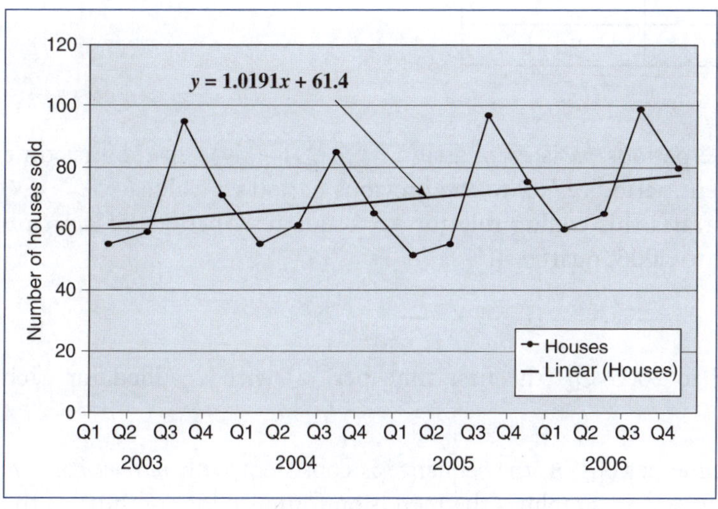

The *Excel* Trendline option automatically uses the sequential *natural numbering* system of $x = 1, 2, 3, 4, 5$, etc. It does not need to be explicitly recorded in the worksheet as is required in the manual approach as used in Table 17.6.

Approach 2 Zero-sum Approach

Any consistent sequential coding system can be chosen to assign values to the time variable, x. A coding system which has manual computational advantages is therefore desirable. The *zero-sum* method is one such system. In this approach, the x time variable is coded in such a way that the *sum of the x-values equals zero*. This is achieved as follows, depending on whether n is odd or even:

n odd

When the number of time periods, n, is *odd*, assign $x = \frac{-[n-1]}{2}$ to the first time period. For each subsequent period, add one to the previous period's x-value.

Table 17.7 *illustrates* this coding rule for $n = 7$ quarterly periods of *caravans sold* from 2005, quarter 1 to 2006, quarter 3.

With $n = 7$ periods:

assign $x = \frac{-(7-1)}{2} = -3$ to 2005 Q1 (the first time period) and add one for each subsequent period.

Table 17.7 Coding scheme for *x* when *n* is odd – Caravan Sales

Period		Caravan sales y	Time x
2005	Q1	94	-3
	Q2	123	-2
	Q3	46	-1
	Q4	102	0
2006	Q1	137	1
	Q2	92	2
	Q3	108	3
			$\boldsymbol{\Sigma x = 0}$

n even

When the number of time periods, n, is *even*, assign $x = (-[n-1])$ to the first time period. For each subsequent period, *add 2* to the previous period's x-value.

Table 17.8 below illustrates this coding rule for $n = 8$ quarterly periods of *caravans sold* from 2005, quarter 1, to 2006, quarter 4.

With $n = 8$ periods:

assign $x = -(8-1) = -7$ to 2005 Q1 (the first time period) with 2 added for each subsequent period.

For any even number of time periods, n, the sequence is consistent with *incremental steps* of +2. This zero-sum coding system simplifies the regression formulae for computing the trend line, since one of the terms in the formulae, namely $\boldsymbol{\Sigma x = 0}$.

Table 17.8 Coding scheme for *x* when *n* is even – Caravan Sales

Period		Caravan sales y	Time x
2005	Q1	94	–7
	Q2	123	–5
	Q3	46	–3
	Q4	102	–1
2006	Q1	137	1
	Q2	92	3
	Q3	108	5
	Q4	99	7
			$\Sigma x = 0$

By replacing Σx with 0 in the regression formulae (see p. 506), the revised formulae for b_0 (y-intercept) and b_1 (gradient coefficient) become:

$$b_1 = \frac{\Sigma xy}{\Sigma x^2} \qquad b_0 = \frac{\Sigma y}{n} \qquad \text{when } \Sigma x = 0$$

This method of coding x is recommended for manual computations only.
It should be noted that trend projections based on the trend line equations derived from different sequential numbering systems will produce different regression coefficient values. However their trend estimates will produce identical results when the appropriate x-value(s) for the coding scheme used, is (are) substituted in the trend equation.

Management interpretation of the trend line

The regression trend line is "free" of cyclical, seasonal and irregular influences. The "other" influences have been removed by trend analysis, leaving only the longer-term trend influence. The "strength" of the trend influence (i.e. growth/decline) can be gauged by the magnitude of the slope coefficient, b_1. A strong (upward/downward) trend is shown by a large positive/negative value of b_1, while values of b_1 close to zero indicate no strong upward/downward pressure on the values of the time series due to trend forces.

17.5 Seasonal Analysis

Seasonal analysis isolates the influence of seasonal forces on a time series.

The **ratio-to-moving-average method** is used to measure and quantify these seasonal influences. This method expresses the seasonal influence as an *index number*. It measures the percentage deviation of the actual values of the time series, y, from a base value that excludes the short-term seasonal influences. These base values of a time series represent the trend/cyclical influences only.

The ratio-to-moving-average method consists of four steps.

Ratio-to-moving-average Method

Step 1 Identify the trend/cyclical movement

The *moving average* approach, as described in section 17.4, is used to isolate the *combined trend/cyclical* components in a time series.

The choice of an appropriate moving average term, *k*, is determined by the number of periods that span the short-term seasonal fluctuations. In most instances, the term, *k*, corresponds to the number of observations that span a one-year period.

Table 17.9 illustrates the appropriate term to use to remove short-term seasonal fluctuations in time series data that occur more frequently than annually.

Table 17.9 Choice of moving average term, *k*, to remove seasonal fluctuations

Time Interval	Appropriate Term (*k*)
Weekly	52-period term
Monthly	12-period term
Bi-monthly	6-period term
Quarterly	4-period term
4-monthly	3-period term
Half-yearly	2-period term

The resultant smoothed moving average series, which reflects the combined trend and cyclical influences, represents a *base measure* of the time series.

To *illustrate*, if quarterly data is given, a 4-period moving average will isolate the trend/cyclical movements in the time series and produce a base set of time series values. These steps include:

- finding the *uncentred* 4-period *moving total* series first
- finding the *centred* 2 × 4-period *moving total* series next, and finally
- dividing the centred 2 × 4-period moving total series by 8 to give the *centred* 4-period *moving average.*

Step 2 Find the seasonal ratios

A seasonal ratio for each period is found by dividing each actual time series value, y, by its corresponding *moving average value* (its base value). This gives the seasonal ratio for each period, i.e.:

$$\text{Seasonal ratio} = \frac{\text{Actual } y}{\text{Moving average } y} \times 100$$

$$= \frac{\text{T} \times \text{C} \times \text{S} \times \text{I}}{\text{T} \times \text{C}} = \text{S} \times \text{I} \times 100$$

A **seasonal ratio** is an *index* that measures the percentage deviation of each actual y (which includes seasonal influences) from its moving average (base) value (which represents trend and cyclical influences only).

This deviation from the base level, which is the trend/cyclical influence (with index = 100), is a measure of the seasonal impact – and to a far lesser extent, irregular forces – on the time series for each time period. (The interpretation of a seasonal ratio is similar to that of a *price relative* as discussed in chapter 16).

Step 3 Produce median seasonal indexes

The seasonal ratios must be *averaged across corresponding periods within the years* to *smooth out* the *irregular component* inherent in the seasonal ratios.

Generally, the *median* is used to find the average of seasonal ratios for corresponding periods within the years. While an arithmetic mean can also be used to average seasonal ratios, the presence of any outliers in the seasonal ratios will distort its value, resulting in an unrepresentative seasonal index. For this reason, the median is preferred for the averaging of the seasonal ratios.

Step 4 Compute adjusted seasonal indexes

Each seasonal index has a base index of 100. Therefore, the sum of the k median seasonal indexes must equal $100 \times k$. If this is not the case, each median seasonal index must be adjusted to a base of 100.

The *adjustment factor* is determined as follows:

$$\text{Adjustment factor} = \frac{k \times 100}{\Sigma\ (\text{Median seasonal indexes})}$$

Each median seasonal index is multiplied by the adjustment factor to ensure a base of 100 for each index.

These *adjusted seasonal indexes* are an (average) *measure of the seasonal influences* on the actual values of the time series for each given time period within a year.

Example 17.6 Valley Estates Quarterly House Sales study

Refer to the quarterly house sales data in **Table 17.6** and reproduced in **Table 17.10** overleaf. The sales director of Valley Estates would like to identify the *impact of quarterly seasonal influences* on house sales.

Excel file: C17.3 – house sales

Management question

Find the *quarterly seasonal indexes* for the house sales data and interpret the results for the sales director of Valley Estates.

Solution

The four-step process to compute the seasonal indexes is shown in Table 17.10 overleaf (steps 1 and 2), Table 17.11 (step 3) and Table 17.12 (step 4) respectively.

Since the time series data given (*house sales*) is *quarterly*, a 4-period term (k = 4) is used to smooth out short-term seasonal and irregular variations (since four periods span a year). Columns (1) to (4) in Table 17.10 show the computation of the **4-period moving average** series (step 1) which is recorded in column (4). This moving average series represents the trend/cyclical component (base level) of house sales by Valley Estates in the Cape Peninsula.

The **seasonal ratios** (step 2) are computed and shown in column (5) of Table 17.11 overleaf.

Table 17.10 Valley Estate House Sales: computation of seasonal ratios (steps 1 and 2)

		(1)	(2)	(3)	(4)	(5)
Period		Houses y	Uncentred 4-quarter moving total	Centred (2 × 4) quarter moving total	4-quarter moving average	Seasonal ratios
2003	Q1	54		–	–	–
	Q2	58		–	–	–
			276			
	Q3	94		553	69,125	**135,99**
			277			
	Q4	70		557	69,625	**100,54**
			280			
2004	Q1	55		553	69,125	**79,57**
			273			
	Q2	61		542	67,75	**90,04**
			269			
	Q3	87		532	66,5	**130,83**
			263			
	Q4	66		520	65	**101,54**
			257			
2005	Q1	49		522	65,25	**75,1**
			265			
	Q2	55		538	67,25	**81,78**
			273			
	Q3	95		557	69,625	**136,45**
			284			
	Q4	74		577	72,125	**102,6**
			293			
2006	Q1	60		590	73,75	**81,36**
			297			
	Q2	64		600	75	**85,33**
			303			
	Q3	99		–	–	–
	Q4	80		–	–	–

Table 17.11 shows the averaging of the seasonal ratios (step 3) using the *median* as a central location measure to derive the median seasonal indexes for each quarter.

Table 17.11 Valley Estate House Sales: median seasonal indexes (step 3)

Year	Quarter 1	Quarter 2	Quarter 3	Quarter 4	Total
2003	–	–	135,99	100,54	
2004	79,57	90,04	130,83	101,54	
2005	75,1	81,78	136,45	102,6	
2006	81,36	85,33	–	–	
Median Seasonal index	**79,57**	**85,33**	**135,99**	**101,54**	**402,43**

In *Excel*, use **=MEDIAN(data range)** to find the median seasonal index for each quarter.

These median seasonal indexes are also called **unadjusted seasonal indexes**.

Finally, Table 17.12 adjusts each median seasonal index to a base of 100 (step 4).

Table 17.12 Valley Estate House Sales: adjusted seasonal indexes (step 4)

Adjustment factor = 400/402,43 = 0,994			
Periods	Median seasonal index	Adjustment factor	Adjusted seasonal index
Quarter 1	79,57	0,994	**79,1**
Quarter 2	85,33	0,994	**84,8**
Quarter 3	135,99	0,994	**135,2**
Quarter 4	101,54	0,994	**100,9**
Total	**402,43**		**400**

Management interpretation of seasonal indexes

Each (adjusted) seasonal index measures the average impact of seasonal influences on the actual values of the time series for a given period within a year.

By subtracting the base index of 100 (which represents the trend/cyclical component) from each seasonal index, the extent of the influence of seasonal forces can be gauged.

For **Example 17.6**, the following interpretation applies:

- In *Quarter 1* of each year, the seasonal index of 79,1 means that, on average, Valley Estates *house sales* are *depressed* by the presence of seasonal forces to the extent of approximately 21%. Alternatively stated, house sales would have been about 26% *higher* ($\frac{21}{79} \times 100$) had seasonal influences not been present.
- *Quarter 2*'s interpretation is similar to that of quarter 1, since the seasonal index is also below 100, namely 84,8.
- In *Quarter 3* of each year, the seasonal index of 135,2 means that, on average, Valley Estates *house sales* are *stimulated* by the presence of seasonal forces to the extent of approximately 35%. Alternatively stated, house sales would have been about 35% *lower* had seasonal influences not been present.
- In *Quarter 4* of each year, seasonal influence is negligible as the seasonal index of 100,9 is almost equal to its base index of 100, which contains only trend and cyclical measurements. Seasonal influences account for less than 1% of Valley Estates' house sales, on average, in Quarter 4.

Excel Template

The *Excel* worksheet file **C17.3 – house sales** can be used as a template to *compute seasonal indexes* for any time series data consisting of four years of quarterly data (i.e. 16 data values).

17.6 Uses of Time Series Indicators

Time series indicators are important planning aids to managers in two ways. They can be used:

- to *de-seasonalise* a time series (i.e. *remove seasonal influences*), and so provide a clearer vision of the longer term trend/cyclical movements; and
- to produce *seasonally-adjusted trend projections* of future values of a time series.

(i) De-seasonalising time series values

The removal of seasonal influences which represent short-term fluctuations in a time series results in a smoother time series, which makes it easier to identify longer-term trend/cyclical movements.

Seasonal influences are removed from a time series by *dividing* the *actual y-value* for each period by its corresponding *seasonal index*.

$$\text{Deseasonalised } y = \frac{\text{Actual } y}{\text{Seasonal index}} \times 100$$

These *de-seasonalised y-values*, which will be measured in the same units as the actual *y*-values, reflect the collective influence of the *trend* and *cyclical* (and to a lesser extent, irregular) *forces only*.

Interpretation of de-seasonalised time series values

The values of a *de-seasonalised time series* show a time series without the influence of (short-term) seasonal forces, allowing attention to be focused on the longer term trend/cyclical movements of the time series.

- If the seasonal index is *less than* 100 (showing that seasonal forces dampen, or reduce, the level of activity of the time series), the *de-seasonalised y-values* will be *inflated* (*higher*) when seasonal influences are removed.
- Conversely, if the seasonal index is *more than* 100 (showing that seasonal forces stimulated, or raised, the level of activity of the time series), the *de-seasonalised y-values* will be *depressed* (*lower*) when seasonal influences are removed.

Example 17.7 Valley Estates Quarterly House Sales study

Refer to the house sales time series data shown in **Table 17.10**. The sales director of Valley Estates would like to observe the *general direction* of house sales *without the effect of short-term seasonal influences.*

Management question

Prepare a *de-seasonalised* time series of the *quarterly house sales* for the sales director of Valley Estates for the period 2003 to 2006. Use the seasonal indexes from Table 17.12 on page 512.

Solution

Figure 17.9 below shows the *de-seasonalised house sales* in column E, together with the plot of the two line graphs (*actual house sales* versus *de-seasonalised house sales*).

Figure 17.9 De-Seasonalised House Sales for Valley Estates

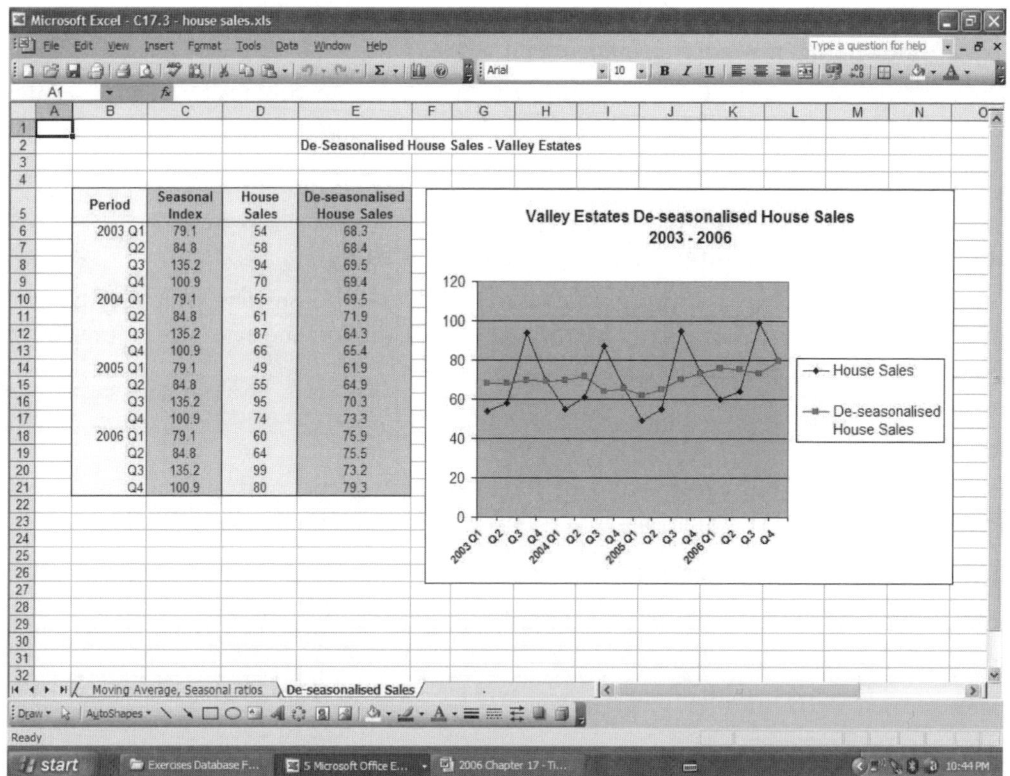

De-Seasonalised House Sales - Valley Estates

Period	Seasonal Index	House Sales	De-seasonalised House Sales
2003 Q1	79.1	54	68.3
Q2	84.8	58	68.4
Q3	135.2	94	69.5
Q4	100.9	70	69.4
2004 Q1	79.1	55	69.5
Q2	84.8	61	71.9
Q3	135.2	87	64.3
Q4	100.9	66	65.4
2005 Q1	79.1	49	61.9
Q2	84.8	55	64.9
Q3	135.2	95	70.3
Q4	100.9	74	73.3
2006 Q1	79.1	60	75.9
Q2	84.8	64	75.5
Q3	135.2	99	73.2
Q4	100.9	80	79.3

Management interpretation

Quarter 1, 2003 house sales, for example, would have been higher at 68 units, instead of the actual sales of 54 units, had seasonal influences not been present. Similarly, house sales for quarter 3, 2004, would have been lower at 64 units, instead of the actual sales of 87 units, had seasonal influences not been present.

In addition, the *de-seasonalised* quarterly house sales *line graph* for Valley Estates shows a very modest growth over the past four years.

(ii) Seasonally-adjusted Trend Projections

Since the actual time series values are assumed to be a function of trend, cyclical, seasonal and irregular movements (i.e. *actual* $y = \boldsymbol{T} \times \boldsymbol{C} \times \boldsymbol{S} \times \boldsymbol{I}$), these components, if known or estimated, can be used to reconstruct values of the actual time series.

However, since only the *trend* and *seasonal* influences can be quantified through time series analysis, only these two influences are used to estimate future values of the actual time series, y.

Step 1 Estimate the trend value of the time series (T)

Estimates of the trend value (**T**) over the forecasting period are found by substituting appropriate x-values of the numerically-coded time variable into the regression-derived trend line equation. The x-values of the future time periods are found by continuing the sequence of x-values into the future.

Step 2 Incorporate the seasonal influence **(S)**

The seasonal influence can be built into the trend value estimates by *multiplying* the trend value (found in *step 1*) by the *seasonal index* for the appropriate time period. This is known as **seasonalising** the *trend value.*

Example 17.8 Valley Estates quarterly House Sales study

Estimate the most likely *seasonally-adjusted trend* values of house sales for Valley Estates for quarters 1, 2, 3 and 4 of 2007. Use the trend line equation and seasonal indexes from **Examples 17.5** and **17.6** respectively.

Solution

Table 17.13 shows the construction of forecasts using trend and seasonal measures derived from time series analysis. The following two-step approach is applied:

Step 1 Estimate the trend values **(T)**

From **Example 17.5**, the straight-line trend equation is given as:

$$T = 61{,}4 + 1{,}019\,x \qquad \text{where} \qquad x = 1 \text{ in 2003 Q1}$$
$$= 2 \text{ in 2003 Q2}$$
$$= 3 \text{ in 2003 Q3, etc.}$$

For the forecasted periods of Ql, Q2, Q3 and Q4 of 2007, the corresponding x-values, shown in Table 17.13, are found by continuing the numeric sequence of x-values (from Table 17.6) to span the forecast periods.

For each forecasted quarter of 2007, substitute the appropriate x-value into the trend line equation, as seen in Table 17.13, to produce the *trend estimate* of house sales.

Table 17.13 Seasonally-adjusted 2007 trend estimates for House Sales

Period		Time x	Trend Equation $T = b_0 + b_1x$	Trend estimate T	Seasonal Index	Seasonally-adjusted Trend Estimates
2007	Q1	17	61,4 + 1,019(17)	78,7	79,1	**62,3**
	Q2	18	61,4 + 1,019(18)	79,7	84,8	**67,6**
	Q3	19	61,4 + 1,019(19)	80,8	135,2	**109,2**
	Q4	20	61,4 + 1,019(20)	81,8	100,9	**82,5**

The resultant values (e.g. 81,8 [or rounded to 82] for quarter 4, 2007) are the expected house sales in the Cape Peninsula by Valley Estates in each quarter of 2007, based on *trend estimates* alone.

Step 2 Seasonalise the trend values (i.e. incorporate the seasonal indexes)

Using the seasonal indexes derived in Table 17.12, the *trend line estimates* for each quarter of 2007 are *multiplied* by their respective *quarterly seasonal indexes* to include seasonal influences in the forecasted values. These values are referred to as **seasonally-adjusted trend estimates**, as shown in the last column of Table 17.13.

Management interpretation

Valley Estates can expect to sell approximately 62 houses in quarter 1 of 2007; 68 houses in quarter 2 of 2007; 109 houses in quarter 3 of 2007; and 83 houses in quarter 4 of 2007.

These statistical forecasts do not include a cyclical or an irregular component. It is assumed that these forces exert a minimal influence on the actual values of the time series. The validity of this forecasting process depends upon the extent to which this assumption holds true. If trend and seasonal forces do account for the majority of the final actual time series values, these statistical forecasts could be of great benefit in practice.

Also, the usefulness and validity of these time series forecasts depend upon the continuation of the historical environmental patterns on which the trend and seasonal indicators are based over the forecasting period. If environmental patterns are reasonably stable, which may be a reasonable assumption in the short to medium future, the forecasted values can be considered reliable, and vice versa. Hence, time series forecasting is of more value for short to medium-term forecasting, as the short to medium-term future is likely to exhibit similar patterns to the immediate past. The longer-term future is less predictable (in terms of environmental forces). Long-term time series forecasting is thus of less value as there is greater uncertainty that historical patterns will continue into the long-term future.

17.7 Summary

This chapter considered an approach involving the analysis of time series data as opposed to cross-sectional data. The analysis and harnessing of time series data is useful for short to medium-term forecasting. The chapter identified and described the nature of each of four possible influences on the values of a time series, *y*. These forces were identified as trend, cyclical, seasonal and irregular influences. The statistical technique of *Time Series Analysis* is used to decompose a time series into these four constituent components, using a *multiplicative model*. Only the trend and seasonal components were examined further.

Trend analysis can be performed either by using the method of *moving averages*, or by fitting a straight line using the *method of least squares from regression analysis*. The *natural numbering* method for coding the time variable, *x*, is the preferred coding scheme, especially if *Excel* is used.

The seasonal component is described by finding *seasonal indexes* using the *ratio-to-moving-average* approach. The interpretation of these seasonal indexes was also covered in the chapter.

Two applications of trend analysis and seasonal indexes, which managers might find useful, were described. First, it was shown how to *de-seasonalise a time series* using seasonal indexes to obtain a clearer vision of the trend of a time series variable such as sales. Finally, the use of time-series analysis to *prepare short to medium-term forecasts* was illustrated using trend line estimates modified by seasonal indexes.

Exercises

17.1 X17.1 – coal tonnage

The following table represents the annual tonnage (in 100 000's) of coal mined in the Limpopo province for 16 consecutive years.

Year	Tonnage	Year	Tonnage	Year	Tonnage	Year	Tonnage
1	118	**5**	132	**9**	160	**13**	191
2	124	**6**	115	**10**	188	**14**	178
3	108	**7**	122	**11**	201	**15**	146
4	120	**8**	148	**12**	174	**16**	161

(i) Compute the 4-yearly moving average of coal tonnage mined.
(ii) Compute the 5-yearly moving average of coal tonnage mined.
(iii) Plot both the 4-yearly and 5-yearly moving averages together with the original data on the same graph.
(iv) Use *Excel's* **Chart Wizard Line** option to produce the plots in (iii).
(v) Describe the pattern of the three line plots.

17.2 X17.2 – franchise dealers

The number of new franchise dealers recorded over 10 periods by the Franchise Association of SA are shown below:

Period	1	2	3	4	5	6	7	8	9	10
New Dealers	28	32	43	31	38	47	40	45	55	42

(i) Draw a time series graph to represent this data.
(ii) Using a trend line of the form $\hat{y} = b_0 + b_1x$, estimate the number of new franchise dealers in periods 11, 12 and 13, based on trend estimates only.

17.3 X17.3 – policy claims

The number of claims per quarter on household policies submitted to the George branch of an insurance company is as follows:

Year	Q1	Q2	Q3	Q4
2003	84	53	60	75
2004	81	57	51	73
2005	69	37	40	77
2006	73	46	39	63

(i) Plot the time series of household policy claims.
(ii) Isolate the trend effect by computing a least squares trend line using the zero-sum method. Comment on the trend in claims.

(iii) Estimate the quarterly seasonal effect on household policy claims. Interpret the seasonal impact.
(iv) Estimate the likely number of claims on household policies for the second quarter of 2007 using a seasonally-adjusted trend measure.

17.4 X17.4 – hotel occupancy

A hotel's monthly occupancy rate (measured as a percentage of rooms available) is reported as follows for a 10-month period:

Months	Occupancy %
Sept 2005	74
Oct	82
Nov	70
Dec	90
Jan 2006	88
Feb	74
Mar	64
Apr	69
May	58
June	65

(i) Produce a line graph of the hotel's occupancy rate per month.
(ii) Fit a least squares trend line to the hotel occupancy rate data.
(iii) What is the trend estimate of the hotel's occupancy rate for July 2006 and August 2006? Comment on your findings.

17.5 X17.5 – electricity demand

Consider the following quarterly demand levels for electricity (in 1 000 megawatts) in Cape Town from 2003 to 2006.

Months	2003	2004	2005	2006
Jan–March	21	35	39	78
Apr–June	42	54	82	114
July–Sept	60	91	136	160
Oct–Dec	12	14	28	40

(i) Plot this time series graphically using *Excel's* **Chart Wizard (Line)**.
(ii) Find the least squares trend line for electricity demand using the sequential numbering systems starting with $x = 1$.
(iii) Find the seasonal index for each quarter.
(iv) Estimate the seasonally-adjusted trend value of likely demand for electricity for Quarters 3 and 4 of 2007.

(v) Re-compute the least squares trend line for electricity demand in (ii) using the **Line** graph and **Add Trendline** option in *Excel.*

17.6 X17.6 – hotel turnover

The seasonal indices and actual quarterly turnover (in R millions) for 2004, 2005 and 2006 in the hotel industry in Cape Town are:

Season	Seasonal Index	2004	2005	2006
Summer	136	568	604	662
Autumn	112	495	544	605
Winter	62	252	270	310
Spring	90	315	510	535

(i) De-seasonalise the hotel industry turnover data for 2004 to 2006.
(ii) Plot both the original and the de-seasonalised quarterly turnover data for the Cape Town hotel industry from 2004 to 2006 on the same axis.
(iii) Derive a trend line equation for the original turnover data using a sequential numbering system starting with $x = 1$ for period 1.
(iv) Estimate the seasonally-adjusted turnover in the Cape Town hotel industry for the summer and autumn seasons in 2007.
(v) Repeat (ii) above using the **Line** graph option in *Excel's* **Chart Wizard**.
(vi) Re-compute the trend line equation in (iii) using *Excel's* **Add Trendline** option in the **Chart Wizard** (**Line**).

17.7 X17.7 – farming equipment

The marketing manager of a company that manufactures and distributes farming equipment (such as combine harvesters, ploughs and tractors) recorded the number of farming units sold quarterly for the period 2003 to 2006.

Quarter	2003	2004	2005	2006
Summer	57	60	65	64
Autumn	51	56	60	62
Winter	50	53	58	58
Spring	56	61	68	70

(i) Find the quarterly seasonal indexes for farming equipment sold.
(ii) Do seasonal forces significantly influence the sale of farming equipment? Comment.
(iii) Derive a least squares trend line for the sales of farming equipment using a sequential numbering system starting with $x = 1$ in period 1.
(iv) Prepare seasonally-adjusted trend estimates of the number of farming units that this company can expect to sell in each quarter of 2007.
(v) Use *Excel* to prepare the quarterly seasonal indexes and derive the seasonally-adjusted trend estimates as required in (iv).

17.8 X17.8 – energy costs

The management of an office complex in central Johannesburg wants to understand the pattern of energy consumption (i.e. energy costs related to heating and air-conditioning) in the complex. They have assembled quarterly data on energy costs for the past three years (in R100 000).

	Quarter			
Year	**Summer**	**Autumn**	**Winter**	**Spring**
2004	2,4	3,8	4	3,1
2005	2,6	4,1	4,1	3,2
2006	2,6	4,5	4,3	3,3

(i) Plot the pattern of energy costs graphically using *Excel's* **Chart Wizard (Line)**.

(ii) Compute seasonal indexes for the complex's energy costs by the ratio-to-moving average method.

(iii) Find the least squares trend line for energy usage using the zero-sum method.

(iv) How much should the financial manager of this office complex budget for energy costs for each quarter of 2007 based on seasonally-adjusted trend estimates.

(v) Re-compute the least squares trend line for energy usage in (ii) using the **Line** graph and **Add Trendline** option in *Excel.*

(vi) Compute the trend line estimates of energy costs for each quarter of 2007 using first, the trend line equation from (iii) and then the trend line equation from (v). What observation can be made about the two sets of trend estimates?

17.9 X17.9 – business registrations

The number of *new business registrations* in the Gauteng region was recorded by the Department of Trade and Industries for the period 2002 to 2006.

	Quarter			
Year	**1**	**2**	**3**	**4**
2002	1 005	1 222	1 298	1 199
2003	1 173	1 371	1 456	1 376
2004	1 314	1 531	1 605	1 530
2005	1 459	1 671	1 762	1 677
2006	1 604	1 837	1 916	1 819

This exercise is to be completed using *Excel* only.

(i) Use *Excel's* **Chart Wizard (Line)** to plot the number of new business registrations in the Gauteng region for the period 2002 to 2006.

(ii) Prepare a four-period centred moving average and plot it on the same axis.

(iii) Compute quarterly seasonal indexes for new business registrations in the Gauteng region. Are new business registrations significantly influenced by seasonal forces? Comment.

(iv) Compute a least square trend line using the **Line** graph and **Add Trendline** option in *Excel*.

(v) Compute the seasonally-adjusted trend estimates of the number of new business registrations in the Gauteng region for the historical data (i.e. from 2002 quarter 1 to 2006 quarter 4).

(vi) Plot the actual time series and the seasonally-adjusted trend estimates from (v) on the same axis. Comment on the closeness of the two time series data.

(vii) Estimate the likely number of new business registrations in the Gauteng region for each of the quarters of 2007 and 2008.

17.10 **X17.10 – engineering sales**

An engineering company estimates its next year's sales to be R48 million. If the company's sales follows the seasonal pattern of sales in the engineering industry (as shown in the table), derive the sales forecast for this company for each quarter of next year.

Quarter	Seasonal Index
1	95
2	115
3	110
4	80

Note: Assume trend and cyclical influences are negligible during the year.

17.11 **X17.11 – table mountain**

The Table Mountain Cable Car Company recorded the following data on the number of tourists (in thousands) who visited Table Mountain, Cape Town in each quarter of 2005 and 2006.

Season	Seasonal Index	2005	2006
Winter	62	18,1	22,4
Spring	89	26,4	33,2
Summer	162	41,2	44,8
Autumn	87	31,6	32,5

(i) Plot the quarterly number of tourists to Table Mountain for 2005 and 2006.

(ii) Calculate the de-seasonalised values for each quarter and plot on the same axis. Comment on the trend in the number of tourists visiting Table Mountain.

(iii) If the projected total number of tourists to visit Table Mountain in 2007 is 150 (in thousands), how many visitors can the Cable Car Company expect to carry for each quarter of 2007?

17.12 X17.12 – gross domestic product

The following table gives the Gross Domestic Product (GDP) for a certain African country from 1996 to 2006:

Year	GDP (R10 millions)
1996	4 510
1997	4 733
1998	6 128
1999	6 174
2000	7 222
2001	7 418
2002	8 412
2003	8 158
2004	9 348
2005	9 348
2006	9 844

(i) Plot the GDP time series using *Excel's* Line option in the Chart Wizard.
(ii) Use the Add Trendline option in the Chart Wizard (Line) to find the least squares trend line for GDP.
(iii) Use this equation to predict the country's GDP for 2008 and 2009.

17.13 X17.13 – pelagic fish

The number of tonnes of pelagic fish caught off the west coast during each of the 3-monthly periods over 4 years are reported by the Department of Marine Resources as follows:

Year	Quarter	Pelagic fish
2003	Jan–Apr	44
	May–Aug	36
	Sept–Dec	34
2004	Jan–Apr	45
	May–Aug	42
	Sept–Dec	34
2005	Jan–Apr	38
	May–Aug	32
	Sept–Dec	27
2006	Jan–Apr	40
	May–Aug	31
	Sept–Dec	28

(i) Compute the 3-period moving average trend of pelagic fish caught off the west coast.
(ii) Plot the actual catches of pelagic fish and the moving average trend on the same graph. Comment on the pattern of pelagic fish catches over the past 4 years.
(iii) Compute the seasonal indexes for each of the 3-monthly periods. Interpret the results.
(iv) Derive the trend line for pelagic fish caught off the west coast for the past 4 years.
(v) Estimate the seasonally-adjusted number of tonnes of pelagic fish that can be expected to be caught off the west coast for each 3-monthly period of 2007.

17.14 X17.14 – share price

A share trader has a policy of selling a share if its share price drops more than one-third of its purchase price. In January, the investor bought shares in Netron (an electronics company) for 90c per share. The table below shows the price of the Netron share at the end of each month.

If the trend in the under-performance of the Netron share price continues, identify, using the least square trend line method, when the investor is likely to sell his holdings in Netron shares.

Month	Share price (c)
January	90
February	82
March	78
April	80
May	74
June	76
July	70

17.15 X17.15 – addo park

The following table reports both the seasonal indexes for all national park visitors and the number of visitors to the Addo National Park near Port Elizabeth on a quarterly basis (in 1 000's).

Season	Seasonal Indexes	2004	2005	2006
Summer	112	196	199	214
Autumn	94	147	152	163
Winter	88	124	132	145
Spring	106	177	190	198

Assume that the seasonal pattern of visitors to the Addo National Park follows the national profile of visitors to all national parks.

(i) Remove the influence of seasonal factors on the number of visitors to the Addo National Park for each of the periods from 2004 to 2006.
(ii) Plot both the original data series and the de-seasonalised data series of the number of visitors to the Addo National Park over the 3-year period on the same axis.
(iii) Is any significant trend evident from the de-seasonalised data? Comment.
(iv) Use *Excel's* **Line** option in the **Chart Wizard** to plot the data in (ii).

17.16 X17.16 – healthcare claims

The following table represents the quarterly value of healthcare claims (in R millions) against all medical health schemes for the period 2003 to 2006.

Year	Quarter 1	Quarter 2	Quarter 3	Quarter 4
2003	11,8	13,2	19,1	16,4
2004	10,9	12,4	22,4	17,8
2005	12,2	16,2	24,1	14,6
2006	12,8	14,5	20,8	16,1

(i) Compute quarterly seasonal indexes for healthcare claims using the ratio-to-moving average method.
(ii) Derive a trend line using the method of least squares.
(iii) Estimate the seasonally-adjusted trend value of healthcare claims for each quarter of 2007.
(iv) Use *Excel's* **Line** graph option from the **Chart Wizard** to plot the actual healthcare claims values and the seasonally-adjusted trend estimates of healthcare claims values.

17.17 X17.17 – financial advertising

The level of advertising expenditure in the financial services sector (i.e. banks, insurance, investments) to promote their products and services has increased steadily in recent years. The annual expenditure levels (in R10 millions) for the financial services sector from 2000 to 2006 are shown in the following table.

Year	2000	2001	2002	2003	2004	2005	2006
Expenditure	9,6	11,8	12	13,6	14,1	15	17,8

(i) Use the least squares regression to compute the trend line equation for advertising expenditure in the financial services sector with $x = 0$ at 2003.
(ii) Predict the level of advertising expenditure for the sector for 2007.
(iii) Use *Excel* to plot a line graph of advertising expenditure in the financial services sector from 2000 to 2006.

(iv) Use the **Add Trendline** option in *Excel* to compute the trend line equation for annual advertising expenditure levels in the financial services sector.
(v) Use *Excel's* trend line equation to estimate advertising expenditure levels from 2000 to 2007 and show these estimates on the same graph as the plot of the original series in (iii).
(vi) Compare the 2007 estimated value derived in (ii) and (v). What do you observe?

17.18 X17.18 – policy surrenders

An insurance company reported the number of policy holders who applied to surrender their endowment policies for each quarter from 2004 to 2006. The insurance company has been communicating with its policy holders over the past 3 years to discourage them from surrendering their policy prior to maturity because of the reduced payout on early surrender.

Year	Q1	Q2	Q3	Q4
2004	212	186	192	205
2005	186	165	169	182
2006	169	158	162	178

Note: Q1 = Jan – Mar; Q2 = Apr – June; Q3 = July – Sept; Q4 = Oct – Dec.

(i) Plot the pattern of surrendered policies from 2004 to 2006 using *Excel's* Line option in the Chart Wizard. Does the company's communication with policyholders appear to be working? Comment.
(ii) Compute the quarterly seasonal indexes using the ratio-to-moving average method. Comment on the seasonal pattern of policy surrenders.
(iii) Derive the least squares trend line for the number of surrendered policies per quarter for the period 2003 to 2006.
(iv) Estimate the number of endowment policies that are likely to be surrendered by policy holders during each of the quarters of 2007 using the seasonal indexes and trend equation computed in (ii) and (iii).

17.19 X17.19 – company liquidations

The Economic Statistics Bureau has recorded the number of company liquidations over 27 time periods as follows:

Period	Liquidations	Period	Liquidations	Period	Liquidations
1	246	**10**	273	**19**	234
2	243	**11**	284	**20**	162
3	269	**12**	305	**21**	240
4	357	**13**	293	**22**	298
5	163	**14**	348	**23**	264
6	154	**15**	423	**24**	253
7	109	**16**	291	**25**	293
8	162	**17**	320	**26**	302
9	222	**18**	253	**27**	188

(i) Use *Excel* to compute both a 3-period and a 5-period moving average time series of company liquidations.

(ii) Plot the original time series of company liquidations and the 3-period and 5-period moving average values on the same graph. Use *Excel's* **Line** graph option in the **Chart Wizard**.

(iii) Comment on the pattern of company liquidations over this time period.

17.20 X17.20 – passenger tyres

Hillstone SA manufactures and sells tyres to the passenger vehicle market in Southern Africa. Their quarterly sales (in 1 000's of units) are shown in the table below.

Their marketing department wishes to apply Time Series Analysis to estimate future quarterly passenger vehicle tyre sales for 2007 and 2008.

Year	Quarter	Tyres sold
2000	Jan–Mar	64 876
	Apr–June	58 987
	July–Sept	54 621
	Oct–Dec	62 345
2001	Jan–Mar	68 746
	Apr–June	66 573
	July–Sept	60 927
	Oct–Dec	71 234
2002	Jan–Mar	78 788
	Apr–June	71 237
	July–Sept	68 098
	Oct–Dec	74 444
2003	Jan–Mar	77 659
	Apr–June	76 452
	July–Sept	73 456
	Oct–Dec	78 908
2004	Jan–Mar	84 563
	Apr–June	81 243
	July–Sept	74 878
	Oct–Dec	86 756
2005	Jan–Mar	91 556
	Apr–June	85 058
	July–Sept	77 035
	Oct–Dec	80 145
2006	Jan–Mar	10 2923
	Apr–June	96 456

(i) Use *Excel* to develop a time series model that Hillstone can use to prepare *seasonally-adjusted trend forecasts* of passenger vehicle tyre sales on a quarterly basis.

(ii) Prepare seasonally-adjusted trend forecast estimates for 2007 and 2008 on a quarterly basis.

(iii) What confidence could the Hillstone management have in the estimates produced? Comment briefly.

17.21 X17.21 – outpatients attendances

The Medical Officer of Health in charge of day clinics in the George district is planning for the expansion of the medical facilities at these clinics based on the growth in demand for the clinics' services.

She therefore asked a statistical analyst to assist in preparing a forecast of future demand for the clinics' services based on the attendance at these clinics over the past 6 years. The Medical Officer was able to supply the analyst with quarterly attendance records for the period 2001 to 2006.

Quarters	Visits
Q1 2001	12 767
Q2	16 389
Q3	19 105
Q4	15 780
Q1 2002	14 198
Q2	19 868
Q3	20 899
Q4	18 304
Q1 2003	14 641
Q2	20 204
Q3	21 078
Q4	16 077
Q1 2004	14 075
Q2	21 259
Q3	20 967
Q4	16 183
Q1 2005	12 412
Q2	21 824
Q3	22 150
Q4	17 979
Q1 2006	17 417
Q2	20 568
Q3	24 310
Q4	23 118

(i) Use *Excel* to conduct a Time Series Analysis (i.e. line plots, seasonal indexes and trend lines) of outpatients attendances at the George day clinics.

(ii) Prepare *seasonally-adjusted quarterly forecasts* of likely outpatients attendances for 2007 and the first half of 2008.

(iii) Draft a brief report to the management of Medical Officer discussing your findings, especially (a) the trend in outpatient attendances and (b) the influence of seasonality on attendances (where quarter 1 is summer and quarter 3 is winter).

17.22 X17.22 – construction absenteeism

The construction industry in the Western Cape is very dependent upon reliable labour to ensure that it meets its project deadlines and avoid incurring late delivery penalties.

The Construction Federation undertook an analysis of the absenteeism levels amongst construction workers over the past 6 years. The number of man-days lost (based on the number of workers absent) (aggregated quarterly) is summarised in the table below.

Quarters	Days_lost
Q1 2001	933
Q2	865
Q3	922
Q4	864
Q1 2002	967
Q2	936
Q3	931
Q4	902
Q1 2003	892
Q2	845
Q3	907
Q4	801
Q1 2004	815
Q2	715
Q3	779
Q4	711
Q1 2005	822
Q2	856
Q3	762
Q4	722
Q1 2006	785
Q2	715
Q3	740
Q4	704

(i) Use *Excel* to conduct a Time Series Analysis of absenteeism levels over the 6-year period. Identify seasonal indexes and produce a trend line of absenteeism levels. Also construct a plot (using the **Chart Wizard**) of the actual time series and the *seasonally-adjusted trend estimates* for the 6 years of historical data.

(ii) Prepare *seasonally-adjusted trend estimates* of absenteeism levels for all quarters of 2007.

(iii) Present your findings in a brief management report.

Chapter

18

Financial Calculations: Interest, Annuities and NPV

Objectives

Financial information for decision making is important in every area of business. An understanding of basic financial calculations, such as *interest* and *annuities*, is essential for investments and loans. The *time value of money* is highlighted in this chapter by using interest and annuity calculations in financial tools, such as the net present value method, which is commonly used to evaluate investment projects.

After studying this chapter, you should be able to:

- explain the concept of simple and compound interest
- perform simple and compound interest calculations
- explain the terms nominal and effective interest rates
- understand the concept of annuities
- distinguish between different types of annuities
- perform various annuity calculations both manually and using *Excel*, and
- apply the net present value method to evaluate investment projects.

18.1 Introduction to Simple and Compound Interest

Interest is the price paid by a borrower for the use of a lump sum of money provided by a lender for a given period of time. It is, alternatively, the bonus received by an investor when a lump sum is deposited for a given period of time.

Interest on any lump sum borrowed or invested is always quoted at a given *rate per cent per annum.* Interest computations are therefore exercises in percentage calculations. Since lump sums can be invested or borrowed for any period of time, interest calculations must also take the element of *time* into account.

There are two methods of working out the interest amount on any lump sum investment or loan. They are:

- *simple* interest
- *compound* interest.

This chapter examines both methods of interest calculation and demonstrates their application to lump sum investments and periodic investment (annuities) situations.

The following terms are used in all interest calculations:

- The principal or *present value* P_v
  This is the *initial lump sum* invested or borrowed.
- The term n
  This is the *duration* of the investment or loan, usually quoted in months or years.
- The rate of interest i
  This rate is always expressed as a *per cent per annum* (e.g. 9% p.a.).
- The amount or *future value* F_v
  This is the total amount of money available or due at the *end* of the investment or loan period. It is the sum of the present value and the accrued interest.

Interest calculation formulae consist of these four components, namely P_v, F_v, i and n. In order to find the value of any one of them, values must be available for the remaining three elements. When applying interest formulae to a problem, the element to be found must always be identified first.

Another important issue in interest calculations is that the quoted *interest rate period* must *coincide* with the *time interval* over which interest accrues over the duration of an investment or loan. This principle is highlighted in the worked examples.

18.2 Simple Interest

If interest is computed on the *original lump sum only* for *each period* over the duration of an investment or a loan, it is termed **simple interest**.

For a lump sum of money P_v invested (loaned) for n periods at a rate of interest of $i\%$ per period, the future value due (owing) F_v at the end of the investment (or loan) period based on simple interest, is defined as:

$$F_v = P_v(1 + in)$$

In each period, interest at the rate of i per cent on the original principal (present value), P_v, accrues. Its accumulation over n periods determines the simple interest amount that has accrued on the investment or the debt.

Example 18.1 Fixed Deposit Investment (Simple Interest)

Mrs Hendricks invested R6 000 at 7 % p.a. for 3 years in a fixed deposit account with the Cape City bank. If simple interest is paid at the end of 3 years on this deposit:

(1) how much money altogether will be paid out to Mrs Hendricks on maturity (i.e. at the end of three years)? and

(2) how much interest was earned over the three years?

Solution

Required to find: The *future value*, F_v, of the fixed deposit investment.

Given P_v = R6 000 (principal invested)
i = 0,07 (rate of interest per annum)
n = 3 (the investment period, in years)

It should be noted that the *interest rate* period and the *term* coincide. They are both expressed in *years*.

Then $F_v = 6\,000\,[1 + (0{,}07)(3)]$
$= 6\,000\,[1 + 0{,}21] = 6\,000\,[1{,}21]$
F_v = R7 260

Management interpretation

(1) Mrs Hendricks will receive R7 260 at the end of three years.

(2) The difference between the *future value*, F_v (R7 260), and the *present value*, P_v (R6 000), of R1 260 is the *amount of simple interest earned* on the R6 000 invested.

Example 18.2 Fixed Deposit Investment (Principal Amount)

How much money should an investor deposit in a fixed deposit account paying 6% p.a. simple interest if she would like to receive R10 000 in four years' time?

Solution

Required to find: The *present value*, P_v, of the investment.

Given F_v = R10 000 (the amount to be received at the end of 4 years)
i = 0,06 (rate of interest *per annum*)
n = 4 (the investment term, in *years*)

Again, note that the *interest rate* period and the *term* coincide, namely that they are both expressed in *years*.

Now	$10\,000$	$= P_v\,[1 + (0{,}06)(4)] = P_v\,[1{,}24]$
Then	P_v	$= \dfrac{10\,000}{1{,}24}$
		$= \text{R}8\,064{,}52$

Management interpretation

The investor must deposit R8 064,52 in the fixed deposit account now in order to receive R10 000 in four years' time, based on simple interest of 6% p.a.

Again, the amount of the simple interest received over this four-year investment period is R1 935,48 (i.e. R10 000 – R8 064,52).

Example 18.3 Student Loan (Simple Interest Rate)

A student borrows R9 000 for three years at a simple interest rate to finance her management studies. If she must repay R11 295 at the end of the three-year loan period, what rate of simple interest per annum was she being charged by the bank?

Solution

Required to find: The *rate of simple interest, i.*

Given	F_v	= R11 295	(the loan amount to be repaid after three years)
	n	= 3	(the term, in *years*)
	P_v	= R9 000	(the initial loan amount)
Now	$11\,295$	$= 9\,000\,[1 + i(3)]$	
	$\frac{11\,295}{9\,000}$	$= [1 + 3i]$	
	$1 + 3i$	$= 1{,}255$	
	$3i$	$= 0{,}255$	
Giving	i	$= 0{,}085$	

Management interpretation

The simple rate of interest charged on the student loan was 8,5% p.a.

Since the *term* of the loan was quoted in units of *years* (i.e. three years), the period of the interest rate found must relate to the same time period. In this instance, the simple interest would be quoted as the rate *per annum.*

Example 18.4 Fixed Deposit Investment (Term of Investment)

An investor deposits R15 609 in a fixed deposit account, which pays 6,25% p.a. simple interest. For how long must the amount be deposited if the investor wishes to withdraw R20 000 at the end of the investment period?

Solution

Required to find: The *term* (*duration*) of the investment, *n*.

Given	P_v	=	R15 609	(the principal amount deposited)
	F_v	=	R20 000	(the maturity value at the end of the term)
	i	=	0,0625	(the interest rate *per annum*)

$$
\begin{aligned}
\text{Now} \quad 20\,000 &= 15\,609\,[1 + 0{,}0625\,(n)] \\
\frac{20\,000}{15\,609} &= [1 + 0{,}0625n] \\
1 + 0{,}0625n &= 1{,}2813 \\
0{,}0625n &= 0{,}2813 \\
\text{Giving} \quad n &= 4{,}5 \text{ years}
\end{aligned}
$$

Management interpretation

The principal of R15 609 must be invested for 4,5 years at 6,25% p.a. simple interest to grow to R20 000 by the end of this investment period.

In all the above examples, the interval over which *simple interest* accrued corresponded to the unit of measure of the *term*. Both are quoted in *years*. Always ensure that the interest rate period coincides with the unit of measure of the term. The following two examples illustrate this requirement.

Example 18.5 Hire Purchase (Simple Interest Rate)

What is the *annual* rate of simple interest on the purchase of a stove costing R2 500 which is to be paid for in three month's time when R75 interest will be charged?

Solution

Required to find: The *rate of simple interest per annum, i.*

Given	F_v	=	R2 575	(R2 500 + R75) (the future value owing in 3 month's time)
	P_v	=	R2 500	(the initial purchase value)
	n	=	0,25	(3 months, expressed in *yearly* terms)

Note: Since the required interest rate must be quoted in percent *per annum*, the term must correspond and also be quoted in units of *years*.

$$
\begin{aligned}
\text{Now} \quad 2\,575 &= 2\,500\,[1 + i\,(0{,}25)] \\
\text{Then} \quad \frac{2\,575}{2\,500} &= [1 + 0{,}25i] \\
1 + 0{,}25i &= 1{,}03 \\
0{,}25i &= 0{,}03 \\
\text{Giving} \quad i &= 0{,}12
\end{aligned}
$$

Management interpretation

The simple rate of interest charged on the stove hire purchase agreement was 12% p.a.

Example 18.6 Short-Term Business Loan (Simple Interest Rate)

An industrial printing company borrowed R75 000 from an investment bank to buy a new hi-tech printer. The bank will charge simple interest on the bridging finance, which must be repaid in 18 months' time. If the printing company repaid R90 750 at the end of the loan period, what rate of simple interest *per annum* was being charged on the loan?

Solution

Required to find: The *rate of simple interest per annum, i.*

Given	F_v	=	R90 750	(the future value owing in 18 month's time)
	P_v	=	R75 000	(the purchase value of the high-tech printer)
	n	=	1,5	(18 months, expressed in *yearly* terms)

Note: Since the required interest rate must be quoted in percent *per annum*, the term must correspond and also be quoted in units of *years*.

Now $90\ 750 = 75\ 000\,[1 + i\,(1{,}5)]$

Then $\frac{90\ 750}{75\ 000} = [1 + 1{,}5i]$

$1 + 1{,}5i = 1{,}21$

$1{,}5i = 0{,}21$

Giving $i = 0{,}14$

Management interpretation

The industrial printing company was charged a simple interest rate of 14% p.a. to finance the hi-tech printer and repay the debt (price plus interest) in 18 months' time.

18.3 Compound Interest

Compound interest is the practice of calculating interest *periodically* and *adding* it to the existing principal *before* each subsequent interest calculation is made.

The interest is said to be **capitalised**. This means that it is made part of the *present value* on which future interest is calculated each time. It is the practice of "*calculating interest on interest*".

The Development of the Compound Interest Formula

The period between two consecutive points in time at which interest is **compounded** is called the **conversion period**. At the end of each conversion period, interest is calculated on the accumulation of the original principal and all previous interest amounts.

This is illustrated in Table 18.1 overleaf. It shows that the *future value* at the end of each conversion period is the *present value* for the next period's interest calculation.

Table 18.1 The development of the compound interest formula

Period	Present value at the beginning of each period	Revised present value at the end of each period (after interest)		
1	P_v	$F_{v1} = F_v(1 + i)$	or	$P_v(1 + i)^1$
2	F_{v1}	$F_{v2} = F_{v1}(1 + i)$	or	$P_v(1 + i)^2$
3	F_{v2}	$F_{v3} = F_{v2}(1 + i)$	or	$P_v(1 + i)^3$
4	F_{v3}	$F_{v4} = F_{v3}(1 + i)$	or	$P_v(1 + i)^4$
5	F_{v4}	$F_{v5} = F_{v4}(1 + i)$	or	$P_v(1 + i)^5$
etc.	etc.	etc.		
n	$F_{v(n-1)}$	$F_{vn} = F_{v(n-1)}(1 + i)$	or	$\mathbf{P_v(1 + i)^n}$

This formula can now be used to find any one of the following elements of a loan or investment where *interest* is *capitalised* at regular intervals, i.e.:

- its future value F_v
- its present value P_v
- its interest rate i
- its term n

(i) Future value

In general, the *compound interest formula* is used to derive the *future value* of an investment or loan after n periods at i% per annum.

Formula

The formula is:

$$F_v = P_v(1 + i)^n$$

Each symbol has the same definition as for simple interest.

Example 18.7 Fixed Deposit Investment (Compound Interest)

Mrs Hendricks invested R6 000 in a fixed deposit account with the Cape City bank for three years at a rate of interest of 7% p.a.

(1) How much will Mrs Hendricks receive upon maturity if interest is *compounded annually*?

(2) How much will Mrs Hendricks receive upon maturity if interest is *compounded quarterly*?

Solution (1)

Required to find: The *future value*, F_v, of the fixed deposit investment.

Given

P_v = R6 000 (principal invested)
i = 0,07 (rate of interest per *annum*)
n = 3 years (the investment period, in *years*)

Since interest is *compounded annually*, both the annual *interest rate* and the *term* must be expressed in annual units (i.e. 7% p.a. and 3 years).

Then $F_v = 6\,000\,(1 + 0{,}07)^3$
$= 6\,000\,(1{,}07)^3 = 6\,000\,(1{,}225043)$

Giving $F_v = \text{R7 } 350{,}26$

Management interpretation (1)

Mrs Hendricks will receive R7 350,26 at the end of three years, based on interest compounded annually.

The difference between the *future value,* F_v (R7 350,26) and the *present value,* P_v (R6 000) of R1 350,26 is the *amount of compound interest earned* on the R6 000 invested.

Solution (2)

Given P_v = R6 000 (principal invested)
i = 0,0175 (rate of interest per *quarter*)
n = 12 quarters (the investment period, in *quarters*)

Since interest is *compounded quarterly*, both the *annual interest rate* and the *term* must be expressed in *quarterly* units. The *annual interest rate* must be divided by 4 ($\frac{0{,}07}{4}$ = 0,0175 per quarter), while the *term* must be multiplied by 4 (3 years × 4 = 12 quarters). Thus an interest rate of 1,75% per *quarter* over 12 *quarters* applies.

Then $F_v = 6\,000\,(1 + 0{,}0175)^{12}$
$= 6\,000\,(1{,}0175)^{12} = 6\,000\,(1{,}231439)$
$F_v = \text{R7 } 388{,}64$

Management interpretation (2)

Mrs Hendricks will receive R7 388,64 at the end of three years, based on interest compounded quarterly.

The difference between the *future value,* F_v (R7 388,64) and the *present value,* P_v (R6 000) of R1 388,64 is the *amount of compound interest earned* on the R6 000 invested.

It can be seen that:

- *compound interest* always *pays more* than *simple interest* for the same capital amount, term and interest rate.

  From **Example 18.1** above, the maturity value when based on simple interest was R7 260, while the maturity value when based on compound interest was R7 350,26 (when compounded annually).

- the *amount of compound interest* earned/paid is *always larger* when the *compounding period* is *more frequent*.

  From **Example 18.7 (1)**, the amount of interest earned when compounded *annually* was R1 350,26, while from **Example 18.7 (2)**, the amount of interest earned when compounded *quarterly* over the same term of three years was R1 388,64. This is R38,38 more as a result of compounding quarterly instead of annually.

(ii) Present value

When the *initial amount* (*present value*) of a loan or an investment where interest is compounded, is unknown, the compound interest formula can be re-arranged to find this *present value* as follows:

Formula

$$P_v = \frac{F_v}{(1 + i)^n}$$

The following example illustrates the calculation of the present value of an investment.

Example 18.8 Fixed Deposit Investment (Monthly Compound Interest)

A father would like to give his daughter a cash gift of R20 000 on her 21st birthday in exactly four years' time. How much must he deposit today in a fixed deposit account which pays 9% p.a. *compounded monthly* to reach his target?

Solution

Required to find: The *present value*, P_v, of an investment.

Given F_v = R20 000 (the maturity value required)
i = 0,0075 (rate of interest per *month*)
n = 48 months (the investment period, in *months*)

Since interest is *compounded monthly*, both the annual interest rate and the term must be expressed in *monthly* units. The annual *interest rate* must be divided by 12 ($\frac{0,09}{12}$ = 0,0075 per month), while the *term* must be multiplied by 12 (4 years × 12 = 48 months). Thus an interest rate of 0,75% per *month* over 48 *months* applies.

Then
$$20\,000 = P_v(1 + 0,0075)^{48}$$
$$20\,000 = P_v(1,431405)$$
$$P_v = \frac{20\,000}{1,431405}$$
$$= \text{R}13\,972,38$$

Management interpretation

The father must deposit R13 972,38 today into a fixed deposit account to receive R20 000 in four years' time at 9% p.a. *compounded monthly*.

(iii) Interest rate

When the *interest rate* of a loan or an investment where interest is compounded, is unknown, the compound interest formula can be re-arranged to find this *interest rate* as follows:

$$i = \sqrt[n]{\frac{F_v}{P_v}} - 1$$

Example 18.9 Interest Payable on Loan (Half-Yearly Compound Interest)

What is the *annual rate of interest* being charged by the Good Hope Bank on a loan of R25 000, if R33 063 is to be repaid in two-and-a-half year's time in full settlement, if interest is *compounded half yearly*?

Solution

Required to find: The *per annum interest rate*, *i*.

Given P_v = R25 000 (the original loan amount)
F_v = R33 063 (the amount to be repaid)
n = 5 half-yearly periods (2,5 years expressed in *half-yearly periods*)

Note: When a value for *i* is found, this will refer to the interest rate *per half year*.

Then $33\,063 = 25\,000\,(1 + i)^5$

$(1 + i)^5 = \frac{33\,063}{25\,000} = 1{,}32252$

$(1 + i) = \sqrt[5]{1{,}32252} = 1{,}0575$ [fifth root of each side]

$i = 1{,}0575 - 1$

giving $i = 0{,}0575$

Management interpretation

The half-yearly interest rate is 5,75%. This translates into an annual interest rate of 11,5% (i.e. 11,5% p.a.).

(iv) Term

To find the *term* of an investment or a loan, the compound interest formula can be rearranged as follows:

$$n = \frac{\log\left(\frac{F_v}{P_v}\right)}{\log(1 + i)}$$

Note: The re-arranged formula requires the calculation of the *logarithm* of a number. The logarithm of a number to the base 10 can be found using the *Excel* function **=LOG(number)**.

Example 18.10 Investment Duration (Quarterly Compound Interest)

If an amount of R86 400 is invested at 8% p.a. compounded *quarterly*, how long will it take to reach R206 500,60?

Solution

Required to find: The *term*, *n*, of the investment.

Given P_v = R86 400 (the original investment amount)
F_v = R206 500,60 (the maturity value)
i = 0,02 (*quarterly* interest rate [i.e. $\frac{0,08}{4} = 0,02$])

Note: When a value for *n* is found, this will refer to the number of *quarterly periods*.

Then
$$206\,500{,}60 = 86\,400\,(1 + 0{,}02)^n$$
$$\frac{206\,500{,}50}{86\,400} = (1{,}02)^n$$
$$(1{,}02)^n = 2{,}390056$$

The term, *n*, can be separated from the number 1,02 by taking the natural logarithm of both sides of the formula, using the *Excel* function **=LOG(1.02)** and **=LOG(2.390056)**

i.e.
$$n\log(1{,}02) = \log(2{,}390056)$$
$$n\,(0{,}0086) = 0{,}378408$$
$$n = \frac{0{,}378408}{0{,}0086}$$

Giving n = 44 quarters (equivalent to 11 years)

Management interpretation

It would take 44 quarters (i.e. 11 years) for an investment of R86 400 to grow to R206 500,60 invested at 8% p.a. compounded quarterly.

18.4 Nominal and Effective Rates of Interest

All deposit and lending institutions quote an annual rate of interest on deposits or amounts loaned. This is called the **nominal** rate of interest.

If interest on a deposit (or a loan) is compounded *more than once per year*, then the real (or *effective*) rate of interest per annum earned (or paid) will be different from the quoted, nominal rate of interest due to the compounded effect.

Effective Rate of Interest

The following formula is used to determine the *effective* rate of interest on any investment or loan when interest is compounded in periods of *less than a year*.

Formula

$$r = \left(1 + \frac{i}{m}\right)^m - 1$$

Where r = the *effective interest rate* per annum
m = the number of *conversion periods* per annum
i = the *nominal interest rate* per annum

Example 18.11 Savings Account Investment (Monthly Compound Interest)

In an advertisement, Absa Bank announced that a savings account for R100 000 or more would pay a nominal rate p.a. of 6,5% capitalised monthly.

Absa stipulated in its advertisement that: "*effective* rates apply for amounts invested for a period of one year, assuming the interest at the nominal rate is constant and capitalised monthly."

Management question

What is the *effective* rate of interest p.a. earned on any deposit in this account?

Solution (manual)

Given i = 0,065 (the nominal interest rate p.a.)
m = 12 months (the number of conversion periods p.a.)

$$
\begin{aligned}
\text{Then} \quad r &= \left(1 + \frac{0{,}065}{12}\right)^{12} - 1 \\
&= (1{,}005417)^{12} - 1 \\
&= 1{,}066972 - 1 \\
&= 0{,}066972 \ (6{,}6972\%)
\end{aligned}
$$

Solution using *Excel*

The function key **=EFFECT(nominal_rate, Npery)** will compute the *effective interest rate* based on a *nominal rate* and the *number of compounding periods* per year (*Npery*).

For *example* (using the above illustration): **=EFFECT(0.065,12)** gives an effective rate of interest of 0,066971852 (i.e. an effective rate of 6,6972% p.a.)

Management interpretation

What is the *effective* rate of interest p.a. earned on any deposit in this account?

This Absa Bank savings account pays an effective 6,6972% p.a. interest on deposits of R100 000 or more.

This means that any amount of R100 000 or more invested for one year would have grown by 6,6972% and not 6,5%.

18.5 Introduction to Annuities

An **annuity** is when a constant amount of money is paid (or received) at *regular intervals* over a period of time.

When money is borrowed and then repaid over time (such as a *property mortgage*); or lump sum investments are withdrawn in fixed amounts at regular intervals (such as a *retirement annuity*), interest is constantly being charged or earned. Annuity calculations therefore involve an interest factor compounded at regular intervals. These series of equal payments could be made yearly, half-yearly, quarterly, monthly, weekly or even daily.

Examples

Common examples of annuities include:

- Regular *monthly contributions* into a pension fund (or provident fund)
- Regular *monthly contributions* to a retirement annuity
- *Monthly* insurance *premiums* on an endowment (or life) policy
- Motor vehicle *lease* (or *repayment*) agreements
- *Monthly mortgage* bond *repayments*
- *Hire-purchase agreements* to settle outstanding debt
- *Unemployment insurance contributions*
- *Short-term personal insurance* policies (car insurance, all risks, house-owners insurance, hospital insurance plans) which can be paid monthly, half-yearly, or annually.

Terminology in annuities

The following terminology is used in all annuity calculations:

- The *future value* of an annuity F_v
  This is the amount of money that has accumulated by the maturity (or expiry) date of an annuity (i.e. when payments/contributions cease). It is equivalent to the sum of all regular payments plus accumulated interest.
- The *present value* of an annuity P_v
  This is a initial lump sum of money which is either deposited or borrowed and which will result in a series of equal payments at regular intervals for a period of time into the future.
- The *duration* (also called the *term*) of an annuity n
- The *payment period* is the time interval between successive *regular payments* of *equal amounts* (i.e. monthly, quarterly, annually). The payment period must always coincide with the period over which interest is compounded.
- The *regular payments* R
  This is the amount of money that must be *deposited or paid* at *each payment period* over the *duration* of the annuity.
- The *rate of interest*, i, which must coincide with the conversion (or compounding) period.

Annuity calculations require finding one of the following:

- The *future value* of an annuity F_v
- The *present value* of an annuity P_v
  or
- The *regular payments* R

The diagrams in Figure 18.1 below illustrate the different concepts of annuities.

Figure 18.1 Schematic view of the concepts of annuities

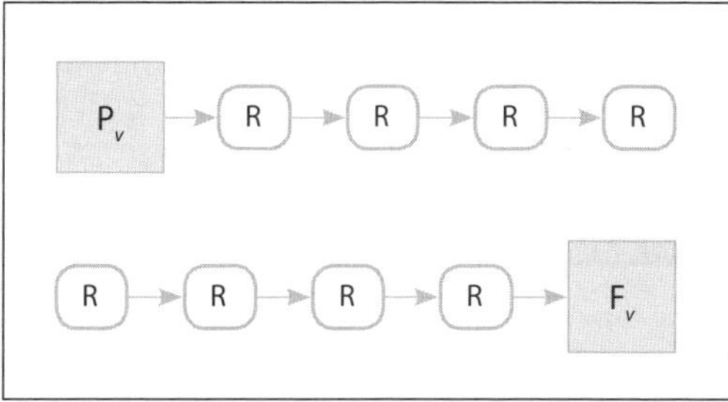

Classification of annuities

Annuities differ according to when the series of regular payments begin. In this regard, there are two broad groupings of annuities. They are:

- *ordinary* annuities, and
- *deferred* annuities.

(i) Ordinary annuities

With **ordinary annuities**, the first of the series of *regular payments* begin in the *first period* of the term of the annuity.

There are two kinds of ordinary annuities:

- ordinary annuity *certain*, and
- ordinary annuity *due*.

An *ordinary annuity certain* is an annuity where the series of regular payments take place at the ***end*** *of each payment period* for a fixed number of periods.

An *ordinary annuity due* is an annuity where the series of regular payments take place at the ***beginning*** *of each payment period* for a fixed number of periods.

This difference in payment practice affects the amount of interest earned or charged on the ordinary annuity.

(ii) Deferred annuities

Where the first of the series of *regular payments* only *begins* at *some future period*, and not immediately, during the term of the annuity, the annuity is known as a **deferred annuity**.

Illustration

A trust fund of R150 000 is instructed to pay the beneficiary, who is currently 12 years of age, regular annual instalments over five years, beginning only when she turns 21 years of age. Since the beneficiary turns 21 years of age in nine years' time, the annuity is said to be deferred for eight years (not nine years). The first payment will occur at the end of the ninth year and four subsequent payments will take place. The beneficiary will receive the final payment from the trust when she is 25 years old.

Both ordinary annuities and deferred annuities are discussed in the following sections.

18.6 Ordinary Annuities Certain

To repeat, the regular payments under an *ordinary annuity certain* occur at the *end* of each payment period.

The following example is given to promote an understanding of the concept of an annuity and its use of compound interest knowledge. However, only the rationale of computing future values of an ordinary annuity certain is illustrated.

Example 18.12 Future Value of an Ordinary Annuity Certain

At the *end* of each year an investor makes 6 equal deposits of R500 each, into an investment account with the Cape City Bank which pays 12% p.a. compounded annually.

Management question

How much will the investor receive after 6 years?

Solution (with explanation)

To determine how much the investor will receive at the end of the sixth year, consider the graphic display of compound interest payments on each regular deposit of R500 over six years as shown in Figure 18.2 below.

Figure 18.2 Illustration of the **future value** of an **ordinary annuity certain**

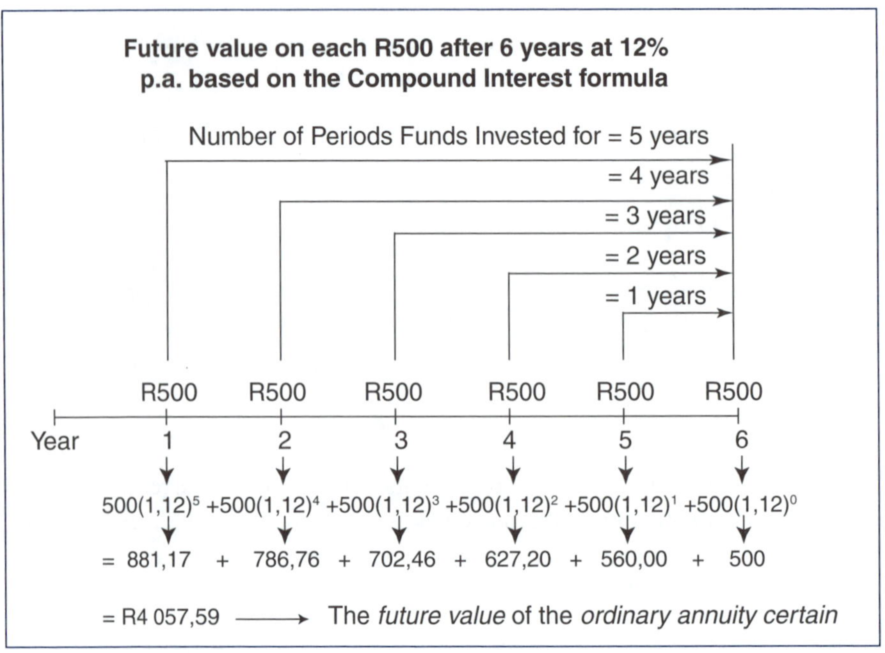

Explanation

- The first deposit of R500 takes place only at the end of year 1. This R500 will earn interest for five years at the rate of 12% p.a. compounded annually.
- The second deposit of R500 takes place at the end of year 2 only, and will earn interest for four years at the rate of 12% p.a. compounded annually.
- The third deposit of R500 takes place at the end of year 3 only, and will earn interest for three years at the rate of 12% p.a. compounded annually, etc.
- The sixth and final deposit of R500 takes place at the end of year 6. It will earn no interest as the full value of the investment (i.e. its *future value*) is due to be paid out on the same day that the final deposit is made.

As noted in the explanation, each regular payment, R, (or deposit instalment) earns interest at a compounded rate for *that portion of the term for which it is invested.*

As seen in the illustration, the *future value* of the *annuity* is the *sum* of all these *regular payments plus* the *compound interest amount* that each instalment has earned over the duration of the annuity.

The following sections derive the future value, F_v, the present value, P_v, and the regular payment, R, of an ordinary annuity certain.

(i) Future value of an ordinary annuity certain

The future value of an ordinary annuity certain can be expressed in a concise mathematical formula as follows:

$$F_v = R\,\frac{(1 + i)^n - 1}{i}$$

Example 18.12

Using the *data*, the *future value* calculations based on the formula are:

Given $i = 0{,}12$ (compounded interest rate p.a.)

$n = 6$ years

$R = 500$ (regular payment amounts)

Then $F_v = 500\,\frac{(1{,}12)^6 - 1}{0{,}12} = 500\,(8{,}11519)$

$= \text{R}4\,057{,}59$

Management interpretation

The investor will receive R4 057,59 at the end of six years after investing R500 per year.

Example 18.13 Education Savings Plan

A father decides to invest R650 at the *end* of each month for five years at 9% p.a. compounded monthly to pay for his son's tertiary education in five years' time.

Management question

What amount of money will be available at the end of five years?

Solution

Since each payment takes place at the *end* of every month, this is an ordinary annuity certain.

Required to find: The *future value*, F_v of an ordinary annuity certain.

Given $R = 650$ (regular monthly instalment)

$i = 0{,}0075$ (interest compounded *monthly*, i.e. $\frac{0{,}09}{12} = 0{,}0075$)

$n = 60$ months (to coincide with the regular payment period) (i.e. 5 years × 12 = *60 months*)

Then
$$F_v = 650\ \frac{(1{,}0075)^{60} - 1}{0{,}0075} = 650\ \frac{0{,}565681^{\cdot}}{0{,}0075}$$
$$= 650\ (75{,}42414)$$
$$= R49\ 025{,}69$$

Management interpretation

The father will have R49 025,69 available at the end of five years to pay for his son's tertiary education.

Example 18.14 Car Purchase Savings Plan

Sam Gumede is planning to buy a new car in two years' time, which he estimates will cost him R140 000. He also estimates that the trade-in value on his current car will be R36 500 in two years' time.

Management question

How much should Sam Gumede *save monthly* in a special savings account with his local bank, which will pay 6,5% p.a. compounded monthly?

Solution

Sam Gumede will require R103 500 (i.e. R140 000 – R36 500 trade-in) in 2 years' time for the purchase of a new car.

Required to find: The *regular payment*, R.

Given $F_v = 103\ 500$ (future value required)

$i = 0{,}005417$ (*monthly* interest rate i.e. $\frac{0{,}065}{12} = 0{,}005417$)

$n = 24$ months (to coincide with the regular payment period) (i.e. 2 years × 12 = 24 *months*)

Then
$$103\ 500 = R\ \frac{(1{,}005417)^{24} - 1}{0{,}005417} = R\ \frac{0{,}138429}{0{,}005417}$$
$$103\ 500 = R\ (25{,}55611)$$

Solve
$$R = \frac{103\ 500}{25{,}55611}$$
$$= 4\ 049{,}91$$

Management interpretation

Sam Gumede would have to save R4049,91 at the end of every month for two years in order to meet the cost of the new car which he hopes to buy at that time.

(ii) Present Value of an Ordinary Annuity Certain

Formula

If the *present value* (initial lump sum) of an ordinary annuity certain is required to generate a regular flow of payments over a fixed period of time, then the following annuity formula is used:

$$P_v = R\,\frac{1-(1+i)^{-n}}{i}$$

It must always be established first from the description of an annuity problem whether present values or future values are being referred to, as this determines which formulae will be selected to solve the problem.

Example 18.15 Retirement Plan (Monthly Compound Interest)

Mr Peterson, who has just retired, would like to receive R5 000 at the *end of every month* for 10 years.

Management question

If money can be invested at 9% p.a. compounded monthly, how much money should he deposit today?

Solution

Required to find: the *present value* of an ordinary annuity certain.

Given $R = 5\ 000$ (regular monthly income)
$i = 0{,}0075$ (interest compounded monthly)
(i.e. 0,09/12 = 0,0075 per *month*)
$n = 120$ months (to coincide with the regular payment period)
(i.e. 10 years × 12 months = 120 *months*)

Then
$$P_v = 5\ 000\,\frac{1-(1{,}0075)^{-120}}{0{,}0075} = 5\ 000\,\frac{1-0{,}407937}{0{,}0075}$$

$$P_v = 5\ 000\,\frac{0{,}592063}{0{,}0075} = 5\ 000\,(78{,}94169)$$

$$P_v = 394\ 708{,}50$$

Management interpretation

Mr Peterson will have to deposit a lump sum of R394 708,50 today to ensure a retirement income of R5 000 per month for the next 10 years, payable at the *end* of each month.

Example 18.16 House Bond Repayment Scheme (Monthly Compound Interest)

Mr Ncube puts down a deposit of R50 000 on a new house costing R540 500. He has raised a mortgage bond for the balance which he is required to pay off in equal monthly instalments over 20 years. Interest is charged at 10,5% p.a. compounded monthly.

Management question

What *regular monthly instalments* will he have to pay at the *end* of each month?

Solution

From the description of the problem, it can be seen that the *present value* formula must be used since the question provides information on the *initial amount outstanding* (i.e. *present value*) and not on a future value.

Required to find: the *regular monthly payments*, R, on the mortgage bond.

Given $P_v = 490\ 500$ (outstanding balance after deposit) (i.e. R540 500 – R50 000 = R490 500)

$i = 0{,}00875$ (interest compounded *monthly*) (i.e. 0,105/12 = 0,00875 per month)

$n = 240$ months (to coincide with the regular payment period) (i.e. 20 years × 12 = 240 *months*)

Then $$490\ 500 = R\frac{1-(1{,}00875)^{-240}}{0{,}00875} = R\frac{1-0{,}12358}{0{,}00875}$$

$$490\ 500 = R\frac{0{,}87642}{0{,}00875} = R\,(100{,}1623)$$

Solve for R $$R = 490\ 500/100{,}1623 = 4\ 897{,}05$$

Management interpretation

Mr Ncube will have to repay R4 897,05 at the end of each month for 20 years to pay off the mortgage bond on his new house.

18.7 Ordinary Annuities Due

An *ordinary annuity due* is an annuity where the series of regular payments take place at the beginning of each payment period for a fixed number of periods.

In such cases where the regular payments are made at the beginning of a payment period, instead of at the end, *an extra period's interest is earned or paid.*

Formulae for finding the *future value*, F_v, and *present value*, P_v, of an ordinary annuity due are similar to those for the ordinary annuity certain cases, but modified to take into account the extra period's interest that is earned or is owing.

Future value of an ordinary annuity due

Thus the *future value*, F_v, for an *ordinary annuity due* is given as:

$$F_v = R\frac{[(1+i)^n - 1](1+i)}{i}$$

The additional term in the *future value* formula is $(1 + i)$ which accounts for the extra period's interest earned or due.

Present value of an ordinary annuity due

Similary, the *present value*, P_v, for an ordinary annuity due is given as:

$$P_v = R\frac{[1-(1+i)^{-n}](1+i)}{i}$$

Again, the additional term in the *present value* formula is $(1 + i)$ which accounts for the extra period's interest earned or due.

Also, prior to performing ordinary annuity due calculations, it must be established whether the problem involves *future values* or *present values* as this determines the choice of the appropriate formula.

Example 18.17 Education Savings Plan (Monthly Compound Interest)

(Example 18.13 modified)

A father decides to invest R650 at the *beginning* of each month for five years at 9% p.a. compounded monthly to pay for his son's tertiary education in five years' time.

Management question

What amount of money will be available at the end of five years?

Solution

Since each payment takes place at the *beginning* of every month, this is an *ordinary annuity due.*

Required to find: the *future value*, F_v, of an ordinary annuity due.

Given			
	R =	650	(regular monthly instalment)
	i =	0,0075	(interest compounded *monthly*, i.e. 0,09/12 = 0,0075)
	n =	60 months	(to coincide with the regular payment period)
			(i.e. 5 years × 12 = 60 *months*)

Using the *future value* formula above for an ordinary annuity due:

Then $$F_v = 650\,\frac{[(1{,}0075)^{60} - 1](1 + 0{,}0075)}{0{,}0075} = 650\,\frac{(0{,}565681)(1{,}0075)}{0{,}0075}$$

$$= 650\,(75{,}98982)$$

$$= \text{R}49\ 393{,}38$$

Management interpretation

The father will have R49 393,38 available to pay for his son's tertiary education in 5 years time.

When compared to **Example 18.13**'s *future value* (of R49 025,69) it can be seen that if the father made deposits at the *beginning* instead of at the end of each month, an additional R367,69 would have accrued to his account from the extra interest earned.

- **Using *Excel's* Future Value**

The following *function key* (f_x) in *Excel* can also be used to compute the *future value* of both an *ordinary annuity certain* and an *ordinary annuity due.*

=FV(rate, nper, pmt, pv, type)

Where *rate* = interest rate for the compounding period
nper = total number of payment periods
pmt = the payment made each period
pv = present value at the beginning of the investment (omit or set *pv* = 0)
type = represents the timing of the regular payments
– if type = 1, payments are made at the *beginning* of each period (i.e. an ordinary annuity due calculation)
– if type = 0, payments are made at the *end* of each period (i.e. an ordinary annuity certain calculation)

Example 18.18

Repeat (a) Example 18.13 and (b) Example 18.17 using Using ***Excel.***

(a) Example 18.13 data.
Using *Excel* to find the F_v of an Ordinary Annuity Certain
=FV(0.0075,60,650,0,0) gives a future value result of R49 025,69.

Interpretation

Based on payments of R650 at the *end* of each month, the father will have R49 025,69 available to pay for his son's tertiary education in five years time.

Interpretation

(b) Example 18.17 data.
Using *Excel* to find the F_v of an Ordinary Annuity Due
=FV(0.0075,60,650,0,1) gives a future value result of R49 393,38.

Interpretation

Based on payments of R650 at the *beginning* of each month, the father will have R49 393,38 available to pay for his son's tertiary education in five years time.

Example 18.19 Retirement Annuity (Quarterly Compound Interest)

Mrs Bosman has won R75 000 in a competition. She decides to invest it in a retirement annuity which will pay her a regular income *quarterly in advance* at 12% p.a. compounded quarterly for 10 years. She will receive her first income cheque the moment she pays her winnings of R75 000 to the Investment Company.

Management question

How much will Mrs Bosman receive quarterly in advance for the next 10 years?

Solution

Since the income is received *quarterly in advance*, this retirement annuity is an *ordinary annuity due*.

Also, since an initial lump sum is paid over, this refers to a *present value* amount, hence the *present value formula* for an ordinary annuity due must be used.

Required to find: the *regular quarterly income*, R, from the retirement annuity.

Given		
	P_v = 75 000	(the initial investment)
	i = 0,03	(interest compounded *quarterly*) (i.e. 0,12/4 = 0,03 per *quarter*)
	n = 40 quarters	(to coincide with the regular quarterly payment period)

Using the *present value* formula, solve for R:

$$75\,000 = R\,\frac{[1-(1+0{,}03)^{-40}](1+0{,}03)}{0{,}03}$$

$$75\,000 = R\,(23{,}80822)$$

Then
$$R = 75\,000/23{,}80822$$
$$R = 3\,150{,}17$$

Interpretation

Mrs Bosman will receive R3 150,17 each *quarter in advance* for 10 years from her retirement annuity.

- **Using *Excel's* Present Value**

The following *function key* (f_x) in *Excel* can also be used to compute the *present value* of both an *ordinary annuity certain* and an *ordinary annuity due*.

=PV(rate, nper, pmt, fv, type)

Where *rate* = interest rate for the compounding period
nper = total number of payment periods
pmt = the payment made/income received each period
fv = future value at the end of the investment (omit or set *fv* = 0)
type = represents the timing of the regular payments
– if type = 1, payments are made at the *beginning* of each period (i.e. an ordinary annuity due calculation)
– if type = 0, payments are made at the *end* of each period (i.e. an ordinary annuity certain calculation)

Example 18.20

Based on Example 18.15 – Using *Excel.*

(a) Example 18.15 data.
Using *Excel* to find the P_v of an Ordinary Annuity Certain.

Solution

=PV(0.0075,120,5000,0,0) gives a *present value* result of R394 708,46.

Management interpretation

To receive a monthly income of R5 000 over 10 years at the *end* of every month, based on a retirement investment at 9% p.a. compounded monthly, Mr Peterson needs to invest an amount of R394 708,46 today.

(b) Example 18.15 data.
Using *Excel* to find the P_v of an Ordinary Annuity Due.

Solution

=PV(0.0075,120,5000,0,1) gives a *present value* result of R397 668,78.

Management interpretation

To receive a monthly income of R5 000 over 10 years at the *beginning* of every month, based on a retirement investment at 9% p.a. compounded monthly, Mr Peterson needs to invest an amount of R397 668,78 today.

Note: A larger initial investment is necessary for an ordinary annuity due because the payments occur sooner (at the *beginning* of a month) and therefore less interest is earned over the duration of the retirement annuity.

18.8 Deferred Annuities

A *deferred annuity* is an annuity of which the *first payment* of the series of regular payments will be made at *some future date*, rather than immediately.

Deferred annuity calculations involve finding either:

- the *present value*, P_v, of the deferred annuity, or
- the *regular payments*, R, made after the period of deferment.

Both values can be found from the same *deferred annuity formula* which is:

$$P_v = R\left(\frac{1-(1+i)^{-(m+n)}}{i} - \frac{1-(1+i)^{-m}}{i}\right)$$

Where
m = number of deferred periods
n = number of payments
i = interest rate per period
R = regular payment amount per period
P_v = present value of the deferred annuity

The *rationale* of the formula is based on two principles:

(i) that an initial lump sum (present value) deposited in an investment account, for example, attracts *compound interest* for the duration of the *deferred period.*

(ii) This compounded future value, F_v, at the end of the deferred period, becomes the new present value, P_v, which is then paid out in regular instalments as an ordinary annuity certain. The ordinary annuity certain formula for present value is used to find these regular payment amounts, R.

Example 18.21 Pension Fund (Deferred Payment)

A R250 000 pension fund is set up for Agnus Mbeki for when she retires after 3 more years of service. The money in the fund must be paid out in 5 *equal annual* instalments to Agnus starting on her retirement date (i.e. she will receive the first instalment on her retirement).

Management question

How much will Agnus receive from each instalment where interest is compounded annually at 8% p.a.?

Solution

Required to find: the *regular payment amount*, R.

Note: Since the first payment only takes place at the end of year 3, the annuity is deferred for 2 years. Payment begins at the end of year 3.

Given
P_v = 250 000 (the initial lump sum)
i = 0,08 (the interest rate p.a.)
m = 2 (the deferred number of periods)
n = 5 (the number of payment periods)

Use the above deferred annuity formula to find the *regular payment amount*, R:

$$250\,000 = R\left[\frac{(1-(1+0{,}08)^{-(2+5)})}{0{,}08} - \frac{(1-(1+0{,}08)^{-2})}{0{,}08}\right]$$

$$250\,000 = R\,[5{,}20637 - 1{,}783265]$$

$$250\,000 = R\,[3{,}423105]$$

Now solve for R $R = 250\,000/3{,}423105$
$R = 73\,033{,}11$

Management interpretation

Agnus Mbeki will receive R73 033,11 at the end of year 3 from now and each year thereafter for another 4 years.

Example 18.22 Education Trust Fund (Deferred Payment)

How much must be deposited in an Education Trust fund today for a schoolgirl such that she will receive R25 000 in 4 years' time and an equal amount for another 4 years thereafter? Assume that interest is compounded annually at the rate of 10 % p.a.

Solution

Required to find: the *present value*, P_v, of the Education Trust fund.

Note: The annuity formula applies from the beginning of year 4, hence the annuity is deferred for 3 years.

Given		
	$R = 25\,000$	(the regular annual payment)
	$i = 0{,}10$	(the interest rate p.a.)
	$m = 3$	(the deferred number of periods)
	$n = 5$	(the number of payment periods)
		(at the end of year 4 and 4 further payments = 5)

Use the above deferred annuity formula to find the *present value* of the deferred annuity, P_v:

$$P_v = 25\,000\left[\frac{(1-(1+0{,}10)^{-(3+5)})}{0{,}10} - \frac{(1-(1+0{,}10)^{-3})}{0{,}10}\right]$$

$$P_v = 25\,000\,[5{,}334926 - 2{,}486852]$$
$$P_v = 25\,000\,[2{,}848074]$$
$$P_v = 71\,201{,}86$$

Management interpretation

The Education trust fund must be set up with an initial investment of R71 201,86 in order to pay a schoolgirl R25 000 for 5 years, starting in 3 years' time.

18.9 Application: The Net Present Value method

To evaluate the profitability of investment decisions for projects, the *time value* of money must be taken into account. This requires that all cash inflows (incomes) and cash outflows (payments) over time must be expressed in *present value* terms to allow for comparisons. This process is called discounted cash flow (DCF) analysis.

The Net Present Value method (NPV) is one DCF approach and is used to assess the profitability of different project alternatives each with their own cash inflows and outflows over time.

The **NPV** of a project is the difference between the present value of all cash inflows and the present value of all cash outflows over the duration of the project.

i.e. NPV = PV (cash inflows) – PV (cash outflows)

The ***decision rule*** for the NPV method of evaluation investment projects is as follows:

1. If NPV > 0, then a project is financially *viable* (profitable). This means that the PV of the cash inflows exceeds the PV of the cash outflows.
2. If NPV = 0, then a project will *break even*. Here the PV of the cash inflows equals the PV of the cash outflows.
3. If NPV < 0, then a project is financially *non-viable* (unprofitable). This means that the PV of the cash inflows is less than the PV of the cash outflows.

To apply the NPV method for project evaluation, a *cost of capital* must be assumed. The cost of capital is the *discount rate* that would be applied to each cash inflow and outflow over time. It represents the '*interest rate*' that the company could earn on the money if it were invested in a savings account.

Example 18.23 New Machinery Evaluation (NPV Approach)

A manufacturing company wants to purchase a new metal stamping machine. Two options are available, machine A and machine B. The expected cash inflow from each machine over 5 years is shown in **Table 18.2**. Machines are scrapped after 5 years. Machine A will cost R228 000 and machine B will cost R344 000 to purchase. Assume a cost of capital of 10% p.a.

Table 18.2 Expected Cash Inflows for each Machine over 5 years

Projected Cash Inflows from Machine Outputs		
Year	**Machine A**	**Machine B**
1	65 000	80 000
2	65 000	80 000
3	65 000	80 000
4	65 000	80 000
5	65 000	80 000
Total	325 000	400 000

Management question

Which machine would be more profitable to purchase?

Solution

The *present value formula* for *compound interest calculations* is used to *discount* each machine's projected cash flow amount to the present period.

To *illustrate*, for machine A:

- the present value of year 1's cash flow is $\frac{65\ 000}{(1{,}01)^1}$ = R59 091
- the present value of year 3's cash flow is $\frac{65\ 000}{(1{,}01)^3}$ = R48 835
- the present value of year 5's cash flow is $\frac{65\ 000}{(1{,}01)^5}$ = R40 360

The present value calculation for all projected cash inflows (incomes) for both machines is shown in Table 18.3.

Table 18.3 Summary of PVs for each machine's cash inflows

Year	Machine A		Machine B	
	Projected Cash Flows	Present Value	Projected Cash Flows	Present Value
1	65 000	59 091	80 000	72 727
2	65 000	53 719	80 000	66 116
3	65 000	48 835	80 000	60 105
4	65 000	44 396	80 000	54 641
5	65 000	40 360	80 000	49 674
Total revenue	**325 000**	**246 401**	**400 000**	**303 263**
	Machine Cost	**228 000**		**344 000**

Based on Table 18.3, the *Net Present Values* (NPV) for each machine are:
Machine A: NPV = R246 401 – R228 000 = R18 401
Machine B: NPV = R303 263 – R344 000 = –R40 737

Management interpretation

Since the NPV for machine A is positive (R18 401) while the NPV for machine B is negative (–R40 737), the management of production company must purchase machine A. If they purchased machine B, they would incur a loss over the 5-year life of the machine.

18.10 Summary

This chapter dealt with two major areas of financial calculations, namely *interest* calculations and *annuity* calculations. A distinction was drawn between the two types of interest calculations, namely *simple interest and compound interest.* Calculations for each interest type require finding one of four values, namely the *present value*, the *future value*, the *rate of interest* or the *term* of an investment or loan. In compound interest calculations, it was emphasised that the interest rate and term must coincide with the conversion (or compounding) period.

This chapter divided *annuities* into *ordinary annuities* where payments begin immediately, and *deferred annuities* where payments commence only after an initial period of deferment. Ordinary annuities are further divided into two types: *ordinary annuities certain* and *ordinary annuities due.* They differ according to the commencement of payments within the first period: the former (ordinary annuities certain) commences payments at the end of the first period, while the latter (ordinary annuities due) starts payments at the beginning of the first period. Ordinary annuity calculations require finding one of three values, namely the *present value* of an annuity, the *future value* of an annuity or the *regular payments. Excel* offers the functions, PV and FV to compute the present value and future values, respectively, of ordinary annuities.

The *net present value* (NPV) method of project evaluations was illustrated as an application of *compound interest* calculation. This approach is extensively used in practice to determine the financial profitability of alternative investment proposals.

Exercises

18.1 An investor deposits R15 000 into a fixed deposit account which pays 8% p.a. The investment is for 5 years.

(i) What is the maturity value of the deposit if simple interest is paid?

(ii) What is the maturity value of the deposit if interest is compounded annually?

(iii) What is the maturity value of the deposit if interest is compounded half-yearly?

18.2 A young couple decide to save to buy a car in 2 year's time. They will invest a fixed sum into a two-year fixed deposit savings account which pays interest at 12% p.a. How much would they need to invest today to have R150 000 at the end of the 2 year's period if

(i) interest is paid annually?

(ii) interest is paid half-yearly?

(iii) interest is paid monthly?

18.3 How long will it take a sum of money to treble itself

(i) at 16% p.a. simple interest?

(ii) at 16% p.a. compound interest, with interest paid annually?

(iii) at 16% p.a. compounded quarterly?

18.4 What amount of money must be invested now so as to accumulate to R10 525 in 30 month's time at:

(i) 14% per annum simple interest?

(ii) 14% per annum interest, compounded annually?

18.5 An investment account is advertised as offering an interest rate of 15% p.a. compounded monthly.

(i) Find the effective interest rate per annum.

(ii) Use the *Excel* function **EFFECT** to find the effective rate.

18.6 The interest rate for an investment is 9% per annum compounded quarterly.

(i) What is the effective interest rate per annum?

(ii) Use the *Excel* function **EFFECT** to find the effective rate.

18.7 An amount of R25 000 is invested at an interest rate of 11% per annum compounded half-yearly for n years. Find the value of n if at the end of this period the investment has accumulated to R58 890.

18.8 R2 000 is invested at 10% per annum compounded half-yearly. After 3 months, the interest rate changes to 12% per annum compounded monthly. Find the value of the investment after 2 years.

18.9 An investment of R7 500 grows to an amount of R10 200 where interest is compounded quarterly over 3 years. What is the annual rate of interest?

18.10 Find the interest rate required for an investment of R5 000 to grow to R8 000 in 4 years if interest is compounded monthly.

18.11 How much must an investor deposit today to withdraw R25 000 after 2 years and 9 months from an investment which pays interest at 9% p.a. compounded quarterly.

18.12 If R21 353,40 is invested at 12% p.a. compounded annually, how long will it take for the capital plus the interest to amount to R30 000?

18.13 If an invested amount is to double in 7 years, find the nominal interest rate at which it must be invested if interest is compounded quarterly.

18.14 A monthly deposit of R1 600 is made at the end of each month into an account at an interest rate of 12% p.a. compounded monthly.

(i) How much is in the account immediately after the fifteenth monthly deposit of R1 600?

(ii) Use the appropriate Excel function (**FV** or **PV**) to compute (i).

(iii) Re-compute (i) and (ii) assuming that the monthly deposit takes place at the beginning of each month.
Note: the final deposit will take place at the beginning of month 15.

18.15 When a sum of money is invested for a period of 9 years with an interest rate of 7% per annum, the difference between the interest earned if calculated using the compound interest method (compounded annually) and the simple interest method is R334,16. What was the capital sum of the money invested?

18.16 A nurse wants to buy a new small car in three year's time. The car she wants to buy currently costs R80 000 but is expected to escalate at a compound rate of 4% per annum. The nurse can invest money at 9% p.a. compounded monthly.

(i) How much would she need to invest at the *end* of each month to purchase the car after 3 years?

(ii) How much would she need to invest at the *beginning* of each month to purchase the car after 3 years?

18.17 A debt of R8 500 is to be settled in equal monthly installments over 3 years beginning at the end of the first month. Interest of 18% p.a. compounded monthly is paid on the debt.

(i) How much must be paid each month to settle the debt?

(ii) How much interest was paid over the period of the debt? What percentage of the original debt does this represent?

18.18 On reaching the age of 60, an employee of Tramcor (Pty) Ltd. has the option of receiving a pension of R8 750 per month for 5 years, payable at the end of each month or taking an equivalent lump sum gratuity on retirement. If an employee who will retire soon decides to take the gratuity, how much will she receive? Assume interest is compounded monthly at 10% p.a.

18.19 Mrs Mabula pays a quarterly premium *in advance* of R750 on an endowment policy with Sun Life Insurance. The term of the policy is 15 years.

(i) How much would she receive on maturity, assuming an interest rate of 14,5% p.a. compounded quarterly?

(ii) Use an appropriate *Excel* function (**PV** or **FV**) to compute (i).

18.20 To save for the future education of their child, a couple are saving R540 at the *end* of every month which they invest in a savings account which carries interest of 12% p.a., compounded monthly. After 24 deposits they increase the payments to R750 at the end of every month.

How much money will be available at the end of nine years from the day they first started to save? (Assume that no withdrawals were made.)

18.21 An investment analyst has told you that it is better to invest R1 000 at the end of every month for one year in a scheme which pays interest of 8,5% p.a. compounded monthly than to invest R3 000 at the end of every quarter in a scheme paying 10% p.a. compounded quarterly over the same period of time.

(i) Would you take his advice and how would you justify your decision?

(ii) Use the appropriate *Excel* function (**PV** or **FV**) to answer question (i).

(iii) If each investment took place at the *beginning* of each month, would the advice still be valid? Justify using the appropriate *Excel* function (**PV** or **FV**). Explain your answer.

18.22 An advertisement for a new 1 600 cc motor vehicle offers the following deal: a deposit of R20 000 and 48 monthly payments in arrears (i.e. at the end of each month) of R2 200 at an interest rate of "prime plus 1%" p.a. compounded monthly. The prime interest rate is currently 8% p.a. The rate of interest will be fixed for the duration of the purchase contract.

(i) Calculate the purchase price of the motor vehicle.

(ii) Use an appropriate Excel function (**PV** or **FV**) to compute (i).

18.23 A couple, who are both working, each invest R500 at the end of each month in a joint savings account which carries interest of 8% p.a. compounded monthly. After two years the interest rate rises to 10% p.a. compounded monthly and the couple continue to pay into the account for a further year.

(i) How much money will be in the account at the end of this period? Assume that no withdrawals were made.

(ii) Use an appropriate *Excel* function (**PV** or **FV**) to compute (i).

18.24 (i) Find the amount in an account after 12 monthly payments of R200 have been made if R300 was withdrawn from the account after 5 months (i.e. at the time of the 5th R200 payment) and again after 10 months (i.e. at the time of the 10th R200 payment). Interest is calculated at 12% p.a. compounded monthly.

(ii) Use an appropriate *Excel* function to assist in the calculation of the amount at the end of the 12-month period.

18.25 A student loan of R26 000 is to be repaid by 12 equal quarterly instalments at an interest rate of 14% p.a. compounded quarterly.

(i) What is the amount of each instalment if each instalment is only paid at the *end* of each quarter?

(ii) What is the amount of each instalment if each instalment must be paid at the *beginning* of each quarter?

(iii) If a student is free to select whether repayments occur at the beginning or at the end of each quarter, which option should be chosen? Why? (Assume funds are available for either option.)

18.26 A business person borrows R30 000 to start a laundry business. The loan must be repaid by 24 equal monthly repayments. The terms of the loan is that the repayments are due only at the end of each month and that the first repayment is due only after 3 years when the business is assumed to be established.

What is the amount of each repayment, assuming an interest rate of 16% p.a. compounded monthly.

18.27 If an investment of R18 000 has grown to R40 697,70 over 5 years where interest is compounded half yearly, what is the nominal rate of interest per annum on the investment?

18.28 A house owner decides to save to build an extension to her house. She plans to save R2 000 at the end of each month and place it into an investment account which pays a fixed interest rate of 12% p.a. compounded monthly.

How long will it take the house owner to save R103 757,98?

18.29 X18.29 – investment options

An investor has R60 000 to invest. He has an option of buying a share in an established long-haul trucking business which transports goods up the West Coast. Alternatively, he can invest his funds into a newly launched laundry business.

Assume a cost of capital of 12% p.a.

The projected cash flows for the next five years are as follows:

	INVESTMENT OPTIONS	
	Trucking	**Laundry**
Initial investment (R)	60 000	60 000
Annual Cash Flow (R)		
year 1	32 000	0
year 2	38 500	7 500
year 3	26 000	45 000
year 4	13 000	37 500
year 5	9 500	55 500

Based on the projected cash-flow values for each investment option, which option should the investor choose? Use the NPV method.

Appendices

APPENDIX 1 – LIST OF STATISTICAL TABLES

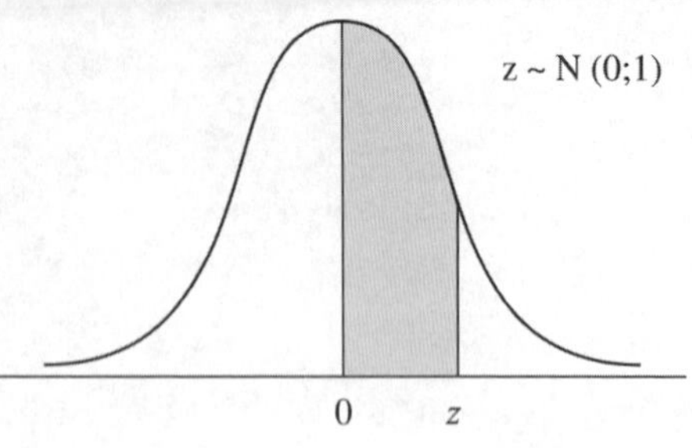

TABLE 1
The standard normal distribution (z)

This table gives the area under the standard normal curve between 0 and z, i.e. $P[0 < Z < z]$

Z	0.00	0.01	0.02	0.03	0.04	0.05	0.06	0.07	0.08	0.09
0.0	0.0000	0.0040	0.0080	0.0120	0.0160	0.0199	0.0239	0.0279	0.0319	0.0359
0.1	0.0398	0.0438	0.0478	0.0517	0.0557	0.0596	0.0636	0.0675	0.0714	0.0753
0.2	0.0793	0.0832	0.0871	0.0910	0.0948	0.0987	0.1026	0.1064	0.1103	0.1141
0.3	0.1179	0.1217	0.1255	0.1293	0.1331	0.1368	0.1406	0.1443	0.1480	0.1517
0.4	0.1554	0.1591	0.1628	0.1664	0.1700	0.1736	0.1772	0.1808	0.1844	0.1879
0.5	0.1915	0.1950	0.1985	0.2019	0.2054	0.2088	0.2123	0.2157	0.2190	0.2224
0.6	0.2257	0.2291	0.2324	0.2357	0.2389	0.2422	0.2454	0.2486	0.2517	0.2549
0.7	0.2580	0.2611	0.2642	0.2673	0.2703	0.2734	0.2764	0.2793	0.2823	0.2852
0.8	0.2881	0.2910	0.2939	0.2967	0.2995	0.3023	0.3051	0.3078	0.3106	0.3133
0.9	0.3159	0.3186	0.3212	0.3238	0.3264	0.3289	0.3315	0.3340	0.3365	0.3389
1.0	0.3413	0.3438	0.3461	0.3485	0.3508	0.3531	0.3554	0.3557	0.3599	0.3621
1.1	0.3643	0.3665	0.3686	0.3708	0.3729	0.3749	0.3770	0.3790	0.3810	0.3830
1.2	0.3849	0.3869	0.3888	0.3907	0.3925	0.3944	0.3962	0.3980	0.3997	0.4015
1.3	0.4032	0.4049	0.4066	0.4082	0.4099	0.4115	0.4131	0.4147	0.4162	0.4177
1.4	0.4192	0.4207	0.4222	0.4236	0.4251	0.4265	0.4279	0.4292	0.4306	0.4319
1.5	0.4332	0.4345	0.4357	0.4370	0.4382	0.4394	0.4406	0.4418	0.4429	0.4441
1.6	0.4452	0.4463	0.4474	0.4484	0.4495	0.4505	0.4515	0.4525	0.4535	0.4545
1.7	0.4554	0.4564	0.4573	0.4582	0.4591	0.4599	0.4608	0.4616	0.4625	0.4633
1.8	0.4641	0.4649	0.4656	0.4664	0.4671	0.4678	0.4686	0.4693	0.4699	0.4706
1.9	0.4713	0.4719	0.4726	0.4732	0.4738	0.4744	0.4750	0.4756	0.4761	0.4767
2.0	0.4772	0.4778	0.4783	0.4788	0.4793	0.4798	0.4803	0.4808	0.4812	0.4817
2.1	0.4821	0.4826	0.4830	0.4834	0.4838	0.4842	0.4846	0.4850	0.4854	0.4857
2.2	0.4861	0.4864	0.4868	0.4871	0.4875	0.4878	0.4881	0.4884	0.4887	0.4890
2.3	0.48928	0.48956	0.48983	0.49010	0.49036	0.49061	0.49086	0.49111	0.49134	0.49158
2.4	0.49180	0.49202	0.49224	0.49245	0.49266	0.49286	0.49305	0.49324	0.49343	0.49361
2.5	0.49379	0.49396	0.49413	0.49430	0.49446	0.49461	0.49477	0.49492	0.49506	0.49520
2.6	0.49534	0.49547	0.49560	0.49573	0.49585	0.49598	0.49609	0.49621	0.49632	0.49643
2.7	0.49653	0.49664	0.49674	0.49683	0.49693	0.49702	0.49711	0.49720	0.49728	0.49736
2.8	0.49744	0.49752	0.49760	0.49767	0.49774	0.49781	0.49788	0.49795	0.49801	0.49807
2.9	0.49813	0.49819	0.49825	0.49831	0.49836	0.49841	0.49846	0.49851	0.49856	0.49861
3.0	0.49865	0.49869	0.49874	0.49878	0.49882	0.49886	0.49889	0.49893	0.49897	0.49900
3.1	0.49903	0.49906	0.49910	0.49913	0.49916	0.49918	0.49921	0.49924	0.49926	0.49929
3.2	0.49931	0.49934	0.49936	0.49938	0.49940	0.49942	0.49944	0.49946	0.49948	0.49950
3.3	0.49952	0.49953	0.49955	0.49957	0.49958	0.49960	0.49961	0.49962	0.49964	0.49965
3.4	0.49966	0.49968	0.49969	0.49970	0.49971	0.49972	0.49973	0.49974	0.49975	0.49976
3.5	0.49977	0.49978	0.49978	0.49979	0.49980	0.49981	0.49981	0.49982	0.49983	0.49983
3.6	0.49984	0.49985	0.49985	0.49986	0.49986	0.49987	0.49987	0.49988	0.49988	0.49989
3.7	0.49989	0.49990	0.49990	0.49990	0.49991	0.49991	0.49991	0.49992	0.49992	0.49992
3.8	0.49993	0.49993	0.49993	0.49994	0.49994	0.49994	0.49994	0.49995	0.49995	0.49995
3.9	0.49995	0.49995	0.49996	0.49996	0.49996	0.49996	0.49996	0.49996	0.49997	0.49997
4.0	0.49997	0.49997	0.49997	0.49997	0.49997	0.49997	0.49998	0.49998	0.49998	0.49998

TABLE 2
The *t* distribution

This table gives the value of $t_{(n)(\alpha)}$ where n is the degrees of freedom i.e. [shaded area] = $P[t \geq t_{(n)(\alpha)}]$

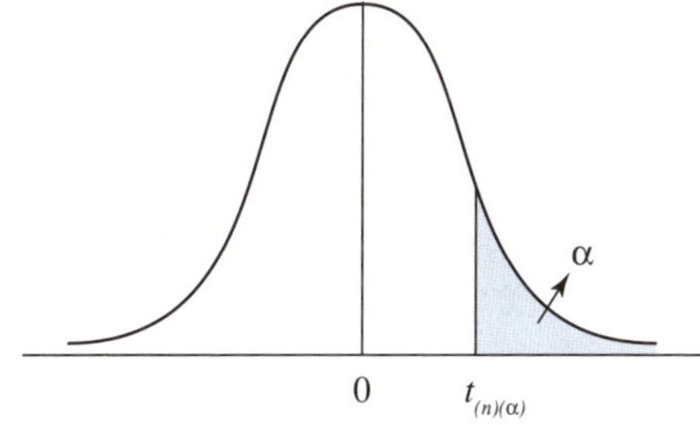

α / df	0.100	0.050	0.025	0.010	0.005	0.0025
1	3.078	6.314	12.706	31.821	63.657	127.322
2	1.886	2.920	4.303	6.965	9.925	14.089
3	1.638	2.353	3.182	4.541	5.841	7.453
4	1.533	2.132	2.776	3.747	4.604	5.598
5	1.476	2.015	2.571	3.365	4.032	4.773
6	1.440	1.943	2.447	3.143	3.707	4.317
7	1.415	1.895	2.365	2.998	3.499	4.029
8	1.397	1.860	2.306	2.896	3.355	3.833
9	1.383	1.833	2.262	2.821	3.250	3.690
10	1.372	1.812	2.228	2.764	3.169	3.581
11	1.363	1.796	2.201	2.718	3.106	3.497
12	1.356	1.782	2.179	2.681	3.055	3.428
13	1.350	1.771	2.160	2.650	3.012	3.372
14	1.345	1.761	2.145	2.624	2.977	3.326
15	1.341	1.753	2.131	2.602	2.947	3.286
16	1.337	1.746	2.120	2.583	2.921	3.252
17	1.333	1.740	2.110	2.567	2.898	3.222
18	1.330	1.734	2.101	2.552	2.878	3.197
19	1.328	1.729	2.093	2.539	2.861	3.174
20	1.325	1.725	2.086	2.528	2.845	3.153
21	1.323	1.721	2.080	2.518	2.831	3.135
22	1.321	1.717	2.074	2.508	2.819	3.119
23	1.319	1.714	2.069	2.500	2.807	3.104
24	1.318	1.711	2.064	2.492	2.797	3.091
25	1.316	1.708	2.060	2.485	2.787	3.078
26	1.315	1.706	2.056	2.479	2.779	3.067
27	1.314	1.703	2.052	2.473	2.771	3.057
28	1.313	1.701	2.048	2.467	2.763	3.047
29	1.311	1.699	2.045	2.462	2.756	3.038
30	1.310	1.697	2.042	2.457	2.750	3.030
31	1.309	1.696	2.040	2.453	2.744	3.022
32	1.309	1.694	2.037	2.449	2.738	3.015
33	1.308	1.692	2.035	2.445	2.733	3.008
34	1.307	1.691	2.032	2.441	2.728	3.002
35	1.306	1.690	2.030	2.438	2.724	2.996
36	1.306	1.688	2.028	2.434	2.719	2.990
37	1.305	1.687	2.026	2.431	2.715	2.985
38	1.304	1.686	2.024	2.429	2.712	2.980
39	1.304	1.685	2.023	2.426	2.708	2.976
40	1.303	1.684	2.021	2.423	2.704	2.971
45	1.301	1.679	2.014	2.412	2.690	2.952
50	1.299	1.676	2.009	2.403	2.678	2.937
60	1.296	1.671	2.000	2.390	2.660	2.915
70	1.294	1.667	1.994	2.381	2.648	2.899
80	1.292	1.664	1.990	2.374	2.639	2.887
90	1.291	1.662	1.987	2.369	2.632	2.878
100	1.290	1.660	1.984	2.364	2.626	2.871
110	1.289	1.659	1.982	2.361	2.621	2.865
120	1.289	1.658	1.980	2.358	2.617	2.860
140	1.288	1.656	1.977	2.353	2.611	2.852
160	1.287	1.654	1.975	2.350	2.607	2.847
180	1.286	1.653	1.973	2.347	2.603	2.842
200	1.286	1.653	1.972	2.345	2.601	2.839
∞	1.282	1.645	1.960	2.327	2.576	2.807

TABLE 3
The Chi-squared distribution (χ^2)

This table gives the value of $\chi^2_{(n)(\alpha)}$ where n is the degrees of freedom i.e. ▒ = $P[\chi^2 > \chi^2_{(n)(\alpha)}]$

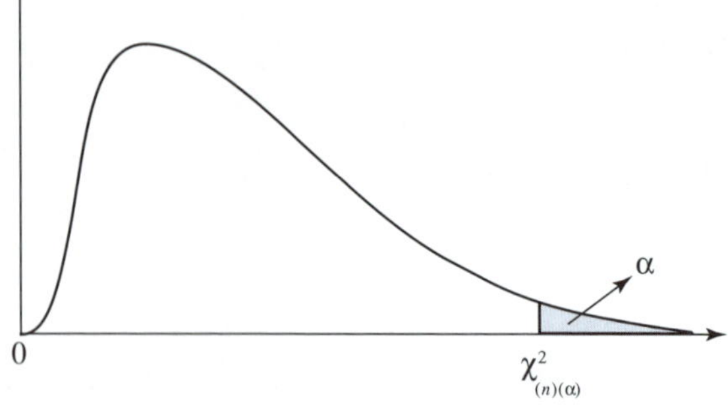

α / df	0.100	0.050	0.025	0.01	0.005	0.0025
1	2.707	3.843	5.026	6.637	7.881	9.142
2	4.605	5.991	7.378	9.210	10.597	11.983
3	6.251	7.815	9.348	11.345	12.838	14.321
4	7.779	9.488	11.143	13.277	14.860	16.424
5	9.236	11.071	12.833	15.086	16.750	18.386
6	10.645	12.592	14.449	16.812	18.548	20.249
7	12.017	14.067	16.013	18.475	20.278	22.040
8	13.362	15.507	17.535	20.090	21.955	23.774
9	14.684	16.919	19.023	21.666	23.589	25.462
10	15.987	18.307	20.483	23.209	25.188	27.112
11	17.275	19.675	21.920	24.725	26.757	28.729
12	18.549	21.026	23.337	26.217	28.300	30.318
13	19.812	22.362	24.736	27.688	29.819	31.883
14	21.064	23.685	26.119	29.141	31.319	33.426
15	22.307	24.996	27.488	30.578	32.801	34.950
16	23.542	26.296	28.845	32.000	34.267	36.456
17	24.769	27.587	30.191	33.409	35.718	37.946
18	25.989	28.869	31.526	34.805	37.156	39.422
19	27.204	30.144	32.852	36.191	38.582	40.885
20	28.412	31.410	34.170	37.566	39.997	42.336
21	29.615	32.671	35.479	38.932	41.401	43.775
22	30.813	33.924	36.781	40.289	42.796	45.204
23	32.007	35.172	38.076	41.638	44.181	46.623
24	33.196	36.415	39.364	42.980	45.558	48.034
25	34.382	37.652	40.646	44.314	46.928	49.435
26	35.563	38.885	41.923	45.642	48.290	50.829
27	36.741	40.113	43.195	46.963	49.645	52.215
28	37.916	41.337	44.461	48.278	50.993	53.594
29	39.087	42.557	45.722	49.588	52.336	54.967
30	40.256	43.773	46.979	50.892	53.672	56.332
31	44.422	44.985	48.232	52.191	55.003	57.692
32	42.585	46.194	49.480	53.486	56.328	59.046
33	43.745	47.400	50.725	54.776	57.648	60.395
34	44.903	48.602	51.966	56.061	58.964	61.738
35	46.059	49.802	53.203	57.342	60.275	63.076
36	47.212	50.998	54.437	58.619	61.581	64.410
37	48.363	52.192	55.668	59.892	62.883	65.739
38	49.513	53.384	56.896	61.162	64.181	67.063
39	50.660	54.572	58.120	62.428	65.476	68.383
40	51.805	55.758	59.342	63.691	66.766	69.699
45	57.505	61.656	65.410	69.957	73.166	76.233
50	63.167	67.505	71.420	76.154	79.490	82.664
60	74.399	79.087	83.305	88.386	91.957	95.357
70	85.529	90.537	95.031	100.432	104.222	107.812
80	96.581	101.885	106.636	112.336	116.329	120.107
90	107.568	113.151	118.144	124.125	128.307	132.262
100	118.501	124.348	129.570	135.815	140.178	144.300
110	129.388	135.487	140.925	147.423	151.958	156.238
120	146.571	152.222	157.389	163.678	168.122	172.351
140	168.618	174.659	180.174	186.875	191.604	196.099
160	190.522	196.926	202.766	209.852	214.845	219.588
180	212.310	219.056	225.200	232.647	237.890	242.866

TABLE 4(a)
F distribution (α = 0.05)

The entries in this table are critical values of F for which the area under the curve to the right is equal to 0.05.

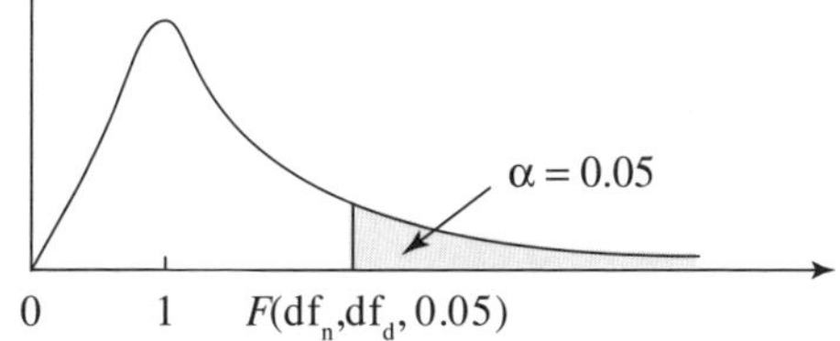

Degrees of Freedom for Denominator (rows) / Degrees of Freedom for Numerator (columns)

	1	2	3	4	5	6	7	8	9	10
1	161.4	199.5	215.7	224.6	230.2	234	236.8	238.9	240.5	241.9
2	18.5	19.0	19.2	19.2	19.3	19.3	19.4	19.4	19.4	19.4
3	10.1	9.55	9.28	9.12	9.01	8.94	8.89	8.85	8.81	8.79
4	7.71	6.94	6.59	6.39	6.26	6.16	6.09	6.04	6.00	5.96
5	6.61	5.79	5.41	5.19	5.05	4.95	4.88	4.82	4.77	4.74
6	5.99	5.14	4.76	4.53	4.39	4.28	4.21	4.15	4.10	4.06
7	5.59	4.74	4.35	4.12	3.97	3.87	3.79	3.73	3.68	3.64
8	5.32	4.46	4.07	3.84	3.69	3.58	3.50	3.44	3.39	3.35
9	5.12	4.26	3.86	3.63	3.48	3.37	3.29	3.23	3.18	3.14
10	4.96	4.10	3.71	3.48	3.33	3.22	3.14	3.07	3.02	2.98
11	4.84	3.98	3.59	3.36	3.20	3.09	3.01	2.95	2.90	2.85
12	4.75	3.89	3.49	3.26	3.11	3.00	2.91	2.85	2.80	2.75
13	4.67	3.81	3.41	3.18	3.03	2.92	2.83	2.77	2.71	2.67
14	4.60	3.74	3.34	3.11	2.96	2.85	2.76	2.70	2.65	2.60
15	4.54	3.68	3.29	3.06	2.90	2.79	2.71	2.64	2.59	2.54
16	4.49	3.63	3.24	3.01	2.85	2.74	2.66	2.59	2.54	2.49
17	4.45	3.59	3.20	2.96	2.81	2.70	2.61	2.55	2.49	2.45
18	4.41	3.55	3.16	2.93	2.77	2.66	2.58	2.51	2.46	2.41
19	4.38	3.52	3.13	2.90	2.74	2.63	2.54	2.48	2.42	2.38
20	4.35	3.49	3.10	2.87	2.71	2.60	2.51	2.45	2.39	2.35
21	4.32	3.47	3.07	2.84	2.68	2.57	2.49	2.42	2.37	2.32
22	4.30	3.44	3.05	2.82	2.66	2.55	2.46	2.40	2.34	2.30
23	4.28	3.42	3.03	2.80	2.64	2.53	2.44	2.37	2.32	2.27
24	4.26	3.40	3.01	2.78	2.62	2.51	2.42	2.36	2.30	2.25
25	4.24	3.39	2.99	2.76	2.60	2.49	2.40	2.34	2.28	2.24
30	4.17	3.32	2.92	2.69	2.53	2.42	2.33	2.27	2.21	2.16
40	4.08	3.23	2.84	2.61	2.45	2.34	2.25	2.18	2.12	2.08
60	4.00	3.15	2.76	2.53	2.37	2.25	2.17	2.10	2.04	1.99
120	3.92	3.07	2.68	2.45	2.29	2.18	2.09	2.02	1.96	1.91
∞	3.84	3.00	2.60	2.37	2.21	2.10	2.01	1.94	1.88	1.83

TABLE 4(a) ***(continued)***

F distribution ($\alpha = 0.05$)

Degrees of Freedom for Denominator	Degrees of Freedom for Numerator								
	12	**15**	**20**	**24**	**30**	**40**	**60**	**120**	∞
1	243.9	245.9	248	249.1	250.1	251.1	252.2	253.3	254.3
2	19.4	19.4	19.4	19.5	19.5	19.5	19.5	19.5	19.5
3	8.74	8.70	8.66	8.64	8.62	8.59	8.57	8.55	8.53
4	5.91	5.86	5.80	5.77	5.75	5.72	5.69	5.66	5.63
5	4.68	4.62	4.56	4.53	4.50	4.46	4.43	4.40	4.37
6	4.00	3.94	3.87	3.84	3.81	3.77	3.74	3.70	3.67
7	3.57	3.51	3.44	3.41	3.38	3.34	3.30	3.27	3.23
8	3.28	3.22	3.15	3.12	3.08	3.04	3.01	2.97	2.93
9	3.07	3.01	2.94	2.90	2.86	2.83	2.79	2.75	2.71
10	2.91	2.85	2.77	2.74	2.70	2.66	2.62	2.58	2.54
11	2.79	2.72	2.65	2.61	2.57	2.53	2.49	2.45	2.40
12	2.69	2.62	2.54	2.51	2.47	2.43	2.38	2.34	2.30
13	2.60	2.53	2.46	2.42	2.38	2.34	2.30	2.25	2.21
14	2.53	2.46	2.39	2.35	2.31	2.27	2.22	2.18	2.13
15	2.48	2.40	2.33	2.29	2.25	2.20	2.16	2.11	2.07
16	2.42	2.35	2.28	2.24	2.19	2.15	2.11	2.06	2.01
17	2.38	2.31	2.23	2.19	2.15	2.10	2.06	2.01	1.96
18	2.34	2.27	2.19	2.15	2.11	2.06	2.02	1.97	1.92
19	2.31	2.23	2.16	2.11	2.07	2.03	1.98	1.93	1.88
20	2.28	2.20	2.12	2.08	2.04	1.99	1.95	1.90	1.84
21	2.25	2.18	2.10	2.05	2.01	1.96	1.92	1.87	1.81
22	2.23	2.15	2.07	2.03	1.98	1.94	1.89	1.84	1.78
23	2.20	2.13	2.05	2.01	1.96	1.91	1.86	1.81	1.76
24	2.18	2.11	2.03	1.98	1.94	1.89	1.84	1.79	1.73
25	2.16	2.09	2.01	1.96	1.92	1.87	1.82	1.77	1.71
30	2.09	2.01	1.93	1.89	1.84	1.79	1.74	1.68	1.62
40	2.00	1.92	1.84	1.79	1.74	1.69	1.64	1.58	1.51
60	1.92	1.84	1.75	1.70	1.65	1.59	1.53	1.47	1.39
120	1.83	1.75	1.66	1.61	1.55	1.50	1.43	1.35	1.25
∞	1.75	1.67	1.57	1.52	1.46	1.39	1.32	1.22	1.00

TABLE 4(b)
F distribution (α = 0.01)

The entries in the table are critical values of F for which the area under the curve to the right is equal to 0.01.

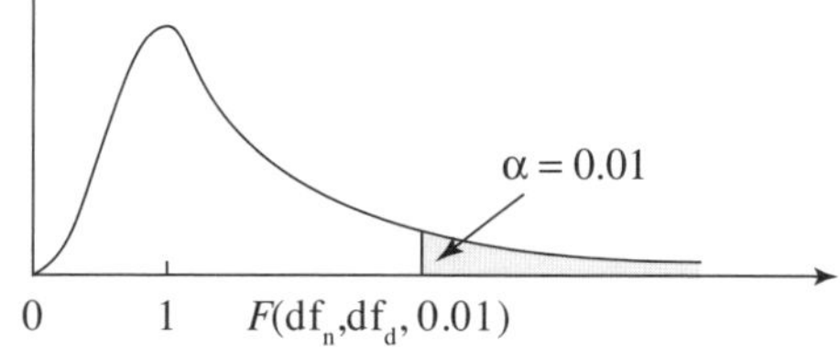

Degrees of Freedom for Numerator (columns); Degrees of Freedom for Denominator (rows)

	1	2	3	4	5	6	7	8	9	10
1	4052	4999.5	5403	5625	5764	5859	5928	5982	6022	6056
2	98.5	99.0	99.2	99.2	99.3	99.3	99.4	99.4	99.4	99.4
3	34.1	30.8	29.5	28.7	28.2	27.9	27.7	27.5	27.3	27.2
4	21.2	18.0	16.7	16.0	15.5	15.2	15.0	14.8	14.7	14.5
5	16.3	13.3	12.1	11.4	11.0	10.7	10.5	10.3	10.2	10.1
6	13.7	10.9	9.78	9.15	8.75	8.47	8.26	8.10	7.98	7.87
7	12.2	9.55	8.45	7.85	7.46	7.19	6.99	6.84	6.72	6.62
8	11.3	8.65	7.59	7.01	6.63	6.37	6.18	6.03	5.91	5.81
9	10.6	8.02	6.99	6.42	6.06	5.80	5.61	5.47	5.35	5.26
10	10.0	7.56	6.55	5.99	5.64	5.39	5.20	5.06	4.94	4.85
11	9.65	7.21	6.22	5.67	5.32	5.07	4.89	4.74	4.63	4.54
12	9.33	6.93	5.95	5.41	5.06	4.82	4.64	4.50	4.39	4.30
13	9.07	6.70	5.74	5.21	4.86	4.62	4.44	4.30	4.19	4.10
14	8.86	6.51	5.56	5.04	4.70	4.46	4.28	4.14	4.03	3.94
15	8.68	6.36	5.42	4.89	4.56	4.32	4.14	4.00	3.89	3.80
16	8.53	6.23	5.29	4.77	4.44	4.20	4.03	3.89	3.78	3.69
17	8.40	6.11	5.19	4.67	4.34	4.10	3.93	3.79	3.68	3.59
18	8.29	6.01	5.09	4.58	4.25	4.01	3.84	3.71	3.60	3.51
19	8.19	5.93	5.01	4.50	4.17	3.94	3.77	3.63	3.52	3.43
20	8.10	5.85	4.94	4.43	4.10	3.87	3.70	3.56	3.46	3.37
21	8.02	5.78	4.87	4.37	4.04	3.81	3.64	3.51	3.40	3.31
22	7.95	5.72	4.82	4.31	3.99	3.76	3.59	3.45	3.35	3.26
23	7.88	5.66	4.76	4.26	3.94	3.71	3.54	3.41	3.30	3.21
24	7.82	5.61	4.72	4.22	3.90	3.67	3.50	3.36	3.26	3.17
25	7.77	5.57	4.68	4.18	3.86	3.63	3.46	3.32	3.22	3.13
30	7.56	5.39	4.51	4.02	3.70	3.47	3.30	3.17	3.07	2.98
40	7.31	5.18	4.31	3.83	3.51	3.29	3.12	2.99	2.89	2.80
60	7.08	4.98	4.13	3.65	3.34	3.12	2.95	2.82	2.72	2.63
120	6.85	4.79	3.95	3.48	3.17	2.96	2.79	2.66	2.56	2.47
∞	6.63	4.61	3.78	3.32	3.02	2.80	2.64	2.51	2.41	2.32

TABLE 4(b) ***(continued)***
F distribution ($\alpha = 0.01$)

Degrees of Freedom for Denominator	Degrees of Freedom for Numerator								
	12	**15**	**20**	**24**	**30**	**40**	**60**	**120**	∞
1	6106	6157	6209	6235	6261	6287	6313	6339	6366
2	99.4	99.4	99.4	99.5	99.5	99.5	99.5	99.5	99.5
3	27.1	26.9	26.7	26.6	26.5	26.4	26.3	26.2	26.1
4	14.4	14.2	14.0	13.9	13.8	13.7	13.7	13.6	13.5
5	9.89	9.72	9.55	9.47	9.38	9.29	9.20	9.11	9.02
6	7.72	7.56	7.40	7.31	7.23	7.14	7.06	6.97	6.88
7	6.47	6.31	6.16	6.07	5.99	5.91	5.82	5.74	5.65
8	5.67	5.52	5.36	5.28	5.20	5.12	5.03	4.95	4.86
9	5.11	4.96	4.81	4.73	4.65	4.57	4.48	4.40	4.31
10	4.71	4.56	4.41	4.33	4.25	4.17	4.08	4.00	3.91
11	4.40	4.25	4.10	4.02	3.94	3.86	3.78	3.69	3.60
12	4.16	4.01	3.86	3.78	3.70	3.62	3.54	3.45	3.36
13	3.96	3.82	3.66	3.59	3.51	3.43	3.34	3.25	3.17
14	3.80	3.66	3.51	3.43	3.35	3.27	3.18	3.09	3.00
15	3.67	3.52	3.37	3.29	3.21	3.13	3.05	2.96	2.87
16	3.55	3.41	3.26	3.18	3.10	3.02	2.93	2.84	2.75
17	3.46	3.31	3.16	3.08	3.00	2.92	2.83	2.75	2.65
18	3.37	3.23	3.08	3.00	2.92	2.84	2.75	2.66	2.57
19	3.30	3.15	3.00	2.92	2.84	2.76	2.67	2.58	2.49
20	3.23	3.09	2.94	2.86	2.78	2.69	2.61	2.52	2.42
21	3.17	3.03	2.88	2.80	2.72	2.64	2.55	2.46	2.36
22	3.12	2.98	2.83	2.75	2.67	2.58	2.50	2.40	2.31
23	3.07	2.93	2.78	2.70	2.62	2.54	2.45	2.35	2.26
24	3.03	2.89	2.74	2.66	2.58	2.49	2.40	2.31	2.21
25	2.99	2.85	2.70	2.62	2.53	2.45	2.36	2.27	2.17
30	2.84	2.70	2.55	2.47	2.39	2.30	2.21	2.11	2.01
40	2.66	2.52	2.37	2.29	2.20	2.11	2.02	1.92	1.80
60	2.50	2.35	2.20	2.12	2.03	1.94	1.84	1.73	1.60
120	2.34	2.19	2.03	1.95	1.86	1.76	1.66	1.53	1.38
∞	2.18	2.04	1.88	1.79	1.70	1.59	1.47	1.32	1.00

APPENDIX 2 – EXERCISE ANSWERS

CHAPTER 1 Statistics in Management

1.1 Random variable: Performance appraisal system used
Population: All JSE companies
Sample: The 68 HR managers surveyed
Sampling unit: a JSE-listed company
A statistic
To allow inferential analysis to be performed with confidence in the findings.

1.2 Random variable: Female magazine readership
Population: All female magazine readers
Sample: The 2000 randomly selected female readers of magazines
Sampling unit: A female
35% – it is a sample statistic (it is derived from the sample)
Inferential statistics – the purpose is to test the belief that market share = 38%.

1.3 3 random variables: weekly sales volumes; number of ads placed; advertising media
Dependent variable – weekly sales volumes
Independent variables - number of ads placed; advertising media
Statistical model building (Aim is to predict sales volumes from frequency and type of advertising used.

1.4 Scenario 1 Inferential statistics
Scenario 2 Descriptive statistics
Scenario 3 Descriptive statistics
Scenario 4 Inferential statistics
Scenario 5 Inferential statistics
Scenario 6 Inferential statistics
Scenario 7 Inferential statistics

CHAPTER 2 Data - Types

2.1 (i) numeric, ratio-scaled, continuous {21,4 year; 34,6 years}
(ii) numeric, ratio-scaled, continuous {416,2m^2 3406,8 m^2}
(iii) categorical, ordinal-scaled, discrete {matric; diploma}
(iv) categorical, nominal-scaled, discrete {married, single}
(v) categorical, nominal-scaled, discrete {Boeing; Airbus}
(vi) categorical, nominal-scaled, discrete {verbal; emotional}
(vii) numeric, interval-scaled, discrete {41; 62}
(viii) categorical, ordinal-scaled, discrete {salary only; commission only}
(ix) (a) categorical, ordinal-scaled, discrete {1 = apple; 2 = orange}
(b) categorical, nominal-scaled, discrete {yes; no}
(c) categorical, nominal-scaled, discrete {train, car}
(d) numeric, interval-scaled, discrete {2; 5}
(x) numeric, ratio-scaled, continuous {12,4 kg; 7,234 kg}
(xi) categorical, nominal-scaled, discrete {Nescafe; Jacobs }

	(xii)	numeric, ratio-scaled, continuous	{26,44 minutes; 38,2 minutes}
	(xiii)	categorical, ordinal-scaled, discrete	{Super; Standard }
	(xiv)	numeric, ratio-scaled, continuous	{R85,47; R2315,22 }
	(xv)	numeric, ratio-scaled, discrete	{75; 23}
	(xvi)	numeric, ratio-scaled, discrete	{5; 38}
	(xvii)	numeric, ratio-scaled, continuous	{10,46 hours; 11,12 hours}
	(xviii)	numeric, interval-scaled, discrete	{2; 6}
	(xix)	numeric, ratio-scaled, discrete	{75; 238}
	(xx)	categorical, nominal-scaled, discrete	{Growth funds; Industrial funds}

2.2 (i) 11 random variables

(ii)

Economic sector	categorical, nominal-scaled, discrete	{Retail}
Head office region	categorical, nominal-scaled, discrete	{Gauteng}
Company size	numeric, ratio-scaled, discrete	{242}
Turnover	numeric, ratio-scaled, continuous	{R3 432 562}
Share price	numeric, ratio-scaled, continuous	{R18,48}
Earnings per share	numeric, ratio-scaled, continuous	{R2,16}
Dividends per share	numeric, ratio-scaled, continuous	{R0,86}
Number of shares	numeric, ratio-scaled, discrete	{12 045 622}
ROI (%)	numeric, ratio-scaled, continuous	{8,64%}
Inflation index (%)	numeric, ratio-scaled, continuous	{6,75%}
Year established	numeric, ratio-scaled, discrete	{1988}

2.3 (i) 20 random variables

(ii)

Gender	categorical, nominal-scaled, discrete	{female}
Home language	categorical, nominal-scaled, discrete	{Xhosa}
Position	categorical, ordinal-scaled, discrete	{middle}
Join	numeric, ratio-scaled, discrete	{1998}
Status	categorical, ordinal-scaled, discrete	{Gold}
Claimed	categorical, nominal-scaled, discrete	{Yes}
Problems	categorical, nominal-scaled, discrete	{Yes}
Yes problem	categorical, nominal-scaled, discrete	{on-line access difficult}
Services – airlines	numeric, interval-scaled, discrete	{2}
Services – car rentals	numeric, interval-scaled, discrete	{5}
Services – hotels	numeric, interval-scaled, discrete	{4}
Services – financial	numeric, interval-scaled, discrete	{2}
Services – telecommunications	numeric, interval-scaled, discrete	{2}
Quality – statements	numeric, interval-scaled, discrete	{2}
Quality – guide	numeric, interval-scaled, discrete	{4}
Quality – centres	numeric, interval-scaled, discrete	{5}
Quality – communication	numeric, interval-scaled, discrete	{2}
Quality – queries	numeric, interval-scaled, discrete	{3}
Quality – product	numeric, interval-scaled, discrete	{4}
Facilities	categorical, ordinal-scaled, discrete	{1 = holiday specials}

2.4 *Financial Analysis data*: mainly numeric (quantitative), ratio-scaled.
Voyager Services Quality data: mainly categorical (qualitative), and when numeric, mainly interval-scaled, discrete (rating responses).

CHAPTER 3 Using *Excel* for Statistical Analysis

Refer to the *Excel* outputs for solution values for each Exercise 3.1 to 3.9.

CHAPTER 4 Summarising Data – Pivot tables and Graphs

4.1 Bar chart
- displays data on a categorical variable;
- categories can be displayed in any order;
- width of the bars is arbitrary (but constant)

Histogram
- displays numeric data;
- intervals must be continuous (joined and in sequence)
- width of bars is determined by the interval width.

4.2 Percentage pie chart (use *Excel*)
True Love 19% Seventeen 29,2% Heat 23,6% Drum 11% You 17,2%

4.3 Percentage bar chart (use *Excel*) Heat = 23,6%

4.4 (i) and (ii) Grades: A 14 (35%) B 11 (27,5%) C 6 (15%) D 9 (22,5%)
(iii) Job grade D = 22,5% of employees

4.5 (i) and (ii)

	< R200	R200–< R250	R250–< R300	R300–< R350	R350–< R400
count	7	4	7	3	3
count (%)	23,3%	13,3%	23,3%	10%	10%
cumulative%	23,3%	36,6%	60%	73,3%	80%

	R400 –< R450	> R450
count	2	4
count (%)	6,7%	13,3%
cumulative %	86,7%	100%

(iii) (a) < R200 = 23,3% (b) < R300 = 66,6%
(c) > R400 = 20% (d) 4 buildings

4.6 (ii) Voelvlei = 26% Wemmershoek and Steenbras = 27,1%

4.7 (ii) Preferences A = 18% B = 10,4% C = 25,6% D = 15,2% E = 30,8%
Most preferred fruit drinks are E (Go Fruit) and C (Yum Yum).

4.8 Toyota = 19,4% Nissan = 12,6% VW = 17,6% Delta = 12,6% Ford =14,8% MBSA = 7,5% BMW = 10,4% MMI = 5,1%
Top 3 car manufacturers (Toyota, VW, Ford) = 51,9%

4.9 (i) Nissan, Volkswagen, MBSA, MMI
(ii) Delta showed a 34,7% increase in sales from first half to second half.

4.10 (i) Daewoo 20 (16%) LG 38 (30,4%) Philips 13 (10,4%) Sansui 30 (24%) Sony 24 (19,2%)
(iii) Philips (only 10,4% of households prefer this brand)
(iv) 30,4% of households own the LG brand.

4.11 (i) 3 = 12 (25%) 4 = 15 (31,25%) 5 = 6 (12,5) 6 = 7 (14,58%) 7 = 5 (10,42%) 8 = 3 (6,25%)
(iii) mode = 4 residential properties

4.12 Most preferred outlet = Butler's Pizza (24%)
Least preferred outlet = Ocean Basket (7,4%)

4.13 (iv) Nationwide - 20 (28,57%)
(v) Nationwide - 47,06% of tourist prefer this airline.
(vi) No, most business travelers prefer to fly with SAA (55,6%)

4.14 (i) Random variable: No. of car occupants
Data type: numeric, ratio, discrete.
(iii) (a) Travel alone – 38,3%
(b) At least 3 occupants – 36,7%
(c) No more than 2 occupants – 63,3%

4.15 (i) Random variable: Distance traveled (*km*)
Data type: numeric, ratio-scaled, continuous.
(iii) (a) Trips between 25 km and 30 km – 9 (18%)
(b) Within 25 km radius – 38 (76%)
(c) Beyond 20 km radius – 24 (48%)
(d) 55% of trips were within 21 km (use =PERCENTILE(data,0.55))
(e) 20% of trips were beyond 26 km (use =PERCENTILE(data,0.8))
(iv) Yes, only 6% of trips are beyond 30 km.

4.16 (iv) Spend between R500 and R600 per month – 7 (14%)
(vi) Spend less than R550 per month – 79% (estimated from graph)
(use =PERCENTRANK(data range,550) which gives 81,6%)
(vii) More than R500 on fuel per month – 15 (30%)

4.17 (ii) Yes – Corsa sales are showing a general upward trend.

4.18 (ii) Volkswagen shows a higher sales level, but a lower growth rate.
Toyota shows a lower sales level, but a higher growth rate.
Choice is not clearcut – suggest choosing Toyota.

4.19 (ii) Yes, there appears to be a moderately strong positive relationship.

4.20 (ii) Yes, there appears to be a moderate to strong positive relationship.

CHAPTER 5 Descriptive Statistics – Central and Non-central Location

5.1 (i) Random variable: Value of meals in a restaurant
Data type: numeric, ratio-scaled, continuous
(ii) $\bar{x}$ = R55,95
(iii) median = R53,00
(iv) mode = R44
(v) Since mean > median, outliers (a few high-valued meals) are present and therefore choose median as a representative central location measure.

5.2 (i) Days absent: $\bar{x}$ = 10,304 days median = 9 days mode = 5 days
(ii) Lower quartile Q_1 = 5,5 days
Upper quartile Q_3 = 15 days
(iii) Since mean > median, outliers (i.e. a few large number of days absent) are present. Hence choose median as a representative central location measure.
The median days absent (9 days) falls within management-prescribed 9 days.

5.3 (i) Bad debts %: $\bar{x}$ = 4,665%
(ii) median = 5,4%
(iv) mode = 2,2%. Difficult to establish its representativeness since its frequency of occurrence is unknown.
(v) Lower quartile Q_1 = 2,6%
Upper quartile Q_3 = 6,1%
(vi) Since mean < median, outliers (i.e. a few companies with low bad debts %) are present. Hence choose median as a representative central location measure. The median bad debts % exceeds 5%, thus send advisory note.

5.4 (i) Turnover (Rand/day): $\bar{x}$ = R1 390,83
(ii) median = R1 404,89
(iii) mode = R1 394,53
(iv) Lower quartile Q_1 = R1 168,18
(v) Upper quartile Q_3 = R1 653,85

5.5 (i) Grocery spend %: $\bar{x}$ = 33,4%
(ii) median = 33,125% lower quartile Q_1 = 24,64%
(iii) Upper quartile Q_3 = 41,5%

5.6 Average price per share in portfolio = R14,29

5.7 Average price of car sold last month = R34 900

5.8 Average annual increase in office rentals = 11,955%

5.9 Average annual increase in sugar price per kg = 6,4556%

5.10 (i) False (ii) False (iii) True (iv) False (v) False

5.11 Statements (iii) and (vi). The mode would be more appropriate.

5.12 Procedure (ii) only.

5.13 (i) Water usage (*kl*/month): $\bar{x}$ = 21,2 kl median = 19,5 kl
mode = 25 kl
(ii) Lower quartile Q_1 = 15 kl Upper quartile Q_3 = 25,75 kl
(iv) Total expected *monthly* usage by suburb = 15 900 kl
Total expected *annual* usage by suburb = 190 800 kl

5.14 (i) Random variable: Value (price) of a veal cordon bleu dish
Data type: numeric, ratio-scaled, continuous
(ii) $\bar{x}$ = R61,25 median price = R59
(iii) modal price = R48 Difficult to establish its representativeness since its frequency of occurrence is unknown.
(iv) Since mean > median, outliers (i.e. a few high-priced dishes) are present. Hence choose median as a representative central location measure.
(v) Upper quartile Q_3 = R68 per dish
(vi) Lower quartile Q_1 = R54,75 per dish
(vii) Lowest price paid at one of the top 10% of restaurants = R72,90
Use (=PERCENTILE(data range,0.9))
(viii) 81,4% of cordon bleu dishes will cost less than R70;
14,8% of cordon bleu dishes will cost less than R52; and
61,5% of cordon bleu dishes will cost less than R64;

5.15 (i) Random variable: Unit selling price of rose buds
Data type: numeric, ratio-scaled, continuous
(ii) $\bar{x}$ = 60,312c
(iii) median = 59,95c
(iv) Sk_p = 0,932 (evidence of moderate positive skewness). Also mean > median.
Choose median as a representative central location measure.
(v) Lower quartile Q_1 = 57,7c
(vi) Upper quartile Q_3 = 62,45c
(vii) 90th percentile selling price = 64,6c
(viii) 10th percentile selling price = 56,6c
(x) 27,9% of all transactions were at or below 58c per rose bud;
88,3% of all transactions were at or below 64c per rose bud.

CHAPTER 6 Descriptive Statistics – Dispersion and Skewness Measures

6.1 (i) Hand luggage weight (kg): $\bar{x}$ = 10,57 kg s = 1,718 kg
(iii) Coefficient of variation: CV = 16,25%
(iv) Low relative variability in hand luggage weights.

6.2 (i) Bicycles sold (units): $\bar{x}$ = 23,6 units median = 22 units
(ii) Range (R) = 21 (note: R = 20 if using *Excel*) s^2 = 43,6
s = 6,603
(iii) Q_1 = 18,25 Q_3 = 28,75
IQR = 10,5 (the range spanning the middle 50% of number of bicycles sold)
(iv) Skewness (approximately) = 0,726939 Positively skewed distribution
(vi) Opening stock next month = 23,6 + 6,6 = 30,2 (30) units.
Will meet demand.

6.3 (i) Glue setting time (minutes): $\bar{x}$ = 24 min s = 4,1833 min
(iii) Coefficient of variation: CV = 17,43%
(iv) No, relative variability is greater than 10%.

6.4 (i) Wage increases (%): $\bar{x}$ = 6,431% median = 6,25%
(ii) s^2 = 1,92096 s = 1,38599
(iii) Lower limit = 3,659% Upper limit = 9,203%
(iv) CV = 21,55% Agreed wage increases moderately consistent.

6.5 (i) CV_1 = 13,8% CV_2 = 14,6575%
(ii) Group 1 is marginally more consistent in their exam scores.

6.6 (i) Fuel bills (R): $\bar{x}$ = R418 median = R398
s^2 = 12926,05 s = 113,6928 Sk_p = 0,6013
(ii) Approx. 68,3% of fuel bills lie between R304,3 and R531,7
Approx. 95,4% of fuel bills lie between R190,6 and R645,4
Approx. 99,7% of fuel bills lie between R76,9 and R759,1
(iii) CV = 27,2% Fuel bills show moderate (not low) variability about the mean.
(iv) Q_1 = R332,5 Q_3 = R502,5 IQR = R170

(v) Min = R256 Q_1 = R332,5 Median = R398 Q_3 = R502,5
Max = R676

(viii) Average consumption per month = 69,67 litres (R418/R6).
Total monthly fuel usage = 1 741 667 litres by 25 000 motorists.

6.7 (i) Service period: $\bar{x}$ = 7 years; median = 6 years; s = 3,8376 years; Sk_p = 0,5526

(iii) Frequency table (frequencies): 21; 30; 24; 15; 8; 2

(iv) Lower limit = 3,162 Upper limit = 10,838 Approx. 68,3%.
Service periods must be normally distributed. The sample data is approximately normal with a slight positive skewness (Sk_p = 0,5526).

(v) ≤ 4 years service = 21,2% Use (=PERCENTRANK(data range,4))
> 12 years service = 14,2% Use (=1-PERCENTRANK(data range,12))

6.8 (i) Random variable: dividend yields (%) data type: numeric, ratio, continuous

(ii) Dividend yields (%): $\bar{x}$ = 4,27% median = 4,1% mode = 2,8%
s = 1,444% Sk_p = 0,259

(iv) Preferred central location measure: Mean (no evidence of significant outliers)

(v) Frequency table (frequencies): 3; 11; 16; 11; 3

(vi) Min = 1,5 Q_1 = 3,175 Median = 4,1 Q_3 = 5,15
Max = 7,6

(viii) Minimum earnings yield of top 10% of companies = 6,17%
(use (=PERCENTILE(data range,0.9))

(ix) % of companies declaring less than 3% dividend yield = 19,7%
(use (=PERCENTRANK(data range,3))

6.9 (i) Rose buds selling price: $\bar{x}$ = 60,312c ; s = 3,1875c; Sk_p = 0,93202

(ii) Coefficient of variation = 5,285%. Low relative variability about mean.

(iii) Q_1 = 57,7c Q_3 = 62,45

(iv) Skewness coefficient = 0,93202 indicates outliers to right. Rule of thumb: 62,45 + 1,5(62,45 – 57,7) = 69,575 shows outliers present. Outliers: 73,5c

(v) Rose buds selling price (edited): $\bar{x}$ = 60,179c; s = 2,9106c; Sk_p = 0,40839
Coefficient of variation = 4,837%.
Lower relative variability about mean.

(vi) Sample mean marginally reduced; lower variability; and data closer to normal distribution.

CHAPTER 7 Basic Probability Concepts

7.1 (i) Mining 45 (18%) Finance 72 (28,8%) IT 32 (12,8%)
Production 101 (40,4%)

(ii) P(Finance) = 28,8% chance

(iii) P(*not* Production) = 59,6% chance

(iv) P(either Mining or IT) = 30,8% chance

(v) (iii) Complementary rule;

(iv) Addition rule for mutually exclusive events.

7.2 (i) A 795 (53%) B 410 (27,3%) C 106 (7,1%) D 189 (12,6%)
(ii) P(Grade A) = 53% chance
(iii) P(either Grade B or Grade D) = 39,9% chance
(iv) P(Export Quality) = P(*not* either Grade C or Grade D) = 80,3% chance
(v) (iii) Addition rule for mutually exclusive events; (iv) Complementary rule.

7.3 (i) Formal Business 6 678 (53%)
Commercial Agriculture 1 492 (11,8%)
Subsistence Agriculture 653 (5,2%)
Informal Business 2 865 (22,7%)
Domestic Service 914 (7,3%)
(ii) P(Domestic Services) = 7,3% chance
(iii) P(either Commercial or Subsistence Agriculture) = 17% chance
(iv) P(Informal trader/Business sector) = 30,2% chance
(v) (iii) Addition rule for mutually exclusive events; (iv) Conditional probability.

7.4 (i) Managerial level categorical, ordinal-scaled, discrete
Qualification type categorical, ordinal-scaled, discrete
(ii) Matric + Division Head = 8 Degree + Section Head = 5
Dept Head = 48
(iii) (a) P(matric) = 38,76% chance (marginal probability)
(b) P(section head and a degree) = 3,88% chance (joint probability)
(c) P(dept head / diploma) = 48% chance (conditional probability)
(d) P(division head) = 21,7% chance (marginal probability)
(e) P(either division head or section head) = 62,79% chance (addition rule for mutually exclusive events)
(f) P(either matric or diploma or degree) = 100% chance (collectively exhaustive events and addition rule for mutually exclusive events)
(g) P(degree / dept head) = 20,83% chance (conditional probability)
(h) P(either division head or diploma or both) = 55,81% chance (addition rule for non-mutually exclusive events)
(iv) See above in (iii)
(v) Yes

7.5 (i) P(cash bonus) = 28% chance (marginal probability)
(ii) P(share option) = 32,33% chance (marginal probability)
(iii) P(production and cash bonus) = 18,7% chance (joint probability)
(iv) P(share option /admin) = 48,57% chance (conditional probability)
(v) P(production /cash bonus) = 66,67% chance (conditional probability)
(vi) P(A = share option / B = an administration) = 48,57% chance
P(A = share option) = 32,33%
Since P(A/B) ≠ P(A), the two events are statistically dependent.
(vii) See above in (i) to (v)

7.6 (i) (a) P(age <30) = 34,33% chance (marginal probability)
(b) P(a production worker) = 53,33% chance (marginal probability)

(c) P(age between 30 and 50) = 41,33% chance
(marginal probability)
(d) P(age >50 /administration) = 44,87% chance
(conditional probability)
(e) P(production or < 30 years, or both) = 67,67%
(addition rule for non-mutually exclusive events)
(ii) No, outcomes from both events can occur simultaneously.
(iii) P(A = age > 50 / B = administration) = 44,87% chance
P(A = age > 50) = 24,33% chance
Since P(A/B) ≠ P(A), the two events are statistically dependent.
(iv) See above in (i)

7.7 (i) P(Professional use) = 32,14% chance (marginal probability)
(ii) P(Nikon user) = 39,29% chance (marginal probability)
(iii) P(Pentax user / Personal use) = 34,21% chance (conditional probability)
(iv) P(A = Pentax user / B = Personal use) = 34,21% chance
P(A = Pentax user) = 32,86% chance
Since P(A/B) ≈ P(A), the two events are statistically *independent*.
(v) P(Canon user and Professional use) = 17,14% chance (joint probability)
(vi) P(either Professional or Nikon or both) = 66,07% chance
(addition rule for non-mutually exclusive events)
(vii) No, outcomes from both events can occur simultaneously i.e. P(A and B) ≠ 0
To illustrate: P(Nikon user and Personal use) = 33,93% (≠ 0)

7.8 (i) P(both A and B failing) = 0,03 (3% chance)
(ii) P(Device will *not* need to be replaced) = 1 – (0,2 + 0,15 – 0.03) = 0,68 (68%)

7.9 (i) 720 (ii) 720 (iii) 288 (iv) 35 (v) 84 (vi) 336
(vii) 20 (viii) 1 (ix) 840

7.10 ${}_{12}C_7$ = 792 different newspaper designs

7.11 ${}_5P_3$ = 60 different displays of 3 soup brands on 5 separate shelves.

7.12 (i) ${}_9C_4$ = 126 portfolios
(ii) P(one particular portfolio) = 1/126 = 0,00794 (0,794% chance)

7.13 P(replacing screws in same holes) = 1/120 = 0,00833 (0,833% chance)

7.14 (i) 120 different selections of 3 attractions from 10 attractions.
(ii) P(any 3 attractions) = 1/120 = 0,00833 (0,833% chance)

7.15 (i) 210 different committee formations
(ii) 420 different committee formations

CHAPTER 8 Probability Distributions

8.1 (i) P(r = 3 / n = 7 p = 0,2) = 0,114688 =BINOMDIST(3,7,0.2,false)

(ii) P(r = 4 / n = 10 p = 0,2) = 0,08808 =BINOMDIST(4,10,0.2,false)

(iii) P($r \leq$ 4 / n = 12 p = 0,3) = 0,723655 =BINOMDIST(4,12,0.3,true)

(iv) P(r = 2 or 3 / n = 10 p = 0,05) = 0,08511
=BINOMDIST(2,10,0.05,false) + BINOMDIST(3,10,0.05,false)

(v) P($r \geq$ 3 / n = 8 p = 0,25) = 0,321457 =1-BINOMDIST(2,8,0.25,true)

(ii) See (i) above for the function key =BINOMDIST(r,n,p,cumulative=true)

8.2 (i) Binomial distribution (only two outcomes; p = 0,2; n trials = 6 stores)

(ii) P(r = 1 / n = 6 p = 0,2) = 0,3932 =BINOMDIST(1,6,0.2,false)

(iii) P($r \leq$ 2 / n = 6 p = 0,2) = 0,9011 =BINOMDIST(2,6,0.2,true)

(iv) P(r = 0 / n = 6 p = 0,2) = 0,2621 =BINOMDIST(0,6,0.2,false)

(v) Mean = 1,2 stores out of stock

8.3 (i) P(r = 0 / n = 12 p = 0,15) = 0,1422 =BINOMDIST(0,12,0.15,false)

(ii) P($r \leq$ 2 / n = 15 p = 0,15) = 0,6042 =BINOMDIST(2,15,0.15,true)

8.4 (i) P(r = 3 / n = 10 p = 0,3) = 0,2668 =BINOMDIST(3,10,0.3,false)

(ii) P(r > 2 / n = 10 p = 0,7) = 0,9984 =1-BINOMDIST(2,10,0.7,true)

8.5 (i) P(r = 1 / n = 8 p = 0,05) = 0,2793 =BINOMDIST(1,8,0.05,false)

(ii) P($r \leq$ 2 / n = 8 p = 0,05) = 0,9942 =BINOMDIST(2,8,0.05,true)

(iii) P(r = 0 / n = 8 p = 0,05) = 0,6634 =BINOMDIST(0,8,0.05,false)

(iv) Average number = 3,2 trucks

8.6 (i) P(r = 6 / n = 6 p = 0,8) = 0,2621 =BINOMDIST(6,6,0.8,false)

(ii) P(r = 2 / n = 6 p = 0,8) + P(r = 3 / n = 6 p = 0,8) = 0,0973
=BINOMDIST(2,6,0.8,false)+BINOMDIST(3,6,0.8,false)

(iii) P($r \leq$ 2 / n = 6 p = 0,2) = 0,9011 =BINOMDIST(2,6,0.2,true)

8.7 (i) P(r = 2 / n = 12 p = 0,2) = 0,2835 =BINOMDIST(2,12,0.2,false)

(ii) P(r = 5 / n = 12 p = 0,2) = 0,0532 =BINOMDIST(5,12,0.2,false)

(iii) P($r \geq$ 6 / n = 12 p = 0,2) = 0,0194 =1-BINOMDIST(5,12,0.2,true)

8.8 (i) (a) P(r < 2 / n = 10 p = 0,1) = 0,7361 =BINOMDIST(1,10,0.1,true)

(b) P(r < 2 / n = 10 p = 0,35) = 0,0859
=BINOMDIST(1,10,0.35,true)

(ii) 182 pensioners (using p = 0,65 (non-heavy readers))

8.9 (i) P(x = 5 / a = 3) = 0,1008 =POISSON(5,3,false)

(ii) P($x \geq$ 4 / a = 3) = 0,3528 =1-POISSON(3,3,true)

(iii) P(x = 0 / a = 3) = 0,0498 =POISSON(0,3,false)

8.10 (i) $P(x \leq 2 / a = 4) = 0{,}2381$ =POISSON(2,4,true)

(ii) $P(x \geq 4 / a = 4) = 0{,}5665$ =1-POISSON(3,4,true)

8.11 (i) (a) $P(x = 1 / a = 6) = 0{,}0149$ =POISSON(1,6,false)

(b) $P(x \leq 3 / a = 6) = 0{,}1512$ =POISSON(3,6,true)

(c) $P(x \geq 3 / a = 6) = 0{,}9380$ =1-POISSON(2,6,true)

(ii) $P(x = 1 / a = 3) = 0{,}1494$ =POISSON(1,3,false)

(iii) Mean (a) = 6 orders per day; Standard deviation = 2,449 orders per day

8.12 (i) $P(x \geq 3 / a = 1{,}8) = 0{,}2694$ =1-POISSON(2,1.8,true)

(ii) $P(x < 4 / a = 1{,}8) = 0{,}8913$ =POISSON(3,1.8,true)

8.13 (i) $P(x \leq 5 / a = 7) = 0{,}3007$ =POISSON(5,7,true)

(ii) $P(x = 6 / a = 7) + P(x = 9 / a = 7) = 0{,}2504$

=POISSON(6,7,false) + POISSON(9,7,false)

(iii) $P(x > 20 / a = 14) = 0{,}0479$ =1-POISSON(20,14,true)

8.14 (i) (a) $P(0 < z < 1{,}83) = 0{,}4664$ =NORMSDIST(1.83)-0.5

(b) $P(z > -0{,}48) = 0{,}6844$ =1-NORMSDIST(–0.48)

(c) $P(-2{,}25 < z < 0) = 0{,}4878$ =0.5-NORMSDIST(–2.25)

(d) $P(1{,}22 < z) = 0{,}1112$ =1-NORMSDIST(1.22)

(e) $P(-2{,}08 < z < 0{,}63) = 0{,}7169$

=NORMSDIST(0.63)-NORMSDIST(–2.08)

(f) $P(z < -0{,}68) = 0{,}2483$ =NORMSDIST(–0.68)

(g) $P(0{,}33 < z < 1{,}5) = 0{,}3039$

=NORMSDIST(1.5)-NORMSDIST(0.33)

8.15 (i) (a) $z = 1{,}3703$ =NORMSINV(0.9147)

(b) $z = -0.08005$ =NORMSINV(1-0.5319)

(c) $z = 1{,}2901$ =NORMSINV(0.5+0.4015)

(d) $z = -2{,}05998$ =NORMSINV(0.5 – 0.4803)

(e) $z = 1{,}2901$ =NORMSINV(1 – 0.0985)

(f) $z = -0{,}66915$ =NORMSINV(0.2517)

(g) $z = -0{,}34008$ =NORMSINV(1-0.6331)

8.16 (i) (a) $P(x < 62) = 0{,}2119$ =NORMDIST(62,64,2.5,true)

(b) $P(x > 67{,}4) = 0{,}0869$ =1-NORMDIST(67.4,64,2.5,true)

(c) $P(59{,}6 < x < 62{,}8) = 0{,}2764$

=NORMDIST(62.8,64,2.5,true)-NORMDIST(59.6,64,2.5,true)

(d) $x = 67{,}167$ =NORMINV(1-0.1026,64,2.5)

(e) $x = 59{,}0023$ =NORMINV(1-0.9772,64,2.5)

(f) $x = 65{,}5297$ (see the two step approach below)

=NORMDIST(60.2,64,2.5,true)+0.6652=0,0643+0.6652=0.729455

=NORMINV(0.729455,64,2.5)

8.17 (i) 2,275% =1-NORMDIST(120,80,20,true)

	(ii)	15,866%	=NORMDIST(60,80,20,true)
	(iii)	74,933 minutes	=NORMINV(1-0.6,80,20)
8.18	(i)	2,8125%	=NORMDIST(1,3.1,1.1,true)
	(ii)	20,6627%	=1-NORMDIST(4,3.1,1.1,true)
		1,4561%	=1-NORMDIST(5.5,3.1,1.1,true)
	(iii)	1,29 years	=NORMINV(.05,3.1,1.1)
8.19	(i)	(a) 3,772%	=1-NORMDIST(300,220,45,true)
		(b) 0,383%	=NORMDIST(100,220,45,true)
		(c) 173,36 litres	=NORMINV(0.15,220,45)
		(d) 257,873 litres	=NORMINV(1-0.2,220,45)
8.20	(i)	(a) 0,008197	=1-NORMDIST(2,1.4,.25,true)
		(b) 0,28814	=0.5-NORMDIST(1.2,1.4,.25,true)
		(c) 0,02275	=NORMDIST(0.9,1.4,.25,true)
		(d) 0,05464	=NORMDIST(1,1.4,0.25,true)-NORMDIST(0.5,1.4,0.25,true)
	(ii)	5,48%	=1-NORMDIST(1.8,1.4,0.25,true)
		6,58 (7) truck drivers	
	(iii)	11,51%	=1-NORMDIST(1.7,1.4,0.25,true)
		41,425 (42) truck drivers	
8.21	(i)	38,755%	=NORMDIST(18,18.2,0.7,true)
	(ii)	18,9255 gms	=NORMINV(0.85,18.2,0.7)
8.22	(i)	0,13326	=NORMDIST(60,70,9,true)
	(ii)	0,01313	=1-NORMDIST(90,70,9,true)
	(iii)	12,0126%	=NORMDIST(60,70,9,true)-NORMDIST(50,70,9,true)
	(iv)	(13,326%) 10,66 customers	=1-NORMDIST(80,70,9,true)
	(v)	mean service = 65,195 minutes	
8.23	(i)	(a) 0, 3085	=1-NORMDIST(235,230,10,true)
		(b) 0,2417	=NORMDIST(245,230,10,true)-NORMDIST(235,230,10,true)
		(c) 0,1586	=NORMDIST(220,230,10,true)
	(ii)	240,36 ml	=NORMINV(1-.15,230,10)
	(iii)	mean fill = 232,8 ml	
8.24	(i)	0,24173	=NORMDIST(34,28,4,true)-NORMDIST(30,28,4,true)
	(ii)	0,158655	=NORMDIST(24,28,4,true)
	(iii)	29,01 months	=NORMINV(0.6,28,4)
	(iv)	21,42 months	=NORMINV(.05,28,4)

CHAPTER 10 Confidence Intervals

10.1 (i) Average no. of employees per SME (95%):
[LL = 22,636 ; UL = 26,164]

(ii) =NORMSINV(0.975) gives z = 1,959964

(iii) =CONFIDENCE(0.05,10.8,144) gives a confidence level = 1,763968 (1,764)

Lower limit = 24,4 – 1,764 = 22,636

Upper limit = 24,4 + 1,764 = 26,164

10.2 (i) Average pallets per order (90%):
[LL = 127,191 ; UL = 136,009]
(ii) =NORMSINV(0.95) gives z = 1,644854
(iii) =CONFIDENCE(0.10,25,87) gives a confidence level = 4,40867 (4,409)
Lower limit = 131,6 – 4,409 = 127,191
Upper limit = 131,6 + 4,409 = 136,009
(iv) Total pallets shipped (on average) [LL = 91 577,76 ;UL = 97 926,24]

10.3 (i) Average car insurance premium (95%):
[LL = R350,61 ; UL = 361,39]
(ii) Average car insurance premium (90%):
[LL = R351,48 ; UL = 360,52]
(iii) =NORMSINV(0.975) gives z = 1,959964
(iv) =CONFIDENCE(0.05,44,256) gives a confidence level = 5,389901 (5,39)
Lower limit = 356 – 5,39 = 350,61
Upper limit = 356 + 5,39 = 361,39
(v) Total premium income (on average)
[LL = R1 051 830 ; UL = R1 084 170]

10.4 (i) Average fill (99%): [LL = 4,9704 litres ; UL = 4,9996 litres]
(ii) Yes. Confidence limits do not include 5,0 litres.
(iii) =NORMSINV(0.995) gives z = 2,575829
(iv) =CONFIDENCE(0.01,.04,50) gives a confidence level = 0,014571 (0,0146)
Lower limit = 4,985 – ,0146 = 4,9704
Upper limit = 4,985 + ,0146 = 4,9996

10.5 (i) Average inventory turnover p.a.(90%):
[LL = 3,5985 times; UL = 4,0015 times]
(ii) =NORMSINV(0.95) gives z = 1,644854
(iii) =CONFIDENCE(0.10,0.6,24) gives a confidence level = 0,201453 (0,2015)
Lower limit = 3,8 – ,2015 = 3,5985
Upper limit = 3,8 + ,2015 = 4,0015

10.6 (i) Average no. of calls per day (95%):
[LL = 155,82 calls; UL = 176,58 calls]
(ii) Average no. of calls per day (99%):
[LL = 152,04 calls; UL = 180,36 calls]
(iv) =TINV(.05,20) gives t = 2,085963
(v) Total calls received over 60 days:
[LL = 9 349,29 calls; UL = 10 594,71 calls]

10.7 (i) Average earnings yield (90%): [LL = 11,40557%; UL = 13,59443%]
(ii) =TINV(.01,27) gives t = 1,703288

10.8 (i) Average fill (99%): [LL = 0,945478 litres; UL = 1,016522 litres]
(ii) Average fill (95%): [LL = 0,955141 litres; UL = 1,006859 litres]
(iv) =TINV(.01,17) gives t = 2,898231
=TINV(.05,17) gives t = 2,109816

10.9 (i) Average farm wages (90%): [LL = R1382,06; UL = R1457,94]
(ii) Average farm wages (99%): [LL = R1359,36; UL = R1480,64]
(iv) =TINV(.10,49) gives t = 1,676551
=TINV(.01,49) gives t = 2,679952
10.10 % of firms meeting equity charter (95%): [LL = 35,16%; UL = 48,84%]
10.11 % of cash-paying customers (95%): [LL = 34,84%; UL = 50,16%]
10.12 % of accounts *not* overdrawn (90%): [LL = 75,1%; UL = 82,16%]
10.13 % of mall shoppers (store mix) (90%) [LL = 35,35%; UL = 44,65%]
10.14 (i) Mean = 9,379 Median = 9 Std dev = 3,364 Skewness = 0,00918
Data approximately normally distributed.
(ii) Mean no. of days absent per year (95%): [LL = 8,1 days ; UL = 10,66 days]
(iii) On average, absenteeism does not exceed 10 (i.e. 11 or more) days p.a.
(iv) =TINV(.05,28) gives t = 2,048407
10.15 (i) Mean = 2,8286 Median = 2,78 Std dev = 0,59985
Skewness = –0,10763
Data slightly negatively skewed. Adequate to assume a normal distribution.
(ii) Mean parcel weights (90%): [LL = 2,675 kg; UL = 2,982 kg]
(iii) On average, parcel weights do not exceed 3 kg.
(iv) =TINV(.10,42) gives t = 1,68195
10.16 (i) Mean = 71,24% Median = 68% Std dev = 14,1227%
Skewness = 0,13907
Data slightly negatively skewed. Adequate to assume a normal distribution.
(ii) Mean cost-to-income ratio (95%): [LL = 67,226%; UL = 75,254%]
(iii) =TINV(.05,49) gives t = 2,009575
(iv) P(x > 75) = P(t > 0,266238) using μ = 71,24% and s = 14,1227%
From *Excel*, use =TINV(0.266238,49,1) to find P(t > 0,266238) = 0,3956
giving P(x > 75) = 0,3956 (39,56% of companies are in violation of the rule).

CHAPTER 11 Single Population Hypotheses Tests

11.1 1. One-sided upper tailed. A = {z > 1,645} *z-stat* = 2,1654
p-value = 0,015178 Reject H_0 at 5% significance level
2. One-sided lower tailed. A = {z < –1,28} *z-stat* = –2,50053
p-value = 0,0062 Reject H_0 at 10% significance level
3. Two-tailed. A = {–2,756 < t < 2,756} *t-stat* = 2,644178
p-value = 0,013077 Do not reject H_0 at 1% significance level
4. One-sided lower tailed. A = {t < –2,718} *t-stat* = –3,4641
p-value = 0,002647 Reject H_0 at 1% significance level
5. Two-tailed. A = {–1,96 < t < 1,96} *z-stat* = –1,70554
p-value = 0,088094 Do not reject H_0 at 5% significance level
11.2 (i) H_0: μ = 85 minutes H_1: $\mu \neq$ 85 minutes
(ii) z-test statistic (since α is known and data are normally distributed)

(iii) *z-stat* = −2,068 *z-crit* = ± 1,96 Reject H_0 (α = 0,05)
(iv) *p-value* = 0,03864 < α = 0,05
(=2*NORMSDIST(−2.068) or
=2*NORMDIST(80.5,85,2.175971,true))

11.3 (i) H_0: $\mu \geq$ 30 minutes H_1: $\mu <$ 30 minutes
(ii) *z*-test statistic (since α is known and data are normally distributed)
(iii) *z-stat* = −1,85472 *z-crit* = −2,33 Do not reject H_0 (α = 0,01)
(iv) *p-value* = 0,031818 > α = 0,01
(=NORMSDIST(−1.85472) or
=NORMDIST(27.9,30,1.132244,true))

11.4 (i) H_0: $\mu \leq$ 72 hours H_1: $\mu >$ 72 hours
z-stat = 1,4695 *z-crit* = 1,28 Reject H_0 (α = 0,10)
(ii) *p-value* = 0,070848 < α = 0,10
(=1-NORMSDIST(1.4695) or
=1-NORMDIST(75.9,72,2.653955,true))

11.5 (i) *z*-test statistic (since α is known)
(ii) *Percentage mark-up* data values are assumed to be normally distributed.
(iii) H_0: $\mu \leq$ 40% H_1: $\mu >$ 40%
z-stat = 2,4315 *z-crit* = 2,33 Reject H_0 (α = 0,01)
(ii) *p-value* = 0,007518 < α = 0,01
(=1-NORMSDIST(2.4315) or
=1-NORMDIST(44.1,40,1.6862,true))

11.6 (i) H_0: μ = 700 gms H_1: $\mu \neq$ 700 gms
t-stat = −1,90476 *t-crit* = ± 2,000 Do not reject H_0 (α = 0,05)
(ii) *p-value* = 0,061378 > α = 0,05 (=TDIST(−1.90476,63,2)
(iii) H_0: $\mu \geq$ 700 gms H_1: $\mu <$ 700 gms
t-stat = −1,90476 *t-crit* = −1,671 Reject H_0 (α = 0,05)
p-value = 0,030689 < α = 0,05 (=TDIST(−1.90476,63,1))

11.7 (i) Assume normality for distribution of weekly sales of pudding
(ii) H_0: $\mu \geq$ R5 500 H_1: $\mu <$ R5 500
t-stat = −1,21141 *t-crit* = −1,333 Do not reject H_0 (α = 0,10)
(iii) *p-value* = 0,121154 > α = 0,10 (=TDIST(−1.21141,17,1))

11.8 (i) H_0: $\mu \leq$ 80 kg H_1: $\mu >$ 80 kg
t-stat = 1,8413 *t-crit* = 1,708 Reject H_0 (α = 0,05)
(ii) *p-value* = 0,038736 < α = 0,05 (=TDIST(1.8413,25,1))

11.9 (i) H_0: $\mu \geq$ 1 litre H_1: $\mu <$ 1 litre
t-stat = −1,1838 *t-crit* = −1,729 Do not reject H_0 (α = 0,05)
(ii) *p-value* = 0,125546 > α = 0,05 (=TDIST(−1.1838,19,1))

11.10 (i) H_0: $\pi \geq$ 0,30 H_1: $\pi <$ 0,30
z-stat = −1,52753 *z-crit* = −1,645 Do not reject H_0 (α = 0,05)
(ii) *p-value* = 0,063315 using (=NORMSDIST(−1.52753))
(iii) *p-value* = 0,063315 using (=NORMDIST(0.265,0.3,0.022913,true))

11.11 (i) H_0: $\pi \leq$ 0,60 H_1: $\pi >$ 0,60
Note: use $p = \frac{96}{150}$ = 0,64 *z-stat* = 1,000 *z-crit* = 1,645
Do not reject H_0 (α = 0,05)

(ii) *p-value* = 0,158655 using (=1-NORMSDIST(1.00))

11.12 (i) $H_0: \pi \leq 0{,}15$ $H_1: \pi > 0{,}15$ $p = \frac{96}{560} = 0{,}171429$

z-stat = 1,420143 *z-crit* = 1,28 Reject H_0 ($\alpha = 0{,}10$)

(ii) *p-value* = 0,077783 using (=1-NORMSDIST(1.420143))

(iii) *p-value* = 0,077783

using (=1-NORMDIST(0.1714,0.15,0.015089,true))

11.13 (i) $H_0: \pi \geq 0{,}90$ $H_1: \pi < 0{,}90$ $p = \frac{260}{300} = 0{,}8667$

z-stat = −1,9245 *z-crit* = −2,33 Do not reject H_0 ($\alpha = 0{,}01$)

(ii) *p-value* = 0,027146 using (=NORMSDIST(−1.9245))

(iii) *p-value* = 0,027146

using (=NORMDIST(0.8667,0.9,0.017321,true))

11.14 $H_0: \mu \geq 75\%$ $H_1: \mu < 75\%$

t-stat = −1,88258 *t-crit* = −1,67655

using (=TINV(0.1,49) Reject H_0 ($\alpha = 0{,}05$)

p-value = 0,03285 < α = 0,05 using (=TDIST(−(−1.88258),49,1))

11.15 (i) Transaction values do not appear to be normally distributed.

(ii) $H_0: \mu \geq$ R150 $H_1: \mu <$ R150

t-stat = −1,93745 *t-crit* = −1,67655

using (=TINV(0.1,49) Reject H_0 ($\alpha = 0{,}05$)

p-value = 0,029233 < α = 0,05 using (=TDIST(−(−1.93745),49,1))

11.16 (i) Transaction values do appear to be normally distributed.

(ii) $H_0: \mu \leq 10$ minutes $H_1: \mu > 10$ minutes

t-stat = 1,241084 *t-crit* = 1,29236

using (=TINV(0.2,79) Do not reject H_0 ($\alpha = 0{,}10$)

p-value = 0,109124 > α = 0,10

using (=TDIST(1.241084,79,1))

11.17 (i) Transaction values do appear to be normally distributed.

(ii) $H_0: \mu \leq 180$ claims $H_1: \mu > 180$ claims

t-stat = 2,274506 *t-crit* = 2,364606 using (=TINV(0.02,99)

Do not reject H_0 ($\alpha = 0{,}01$)

p-value = 0,012547 > α = 0,01 using (=TDIST(2.274506,99,1))

11.18 (i) Pivot table frequencies: Sun = 19; Guardian = 42; Mail = 31;

Voice = 28

(ii) $H_0: \pi \geq 0{,}40$ $H_1: \pi < 0{,}40$ $p = \frac{42}{120} = 0{,}35$

z-stat = −1,11803 *z-crit* = −1,64485

Do not reject H_0 ($\alpha = 0{,}05$)

p-value = 0,131776 using (=NORMSDIST(−1.11803))

11.19 (i) Pivot table frequencies: Low = 72; Moderate = 64; High = 34

(ii) $H_0: \pi \leq 0{,}15$ $H_1: \pi > 0{,}15$ $p\,(\text{High}) = \frac{34}{170} = 0{,}20$

z-stat = 1,825742 *z-crit* = 2,326348

Do not reject H_0 ($\alpha = 0{,}01$)

p-value = 0,033945 using (=1-NORMSDIST(1.825742))

CHAPTER 12 Hypotheses Tests for Difference between Two Populations

12.1 (i) Assumptions: normally distributed populations; with equal variances

(ii) $H_0: \mu_M = \mu_R$ $H_1: \mu_M \neq \mu_R$

t-stat = −1,516098 *t-crit* (0.025,41) = ±2,01954

Do not reject H_0

p-value = 0,13717 > α = 0,05 using (=TDIST(−(−1.516098),41,2))

No evidence to reject H_0 in favour of H_1 at the 5% significance level. Hence conclude that there is no difference in mean earnings yields between the manufacturing and retailing sectors.

12.2 (i) $H_0: \mu_D \geq \mu_{ND}$ $H_1: \mu_D < \mu_{ND}$

t-stat = −1,379208 *t-crit* (0.10,61) = −1,29558 Reject H_0

Weak evidence in favour of H_1 at the 10% significance level. Hence conclude that the mean age of DIY consumers is significantly lower than the mean age of non-DIY consumers.

(ii) *p-value* = 0,08643 < α = 0,10 using (=TDIST(−(−1.379208),61,1))

(iii) *t-stat* = −1,379208 *t-crit* (0.05,61) = −1,670219

Do not reject H_0.

No evidence to reject H_0 in favour of H_1 at the 5% significance level. Hence there is no difference in mean ages between DIY's and non-DIY consumers.

12.3 (i) $H_0: \mu_B \leq \mu_T$ $H_1: \mu_B > \mu_T$

t-stat = 2,154389 *t-crit* (0.01,56) = 2,3948 Do not reject H_0

No evidence to reject H_0 in favour of H_1 at the 1% significance level. Hence there is no difference in mean commuting times between bus and train commuters.

p-value = 0,017763 > α = 0,01 using (=TDIST(2.154389,56,1))

(ii) Since there is no difference in mean commuting times, both services should prioritized for upgrading to speed up commuting times.

12.4 $H_0: \mu_M = \mu_V$ $H_1: \mu_M \neq \mu_V$ Note: use z since σ's known

z-stat = 1,55989 *z-crit* (0.025) = ±1,96 Do not reject H_0

p-value = 0,118786 > α = 0,05

using (=(1-NORMSDIST(1.55989))*2)

No evidence to reject H_0 in favour of H_1 at the 5% significance level. Hence conclude that there is no difference in mean month-end balances between Mastercard and Visa credit card holders.

12.5 $H_0: \mu_A \leq \mu_{NA}$ $H_1: \mu_A > \mu_{NA}$ Note: use z since σ's known

z-stat = 2,113409 *z-crit* (0.05) = 1,645 Reject H_0

p-value = 0,017283 < σ = 0,05

using (=1-NORMSDIST(2.113409))

There is strong evidence to reject H_0 in favour of H_1 at the 5% significance level. Hence conclude that the mean job satisfaction score of attendees is significantly higher than the mean job satisfaction scores of non-attendees. The job enrichment workshops are beneficial to employees.

12.6 (i) Explorer Fund: 95% confidence limits: (11,236 days ; 13,564 days)

(ii) $H_0: \mu_G \geq \mu_E$ $H_1: \mu_G < \mu_E$ Note: use z since σ's known

z-stat = –1,53669 *z-crit* (0.05) = –1,645 Do not reject H_0
No evidence to reject H_0 in favour of H_1 at the 5% significance level. Hence conclude that the mean settlement times of claims is the same between the two Medical Funds.
(iii) *p-value* = 0,062184 > α = 0,05 using (=NORMSDIST(–1.53669))

12.7 H_0: $\mu_E \leq \mu_G$ H_1: $\mu_E > \mu_G$ *t-stat* = 1,70529 *t-crit* (0.05,8) = 1,86
Do not reject H_0
No evidence to reject H_0 in favour of H_1 at the 5% significance level. Hence baking times of gas ovens are not quicker, on average, than electric ovens.
p-value = 0,063267 > α = 0,05 using (=TDIST(1.70529,8,1))

12.8 (i) Assumptions: Normality (examine histograms of each sample); Equal variances (compare sample variances; if their ratio < 3, assume equality).
(ii) H_0: $\mu_C \leq \mu_D$ H_1: $\mu_C > \mu_D$ *t-stat* = 1,461439
t-crit (0.10,31) = 1,309 Reject H_0
There is sufficient evidence to reject H_0 in favour of H_1 at the 10% significance level. Hence the average order value at the Cape Town branch is significantly greater than the average order value at the Durban branch.
(iii) *p-value* = 0,076979 < α = 0,10 using (=TDIST(1.461439,31,1))
(iv) *t-stat* = 1,461439 *t-crit* (0.05,31) = 1,696 Do not reject H_0
No evidence to reject H_0 in favour of H_1 at the 5% significance level. Hence conclude that there is no difference in the average order values between the Cape Town branch and the Durban branch.
(v) More confidence in the 5% significance level hypothesis test. This test requires the sample evidence to be stronger (i.e. the sample mean differences in *order values* must be greater) before H_0 is rejected in favour of H_1.

12.9 H_0: $\mu_P \geq \mu_B$ H_1: $\mu_P < \mu_B$ $\bar{x}_p$ = 23,75 $\bar{x}_b$ = 27,375
t-stat = –1,36772 *t-crit* (0.05,14) = –1,761 Do not reject H_0
Also *p-value* = 0,096477 > α = 0,05 using (=TDIST(–(–1.36772,14,1))
No evidence to reject H_0 in favour of H_1 at the 5% significance level. Hence conclude that the average weekly sales of fruit juice are the same for the different package designs.

12.10 (i) Machine 1: Normality assumption is satisfied. Histogram is only slightly skewed to right. See also its skewness coefficient = 0,3311
(ii) Machine 2: 95% confidence limits (3,52% ; 3,81%)
(iii) H_0: $\mu_2 \geq$ 3,75% H_1: $\mu_2 <$ 3,75%
t-stat = –1,15143 *t-crit* (0.05,29) = 21,699 Do not reject H_0
Also *p-value* = 0,12948 < α = 0,05
using (=TDIST(–(–1.15143,29,1))
No evidence to reject H_0 in favour of H_1 at the 5% significance level. Hence conclude that the mean daily percentage scrap produced by machine 2 is at least 3,75% (i.e. 3,75% or more). Machine 2 must be fully serviced.
(iv) H_0: $\mu_1 \geq \mu_2$ H_1: $\mu_1 < \mu_2$
t-stat = –1,7027 *t-crit* (0.05,78) = –1,6646 Reject H_0

There is sufficient evidence to reject H_0 in favour of H_1 at the 5% significance level. Hence machine 1 produces significantly less daily percentage scrap, on average, than machine 2.

(v) *p-value* = 0,0463 < α = 0,05 using (=TDIST(–(–1.7027),78,1))

12.11 (i) Normality assumption is adequately satisfied for both purification plants. Both histograms are sufficiently normally distributed.

(ii) s^2 = 1,56 (Plant 1); s^2 = 1,47 (Plant 2); Equal variances assumption satisfied.

sk_p = 0,0302 (plant 1) and sk_p = –0,193 (plant 2). Skewness is negligible.

(iii) $H_0: \mu_F \leq 27$ $H_1: \mu_F > 27$

t-stat = 1,79577 *t-crit* (0.01,23) = 2,49987 Do not reject H_0

Also *p-value* = 0,04284 > α = 0,01 using (=TDIST(1.79577,23,1))

No evidence to reject H_0 in favour of H_1 at the 1% significance level. Hence conclude that the mean impurities level at the Free State purification plant does not exceed 27 parts per million. Water is of an acceptable standard.

(iv) KZN Plant: 99% confidence limits (25,826 parts; 27,0705 parts)

Since the claimed average level of impurities of 25,5 parts per million is not included in confidence interval, reject the claim at 1% significance level.

(v) $H_0: \mu_F \leq \mu_K$ $H_1: \mu_F > \mu_K$

t-stat = 2,97635 *t-crit* (0.01,51) = 2,4017 Reject H_0

There is strong evidence to reject H_0 in favour of H_1 at the 1% significance level. Hence conclude that the KZN purification plant produces water of a higher quality (i.e. lower mean impurities per million) than the Free State purification plant.

(vi) *p-value* = 0,002226 < α = 0,01 using (=TDIST(2.976351,51,1))

12.12 (i) $H_0: \mu_F = \mu_Y$ $H_1: \mu_F \neq \mu_Y$

t-stat = 1,784 *t-crit* (0.025,40) = ±2,021 Do not reject H_0

p-value = 0,082 > α = 0,05 using (=TDIST(1.784,40,2))

No evidence to reject H_0 in favour of H_1 at the 5% significance level. Hence conclude that the mean quercetin levels are the same in both brands of rooibos tea.

(ii) $H_0: \mu_F \leq \mu_Y$ $H_1: \mu_F > \mu_Y$

t-stat = 1,784 *t-crit* (0.05,40) = 1,6839 Reject H_0

p-value = 0,041 < α = 0,05 using (=TDIST(1.784,40,1))

There is strong evidence to reject H_0 in favour of H_1 at the 5% significance level. Hence conclude that the mean quercetin level of Freshpak rooibos tea is significantly higher than that of Yellow Label rooibos tea.

12.13 (i) $H_0: \mu_K \leq 28$ $H_1: \mu_K > 28$

t-stat = 2,0639 *t-crit* (0.05,20) = 1,7247 Do not reject H_0

Also *p-value* = 0,06024 > α = 0,05 using (=TDIST(1.62186,20,1))

Reject H_0 in favour of H_1 at the 5% significance level.

Hence conclude that the mean fat content of meat supplied by the Little

Karoo producer does exceed 28 gms/kg. The consignment should not be accepted.

(ii) $H_0: \mu_N \geq \mu_K$ $H_1: \mu_N < \mu_K$
t-stat = –2,0186 *t-crit* (0.01,46) = –2,410189 Do not reject H_0
p-value = 0,024688 > α = 0,01 using (=TDIST(–(–2.0186,46,1))
No evidence to reject H_0 in favour of H_1 at the 1% significance level. Hence conclude that the mean fat content between the Namibian and Little Karoo meat producers is the same. No justification to sign an exclusive contract with the Namibian meat producer.

12.14 $H_0: \mu_P \leq \mu_W$ $H_1: \mu_P > \mu_W$
z-stat = 1,37719 *z-crit* (0.5) = 1,645 Do not reject H_0
p-value = 0,084226 > α = 0,05 using (=1-NORMSDIST(1.37719))
No evidence to reject H_0 in favour of H_1 at the 5% significance level. Hence conclude that the percentage of households who would prefer Fruit Puffs is not significantly larger than the percentage of households who would prefer the Fruity Wheat. The manager's belief is not justified.

12.15 (i) $H_0: \mu_M = \mu_F$ $H_1: \mu_M \neq \mu_F$
z-stat = 2,4394 *z-crit* (0.5) = ±1,96 Reject H_0
There is overwhelming evidence to reject H_0 in favour of H_1 at the 5% significance level. Hence conclude that there is a significant difference in the percentage of males and females enjoying jazz music. The evidence indicates that males tend to prefer jazz more than females.

(ii) *p-value* = 0,014712 < α = 0,05
using (=(1-NORMSDIST(2.4394))*2)

12.16 (i) $H_0: \mu_S \geq \mu_E$ $H_1: \mu_S < \mu_E$
z-stat = –1,79594 *z-crit* (0.5) = –1,645 Reject H_0
There is strong evidence to reject H_0 in favour of H_1 at the 5% significance level. Hence conclude that a significantly larger percentage of Elite cheque accounts than Status cheque accounts are overdrawn.

(ii) *p-value* = 0,03625 < α = 0,05 using (=NORMSDIST(–1.795936))

12.17 $H_0: \mu_{difference} \geq 0$ $H_1: \mu_{difference} < 0$ where $x_{\text{difference}} = (x_{\text{before}} - x_{\text{after}})$
t-stat = –1,87617 *t-crit* (0.05,11) = –1,7958 Reject H_0
Also *p-value* = 0,0437 < α = 0,05
using (=TDIST(–(–1.87617),11,1))
There is strong evidence to reject H_0 in favour of H_1 at the 5% significance level. Hence conclude that the average weekly sales for the disinfectant product are greater after the campaign than before the campaign. The campaign has been effective in raising average weekly sales of the product.

12.18 (i) Not independent – the same employee is measured before and after the programme. Hence the two sets of sample data values are not independent.

(ii) $H_0: \mu_{difference} \geq 0$ $H_1: \mu_{difference} < 0$
where $x_{\text{difference}} = (x_{\text{before}} - x_{\text{after}})$
t-stat = –2,120346 *t-crit* (0.05,17) = –1,739606 Reject H_0

Also *p-value* = 0,02449 < α = 0,05
using (=TDIST(–(–2.120346),17,1))
There is strong evidence to reject H_0 in favour of H_1 at the 5% significance level. Hence conclude that the average performance score of workers is significantly higher after the workshop than before it. The workshop programme has been effective in raising worker performance.

12.19 (i) H_0: $\mu_{difference} \leq 0$ H_1: $\mu_{difference} > 0$
where $x_{\text{difference}} = (x_{\text{year ago}} - x_{\text{current}})$
t-stat = 2,092457 *t-crit* (0.05,9) = 1,8331 Reject H_0
There is strong evidence to reject H_0 in favour of H_1 at the 5% significance level. Hence conclude that the average debt ratio is significantly lower today (currently) than it was a year ago. The prime rate increase has been effective in reducing the average household debt ratio.

(ii) The data on the paired differences in normally distributed.

(iii) *p-value* = 0,03296 < α = 0,05 using (=TDIST(2.092457),9,1))

12.20 (i) H_0: $\mu_F \leq \mu_M$ H_1: $\mu_F > \mu_M$
t-stat = 1,739739 *t-crit* (0.05,43) = 1,681 Reject H_0
Also *p-value* = 0,04453 < α = 0,05
using (=TDIST(1.739739,43,1))
There is strong evidence to reject H_0 in favour of H_1 at the 5% significance level. Hence conclude that females have paid more, on average, for their jeans than males.

(ii) H_0: $\mu_W = \mu_L$ H_1: $\mu_W \neq \mu_L$
t-stat = 0,918721 *t-crit* (0.05,36) = 1,6883 Do not reject H_0
Also *p-value* = 0,182178 > α = 0,05
using (=TDIST(0.918721,36,1))
No evidence to reject H_0 in favour of H_1 at the 5% significance level. Hence conclude that there is no difference in the average price of Wrangler and Levis jeans.

(iii) H_0: $\mu_{Lee} \leq \mu_{Levi}$ H_1: $\mu_{Lee} > \mu_{Levi}$
t-stat = 1,817946 *t-crit* (0.05,26) = 1,7056 Reject H_0
Also *p-value* = 0,0403 < α = 0,05 using (=TDIST(1.817946,26,1))
There is strong evidence to reject H_0 in favour of H_1 at the 5% significance level. Hence conclude that customers who purchase Lee branded jeans are older, on average, than customers who purchase Levis branded jeans.

(iv) P(females) = $\frac{7}{21}$ = 33,3% P(males) = $\frac{14}{24}$ = 58,33%

(v) H_0: $\mu_F = \mu_M$ H_1: $\mu_F \neq \mu_M$
z-stat = –1,67705 *z-crit* (0.025) = ±1,96 Do not reject H_0
Also *p-value* = 0,09353 > α = 0,05
using (=NORMSDIST(–1.67705)*2)
No evidence to reject H_0 in favour of H_1 at the 5% significance level. Hence conclude that females and males equally prefer Levis jeans.

CHAPTER 13 Chi Squared Tests

13.1 (ii) H_0: No association (independent)
H_1: An association (not independent)
χ^2-*stat* = 5,0428 χ^2-*crit* = 4,605 Reject H_0 (α = 0,10)
(iii) *p-value* = 0,0803 (=CHIDIST(5.0428,2))

13.2 (ii) p_1 = "Yes/full-time" = 24,3% p_2 = "Yes/at-home" = 18,52%
H_0: No association (independent)
H_1: An association (not independent)
or $H_0: \pi_1 = \pi_2$ $H_1: \pi_1 > \pi_2$
χ^2-*stat* = 1,7544 χ^2-*crit* = 3,8415 Do not reject H_0 (α = 0,05)
(iii) *p-value* = 0,1853 (=CHIDIST(1.7544,1))

13.3 (ii) H_0: No association (independent)
H_1: An association (not independent)
χ^2-*stat* = 14,6247 χ^2-*crit* = 13,277 Reject H_0 (α = 0,01)
(iii) *p-value* = 0,0055 (=CHIDIST(14.6247,4))

13.4 (i) p_1= "Yes/ECape"= 16% p_2 = "Yes/WCape"= 10,4%
p_3 = "Yes/KZN" = 25%
$H_0: \pi_1 = \pi_2 = \pi_3$ H_1: At least one π_i differs (i = 1, 2, 3)
(ii) χ^2-*stat* = 7,5954 χ^2-*crit* = 9,210 Do not reject H_0 (α = 0,01)
(iii) H_0: Sports news readership is independent of region
H_1: Not independent
(iv) *p-value* = 0,0224 (=CHIDIST(7.5954,2))

13.5 (ii) H_0: No association (independent)
H_1: An association (not independent)
χ^2-*stat* = 4,803 χ^2-*crit* = 4,605 Reject H_0 (α = 0,10)
(iii) *p-value* = 0,0906 (=CHIDIST(4.803,2))
(iv) p_1 = "male/spin" = 55,4% p_2 = "male/swim" = 54,3%
p_3 = "male/circuit" = 75%
$H_0: \pi_1 = \pi_2 = \pi_3$ H_1: At least one π_i differs (i = 1, 2, 3)
(v) χ^2-*stat* = 4,803 χ^2-*crit* = 5,991 Do not reject H_0 (α = 0,05)
Conclusion changes to "do not reject H_0" as $\chi^2 -$ *crit* = 5,991 > $\chi^2 -$ *stat* = 4,803
Also *p-value* = 0,0906 > 0,05

13.6 (i) daily = 29%; 3/4 times = 30,6%; twice = 34,4%;
only once = 15%
(ii) H_0: Shopping profile as per manager's belief
H_1: Profile differs
or H_0: π_1 = 0,25 π_2 = 0,35 π_3 = 0,30 π_4 = 0,10
H_1: At least one π_i differs
χ^2-*stat* = 8,501 χ^2-*crit* = 7,815 Reject H_0 (α = 0,05)
(iii) *p-value* = 0,0367 (=CHIDIST(8.501,3))

13.7 (i) H_0: No change in 2004 equity portfolio mix
H_1: 2007 portfolio mix differs
χ^2-*stat* = 7,4074 χ^2-*crit* = 7,815 Do not reject H_0 (α = 0,05)
(ii) *p-value* = 0,059986 (=CHIDIST(7.4074,3))

13.8 (i) H_0: No change in payment method
H_1: Payment method has changed
χ^2-*stat* = 14,8911 χ^2-*crit* = 5,991 Reject H_0 (α = 0,05)
(ii) *p-value* = 0,000584 (=CHIDIST(14.8911,2))
13.9 (i) H_0: Limpopo same as national sales profile
H_1: Limpopo sales profile differs
χ^2-*stat* = 6,9136 χ^2-*crit* = 5,991 Reject H_0 (α = 0,05)
(ii) *p-value* = 0,031531 (=CHIDIST(6.9136,2))
13.10 (ii) sample mean = 10,324 minutes sample std dev = 2,333 minutes
n = 80
(iii) H_0: Flight delay times are normally distributed (μ = 10,324 min; α = 2,333)
H_1: Flight delay times do not follow this normal distribution
expected normal probabilities
$P(x < 5) = 0{,}011253$ $P(5 < x < 7{,}5) = 0{,}10184$
$P(7{,}5 < x < 10) = 0{,}33173$ $P(10 < x < 12{,}5) = 0{,}3797$
$P(12{,}5 < x < 15) = 0{,}15296$ $P(15 < x < 17{,}5) = 0{,}02147$
χ^2-*stat* = 1,1397 χ^2-*crit* = 7,815 Do not reject H_0 (α = 0,05)
(iv) *p-value* = 0,7675 (=CHIDIST(1.1397,3))
13.11 (i) H_0: No. of sales per day follows a Binomial distribution with p = 0,40
H_1: No. of sales per day does not follow a Binomial distribution with p = 0,40
$P(x = 0) = 0{,}216$ $P(x = 1) = 0{,}432$ $P(x = 2) = 0{,}288$
$P(x = 3) = 0{,}064$
χ^2-*stat* = 10,39063 χ^2-*crit* = 5,991 Reject H_0 (α = 0,05)
(iv) *p-value* = 0,005542 (=CHIDIST(10.39063,2))
13.12 (i) H_0: Absenteeism rate follows a Poisson distribution with a = 2
H_1: Absenteeism rate does not follows a Poisson distribution with a = 2
$P(x = 0) = 0{,}13534$ $P(x = 1) = 0{,}27067$ $P(x = 2) = 0{,}27067$
$P(x = 3) = 0{,}18045$ $P(x = 4) = 0{,}09022$ $P(x \geq 5) = 0{,}05265$
χ^2-*stat* = 15,30357 χ^2-*crit* = 9,488 Reject H_0 (α = 0,05)
(ii) *p-value* = 0,004111 (=CHIDIST(15.30357,4))
13.13 (ii) p_1 = "present/Cape" = 62% p_2 = "present/Gauteng" = 75,7%
p_3 = "present/Free State" = 67,1% p_4 = "present/KZN" = 72,7%
$H_0: \pi_1 = \pi_2 = \pi_3 = \pi_4$ H_1: At least one π_i differs (i = 1, 2, 3, 4)
(iii) χ^2-*stat* = 6,5169 χ^2-*crit* = 6,2514 Reject H_0 (α = 0,10)
(iv) H_0: No association between preference for a compensation plan and province
H_1: Preference does vary according to province (there is an association)
(v) *p-value* = 0,088998 (=CHIDIST(6.5169,3))
(vi) χ^2-*stat* = 6,5169 χ^2-*crit* = 7,815 Do not reject H_0 (α = 0,05)
Conclusion changes to "do not reject H_0" as χ^2-*crit* = 7,815 > χ^2-*stat* = 6,5169
Also *p-value* = 0,088998 > 0,05

13.14 (ii) H_0: No association (independent)
H_1: An association (not independent)
χ^2-*stat* = 10,0812 χ^2-*crit* = 9,488 Reject H_0 (α = 0,05)
(iv) *p-value* = 0,0391 (=CHIDIST(10.0812,4))
(v) p_1 = "mechanical/morning" = 61,8%
p_2 = "mechanical/afternoon" = 46,5%
p_3 = "mechanical/night" = 36,6%
H_0: $\pi_1 = \pi_2 = \pi_3$ H_1: At least one π_i differs (i = 1, 2, 3)
χ^2-*stat* = 10,0812 χ^2-*crit* = 9,488 Reject H_0 (α = 0,05)
Also *p-value* = 0,0391 $<$ 0,05

13.15 (iii) H_0: No association (independent)
H_1: An association (not independent)
χ^2-*stat* = 5,5525 χ^2-*crit* = 4,6052 Reject H_0 (α = 0,10)
(iv) p_1 = "female/sport" = 25,45% p_2 = "female/social" = 44,44%
p_3 = "female/business" = 29,03%
H_0: $\pi_1 = \pi_2 = \pi_3$ H_1: At least one π_i differs (i = 1, 2, 3)
χ^2-*stat* = 5,5525 χ^2-*crit* = 4,6052 Reject H_0 (α = 0,10)
Also *p-value* = 0,0623 $<$ 0,10
(v) *p-value* = 0,0623 (=CHIDIST(5.5525,2))

13.16 (iii) H_0: No change in pattern of vehicle loans
H_1: There is a pattern change
(iv) χ^2-*stat* = 13,9 χ^2-*crit* = 9,488 Reject H_0 (α = 0,05)
(ii) *p-value* = 0,007621 (=CHIDIST(13.9,4))

13.17 (iii) H_0: Milk type purchased is independent of consumer's health-conscious status (there is no association)
H_1: Milk type purchased and consumer's health-conscious status are dependent (there is an association)
χ^2-*stat* = 7,5831 χ^2-*crit* = 5,991 Reject H_0 (α = 0,05)
(iv) p_1 = "yes/fat-free" = 80% p_2 = "yes/low fat" = 60%
p_3 = "yes/full cream" = 42,3%
H_0: $\pi_1 = \pi_2 = \pi_3$ H_1: At least one π_i differs (i = 1, 2, 3)
χ^2-*stat* = 7,5831 χ^2-*crit* = 5,991 Reject H_0 (α = 0,05)
(v) *p-value* = 0,0226 (=CHIDIST(7.5831,2))

CHAPTER 14 Analysis of Variance

14.1 (i) Sample means (l/100km): Peugeot = 6,48 VW = 7,325
Ford = 6,88
(ii) H_0: $\mu_1 = \mu_2 = \mu_3$ H_1: At least one μ_i differs
F-stat = 4,2343 *F-crit* (0.05,2,11) = 3,9823 Reject H_0
At least one make of motor vehicle has a different mean consumption level. By inspection, Peugeot is the most fuel efficient motor vehicle of those tested.
(iii) *p-value* = 0,043282 $< \alpha$ = 0,05 using (=FDIST(4.2343,2,11))
(iv) *F-stat* = 4,2343 *F-crit* (0.01,2,11) = 7,20571
p-value = 0,043282 $> \alpha$ = 0,01
Do not reject H_0. There is no difference in the mean consumption levels. Hence all makes are equally fuel efficient.

14.2 (i) Normality. Equal variances.
(ii) $H_0: \mu_A = \mu_B = \mu_C$ H_1: At least one μ_i differs
F-stat = 2,7995 *F-crit* (0.05,2,18) = 3,5546 Do not reject H_0
No difference in mean sales. All package designs are equally effective.
(iii) *p-value* = 0,087378 > α = 0,05 using (=FDIST(2.7995,2,18))

14.3 (i) $H_0: \mu_X = \mu_Y = \mu_Z$ H_1: At least one μ_i differs
F-stat = 2,574038 *F-crit* (0.10,2,24) = 2,538332 Reject H_0
At least one bank has a different mean service rating score. By inspection, Bank X has the highest mean service rating score (marginal evidence).
(ii) *p-value* = 0,097099 < α = 0,10 using (=FDIST(2.574038,2,24))
(iii) *F-stat* = 2,574038 *F-crit* (0.05,2,24) = 3,402826
p-value = 0,097099 > α = 0,05 Do not reject H_0
All banks have equal mean service rating scores.

14.4 (i) $H_0: \mu_B = \mu_W = \mu_S = \mu_T$ H_1: At least one μ_i differs
F-stat = 3,719882 *F-crit* (0.05,3,26) = 2,975154 Reject H_0
Shelf height and product sales are *not* statistically independent. At least one shelf height generates a different mean sales level. By inspection, shelves at waist and shoulder height generate higher mean sales.
(ii) *p-value* = 0,023807 < α = 0,05 using (=FDIST(3.719882,3,26))

14.5 (i) $H_0: \mu_I = \mu_R = \mu_F = \mu_M$ H_1: At least one μ_i differs
(ii) *F-stat* = 3,075703 *F-crit* (0.05,3,76) = 2,724944 Reject H_0
Earnings yields and Economic sector are *not* statistically independent. At least one Economic sector has a different mean earnings yield. By inspection, the Financial and Mining sectors have the higher mean earnings yields.
(iii) Equal variances assumption appears satisfied (max var/min var < 3); Independent sectors implies that samples are independent.
(iv) *p-value* = 0,032584 < α = 0,05 using (=FDIST(3.075703,3,26))

14.6 (i) $H_0: \mu_S = \mu_A = \mu_T$ H_1: At least one μ_i differs
(ii) *F-stat* = 3,390651 *F-crit* (0.05,2,57) = 3,158843 Reject H_0
Advertising strategy and sales are *not* statistically independent. At least one advertising strategy produces a different mean sales level. By inspection, the "Sophisticated" strategy appears to make the largest mean sales impact.
(iii) *p-value* = 0,040614 < α = 0,05 using (=FDIST(3.390651,2,57))
(iv) $H_0: \mu_S = \mu_T$ $H_1: \mu_S \neq \mu_T$
t-stat = 0,831576 *t-crit* (0.05,38) = 2,024394 Do not reject H_0
No difference in mean deodorant sales between the two advertising strategies.
(v) *p-value* = 0,410843 > α = 0,05 using (=TDIST(0.831576,38,2))
(vi) Management can adopt either the "Sophisticated" or the "Trendy" strategy.
Statistically there is no difference in their mean sales impact (α = 0,05).

14.7 (i) $H_0: \mu_A = \mu_B = \mu_C$ H_1: At least one μ_i differs
F-stat = 3,287879 *F-crit* (0.10,2,12) = 2,806796 Reject H_0
Mean processing time is affected by machine type (i.e. *not* independent). At least one machine has a different mean processing time. By inspection, machine A appears to have the fastest mean processing time.

(ii) $H_0: \mu_A = \mu_B$ $H_1: \mu_A \neq \mu_B$
t-stat = 0,437595 *t-crit* (0.10,8) = 1,859548 Do not reject H_0
No difference in mean processing times between machines A and B.

(iii) Management can choose either machine A or machine B, but not machine C.
Statistically, no difference exists in A or B's mean processing times (α = 0,10).

(iv) Anova: *p-value* = 0,072679 < α = 0,10
using (=FDIST(3.287879,2,12))
t-test: *p-value* = 0,673253 > α = 0,10
using (=TDIST(0.437595,8,2))

14.8 (i) Sample means: T = 73,83 C = 78,07 B = 69,73 M = 76,37
By inspection, mean differences appear to exist; and the Banking sector appears to be the sector with the lowest risk i.t.o leverage ratio.

(ii) Skewness coefficient: T (0,0097); C (0,051); B (0,1033); M (–0,8573).
Normality assumption appears violated only in the Manufacturing sector.
Equal variances assumption appears satisfied (max var/min var < 3).

(iii) $H_0: \mu_T = \mu_C = \mu_B = \mu_M$ H_1: At least one μ_i differs
F-stat = 2,848554 *F-crit* (0.05,3,116) = 2,682809 Reject H_0
Leverage ratios and Economic sector are *not* statistically independent. At least one Economic sector has a different mean leverage ratio. By inspection, the Banking sector has the lowest mean leverage ratio.

(iv) $H_0: \mu_T = \mu_B$ $H_1: \mu_T \neq \mu_B$
t-stat = 1,346856 *t-crit* (0.05,58) = 2,001717 Do not reject H_0
Equal mean leverage ratios between the Technology and Banking sectors.

(v) The investor can choose to invest in either Technology or Banking equities.
Statistically there is no difference in their mean leverage ratios (α = 0,05).

(vi) Anova: *p-value* = 0,040552 < α = 0,05
using (=FDIST(2.848554,3,116))
t-test: *p-value* = 0,183266 > α = 0,05
using (=TDIST(1.346856,58,2))

14.9 (i) Sample means: OJ = 9 L = 8,75 RP = 9,2 AV = 8,85
By inspection, mean differences appear to exist with On-the-Job and Role Play training methods producing the higher mean performance scores.

(ii) H_0: $\mu_{OJ} = \mu_L = \mu_{RP} = \mu_{AV}$ H_1: At least one μ_i differs
F-stat = 3,478697 *F-crit* (0.05,3,52) = 2,7826 Reject H_0
Performance scores and training methods are *not* statistically independent. At least one training method has a different mean performance score. By inspection, Role Play and On-the-Job training methods produce the higher mean performance scores.

(iii) H_0: $\mu_{OJ} = \mu_{RP}$ H_1: $\mu_{OJ} \neq \mu_{RP}$
t-stat = –1,607436 *t-crit* (0.05,26) = –2,05553 Do not reject H_0
Equal mean performance scores between On-the-Job and Role Play methods.

(iv) The HR manager can select between On-the-Job and Role Play training. Statistically there is no difference in their mean performance scores (α = 0,05).

(v) Anova: *p-value* = 0,02229 < α = 0,05
using (=FDIST(3.478697,3,52))
t-test: *p-value* = 0,1200365 > α = 0,05
using (=TDIST(–(–1.607436),26,2))

CHAPTER 15 Regression Analysis

Part 1: Simple Linear Regression and Correlation Analysis

15.1 (i) Strong positive association
(ii) $\hat{y}$ = 18,916 + 1,112x for 20 ≤ x ≤ 40
(iii) r^2 = 0,6516
(iv) *y(estimated)* = 46,716 (expected output of 47 units)

15.2 (i) Very strong positive association
(ii) $\hat{y}$ = 4,333 + 1,4167x for 3 ≤ x ≤ 8
(iii) r = 0,8552
(iv) r^2 = 0,7313
(iv) *y(estimated)* = 12,833 (expected earnings yield %)

15.3 (i) x = interest rate y = loan applications
(ii) Strong negative association
(iii) r = –0,8302
(iv) H_0: ρ = 0 H_1: ρ ≠ 0 *t-stat* = –4,4677 *t-crit* = ±2,262
Reject H_0
(v) *p-value* = 0,00156
(vi) $\hat{y}$ = 48,991 – 3,9457x for 5,5 ≤ x ≤ 8,5
(vii) b_1 = –3,9457
a 1% increase in interest rates will lead to 3,95 fewer loan applications.
(viii) *y(estimated)* = 25,32 (25 expected number of loan applications)

15.4 (i) x = machine age (years) y = annual maintenance cost
(ii) Very strong positive association
(iii) r = 0,870028
(iv) H_0: ρ = 0 H_1: ρ ≠ 0 *t-stat* = 5,58 *t-crit* = 2,228 Reject H_0
(v) *p-value* = 0,000343

(vi) $\hat{y} = 12{,}627 + 5{,}8295x$ for $1 \leq x \leq 8$
(vii) $b_1 = 5{,}8295$
For every additional year, the maintenance cost goes up by R5,8295.
(viii) *y(estimated)* = R41,77 (expected maintenance costs)

15.5 (i) Moderate positive association
(ii) $r = 0{,}5194$
(iii) H_0: ρ = 0ρ H_1: ρ ≠ 0 *t-stat* = 1,922 *t-crit* = 2,228
Do not reject H_0
(iv) *p-value* = 0,0835
(v) $\hat{y} = 60{,}1032 + 2{,}7168x$ for $4 \leq x \leq 9$
y(estimated) = 81,84 (expected performance rating score)

15.6 (i) $r = 0{,}7448$
(ii) H_0: ρ = 0 H_1: ρ ≠ 0 *t-stat* = 3,3484 *t-crit* = 2,262
Reject H_0
(iii) $\hat{y} = 14{,}4174\ 1\ 0{,}729x$ for $34 \leq x \leq 65$
(iv) *y(estimated)* = 56,7% (expected election percentage)
(v) *y(estimated)* = 74,2% (extrapolated estimate – outside domain of x)

15.7 (i) x = capital investment y = return on investment
(iii) $r = 0{,}4145$
$\hat{y} = 1{,}2741 + 0{,}0678x$ for $21{,}1 \leq x \leq 79{,}5$
(iv) $r^2 = 0{,}1718$
(v) H_0: ρ = 0 H_1: ρ ≠ 0 *t-stat* = 2,9865 *p-value* = 0,004645
Reject H_0
(vi) $b_1 = 0{,}0678$
For every 1% change (up/down) in capital investment, roi will change (up/down) by 0,0678.
(vii) There is a 95% chance that the interval from 0,022% to 0,1136% covers the actual coefficient of capital investment. It is a highly significant variable.
(viii) *y(estimated)* = 5,005 (expected return on investment).

15.8 (i) x = council valuations y = market values
(iii) $r = 0{,}7810$
$\hat{y} = 71{,}362 + 1{,}0151x$ for $48 \leq x \leq 154$
(iv) $r^2 = 0{,}61$
(v) H_0: ρ = 0 H_1: ρ ≠ 0 *t-stat* = 7,70975
p-value = 0,00000000275 Reject H_0
(vi) $b_1 = 1{,}0151$
For every R1 change (up/down) in council valuations, the market value of a property will change (up/down) by R1,0151.
(vii) There is a 95% chance that the interval from 0,7486 to 1,2817 covers the actual coefficient of council valuations. It is a highly significant variable.
(viii) *y(estimated)* = R172,87 (expected market value in R1000's)

Part 2: Multiple Regression Analysis

15.9 (i) x_1 = risk factor x_2 = expense ratio y = mutual fund returns
(iv) $\hat{y} = 17{,}5535 + 0{,}9969x_1 - 1{,}1183x_2$

(v) $R^2 = 0{,}6597$
(vi) $H_0: \rho^2 = 0$ $H_1: \rho^2 > 0$ *F-stat* = 11,6325 *p-value* = 0,00155
Reject H_0
(viii) Risk factor: $H_0: \beta_1 = 0$ $H_1: \beta_1 \neq 0$ *t-stat* = 1,582
p-value = 0,1395 Do not reject H_0
Expense ratio: $H_0: \beta_2 = 0$ $H_1: \beta_2 \neq 0$ *t-stat* = –1,941
p-value = 0,076 Do not reject H_0
(ix) *y(estimated)* = 19,85% (expected return)

15.10 (iii) $\hat{y} = 37{,}28305 + 0{,}5241x_1 + 1{,}8042x_2$ x_1 = # of visitors
x_2 = # of conferences
(iv) $R^2 = 0{,}483163$
(v) $H_0: \beta_1 = \beta_2 = 0$ H_1: At least one $\beta_i \neq 0$ *F-stat* = 9,8159
p-value = 0,00097 Reject H_0
(vi) $b_1 = 0{,}5241$
For one more/less visitor (in 10 000's), occupancy rises/falls by 0,241%
$b_2 = 1{,}8042$
For one more/less conference, occupancy rises/falls by 1,8042%
(vii) Visitors: $H_0: \beta_1 = 0$ $H_1: \beta_1 \neq 0$ *t-stat* = 2,1327
p-value = 0,0449 Reject H_0
Conferences: $H_0: \beta_2 = 0$ $H_1: \beta_2 \neq 0$ *t-stat* = 3,637
p-value = 0,00154 Reject H_0
(viii) Conferences – since its *p-value* (= 0,00154) is more significant
(<< 0,0449)
(ix) *y(estimated)* = 72,389% (expected occupancy level of hotels)

15.11 (iii) $\hat{y} = 33{,}2653 + 0{,}1264x_1 - 0{,}209x_2 - 0{,}3229x_3$
x_1 = tenure x_2 = job satisfaction x_3 = organization commitment
(iv) $R^2 = 0{,}57166$
(v) $H_0: \beta_1 = \beta_2 = 0$ H_1: At least one $\beta_i \neq 0$ *F-stat* = 7,1178
p-value = 0,00297 Reject H_0
(vi) $b_1 = 0{,}1264$
For one more/less month of tenure, absenteeism changes by 0,1264 days
$b_2 = -0{,}209$
A one unit change in the job satisfaction index *inversely* changes absenteeism by 0,209 days.
$b_3 = -0{,}3229$
A one unit change in the organizational commitment index *inversely* changes absenteeism by 0,3229 days.
(vii) Tenure: $H_0: \beta_1 = 0$ $H_1: \beta_1 \neq 0$ *t-stat* = 2,1374
p-value = 0,0484 Reject H_0
Satisfaction: $H_0: \beta_2 = 0$ $H_1: \beta_2 \neq 0$ *t-stat* = –1,467 *p-value* = 0,1618
Do not reject H_0
Commitment: $H_0: \beta_3 = 0$ $H_1: \beta_3 \neq 0$ *t-stat* = –3,079
p-value = 0,0072 Reject H_0
(viii) Commitment – since its *p-value* (= 0,0072) is the most significant.
(ix) *y(estimated)* = 9,504 days (expected number of days absent)

15.12 (iii) $\hat{y} = 190{,}4548 + 2{,}17954x_1 + 2{,}61x_2 - 23{,}753x_3 + 4{,}11878x_4$
x_1 = adspend x_2 = reps x_3 = competing brands
x_4 = crime index

(iv) $R^2 = 0{,}7632$

(v) $H_0: \beta_1 = \beta_2 = 0$ H_1: At least one $\beta_i \neq 0$ *F-stat* = 16,925
p-value = 0,00000243 Reject H_0

(vi) $b_1 = 2{,}17954$
For a unit change in adspend, lock sales will change by 2,179 units
$b_2 = 2{,}61$
For one more/less sales representative, lock sales will rise/fall by 2,61 units
$b_3 = -23{,}753$
Every additional brand available reduces sure-safe lock sales by 23,753 units.
$b_4 = 4{,}11878$
A unit increase in the crime index increases lock sales by 4,11878 units.

(vii) Adspend: $H_0: \beta_1 = 0$ $H_1: \beta_1 \neq 0$ *t-stat* = 0,4223
p-value = 0,6771 Do not reject H_0
Reps: $H_0: \beta_2 = 0$ $H_1: \beta_2 \neq 0$ *t-stat* = 3,2002
p-value = 0,0043 Reject H_0
Brands: $H_0: \beta_3 = 0$ $H_1: \beta_3 \neq 0$ *t-stat* = –5,809
p-value = 0,00000912 Reject H_0
Crimedex: $H_0: \beta_4 = 0$ $H_1: \beta_4 \neq 0$ *t-stat* = 1,731
p-value = 0,09816 Do not reject H_0

(viii) Brands – since its *p-value* (= 0,00000912) is the most significant.

(ix) *y(estimated)* = 155,32 (155 locks) (expected sales level of sure-safe locks)

CHAPTER 16 Index Numbers

16.1 (i) Price relatives: A = 120 B = 113,3 C = 116,7
(ii) Composite Price Index (using both methods) = 115,4

16.2 (i) Quantity relatives: A = 70 B = 105,45 C = 125
(ii) Composite Quantity Index (using both methods) = 104,5
(iii) Volume of motorcycle sales have increased by only 4,5%.

16.3 (i) Price relative (ISDN): (2005) 90 (2006) 80
(ii) Composite Price Index: (2005) 104,71 (2006) 98,87
(iii) Composite Quantity Index: (2005) 123,73 (2006) 133,52

16.4 (i) Composite Salary (Price) Index (2007): 120,46
(ii) Salary relatives: Programmers have shown the largest salary increase.
Systems analyst = 119,05 Programmer = 124,14 Network manager = 116,67

16.5 (i) Staff relatives: Systems analysts have shown the largest increase in staff.
Systems analyst = 127,38 Programmer = 85,42 Network manager = 110,34
(ii) Composite Staff (Quantity) Index (2007): 109,14

16.6 (i) Price relatives (2006): HQ26 = 11,02 HQ32 = 95,22
(ii) Composite Price (Cost) Index: (2005) = 100,82 (2006) = 98,82

(iii) Overall costs increased marginally by 0,82% in 2005 from 2004.
From 2004 to 2006, overall costs decreased by 1,18%.

(iv) Composite Link relatives: (2005) 100,82 (2006) 98,02

16.7 (i) Re-based to 2005 78,6 85,7 89,3 97,3 101,8 **100** 102,7

(ii) Link relatives 100 109,1 104,2 109,0 104,6 98,2 102,7

16.8 (i) Federal (base = 2005) 84,4 87,2 91,4 93,8 **100** 101,6
Baltic (base = 2005) 89,7 96,7 94,0 95,7 **100** 103,0

(ii) Federal = 9,4% increase; Baltic = 6,4% (6,3/98,2%) increase only.

(iii) Link relatives
Federal 100 103,4 104,8 102,6 106,6 101,6
Baltic 100 107,9 97,1 101,8 104,5 103,0

(iv) Baltic = 3% increase; Federal = 1,6% increase only.

(v) Geometric mean: Federal = 1,031446 (3,1446%);
Baltic = 1,02327 (2,327%)

(vi) Federal Insurance's claims grew by an average of 3,1446% annually between 2001 and 2006.

16.9 (i) Price relatives: Milk = 108,2 Bread = 104,7 **Sugar = 111,9**
Maize = 106,5

(ii) Composite Price Index (2007) = 107,4 (overall 7,4% price increase from '04)

(iii) Quantity relatives: Milk = 83,8 Bread = 114,3 **Sugar = 71,4**
Maize = 110,3

(iv) Composite Consumption Index (2007) = 93,8 (overall 6,2% drop in consumption from '04)

16.10 (i) Price relatives (2007)
Electricity = 106,1 Sewage = 116,1 Water = 120,7
Telephone = 85,5

(ii) Composite Price Index: (2006) = 100,3 (2007) = 97,5

(iii) In 2006, overall utility costs increased by 0,3%, while in 2007 overall utility costs decreased by 2,5% from 2005.

16.11 (i) Consumption relatives (2007)
Electricity = 131,1 Sewage = 94,1 Water = 127,7
Telephone = 124,9

(ii) Composite Consumption Index: (2006) = 113,1 (2007) = 127,7

(iii) Relative to 2005, overall usage of utilities increased by 13,1% in 2006. Also households used 27,7% more of utilities in 2007 than they did in 2005.

16.12 (i) Re-based to 2004 90,7 86 93,5 95,3 **100** 108,4 104,7

(iii) From 2004 to 2006: 4,7% increase

(iv) Link relatives 100 94,9 108,7 102,0 104,9 108,4 96,6
Largest annual increase of 8,7% from 2001 to 2002.

(v) Geometric mean: Leather cost = 102,075 (2,075% average increase per year)

16.13 (i) CPI-adjusted salaries: R302,1 R306 R309,6 R313,5 R302,5 R314,3 R308,3

(ii) Salaries were below base period salaries in 2001 and 2005
(iii) Salary link relatives 100 106,6 105,2 108,1 105,2 108,2 103,5
CPI link relatives 100 105,2 104 106,7 109,0 104,1 105,5
Salary adjustments fell below CPI increases in 2005 and 2007.

16.14 (i) Re-based to 2004: 83,2 85,7 87,8 92,4 95,3 **100** 102,5 106,3
(iii) Link relatives: 100 102,95 102,46 105,2 103,14 104,98 102,46 103,77
(iv) Budgets: R5 000 000; R5 147 679; R5 122 951; R5 260 000; R5 156 844; R5 248 848; R5 122 915; R5 188 518

16.15 (i) Price relatives (2006):
Java = 115,3 Colombia = 115,6 Sumatra = 15,7
Mocha = 110,5
(ii) Composite Price Index (2006) = 113,9
(iii) Cheaper. Coffee imports have increased by only 13,9% since 2003.
(iv) Composite Quantity Index (2006) = 109,5

16.16 (i) Composite Quantity Index (2006) = 118,34 (18,34% increase since 2004)
(ii) Quantity relatives (2006):
GP's = 150 Specialists = 83,33 **Dentists = 150** Medicines = 140
(iii) Composite Price Index (2006) = 111,6

16.17 (i) Quantity relatives (2006): Trainer = 114,6 Balance = 120
Dura = 88,9
Dura's sales volume is down by 11,1% from 2005.
(ii) Composite Quantity (Volume) Index (2006) = 110,83 (10,83% increase)
Overall sales volumes do not meet the required growth of 12% per annum.

16.18 (i) Re-based to 2002:
71,28 82,82 87,24 94,16 96,72 **100** 101,78 104,7 109,34 114,4
(ii) Link relatives:
100 116,2 105,34 107,92 102,73 103,39 101,78 102,87 104,42 104,63

16.19 (i) Price relatives (Cruiser model) 100 102,1 106,6 111,7 121,9
(ii) Composite Price Index: 100 104,0 109,2 113,5 121,7
(iii) On average, motorcycle prices have increased by 21,7% from 2003 to 2007.
(iv) Link relatives (Classic model) 100 107,6 102,3 100,9 106,4
(v) Composite Quantity Index: 100 84,1 93,2 120,7 121,3
(vi) Motorcycle sales volumes have risen by 21,3% from 2003 to 2007.

16.20 (i) Cost relative index series (Passenger tyres) (base = January 2006)
100 100,8 100 103,5 104 102,6 107,2 111,1 109,1 105,7 106,3 95,1
(ii) Composite Cost Index series (base = January 2006)

100 98,0 97,4 99,8 100,3 99,3 103,4 105,9 104,2
102,7 102,8 96,8

Overall monthly production costs have fluctuated from 3,2% below to 5,9% above January 2006 costs.

(iii) Link relative index series (Light Truck Radial tyres)
100 96,1 100 100,6 99,9 100,1 103,5 99,6 100 99,9
100,1 100,2

(iv) Composite Volumes index series (base = January 2006)
100 133,7 123 106,8 141,6 138,3 156,5 146,4 138,3
143,7 129,2 53,2

Production volumes have fluctuated between 6,8% to 56,5% higher than January 2006 volumes between February and November. In December, output has slumped by 46,8% from January 2006 levels (due presumably to factory closings for holiday period).

Monthly production volumes of tyres are more volatile than production costs.

CHAPTER 17 Time Series Analysis

			3	4	5	6	7	
17.1	(i)	4-yearly moving average:	119,25	119,875	120,5	125,75	132,75	...
	(ii)	5-yearly moving average:	120,4	119,8	119,4	127,4	135,4	...

(v) Pattern: upward cyclical trend

17.2 (ii) y(trend) = 29 + 2,0182x x = 11 y(trend) = 51,89 (52);
x = 12 y(trend) = 53,97 (54); x = 13 y(trend) = 56,06 (56)

17.3 (ii) y(trend) = 61,125 – 0,60882x where x = –1 in Q4, 2004;
x = + 1 in Q1, 2005

(iii) Seasonal indexes: Q1 = 121,4 Q2 = 79,7 Q3 = 78,7
Q4 = 120,2

(iv) Estimated number of claims in Q2, 2007: (x = 19)
y(trend-adj) = 39,5 (40)

17.4 (ii) y(trend) = 84,933 – 2,097x where x = 1 in Sept 2005;
x = 2 in Oct 2005

(iii) Estimated occupancy rate (%):
July 2006 (x = 11) y(est) = 61,866%;
Aug 2006 (x = 12) y(est) = 59,769%

17.5 (ii) y(trend) = 20,8 + 4,95x where x = 1 in Q1 2003;
x = 2 in Q2 2003

(iii) Seasonal indexes: Q1 = 77,97 Q2 = 115,98
Q3 = 175,61 Q4 = 30,44

(iv) Estimated electricity demand (1000 mw):
Q3 2007 (x = 19) y(est) = 201,69 mw;
Q4 2007 (x = 20) y(est) = 36,47 mw

17.6 (i)

2004	Summer	417,6	Autumn	442	Winter	406,5	Spring	350
2005	Summer	444,1	Autumn	485,7	Winter	435,5	Spring	566,7
2006	Summer	486,8	Autumn	540,2	Winter	500	Spring	594,4

(iii) y(trend) = 435,64 + 5,6713x where x = 1 (Summer '04) ; x = 2 (Autumn '04)
(iv) Estimated hotel industry turnover (R millions): Summer '07 (x = 13) y(est) = R692,74; Autumn '07 (x = 14) y(est) = R576,84

17.7 (i) Seasonal indexes:
Summer = 107,4 Autumn = 97 Winter = 92,63
Spring = 102,97
(ii) Seasonal forces have a moderate quarterly influence.
(iii) y(trend) = 52,05 + 0,8544x where x = 1 (Summer '03) ; x = 2 (Autumn '03)
(iv) Estimated farming units sales (units) (2007): Summer = 71,5 (72)
Autumn = 65,41 (66) Winter = 63,25 (64) Spring = 71,19 (72)

17.8 (ii) Seasonal indexes:
Summer = 73 Autumn = 119,5 Winter = 117.6 Spring = 90
(iii) y(trend) = 3,5 + 0,03007x where x = –1 (Autumn '05); x = 1 (Winter '05)
(iv) Estimated energy costs (R100 000) (2007):
Summer = R2,84 Autumn = R4,7215 Winter = R4,7172
Spring = R3,6642
(v) y(trend) = 3,1091 + 0,0601x where x = 1 (Summer '04) ; x = 2 (Autumn '04)
(vi) Trend estimated values are identical for both trend lines.

17.9 (iii) Seasonal indexes: Q1 = 91,72 Q2 = 103,46 Q3 = 106,41
Q4 = 98,41
(iv) y(trend) = 1078,2 + 39,338x where x = 1 (Q1 2002); x = 2 (Q2 2002)
(vii) Estimates (2007) 1747; 2011; 2110; 1990; (2008) 1891; 2174; 2278; 2145

17.10 Estimated Quarterly Sales: Q1 = R11,4; Q2 = R13,8; Q3 = R13,2; Q4 = R9,6

17.11 (ii) (2005) 29,19; 29,66; 25,43; 36,32 (2006) 36,13; 37,30; 27,65; 37,36
(iii) Estimated visitors (2007) Q1 = 23,25 Q2 = 33,375 Q3 = 60,75
Q4 = 32,625

17.12 (ii) y(trend) = 4120,6 + 544,98x where x = 1 (1996); x = 2 (1997)
(vii) Estimates (2008) R11 205,34 (2009) R11 750,32

17.13 (iii) Seasonal indexes: Period 1 = 112,65 Period 2 = 97,79
Period 3 = 89,56
(iv) y(trend) = 42,621 – 1,0315x where x = 1 (P1 2003); x = 2 (P2 2003)
(vii) Estimates (2007) P1 = 32,907 P2 = 27,558 P3 = 24,313

17.14 y(trend) = 89,429 – 2,7143x where x = 1 (Jan); x = 2 (Feb)
Selling policy: If share price falls below 60c.

	Estimates (c): Aug = 67,71c Sept = 65c Oct = 62,286 Nov = 59,572 Sell Netron shares in November.
17.15 (i)	De-seasonalised number. of visitors 2004 Summer 175 Autumn 156,4 Winter 140,9 Spring 167 2005 Summer 177,7 Autumn 161,7 Winter 150 Spring 179,2 2006 Summer 191,1 Autumn 173,4 Winter 164,8 Spring 186,8
17.16 (i)	Seasonal indexes: Q1 = 70,37 Q2 = 89,19 Q3 = 136,28 Q4 = 104,15
(ii)	y(trend) = 14,2 + 0,2066x where x = 1 (Q1 2003); x = 2 (Q2 2003)
(iii)	Health claim value estimates (in R millions) (2007) Q1 = R12,46 Q2 = R15,98 Q3 = R24,7 Q4 = R19,09
17.17 (i)	y(trend) = 13,414 + 1,1821x where x = –1 (2002); x = 0 (2003); x = 1 (2004)
(ii)	Advertising expenditure estimate (2007): R18,143 (using trend line in (i))
(iv)	y(trend) = 8,6857 + 1,1821x where x = 1 (2000); x = 2 (2001); x = 3 (2002)
(v)	Advertising expenditure estimate (2007): R18,1425 (using *Excel's* trend line)
(vi)	Trend estimates from both trend line equations are identical.
17.18 (ii)	Seasonal indexes: Q1 = 100,77 Q2 = 93,62 Q3 = 97,99 Q4 = 107,62
(iii)	y(trend) = 203,42 – 3,5524x where x = 1 (Q1 2004); x = 2 (Q2 2004)
(iv)	Policy surrender estimates (2007): Q1 = 158,45 Q2 = 143,88 Q3 = 147,12 Q4 = 157,75
17.19 (i)	3-period moving average: (period 2) 252,7; 289,7; 263,0; 224,7; 142; 141,7 5-period moving average: (period 3) 255,6; 237,2; 210,4; 189,0; 162; 184,0
17.20 (i)	Seasonal indexes: Q1 = 107,76 Q2 = 100,61 Q3 = 90,72 Q4 = 100,91 y(trend) = 58 114 + 1302x where x = 1 (Q1 2000); x = 2 (Q2 2000)
(ii)	Passenger tyre sales estimates: (2007): Q1 = 103 312 Q2 = 97 767 Q3 = 89 337 Q4 = 100 686 (2008): Q1 = 108 924 Q2 = 103 007 Q3 = 94 062 Q4 = 105 941
(iii)	High confidence in estimates as trend and seasonal patterns are very stable.

17.21 (i) Seasonal indexes: Q1 = 79,10 Q2 = 110,69 Q3 = 117,46
Q4 = 92,75
y(trend) = 15 591 + 224,66x where x = 1 (Q1 2001);
x = 2 (Q2 2001)
(ii) Outpatients attendance estimates:
(2007): Q1 = 16 675 Q2 = 23 723 Q3 = 25 438
Q4 = 20 295
(2008): Q1 = 17 486 Q2 = 24 718

17.22 (i) Seasonal indexes: Q1 = 104,21 Q2 = 96,98 Q3 = 102,88
Q4 = 95,93
y(trend) = 952,75 – 9,917x where x = 1 (Q1 2001);
x = 2 (Q2 2001)
(ii) Construction employees' absenteeism estimates (days lost):
(2007): Q1 = 734 Q2 = 674 Q3 = 705 Q4 = 648

CHAPTER 18 Financial Calculations

18.1 (i) F_v = R21 000
(ii) F_v = R22 039,92
(iii) F_v = R22 203,66
18.2 (i) P_v = R119 579,10
(ii) P_v = R118 814
(iii) P_v = R118 134,90
18.3 (i) n = 12,5 years
(ii) n = 7,40205 years
(iii) n = 7,002756 years (28,011 quarters)
18.4 (i) P_v = R7 796,30
(ii) P_v = R7 585,08
18.5 (i) r = 16,0755% p.a.
(ii) =EFFECT(.15,12) gives 0,160755 (16,0755% p.a.)
18.6 (i) r = 9,3083% p.a.
(ii) =EFFECT(.09,4) gives 0,093083 (9,3083% p.a.)
18.7 n = 8,001337 years
18.8 F_v = R2 525,65
18.9 i = 10,3819% p.a.
18.10 i = 11,8078% p.a.
18.11 P_v = R19 572,37
18.12 n = 3 years
18.13 i = 10,0257% p.a.
18.14 (i) F_v = R25 755,03
(ii) =FV(.01,15,1600) gives R25 755,03
(iii) F_v = R26 012,58
(iv) =FV(.01,15,1600,,1) gives R26 012,58
18.15 P_v = R1 603
18.16 (i) R (regular payment) = R2 186,71 (deposit at end of month)
(ii) R (regular payment) = R2 170,43 (deposit at beginning of month)
18.17 (i) R (monthly payment – at end of month) = R307,30
(ii) Interest paid = R2 562,63 ; 30,1486%

18.18 P_v = R411 821,98
18.19 (i) F_v = R160 149,71
(ii) *Excel* function key: =FV(0.03625,60,750,,1)
18.20 R131 603,17
18.21 (i) At *end* of period: F_v = R12 478,72; Quarterly: F_v = R12 457,55
Monthly investment scheme is better.
(ii) *Excel* function key: Monthly: =FV(0.0070833,12,1000) = R12 478,72
Quarterly: =FV(0.025,4,3000) = R12 457,55
(iii At *beginning* of period: F_v = R12 567,11; Quarterly: F_v = R12 768,99
Quarterly investment scheme is better.
Excel function key: Monthly: =FV(0.0070833,12,1000,,1)
= R12 567,11
Quarterly: =FV(0.025,4,3000,,1) = R12 768,99
18.22 (i) Purchase price = R88 406,52 + R20 000 = R108 406,52
(ii) *Excel* function key: Monthly: =PV(0.0075,48,2200) = R88 406,52
18.23 (i) F_v = R41 214,30
(ii) For first 2 years: =FV(0.006667,24,1000) = R25 933,19
Compound interest for 1 year: =25 933,19$(1+0.008333)^{12}$
= R28 648,73
For year 3: =FV(0.008333,12,1000) = R12 565,57
Total funds available: R28 648,73 + R12 565,57 = R41 214,30
18.24 (i) F_v = R1 908,83
(ii) For the first 5 months: =FV(0.01,5,200) = R1 020,20
Compounded for 7 months: 720,20$(1+.01)^7$ = R772,15
For months 6 to 10: =FV(0.01,5,200) = R1 020,20
Compounded for 2 months: 720,20$(1+.01)^2$ = R734,68
For remaining 2 months: =FV(0.01,2,200) = R402,00
Balance at end of 12 months: R772,15 + R734,68 + R402
= R1 908,83
18.25 (i) R (repayment at end of each quarter) = R2 690,58
(ii) R (repayment at beginning of each quarter) = R2 599,60
(iii) Choose to repay at beginning of quarter as total repayment is less.
18.26 R (repayment beginning after 3 years) = R2 366,32
18.27 nominal interest rate: i = 17% p.a.
18.28 n = 42 months (3 years and 6 months)
18.29 NPV (Trucking) = R31 421,97 NPV (Laundry) = R33 333,18
Since NPV (Laundry) > NPV (Trucking) recommend laundry investment.

APPENDIX 3: LIST OF KEY FORMULAE

MEASURES OF CENTRAL LOCATION

Arithmetic mean

Ungrouped data

$$\bar{x} = \frac{\sum_{i=1}^{n} x_i}{n}$$

Grouped data

$$\bar{x} = \frac{\sum_{i=1}^{m} f_i x_i}{n}$$

Mode

Grouped data

$$M_o = O_{mo} + \frac{c(f_m - f_{m-1})}{2f_m - f_{m-1} - f_{m+1}}$$

Median

Grouped data

$$M_e = O_{me} + \frac{c\left[\frac{n}{2} - f(<)\right]}{f_{me}}$$

Lower quartile

Grouped data

$$Q_1 = O_{q1} + \frac{c\left(\frac{n}{4} - f(<)\right)}{f_{q1}}$$

Upper quartile

Grouped data

$$Q_3 = O_{q3} + \frac{c\left(\frac{3n}{4} - f(<)\right)}{f_{q3}}$$

Geometric mean

Ungrouped data

$$\text{G.M.} = \sqrt[n]{x_1 \times x_2 \times x_3 \times \ldots \times x_n}$$

Weighted arithmetic mean

Grouped data

$$\text{weighted } \bar{x} = \frac{\sum f_i x_i}{\sum f_i}$$

MEASURES OF DISPERSION

Range

Ungrouped data

Range = Maximum value − Minimum value + 1

$= x_{max} - x_{min} + 1$

Grouped data

Range = Upper limit (highest class) − Lower limit (lowest class)

Interquartile range

Interquartile Range = $Q_3 - Q_1$

Quartile deviation

Quartile Deviation (Q.D.) = $\frac{Q_3 - Q_1}{2}$

Variance

Mathematical – ungrouped data

$$S_x^2 = \frac{\sum (x_i - \bar{x})^2}{(n-1)}$$

Computational – ungrouped data

$$S_x^2 = \frac{\sum x_i^2 - n\bar{x}^2}{(n-1)}$$

Standard deviation

$$S_x = \sqrt{S_x^2}$$

Coefficient of variation

$$CV = \frac{S_x}{\bar{x}} \times 100\%$$

Pearson's coefficient of skewness

$$Sk_p = \frac{3\,(\text{Mean} - \text{Median})}{\text{Standard deviation}}$$

$$Sk_p = \frac{(\text{Mean} - \text{Mode})}{\text{Standard deviation}}$$

PROBABILITY CONCEPTS

Conditional probability $P(A/B) = \frac{P(A \cap B)}{P(B)}$

Addition rule
Non mutually exclusive events
$P(A \cup B) = P(A) + P(B) - P(A \cap B)$

Mutually exclusive events
$P(A \cup B) = P(A) + P(B)$

Multiplication rule
Statistically dependent events
$P(A \cap B) = P(A/B) \times P(B)$

Statistically independent events
$P(A \cap B) = P(A) \times P(B)$

Permutations $_{n}P_{r} = \frac{n!}{(n-r)!}$

Combinations $_{n}C_{r} = \frac{n!}{r!\,(n-r)!}$

PROBABILITY DISTRIBUTIONS

Binomial distribution
$P(r) = {_{n}C_{r}}\, p^{r} q^{(n-r)}$ for $r = 0, 1, 2, 3, \ldots, n$

$P(r\ \textit{successes}) = \frac{n!}{r!\,(n-r)!}\, p^{r} q^{(n-r)}$ for $r = 0, 1, 2, 3, \ldots, n$

Binomial descriptive measures
Mean $\mu = np$
Standard deviation $\sigma = \sqrt{npq}$ where $q = 1 - p$

Poisson distribution
$P(x) = \frac{e^{-a} a^{x}}{x!}$ for $x = 0, 1, 2, 3 \ldots$

Poisson descriptive measures
Mean $\mu = a$
Standard deviation $\sigma = \sqrt{a}$

Standard normal probability $z = \dfrac{x - \mu_x}{\sigma_x}$

CONFIDENCE INTERVALS

Single mean *n large; variance known*

$$\bar{x} - z\frac{\sigma_x}{\sqrt{n}} \leq \mu_x \leq \bar{x} + z\frac{\sigma_x}{\sqrt{n}}$$

(lower limit) (upper limit)

n small; variance unknown

$$\bar{x} - t_{(\alpha)(n-1)}\frac{s_x}{\sqrt{n}} \leq \mu_x \leq \bar{x} + t_{(\alpha)(n-1)}\frac{s_x}{\sqrt{n}}$$

(lower limit) (upper limit)

Single proportion

$$p - z\frac{\sqrt{pq}}{n} \leq \pi \leq p + z\frac{\sqrt{pq}}{n}$$

(lower limit) (upper limit)

HYPOTHESES TESTS

Single mean *Variance known*

$$z_{stat} = \frac{\bar{x} - \mu_x}{\frac{\sigma_x}{\sqrt{n}}}$$

Variance unknown; n small

$$t_{stat} = \frac{\bar{x} - \mu_x}{\frac{s_x}{\sqrt{n}}}$$

Single proportion

$$z_{\text{stat}} = \frac{p - \pi}{\sqrt{\frac{\pi(1-\pi)}{n}}}$$

Difference between two means

Variances known

$$z_{\text{stat}} = \frac{(\bar{x}_1 - \bar{x}_2) - (\mu_1 - \mu_2)}{\sqrt{\frac{\sigma_1^2}{n_1} + \frac{\sigma_2^2}{n_2}}}$$

Variances unknown; n_1 and n_2 small

$$t_{\text{stat}} = \frac{(\bar{x}_1 - \bar{x}_2) - (\mu_1 - \mu_2)}{\sqrt{\frac{s^2}{n_1} + \frac{s^2}{n_2}}} \quad \text{where } s^2 = \frac{(n_1 - 1)s_1^2 + (n_2 - 1)s_2^2}{n_1 + n_2 - 2}$$

Differences between two proportions

$$z_{\text{stat}} = \frac{(p_1 - p_2) - (\pi_1 - \pi_2)}{\sqrt{\hat{\pi}(1-\hat{\pi})\left(\frac{1}{n_1} + \frac{1}{n_2}\right)}}$$

$$\text{where } \hat{\pi} = \frac{x_1 + x_2}{n_1 + n_2};\ p_1 = \frac{x_1}{n_1};\ p_2 = \frac{x_2}{n_2}$$

Chi-square

$$\chi^2_{\text{stat}} = \sum \frac{(f_o - f_e)^2}{f_e}$$

INDEX NUMBERS

Price relative

$$\text{Price relative} = \frac{p_1}{p_0} \times 100\%$$

Laspeyres price index

Weighted aggregates method

$$\text{Laspeyres price index} = \frac{\sum(p_1 \times q_0)}{\sum(p_0 \times q_0)} \times 100\%$$

Laspeyres price index

Weighted average of relatives method

$$\text{Laspeyres price index} = \frac{\sum\left[\left(\frac{p_1}{p_0}\right) \times 100 \times (p_0 \times q_0)\right]}{\sum(p_0 \times q_0)}$$

Unweighted price index Price index (unweighted) = $\frac{\sum p_1}{\sum p_0} \times 100\%$

Quantity relative Quantity relative = $\frac{q_1}{q_0} \times 100\%$

Laspeyres quantity index *Weighted aggregates method*

Laspeyres quantity index = $\frac{\sum (p_0 \times q_1)}{\sum (p_0 \times q_0)} \times 100\%$

Laspeyres quantity index *Weighted average of relatives method*

Laspeyres quantity index = $\frac{\sum \left[\left(\frac{q_1}{q_0}\right) \times 100 \times (p_0 \times q_0)\right]}{\sum (p_0 \times q_0)}$

REGRESSION AND CORRELATION

Formula $\hat{y} = b_0 + b_1 x$

Coefficients $b_1 = \frac{n\sum xy - \sum x \sum y}{n\sum x^2 - (\sum x)^2}$

$b_0 = \frac{\sum y - b_1 \sum x}{n}$

Pearson's correlation coefficient $r = \frac{n\sum xy - \sum x \sum y}{\sqrt{\left[n\sum x^2 - (\sum x)^2\right] \times \left[n\sum y^2 - (\sum y)^2\right]}}$

TIME SERIES ANALYSIS

Regression trend coefficients $b_1 = \frac{\sum xy}{\sum x^2}$

$b_0 = \frac{\sum y}{n}$ when $\sum x = 0$

FINANCIAL CALCULATIONS

Simple interest $F_v = P_v(1 + in)$

Compound interest $F_v = P_v(1 + i)^n$

Effective rate of interest $r = \left(1+\frac{i}{m}\right)^m - 1$

Ordinary annuity certain

$$F_v = R\frac{(1+i)^n - 1}{i}$$

$$P_v = R\frac{1-(1+i)^{-n}}{i}$$

Ordinary annuity due

$$F_v = R\frac{\left[(1+i)^n - 1\right](1+i)}{i}$$

$$P_v = R\frac{[1-(1+i)^{-n}](1+i)}{i}$$

Deferred annuity

$$P_v = R\left(\frac{1-(1+i)^{-(m+n)}}{i} - \frac{1-(1+i)^{-m}}{i}\right)$$

Index

D

E

F

G

H

I

Q

R

S

W

X

Y

Z